A Reference Guide to
Television's *Bonanza*

A Reference Guide to Television's *Bonanza*

Episodes, Personnel and Broadcast History

by BRUCE R. LEIBY *and* LINDA F. LEIBY

McFarland & Company, Inc., Publishers

Jefferson, North Carolina, and London

The present work is a reprint of the library bound edition of A Reference Guide to Television's *Bonanza*: Episodes, Personnel and Broadcast History, *first published in 2001 by McFarland.*

LIBRARY OF CONGRESS CATALOGUING-IN-PUBLICATION DATA

Leiby, Bruce R.
  A reference guide to television's *Bonanza* : episodes, personnel and broadcast history / by Bruce R. Leiby and Linda F. Leiby.
      p.   cm.
  Includes bibliographic references and index.

  ISBN 0-7864-2268-8 (softcover : 50# alkaline paper) ∞

  1. Bonanza (Television program).   I. Leiby, Linda F., 1947–
II. Title.
PN1992.77.B59L45   2005
791.45'72 — dc21   2001031500

British Library cataloguing data are available

On the cover: Cast of *Bonanza*, 1959–1973 (Photofest); pistol, pocket watch and background ©2005 Photospin; horseshoe ©2005 Clipart.com

Manufactured in the United States of America

McFarland & Company, Inc., Publishers
  Box 611, Jefferson, North Carolina 28640
    www.mcfarlandpub.com

To the stars and their families,
and to the memories of our parents,
Margaret and Edward Leiby and Mae and Clyde Flounders

Acknowledgments

The authors would like to thank the following people and organizations for their kind assistance in the preparation of this work:

James Robert Parish, Howard and Ron Mandelbaum (Photofest), David Greenland, Bing Russell, Sul Ross University, Lisgar Collegiate Institute and the Philadelphia Free Library.

Contents

Contents

Preface

Over the years, since its inception in 1959, *Bonanza* has provided quality programming and wholesome entertainment to millions of viewers world wide. It was the second longest running TV Western, surpassed only by *Gunsmoke*, surviving for 14 seasons and three TV films. It lives on in reruns, reaching loyal fans and acquiring new ones.

Bonanza's legion of fans meet frequently at the theme park near Lake Tahoe to exchange memorabilia and relive their favorite memories.

The purpose of this book is to provide an in-depth chronicle of the series and its stars to be used by libraries, researchers and those interested in classic television.

Part I gives a brief history of Virginia City, as many of the early episodes were based on real events and people. The second half of the section includes the history of the show itself.

Part II provides cast members and the years they were connected with the show. It gives the technical credits as well. The episodes are broken down into seasons providing writer, director, producer, executive producer (where appropriate), supporting cast, synopsis, review (where available) and a note for each show. Each episode is numbered sequentially and preceded by an E. Following the episodes, the three movies are chronicled with the same information.

In Part III, biographies of *Bonanza*'s four stars are preceded by a description of the character they played. At the end of the Biography, the star's media credits are provided. Each is numbered and preceded by the star's initials.

Part IV provides the same sort of information for the supporting cast.

1

Various appendices follow Part IV. Appendix A supplies the known awards, honors and memberships received by the show, David Dortort and each of the stars and supporting players. Each is numbered and preceded by AHM.

Appendix B deals with *Bonanza* collectibles which are numbered and preceded by a BC. Appendix C is a discography and provides the numerous recordings on which the *Bonanza* theme appears. It gives the title of the recording on which it appears, label, artist, date and whether the version was instrumental or vocal. The format (45, LP, CD, or cassette) is also noted. Following the theme song, the cast albums are chronicled with title, label and year. Songs are listed by side with singer and recording date for each song (as well as technical credits). A *Bonanza* discography is provided for David Rose and a full one is given for the stars and supporting players. Where appropriate, charted records are noted. Recordings are numbered and preceded by a D. Appendix D lists products and causes endorsed by the stars. Each is numbered and preceded by an EN. Appendix E includes the lists of the A.C. Nielsen's "top ten" shows (by season) on which *Bonanza* appeared. It also ranks Westerns by season as well as overall Western ratings. Each is numbered and preceded by an R. Appendix F lists sheet music on which the stars were pictured. Each is numbered and preceded by an SM.

The last appendix (G) provides a videolog for the series episodes, the *Bonanza* films and the video releases for the stars and supporting cast. Included are the names of the various companies releasing the videos with number, format and year of release. When release year was unavailable, the film's release date was used. Each video number is preceded by a V.

Following the discography is a bibliography divided into two parts, the first listing newspaper and magazine references and the second listing books. A general index concludes the book.

The authors hope this work will provide the reader with useful information and the researcher a foundation on which to further their research. We welcome any additions or corrections and will make every effort to incorporate them in any future editions.

PART I

The History of *Bonanza*

Creator David Dortort was particularly interested in the time period of the late 1850s and especially the big bonanza strikes that were found on the Comstock Lode.

In Western Nevada in 1859, rich veins of silver and gold were unearthed. Prospector Henry T. Comstock took credit for the find although other miners had made discoveries several years before.

Pioneers seeking instant wealth flooded the area, setting up mining camps that would eventually evolve into Virginia City, Nevada, a rowdy and dangerous place.

Dortort opted to tell his story in this time period, placing the Cartwrights on a cattle ranch away from the greed of the city yet close enough to involve Virginia City in his tales of taming the new frontier from the viewpoint of the Cartwright clan.

The Real Virginia City

In the Beginning

Ten years before there was a Virginia City, the word of California gold spread across the land and several forty-niners passed through the edge of the eastern Sierra in what was known as western Utah Territory. Many lingered long enough to find some gold, but the riches of California lured them onward. Along the way, they discussed their finds and, the next year, prospectors

3

returned to the area which they would name Washoe after the Wa-Sha-Shu Indians. Enough gold was found to keep them in the area and a small settlement called Johntown sprang up.

No one would have guessed that, in a short period, Virginia City would evolve into the West's wealthiest town and would have a big influence on the nation's history.

Enter Henry T. Comstock

In the winter of 1859, prospectors stayed in Johntown awaiting a thaw so that mining could resume. In January, the thaw came and a group of prospectors, including James "Old Virginny" Finney (for whom Virginia City was named), headed up a hill where gold was found. They named the place Gold Hill.

Two Irishmen, Peter O'Reilly and Patrick McLaughlin, left Gold Hill to explore the top of a canyon. Needing water for their rockers, they uncovered a spring. In that first shovel full of dirt was gold and some "blue stuff." Their find would eventually yield $20,000,000.

They were thrilled at their discovery until Henry T. "Old Pancake" Comstock showed up claiming the right to the spring and the trench they had found. Of course he held no such rights. He conned the Irishmen out of their discovery but agreed to cut them in if they would continue working the mine for him. He was a man interested in attaining riches without working for them. His continued referral to the discoveries within 160 acres as "his" led to what became known as the Comstock Lode.

Silver and Lost Fortunes

Two men, Stone and Harrison, approached Comstock in June 1859 and inquired about the "blue stuff." Comstock considered the "blue stuff" a hindrance. Stone and Harrison were curious and to their surprise, when they had it assayed, found that the sample contained silver sulfide valued at $3,000 a ton for silver and $800 a ton for gold. Investors promised to keep this a secret. But after they told close friends, the word leaked out and the West became deluged with prospectors seeking instant wealth.

Ironically, Pat McLaughlin sold his interest in the property for $3,500 (the investment was making $400 daily on surface diggings alone). He died earning $40 a month cooking on a ranch in Montana.

Henry Comstock sold his share for $11,000 and bought a general store which failed because of his poor business skills. He committed suicide.

Pat O'Reilly earned $40,000 but lost it all investing in mining stocks.

He ended his days in an insane asylum and when he died he was buried in a pauper's field.

Old Virginny sold his interest for a horse and a bottle of whiskey. He died after falling from his horse in Gold Canyon.

The Paiutes

During the winter of 1859-60, many of the prospectors became ill and died because of bad water, weather and hunger. They went into the hills and took nuts from the Pion trees and killed animals needed by the Paiutes. The Indian leaders sought revenge against the advice of Chief Winnemucca.

In 1860, war broke out after three white men took two Paiute girls captive. Several Paiute warriors rescued the girls at a trading post on the Carson River. They burned the post and killed the men who had taken the girls. Word got back to Virginia City and 100 rowdy men headed for the Paiute village at Pyramid Lake. To their surprise, they were ambushed and 76 of them were killed. The people of Virginia City enlisted the help of the U.S. Army, who attacked the encampment at Pyramid Lake where 160 Indians were cut down. The survivors fled. The troops remained, building Fort Churchill. Other outposts sprang up all over Nevada to protect the settlers from the Indians.

The Pony Express

Russell, Majors and Waddell owned a freight and express company and wanted a government contract to deliver the mail between St. Joseph, Missouri, and Sacramento, California. Their idea was to transport the mail 2,000 miles in ten days, which beat their competitors (the Overland Mail Company) by half.

They formed the Pony Express in April 1860. The riders needed to be 18 or younger and weigh no more than 135 pounds. The equipment weighed 13 pounds. The rider could only take with him a knife and repeating revolver. They would earn $50–150 a month. The company charged $5 for every half-ounce letter and $3.50 for every ten-word telegram.

Eighty riders were always in use, 40 going east and 40 west. Fresh horses were needed. Five hundred of the fastest horses were selected.

Home stations were set up at intervals of 30 miles and swing stations every ten. The men changed horses every ten miles, thus averaging three horses. They had two minutes to make their switch. Eventually riders rode 75 miles making switches every ten. Runs were even made in winter. The rides were dangerous either due to the weather or attacking Indians.

The idea was a sound one but not a financial success, causing the Pony Express to go belly up only 18 months later, in October 1861, just as the Overland Telegraph construction was completed.

Mining Conditions

As the shafts deepened, traditional equipment and techniques became outdated. Hoisting equipment no longer was efficient and timbering methods began to fail, resulting in frequent cave-ins. Fresh air was not getting into the lower depths of the shafts.

In 1861, Phillip Diedeshiemer, a young engineer, was brought in to work on the timbering problem. He came up with square-set timbering which revolutionized support systems, allowing endless extensions to be added in any direction and to depths unknown. Diedeshiemer got so involved in his work, he neglected to have his invention patented. He earned little for his discovery, although he stayed on as a consultant and became well-off.

Not only was air foul for those who worked at the end of the tunnels, but at 2,200 feet temperatures reached between 120 and 140 degrees. The problem was solved, in part, with Root Blowers — power air pumps. These pumps did not totally take care of the problem and forced the men working at the lowest levels to strip to the waist and work for 15-minute intervals.

High-speed hoisting cages helped get men and equipment quickly down into the shafts and six-ton loads of ore out of the mines. Mules (called Washoe Canaries) pulling underground railroad cars, explosives, pneumatic drills and ice water. Equipment to communicate between levels of the mine and those on the surface was also used.

By 1863, claims overlapped to the point where each claim was owned three or four times. This was due to poor records, vague laws and lack of enforcement. The court dockets were jammed with lawsuits claiming rightful ownership. Lawyers were bountiful and courts corrupt.

Life on the Comstock Improves

Tents were quickly replaced by wooden buildings despite the outrageous cost of lumber. A lot cost up to $1500 without a valid deed. Houses were built and bought as soon as erected.

Businesses soon appeared on the main street along with wooden sidewalks and graded city streets. Most residences were inexpensively built and had modest furnishings. The average wages for miners was $4 (75¢ elsewhere) a day but a pound of coffee was 30¢, fresh beef ran between 10¢ to 25¢ a pound, a gallon of whiskey cost $4, oysters were $3.25 a dozen and a steak dinner in a restaurant cost 20¢. Class distinction was in evidence and determined in which area different things were located.

Plight of the Chinese

Upon completion of the transcontinental railroad, the initial group of Chinese arrived in Virginia City. They were treated as inferior beings,

Inside the Chollar Mine, Virginia City. The mine started operation in 1861. (Photograph by Linda F. Leiby.)

unable to testify in court, send their children to public schools, hold claims or work in the mines. Miners showed their prejudice by chasing the Chinese into the brush after learning the Virginia & Truckee Railroad had offered them jobs.

The Chinese lived in poverty within a five-block radius where opium dens and gambling were abundant. Their homes were constructed of scrap wood and paper. They were hard workers putting in 16- to 24-hour days as laborers, chopping wood, operating laundries or selling vegetables. The wealthier miners hired them as servants.

Julia Bulette

Julia Bulette, a high-class madame, came to Virginia City in 1859. Since men way outnumbered women, she entered the "world's oldest profession."

Within a year, Julia opened her luxurious Julia's Palace where she employed six girls. Spending a night with Julia might run $1,000. She exhibited beauty, wit, charm and good taste.

When the Paiutes threatened to attack Virginia City, the women were moved to Carson City but Julia remained to support the men.

When influenza hit Virginia City, Julia offered the use of her palace as a hospital and even raised money by pawning jewelry and other personal items.

After the fever was over, the men rewarded her by making her an honorary member of Fire Engine Company No. 1 and by giving her name to a Virginia & Truckee railroad car. Despite being snubbed by the women, she would accompany the men to fires to make coffee for them.

In 1867, Jean Millain robbed and strangled Julia. Everything closed the day of her funeral. The fire company marched behind the silver-handled casket and a brass band played "The Girl I Left Behind Me" and led the way to the cemetery at the east end of town where she was buried — but not in the same area as "respectable people."

Jean Millain was arrested in 1868. The women who visited him in jail considered him a hero but Virginia City celebrated his hanging on April 24, 1869.

Samuel Clemens and the Territorial Enterprise

Samuel Clemens and his brother Orion headed by stagecoach for Nevada in July 1861. Orion was to become Secretary for the Nevada Territory. Clemens failed at mining and turned to writing humorous accounts of his experiences in the West, using the pen name Josh. The *Territorial Enterprise* was the most noted paper in Virginia City and offered Clemens a job paying $25 a week. Clemens walked 60 miles from Aurora (where he was working) to Virginia City.

During the two years he stayed with the paper, he chose the pen name Mark Twain. His career was helped along by fellow writer William Wright (Dan De Quille), who helped Twain with hoaxes. When things became dull, they spiced them up by exaggeration or making up something that would attract the reader's attention.

The Bankers Take Control

Nevada achieved statehood in 1864. By 1865, the shafts had gone as deep (400-500 feet) as they could without acquiring more expensive equipment and building more mills to refine the ore.

Miners felt they had extracted as much ore as they could and began to move on to more productive areas. Merchants followed, and stockholders refrained from further investments in the mines. William Ralston, a cashier at the Bank of California, sent William Sharon to Virginia City to take charge

The building on the right is Julia Bulette's Palace. (Photograph by Linda F. Leiby.)

of the situation. His determination, greed and ruthlessness compelled him to study mining and become an expert. Ralston's Ring was formed and was in power for seven years.

Sharon made loans at low interest rates, thus spurring borrowing and encouraging miners to dig deeper for ore. He accepted stocks from the miners and mills as collateral and stored them in the bank's vaults. He became very popular until loans became due. When the miners were unable to pay, Sharon took control of mines, mills, and timberland. Sharon, Ralston and bank president D.O. Mills became owners of the Union Mill & Mining Company and took control of the more prosperous property now owned by the bank.

Sharon also built a line of the Virginia & Truckee Railroad between the mines and mills going from Virginia City, Carson River and Carson City.

John Mackay, who had joined the Comstock in 1860, held major shares of stock in the bigger mines and earned profits for those outside of Ralston's Ring. John and his partners James Fair, James Flood and William O'Brien

The Territorial Enterprise, *Nevada's first newspaper, was established in 1858. (Photograph by Linda F. Leiby.)*

began to give Sharon a taste of his own medicine by taking away the control of the Bank of California's Hale & Norcross Mine. Earnings from their Kentucky Mine enabled Mackay to quietly purchase the Consolidated Virginia Mine located under downtown Virginia City. It was the granddaddy of ore bodies. Mackay and his partners opened their own San Francisco bank which was, in part, responsible for causing a run on the Bank of California. Ralston was ousted and he drowned that day in San Francisco Bay. Leadership of the bank was taken over by Sharon.

The Great Fire and Prosperity

In 1875, fire broke out in Virginia City and burned down 33 blocks, 10 square blocks of which were in the heart of town. The wealth earned from mining rebuilt the city bigger and better then before.

The year 1876 was the city's peak year with over 23,000 residents (half of Nevada's population). Virginia City was reconstructed with brick and stone buildings and became tame and civilized. The leading citizens were respectable, wealthy, dignified and important. Champagne, caviar, Paris gowns, a German tailor and jewelry stores with diamonds were all a part of city life. Wealthy citizens had mansions where anything that was metal was made out of silver.

In 1877, there were 150 grocery and dry good stores, four banks, six churches, one Chinese Temple, 30 carpenters, three doctors, two horse doctors, 150 saloons and six breweries.

Piper's Opera House was one of the finest examples of culture in Virginia City. Italian operas, Shakespearean plays and vaudeville acts were presented. Famous performers appeared, including Edwin Booth and Houdini. But the best loved was a performer named Adah Menken. If the miners liked a performer, they tossed silver coins or gold nuggets on stage. Adah was presented with a 50-ounce brick of silver bullion, polished and engraved.

Virginia City, at least for a short time, was known worldwide and was of such importance that New York and San Francisco newspapers set up offices in the city.

Decline and Rebirth

Around 1878, the Comstock Lode was pretty much depleted and it took a few more years to convince the last diehard investors. In the 20 years of the lode, it is estimated that some $320,000,000-750,000,000 in precious metal was uncovered.

Many moved on to other adventures, leaving Virginia City to fade away, but she refused to give up. There was still a little more digging and a new cyanide process was used to recover ore. In 1935, the price of gold brought renewed interest in mining.

Paul Smith, a New York hotel man, arrived in 1937 and helped perk up

Top: *The John MacKay Mansion in Virginia City.* Bottom: *The Bucket of Blood Saloon restored in 1876. (Photographs by Linda F. Leiby.)*

Top: *Piper's Opera House, a center of Virginia City culture.* Bottom: *Virginia City today. (Photographs by Linda F. Leiby.)*

the economy by setting up museums, selling merchandise he'd had kids round up, and by giving walking tours of Piper's Opera House for 15¢.

World War II caused mining to stop and by 1950, Virginia City seemed to be headed downhill again. When Lucius Beebe and Charles Clegg, who were from New York and wrote about the American West, came to Virginia City, they became enchanted with the area. They re-started the _Territorial Enterprise_ and sent copies around the world in an attempt to revive the business area.

The popularity of TV's _Bonanza_ brought tourists to the area in droves. The residents refurbished the city and today more than 3,000,000 visitors a year come to the area.

The Show's History

The classic Western series _Bonanza_ was the brainchild of writer-producer David Dortort, who was born in Brooklyn, New York, on October 23, 1918. He enjoyed learning and at the age of 15 enrolled at New York's City College. It was there that he took particular interest in geography. At 17, he traveled around the country. During his travels, he became interested in the nation's history, and was especially intrigued by the period of the Old West.

Dortort returned to college where he assumed the responsibilities of editor of his college's literary magazine. He graduated in 1936. He completed two novels (one of which was _Burial of the Fruit_, based on his youth) and several short stories prior to turning his talents to writing film and television scripts.

Dortort served as president of the Writers Guild of America, West (television branch), three terms in a row.

John Payne, star of NBC's _The Restless Gun_, approached Dortort about producing the show. With _The Restless Gun_ he gained the distinction of being the first writer to produce a television series. It was one of TV's better Westerns at the time. The show was in its second season when Payne tired of doing a weekly series. He was also in a legal dispute with Universal Studios. He decided not to return for a third season. This would soon free Dortort to pursue other projects.

NBC wanted to produce its own shows rather than relying upon other companies to supply their programs. Westerns were doing well at the time, so it was a logical choice for the network to choose this genre to pit against the successes of competing networks.

The network thought _The Restless Gun_ had quality and good ratings so it made sense to approach Dortort to develop their one hour show. "The network came to me early in 1959 and asked if I had an idea for a show," recalled Dortort. "I told them I thought I did."[1] Dortort forged ahead not only developing a new program but completing scripts for the remainder of *The Restless Gun* season. He quickly decided on a format that would differ from the usual one-man hero and his gun — that of a father and three sons. The inspiration for *Bonanza* came from *King Arthur and the Knights of the Round Table* and the whole idea of *Camelot*. The father figure replaced the king; his sons were the knights.

Dortort was given a free hand. He was especially interested in the late 1850s (the Comstock and Civil War era) as well as the rise of Virginia City. Dortort felt that this period was colorful and played an important part in America's history and thus chose it as the setting of his stories.

He thought the relationship of a father and his sons had a lot of possibilities. The homestead was called the Ponderosa, named for the Ponderosa pines that grew in the area. Things would revolve around the 1,000 square mile ranch which would later be considered by some as the fifth cast member. *Bonanza* became the first "property Western" and would later be followed by *The High Chaparral* (also produced by Dortort) and *The Big Valley*.

The character of Hoss (Norwegian for "big friendly man") was the first to be cast. Dortort had used Dan Blocker as an extra on *The Restless Gun* and, recognizing his talent, had him return as a guest star. He would play the middle son as a big, gentle man who would appeal to children of all ages. Michael Landon had been cast in the pilot of *The Restless Gun* and was chosen to play the youngest son who was impulsive, hot-headed — and the romantic interest appealing to the teenage viewers. The two characters were modeled after Blocker and Landon.

Dortort had seen Lorne Greene on an episode of *Wagon Train* entitled "The Vivian Carter Story" and felt the actor displayed the qualities he was looking for in the role of Ben Cartwright — a stern but loving father. Greene fashioned the character after his own father and would go on to represent a father figure to many fans. His character appealed to the older members of the audience. "When I created the show, I wanted to put a father on television who wasn't a buffoon or an incompetent," said Dortort in a *Look* magazine interview.[2]

Guy Williams was considered for the role of Adam but, by the time *Bonanza* got underway, he had already signed to star in Disney's *Zorro*. Dortort hired Pernell Roberts to play Adam, the oldest son. Adam was sensitive, serious, intellectual, and most likely the one to take over the Ponderosa. He would appeal to the college co-ed segment of viewers.

The network executives objected to Dortort's choices as the four actors were not the big marquee names they felt were necessary to draw sponsors for the big-budgeted show ($100,000-150,000 per week). He eventually convinced the powers-that-be to accept his casting.

After getting his cast, Dortort went to NBC with his plans. The first was to film *Bonanza* in color. The network balked as they wanted stars to appear on the show and the cost of color would take a big chunk of the weekly budget. The network eventually gave into Dortort's demands, accepting a guest cast of unknowns he would hand pick.

Dortort wanted to shoot on location but was forced to compromise and do an annual shoot in California's Sierra Nevada mountains to get exterior footage representing the Ponderosa. The use of color helped the sales of many color TV sets by RCA (NBC's parent company).

Paramount Studios was chosen for filming by Dortort because of its two-story Western set that served as the site for Virginia City until the 1969-70 season. It would also be used in *The Trap* starring Lorne Greene and Michael Landon's *Little House on the Prairie*, eventually being torn down in 1979. NBC rented the town and Stages 16 and 17 for a hefty price. Interior sets were constructed on these soundstages under the direction of Hal Pereira, Earl Hedrick and Dortort. Hedrick was also credited for the creation of the map that was seen burning in each episode. Grace Gregory was responsible for decorating the sets. Several duplicates of the casts' costumes were created so that they could wear the same outfit in each episode (in order for stock footage to be used when needed in other shows).

Wally Westmore was chosen as makeup artist. Because he was not crazy about the television medium, he delegated many of his duties to his brother Frank. It was Frank who was given the responsibility of getting the makeup to appear the right shade when photographed in color. The arc lamps used to light the set were hot and caused problems with the makeup and wardrobe. The problem was solved by color technician Alex Quiroga, who finally persuaded the studio to use only two arc lamps instead of ten.

Although surrounded by the best production staff, Dortort kept his hand in almost every phase of the operation.

Alan Livingston, NBC's vice-president in charge of programming, asked his brother Jay Livingston and Jay's partner Ray Evans to write the theme song for *Bonanza*. They agreed to write it for $750 plus $750 more if the series sold. They felt that the title *Bonanza* did not make sense as the ranch was called the Ponderosa and they found it difficult to write the lyrics. The song would become one of television's best-known themes, at least instrumentally. The four stars were to have sung the song riding out of Virginia City but the final take was without lyrics. Lorne Greene later recorded the song (with lyrics) on his 1964 album *Welcome to the Ponderosa*.

Dortort did not like the lyrics but agreed to use the song in the opening and closing as long as David Rose did not have to include it in the episodes. Dortort felt that the power of music was essential in film. Rose was given a 35-musician orchestra. The series thus had the richest sounds of the time period. Rose scored most of the episodes.

The first color Western, *Bonanza* premiered on Saturday, September 12, 1959 (there were 30 Westerns on the air the time). It received bad reviews. Because the network owned and had a financial interest in the show, it was not canceled. It had been given only six months to put things together before its first air date and was experiencing problems getting good scripts. Even the cast was unhappy with the material.

In 1961, Chevrolet was responsible for the show's move to Sunday nights (replacing *The Dinah Shore Show*), where it found a growth in popularity. In 1961, Lorne Greene had a hand in helping *Bonanza* succeed by threatening to quit if changes were not made in his character. He wanted to go from the Bible-quoting Ben Cartwright to a man showing warmth and strength and having a sense of humor — in short, more of a human being. He also wanted to have a warmer relationship with his sons and he suggested easing up on their over-protective attitude towards the Ponderosa.

Although Dortort wrote or co-wrote only four scripts in the first season, he had input on most of the shows (without credit) and would do so for most of the series. Before shooting began on an episode, Dortort had spent several weeks (give or take) with the writer, and he would work with the director for at least three days going over the script so that there would be no doubt as to what was to be done. It was his way of fine-tuning the show in an effort to make the material the best he could.

The plots, especially in the first several seasons, relied heavily on historical events and characters. Many of the events, however, could not have taken place during the time period of the stories. These inaccuracies did not seem to matter to fans. Dortort tried to incorporate historical facts in his fictional plots and characters. He believed that education should be a part of entertainment. *Bonanza* gave many writers and actors their first television breaks. The stories were to feature the Cartwright family as a group or individually. Even when the plot concerned a guest star, the Cartwrights were not to be passive onlookers. The problem and its solution was to be that of the Cartwrights. The boys often battled each other, but when the chips were down they stood united.

Despite the time period in which *Bonanza* was set, it dealt with themes that were current issues — racial prejudice, mercy killing, and problems of conscience. They also did love stories and even showed the lighter side of the Old West by lacing stories with comedy. The cast had no problems switching from drama to comedy. Michael Landon said that the network was not happy when they did a comedy episode but, with the show's growth in popularity, they did not interfere.

Bill and Joyce Anderson, who would later develop the idea of the Ponderosa

Ranch Theme Park, arrived at Incline Village in the early 1960s. Bill supplied a large development company with needed equipment. They also opened riding stables which would house horses used by _Bonanza_ while filming there. When accepting their roles, the cast claimed to be able to ride. None of the four stars were good riders. Blocker and Landon were sent to the stables for additional instruction after Blocker hurt his shoulder falling off his horse. Landon said Greene was a novice rider and that they all were unable to keep control of their horses while riding in a Rose Bowl Parade. The horses used in the series were rented from Fat Jones, who owned a North Hollywood ranch. Ben's horse was named Buck, Joe's was Cochise and Hoss was Chub. (No name was known for Adam's horse). In 1965, six film horses, including Cochise, were destroyed because they were mutilated by looters. The 12-year-old Cochise had been valued at $3,000. The replacement pinto had blacker markings then its predecessor and would later die from a heart attack.

By 1961, the Western was slipping in the ratings. _Bonanza_ survived because Dortort had wisely included elements in the show not normally seen in most Westerns.

Landon expressed a desire to write and direct. He persuaded Dortort to give him a chance. The producer supplied Michael with a number of old scripts to study. The idea for his first script "The Gamble" came to him during the 1962–63 season after production had shut down for the week. "We were told to take the next week off," Landon recalled. "Something about not having a suitable script."[3] He spent the weekend handwriting a story about the Cartwrights being accused of a bank robbery in another town. He showed up on Monday and handed Dortort the script. Frank Chase and Dortort helped Landon polish his story, after which shooting began.

Before _Bonanza_ left the air, Landon had written some 30 scripts and directed a dozen episodes, including his directorial debut "To Die in Darkness" (which he also wrote). His favorite episode that he wrote and directed was entitled "The Wish." Cinematographer Ted Voigtlander took Landon under his wing to teach him about camerawork and lighting.

Bonanza continued to grow rapidly in popularity. For ten of the 14 years, it remained in the top ten. Between 1964 and 1967 it became the most-watched program in the United States. A rumor had it that President Lyndon Johnson did not schedule his speeches during the show's time slot. Over 450 Bonanza Boosters (a fan club) formed across the country. The show became as popular overseas and included Queen Elizabeth II among its fans. The popularity spawned two albums (_Bonanza: Ponderosa Party Time_ and _Bonanza: Christmas on the Ponderosa_) as well as recordings by each of the cast members. The largest output was by Lorne Greene. Other _Bonanza_ merchandise included novels, comics, toys, board games, coloring books and lunch boxes which were sought after by younger fans. These items are valuable collectibles today. _Bonanza_ managed to kill its competition *Perry Mason* and *The Judy Garland Show.* During its peak period, over 5,000 letters poured in weekly.

Many famous celebrities asked to be on the show. With popularity came spoofs, including a Bob Hope–Bing Crosby sketch shot in the Ponderosa living room. ABC's *Maverick* also did a spoof on November 11, 1961: "Three Queens Full," where Jim Backus played Joe Wheelwright and lived on the Subrosa with his three sons Henry, Moose and Small Paul.

The September 1962 issue of *Mad* satirized the show as "Bananaz." The characters were called Pa, Yves, Ox and Short Mort Cartwheels and they lived on the Pawnderosa. The show also received a satirical playing on the cartoon *The Flintstones* and were known as the Cartrocks from the Rockarosa.

From the start, Pernell Roberts seemed unhappy doing a weekly series — acting as if it were beneath him. He felt that the time restraint of churning out a show every six days did not allow for character or plot development. He did not join in with the activities of his fellow colleagues, preferring to remain aloof. He complained about the quality of the scripts but appeared happier when the episode featured his character. He felt he was stagnating. He claimed the tension between himself and Michael Landon was the result of a misunderstanding. Roberts told Landon "that he was perpetuating bad acting habits ... that he was not getting the fullest potential from his talent ... that he wasn't developing himself.... Somehow he took it as a personal attack. He never forgot. I'm sorry."[4]

Roberts wanted to leave the show before 1965, but relented after NBC told him he would never work anywhere again. He claimed, to save his sanity, he would walk through his part. When Pernell threatened to leave the show, the character of Cousin Will Cartwright (Guy Williams) was created to fill the void if Roberts made good his threats. When Roberts could not get out of his contract, Dortort hoped that Adam and Laura (Kathie Browne) would marry and that the three characters would remain. He thought that Adam's marriage would expand Roberts' role and appease him.

But there was concern that the audience would not accept the marriage. Landon did not believe Will's character was a necessary addition to the cast and Greene agreed. Dortort wanted to find out how the public felt about Adam's marriage before he proceeded with additional scripts. After looking at thousands of fan letters, it was concluded by Dortort that the public wanted the Cartwrights to remain single. Williams and Browne remained on the show until May rather than depart as originally planned on March 22.

When Nevada celebrated its centennial, they made the stars honorary citizens. Only Greene, Blocker and Landon attended the ceremony.

"You've got to keep an actor happy if you want a great performance from him," Dortort said. "We offered [Roberts] more money, allowed him time off to do plays, everything."[5] The circumstances surrounding Roberts' departure after the 1964-65 season are known only to himself and it is a topic he wishes not to talk about. All he ever said was that he had grown tired of the character. Dortort felt Pernell was good and was willing to forgive his behavior if he changed his mind and returned to the show. The storyline allowed for the opportunity for his return.

In the fall of 1965, NBC aired "The Hostage" without commercials, using all the commercial time at the end to introduce Chevrolet's 1965 models. It had been tried in 1964 with success but was never attempted again.

Fans arrived at Incline Village looking for the Ponderosa seen on the burning Nevada map each Sunday but were disappointed to learn it did not exist. Bill Anderson approached NBC, Greene, Blocker and Landon with the idea of constructing such a ranch. He asked them to help back the project. They consented and in the summer of 1967 the Ponderosa Ranch was opened to the public. From 1967 to 1973 and later (for the recent TV movies), shooting frequently took place inside the ranch house and around Lake Tahoe as well as numerous other locations.

"Ride the Wind" was the show's first two-part episode. It concerned the Pony Express and received a citation from the U.S. Postal Service. "Ride the Wind" was released to foreign theaters in 1967.

In 1967, Dortort was credited as creator and executive producer because he was now involved not only with *Bonanza* but with a new series, *The High Chapparral*. He intended for the two casts to appear on each others shows but the plan never materialized.

A number of regulars were cast over the years. Victor Sen Yung (Hop Sing) joined the show during the first season, appearing in 14–18 episodes per year. He played the Cartwrights' indispensable cook and would stay with the show until the end of the run. Sheriff Roy Coffee (Ray Teal) became the law in Virginia City from 1960–1972. Deputy Clem Foster (Bing Russell) joined the cast during the fourth season to help Coffee. The two characters rarely appeared on the same episode. By the show's end, Clem was the only lawman in Virginia City. Before being cast as Clem, Russell had previously appeared in the episode "The Long Night."

While working on *The High Chaparral*, Dortort spotted David Canary filming a barroom scene with Paul Newman in the film *Hombre*. It was then that Dortort knew he had the Ponderosa's new foreman. It did not take long for Canary to fit in.

Lou Frizzel appeared in the episodes "The Mark of Guilt" and "The Lady and the Mark" as a guest star before being introduced as Dusty Rhoades in "The Horse Traders." He would leave the show in 1972.

Bonanza had the rare distinction of being one of the few shows to get better as it progressed.

When the twelfth season opened on September 13, 1970, changes had been made to the opening credits, and to Virginia City. A new theme, David Rose's "The Big Bonanza," replaced the original theme. Instead of the burning map, each Cartwright had their own action shots. Rose had delegated scoring chores to Harry Sukman in 1969.

Paramount Studios' production costs kept going up and *Bonanza* was able to make a better deal with Warner Bros. It was on these same streets that *Maverick* had spoofed *Bonanza* some nine years earlier. In "The Night Virginia City Died," the season's opening episode, the town was burned down by an arsonist (Clem's fiancée). Associate producer and writer John Hawkins wrote the story to explain Virginia City's new look. The viewers were the only ones who knew the arsonist's identity as she was killed by one of her own fires.

The character of Jamie Hunter (Mitch Vogel) was introduced in the episode "A Matter of Faith." The character was created to bring back the warmth lost after Ben's sons grew up. It would introduce problems that teenagers experienced. Before being cast as Jamie, Vogel had appeared in "The Real People of Muddy Creek."

Richard Thomas appeared in the episode "The Weary Willies" and Dortort wanted to add him to the cast, but the network brass told the producer there was not enough money in the budget for a new character.

After Dan Blocker's May 13, 1972, death the ratings began to decline and Greene and Landon felt that it would soon be the end of *Bonanza*. In addition to Blocker's death, other problems beset the series. Chevrolet dropped its sponsorship and NBC was not happy with the ratings. The show moved to Tuesday evenings. NBC paved the way for the change by airing reruns under the title *Ponderosa*.

"I begged the network not to move us," Dortort said, "that people were used to seeing us on Sunday after so many years."[6] The network told Dortort that other programs were eager for the Sunday time period.

David Canary had left the series at the end of the 1969-70 season to pursue writing and directing. "Two things happened just before I was asked to come back to *Bonanza* that made up my mind," Canary explained. "First, a pilot called *The Young Prosecutors* ... didn't get sold, then I heard that one of the very top filmmakers was having trouble raising money for his next picture. If he couldn't do it, I sure as hell wasn't going to be able to. So I came back."[7] He returned to *Bonanza* with the intention of getting a chance to write and direct some of the show's episodes, but the opportunity never presented itself.

David Rose's new theme was dropped in favor of the more familiar Livingston-Evans theme. Rose had won an Emmy for scoring the episode "The Love Child" and had been particularly proud of his score for the two-part

"Ride the Wind." He was also known for the themes for *The High Chaparral, Father Murphy, Little House on the Prairie* and *Highway to Heaven.*

Tim Matheson (Griff King) was added to the cast to appeal to Tuesday's younger viewers. He had been seen by Dortort in the 1969-70 season of *The Virginian.*

Landon and Greene found that their first day back on the set, following Blocker's death, to be hard and that everyone had to force themselves to be in good humor.

On a Monday, the cast was notified that *Bonanza* had been canceled and that shooting would end on Wednesday. Greene was annoyed at the short notice, figuring that after such a long run, they deserved more notice. Dortort asked that they at least be given permission to complete the season but his request met deaf ears.

The second longest running Western (*Gunsmoke* was the longest) had finally come to an end after 14 seasons. By 1973, *Bonanza* had been viewed by 480,000,000 viewers in 97 countries and had been dubbed in dozens of foreign languages.

By 1973, early episodes had been running in syndication on channels like TBS and the Family Channel. NBC never repeated any of the episodes from the last season and they were not seen again until shown on the Family Channel in 1988. After a number of years, TBS dropped *Bonanza* but the show continued to be aired on the Family Channel until it changed its entire lineup on August 15, 1998. The PAX Channel began airing *Bonanza* on September 5, 1998, starting with its first episode.

Some 15 years after *Bonanza's* cancellation, *Bonanza: The Next Generation* (1988) aired as a movie intended as a pilot for a series sequel. Greene had died before shooting began and John Ireland (as Ben's brother Aaron) took on the starring role. Michael Landon, Jr., played Benji, Little Joe's son, and Gillian Greene (Lorne's daughter) was featured as Jennie Sills. It did not sell and in 1992, Dortort tried *Bonanza: Legends of the Ponderosa* as a new series. Michael Landon, Jr., stayed on as Benji and Ben Johnson starred as an old friend of Ben's. Landon, Jr., was to write and direct many of the 26 episodes. "*Bonanza* was where my father got all of his breaks and wrote and directed and learned his craft," Landon, Jr., explained.[8]

Dortort felt the show deserved another chance and in the spring of 1993 *Bonanza: The Return* began production and was scheduled to air on NBC on Sunday, November 28, 1993, at 9 P.M. It was filmed at Lake Tahoe, Nevada, at the Bonanza Ranch Theme Park. A tribute, *Back to Bonanza*, preceded the TV movie at 7 P.M. Pernell Roberts was asked by Dortort to host the special, and Roberts turned him down. Landon, Jr., and Dirk Blocker shared the hosting duties. The special and film appeared on the Nielsen top ten.

A final film, *Bonanza: Under Attack* aired on NBC on January 15, 1995.

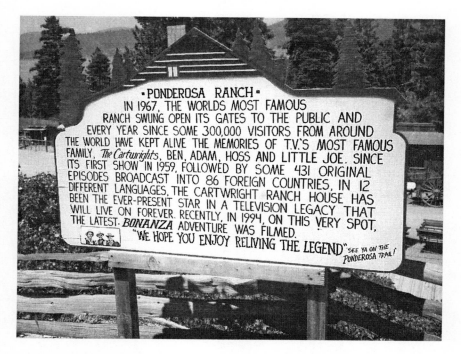

Sign located at the Ponderosa Theme Park. (Photograph by Linda F. Leiby.)

Landon, Jr., returned as Benji and Dirk Blocker, who played journalist Walter Finster in *Bonanza: The Return*, reprised his role in this 1995 TV film. To date this has been the last *Bonanza* project. Dortort had discussed doing three or four movies a year similar to the *Perry Mason* revivals and mention was made of doing a *Bonanza* Broadway musical, but as of this writing neither of these projects have surfaced.

Regardless, *Bonanza* lives on in reruns. Millions of visitors travel to the area yearly to visit the real Virginia City which was revived, in part, due to *Bonanza* and to visit the Ponderosa Ranch and its reconstructed Old West town. They come to enjoy the happy memories and relive the legend that was known as *Bonanza*.

NOTES

1. Greeneland, David. *Bonanza: A Viewer's Guide.* R & G Productions, 1997.
2. Poppy, John. "Worldwide Lure of *Bonanza. Look.* December 1, 1964.
3. Yoggy, Gary. *Riding the Video Range.* McFarland, 1995.
4. Shapiro, Melany. *Bonanza: The Unofficial Story of the Ponderosa.* Pioneer Books, 1993.

5. Greeneland, David. *Bonanza: A Viewer's Guide*. R & G Productions, 1997.
6. *Ibid.*
7. Shapiro, Melany. *Bonanza: The Unofficial Story of the Ponderosa*.
8. Sackett, Susan. *Primetime Hits*. Billboard, 1993.

PART II

Episode Guide

The following section provides a guide for 430 episodes comprising 431 hours of programming. A list of the regular cast (with character), the years spent with the series, and the show's credits are also given. The episodes are divided into seasons and for each the air date, writer, director, producer and executive producer (where applicable) are provided as well as a review (when available). The episode is preceded by an E and a number. An asterisk (*) indicates video availability.

Cast: Lorne Greene (Ben Cartwright 1959–1973); Pernell Roberts (Adam Cartwright 1959–1965); Dan Blocker (Hoss "Eric" Cartwright, 1959–1972); Michael Landon ("Little" Joe Cartwright, 1959–1973); Victor Sen Yung (Hop Sing, 1959–1973); Ray Teal (Sheriff Roy Coffee, 1960–1972); Bing Russell (Deputy Clem Foster, 1963–1973); David Canary ("Candy" Canaday, 1967–1970, 1972–1973); Mitch Vogel (Jamie Hunter Cartwright, 1970–1973); Lou Frizzell (Dusty Rhoades, 1970–1973); Guy Williams (Will Cartwright, 1964); Tim Matheson (Griff King, 1972–1973).

Credits: *Creator:* David Dortort. *Producers:* Robert Blees, Richard Collins, David Dortort, John Hawkins. *Directors:* Lewis Alies, Lewis Allen, Robert Altman, Richard Bartlett, Leon Benson, Bruce Bilson, Ralph E. Black, George Blair, John Brahm, Robert Butler, Thomas Carr, James B. Clark, William F. Claxton, Chris Christenberry, Nicholas Colasanto, Alan Crosland, Jr., Marc Daniels, Herschel Daugherty, Don Daves, William Dario Faralla, Felix Feist, John Florea, Robert L. Friend, Alvin Ganzer, Tay Garnett, Maury Geraghty, Murray Golden, Robert Gordon, Charles F. Hass, Harry Harris, Jr., Gunnar Hellstrom, Paul Henreid, Jesse Hibbs, Joseph Kane, Alf Kjellin,

Michael Landon, Paul Landres, Philip Leacock, Joseph H. Lewis, Josef Leytes, Arthur Lubin, Edward Ludwig, Gerald Mayer, David Orrick McDearmon, Don McDougall, Bernard J. McEveety, Vincent McEveety, Dick Moder, Irving J. Moore, Michael Moore, Hollingsworth Morse, Arthur H. Nadel, Paul Nickell, James Nielson, Christian Nyby, Gerd Oswald, Leo Penn, Joseph Pevney, John Peyser, Don Richardson, John Rich, Seymour Robbie, Sutton Roley, Charles R. Rondeau, Richard G. Safarian, Joseph Sargent, Robert Sparr, R. G. Springsteen, Herbert L. Strock, E. W. Swackhammer, Jacques Tourneur, Robert Totten, Virgel W. Vogel, Nick Webster, William Wiard, William Whitney, James P. Yarborough, Jean Yarbrough. *Writers:* Ed Adamson, Stanley Adams, Jerry Adelman, James Amesbury, U. S. Andersen, Anne Howard Bailey, Bill Ballinger, S. H. Barnett, Bill Barrett, Richard Barrett, Robert V. Barron, Juanita Bartlett, John Tucker Battle, Arnold Belgard, Jessica Benson, Louis Bercovitch, A. I. Bezzerides, Walter Black, Raphael D. Blau, William Blinn, Robert Bloomfield, Harold Jack Bloom, True Boardman, Joseph Bonaduce, William Bruckner, Robert Buckner, Jess Carneol, Dick Carr, Borden Chase, Frank Chase, Cy Chermak, John M. Chester, Suzanne Clauser, Lewis Clay, Frank Cleaver, Richard Collins, Kelly Covin, Gene L. Coon, William R. Cox, Oliver Crawford, Arthur Dales, Tom Davison, Gordon T. Dawson, Edward DeBlasio, Paul Leslie Dell, Joy Dexter, Meyer Dolinsky, David Dortort, Warren Douglas, William Driskill, John T. Dugan, Robert Duncan, Wanda Duncan, John Dunkel, Sidney Ellis, Fred Ferenberger, Matilda Ferro, Theodore Ferro, Michael Fessier, Michael Fisher, Jeffrey Fleece, John Florea, Jr., D. C. Fontana, Frederic Louis Fox, Robert Fresco, John Furia, Jr., Milton S. Gelman, George W. George, Judith George, Wally George, Peter Germano, Elliot Gilbert, Jackson Gillis, Mel Goldberg, Murray Golden, Charles Goodwin, Robert L. Goodwin, Leo Gordon, William P. Gordon, Morris Lee Green, Herman Groves, Alf Harris, John Hawkins, Ward Hawkins, George Lovell Hayes, Leonard Heideman, Arthur Heinemann, Shirl Hendrix, Helen B. Hicks, Lois Hire, Herman Hoffman, Joseph Hoffman, Jean Holloway, Robert I. Holt, Clair Huffacker, Don Ingalls, Clifford Irving, Norman Jacob, William Jerome, John A. Johns, John Joseph, Herbert Kastle, Norman Katkov, John T. Kelley, William Kelley, Paul King, Jonathan Knopf, William Koenig, Chester Krumholtz, Richard Landau, Michael Landon, Charles Lang, David Lang, William Douglas Langsford, Gil Lasky, Anthony Lawrence, William F. Leicester, Kay Leonard, Norman Lessing, Seeley Lester, Melvin Levy, Mort R. Lewis, Paul R. Link, Stephen Lord, Jack McClain, Richard P. McDonough, Leslie McErlaine, Brian McKay, Colin McKenzie, Steve McNeil, Steve McNill, Larry Markes, William Marks, Laurence Mascot, Esther Mayesh, Mark Michaels, Jack Miller, Richard N. Morgan, Donn Mullally, Joel Murcott, Dick Nelson, E. Jack Newman, Richard Newman, Eric Norden, R. Kamer Norris, Peter Packer, Jo Pagano, Marion

Parsonett, E. M. Parsons, Paul Leslie Peil, Samuel A. Peoples, Rod Peterson, Denne Petticlerc, Ken Pettus, Lee Pickett, Robert Pirosh, Abe Polsky, William D. Powell, June Randolph, William Raynor, Lewis Reed, Dean Riesner, Stanley Roberts, Jack Rumler, Robert Sabaroff, B. W. Sandefur, Donald S. Sanford, Alvin Sapinskey, Carol Saraceno, George Schneck, Paul Schneider, Harold Schumate, S. S. Schweiter, Tom Seller, Richard Shapiro, Alex Sharp, Olney Sherman, Barney Slater, George E. Slavin, Jack B. Sowards, George Stackalee, Douglas Day Stewart, H. B. Stone, Jr., Joseph Stone, N. B. Stone, Jr., William L. Stuart, Sandy Summerhays, Hazel Swanson, Harold Swanton, Don Tait, Nat Tanchuck, Mary Teri Taylor, Frank Telford, Mort Thaw, Palmer Thompson, Robert E. Thompson, Thomas Thompson, Ken Trevey, Karl Tunberg, Jack Turley, John Twist, Dan Ullman, Frank Unger, James Van Wagner, Lois Vittes, Ric Vollaeret, George Waggner, Al C. Ward, Arthur Weigarten, Halsted Welles, Robert Lyon Welsch, Richard Wendley, Carey Wilber, Myles Wilder, Martha Wilkerson, Anthony Wilson, Lewis Wood, Preston Wood, Robert Vincent Wright, William H. Wright, Gerry Prince Young, Mort Zarkoff. *Music:* Raoul Kraushaar, David Rose, Walter Scharf, Harry Sukman. *Theme Music "Bonanza":* Ray Evans, Jay Livingston. *Music Supervisor:* William Lava. *Art Directors:* Preston Ames, Carl Anderson, John Burch, Earl Hedrick, Hal Pereira. *Set Decorators:* Sam Comer, Grace Gregory. *Photographers:* Haskell Boggs, Walter H. Castle, Lester Shorr, William Snyder, Ted Voigtlander, William F. Whitney. *Makeup:* Frank Westmore, Wally Westmore. *Associate Producers:* John Hawkins, James W. Lane, Thomas Thompson. *Production Supervisors:* John Banes, Kent McCray. *Production Executives:* James W. Lane, Robert Stillman. *Story Consultants:* Frank Cleaver, Leonard Heideman, Richard P. McDonagh. *Unit Production Manager:* Andrew J. Durkus. *Hair Stylist:* Nellie Manley. *Casting Supervisor:* William Maybery. *Story Editor:* Thomas Thompson. *Editors:* Marvin Coil, Everett Douglas, Ellsworth Hoagland, George Walters. *Assistant Directors:* Ralph E. Black, J. Walter Daniels, Bud Drill, Dale Hutchinson, Charles L. Scott, Jack Voglin. *Sound Recording:* Lyle Figland, Harold Lewis, Winston Leverett, Harry Lindgren, Joel Moss, John Wilkinson. *Technical Advisors:* Harry Cook, Dave Kashner.

The following are the days and times on which *Bonanza* aired during its 14-year run: September 1959–September 1961: NBC, Saturday 7:30–8:30 P.M.; September 1961–May 1972: NBC, Sunday 9:00–10:00 P.M.; May 1972–August 1972: NBC, Tuesday 7:30–8:30 P.M.; September 1972–January 1973: NBC, Tuesday 8:00–9:00 P.M.

First Season
(September 12, 1959–April 3, 1960)

*E1. *A Rose for Lotta* (September 12, 1959)

Credits: *Writer:* David Dortort. *Director:* Edward Ludwig. *Producer:* David Dortort. **Starring:** Lorne Greene, Pernell Roberts, Dan Blocker, Michael Landon. **Supporting Cast:** Yvonne DeCarlo (Lotta Crabtree); George MacReady (Alpheus Troy); Barry Kelley (Aaron Hopper); Willis Bouchey (George Garvey); Christopher Dark (Langford Pool); Victor Sen Yung (Hop Sing); Sammee Tong (Hop Ling); Ned Glass (Coach Driver).

Synopsis: Alpheus Troy needs trees from the Ponderosa in his mining business but Ben will not sell. Undaunted, Troy acquires the services of actress Lotta Crabtree to entice Joe Cartwright to her room, where Alpheus plans to kidnap him as ransom for the trees. Lotta's wagon loses a wheel on the Ponderosa. The Cartwrights fix it and Joe escorts her back to town. After the show, Joe and Lotta talk about New Orleans and Joe's mother, Marie, in her room. Two men enter and a fight ensues.

Review: *Variety* (September 16, 1959): The reviewer felt that "for all its pretentions [*Bonanza*] proves to be little more than a patchwork of stock oater ideas without a fresh twist to distinguish it.... It had a pathetically overworked storyline that was predictable and cliche-ridden.... The show received capable performances from its regulars, Lorne Greene, Pernell Roberts, Dan Blocker, and Landon, but they play stock roles and there's little opportunity for anyone to do a standout job.... *Bonanza* at this point doesn't show much promise of living up to its name."

Note: Location filming took place in Los Angeles and the surrounding area. The real Lotta Crabtree would have been 12 in 1859, the time period of this episode.

E2. *The Sun Mountain Herd* (September 19, 1959)

Credits: *Writers:* Gene L. Coon, David Dortort. *Director:* Paul Landres. *Producer:* David Dortort. **Starring:** Lorne Greene, Pernell Roberts, Dan Blocker, Michael Landon. **Supporting Cast:** Barry Sullivan (Mark Burdette); Leo Gordon (Early Thorne); Bel Nelson (Glory); Karl Swenson (Carl Harris); Harry Bartell (Winnemucca); Ron Soble (Tokwa); Jeanne Bates (Stella Harris); Robin Warga (Michael Harris); Jay Hector (Harold Harris); Zon Murray (Miner).

Synopsis: Mark Burdette and Early Thorne arrive in Virginia City planning to get rich by killing Indian herds of antelope and charging the miners $10 a pound for the meat. When Ben discovers Chief Winnemucca and another Indian are stealing Ponderosa cattle, he catches onto what Burdette and Thorne are doing. He thwarts their plans by selling cattle for $20 each. Dressing as Indians, Burdette and Thorne attack miners who are buying cattle from Ben.

Note: The exterior footage was shot at Iverson Movie Ranch. This episode was based on actual events and was narrated by Lorne Greene.

E3. *The Newcomers* (September 26, 1959)

Credits: *Writer:* Thomas Thompson. *Director:* Christian Nyby. *Producer:*

David Dortort. **Starring:** Lorne Greene, Pernell Roberts, Dan Blocker, Michael Landon. **Supporting Cast:** Inger Stevens (Emiley Pennington); John Larch (Blake McCall); Robert Knapp (John Pennington); Charles Maxwell (Krug); George J. Lewis (Jose Moreno); Byron Foulger (Justin Flannery); Diane Grey (Wyoming); Jon Lormer (Doc Riley); Martin Mason (1st Miner); Troy Melton (Merrill).

Synopsis: Blake McCall and his partner John Pennington are headed across the Ponderosa. Ben is concerned because they are in the business of hydraulic mining and he is afraid his land will be damaged. He demands they leave his property. John assures Ben they are only bringing his sister Emily (Blake's fiancée) to a climate better suited for her respiratory disease.

McCall is really interested in the land and has his men ambush Mr. Flannery, a botanist, who is traveling with them. The Cartwrights are blamed for his murder.

Note: Before this episode was aired, the public, cast, area brass and network representatives attended a preview at the Granada Theatre in Reno, Nevada. Location filming took place at Big Bear, California. Exterior footage of the ranch house was shown for the first time in this episode.

E4. *The Paiute War* (October 3, 1959)

Credits: *Writer:* Gene L Coon. *Director:* Paul Landres. *Producer:* David Dortort. **Starring:** Lorne Greene, Pernell Roberts, Dan Blocker, Michael Landon. **Supporting Cast:** Jack Warden (Mike Wilson); Anthony Caruso (Chief Winnemucca); Mike Forest (Young Winnemucca); Walter Coy, Douglas Kennedy, Howard Petrie, Peter Coe, George Keymas, Michael Ryan, I. Stanford Jolley, Gregg Martell.

Synopsis: Four Paiutes ride into the Wilson Trading Post and proprietor Jack Wilson keeps and mistreats the two women. Adam and a brave rescue them and Wilson flees to avoid punishment.

When Indian raids are made on wagons and small ranches, Wilson accuses the Paiutes. In reality, the Bannock Indians are responsible. Ben and Adam convince the townspeople to ride with them to talk to Winnemucca. Wilson shoots an Indian which results in a battle between the militia and the Paiutes. Adam is taken hostage by the indians.

Note: The Pyramid Lake War in May-June of 1860 was the basis for this episode. Location filming of the battle scenes took place at Iverson Movie Ranch.

*E5. *Enter Mark Twain* (October 10, 1959)

Credits: *Writer:* Harold Shumate. *Director:* Paul Landres. *Producer:* David Dortort. **Starring:** Lorne Greene, Pernell Roberts, Dan Blocker, Michael Landon. **Supporting Cast:** Howard Duff (Samuel Langhorn Clemens); John Litel (Judge Yerrington); Dorothy Green (Minaie); Victor Sen Yung (Hop Sing); Ann Whitfield (Rosemary); Percy Helton (Blurry Jones); Patrick McVey (Bill Raleigh); Edmund Lyon, Lane Bradford, Arthur Lovejoy, Robert Carson.

Synopsis: Samuel Clemens has arrived in Virginia City and takes a job with the *Territorial Enterprise*. After he hears about the sighting of a wild man on the Ponderosa, he writes a story in the paper. The article draws curiosity seekers to the ranch, much to the annoyance of the Cartwrights.

The wild man turns out to be a young woman, Rosemary Larson. She had witnessed some men kill her father. Uncovering the true identity of the "wild man," the Cartwrights demand Clemens write a retraction to keep people off the Ponderosa. Sam composes an unsatisfactory retraction.

When Clemens begins writing negative articles on political candidate, Judge Yerrington he is hit on the head as a warning to stop the articles.

Note: Sam Clemens was hired as a reporter in Virginia City in 1862–1864 by Territorial Enterprise owners Joseph T. Goodman and Dennis McCarthy.

E6. *The Julia Bulette Story* (October 7, 1959)

Credits: *Writer:* Al Ward. *Director:* Christian Nyby. *Producer:* David Dortort. **Starring:** Lorne Greene, Pernell Roberts, Dan Blocker, Michael Landon. **Supporting Cast:** Jane Greer (Julia Bulette); Alexander Scourby (John Millain); Victor Sen Yung (Hop Sing); Harry Seymour (Piano Player); Robert J. Stevenson (George Romley); Kem Dibbs (Sheriff Olins); Roy Engel, Kay Kuter, Mary Munday, Rush Williams, Robert B. Williams.

Synopsis: Joe defends saloon owner Julia Bulette from a Frenchman. To thank him, she invites him to dinner. Joe becomes enchanted by her due in part to her being a Frenchwoman from New Orleans (as was his mother). The two are frequently seen together and become the talk of the town. Ben is not pleased with the relationship because of her past and the differences in their ages. He asks Julia to stop seeing Joe. She agrees but later changes her mind.

When a doctor announces a scarlet fever epidemic, Julia offers her help and the use of her saloon to take care of the sick. After the epidemic, the Sheriff rides to the Ponderosa to announce that Julia has been stabbed and robbed.

Note: Julia Bulette did offer her saloon to help the sick during an epidemic and was murdered by Jean Millain in 1867.

E7. *The Saga of Annie O'Toole* (October 24, 1959)

Credits: *Writer:* Thomas Thompson. *Director:* Joseph Kane. *Producer:* David Dortort. **Starring:** Lorne Greene, Pernell Roberts, Dan Blocker, Michael Landon. **Supporting Cast:** Ida Lupino (Annie O'Toole); Alan Hale, Jr. (Swede Lundberg); John Patrick (Kevin O'Toole); Harry Lascoe (Gregory Spain); Richard Reeves (Clayton); Ollie O'Toole (Simpson); Victor Sen Yung (Hop Sing).

Synopsis: Annie O'Toole arrives in the Washoe to take over a mining claim that her fiance Swede Lundberg had filed for her. Meanwhile, her father "Himself" dies and is buried by Hoss. When Annie thanks him by cooking a meal, the miners are attracted by the smell of the food. Adam convinces her to open a restaurant to feed the men.

Swede arrives and tells Annie he sold one of the two claims to Gregory Spain but can not remember which one. Spain is sure she is on his property. Ben sets up a miner's court to decide who is the rightful owner.

Note: Location filming took place at Bronson Canyon in Griffith Park. Pernell Roberts did a voiceover.

E8. *The Philip Diedeshiemer Story* (October 31, 1959)

Credits: *Writer:* Thomas Thompson. *Director:* Joseph Kane. *Producer:* David Dortort. **Starring:** Pernell Roberts, Dan Blocker. **Supporting Cast:** John Beal

(Philip Diedeshiemer); Mala Powers (Helene); R. G. Armstrong (Andrew Holloway); Charles Cooper (Gil Fenton); Paul Birch (Tregalis); Mae Marsh.

Synopsis: A number of deadly cave-ins have beset the Ophir Mine. Superintendent Gil Fenton blames owner Andrew Holloway (his future father-in-law) for not spending the money to make the mine safe. German engineer Philip Diedeshiemer is brought in to have a look at the situation. Gil and Adam join him

Replica of the square-set system designed by Philip Diedshiemer. (Photograph by Linda F. Leiby.)

in the mine when another cave-in occurs. Hoss comes to their rescue but Gil does not make it out alive.

Diedeshiemer comes up with a square-set timbering system but Holloway and the other miners refuse to implement it, not wanting to absorb the cost. Adam and Philip secretly install the system. The mine owners learn about their plans and come to stop them.

Note: Philip Diedeshiemer invented the square-set system, on which this episode is based, in December 1860.

E9. *Mr. Henry Comstock* (November 7, 1959)

Credits: *Writer:* David Dortort. *Director:* John Brahm. *Producer:* David Dortort. **Starring:** Lorne Greene, Pernell Roberts, Dan Blocker, Michael Landon. **Supporting Cast:** Jack Carson (Henry T. P. Comstock); Joanna Sages (Princess Saratuchee); Terence De Marney (Pat O'Reilly); Jack Mathers (Heck Turner); Richard Cutting (Old Virginny); Bruce Gordon (Winnemucca); Charles Wagenheim (Pike); John Dierkes (Pat McLaughlin); Abel Fernandez (Lean Knife).

Synopsis: After rescuing Henry Comstock from four men, the Cartwrights invite him to the Ponderosa for dinner. Henry leaves for Washoe to sell whiskey to the miners. When two men discover gold, Comstock claims ownership of the land where the gold was uncovered.

Joe has met Saratuchee, daughter of Chief Winnemucca, and has taken a liking to her. Saratuchee secretly agrees to meet Joe later and go with him to a dance. Hoss and Joe are enjoying themselves at the dance when Chief Winnemucca and his braves arrive to take his daughter home.

Comstock's partner announces a gold strike. Henry takes advantage of the miners by selling stock at $100 a share.

Note: The evolution of Virginia City and the Comstock Lode, in 1859, was the basis for this episode.

E10. *The Magnificent Adah* (November 14, 1959)

Credits: *Writer:* Donald S. Sanford. *Director:* Christian Nyby. *Producer:* David Dortort. **Starring:** Lorne Greene, Pernell Roberts, Dan Blocker, Michael Landon. **Supporting Cast:** Ruth Roman (Adah Menken); Don Megowan (John C. Regan); Victor Sen Yung (Hop Sing); Hal K. Smith (Watkyns); Mauritz Hugo (Hotel Manager); William Mims, Fay Roope, Nancy Root.

Synopsis: Adam, Hoss and Joe sneak into Virginia City to see actress Adah Menken at the Piper's Opera House in the play *Mazeppa*. The young Cartwrights go to the saloon after the show and are surprised to learn that Adah is an old friend of Ben's.

When Ben takes a room at the hotel to protect Adah from a former lover, boxer John Regan, Ben's sons suspect he has become interested in the actress. Each, in turn, try to discover her intentions.

E11. *The Truckee Strip* (November 21, 1959)

Credits: *Writer:* Herman Groves. *Director:* Christian Nyby. *Producer:* David Dortort. **Starring:** Lorne Greene, Pernell Roberts, Dan Blocker, Michael Landon.

Supporting Cast: James Coburn (Pete Jessup); Carl Benton Reid (Luther Bishop); S. John Launer (Jason Cauter); Adrienne Hayes, Charles Horvath, John Merrick, Peter Chong, Jim Hayward.

Synopsis: The Cartwrights and Luther Bishop are feuding over a piece of land between their ranches. Jason Cauter, a wealthy man, is interested in the property for its timber but Bishop refuses to sell him any.

Cauter, with the help of Pete Jessup (one of Bishop's men), decides to stir things up by cutting a tree on the strip. While chasing one of the culprits, Joe runs across Amy Bishop. They meet at the same spot several times and fall in love, planning to marry despite their families' dispute. Jessup continues causing trouble by rustling Bishop's horses and blaming the Cartwrights.

Note: Location filming took place around Big Bear, California.

E12. *The Hanging Posse* (November 28, 1959)

Credits: *Writer:* Carey Wilbur. *Director:* Christian Nyby. *Producer:* David Dortort. **Starring:** Lorne Greene, Pernell Roberts, Dan Blocker, Michael Landon. **Supporting Cast:** Onslow Stevens (Flint Johnson); Adam Williams (Blackie Marks); Arthur Hunnicutt (Piute); Ray Hemhill (Buck); Alan Reed, Jr., Ron Haggerty, Robert Kline, Dick Rich, George Sawaya, Evelyn Scott, Barbara Pepper.

Synopsis: Three men ride onto the Johnson ranch in search of food. Blackie shoots and kills the rancher's wife. When Flint Johnson forms a posse, Joe and Adam join up, fearing he is planning to avenge his wife's murder rather than bring the culprits to trial.

E13. *Vendetta* (December 5, 1959)

Credits: *Writer:* Robert E. Thompson. *Director:* Joseph Kane. *Producer:* David Dortort. **Starring:** Lorne Greene, Pernell Roberts, Dan Blocker, Michael Landon. **Supporting Cast:** Mort Mills (Carl Morgan); Simon Scott (Tom Pryor); William Quinn (Doc Travis); William Pullen (Sheriff Toller); Steve Rowland (Billy Morgan).

Synopsis: After Adam and Joe leave for Sacramento to buy cattle, Ben and Hoss head for the bank but walk in on a robbery. When Hoss comes to the aid of the teller, Ben is shot but manages to wound Billy Morgan.

The Sheriff rides out after the Morgans but walks into a trap and is killed. Billy succumbs to his injuries and Carl Morgan seeks revenge on Ben and the town.

E14. *The Sisters* (December 12, 1959)

Credits: *Writer:* Carey Wilbur. *Director:* Christian Nyby. *Producer:* David Dortort. **Starring:** Lorne Greene, Pernell Roberts, Dan Blocker, Michael Landon. **Supporting Cast:** Buddy Ebsen (Sheriff Standers); Fay Spain (Sue Ellen Terry); Victor Sen Yung (Hop Sing); Malcolm Atterbury (Ol' Virginny); Jean Willes, John Stephenson, Charles Meredith, Clarke Alexander.

Synopsis: Adam has taken a liking to Sue Ellen Terry and gets into a duel to defend the saloon girl's honor. He takes her to the Ponderosa for dinner where she tries to impress Ben with made-up stories about her background. When Adam takes Sue Ellen home, she is ambushed and killed. He is arrested for her murder.

E15. *The Last Hunt* (December 19, 1959)

Credits: *Writer:* Donald S. Sanford. *Director:* Christian Nyby. *Producer:* David Dortort. **Starring:** Lorne Greene, Pernell Roberts, Dan Blocker, Michael Landon. **Supporting Cast:** Chana Eden (Shoshone Girl); Steven Terrell (Jason Kyle); Carlyle Mitchell (Doctor); Raymond Bailey (Sumner Kyle); Victor Sen Yung (Hop Sing).

Synopsis: While Hoss and Joe are in the mountains hunting big horn sheep, an Indian girl in search of her husband sneaks into their camp and collapses as she is about to have a baby. Joe and Hoss build a lean-to where she gives birth to a blue-eyed baby boy, which means the father is white. As a blizzard is approaching, they are anxious to get off the mountain and back to the Ponderosa.

The next morning, the girl and the baby are almost taken by six Shoshone Indians in attempt to return the girl to her father, the chief.

Note: Location filming took place at Big Bear, California.

E16. *El Toro Grande* (January 2, 1960)

Credits: *Writer:* John Tucker Battle. *Director:* Christian Nyby. *Producer:* David Dortort. **Starring:** Lorne Greene, Pernell Roberts, Dan Blocker, Michael Landon. **Supporting Cast:** Ricardo Cortez (Don Xavier Losaro); Barbara Luna (Cayetena Losaro); Armand Alzamora (Edwardo Montalban); Jose Gonzalez Gonzalez (Valiente); Alma Bettram (Maria Teresa); Alan Roberts (Epiphania); Penny Santon (Esmerelda); Tina Menard, Ralph Moody, Rodd Redwing, Don Kelly, Duane Cress.

Synopsis: Hoss and Joe leave for Monterey with $15,000 to buy "El Rojo Grande" (big red bull) from Don Xavier Losaro. After dinner, they go to look at the bull but find it missing as a small Mexican boy has taken his pet to protect him.

The next morning, El Rojo Grande is loaded onto a wagon with the boy. Later that night, the lad's parents arrive. After supper, Don's daughter Cayetena is discovered as a stowaway. She has come to marry Joe. Don Xavier arrives with Cayentena's fiance Edwardo Montalban, who challenges Joe to a duel.

E17. *The Outcast* (January 9, 1960)

Credits: *Writer:* Thomas Thompson. *Director:* Lewis Allen. *Producer:* David Dortort. **Starring:** Lorne Greene, Pernell Roberts, Dan Blocker, Michael Landon. **Supporting Cast:** Susan Oliver (Leta Malvet); Jack Lord (Clay Renton); Edward C. Platt (Harvey Bufford); Mark Allen (Garth) Irene Tedrow, Robert Lieb, Joel Ashley.

Synopsis: The Cartwrights ride into town to find that Leta Malvert's father and brother have been hung for murder. The townspeople snub her. Needing someone to trust, she takes up with outlaw Clay Renton against the Cartwrights' advise.

When plans to steal the Ponderosa's payroll fail, Clay and his men rob Bufford's store of $50 during Virginia City's bazaar.

E18. *House Divided* (January 16, 1960)

Credits: *Writer:* Al C. Ward. *Director:* Lewis Allen. *Producer:* David Dortort. **Starring:** Lorne Greene, Pernell Roberts, Dan Blocker, Michael Landon. **Supporting Cast:** Cameron Mitchell (Fred Kyle); Stacy Harris (Regis); Mickey

Simpson (Northern Miner); John Locke (Southern Miner); Marianne Stewart (Lily); Howard Wendell (Mine Owner); John Anderson, Dan Riss, Kenneth MacDonald, Stafford Repp, Barry Cahill.

Synopsis: Seeking silver and gold to support the cause of the Confederacy, Fred Kyle arrives in Virginia City. He asks Joe to introduce him to the mine owners. Joe becomes enchanted by Kyle after learning he was an old friend of his mother's in New Orleans.

Adam becomes aware of what is going on and tells Ben. Friction develops between the two brothers as Joe defends Kyle.

*E19. *The Gunman* (January 23, 1960)

Credits: *Writer:* Carey Wilbur. *Director:* Christian Nyby. *Producer:* David Dortort. **Starring:** Dan Blocker, Michael Landon. **Supporting Cast:** Ellen Corby (Lora Doone Mayboy); Douglas Spencer (Alonzo McFadden); Henry Hull (B. Bannerman Brown); Jonathan Gilmore (Anse Hadfield); George Mitchell (Jubal); King Donovan, Dennis Holmes, Ann Graves, Jenny Maxwell, Billy McLean, Dorothy Neumann, Jody Fair, Dorothy Crehan.

Synopsis: While buying cattle in Texas, Joe and Hoss head for Keowa Flats to have a drink. Claiming to know the Slade Brothers, the town drunk identifies Hoss and Joe as the gunmen because they are lookalikes. The Cartwrights explain who they are but no one believes them and they are arrested.

Believing they are the Slades, Alonzo McFadden helps them to escape and employs them to do away with Anse Hadfield, with whom he is feuding. They resist but are given the option to do the job or hang.

Note: The roles of Big Jake Slade and Shorty Jim Slade were portrayed by Dan Blocker and Michael Landon.

*E20. *The Fear Merchants* (January 30, 1960)

Credits: *Writers:* Frank Unger, Thomas Thompson. *Director:* Lewis Allen. *Producer:* David Dortort. **Starring:** Lorne Greene, Pernell Roberts, Dan Blocker, Michael Landon. **Supporting Cast:** Gene Evans (Andrew Fulmer); Victor Sen Yung (Hop Sing); Pat Michon (Sally Ridley); Helen Westcott (Amanda Ridley); Ray Stricklyn (Billy Wheeler); Christopher Dark (Jesse Tibbs); Guy Lee (Jimmy Chong); Frank Ferguson, Philip Ahn, Arthur Space, Gregg Barton, Alexander Campbell, Peter Chong.

Synopsis: After Hop Sing and his family experience some trouble, Ben goes to mayoral candidate Andy Fulmer, whose campaigning is prejudicial against the Chinese.

Jimmy Chong, Hop Sing's nephew, works in Mr. Ridley's livery stable. When one of Fulmer's men bothers Sally Ridley, Jimmy comes to her defense. Ridley confronts Sally and Jimmy, and she is accidentally shot. At the inquest, Jimmy is held over for trial on murder charges.

*E21. *The Spanish Grant* (February 6, 1960)

Credits: *Writers:* Leonard Heideman, David Dortort, Morris Lee Green. *Director:* Christian Nyby. *Producer:* David Dortort. **Starring:** Lorne Greene, Pernell

Ponderosa Ranch House. (Photograph by Linda F. Leiby.)

Roberts, Dan Blocker, Michael Landon. **Supporting Cast:** Patricia Medina (Rosita Morales); Sabastian Cabot (Don Antonio Luga); Paul Picerni (Sanchez); Michael Ragan (High Card Smith); Victor Sen Yung (Hop Sing); Celia Lovsky, Ned Wever, Salvador Baguez, John Merrick, Claudia Bryar, Stuart Randall, Genaro Gomez.

Synopsis: Luga and Sanchez want a large section of Nevada territory which includes a part of the Ponderosa and acquire the services of Rosita Morales to help them with their unscrupulous plans. Upon her arrival in Virginia City, Rosita pretends to be Isabella Maria Inez de la Cuesta, heir to the de la Cuesta land grant.

Ben becomes concerned about the validity of Isabella's claim. He becomes especially suspicious when a rancher is killed by Luga after refusing to give up his land.

*E22. *Blood on the Land* (February 13, 1960)

Credits: *Writer:* Robert E. Thompson. *Director:* Felix Feist. *Producer:* David Dortort. **Starring:** Lorne Greene, Pernell Roberts, Dan Blocker, Michael Landon. **Supporting Cast:** Everett Sloane (Jeb Drummond); Ray Daley (Billy); Tom Reese (Burton); Ken Lynch, Jerry Oddo, Glen Holtzman.

Synopsis: On his way to market, Jeb Drummond brings his flock of sheep onto the Ponderosa, allowing them to graze as they go. The Cartwrights find Drummond and, fearing the sheep will damage the land, order him to leave. Seeing the possibilities of the Ponderosa, he decides to take the land for himself.

When the Cartwrights learn Drummond is still on the Ponderosa, Adam wants to go to the Sheriff but is vetoed by his father. The four ride out to confront Drummond but Adam is taken hostage.

*E23. *Desert Justice* (February 20, 1960)

Credits: *Writer:* Donald S. Sanford. *Director:* Lewis Allen. *Producer:* David Dortort. **Starring:** Lorne Greene, Pernell Roberts, Dan Blocker, Michael Landon. **Supporting Cast:** Claude Akins (Marshall Emmett Dowd); Wesley Lau (Dave Walker); Fintan Meyler (Andrea); Ron Hayes (Hurd Cutler); John Wengraf (Dr. Strasser); Bud Osborne (Charlie); Bill Wright (Bailey); Tom Greenway.

Synopsis: Dave Walker, one of Ben's hired hands, is arrested by Marshall Emmett Dowd for murdering a paymaster and causing the death of Dowd's wife.

Dowd puts the shackled Dave onto the stage which is headed for Los Angeles. Because Adam and Hoss found their friend beaten in his cell, they decide to accompany him on the trip to insure his safe arrival.

*E24. *The Stranger* (February 27, 1960)

Credits: *Writers:* Leonard Heideman, Oliver Crawford. *Director:* Christian Nyby. *Producer:* David Dortort. **Starring:** Lorne Greene, Pernell Roberts, Dan Blocker, Michael Landon. **Supporting Cast:** Lloyd Nolan (Charles Leduque); Robert Foulk (Sheriff); Joan Staley (Dixie); Hal Baylor (Tom Cole); Charles Tannen (Clerk); Donald Foster (Alfred Gibbons); Arthur Shields, Elizabeth York, Jomarie Pettit, Hank Worden.

Synopsis: Reading in the paper that Ben is running for governor of Nevada, Charles Leduque, a New Orleans police inspector who blames him for his bad leg, comes to Virginia City in an attempt to force Ben to withdraw from the governorship race. He presents a warrant for his arrest for the 20-year-old murder of La Roche, who blackmailed Marie about her past and was killed by Ben in a fair fight.

*E25. *Escape to Ponderosa* (March 5, 1960)

Credits: *Writers:* Robert E. Thompson, Bill Barrett. *Director:* Charles F. Haas. *Producer:* David Dortort. **Starring:** Lorne Greene, Pernell Roberts, Dan Blocker, Michael Landon. **Supporting Cast:** Joe Maross (Sutton); Gloria Talbott (Neda); Grant Williams (Tyler); James Parnell (Mertz); Chris Alcaide (Captain Bolton); Dayton Lummis (Colonel Metcalfe); Sherwood Price (Corporal).

Synopsis: Mertz, Sutton and Tyler escape from the Army stockade and are being tracked by Captain Bolton. The captain searches the Ponderosa for the escapees.

Leaving Mertz behind, Sutton tells Tyler that they can hide out at his girlfriend Neda's ranch. Meanwhile Mertz refuses to divulge the whereabouts of his cohorts and is beaten relentlessly by Bolton. When Ben reports Bolton's brutality to Colonel Metcalfe, the Colonel backs up the Captain but warns Bolton to watch his step.

*E26. *The Avenger* (March 19, 1960)

Credits: *Writer:* Clair Huffacker. *Director:* Christian Nyby. *Producer:* David Dortort. **Starring:** Lorne Greene, Pernell Roberts, Dan Blocker, Michael Landon. **Supporting Cast:** Vic Morrow (Lassiter); Jean Allison (Sally); Dan White (Jackson); Bern Bassey (Giles); Nestor Paiva (Thornton); Robert Griffin (Sheriff Hansen); Richard Devon, James Anderson, Harry Swoger, Ian Wolfe, Eugene Martin, Bill Catching, Robert Brubaker.

Synopsis: Ben and Adam are in jail for the murder of Sally's father. As the hanging approaches, Hoss and Joe make one last attempt to get Sally to change her testimony but to no avail. Hawkins and his men thwart their efforts to have a petition signed to stop the hanging.

Lassiter arrives to see if the men in jail are responsible for the lynching of his father. Realizing that Ben and Adam are not the ones he is looking for, he sides with the Cartwrights.

Note: This was the pilot for an unsold spinoff.

E27. *The Last Trophy* (March 26, 1960)

Credits: *Writer:* Bill Ballinger. *Director:* Lewis Alies. *Producer:* David Dortort. **Starring:** Lorne Greene, Pernell Roberts, Dan Blocker, Michael Landon. **Supporting Cast:** Hazel Court (Lady Beatrice Dunsford); Edward Ashley (Lord Marion Dunsford); Bert Freed (Simon Betcher); Ken Mayer (Whitey).

Synopsis: Lord Marion and Lady Beatrice Dunsford, who knew Ben back in New Orleans, arrive at the Ponderosa and reminisce about the past.

When Adam intervenes for Lord Marion, who refuses to defend himself against Simon Betcher, Lady Beatrice thinks her husband is a coward. Adam and the Dunsfords embark on a cougar hunt, at Ben's suggestion, to help Marion's confidence.

E28. *San Francisco* (April 2, 1960)

Credits: *Writer:* Thomas Thompson. *Director:* Arthur Lubin. *Producer:* David Dortort. **Starring:** Lorne Greene, Dan Blocker, Michael Landon. **Supporting Cast:** Robert Nichols (Johnny); O. Z. Whitehead (Hamp); Murvyn Vye (Cut-Rate Joe); Victor Sen Yung (Hop Sing); Kathleen Crowley (Kathleen); David White (Mr. Pendleton/Shanghai Pete); Richard Deacon (Captain Shark); Herb Vigran (Bartender); Tor Johnson (Busthead Brannigan); James Hong, Stephen Roberts, Michael Ross, Donnelly Rhodes.

Synopsis: After a cattle drive, the Cartwrights and two hands, Johnny and Hemp, vacation in San Francisco. Ben warns them to stay out of trouble but the hands are shanghaied. With the help of Hop Sing and his cousins, the others search for the missing men to no avail.

Ben goes into Alexander Pendleton's saloon in search of information but he too is shanghaied.

*E29. *Bitter Water* (April 9, 1960)

Credits: *Writer:* Harold Jack Bloom. *Director:* George Blair. *Producer:* David Dortort. **Starring:** Lorne Greene, Pernell Roberts, Dan Blocker, Michael Landon. **Supporting Cast:** Don Dubbins (Tod McKaren); Merry Anders (Virginia); Robert F. Simon (Len Keith); Ken Becker (Tucker); Rhys Williams.

Synopsis: Miner Len Keith is interested in land owned by rancher Andy McKaren that adjoins the Ponderosa. Tod McKaren encourages his father to sell as he and Keith's daughter Virginia are lovers and her father has promised to make him a partner.

Ben reminds his friend Andy that mining would pollute the water on his ranch. The rancher tells Len that his land is not for sale. The miner, intent on getting what he wants, slips some cattle, sick with tick fever, onto the Ponderosa in an effort to cause a rift between the McKarens and the Cartwrights.

*E30. *Feet of Clay* (April 16, 1960)

Credits: *Writer:* John Florea, Jr. *Director:* Arthur Lubin. *Producer:* David Dortort. **Starring:** Lorne Greene, Pernell Roberts, Dan Blocker, Michael Landon. **Supporting Cast:** David Ladd (Billy Allen); Logan Field (Vance Allen); Robert Tetrick (Pike); Victor Sen Yung (Hop Sing); Tom Greenway, Guy Prescott, Philip Grayson, John Eldredge, Riza Royce.

Synopsis: After Billy Allen's mother is buried, he goes to the Ponderosa to stay until his uncle arrives. While there, Billy grows quite fond of Hoss.

Vance Allen, Billy's father, and Pike escape from prison and they commit a stage robbery and murder. While lying low for 48 hours, Vance heads to the Ponderosa to get his son. He asks Billy to meet him at their special cave with food. Hoss hears the boy slip out at night and trails him. After Vance sends his son back to the ranch, Hoss confronts him and is forced to kill the boy's father. Hoss tells the boy what he has done and Billy says he hates him, which devastates Hoss.

On the way to town with Vance's body, Hoss and Billy meet up with Pike. He tells Hoss to guide him through the mountains or he will kill the boy.

Note: David Ladd is Allan Ladd's son.

E31. *Dark Star* (April 23, 1960)

Credits: *Writer:* Thomas Thompson. *Director:* Lewis Allen. *Producer:* David Dortort. **Starring:** Lorne Greene, Pernell Roberts, Dan Blocker, Michael Landon. **Supporting Cast:** Hugo Haas (Zurka); Susan Harrison (Tirza); Arthur Batanides (Sipro); Lili Valenty (Bruja); Grandon Rhodes (Doctor); Argentina Brunetti.

Synopsis: Hoss and Little Joe are wolf hunting when they come across Tirza, a gypsy, and return with her to the Ponderosa. Claiming to be a witch, she tells Joe that she will cause only trouble for him.

Ben finds her family on the Ponderosa and tells them to pick up the girl. They decline because they also consider her to be a witch. Little Joe cares deeply for her and is unconcerned about her being a witch.

Note: This marked the first of many appearances of Grandon Rhodes in the role of the town doctor.

*E32. Death at Dawn (April 30, 1960)

Credits: *Writer:* Lawrence Mascot. *Director:* Charles F. Haas. *Producer:* David Dortort. **Starring:** Lorne Greene, Pernell Roberts, Dan Blocker, Michael Landon. **Supporting Cast:** Robert Middleton (Sam Bryant); Nancy Deale (Beth Cameron); Gregory Walcott (Farmer Perkins); Morgan Woodward (Sheriff Biggs); Wendell Holmes (Judge Scribner); Paul Carr (McNeil); Peter Leeds (Norton); Hugh Sanders (Dr. Brah); Rick Marlowe, Anthony Jockim, Bill Edwards.

Synopsis: Mr. Cameron, a store owner, is murdered by Farmer Perkins after refusing to buy protection from him. Beth Cameron witnessed her husband's killing but is terrified to testify. Crime boss Sam Bryant bails out his hired gunman.

The Cartwrights are deputized and offer protection to Beth Cameron if she agrees to tell what she witnessed. After Perkins is found guilty and sentenced to the gallows, Bryant's men take Ben hostage. Sheriff Biggs receives a warning that if Perkins is put to death, Ben will be too.

Note: Nancy Deale later became Lorne Greene's second wife.

Second Season
(September 10, 1960–June 3, 1961)

E33. *Showdown* (September 10, 1960)
Credits: *Writer:* Dean Riesner. *Director:* Lewis Allen. *Producer:* David Dortort. **Starring:** Lorne Greene, Pernell Roberts, Dan Blocker, Michael Landon. **Supporting Cast:** Ben Cooper (Sam Kirby); Jack Lambert (Pardo); Ray Teal (Sheriff Roy Coffee); Jody Warner (Ellie); John Maxwell (Tom McClure); Norman Leavitt (Telegrapher); Red Morgan.

Synopsis: Sam Kirby and four others rob the Virginia City bank. Sam is then hired to break in horses on the Ponderosa. His presence on the ranch enables him to keep an eye on the sheriff and the posse's movements.

Joe becomes suspicious after hearing from a ranch hand that Sam and two men were seen in town the night of the robbery.

The Cartwrights invite Sam to a picnic where a fight breaks out between Joe and Sam over Ellie McClure. Joe rides out after Sam to apologize. Following him into the outlaw's camp, Joe is taken captive.

Review: *Variety* (September 14, 1960): The reviewer thought the "episode came off effectively once the slow start was digested." The acting and direction "were up to pro standards" and the four leads "each made an excellent contribution." The summation: "*Bonanza* appears to have a good workable concept riding for it."

Note: Ray Teal made his first appearance as Sheriff Roy Coffee.

E34. *The Mission* (September 17, 1960)
Credits: *Writer:* Robert E. Thompson. *Director:* James Neilson. *Producer:* David Dortort. **Starring:** Lorne Greene, Pernell Roberts, Dan Blocker. **Supporting Cast:** Henry Hull (Charlie Trent); John Dehner (Capt. Pender); Peter Whitney (Lt. Cutter); Harry Carey, Jr. (Corporal Burton); Don Collier (Sergeant); Lane Bradford (Buck); Dale Van Sickel (Morgan); Don Rhodes (Latigo); Mike Ragan (Kelly); Ray Hemphill (Johnson); Robert Adler (O'Hara); Leo Needham (Bank Clerk).

Synopsis: Charlie Trent takes to the bottle because he blames himself for the deaths of soldiers under his command several years before.

After Captain Pender fires his scout, Lieutenant Cutter, Hoss recommends Charlie for the job. Charlie agrees to take the position only if Hoss accompanies him.

Planning to steal the Army gold shipment, Cutter and his men follow the Army patrol into the desert.

*E35. *Badge without Honor* (September 24, 1960)

Credits: *Writer:* John Twist. *Director:* Arthur Lubin. *Producer:* David Dortort. **Starring:** Lorne Greene, Pernell Roberts, Dan Blocker, Michael Landon. **Supporting Cast:** Dan Duryea (Gerald Eskith); Fred Beir (Jason Blaine); Christine White (Mariette); Wendell Holmes (Judge Rand); Richard Warren (Gid Clevenger); James Hong (Cousin); Bob Miles, Jr. (Bill Clevenger).

Synopsis: Arriving in Virginia City, Gerald Eskith, a deputy marshal, has come to escort Jason Blaine to San Francisco in order for him to give testimony at the trial of the Murdock gang.

Fearing for his friend's life, Adam goes to a local judge to stop Eskith from taking Blaine. After his request is denied, Adam accompanies the marshal and his friend.

E36. *The Mill* (October 1, 1960)

Credits: *Writer:* Halsted Welles. *Director:* John Rich. *Producer:* David Dortort. **Starring:** Lorne Greene, Pernell Roberts, Dan Blocker, Michael Landon. **Supporting Cast:** Claude Akins (Ezekiel); Harry Townes (Tom Edwards); Dianne Foster (Joyce Edwards).

Synopsis: Tom Edwards, who has been accidentally crippled, puts the blame on Ben. Feeling sorry for himself, he starts drinking and gambling. He then falls under the control of Ezekiel, his hired hand.

In an attempt to help their friend feel better about himself, the Cartwrights construct a mill on his property.

To maintain his control over Tom, Ezekiel rekindles Tom's contempt for the Cartwrights.

E37. *The Hopefuls* (October 8, 1960)

Credits: *Writer:* E. Jack Newman. *Director:* James Nielson. *Producer:* David Dortort. **Starring:** Lorne Greene, Pernell Roberts, Dan Blocker, Michael Landon. **Supporting Cast:** Larry Gates (Jacob Darien); Patricia Donahue (Regina Darien); Dennis Patrick (Sam Bord); Charles Maxwell (Shenandoah); Jason Johnson, Paul Genge, Clarence Straight, Richard Reeves, Tom Newman, Clegg Hoyt, Hank Patterson.

Synopsis: A Quaker wagon train led by Jacob Darien stops in Virginia City on its way to Slatersville. When Jacob and his daughter Regina are accosted by two drunks, Adam and gambler named Sam Bord come to their rescue.

Adam, who has taken a liking to Regina, joins Sam to escort the wagon train. That night they make camp on the Ponderosa, where they are met by the other three Cartwrights. Jacob tells them of their dreams to buy land with their life savings.

When the wagon train leaves, Hoss joins his brother. Meanwhile, Sam and his gang are planning to rob the train.

E38. *Denver McKee* (October 15, 1960)

Credits: *Writers:* Fred Freiberger, Steve McNeill. *Director:* Jacques Tourneur. *Producer:* David Dortort. **Starring:** Lorne Greene, Pernell Roberts, Dan Blocker,

Michael Landon. **Supporting Cast:** Franchot Tone (Denver McKee); Natalie Trundy (Connie McKee); Ken Mayer (Miles); Stephen Courtleigh (Harley); William Fawcett (Pete Redford); Jack Lester (Johnson); Pete Robinson (Fleming); Bob Barker (Mort); Jim Galante.

Synopsis: Denver McKee, a retired lawman and friend of the Cartwrights, is awaiting the return of his daughter Connie from the East, where she had been attending school.

Ben goes to Denver's to ask for his help in tracking a gang of outlaws who have been terrorizing the area.

Pete Redford, the latest target in a string of robberies, dies after identifying one of the four men as having red hair.

After Ben, Adam and Hoss search the High Sierras, Hoss discovers tracks which indicate that the outlaws have doubled back. Ben suspects that the robbers may be one of their own neighbors.

*E39. *Day of Reckoning* (October 22, 1960)

Credits: *Writers:* Leonard Heideman, R. Kamer Norris. *Director:* Richard H. Bartlett. *Producer:* David Dortort. **Starring:** Lorne Greene, Pernell Roberts, Dan Blocker, Michael Landon. **Supporting Cast:** Ricardo Montalban (Indian Matsou); Madlyn Rhue (Itoya Matsou); Karl Swenson (Ike Daggett); Anthony Caruso (Lagos); Roy Engel, Gail Bonney.

Synopsis: Matsou, a Banuk Indian, prevents his brother Lagos from killing Ben. When Matsou brings the wounded Ben back to the Ponderosa, he is rewarded with a piece of farm land next to Ike Daggett, who despises Indians. For the sake of his wife Itoya and his forthcoming child, Matsou tries to live the life of a white man.

Several months later, Lagos, who is now the chief, declares war. When Matsou goes to warn Ike, his neighbor fails to heed the warning.

E40. *The Abduction* (October 29, 1960)

Credits: *Writer:* Herman Groves. *Director:* Charles F. Haas. *Producer:* David Dortort. **Starring:** Lorne Greene, Pernell Roberts, Dan Blocker, Michael Landon. **Supporting Cast:** Gerald Mohr (Philip Reed); Jackie Russell (Jennifer Beale); Barbara Lawrence (Della); Jerry Oddo (Gerner); Robert Maffei (Bull Wyatt); Theodore Marcuse, Bob Hopkins, Mary Orozco, Laurie Mitchell, Stafford Repp.

Synopsis: When a carnival comes to Virginia City, Joe and Hoss escort Jennifer Beale and Harriet to see the different acts. Jennifer sneaks off and runs into owner Philip Reed. When he invites her to his wagon, Gerner enters and suggests that she be held for a million dollar ransom.

Meanwhile Joe, Hoss and Harriet search for the missing Jennifer. After splitting up, Joe is attacked by four roustabouts and his gun is stolen.

When Reed's girlfriend Della stops Joe telling him that Jennifer is still at the carnival, she is killed from ambush with Little Joe's gun.

Note: This episode was shot in its entirety on a Paramount soundstage.

E41. *Breed of Violence* (November 5, 1960)

Credits: *Writer:* David Lang. *Director:* John Florea. *Producer:* David Dortort.

Starring: Lorne Greene, Pernell Roberts, Dan Blocker, Michael Landon. **Supporting Cast:** John Ericson (Vince Dagen); Myrna Fahey (Dolly Kincaid); Val Avery (Sheriff Kincaid); Hal Baylor (Clegg); Norm Alden (Poke); Paul Lukather, Stuart Randall, Charles Wagenheim.

Synopsis: Sheriff Kincaid of Mormon Flats keeps a tight rein on his daughter Dolly because of the fact that her mother had run away.

While Adam, Hoss and Joe are hunting the wolves that have been attacking their livestock, Dolly rides out to meet Vince Dagen who, along with his gang, has robbed the bank.

To get help with the wolves, Hoss and Joe ride to see Mr. Traeger, a tracker, but are taken prisoners by Dagen, who has killed Traeger.

*E42. *The Last Viking* (November 12, 1960)
Credits: *Writer:* Anthony Lawrence. *Director:* John Florea. *Producer:* David Dortort. **Starring:** Lorne Greene, Pernell Roberts, Dan Blocker, Michael Landon. **Supporting Cast:** Neville Brand (Gunnar Borgstrom); Sonya Wilde (Carrie McClane); Al Ruscio (Vaca); Louis Mercier (Duzzag); Ric Marlow (Morgan); Herbert C. Lytton (Abe McClane).

Synopsis: The Cartwrights are visited by Gunnar Borgstrom, Hoss' uncle. During dinner, Gunnar speaks of his exploits and of his sister Inger (Ben's second wife). After Gunnar talks to Hoss about his mother, he leaves for the Comanchero camp.

Upon his arrival, Gunnar gets into a fight with Vaca over raiding the Ponderosa. A decision is made to raid the McClain ranch instead.

During the raid, Abe McClain is wounded. His niece Carrie and Joe, who had been helping out, are taken prisoners.

*E43. *The Trail Gang* (November 26, 1960)
Credits: *Writer:* Carey Wilber. *Director:* John Rich. *Producer:* David Dortort. **Starring:** Lorne Greene, Dan Blocker. **Supporting Cast:** Dick Davalos (Johnny Logan); James Westerfield (Sheriff Logan); Edgar Buchanan (Hallelujah Hicks); Robert J. Wilke (Brazos); Linda Lawson (Melinda); Richard Devon, Harry Antrim.

Synopsis: Seeking vengeance upon the lawman responsible for his imprisonment, outlaw Johnny Logan poses as "Sam Jackson" and hires on as a drover on a Ponderosa cattle drive. He has chosen the drive because its destination is the town where the lawman lives.

E44. *The Savage* (December 3, 1960)
Credits: *Writers:* Joseph Stone, Paul King. *Director:* James Neilson. *Producer:* David Dortort. **Starring:** Pernell Roberts. **Supporting Cast:** Anna-Lisa (White Indian Woman); Hal Jon Norman (Chato); Vic Millan (Dako); Larry Chance (Haddon); Henry Wills (McGregor); Frank Sentry (Iowa); Bob Wienskjo (Kaska); Maurice Jara (Tolka).

Synopsis: Shoshone Indians kill trappers McGregor and Haddon when they cross the Indians' sacred land.

Headed for Nevada City, Adam comes across the dead men. He sights a white woman whom the Indians believe to possess special powers. Realizing that the white buffalo woman is human, she is almost put to death. While trying to save her, Adam is struck by an arrow.

Note: Location shooting took place at Hollywood's Franklin Lake and Iverson's Movie Ranch.

*E45. *Silent Thunder* (December 10, 1960)

Credits: *Writer:* John Furia. *Director:* Robert Altman. *Producer:* David Dortort. **Starring:** Lorne Greene, Michael Landon. **Supporting Cast:** Stella Stevens (Ann Croft); Albert Salmi (Albie); Kenneth MacKenna (Sam Croft); James Griffith (Preacher); Sherwood Price (Eb); Harry Swoger (Tom).

Synopsis: On his way back from Placerville, Joe stops to visit Sam Croft and his daughter Annie, a deaf-mute. He starts teaching her sign language from a book. Albie, a hired hand, often forces his attentions on her.

Annie continues to learn, which upsets her father, who feels that she has fallen in love with Joe. After Annie kisses Joe, she runs away.

Joe goes looking for her. What he finds is Albie, who pushes Sam off a cliff.

*E46. *The Ape* (December 17, 1960)

Credits: *Writer:* Gene L. Coon. *Director:* James P. Yarborough. *Producer:* David Dortort. *Associate Producer:* Thomas Thompson. **Starring:** Lorne Greene, Pernell Roberts, Dan Blocker, Michael Landon. **Supporting Cast:** Cal Bolder (Arnie Gurne); Karen Sharpe (Shari); Leonard Nimoy (Freddie); Ray Teal (Sheriff Roy Coffee); Rodolfo Hoyos (Mexican); Charles Tannen (Bartender).

Synopsis: When Shari insults Arnie, a huge, slow-witted man, he fights Hoss.

After the fight, Hoss takes Arnie home to an old shack where he learns of the man's dream of owning his own farm. Hoss hires him to work on the Ponderosa despite the objections of his brothers. Hoss says that he can help Arnie to control his temper. Later, a squatter is found with his neck broken.

That night Hoss and Arnie are in the saloon where Arnie buys Shari a necklace. After spurning his advances once more, Shari is strangled accidentally.

*E47. *The Blood Line* (December 31, 1960)

Credits: *Writers:* William Raynor, Myles Wilder. *Director:* Lewis Allen. *Producer:* David Dortort. **Starring:** Lorne Greene, Pernell Roberts, Michael Landon. **Supporting Cast:** Lee Van Cleef (Appling); Jan Sterling (Dianne Jordan); David Macklin (Todd Grayson); Ray Teal (Sheriff Roy Coffee); Norman Leavitt (Bert); Allan Lane (Luke Grayson); Thomas B. Henry (Jenkins); Ed Prentiss, Dan Riss.

Synopsis: Ben kills a drunken Luke Grayson in self defense. When Luke's teenage son Todd arrives in Virginia City for his father's funeral, he swears to take vengeance on his father's killer.

E48. *The Courtship* (January 7, 1961)

Credits: *Writer:* Richard N. Morgan. *Director:* James P. Yarborough. *Producer:* David Dortort. *Associate Producer:* Thomas Thompson. **Starring:** Lorne Greene,

Pernell Roberts, Dan Blocker, Michael Landon. **Supporting Cast:** Julie Adams (Helen Layton); Marshall Reed (Hammond); Lyle Talbot (Sugar Daddy); Paul Dubov (Dealer).

Synopsis: After hearing of the death of his old friend Josh Layton, Ben asks Little Joe and Hoss to visit Josh's widow Helen in Sacramento.

Upon their arrival, Hoss urges her to accompany them back to the Ponderosa. Along the way, Helen accepts Hoss's marriage proposal.

When Adam comes back from San Francisco, he informs Ben that Helen is addicted to gambling. When Hoss is told about Helen, he comes to her defense, refusing to accept the truth.

*E49. *The Spitfire* (January 14, 1961)

Credits: *Writer:* Ward Hawkins. *Director:* William Dario Faralla. *Producer:* David Dortort. **Starring:** Lorne Greene, Pernell Roberts, Dan Blocker, Michael Landon. **Supporting Cast:** Katherine Warren (Maud Hoad); Don Harvey (Jeb Hoad); Jack Elam (Dodie); Anita Sands (Willow); Steven Terrell (Bud Harvey); Ray Teal (Sheriff Roy Coffee).

Synopsis: After warning Zeb Hoad and his daughter Willa about setting a prairie fire, Joe is forced to kill Zeb in self defense. Returning home with Willa in tow, Joe tells Ben what happened.

While cleaning up Willa, she screams that her family will come and wreak vengeance on the Cartwrights.

After Adam is shot in the leg, Sheriff Roy Coffee arrives to tell Ben that the Hoads are in the area.

E50. *The Bride* (January 21, 1961)

Credits: *Writer:* Richard Newman. *Director:* Alvin Ganzer. *Producer:* David Dortort. *Associate Producer:* Thomas Thompson. **Starring:** Lorne Greene, Pernell Roberts, Dan Blocker, Michael Landon. **Supporting Cast:** Suzanne Lloyd (Jennifer Lane); John McIntire (Sheriff Mike Latimer); Adam West (Frank Milton); William Mims (Eb Bailey).

Synopsis: While Ben is away, a woman arrives at the Ponderosa claiming to be Mrs. Ben Cartwright.

When Ben returns home, he is introduced to his "wife" but he is shocked as he has never met her. After she tells them that her "Ben" borrowed $4,000 to buy cattle in Crater Plain, the Cartwrights decide to return there with her.

On the way, an old miner, Ned Birch, allows them to water their horses. When Ned is found murdered, Ben is arrested because of a letter found on the body.

E51. *Bank Run* (January 28, 1961)

Credits: *Writer:* N. B. Stone, Jr. *Director:* Robert Altman. *Producer:* David Dortort. **Starring:** Lorne Greene, Pernell Roberts, Dan Blocker, Michael Landon. **Supporting Cast:** Ian Wolfe (Harrison); Walter Burke (Tim O'Brien); Dan Tobin (Finch); Wynn Pearce (Teller); Owen Bush, Arnold Merritt, Howard Wendell, Carl Milletaire, Mickey Finn.

Synopsis: Overhearing banker Harrison's plans to file bankruptcy, Joe learns that he plans to abscond with the bank assets. He also discovers that Harrison plans to use the money to purchase a silver mine.

Actual clothes worn by Dan Blocker and Michael Landon. (Photograph by Linda F. Leiby.)

Telling Hoss, they decide to thwart Harrison's plans by stealing the money and depositing it in a different bank. They soon find themselves wanted by the law.

E52. *The Fugitive* (February 4, 1961)

Credits: *Writer:* Richard Landau. *Director:* Lewis Allen. *Producer:* David Dortort. **Starring:** Lorne Greene, Pernell Roberts. **Supporting Cast:** Ziva Rodann (Maria); James Best (Carl); Will Wright (Will Reagan); Frank Silvera (El Jefe);

Arthur Batanides (Pablo); Veda Ann Borg (Beulah); Salvador Baguez (Gomez); Alex Montoya (Juan).

Synopsis: When a previous foreman, Will Reagan, receives notification from Mexico of his son Carl's death, he persuades Adam to head to Plata to learn the truth about his son.

At first Adam gets no answers but is finally told that Carl was murdered while attempting to break out of jail.

When Adam goes back to his room, he finds two men who order him home and beat him up to prevent him from finding out the real truth.

E53. *Vengeance* (February 11, 1961)

Credits: *Writer:* Marion Parsonett. *Director:* Dick Moder. *Producer:* David Dortort. **Starring:** Lorne Greene, Pernell Roberts, Dan Blocker, Michael Landon. **Supporting Cast:** Adam Williams (Red Twilight); Beverly Tyler (Mary); Keith Richards (Willie Twilight); Olan Soule (Hotel Clerk); Robert E. Griffin (Sheriff); Roy Engel (Doc Tolliver).

Synopsis: Hoss is loading a wagon when there are shots from Willie, who is drunk. When Hoss pushes him, he hits a post and dies. Hoss goes off by himself because he feels responsible for Willie's death.

Willie's brother Red comes to town and learns that Hoss was responsible for his brother's death. As no charges were filed against Hoss, Red decides to take matters into his own hands by stalking him.

When Hoss does not return home, Joe and Adam set out to search for him. Meanwhile, Hoss has been shot from ambush and left to die.

E54. *Tax Collector* (February 18, 1961)

Credits: *Writer:* Arnold Belgard. *Director:* William Witney. *Producer:* David Dortort. **Starring:** Lorne Greene, Dan Blocker, Michael Landon. **Supporting Cast:** Eddie Firestone (Jock Henry); Kathie Browne (Ellen); Victor Sen Yung (Hop Sing); Russ Conway (Dave Hart); Charles Watts (Ellery); Florence MacMichael, Maudie Prickett, Henry Corden.

Synopsis: Jock Henry finally gets a job as assistant tax collector. Because he gets two percent commission, he over-assesses the property of the citizens of Virginia City. His first call is on the Ponderosa, where he tells Ben that he owes over $1,600 in taxes — a major increase from last year.

Because of his enthusiasm for his work, Jock forgets about his wife Ellen and horse Sally, who are both expecting. At the urging of Ellen and the citizens of Virginia City, the Cartwrights come up with a plan to force Jock to resign.

E55. *The Rescue* (February 25, 1961)

Credits: *Writer:* Steve McNeil. *Director:* William Dario Faralla. *Producer:* David Dortort. **Starring:** Lorne Greene, Pernell Roberts, Dan Blocker, Michael Landon. **Supporting Cast:** Burt Douglas (Jack Tatum); Leif Erickson (Josh Tatum); Richard Coogan (Jake Moss); Victor Sen Yung (Hop Sing); Ron Hayes (Johnny Reed); Joe Partridge (Gus Tatum); Lane Bradford.

Synopsis: When Ben arrives on the Tatum spread, he finds a steer hide. He then gets into a fight with Josh Tatum. Ben returns to the ranch. Seeing their father's condition, the boys feel that Ben is getting on in years and should slow down.

They offer to search for the cattle rustlers while Ben remains at the ranch. They track the thieves into a box canyon. When they dismount, Hoss' leg is wounded. Their horses run off, leaving them stranded without supplies.

Note: Location shooting took place at Iverson's Movie Ranch.

*E56. *The Dark Gate* (March 4, 1961)

Credits: *Writer:* Ward Hawkins. *Director:* Robert Gordon. *Producer:* David Dortort. **Starring:** Lorne Greene, Pernell Roberts, Dan Blocker, Michael Landon. **Supporting Cast:** James Coburn (Ross Marquett); Cece Whitney (Mrs. Delphine Marquett); Med Florey (Monk); Harry Dean Stanton (Billy Todd); Ray Teal (Sheriff Roy Coffee); James Anderson, Joe di Reda, Donald Foster, Roy Engel, John Mitchum, Rush Williams.

Synopsis: When Ross Marquett starts acting strangely, Adam becomes concerned. Ross beats his wife Delphine because he believes that she has become involved with Adam.

Ross has also become a member of a ruthless gang intent on stealing a gold shipment. Adam might become the next target of Ross' madness.

Note: Red Rock Canyon is seen in the climax.

E57. *The Duke* (March 11, 1961)

Credits: *Writers:* William R. Cox, Theodore and Matilda Ferro. *Director:* Robert Altman. *Producer:* David Dortort. *Associate Producer:* Thomas Thompson. **Starring:** Lorne Greene, Dan Blocker, Michael Landon. **Supporting Cast:** Maxwell Reed (Duke); J. Pat O'Malley (Limey); Randy Stuart (Marge); Jason Evers (J. D. Lambert); Ray Teal (Sheriff Roy Coffee); Al Christy (Bartender).

Synopsis: Duke, a prizefighter, arrives in Virginia City with his manager Limey, in search of their next challenger.

That night at dinner, Ben warns his sons to stay away from the fighter.

As a result of the beating of J.D., Ben sends a telegram to Adam to bring back Bonicia Boy to fight the Duke. A week later, Ben still has not heard from Adam and the fighter.

After Limey is beaten up by the Duke, Hoss is forced to step into the ring to settle the score.

E58. *Cutthroat Junction* (March 18, 1961)

Credits: *Writer:* Nat Tanchuck. *Director:* Dick Moder. *Producer:* David Dortort. **Starring:** Lorne Greene, Pernell Roberts, Dan Blocker, Michael Landon. **Supporting Cast:** Robert Lansing (Jed Trask); Shirley Ballard (Belle Trask); Richard Wessel, John Harmon, J. Edward McKinley, Dan White, Bob Anderson, Jim Hayward, Robert Adler, Bob Miles.

Synopsis: Ben and the townsmen are upset because the Sierra Stage Line is not getting the mail and supplies through.

Trask, a troubleshooter for the line, rides through town on his way to Latigo to take care of the problem. Ben volunteers the Cartwrights to go along.

When they arrive in Latigo, Ben and Trask start to straighten out the mess when Joe comes in telling them that the barn is loaded with mail and supplies.

A letter which arrives on the stage notifies Trask that he has been relieved of his duties after having worked for them for ten years. Irate over the loss of his job, Trask vows to wreck the Sierra Stage Line all over again.

E59. *The Gift* (April 1, 1961)

Credits: *Writers:* Denne Petticlerc, Thomas Thompson. *Director:* William Witney. *Producer:* David Dortort. **Starring:** Lorne Greene, Pernell Roberts, Dan Blocker, Michael Landon. **Supporting Cast:** Martin Landau (Emeliano); Jim Davis (Sam Wolfe); Jack Hogan (Cash); Joe Yrigoyen (Cayetano); Robert Christopher, Felipe Turich, Bob Miles.

Synopsis: Having picked up a white Arabian stallion, purchased as a present for Ben's birthday, Joe and Emeliano cross the desert. En route, they run into trouble with Cochise, who is leading his tribe into battle.

Running low on supplies, they seek aid from Sam Wolfe and his Comancheros. Wolfe agrees to help only if he can have the stallion.

Note: Red Rock Canyon is the setting for this episode.

E60. *The Rival* (April 15, 1961)

Credits: *Writer:* Anthony Lawrence. *Director:* Robert Altman. *Producer:* David Dortort. **Starring:** Lorne Greene, Pernell Roberts, Dan Blocker, Michael Landon. **Supporting Cast:** Peggy Ann Garner (Cameo Johnson); Charles Aidman (Jim Applegate); Ray Teal (Sheriff Roy Coffee); Robert McQueeney (Gideon); Joe DeSantis, Orville Sherman, Bill Clark, Charlene Brooks.

Synopsis: Walking home after a date with Cameo Johnson, Hoss sees Jim Applegate and four other men leaving the area. Coming up to a cabin, Hoss discovers a murdered couple.

When a posse is sent out to search for the killers, they spot the five men. There is a shoot-out and Jim Applegate gets away.

The next morning, Roy finds Applegate at Cameo's and takes him into custody. Jim maintains his innocence but Hoss has his doubts. After serving Applegate his dinner, Roy is knocked out, enabling Jim to escape.

E61. *The Infernal Machine* (April 22, 1961)

Credits: *Writer:* Ward Hawkins. *Director:* William Witney. *Producer:* David Dortort. **Starring:** Lorne Greene, Dan Blocker, Michael Landon. **Supporting Cast:** Eddie Ryder (Daniel Pettibone); Willard Waterman (Throckmorton); June Kenney (Robin); Nora Hayden (Big Red); George Kennedy (Pete Long); Ray Teal (Sheriff Roy Coffee).

Synopsis: Intrigued by his friend Daniel Pettibone's horseless carriage, Hoss decides to put money into the project. When they try to get the townspeople to invest, Hoss and Daniel are ridiculed.

Trouble starts when Throckmorton arrives in town putting $1,000 into the invention, thus causing others to join the venture. Unbeknownst to the other investors, Throckmorton plans to abscond with the money.

E62. *Thunderhead Swindle* (April 29, 1961)
    Credits: *Writer:* Gene L. Coon. *Director:* Dick Moder. *Producer:* David Dor-
tort. **Starring:** Lorne Greene, Dan Blocker, Michael Landon. **Supporting Cast:**
Parley Baer (Jack Cunningham); Walter Coy (Frank Furnas); Ross Elliott (Watkins);
Judson Pratt (Jim Bronson); Ray Teal (Sheriff Roy Coffee); Vito Scotti.
    Synopsis: The Cartwrights catch some miners poaching cattle because they
are hungry and out of work. To help feed their families, Ben donates some beef.
    New owners Jack Cunningham and Frank Furnas declare a silver strike at the
Thunderhead Mine. After learning from the former owner Jim Bronson that the
mine is depleted, Ben becomes suspicious. Upon further investigation, Ben believes
that silver from another mine has been placed in the Thunderhead.
    Note: Location filming took place at Bronson Canyon.

E63. *The Secret* (May 6, 1961)
    Credits: *Writer:* John Hawkins. *Director:* Robert Altman. *Producer:* David
Dortort. *Associate Producer:* Thomas Thompson. **Starring:** Lorne Greene, Pernell
Roberts, Dan Blocker, Michael Landon. **Supporting Cast:** Russell Collins (John
Hardner); Graham Denton (Jake Parson); Stephen Joyce (Jerome Bell); Sherwood
Price (Pete Parson); Pat Michon (Betty May); Dayton Lummis (Hiram); Morgan
Woodward (Deputy Conlee); Bob Harris (Bill Parson); Roy Engel, Bill Edwards.
    Synopsis: Jake Parson tells Ben that he would like to give Joe and his daugh-
ter Mary a small spread as a wedding present. Joe is confused, knowing nothing
about the situation. Mary's two brothers ride, in saying that they found Mary's
dead body.
    John Hardner, Joe's best friend, claims to have seen Joe and Mary together
shortly before her death. Joe maintains that he had not been with her the night she
died. Mary's family insists that she had plans to run away with Joe to be married.
Deputy Conlee arrests Joe for her murder.

E64. *The Dream* (May 20, 1961)
    Credits: *Writers:* Jack McClain, James Van Wagner. *Director:* Robert Altman.
Producer: David Dortort. **Starring:** Lorne Greene, Pernell Roberts, Dan Blocker,
Michael Landon. **Supporting Cast:** Sidney Blackmer (Major John Cayley); Burt
Douglas (Bill Kingsley); Stuart Nisbet (Sgt. Hines); Diana Milay (Diana Cayley);
Jonathan Hole (Hershell).
    Synopsis: Arriving from the East, Major John Cayley, a friend of Ben's, heads
for the Ponderosa. Ben consents to allow him the use of the ranch to carry on his
balloon test flights that he is conducting in connection with the Army.
    After Diana Cayley arrives in town, she leaves for the ranch with Adam. She
surprises her father and demands to know what he is up to.
    Unbeknown to Ben, the major and his two men are absent without leave from
the Army and plan to rob the bank.

E65. *Elizabeth, My Love* (May 27, 1961)
    Credits: *Writer:* Anthony Lawrence. *Director:* Lewis Allen. *Producer:* David
Dortort. **Starring:** Lorne Greene, Pernell Roberts, Dan Blocker, Michael Landon.

Supporting Cast: Geraldine Brooks (Elizabeth); Torin Thatcher (Captain Stoddard); Berry Kroeger (Mandible); Richard Collier (Otto); Alex Sharpe (Blackner); Bob Hopkins (Mariner); Molly Roden (Mrs. Callahan); Max Slaten (Bartender); John Close (Bell); Jack Rice (Van Meer); Selmer Jackson, Bill Quinn, Ted Knight.

Synopsis: When Adam becomes seriously ill, Ben keeps an all-night vigil and reflects back, remembering Adam's mother, Elizabeth.

After losing his commission, a ship captain and Ben open a ship's chandlery. Shortly after the shop is opened, Ben and Elizabeth are married.

Unhappy over his situation, Stoddard begins drinking and almost decides to take over the helm of a slave ship.

After overhearing an argument between her father and Ben, Elizabeth collapses. She is put to bed to await the birth of their first child.

E66. *Sam Hill* (June 3, 1961)

Credits: *Writer:* David Dortort. *Director:* Robert Altman. *Producer:* David Dortort. **Starring:** Lorne Greene, Pernell Roberts, Dan Blocker, Michael Landon. **Supporting Cast:** Claude Akins (Sam Hill); Ford Rainey (Colonel Tyson); Edgar Buchanan (John Henry Hill); Robert Ridgely (Billy Joe); Caroline Richter (Lonesome Lil); Howard Wendell (Willis); Mickey Simpson (Bartender); Richard Bartell (Hathaway); Nesdon Booth (Hotel Clerk).

Synopsis: Blacksmith Sam Hill has the reputation of being physically powerful and stubborn. However, he possesses one weak point: the land containing his mother's grave.

Trouble begins when Colonel Tyson buys the land from Sam's father, John Henry. Infuriated, Sam is determined that no one else will own the land.

Note: This was the pilot for an unsold spinoff.

Third Season
(September 24, 1961–May 20, 1962)

E67. *The Smiler* (September 24, 1961)

Credits: *Writer:* Lewis Reed. *Director:* Thomas Carr. *Producer:* David Dortort. **Starring:** Lorne Greene, Pernell Roberts, Dan Blocker, Michael Landon. **Supporting Cast:** Herschel Bernardi (Clarence Bolling); Catherine McLeod (Mrs. McClure); Bill Zuckert (Gilbert); Hy Terman (Arthur Bolling); Scatman Crothers (Jud); Robert Foulk (Deputy); Ray Teal (Sheriff Roy Coffee).

Synopsis: Hoss comes to the defense of widow McClure when Arthur Bolling, who has been drinking, speaks to her disrespectfully. During a struggle, Hoss accidentally kills him.

Although the widow's account of what happened clears Hoss of any wrongdoing, he continues to believe that he is responsible.

Clarence Bolling arrives in town to bury his brother. Learning what had happened, he claims that he does not want to cause any trouble and that he does not hold Hoss responsible. But deep down he is harboring a grudge and plans to make Hoss pay for his brother's death.

Review: *Variety* (September 27, 1961): The critic thought that the episode was "uncommonly slow," that the script by Lewis Reed was "poor" and that guest star Herschel Bernardi "was good in a bad role." "*Bonanza* is formula stuff, but it is highly likely that a western can do quite well for itself on Sunday nights."

E68. *Springtime* (October 1, 1961)

Credits: *Writer:* John Furia, Jr. *Director:* Christian Nyby. *Producer:* David Dortort. **Starring:** Lorne Greene, Pernell Roberts, Dan Blocker, Michael Landon. **Supporting Cast:** John Carradine (Jebediah); John Qualen (Parley); Jena Engstrom (Ann); Claude Johnson (Paul); Denver Pyle (Theodore).

Synopsis: While Adam, Hoss and Joe are horsing around, Ben arrives with an old friend, Jebediah. During the scuffle, Joe hurls some wood toward his brothers, striking Jebediah unintentionally on the foot.

Seizing the chance, he cons the Cartwrights into conducting his business for him. He gets Adam to throw Theodore and his wife off their land for defaulting on their mortgage. Then he sends Hoss with a bill of sale to purchase land from a young married couple, because Jebediah wants to use it to fatten up his livestock. Finally Joe has to evict a man off a piece of land belonging to Jebediah.

*E69. *The Honor of Cochise* (October 8, 1961)

Credits: *Writer:* Elliott Arnold. *Director:* Don McDougall. *Producer:* David Dortort. **Starring:** Lorne Greene, Pernell Roberts, Dan Blocker, Michael Landon. **Supporting Cast:** Jeff Morrow (Cochise); DeForest Kelley (Captain Moss Johnson); Al Ruscio (Delgado); Stacy Harris (Colonel Clinton Wilcox); Bing Russell (Major Reynolds).

Synopsis: While the Cartwrights make camp, Captain Moss Johnson rides in, chased by Cochise and his warriors. After the Indians run off their horses, Ben tells Cochise that they will not hand over Johnson.

When Adam sneaks out to get water, he is wounded and is brought back to camp by Joe.

Cochise wants to talk to Ben, who goes out to meet him. He is told by Cochise that Johnson signed a treaty with some Apaches but poisoned their food.

Ben returns to camp and confronts the captain, who claims that he was only following orders. To save Adam's life, Hoss and Joe want to turn Johnson over to the Apaches. Ben vetoes the idea. He decides that he is going to try to get to Fort Churchill for a doctor for Adam and a commanding officer to arrest Johnson, but he is captured.

E70. *The Lonely House* (October 15, 1961)

Credits: *Writer:* Frank Chase. *Director:* William Witney. *Producer:* David Dortort. **Starring:** Lorne Greene, Michael Landon. **Supporting Cast:** Paul Richards (Trock); Faith Domergue (Lee Bolden); Jim Beck (Gavin); Vito Scotti (Pooch); Ray Hemphill.

Synopsis: Ben sends Joe to the bank with a draft for Mrs. Lee Bolden. While there, the bank is robbed by Trock and his partners Gavin and Pooch. After the teller wounds Trock, Joe knocks him out.

Joe rides to Lee Bolden's house and tells her about the bank robbery. That night after dinner, Lee tells Joe how lonely she is since her husband, a doctor, died of Typhoid fever. Invited to stay because of a storm, Joe goes into the barn and finds Trock. He takes Joe at gunpoint into the house. Lee tells Trock that the bullet must be removed in order to save his life. He warns both of them not to try anything or he will kill both of them.

E71. *The Burma Rarity* (October 22, 1961)

Credits: *Writer:* H. B. Stone, Jr. *Director:* William Witney. *Producer:* David Dortort. **Starring:** Lorne Greene, Pernell Roberts, Dan Blocker, Michael Landon. **Supporting Cast:** Beatrice Kay (Clementine Hawkins); Wally Brown (Henry Morgan); Dave Willock (Phil Axe); Victor Sen Yung (Hop Sing); Ray Teal (Sheriff Roy Coffee); James Griffith, Charles Watts, Howard Wright, William Keene, Joan Staley, Nestor Paiva.

Synopsis: Hoss brings in a letter from a Texas judge about arranging for a place to stay for Wally Brown and Phil Axe. The boys suggest the Widow Hawkins boarding house. When Ben and Adam introduce Brown and Axe to Clementine, she agrees to take them in as boarders.

Mayoral candidate Sam and the banker show Clementine, Brown and Axe some land they call Sunny Acres. To raise money for the property, they must sell a large emerald, the Burma Rarity, to Clementine. After selling the gem, the two cons switch the real one for a fake.

E72. *Broken Ballad* (October 29, 1961)

Credits: *Writer:* John T. Kelley. *Director:* Robert Butler. *Producer:* David Dortort. **Starring:** Lorne Greene, Pernell Roberts, Dan Blocker, Michael Landon. **Supporting Cast:** Robert Culp (Ed Payson); Ray Daley (Billy Buckley); Dabbs Greer (Will Cass); Abbagail Shelton (Sally); Robert Christopher (Cahill); Richard Rosmini (Jamie); Cosmo Sardo (Bartender); John Graham.

Synopsis: Ed Payson arrives in Virginia City to settle on his father's ranch. He has returned after being imprisoned for killing David, the son of shopkeeper Will Cass. After Payson is refused service at the store, Adam pays for his order, threatening to pull the Ponderosa account.

The townspeople and Cass are determined to get rid of Payson. In an attempt to cause Payson to lose his ranch, Cass decides to pay the $800 owed in back taxes but is thwarted by Adam, who becomes Ed's friend.

Billy Buckley becomes jealous over Payson's attentions towards Sally Cass. He practices with a handgun with the intentions of challenging his rival Ed.

E73. *The Many Faces of Gideon Flinch* (November 5, 1961)

Credits: *Writer:* Robert Vincent Wright. *Director:* Robert Altman. *Producer:* David Dortort. **Starring:** Lorne Greene, Pernell Roberts, Dan Blocker, Michael Landon. **Supporting Cast:** Ian Wolfe (Gideon Flinch); Sue Ane Langdon (Jennifer); Harry Swoger (Bullethead Burke); Arnold Stang (Jake the Weasel); Ray Teal (Sheriff Roy Coffee); Joe Turkel, Robert Jordan, Robert Foulk, Clem Bevans, Burt Mustin, Rickey Kelman, Charles Horvath, George Dunn, Owen Bush.

Synopsis: The stage arrives in Virginia City carrying Gideon Flinch and his niece Jennifer. Flinch tells Roy Coffee that Bullethead Burke is out to kill him because of $5,000 that he had invested and lost.

At the hotel, Jennifer tells her uncle that she has a plan to hide and protect him from Burke. She then hides Gideon in an old cabin.

Since Burke and Flinch have never met, Jennifer persuades Hoss to pose as her uncle. As Joe has his eye on Jennifer, he devises a plan to substitute himself for Hoss. Little Joe has no idea what trouble awaits him.

E74. *The Friendship* (November 12, 1961)

Credits: *Writer:* Frank Chase. *Director:* Don McDougall. *Producer:* David Dortort. **Starring:** Lorne Greene, Pernell Roberts, Dan Blocker, Michael Landon. **Supporting Cast:** Dean Jones (Danny Kidd); Janet Lake (Ann Carter); Edward Faulkner (Bob Stevens); Norm Alden (Teller); Rusty Lane (Warden); Stafford Repp (Carter); Roy Wright.

Synopsis: Joe is checking on a chain gang working on the Ponderosa. His horse is startled, causing Joe to be dragged along the ground. He is rescued by Danny Kidd, who has been in prison for ten years. As a reward, Ben is able to get Danny a parole making Joe accountable for Danny's behavior.

At a party given for Mr. Carter and his daughter Ann, two hands inform him about Danny's past. The next day, when Ann comes to visit Danny, her blouse is accidentally ripped when he returns her kiss. Misunderstanding what has happened, Joe threatens to send Danny back to prison. Danny panics and hits Joe over the head.

E75. *The Countess* (November 19, 1961)

Credits: *Writers:* William R. Cox, William D. Powell. *Director:* Robert Sparr. *Producer:* David Dortort. **Starring:** Lorne Greene, Pernell Roberts, Dan Blocker, Michael Landon. **Supporting Cast:** Maggie Hayes (Linda Chadwick); John Alderson (Montague); Dan Sheridan (Kelly); Dick Wittinghill, Orville Sherman, Michael Ross, Norman Leavitt, Robert Ridgely.

Synopsis: Lady Linda Chadwick and Montague arrive in Virginia City and are met by Ben, Hoss and Joe. After the luggage is loaded, everyone heads for the Ponderosa. After dinner, she presents Ben with an oil painting of the two of them from 20 years before. The next morning, Ben takes Linda for a buggy ride to see Lake Tahoe. She tells him that she is sorry that she had rejected him 20 years earlier.

Trouble begins when miners and lumberjacks both demand money after each work day. With a rumor circulating that he is low on funds, Ben is turned down for a bank loan. When Lady Chadwick offers to bail him out of his troubles, he turns her down.

Note: Location shooting took place at Incline Village.

E76. *The Horse Breaker* (November 26, 1961)

Credits: *Writer:* Frank Chase. *Director:* Don McDougall. *Producer:* David Dortort. **Starring:** Lorne Greene, Pernell Roberts, Dan Blocker, Michael Landon. **Supporting Cast:** Ben Cooper (Johnny Lightly); Addison Richards (Dr. Kay); Sue

Randall (Ann Davis); R. G. Armstrong (Nathan Clay); Don Burnett (Gordie); John Cole (Gunnar).

Synopsis: Johnny Lightly is paralyzed while breaking horses for the Cartwrights. Dr. Kay sends Ann Davis to help with his exercises. On the way back from a doctor's visit, he and Ben are stopped by Nathan Clay, who blames Ben for the death of his son.

After Adam, Hoss and Joe leave on a cattle drive, the Clays barge into the house pouring coal oil over the living room floor and threatening to set the house ablaze.

E77. *Day of the Dragon* (December 3, 1961)

Credits: *Writer:* John T. Dugan. *Director:* Don McDougall. *Producer:* David Dortort. **Starring:** Lorne Greene, Pernell Roberts, Dan Blocker, Michael Landon. **Supporting Cast:** Lisa Lu (Su Ling); Richard Loo (General Tsung); Mort Mills (Gordon); Harry Lauter (Barrett); Philip Ahn (Kam Lee).

Synopsis: Joe wins a poker game from Barrett and Gordon. His winnings include a Chinese girl named Su Ling. After he gets a bill of sale for the girl, Joe tries to release her but she insists on remaining with him.

When they return to the Ponderosa, Joe explains to Ben about Su Ling's life in China and being owned by General Tsung. Ben offers to pay her passage back to China but she insists on staying at the ranch.

That night, Gordon and Barrett are taken prisoners by General Tsung, who demands to know where he can find Su Ling. After telling him where she is, Gordon is killed.

General Tsung rides to the ranch demanding that the Cartwrights return Su Ling.

E78. *The Frenchman* (December 10, 1961)

Credits: *Writer:* Norman Lessing. *Director:* Christian Nyby. *Producer:* David Dortort. **Starring:** Lorne Greene, Pernell Roberts, Dan Blocker, Michael Landon. **Supporting Cast:** Andre Philippe (Francois Villon); Erika Peters (Eloise); Robert J. Stevenson (Proprietor); Victor Sen Yung (Hop Sing); Ray Teal (Sheriff Roy Coffee).

Synopsis: Francois Villon and his sister Eloise arrive in Virginia City. He insists that he has come back from the Fifteenth Century as the poet Villon.

When Hoss shows his skepticism, the poet provokes him into a duel. With the challenge left undecided, the Villons accompany Hoss to the Ponderosa. The Cartwrights find themselves infatuated with the poet's sister.

After robbing the Cartwrights, Villon insists on being punished as was the real Francois Villon.

E79. *The Tin Badge* (December 17, 1961)

Credits: *Writer:* Don Ingalls. *Director:* Lewis Allen. *Producer:* David Dortort. **Starring:** Lorne Greene, Pernell Roberts, Dan Blocker, Michael Landon. **Supporting Cast:** Vic Morrow (Ab Brock); Karen Steele (Sylvia Ann); John Litel (Major Goshen); Robert Fortier (Higgler); Bill Catching (Virgil); Stephen Chase (Bankey).

Synopsis: Joe rides into the town of Rubicon, where Brock and Mayor Goshen want him to wear the sheriff's badge for two weeks while the sheriff is away. Unsure of what to do, he returns home to tell Ben who does not like the idea. After Adam and Hoss laugh at him, Joe storms out, determined to take the job.

Two men, dressed in black, register at the hotel. They were hired by Brock and the mayor to kill a man getting off the stage because he knew Brock under a different name.

E80. *Gabrielle* (December 24, 1961)

Credits: *Writer:* Anthony Lawrence. *Director:* Thomas Carr. *Producer:* David Dortort. **Starring:** Lorne Greene, Pernell Roberts, Dan Blocker, Michael Landon. **Supporting Cast:** Diane Montford (Gabrielle Wickham); John Abbott (Zachariah Wickam); Kevin Hagen (Everett Pastor); Victor Sen Yung (Hop Sing); Evelyn Scott, Mike McGreevey, Selmer Jackson.

Synopsis: Hoss and Joe come across a wrecked wagon containing two dead people and a 12-year-old blind girl named Gabrielle. Back at the Ponderosa, she tells the Cartwrights that she and her parents had been on their way to find her grandfather, Zachariah.

Joe and Hoss take her to visit him but, after getting shot at, they are ordered off of Mt. Davidson by Zachariah.

The Cartwrights decide that Gabrielle should live with the Pastors. Their son Jeremy takes Gabrielle back up the mountain but he is scared off by the hermit. This leaves the girl alone on the mountain with the embittered old man.

Note: Location shooting took place at Incline Village. Songs sung at a Christmas party were "Joy to the World" and "O Come All Ye Faithful."

E81. *Land Grab* (December 31, 1961)

Credits: *Writer:* Ward Hawkins. *Director:* David Orrick McDearmon. *Producer:* David Dortort. **Starring:** Lorne Greene, Pernell Roberts, Dan Blocker, Michael Landon. **Supporting Cast:** John McGiver (Colonel Bragg); George Mitchell (Mike Sullivan); Don Wilbanks (Jack); Lisette Loze (Lisete Belrose); Victor Sen Yung (Hop Sing); Ray Teal (Sheriff Roy Coffee).

Synopsis: Joe and Ben discover three men building a cabin on the Ponderosa. One of the men, Mike Sullivan, tells Ben that he has a deed signed by John Poke. They also discover two women and Mr. and Mrs. Belrose, who also make the same claim.

Colonel Bragg arrives on the Ponderosa to pay a visit to his old friend Ben. The Colonel feels that the homesteaders are trespassers.

When the Cartwrights try to force the settlers off the Ponderosa, they become defensive. Determined more than ever to keep their land, the settlers will stop at nothing to hold onto it, including murder.

E82. *The Tall Stranger* (January 7, 1962)

Credits: *Writer:* Ward Hawkins. *Director:* Don McDougall. *Producer:* David Dortort. **Starring:** Lorne Greene, Pernell Roberts, Dan Blocker, Michael Landon. **Supporting Cast:** Sean McClory (Mark Connors); Kathie Browne (Margie Owens);

Famous fireplace at the ranch house. (Photograph by Linda F. Leiby.)

Jacqueline Scott (Kathy); Russell Thorson (Owens); Ed Prentiss, Dorothy Neumann, Forrest Taylor, Robert Ridgely, Bart Carlon, Henry Wills.

Synopsis: Hoss takes Margie on a buggy ride and awkwardly asks for her hand in marriage. He wants to announce their engagement at a Saturday night party at the Ponderosa but she wants him to ask her father first.

Going to the Owens' house to ask her father for his daughter's hand, Hoss finds Mark Connors entertaining them with stories of his travels.

At the party, Hoss presents Margie with June Bug, a horse, as an engagement gift. The next day, Margie tells Hoss that she is sorry that she can not marry him because she is going to marry Connors.

Months after the wedding, her father comes to the ranch telling Hoss that Margie's marriage is in trouble and that he has only heard from Connors demanding money.

E83. *The Lady from Baltimore* (January 14, 1962)

Credits: *Writer:* Elliot Arnold. *Director:* John Peyser. *Producer:* David Dortort. **Starring:** Lorne Greene, Pernell Roberts, Dan Blocker, Michael Landon. **Supporting Cast:** Mercedes McCambridge (Deborah Banning); Hayden Rorke (Horace Banning); Audrey Dalton (Melinda Banning); Robert Adler.

Synopsis: Ben meets the stage bringing Deborah Banning and her daughter Melinda. He escorts them back to the Ponderosa. Melinda tells her mother that she does not want to marry Little Joe as her mother has planned. Her mother does not want her to make the same mistake she did by marrying a loser like her father, Horace.

Horace arrives at the ranch, surprising Deborah. He informs her that he has lost his job. She orders him to leave after telling him about Melinda's impending marriage to Joe. He is warned that if he interferes with the wedding plans, she will kill him.

E84. *The Ride* (January 21, 1962)

Credits: *Writer:* Ward Hawkins. *Director:* Don McDougall. *Producer:* David Dortort. **Starring:** Lorne Greene, Pernell Roberts, Dan Blocker, Michael Landon. **Supporting Cast:** Jan Merlin (Bill Enders); Ray Teal (Sheriff Roy Coffee); Grace Gaynor (Mary Enders); Hal Baylor (Stewart); Chubby Johnson (Toby Barker); Bob Harris.

Synopsis: The Goat Springs stage is robbed by a man wearing a hood and manager Toby Barker is murdered. Adam is positive that the robber was Bill Enders, with whom he co-owns a mine. Because his friend Bill is so well thought of in Virginia City, Adam cannot prove his suspicions.

Enders was seen in Virginia City an hour and a half after the murder and no one feels that he could have made the ride in that short a period. To prove them wrong, Adam decides that he has to go on the ride himself.

E85. *The Storm* (January 28, 1962)

Credits: *Writer:* Denne Petticlerc. *Director:* Lewis Allen. *Producer:* David Dortort. **Starring:** Lorne Greene, Pernell Roberts, Dan Blocker, Michael Landon. **Supporting Cast:** Frank Overton (Captain Matthew White); Brooke Hayward (Laura White).

Synopsis: After Ben escorts Laura and her father Captain Matthew White to the Ponderosa, the captain tells him of his leave of absence from the sea.

The next day, Joe takes Laura for a buggy ride to see the Ponderosa. Along the way, they stop at a small run-down cabin that will someday be his. As a result of a storm, they are forced to spend the night.

Upon their return home, Joe is punched by Matthew. Joe realizes that he and Laura are in love.

Ben speaks to Matthew about the impending marriage but is met by strong resistance.

E86. *The Auld Sod* (February 4, 1962)

Credits: *Writer:* Charles Lang. *Director:* William Witney. *Producer:* David Dortort. **Starring:** Lorne Greene, Pernell Roberts, Dan Blocker, Michael Landon.

Supporting Cast: Cheerio Meredith (Nellie Lynch); James Dunn (Danny Lynch); Jeff DeBenning (Higgins); Howard Wright (Howie); Keith Richards, Jack Carr, Pete Robinson, Norman Leavitt.

Synopsis: When the Cartwrights return with a newly purchased bull, they find a clean house and a women sleeping in one of the beds.

To find out the woman's identity, they search her satchel, learning that she is Nellie Lynch. She then tells Ben that her son Danny owns the Ponderosa.

Ben bails Danny Lynch out of jail. After learning that his mother has arrived from Ireland, Danny confesses that he had written her of his ownership of the Ponderosa.

The Cartwrights go along with the charade; agreeing to pretend to work for Danny for a two-week period.

E87. *Gift of Water* (February 11, 1962)

Credits: *Writer:* Borden Chase. *Director:* Jesse Hibbs. *Producer:* David Dortort. **Starring:** Lorne Greene, Pernell Roberts, Dan Blocker, Michael Landon. **Supporting Cast:** Royal Dano (Mr. Ganther); Pam Smith (Lindy Ganther); Majel Barrett (Mrs. Ganther); James Doohan (Bill Collins); Kay Stewart (Mrs. Collins); Paul Birch (Kent).

Synopsis: A drought forces farmers to pick up stakes and head to lusher property closer to the Ponderosa. Neighboring ranchers become vigilantes in order to stop the farmers. Trying to end the violence, the Cartwrights join forces with Mr. Ganther to find water.

E88. *The Jack Knife* (February 18, 1962)

Credits: *Writer:* Frank Chase. *Director:* William Witney. *Producer:* David Dortort. **Starring:** Lorne Greene, Pernell Roberts, Dan Blocker, Michael Landon. **Supporting Cast:** Bethel Leslie (Ann Grant); John Archer (Matthew Grant); Donald Losby (Jody Grant); Robert H. Harris (Chad); Robert Karnes.

Synopsis: Adam takes Matthew Grant home to Oak Meadow after finding him hurt. At the house, Adam tends Matthew's wounds because the man's wife Ann is reluctant to do so. She then asks Matthew why he has come back.

After dinner, Adam tells Matthew that he is looking for 30 head of cattle that were rustled.

The next day, Adam and Matt's son Jody are working at the ranch when two men ride up looking for Grant. Matthew wants to know about the cattle and his share of the money.

The two men seem suspicious of Adam working on the ranch. They suggest another heist of 150 head of Cartwright cattle but want him to get rid of Adam.

E89. *The Guilty* (February 25, 1962)

Credits: *Writer:* Clifford Irving. *Director:* Lewis Allen. *Producer:* David Dortort. **Starring:** Lorne Greene, Pernell Roberts, Dan Blocker, Michael Landon. **Supporting Cast:** Lyle Bettger (Lem Partridge); Charles Maxwell (Jack Groat); Ann Benton (Caroline); Edward C. Platt (Wade); Ray Teal (Sheriff Roy Coffee); Jack Easton, Jr.

Synopsis: Retired Sheriff Lem Partridge, a neighbor of Ben's, runs into Jack Groat, whom he had sent to jail ten years before for killing his own wife.

The next day at the land office, after being provoked by Grant, Jimmy Partridge is killed while going for Ben's gun. Lem Partridge holds Ben responsible for his son's death because he failed to try to stop the shooting.

E90. *The Wooing of Abigail Jones* (March 4, 1962)

Credits: *Writer:* Norman Lessing. *Director:* Christian Nyby. *Producer:* David Dortort. **Starring:** Lorne Greene, Pernell Roberts, Dan Blocker, Michael Landon. **Supporting Cast:** Vaughn Monroe (Hank Meyers); Eileen Ryan (Abigail Jones); Norma Varden (Ma Nutley); Diana Darrin (Margie); Robert J. Stevenson.

Synopsis: Hank Meyers, a ranch hand, is in love with schoolteacher Abigail Jones, but she wants to be courted.

Trying to help their friend, Hoss and Joe try various things, including getting Hank to place his coat over a mud puddle. But Abigail slips and falls in the mud.

That night, Hoss and Joe overhear Hank singing to his horse. With Adam's help, they decide to teach him the correct way to sing. When all else fails, they coerce Adam into doing the singing for Hank. He hides while Hank pretends to serenade Abigail. Hearing a noise, she comes out to investigate. Finding only Adam, she is sure he loves her and she proposes.

E91. *The Lawmaker* (March 11, 1962)

Credits: *Writers:* Dick Nelson, John A. Johns. *Director:* Christian Nyby. *Producer:* David Dortort. **Starring:** Lorne Greene, Pernell Roberts, Dan Blocker, Michael Landon. **Supporting Cast:** Arthur Franz (Asa Moran); Ray Teal (Sheriff Roy Coffee); Les Tremayne (Judge Jackson); Charles Briggs (Charlie Fitch); John Mitchum (Lou Palmer); Rosalind Roberts, Roy Engel, Bob Miles, J. P. Catching.

Synopsis: When Roy Coffee interrupts an express office robbery, his leg is injured. Before leaving on the stage for San Francisco on business, Roy asks Ben to be his replacement. Ben turns him down and suggests Asa Moran instead.

Asa and his deputy Charlie are on patrol when they spot two horses outside the freight office. They order the men to come out, and Asa kills them both.

After Lou, one of their hired hands, is arrested and beaten, the Cartwrights ride to town to confront Asa. When Adam talks to Charlie about Asa's actions, he tells him what happened at the express office. Asa comes in and hits Adam over the head and takes him to jail. He tells Charlie to leave the cell door open so that Adam can be shot while trying to escape.

E92. *Look to the Stars* (March 18, 1962)

Credits: *Writers:* Robert Fresco, Paul R. Link. *Director:* Don McDougall. *Producer:* David Dortort. **Starring:** Lorne Greene, Pernell Roberts, Dan Blocker, Michael Landon. **Supporting Cast:** Douglas Lambert (Albert Michelson); William Schallert (Mr. Norton); Joe DeSantis (Samuel Michelson); Penny Santon (Rosalie Michelson); Salvador Baguez, Booth Colman, Wallace Rooney, Richard Vera.

Synopsis: After Ben is thrown from the back of a wagon as a result of Albert Michelson's telescope experiment, he is taken into Samuel Michelson's shop. When

Sam scolds his son for almost killing Ben, his mother says that he will be a scientist someday. Ben and Adam are then told that Albert has been expelled from school.

Ben goes to see about an application for Albert to go to West Point but learns the appointments are filled. He then finds out that Annapolis is having entrance exams in two weeks. After Mr. Norton, the teacher, refuses to tutor Albert, Ben talks Adam into the job.

Later, when Mr. Norton visits the Michelson's store, he is questioned about why Albert was asked to leave school. Informed about the entrance test for Annapolis, Mr. Norton tells the Michelsons that Albert does not belong there.

Note: In 1907, Albert Michelson received the first Nobel Prize in Science awarded to an American. The prize was for the measurement of light waves.

E93. *The Gable* (April 1, 1962)

Credits: *Writers:* Michael Landon, Frank Cleaver. *Director:* William Witney. *Producer:* David Dortort. **Starring:** Lorne Greene, Pernell Roberts, Dan Blocker, Michael Landon. **Supporting Cast:** Charles McGraw (Sheriff Gains); Ben Johnson (Stan); Robert Sampson (Artie); Raymond Greenleaf (Judge); Jan Harrison, Joey Walsh, I. Stanford Jolley, Robert Foulk, Morris Ankrum.

Synopsis: The Cartwrights ride into a small town late at night after a long cattle drive. After putting up their horses, Artie, the stable owner, overhears them talking about the $30,000 that they are carrying.

Three hooded men rob the bank, killing the banker. When the sheriff is informed of the crime, he comes to the stables to arrest the Cartwrights. On the way to the jail, he tells everyone that they will get a fair trial the next day.

At the trial, a young man, testifies about the robbery. He describes the brand on the saddle bags and the size of the robbers. After further testimony, the Cartwrights are found guilty and sentenced to hang.

Note: Location filming took place at Iverson's Movie Ranch.

*E94. *The Crucible* (April 8, 1962)

Credits: *Writer:* John T. Dugan. *Director:* Paul Nickell. *Producer:* David Dortort. **Starring:** Lorne Greene, Pernell Roberts, Dan Blocker, Michael Landon. **Supporting Cast:** Lee Marvin (Peter Kane); Howard Ledig (Frank Preston); Barry Cahill (Jim Gann); William Edmondson, Roy Barcroft, Paul Barselow.

Synopsis: After leaving Joe in Eastgate, Adam is robbed by Preston and Gann of $5,000, his horse and supplies and left on foot. He starts walking and staggers into Peter Kane's camp. Over some food and water, Adam tells Kane that he is angry about the men who left him to die.

Adam wants to borrow Kane's mule. He is told that if he works the mine claim for three days he will be allowed to borrow the animal.

Adam and Kane work the mine with Adam doing most of the labor. When Adam decides that it is time to leave, Kane kills the mule, deciding to use Adam as a replacement. The deranged man continues to torment Adam in order to drive him to kill.

E95. *Inger, My Love* (April 15, 1962)

Credits: *Writers:* Frank Cleaver, David Dortort, Anthony Lawrence. *Director:* Lewis Allen. *Producer:* David Dortort. **Starring:** Lorne Greene, Pernell Roberts,

Dan Blocker, Michael Landon. **Supporting Cast:** Inga Swenson (Inger); James Philbrook (McWhorter); Jeremy Slate (Gunnar); Johnny Stephens, Taggart Casey, Harlan Warde, Charles Fredericks, Helen Brown, Nolan Leary.

Synopsis: During a storm, Ben is worried because Hoss is late for his own birthday party. He remembers the first time he met Hoss's mother, Inger.

When Ben and young Adam arrive in Galesburg, Illinois, Ben eventually gets work in McWharter's saloon. Inger begs her brother Gunnar to take more interest in their store but he is only interested in gambling and drinking.

Several days later, Ben, Inger and Adam go on a picnic where she tells of her memories of Sweden. Then Gunnar arrives to demand that Inger get back to town and to stay away from Ben.

After Ben is fired from his job, he loads his wagon preparing to leave. Inger then offers him a job in the store. After Ben agrees to take the job, he proposes to her.

Note: As a result of a riding accident, Dan Blocker appears at the end of this episode with his arm in a sling.

E96. *Blessed Are They* (April 22, 1962)

Credits: *Writers:* Borden Chase, Frank Cleaver. *Director:* Don McDougall. *Producer:* David Dortort. **Starring:** Lorne Greene, Pernell Roberts, Dan Blocker, Michael Landon. **Supporting Cast:** Robert Brown (Reverend); Leslie Wales (Peggy); Ford Rainey (Clarke); Irene Tedrow (Mrs. Mahan); Rory O'Brien (Kenny); Walter Sande, Amzie Strickland, Robert Brubaker, Robert Foulk, Tracy Stratford, Arthur Peterson.

Synopsis: The town is divided by the Mahan-Clarke feud over who will take care of two children left without parents. Ben is forced to try to bring the situation to an acceptable conclusion before things get out of hand.

E97. *The Dowry* (April 29, 1962)

Credits: *Writer:* Robert Vincent Wright. *Director:* Christian Nyby. *Producer:* David Dortort. **Starring:** Lorne Greene, Pernell Roberts, Dan Blocker, Michael Landon. **Supporting Cast:** Luciana Paluzzi (Michelle Dubois); Steven Geray (Alexander Dubois); Lee Bergere (Ricardo Fernandez); Ken Mayer (Crusty); Roy Engel (Doctor).

Synopsis: The stage is robbed by three men who take a metal box from Alexander Dubois. Dubois is wounded when he fires back at the outlaws.

After learning that her father will be all right, Michelle expresses concern over her missing dowry valued at $100,000. Ricardo Fernandez informs them that without the dowry, the marriage cannot take place.

Adam and Hoss track down the bandits. As they chase them, the chest is dropped. When they get back to the ranch, Ben discovers that the jewels are fake.

That night, the three bandits sneak back into Alexander's room trying to steal the box. When Alexander shoots at them, they drop it. The Cartwrights chase the outlaws, but they escape.

E98. *The Long Night* (May 6, 1962)

Credits: *Writers:* George Stackalee, E. M. Parsons. *Director:* William Witney. *Producer:* David Dortort. **Starring:** Lorne Greene, Pernell Roberts, Michael Landon.

Supporting Cast: James Coburn (Trace); Bing Russell (Poindexter); Jack Chaplain (Billy McCord); William Bramley (Townsend); Whit Bissell (Neighbor); Frank Ferguson, Paul Dubov, Dorothy Adams, E. J. Andre, Eric Barnes, Al Avalon.

Synopsis: After making a cattle deal, Adam heads to Genoa with a check for $5,000.

Meanwhile, two escaped prisoners, Trace and Poindexter, are trying to break their chains. When Brubaker, the guard, catches up with them, they get the drop on him and Trace exchanges clothes with the guard.

Later, in the town of Bowleg, the Sheriff is organizing a posse to search for the escaped men. On the way, Adam is stopped by Poindexter who orders him, at gunpoint, to swap clothes. he then rides away with Adam following.

After Adam catches up with Poindexter, he is fired at and forced to kill him before they can change clothes. When Trace rides up, he does not believe Adam's account of what happened. Trace demands that Adam turn over the money or he will kill him.

E99. *The Mountain Girl* (May 13, 1962)

Credits: *Writer:* John Furia, Jr. *Director:* Don McDougall. *Producer:* David Dortort. **Starring:** Lorne Greene, Pernell Roberts, Dan Blocker, Michael Landon. **Supporting Cast:** Nina Shipman (Trudy Harker); Carl Benton Reid (Josiah Harker); Warren Oates (Paul); Nancy Hadley (Stephanie); Will Wright (Seth); Mary Treen (Annie).

Synopsis: While Joe is riding in the hills, he comes across Seth, an old man lying in the road. When he helps Seth to return to his camp, he finds out that the man has a granddaughter named Trudy. Seth tells Trudy about her family, the Harkers, in San Francisco. Before dying, he makes them promise to find the Harkers so that Trudy will have a home. After saying good bye to Paul, who is in love with her, they return to the Ponderosa.

Later Ben receives a wire stating that the Harkers will arrive in two weeks. Realizing that she may not fit in, Trudy gets Joe to teach her how to be a lady.

Note: Dan Blocker's shoulder was still in a sling as this episode was completed (after "Inger, My Love").

E100. *The Miracle Maker* (May 20, 1962)

Credits: *Writers:* Frank Cleaver, Lewis Wood. *Director:* Don McDougall. *Producer:* David Dortort. **Starring:** Lorne Greene, Dan Blocker, Michael Landon. **Supporting Cast:** Ed Nelson (Garth); Patricia Breslin (Susan Blanchard); Mort Mills (Thorne); Jean Inness (Aunt Celia); Tol Avery (Dr. Moore); Raymond Bailey (Sam Blanchard); Bill Quinn, Robert Adler.

Synopsis: Because of Hoss' shoulder injury, Susan Blanchard is forced to drive the buggy home. There is an accident in which her father is killed and she is left unable to walk.

Later, at Susan's house, a specialist says that there seems to be nothing wrong with her legs. Hoss, feeling responsible for her accident, assures her that he will find some way to help her.

After Hoss sees Garth healing Thorn, who is a cripple, he gets him to pay a visit to Susan. Garth assures her that he can cure her. During his treatments, Garth realizes that he has fallen in love with Susan and proposes marriage.

When Thorn asks Garth for some of Susan's money, they have a falling out. Feeling betrayed, Thorn tells Hoss that Garth is a fake. Hoss vows to keep Susan from marrying Garth.

Fourth Season
(September 23, 1962–May 26, 1963)

E101. *The First Born* (September 23, 1962)
Credits: *Writers:* Judith and George W. George. *Director:* Don McDougall. *Producer:* David Dortort. **Starring:** Lorne Greene, Pernell Roberts, Dan Blocker, Michael Landon. **Supporting Cast:** Barry Coe (Clay Stafford); Ray Teal (Sheriff Roy Coffee); Eddy Waller (Harry); Don Beddoe (Stan Perkins); Mike Ragan (Miner); Robert Karnes (Miner); Ben Erway (Cashier).

Synopsis: Ben, Hoss and Little Joe are in town hiring men for a round-up. Harry and another man, Clay Stafford, are both hired. Clay tells Joe that he was born in New Orleans. During the round-up, Clay volunteers to go back to the ranch to help Joe with supplies. While there, he asks Joe what he remembers about his mother. Joe shows him a picture.

Saturday night, while playing poker, Clay shoots and kills a miner when he is accused of cheating.

Clay is getting ready to leave the next day when Joe asks him to stay. Clay then announces that he and Joe are really half brothers. Adam, skeptical of Clay's claim, sends a wire to New Orleans to verify his story.

Review: *Variety* (September 26, 1962): "[D]espite the doses of soap sentimentality there were winning moments in the script…. [The Leads] make an excellent combo."

Note: Location shooting took place at Incline Village. At the end of the show, Lorne Greene asked viewers to be sure to tune in the following week to see the new Chevrolet models.

E102. *The Quest* (September 30, 1962)
Credits: *Writers:* John Joseph, Thomas Thompson. *Director:* Christian Nyby. *Producer:* David Dortort. **Starring:** Lorne Greene, Pernell Roberts, Dan Blocker, Michael Landon. **Supporting Cast:** Grant Richards (Will Poavey); James Beck (Dave Donovan); Frank Gerstle (Weber); Dan Riss (Crawford); Charles Seel (Hawkins); Grandon Rhodes, Harry Lauter.

Synopsis: To prove his independence, Joe stays up all night working on an idea for a lumber contract and refuses Hoss and Adam's assistance. Ben tells Joe not to let his pride keep him from asking for help.

Joe arrives at the bid sight with Dave Donovan. He wins the contract, beating out Will Poavey, who has become very upset. After going to the bank to post a $5,000 performance bond, Joe leaves Donovan to hire a crew. He entices each man by giving them a bottle. After work begins on the flume, Joe heads out to get more horses, leaving Donovan in charge. When Joe returns, he finds him gambling and drinking. After being fired, Donovan is hired by Poavey to stop Joe.

Note: Location shooting took place at Incline Village. This episode ran without commercials in order for the sponsor, Chevrolet, to introduce its new models at the end of the show.

E103. *The Artist* (October 7, 1962)

Credits: *Writer:* Frank Chase. *Director:* Don McDougall. *Producer:* David Dortort. **Starring:** Lorne Greene, Pernell Roberts, Dan Blocker, Michael Landon. **Supporting Cast:** Dan O'Herlihy (Matthew Raine); Virginia Grey (Ann Loring); Arch Johnson (Gavin); William Keene (Stevens); S. John Launer (Buyer); Frank Chase, Ralph Montgomery.

Synopsis: Recluse Matthew Raine, a sightless artist, becomes friends with Ben.

Ben is asked by Ann Loring, who loves Raine, to extend his visit in order to help Mathew to feel better about himself. After the two spend many hours together, Raine's disposition seems to improve. But when someone wants to buy a painting, Raine gets upset nearly destroying his studio.

Gavin, who works for Raine, has resented him for years and decides to sell all of Matthew's works of art.

E104. *A Hot Day for a Hanging* (October 14, 1962)

Credits: *Writers:* Preston Wood, Elliott Arnold. *Director:* William F. Claxton. *Producer:* David Dortort. **Starring:** Lorne Greene, Dan Blocker. **Supporting Cast:** Denver Pyle (Sheriff Tom Stedman); Olive Sturgess (Mary Ann); Roy Roberts (Fillmore); Terry Becker (Shukie); Kelly Thordsen (Larsen); John Harmon, Gene Roth, Rayford Barnes, Lane Bradford, John Mitchum, Robert Carson.

Synopsis: Hoss is taking $12,000 in cash to Ben in order to make a land deal. On his way through the town of Duchman Flats, he is apprehended by Sheriff Stedman and charged with bank robbery and murder. The widow of the slain teller forces the only witness to make a positive identification.

The men of the town decide that a hanging is faster than waiting for a trial. After the banker talks them out of it, he sends a telegram to Ben. When two strangers try to rob the safe in the sheriff's office, the townspeople believe that they were trying to break Hoss out of jail. They begin to talk again of lynching Hoss.

E105. *The Deserter* (October 21, 1962)

Credits: *Writer:* Norman Lessing. *Director:* William Witney. *Producer:* David Dortort. **Starring:** Lorne Greene, Pernell Roberts, Dan Blocker. **Supporting Cast:** Claude Akins (Col. Edward J. Dunwoody); Robert Sampson (Bill Winters); Gale Garnett (Maria); Anthony Caruso (Keokuk); George Keymas (Running Wolf); Hal Jon Norman, Andrea Darvi, Robert Carricart, Ricky Branson.

Synopsis: Army Colonel Edward Dunwoody arrives at the Ponderosa looking for a deserter. Being shown a picture, the Cartwrights realize that it is Billy

Winters, a neighbor. It seems that he had warned the Indians of an attack ordered by his father, the colonel, ten years before.

The Shoshones take Bill away for trying to save his wounded father's life. Later, Maria, Bill's wife, comes to Ben for help because the Indians have sentenced Bill to death.

E106. *The Way Station* (October 29, 1962)

Credits: *Writer:* Frank Cleaver. *Director:* Lewis Allen. *Producer:* David Dortort. **Starring:** Pernell Roberts. **Supporting Cast:** Robert Vaughn (Luke Martin); Dawn Wells (Marty); Trevor Bardette (Jesse); Dorothy Green (Lucy); Walter Reed, Raymond Guth, Keith Richards.

Synopsis: Adam rides into a way station to escape an on-coming storm. Marty and her grandfather, Jesse, invite him to spend the night in the barn. After supper, Marty comes to the barn to talk to Adam and to get her books about distant places.

Later, Cody comes in also looking for shelter. Marty asks him to take her with him to Mexico.

When a stagecoach carrying two passengers pulls in four hours late, one of them recognizes Cody as the outlaw, Luke Martin. After Luke confiscates all of the guns, Adam learns that he is wanted for murder and has a bounty of $5,000 on his head.

E107. *The War Comes to Washoe* (November 4, 1962)

Credits: *Writer:* Alvin Sapinsky. *Director:* Don McDougall. *Producer:* David Dortort. **Starring:** Lorne Greene, Pernell Roberts, Dan Blocker, Michael Landon. **Supporting Cast:** Harry Townes (Judge Terry); Joyce Taylor (Morvath Terry); Barry Kelley (Stewart); Alan Caillou (Cragsmuir); David Whorf, Wallace Roney, Harry Swoger, Marshall Reed.

Synopsis: At a Ponderosa party, Ben asks Shakespearean actor Walter Cragsmuir to give a reading. Trouble begins when he is interrupted by a drunk singing "Dixie."

Ben goes to town where he witnesses a confrontation between Bill Stewart and Judge Terry. Ben tells the judge that he believes the Comstock should be part of the Union and plans to vote that way.

Receiving a telegram, Terry and his daughter Morvath go to the Ponderosa to inform Ben that he has to send two delegates to the statehood convention. Since Hoss and Adam are away marking trees for a lumber contract, Joe gets the job by default. When Joe and Morvath, who have fallen in love, come into the house, he is told about being selected as a delegate. He does not want the position but Ben tells him that it is his civic responsibility.

That night, when Adam and Hoss make camp, they discover the dead body of Peters, Cragsmuir's aide. Adam finds a letter from Cragsmuir which indicates a conspiracy.

Note: Location shooting took place at Incline Village. This episode was based on the real-life events of British spy Bill Stewart.

E108. *Knight Errant* (November 18, 1962)

Credits: *Writer:* Joseph Hoffman. *Director:* William F. Claxton. *Producer:*

David Dortort. **Starring:** Lorne Greene, Pernell Roberts, Dan Blocker, Michael Landon. **Supporting Cast:** John Doucette (Walter Prescott); Judi Meredith (Lotty); Ray Teal (Sheriff Roy Coffee); Phil Chambers (Dick Thompson); Roy Engel (Doctor); Tyler McVey (Townsman); Tina Menard (Francesca); George Robotham (Frank); Gil Perkins (Whitney).

Synopsis: Ben and Hoss ride into town where they learn that Walter Prescott is about to pick up his mail order bride. He is so excited that his leg is broken when he is hit by a wagon, which prevents him from getting his bride. Hoss then agrees to go get her.

The next day Ben, Joe and Adam arrive at Walter's ranch for the wedding. After Lotty is introduced to Walter, he accuses Hoss of falling in love with her because she will not marry him. When Walter asks the Cartwrights to leave, Lotty runs after Hoss, begging him to take her with him.

After Walter takes Lotty to the hotel in town, he begins drinking in the saloon. When he sees Hoss in town, Prescott decides to put a $3,000 bounty on his head for wife stealing.

E109. *The Beginning* (November 25, 1962)

Credits: *Writer:* Preston Wood. *Director:* Christian Nyby. *Producer:* David Dortort. **Starring:** Lorne Greene, Michael Landon. **Supporting Cast:** Carl Reindel (Billy Horn); Ken Lynch (Milton Tanner); Ray Teal (Sheriff Roy Coffee); Robert Burton (Lewis); Raymond Bailey, Francis De Sales, Lon Dean.

Synopsis: While the Cartwrights and a posse are chasing Indians who are stealing horses, a young man sneaks into their camp. They soon discover that he is white and his name is Billy Horn. He tells them that his father's name was Matt. Roy wants to lock him up but Ben insists that he come to stay on the Ponderosa.

Ben's lawyer Ned Lewis informs him that Milt Tanner is filing title claiming part of the Ponderosa. Ned also tells Ben that his title is questionable and if taken to court he will probably lose. Ben meets with Lewis and Tanner who have a proposition about the timber rights, but they end up irritating Ben.

Ben and Joe try to explain the legal system to Billy, but he has trouble understanding it. Billy tells Joe what he had learned from his mother and also tries to sort out what he has learned from the Indians and whites. Billy rides to Tanner's house, where Tanner threatens him.

E110. *The Deadly Ones* (December 2, 1962)

Credits: *Writers:* Dene Petticlerc, N. B. Stone, Jr. *Director:* William Witney. *Producer:* David Dortort. **Starring:** Lorne Greene, Michael Landon. **Supporting Cast:** Will Kuluva (General Diaz); Leo Gordon (Forsythe); Lee Farr (Sims); Jena Engstrom (Molly).

Synopsis: Joe is shot in the back by Forsythe, one of General Diaz's men. They ransack the house as Ben rides in. Taken hostage, Ben is denied a doctor for Joe. Diaz, knowing something of wounds, removes the bullet.

Explaining that he is there to steal a heavily guarded gold shipment, the general forces Ben to escort them through the back country. After being punished for shooting Joe, Forsythe plots with Pablo to double-cross Diaz and take the gold for themselves.

Gun rack at the ranch house. (Photograph by Linda F. Leiby.)

E111. *Gallagher's Sons* (December 9, 1962)

Credits: *Writer:* Dick Nelson. *Director:* Christian Nyby. *Producer:* David Dortort. **Starring:** Dan Blocker. **Supporting Cast:** Eileen Chesis (Will Gallagher); Larrian Gillespie (Charlie Gallagher); Robert Strauss (Blake); Craig Curtis (Tully); Tom Greenway (Sheriff); Chubby Johnson (Sam); Victor French (Conn); Ken Mayer, Bill Henry.

Synopsis: After Hoss buries the father of Will and Charlie, he promises to take them to their Aunt Cloe. The girls pack their belongings, including a bag of stolen money. Hoss later finds out that their real names are Wilamena and Charlotte.

After Hoss is arrested in Cantill for kidnapping, the two girls leave on the stage. Scared by one of their father's partners, Will and Charlie return on horseback.

Hoss is released from jail and the sheriff is on the lookout for the men who robbed the freight office of $34,000. Trouble really begins when Hoss and the girls cross the desert on their way to Furnace Wells.

E112. *The Decision* (December 16, 1962)

Credits: *Writers:* Frank Chase (Teleplay), Norman Jacobs (Story). *Director:* William F. Claxton. *Producer:* David Dortort. **Starring:** Lorne Greene, Pernell Roberts, Dan Blocker, Michael Landon. **Supporting Cast:** DeForest Kelley

(Dr. Johns); John Hoyt (Judge Grant); Lisabeth Hush (Karen Johns); Walter Sande (Sheriff); Eddie Quillan (Culp); Will J. White.

Synopsis: While on a cattle drive, Hoss is seriously injured in a horse accident. Ben takes him to the nearest town in search of medical aid.

Ben finds the only available doctor has been jailed and sentenced to hang. He then goes to Judge Grant to get him to release the doctor to tend his son. He denies Ben's request as he holds Dr. Johns responsible for the death of his wife during surgery.

E113. *The Good Samaritan* (December 23, 1962)

Credits: *Writer:* Robert Bloomfield. *Director:* Don McDougall. *Producer:* David Dortort. **Starring:** Lorne Greene, Dan Blocker. **Supporting Cast:** Jeanne Cooper (Abigail Hinton); Don Collier (Wade Tyree); Noreen DeVita (Bonnie Hinton); Roy Engel (Doctor).

Synopsis: When his girlfriend walks out on him, Wade Tyree feels sorry for himself. Widow Abigail Hinton and her daughter Bonnie were also deserted by a male friend who often gambled.

Feeling sorry for them, Hoss helps the two get together. They marry out of loneliness rather than love. The more Hoss does Wade's work for him, the less he does for himself, putting the marriage in danger of failure.

E114. *The Jury* (December 30, 1962)

Credits: *Writer:* Robert Vincent Wright. *Director:* Christian Nyby. *Producer:* David Dortort. **Starring:** Lorne Greene, Pernell Roberts, Dan Blocker. **Supporting Cast:** Jack Betts (Jamie Wren); Ray Teal (Sheriff Roy Coffee); James Bell (Olson); Don Haggerty (Murdock); Arthur Space (Judge Crane); Tol Avery (Breese); Bobs Watson, Byron Foulger, Sara Haden, Bob Harris, Michael Hinn.

Synopsis: Jury member Hoss is the only hold-out for a "not guilty" verdict. Jamie Wren is accused of the murder and robbery of Mr. Olson. Later, at the saloon, the murdered man's brother accuses Hoss of paying for his drink with stolen money. The townspeople now think that Wren is guilty and Hoss has taken a bribe. After Jamie escapes from jail, Hoss asks Adam to investigate the two crimes.

E115. *The Colonel* (January 6, 1963)

Credits: *Writer:* Preston Wood. *Director:* Lewis Allen. *Producer:* David Dortort. **Starring:** Lorne Greene, Dan Blocker, Michael Landon. **Supporting Cast:** John Larkin (Col. Frank Medford); Helen Westcott (Emily Colfax); Warren Kemmerling (Asa Flanders); Edward Platt (Will Flanders); Mary Wickes (Martha); Lindsay Workman, Phil Chambers.

Synopsis: Colonel Frank Medford, a friend of Ben's from their Army days, arrives in Virginia City. When Ben comes to meet him, Medford realizes that his old friend is rich. Finding himself not in the same financial situation, Frank lies to Ben about his upcoming business ventures. Trouble begins when he claims that one of his business ventures deals with a railroad survey that he is preparing for Ben.

E116. *Song in the Dark* (January 13, 1963)

Credits: *Writers:* Judith and George W. George. *Director:* Don McDougall. *Producer:* David Dortort. **Starring:** Lorne Greene, Pernell Roberts, Dan Blocker, Michael Landon. **Supporting Cast:** Gregory Walcott (Danny Morgan); Edward Andrews (Rev. William Johnson); Virginia Christine (Mary); Mort Mills (Deputy); Harry Swoger, James Tartan.

Synopsis: When the widow Baker is found robbed and murdered, the chief suspect is Danny Morgan. The evidence points to him because he was heard singing and playing his guitar near the scene of the crime. Also, his arm is scratched, and human skin was discovered beneath her nails.

Adam believes that his friend Danny is innocent because Danny had rescued him when he was out of his head with fever. He sets out to prove Danny's innocence.

E117. *Elegy for a Hangman* (January 20, 1963)

Credits: *Writers:* E. M. Parsons (Teleplay & Story), Shirl Hendrix (Teleplay). *Director:* Hollingsworth Morse. *Producer:* David Dortort. **Starring:** Lorne Greene, Pernell Roberts, Dan Blocker, Michael Landon. **Supporting Cast:** Keir Dullea (Bob Jolley); Otto Kruger (Judge Harry Whitaker); Kevin Hagen (Hobie Klinderman); William Zuckert (Senator Cal Prince); Ray Teal (Sheriff Roy Coffee); Ron Soble, Roy Engel.

Synopsis: A stranger, Bob Jolley, arrives in Virginia City to accuse a drunken Judge Harry Whitaker of sending his innocent father, Carl, to the gallows. Adam defends the judge's honor because of his long friendship with the Cartwrights. After Adam talks with Jolley, he begins to believe his story.

Upon further investigation, Adam discovers that Senator Cal Prince and Hobie Klinderman as well as the judge might have had a lot to gain from Carl Jolley's murder. In an attempt to learn what really happened, Adam organizes an informal meeting in the saloon.

E118. *Half a Rogue* (January 27, 1963)

Credits: *Writer:* Arnold Belgard. *Director:* Don McDougall. *Producer:* David Dortort. **Starring:** Lorne Greene, Pernell Roberts, Dan Blocker, Michael Landon. **Supporting Cast:** Slim Pickens (Jim Leyton); Judson Pratt (Nelson); Bing Russell (Deputy Clem Foster); Victor Sen Yung (Hop Sing); John Milford (Jelke).

Synopsis: While Hoss is out riding, Jim Leyton takes a shot at him. After Leyton demands that Hoss get off his horse, he collapses. When Leyton comes to at the Ponderosa, he introduces himself as "Jim Smith."

The next day, Cal Stacy and his lawyer ride in, claiming that Jim Leyton is wanted for robbery and murder. They also claim that he escaped from jail. After Hoss talks to Clem, Jim is placed in Hoss' custody. Cal rides in to check on Jim and is attacked.

Clem comes to see Ben, telling him that he has found the body of Leyton's partner Carter, who has been shot in the back. He wants Jim to turn himself in.

Note: This episode marks the first time that Bing Russell appeared as Deputy Clem Foster.

E119. *The Last Haircut* (February 3, 1963)

Credits: *Writer:* Charles Lang. *Director:* William F. Claxton. *Producer:* David

Dortort. **Starring:** Lorne Greene, Pernell Roberts, Dan Blocker, Michael Landon. **Supporting Cast:** Perry Lopez (Duke Miller); Jered Barkley (Cal); Rex Holman (Otie); Ray Teal (Sheriff Roy Coffee); Alex Montoya (Carlos); John Harmon (Barber); Chubby Johnson, John Archer, Rafael Lopez, Howard Wendell, Willis Bouchey, Shelby Grant, Joe Higgins.

Synopsis: Joe is waiting to get a haircut with Sheriff Coffee and Carlos Rodriguez. It is finally Joe's turn when Duke Miller pulls a gun, demanding to be next. After Joe gets up, Carlos takes his place. After Duke kills Carlos and hits Joe over the head, he sits in the barber chair.

Later, at the ranch, Adam and Hoss tell Joe that two of the men were in jail. Joe then identifies Duke Miller and almost strangles him. Paco, Carlos' son, tells Joe that there was nothing Joe could have done.

After a Carson City trial, Duke and his two friends are found not guilty. The judge warns everyone that if Duke Miller is killed, they will be tried and hung.

E120. *Marie, My Love* (February 10, 1963)

Credits: *Writers:* Anthony Lawrence (Story & Teleplay), Anne Howard Bailey (Story). *Director:* Lewis Allen. *Producer:* David Dortort. **Starring:** Lorne Greene, Pernell Roberts, Dan Blocker, Michael Landon. **Supporting Cast:** Felicia Farr (Marie); Eduard Franz (Marius Angeville); George Dolenz (D'Arcy); Lily Valenty, Richard Angarola, Jean Del Val.

Synopsis: Joe is injured when his horse stumbles and falls, and Ben remembers that Joe's mother Marie died the same way.

Ben is in New Orleans visiting Marius Angeville, a friend of Jean, to tell him of his death. He also tells Jean's mother and wife about DeMarigny dying.

Marius later takes Ben to visit Marie at a gambling house to speak to her about Jean, but she will not listen.

The next morning, Ben goes to her home where he tells her that Jean died after saving his life. She informs him that her infant son died of a fever and that she was disgraced when Jean ran away. Marius asks for Ben's help with Marie but he does not want to get involved

Darius meets with Jean's mother, who is upset with Ben's interference. She is afraid he might find out that Marie's child is not dead. She also wants him out of New Orleans.

That night, Marius and Ben enter the gambling house to discuss the selling of his furs. While playing poker with Darius, Ben is accused of cheating and is challenged to a duel.

E121. *The Hayburner* (February 17, 1963)

Credits: *Writer:* Alex Sharp. *Director:* William F. Claxton. *Producer:* David Dortort. **Starring:** Lorne Greene, Pernell Roberts, Dan Blocker, Michael Landon. **Supporting Cast:** William Demarest (Enos Milford); Ellen Corby (Cora); Howard Wright (Sam); Percy Helton (Lafe); Paul Bryar (Horse Trader).

Synopsis: When Hoss enters a poker game, he is forced to ante up a thoroughbred race horse to cover his bet. He and Adam have just purchased the animal as an entry in the Virginia City Sweepstakes.

Joe has been earning a great deal of money working for Enos Milford. To get the horse back, Adam and Hoss must borrow $160 from Joe. They will get the money when they agree to Joe's demands.

Things become more complicated when Joe rides Milford's entry in the race, competing against his brothers.

E122. *The Actress* (February 24, 1963)

Credits: *Writer:* Norman Lessing. *Director:* Christian Nyby. *Producer:* David Dortort. **Starring:** Lorne Greene, Pernell Roberts, Dan Blocker, Michael Landon. **Supporting Cast:** Patricia Crowley (Julia Grant); Joey Scott (Tommy Grant); Lester Matthews (Forrester); Robert J. Stevenson (Larkin); Victor Sen Yung (Hop Sing); John Rodney (Edwin Booth); Robert Hoy.

Synopsis: Julia Grant and her son Tommy come to the ranch looking for Ben about a teaching job that she was denied because she is a woman. That night after dinner, she tells the Cartwrights that she believes in teaching the classics. Tommy announces that his mother is an actress and that she sings in saloons to make a living.

The next day on a picnic, Julia sings "Early One Morning." She kisses Joe but then stops, telling him that she badly wants to be an actress and cannot afford to fall in love with him.

That night, Joe suggests that she take a job at the finest saloon in Virginia City at $50 a week. On opening night she sings "Go West Young Gal" but when a fight breaks out, Joe defends her honor. The next day, the saloon owner demands that Joe pay the damages and Julia's salary.

Telling Joe that Edwin Booth is coming to town, Adam says he will be able to arrange a private audition. Julia is thrilled.

E123. *A Stranger Passed This Way* (March 3, 1963)

Credits: *Writer:* William L. Stuart. *Director:* Lewis Allen. *Producer:* David Dortort. **Starring:** Lorne Greene, Pernell Roberts, Dan Blocker, Michael Landon. **Supporting Cast:** Signe Hasso (Christina Vandervoort); Robert Emhardt (Klass Vandervoort); Addison Richards (Dr. Hickman); Robert Carricart (Don Escobar); Dan White (Stableman).

Synopsis: After making a horse deal, Hoss is on the way to Placerville when he is robbed and hit over the head. The next morning, he is picked up by the Vandervoorts but passes out.

After Ben finds out that Hoss has not returned, he goes looking for him. Later, Hoss wakes up at the Vandervoorts and realizes that he has no memory.

That night, Ben finds the picture of Hoss' mother, which had been dropped during the robbery. He then arrives at the Vandervoorts but he is told that Hoss is not there. It seems that Mrs. Vandervoort has adopted Hoss as a replacement for her dead son Hendrick.

E124. *The Way of Aaron* (March 10, 1963)

Credits: *Writer:* Raphael D. Blau. *Director:* Murray Golden. *Producer:* David Dortort. **Starring:** Lorne Greene, Pernell Roberts. **Supporting Cast:** Aneta

Corseaut (Rebecca Kaufmann); Ludwig Donath (Aaron Kaufmann); Jason Wingreen (Hank); Harry Dean Stanton (Stiles); Sarah Selby (Mrs. Cardiff).

Synopsis: Jewish peddler Aaron Kaufmann is displeased that his daughter Rebecca is seeing Adam. Despite her love and respect for her father, she is intrigued by the outside world and with Adam, regardless of their religious differences.

Paying a call on the Kaufmanns, Adam discovers them at a campsite as the sabbath came before they could reach home. Concerned about the safety of the Kaufmanns, Adam makes camp nearby. Two thieves raid the campsite, taking Aaron and Rebecca prisoners to persuade them to hand over their valuables.

E125. *A Woman Lost* (March 17, 1963)

Credits: *Writer:* Frank Chase. *Director:* Don McDougall. *Producer:* David Dortort. **Starring:** Lorne Greene, Pernell Roberts, Dan Blocker, Michael Landon. **Supporting Cast:** Ruta Lee (Rita "Dolly" Marlow); Don Megowan (Mase Sindell); Harry Hickox (Dink Martin); Roger Torrey (Tiny Mac); Bern Hoffman (Fisherman); Dick Miller (Sam); Bill Edwards, Don Kennedy, John Indrisano.

Synopsis: In San Francisco, Ben prevents a drunken saloon singer Rita Marlow ("Dolly") from being attacked. She recognizes Ben and tells him that her husband, son and daughter had been killed in a hotel fire.

When she is discharged, Ben takes her home to the Ponderosa for a month. In Virginia City, Ben and Rita stop for a drink and are served by Mase Sindell, an exprize fighter.

While Mase is at the ranch to fix a chair, Dink Martin and Tiny Mac try to persuade him to return to the ring but he refuses. When Rita goes to town for a drink, Deek offers her $200 to see that Mase gets into the ring. Mase falls in love with Rita. In need of money, she talks him into fighting Tiny.

*E126. *Any Friend of Walter's* (March 24, 1963)

Credits: *Writer:* Lois Hire. *Director:* John Florea. *Producer:* David Dortort. **Starring:** Pernell Roberts, Dan Blocker, Michael Landon. **Supporting Cast:** Arthur Hunnicutt (Obie); Steve Brodie (Macie); Vic Werber (Teague); James Luisi (Willard); Katie Barrett (Bessie Sue); Robert Foulk.

Synopsis: On his way back from a cattle drive, Hoss intends to visit his girlfriend Bessie Sue. He never reaches his destination because he is shot at by outlaws. He takes cover in an old shack belonging to Obie and his dog Walter. The thieves are after the gold hidden in the cabin.

E127. *Mirror of a Man* (March 31, 1963)

Credits: *Writer:* A. I. Bezzerides. *Director:* Lewis Allen. *Producer:* David Dortort. **Starring:** Lorne Greene, Dan Blocker, Michael Landon. **Supporting Cast:** Ron Hayes (Jud Lally/Homer Barnes/Rube Barnes); Nancy Rennick (Amelia); Ford Rainey (Luke Barnes); Tris Coffin (Ralph Austin); Joseph Breen (Sol); Kathleen O'Malley (Janey); Eugene Martin (Tobey).

Synopsis: Unbeknown to the Cartwrights, Jud Lally, who works for them, is really outlaw Homer Barnes. Amelia, who is married to Jud, is also unaware of his true identity.

Trouble begins when Rube Barnes arrives. Being identical twins, Jud reluctantly switches places with him. Rube accompanies Joe to Carson City to take the Arabian stallion that they are there to get. To prevent his son Jud from revealing Rube's plans, Luke Barnes keeps Jud and Amelia hostages.

E128. *My Brother's Keeper* (April 7, 1963)

Credits: *Writer:* Seeley Lester. *Director:* Murray Golden. *Producer:* David Dortort. **Starring:** Lorne Greene, Pernell Roberts, Dan Blocker, Michael Landon. **Supporting Cast:** Carolyn Kearney (Sheila); Brendon Dillon (Emmett); Ken Lynch (Dowd); Addison Richards (Doctor); Jason Johnson (Vince).

Synopsis: A wolf attacks Little Joe, and Adam accidentally hits his brother while firing at the wolf. On the way back to the ranch, they meet the Reardons and use their wagon to get Joe home. Adam, distraught over what happened, plans to leave the ranch and go back to the more civilized East.

Hoss rides to Genoa for medicine. Meanwhile, Adam removes the bullet. When Hoss is returning with the medicine, rancher Dowd steals it, demanding a $3,000 ransom for damages caused by Joe's stampeding horse.

E129. *Five Into the Wind* (April 21, 1963)

Credits: *Writer:* Meyer Dolinsky. *Director:* William F. Claxton. *Producer:* David Dortort. **Starring:** Lorne Greene, Dan Blocker, Michael Landon. **Supporting Cast:** Kathleen Crowley (Lory Hayden); Betsy Jones-Moreland (Nora Whiteley); Kelly Thordsen (Howard Benson); Mario Alcaide (Roberto deSorto); Dabbs Greer (Mr. Henshaw).

Synopsis: On a stage, Benson, a fur trader, shares his beef jerky with Joe and the other passengers and tells them that he is carrying $5,000 in cash. When the driver becomes ill, Joe takes over the reins but cannot stop the team and the stage overturns. When Joe suggests that they stay on the road, Benson overrules him and suggests a shortcut. They start walking and soon arrive at a line shack just as a storm arrives.

That night, Joe discovers that Benson has been stabbed to death and his $5,000 is missing. When he is found bending over the body, Joe is accused of the crime by the other passengers.

Note: Location filming took place at Griffith Park.

E130. *Saga of Whizzer McGee* (April 28, 1963)

Credits: *Writer:* Robert Lyon Welsch. *Director:* Don McDougall. *Producer:* David Dortort. **Starring:** Lorne Greene, Dan Blocker. **Supporting Cast:** George Brenlin (Whizzer McGee); Jeanne Bal (Melissa); Med Flory (Otis); Burt Mustin (Mashburn); Hal Baylor (Big Red).

Synopsis: Whizzer McGee has grown resentful after being ridiculed about his size. Hoss feels sorry for him and assists him in securing work at a mercantile establishment.

Whizzer begins to see Melissa, a saloon entertainer. Unbeknownst to him, she and Otis are lovers and plan a bank robbery. But they need access to Whizzer's room, which is next to the bank.

E131. *Thunder Man* (May 5, 1963)

Credits: *Writer:* Lewis Reed. *Director:* Lewis Allen. *Producer:* David Dortort. **Starring:** Lorne Greene, Pernell Roberts, Dan Blocker, Michael Landon. **Supporting Cast:** Simon Oakland (William Poole); Evelyn Scott (Mrs. Gibson); Harvey Stephens (Uncle Fred Wilson); Bing Russell (Deputy Clem Foster); Bill Quinn (Doctor); Toby Michaels.

Synopsis: Fred Wilson and his niece Ann are on their way to the Ponderosa when their wagon breaks down. When her uncle collapses, Ann goes for help and runs into Poole, who attacks and kills her. After Fred is taken to the doctor's, a search is made for Ann. The next day, Ben finds her body.

In town, William Poole talks to Ben about his nitro glycerin demonstration. Joe then feels that Fred Wilson's life is in danger and that he would be safer at the ranch.

The next day, Poole holds his demonstration. Mrs. Gibson hires him to clear some land after he completes his work for the Cartwrights but he decides to take her job first.

Before dying as a result of a stroke, Fred indicates that the killer of his niece sang a song called "New Orleans Woman."

E132. *Rich Man, Poor Man* (May 12, 1963)

Credits: *Writer:* Richard P. McDonough. *Director:* John Florea. *Producer:* David Dortort. **Starring:** Lorne Greene, Dan Blocker, Michael Landon. **Supporting Cast:** John Fiedler (Claude Miller); Florence Sundstrom (Daisy); J. Pat O'Malley (Clancy); Jay Lavin (Slauson); Ken Mayer, Philip Chambers, Ken Drake, Clegg Hoyt, Bill Hickman.

Synopsis: After Claude Miller strikes it rich, he is no longer ridiculed by the citizens of Virginia City. He gets back at them by securing control of their mortgages with the help of his business manager, Deputy Slauson. Joe, Hoss and Daisy try to get Claude to be reasonable.

Unbeknownst to Claude, Slauson has taken over control of his business affairs with the intent of swindling him out of his money.

Note: Location filming took place in Bronson Canyon.

*E133. *The Boss* (May 19, 1963)

Credits: *Writers:* Leo Gordon, Paul Leslie Dell. *Director:* Arthur H. Nadel. *Producer:* David Dortort. **Starring:** Lorne Greene, Pernell Roberts, Dan Blocker, Michael Landon. **Supporting Cast:** Carroll O'Connor (Tom Slayden); Judee Morton (Karen Slayden); Denver Pyle (Sheriff); Phil Ober (Oliver); Chris Alcaide (Gus Hanna); William Tannen (Durra); Roy Engel (Doctor); Dan White.

Synopsis: After driving out all hauling competition, Tom Slaydon has the citizens of Virginia City just where he wants them. Joe tries to transport his own supplies but is gunned down by Slayden's men. When Ben has Tom arrested, he retaliates by cutting off the town's access to all deliveries.

E134. *Little Man–Ten Feet Tall* (May 26, 1963)

Credits: *Writers:* Eric Norden, Frank Arno. *Director:* Lewis Allen. *Producer:*

David Dortort. **Starring:** Lorne Greene, Pernell Roberts, Dan Blocker, Michael Landon. **Supporting Cast:** Ross Martin (Nick Biancci); Michael Davis (Mario Biancci); Denver Pyle (Sheriff); James Anderson (Al); Lane Bradford (Todd); Bern Hoffman (Bartender).

Synopsis: Adam and Hoss are in the saloon talking about their father's party when Nick Biancci and his son Mario come in looking for work. After Mario plays the guitar, Nick passes the hat, but Al and Todd cause trouble by smashing the guitar. Adam and Hoss force them to pay $100 for the damaged instrument.

The next day, Adam arrives at the ranch with the Bianccis. Nick decides to prepare the food for the party. That night, Ben is surprised at the celebration. He receives gifts of clothes, a saddle and a rifle. After he thanks everyone, Adam introduces Mario, who plays the guitar while Todd and Al watch from outside. Later, Todd and Al demand that Nick return their money but he refuses because it is needed for Mario's musical education.

Ben asks Nick to stay at the Ponderosa to cook. As Mario helps Hoss with his chores, he looks up to him. He wants to be more like Hoss than his father because he considers Nick a coward.

Note: This marked the first of many appearances of Bern Hoffman as the bartender.

Fifth Season
(September 22, 1963–May 24, 1964)

E135. *She Walks in Beauty* (September 22, 1963)

Credits: *Writer:* William L. Stuart. *Director:* Don McDougall. *Producer:* David Dortort. **Starring:** Lorne Greene, Pernell Roberts, Dan Blocker, Michael Landon. **Supporting Cast:** Gena Rowlands (Ragan Miller); Jeanne Cooper (Emilia); Phil Chambers, Robert Adler, Craig Duncan.

Synopsis: Ragan arrives on the stage and goes to see her sister Emilia, who allows her to stay only if she does things her way. After Emilia asks Ben about investing in his mining venture, she introduces Ben and Hoss to Ragan.

The next day, after Hoss and Ragan go on a buggy ride, they have dinner at the Ponderosa. Ragan tells her sister that she thinks Hoss wants to marry her.

When Adam comes home from San Francisco, he is introduced to Ragan. She wants Hoss but will have to keep Adam from interfering. Amelia is worried because she does not want to lose her deal with Ben. Ragan talks to Adam about her life, telling him that she has not enticed Hoss and insists her past is behind her. After Hoss sees Ragan kissing Adam, he gets upset but will not listen to the truth about her past.

Review: *Variety* (September 25, 1963): The critic thought that the season opener was "a week entry" and that William L. Stuart's script was "cliche ridden." It was felt that director Don McDougall "paced the tired romance as best he could, pinching the stereotype goings on with as much humor as possible." Greene's performance "was solid and winning as ever" and Roberts and Landon "played their minor roles well."

E136. *A Passion for Justice* (September 29, 1963)

Credits: *Writer:* Peter Packer. *Director:* Murray Golden. *Producer:* David Dortort. **Starring:** Lorne Greene, Pernell Roberts, Dan Blocker, Michael Landon. **Supporting Cast:** Jonathan Harris (Charles Dickens); Victor Maddern (Dan); Frank Albertson (Sam Walker); Charles Irving ((Rogers); Ray Teal (Sheriff Roy Coffee); Sydney Smith, E. J. Andre, Don Washbrook, Alice Frost, James Stone, Clegg Hoyt.

Synopsis: The townspeople are displeased with their favorite author Charles Dickens' attitude when he arrives in Virginia City. He is annoyed with Sam Walker for printing portions of his literary works and not getting his consent. When Dickens gets a message requesting that he go to the newspaper office, he finds the place ransacked.

Sheriff Coffee is forced to take him into custody. When a jury renders a guilty verdict, Dickens is made to pay a $1,000 fine. As a matter of principle, he is determined not to pay the fine even if it means going to jail.

E137. *Rain from Heaven* (October 6, 1963)

Credits: *Writer:* Robert Vincent Wright. *Director:* Lewis Allen. *Producer:* David Dortort. **Starring:** Lorne Greene, Pernell Roberts, Dan Blocker, Michael Landon. **Supporting Cast:** John Anderson (Tulsa Weems); Mickey Sholdar (Jube Weems); Claudia Bryar (Mrs. Weems); Ray Teal (Sheriff Roy Coffee); Eileen Chesis (Mary Beth Weems); Bing Russell (Deputy Clem Foster); Phil Chambers, Herb Lytton, Mary Newton.

Synopsis: When Virginia City is in the midst of a drought, Tulsa Weems agrees to make it rain for the fee of $200. The townspeople try to raise the money but have to go to Ben to come up with the $30 balance. Not trusting rainmakers, Ben turns them down.

After refusing Ben's offer of help, Tulsa pulls a gun on him and is arrested. His family goes to stay on the Ponderosa where it is learned that daughter Mary Beth has typhoid fever.

E138. *Twilight Town* (October 13, 1963)

Credits: *Writer:* Cy Chermack. *Director:* John Florea. *Producer:* David Dortort. **Starring:** Lorne Greene, Pernell Roberts, Dan Blocker, Michael Landon. **Supporting Cast:** Davey Davison (Louise Corman); Michael Mikler (Mathews); Doris Dowling (Kathy); Stacy Harris (Corman); Walter Coy (Masterson); Andy Albin, Don Dillaway, Joseph Breen.

Synopsis: In the desert, Joe is robbed, knocked out and his horse stolen. Coming across Martinville, a deserted ghost town, he collapses. When he comes to, he is being treated by Louise Corman, who will not tell him what is going on. He then meets Mrs. Oberon, the late sheriff's wife, who warns Joe to leave town. Joe is well enough to leave but has to find the man who took his horse and $2,000.

The men of the town want him to be the sheriff and, when he refuses, no one will sell him a horse. Louise tells Joe that they are being held prisoners in town by an outlaw, Felix Mathews, who is coming back that night. Joe finally agrees to take the job if the townspeople will back him up.

E139. *The Toy Soldier* (October 20, 1963)

Credits: *Writer:* Warren Douglas. *Director:* Tay Garnett. *Producer:* David Dortort. **Starring:** Lorne Greene, Pernell Roberts, Dan Blocker, Michael Landon. **Supporting Cast:** Phillip Abbott (James Callan); Morgan Woodward (McDermott); Trevor Bardette (Scotty); Donna Martell (Esther Callan); Michael Keep, Quinn Redeker.

Famous staircase leading to the second floor. (Photograph by Linda F. Leiby.)

Synopsis: In Sheephead, Adam encounters artist James Callan, who is married to an Indian. Rancher McDermott feeds on Callan's drinking problem, forcing him to part with his paintings for the price of a bottle and smaller rations of food for the Paiutes.

Adam devises a plan to allow the Indians to herd cattle: He permits them to retain part of the herd. Trouble begins when McDermott's hired hands take the livestock and change the brands.

E140. *A Question of Strength* (October 27, 1963)

Credits: *Writer:* Frank Cleaver. *Director:* Don McDougall. *Producer:* David Dortort. **Starring:** Lorne Greene, Pernell Roberts, Dan Blocker. **Supporting Cast:** Ilka Windish (Mother Veronica); Judy Carne (Sister Mary Kathleen); Raymond Guth (Toby); John Kellogg (Stager); James Jeter (Wilson); I. Stanford Jolley (Sam).

Synopsis: Hoss goes to Denver on the stage with two nuns, Sister Mary Kathleen and Mother Veronica. The stage is attacked by two bandits and is wrecked. Hoss comes to while two outlaws are searching the luggage. They take his $200 and the nun's $10,000, which was meant for a hospital in Denver.

The next day, they arrive at a way station and find one of the men wounded. To find out what happened to the other man and the money, Mother Veronica decides to operate.

E141. *Calamity Over the Comstock* (November 3, 1963)

Credits: *Writer:* Warren Douglas. *Director:* Charles R. Rondeau. *Producer:* David Dortort. **Starring:** Lorne Greene, Pernell Roberts, Dan Blocker, Michael Landon. **Supporting Cast:** Stefanie Powers (Calamity Jane); Christopher Dark (Doc Holiday); Fifi Dorsay (Babette); Bern Hoffman (Bartender); Russ Bender (Walt); Big John Hamilton (Miner).

Synopsis: When Joe is being chased by Paiutes, he comes across two wagons. One of the drivers is attacked by an Indian. Before he dies, the man asks Joe to take care of Cal. Later, the young boy blames Joe for what happened but then apologizes. Cal then gets mad when Joe realizes that he is a girl.

Back at the Ponderosa, she tells the Cartwrights that her name is Calamity Jane Canary, but when she tries to tell Joe that she likes him he falls asleep. The next day, in town, Joe is introduced to Johnny, her boyfriend, who says his name is Doc Holiday. Calamity tells Doc that she will not go away with him. Doc says that he will kill anyone who takes Cal away.

Note: David Canary claimed to be a descendant of the real Calamity Jane.

E142. *Journey Remembered* (November 10, 1963)

Credits: *Writer:* Anthony Lawrence. *Director:* Irving J. Moore. *Producer:* David Dortort. **Starring:** Lorne Greene, Dan Blocker. **Supporting Cast:** Inga Swenson (Inger Cartwright); Gene Evans (Lucas Rockwell); Kevin Hagen (Simon); Johnny Stephens (Little Adam); Dee Carroll (Rachel); Ken Lynch (Wilkes); John Frederick (Payne); Kathleen O'Malley (Mrs. Payne).

Synopsis: While Hoss is helping a mare give birth, Ben reflects back to the time he crossed the prairie with little Adam and Inger.

The wagon master, Wilkes, is constantly drinking and Ben tells him that he will not get paid if they do not get to Ash Hollow in time to meet the main wagon train. That night, after Wilkes is threatened by Rockwell for owing him money, he is shot and killed.

The next morning, when the men ask Rockwell to lead them West, he agrees but sets a grueling pace. As they enter Indian country, Inger gives birth to a son, Eric, whom Adam calls Hoss.

E143. *The Quality of Mercy* (November 17, 1963)

Credits: *Writer:* Peter Packer. *Director:* Joseph H. Lewis. *Producer:* David Dortort. **Starring:** Lorne Greene, Pernell Roberts, Dan Blocker, Michael Landon. **Supporting Cast:** Richard Rust (Seth Pruitt); Nancy Rennick (Sara); Kitty Kelly (Mrs. Gibbons); Ed Prentice (Minister); Bob Miles (Card Player); Bill Clark (John Dagliesh).

Synopsis: After hearing an explosion, Joe heads for the mine and finds one of the men dead. Another man, Seth, claims that he was forced to kill him so he would not suffer. Seth wants Joe to tell Sarah that her father died in the accident. After the funeral, Joe goes to see Sarah and invites her to stay at the Ponderosa. Joe takes her for a ride where they reminisce about their youth.

When Seth comes back from a trip to San Francisco, Sarah decides to return home. Joe begins to question if the death of Sarah's father was really a mercy killing and if the explosion was purposely set.

E144. *The Waiting Game* (December 8, 1963)

Credits: *Writer:* Ed Adamson. *Director:* Richard G. Safarian. *Producer:* David Dortort. **Starring:** Lorne Greene, Pernell Roberts, Dan Blocker. **Supporting Cast:** Kathie Browne (Laura Dayton); Katie Sweet (Peggy Dayton); Jacqueline Loughery (Rita); Wade Preston (Frank Dayton); Bill Quinn (Clinton); Craig Duncan (Driver).

Synopsis: Hoss and Adam are greeted by Peggy, who is waiting for her father to come home. After Frank Dayton talks to Adam and Hoss, he is killed when he tries to get his horse to jump a fence.

Four months later, after Adam finds Laura at Frank's grave, he walks her home. Adam realizes that Peggy still does not know that her father is dead.

Later, at Laura's ranch, she tries to explain how she has tried to shield Peggy from pain. Adam says that her daughter can adjust because *he* had to when he was young.

Note: Location shooting took place at Golden Oak Ranch.

E145. *The Legacy* (December 15, 1963)

Credits: *Writer:* Anthony Wilson. *Director:* Bernard E. McEvetty. *Producer:* David Dortort. **Starring:** Lorne Greene, Pernell Roberts, Dan Blocker, Michael Landon. **Supporting Cast:** Robert H. Harris (Dormann); Sandy Kevin (Billy); James Best (Page); Phillip Pine (Gannon); Ray Teal (Sheriff Roy Coffee); Jeanne Baird (Jeannie); Percy Helton, Rory Stevens, Dayton Lummis, James Doohan, Will J. White, John Mitchum.

Synopsis: When Ben and Joe spot a poacher, Ben rides after him. He orders the man from behind a bush but is shot twice. Meanwhile, Billy, Page, and Gannon are camping when Ben's horse comes in. They decide to run because they just got out of prison and are afraid of being accused of murder.

The boys set out to search for Ben. After finding their father's horse, Adam, Hoss and Joe go to Roy with their suspicions that Ben might have been killed. They ride out to track the three responsible men.

*E146. *Hoss and the Leprechauns* (December 22, 1963)

Credits: *Writer:* Robert V. Barron. *Director:* John Florea. *Producer:* David Dortort. **Starring:** Lorne Greene, Pernell Roberts, Dan Blocker, Michael Landon. **Supporting Cast:** Sean McClory (Prof. McCarthy); Frank DelFino (Timothy); Ray Teal (Sheriff Roy Coffee); Robert Sorrells (Charles); Clegg Hoyt (Dorsel); Billy Curtis, Roger Arroya, Nels Nelson, Harry Monte, Felix Silla.

Synopsis: After Hoss saves a little man dressed in green from a bear, he discovers the chest of gold that the man has just hidden. When he brings it back to the ranch, he tells them how he got it. After hearing the story, Ben, Adam and Joe think he is crazy. That night, a group of the Little People follow Hoss and take the chest back.

When Mr. McCarthy arrives, he tells the townspeople about the Leprechaun legend. Trouble begins when the townspeople arrive on the Ponderosa looking for little men and their gold.

E147. *The Prime of Life* (December 29, 1963)

Credits: *Writer:* Peter Packer. *Director:* Christian Nyby. *Producer:* David Dortort. **Starring:** Lorne Greene, Pernell Roberts, Dan Blocker, Michael Landon. **Supporting Cast:** Jay C. Flippen (Barney Fuller); Melora Conway (Martha); Ralph Moody (Gabe); Raymond Guth (Watts); Victor Sen Yung (Hop Sing); Butch Patrick, Roy Engel, Roy Jenson, Dan Riss.

Synopsis: To secure a lumber contract to build a railroad trestle, Ben must beat out his competition, Barney Fuller. When Gabe Fletcher is crushed to death by a piece of faulty equipment, Ben feels responsible. He sulks around the ranch, forcing his sons to complete the contract. Fuller, taking advantage of the situation, entices hands away from the Ponderosa.

E148. *The Lila Conrad Story* (January 5, 1964)

Credits: *Writers:* Preston Wood, George Waggner. *Director:* Tay Garnett. *Producer:* David Dortort. **Starring:** Pernell Roberts, Michael Landon. **Supporting Cast:** Andrew Duggan (Judge Knowlton); Patricia Blair (Lila Conrad); Cathy O'Donnell, Don Haggerty, Lindsay Workman, Stuart Randall, Scott Peters, Don O'Kelly, Don Wilbanks.

Synopsis: While defending herself against Dolph Rimbeau, Lila Conrad is forced to kill him. Because she is a dance hall girl, the townspeople believe she is guilty of murder. To keep from being hanged, Lila escapes in a Cartwright supply wagon. The Cartwrights find her and take her to Virginia City to face trial but must deal with vindictive citizens bent on seeing her go to the gallows.

Note: Location shooting took place at Golden Oaks Ranch.

E149. *Ponderosa Matador* (January 12, 1964)

Credits: *Writer:* Alex Sharp. *Director:* Don McDougall. *Producer:* David Dortort. **Starring:** Lorne Greene, Pernell Roberts, Dan Blocker, Michael Landon. **Supporting Cast:** Marianna Hill (Delores Tenino); Nestor Paiva (Senor Tenino); Frank Ferguson (Jigger); Tol Avery (Troutman); Mike Ragan (Saloon Keeper).

Synopsis: Joe and Hoss are practicing bullfighting when Ben comes in wanting to know who is going to look after Delores, the daughter of his guest Senor Tenino. When they arrive, the boys vie to get her attention. Adam gets the edge when he entertains her with his guitar and poetry recitals.

After dinner, Adam and Delores tease Hoss and Joe about their bullfighting. When they start arguing, Adam sneaks off with the girl for a ride.

After Delores tells them that she likes men of action, Hoss decides that Joe should compete in a bullfight at the rodeo.

E150. *My Son, My Son* (January 19, 1964)

Credits: *Writer:* Denne Petticlerc. *Director:* William F. Claxton. *Producer:* David Dortort. **Starring:** Lorne Greene, Pernell Roberts, Dan Blocker, Michael Landon. **Supporting Cast:** Teresa Wright (Katherine Saunders); Dee Pollock (Eden); Sherwood Price (Miller); Victor Sen Yung (Hop Sing); Zon Murray.

Synopsis: Ben invites Katherine Saunders to dinner. On the way back to the Ponderosa, they talk about her son, Eden. It seems that he had run away after his trial three years before. Katherine also tells him that she is still picking up the pieces after her husband's death. After dinner, they decide to announce their engagement. When Adam arrives, he tells Ben that Eden is back and wanted for murdering his old girlfriend.

Note: Bronson Canyon was used in filming the climax.

E151. **Alias Joe Cartwright** (January 26, 1964)

Credits: *Writer:* Robert Vincent Wright. *Director:* Lewis Allen. *Producer:* David Dortort. **Starring:** Lorne Greene, Dan Blocker, Michael Landon. **Supporting Cast:** Michael Landon (Angus Borden); Keenan Wynn (Sgt. O'Rourke); Douglas Dick (Capt. Murced); Joseph Turkel (Private Peters); Owen Bush (Dugan); Hugh Sanders (Billings); Dave Willock (Weems); Bill Yeo.

Synopsis: When Joe makes camp for the night, a man sneaks in, knocking him out. After stealing his clothes, he pours whiskey all over him.

When Joe wakes up the next morning, Sgt. O'Rourke and his patrol ride in and arrest him as a deserter. They then take him to Fort Meade where Joe tells Capt. Murced his story. Murced insists that Joe is Angus Borden. O'Rourke is then ordered to place Joe under arrest, but becomes suspicious of the captain when he orders Joe's immediate execution.

Note: Location shooting took place at Vasquez Rocks.

E152. *The Gentleman from New Orleans* (February 2, 1964)

Credits: *Writer:* William Bruckner. *Director:* Don McDougall. *Producer:* David Dortort. **Starring:** Lorne Greene, Dan Blocker, Michael Landon. **Supporting Cast:** John Dehner (Jean Lafitte); Sheldon Allman (Betts); Jean Willes (Molly); Harry

Swoger (Amos Whittaker); Bern Hoffman (Bartender); Ray Teal (Sheriff Roy Coffee); Joan Connors.

Synopsis: Hoss is in the saloon when two saloon girls get into a fight over an old man. While the damages pile up, he tells everyone that he is Jean Lafitte. When he is arrested, Hoss decides to bail him out and pay the damages.

Jean walks out to the Ponderosa to visit Hoss, giving him a "ruby" and asking for food and shelter. Ben agrees to let him stay.

That night, while Lafitte is entertaining everyone at the saloon, Amos Whitaker tells Hoss that he does not remember anything about the money that Hoss claims is owed him.

The next morning, Roy comes to the ranch telling everyone that Whitaker and his foreman Tully were found murdered. Lafitte is arrested because he had threatened Amos Whitaker the night before.

*E153. *The Cheating Game* (February 9, 1964)
  Credits: *Writer:* William L. Stuart. *Director:* Joseph Sargent. *Producer:* David Dortort. **Starring:** Lorne Greene, Pernell Roberts. **Supporting Cast:** Kathie Browne (Laura Dayton); Peter Breck (Ward Bannister); Katie Sweet (Peggy Dayton); Lee Henry, Roy Barcroft, Lincoln Demyan, Lew Brown, Norman Leavitt, Charles Seel, Robert Broyles.
  Synopsis: Laura Dayton and Adam are romantically involved. She becomes angered when he discharges her foreman when he fails to properly look after her ranch. She takes it upon herself to employ Ward Bannister. Ward tells her he was a friend of her deceased husband and hands over a $10,000 policy her husband had taken out on himself. A man named Canfield conspires with Bannister to sell Laura stock in a railroad.

*E154. *Bullet for a Bride* (February 16, 1964)
  Credits: *Writer:* Tom Seller. *Director:* Tay Garnett. *Producer:* David Dortort. **Starring:** Lorne Greene, Pernell Roberts, Dan Blocker, Michael Landon. **Supporting Cast:** Marlyn Mason (Tessa Caldwell); Denver Pyle (Mr. Caldwell); Steve Harris (Lon Caldwell); Grandon Rhodes (Doctor); John Matthews (Clergyman); Gail Bonney.
  Synopsis: While Adam and Joe are tracking a cougar, Joe takes aim at the animal but hits a girl, Tessa, instead. She becomes blinded as a result. He blames himself for what happened and the Caldwells are taken in by the Cartwrights.

Several days later, Tessa is taken on a ride by Joe, who apologizes to her. She tells him that her father is always looking for the pot of gold at the end of the rainbow. At dinner, Mr. Caldwell tells everyone about a new job and Tessa's fiance in California, but she wants to know why he is lying. Her father tells her that he feels that the Cartwrights owe them and that he has found his pot of gold.
  Note: Location shooting took place at Golden Oaks Ranch.

E155. *King of the Mountain* (February 23, 1964)
  Credits: *Writer:* Robert Sabaroff. *Director:* Don McDougall. *Producer:* David Dortort. **Starring:** Lorne Greene, Dan Blocker. **Supporting Cast:** Slim Pickens

(Jim Leyton); Laurie Mitchell (Julie); Robert Middleton (Grizzley); Byron Foulger (Parson); Billy M. Greene (Storekeeper); Ray Hemphill, Bruce McFarlane.

Synopsis: Jim Leyton sends a letter to Hoss asking him to be his best man. Ben then gives Hoss a set of matched ponies for a wedding present.

Leyton takes Hoss to his cabin where introductions are made with his fiancée Julie and her father Grizzley. Grizzley and Leyton then get into an argument over a piece of land that they both lay claim to. After Julie gets upset, Hoss suggests that Jim give the land to Grizzley, but he will not sell. Trouble begins when they try to find a third party to arbitrate the land dispute.

E156. *Love Me Not* (March 1, 1964)

Credits: *Writer:* Frank Cleaver. *Director:* Tay Garnett. *Producer:* David Dortort. **Starring:** Lorne Greene, Pernell Roberts, Dan Blocker, Michael Landon. **Supporting Cast:** Anjanette Comer (Joan); Jack Bighead (Chief); Gene Tyburn (Tom); Victor Sen Yung (Hop Sing); Ray Hemphill, Bill Yeo, Wynn Pearce.

Synopsis: On their yearly trip to the Paiute village, Ben and Adam give the chief a pocket watch as a sign of friendship. In return, they are presented with a white woman the Indians had captured a number of years ago. Refusal of the chief's gift would mean death for the girl.

*E157. *The Pure Truth* (March 8, 1964)

Credits: *Writer:* Lois Hire. *Director:* Don McDougall. *Producer:* David Dortort. **Starring:** Lorne Greene, Pernell Roberts, Dan Blocker, Michael Landon. **Supporting Cast:** Glenda Farrell (Looney); Stanley Adams (Sheriff Tate); Lloyd Corrigan (Simmons); Jay Lanin (Ward); Raymond Guth, Olan Soule, Maudie Prickett.

Synopsis: To help control Hoss' spring fever, Ben persuades Roy to let Hoss help out while Clem is out of town. His clumsiness results in the breaking of Roy's gun hand. Feeling responsible, Hoss volunteers to get Roy's prisoner in Rimrock. Inadvertently, he arrives in Red Rock to find the bank has been held up. Being the only outsider in town, he is arrested for the crime.

E158. *No Less a Man* (March 15, 1964)

Credits: *Writer:* Jerry Adelman. *Director:* Don McDougall. *Producer:* David Dortort. **Starring:** Lorne Greene, Pernell Roberts, Dan Blocker, Michael Landon. **Supporting Cast:** Parley Baer (Armistead); Bill Zuckert (Browning); John Kellogg (Wagner); Justin Smith (Carter); Ray Teal (Sheriff Roy Coffee); Billy Corcoran, Adrienne Marden, Ed Faulkner, Ed Prentice, Bill Clark, Joseph Breen, Rush Williams, Bob Miles.

Synopsis: The citizens and leaders of Virginia City have lost faith in Sheriff Roy Coffee's ability to handle his job. They would like to see someone younger in the position. Adam is asked to assist him. It is up to Roy to prove he is still fit for the job and to bring the treacherous Wagner gang to justice.

E159. *Return to Honor* (March 22, 1964)

Credits: *Writer:* Jack Turley. *Director:* Don McDougall. *Producer:* David Dortort. **Starring:** Lorne Greene, Pernell Roberts, Dan Blocker, Michael Landon.

Supporting Cast: Guy Williams (Will Cartwright); Arch Johnson (Butler); Robert J. Wilke (Marshall); Hugh Sanders (Doctor); Gregg Palmer (Gannett); Bill Clark (Jenner); I. Stanford Jolley (Bixby); Ralph Montgomery (Bartender); James Tartan.

Synopsis: Will Cartwright rides into a town with Jenner following close behind. In an alley, Jenner demands that Will give him two stolen engraving plates. After Jenner is killed in a gunfight, Will trades identification with him but is wounded when he rides away.

Ben receives a telegram from Pine City saying that his nephew Will has been killed. When Ben arrives in Pine City, he is met by Sheriff Hollister, who informs him that the killer has not been found yet. Ben then signs all the paperwork to release the body and his personal effects. When Ben goes to the cemetery to pay his last respects at the grave, he is shot at.

E160. The Saga of Muley Jones (March 29, 1964)

Credits: *Writers:* Alex Sharp, Robert V. Barron (Adaptation). *Director:* John Florea. *Producer:* David Dortort. **Starring:** Lorne Greene, Dan Blocker. **Supporting Cast:** Bruce Yarnell (Muley Jones); Jesse White (Esky); Jerome Cowan (Thornbridge); Ken Drake (Brave Pony); Strother Martin (Urey); Bern Hoffman (Bartender); Ralph Moody (Chief); Ray Teal (Sheriff Roy Coffee); Billy M. Greene.

Synopsis: Cousin Muley Jones visits the Ponderosa. He enjoys playing the guitar and singing. Unfortunately, when he opens his mouth, glass shatters. Indian agent Thornbridge pays a visit to the Cartwrights. When Thornbridge and Chief White Bear are about to hold a pow-wow, Muley breaks out in song. The Indians think Thornbridge is firing upon them when they hear some glass shatter.

E161. *The Roper* (April 5, 1964)

Credits: *Writer:* Peter Packer. *Director:* John Florea. *Producer:* David Dortort. **Starring:** Lorne Greene, Pernell Roberts, Dan Blocker, Michael Landon. **Supporting Cast:** Guy Williams (Will Cartwright); Scott Marlowe (Lee Hewitt); Julie Sommers (Emma); John Hubbard (Doctor); James Beck (Dolph); Ray Teal (Sheriff Roy Coffee); Corey Allen, Donald Elson, Barbara Morrison, Armand Alzamora, Stephen Holmes.

Synopsis: While the Cartwrights are off on a cattle drive, Will Cartwright considers heading out on his own. His plans are put on hold when an Army lieutenant and injured outlaw Lee Hewitt ride up. Will rides for the doctor. Hewitt's gang raids the ranch and decide to stay put until Ben returns and opens his safe. Will knows Lee will not leave anyone alive and decides to play along with the outlaws.

E162. *A Pink Cloud Comes from Old Cathay* (April 12, 1964)

Credits: *Writer:* Lewis Clay. *Director:* Don McDougall. *Producer:* David Dortort. **Starring:** Lorne Greene, Pernell Roberts, Dan Blocker, Michael Landon. **Supporting Cast:** Marlo Thomas (Tai Li); Benson Fong (Na Shan); Philip Ahn (Wang Sai); William Fawcett (Rafe); Victor Sen Yung (Hop Sing); Mike Ragan, Phil Chambers.

Synopsis: Ben addresses a group of men who are celebrating the halfway point in the railroad spur line. The Cartwrights return to the ranch where they find a

Wells Fargo wagon. Hoss ordered fireworks, but gets a Chinese girl named Tai Li instead. After Ben pays the $40 freight charges, she is introduced to Hop Sing. She soon has him asking for a raise. Tai Li continues to cause trouble when she appoints herself as a spokesperson for the ranch hands.

Na Shan, the railroad foreman, arrives and claims her as his mail order bride, but she will not go with him. Na Shan thinks that Hoss has put her under a spell.

E163. *The Companeros* (April 19, 1964)

Credits: *Writer:* Ken Pettus. *Director:* William F. Claxton. *Producer:* David Dortort. **Starring:** Lorne Greene, Michael Landon. **Supporting Cast:** Guy Williams (Will Cartwright); Faith Domergue (Carla); Frank Silvera (Mateo); Rico Alaniz (Pacheco); Anthony Carbone (Vicente); Rudolfo Hoyos (Luis); Pepe Hern (Macimo); Joe Yrigoyen (Santos); Roy Engel (Doctor).

Synopsis: Mateo Ibara is injured while on the Ponderosa. Carla and her husband are asked to stay on the ranch while he recuperates. Will and Mateo had met during a battle in Juarez, Mexico. Ibara prevented a firing squad from killing Will. He seriously considers Mateo's invitation to accompany him back to Mexico but Ben becomes suspicious of Ibara's motives.

E164. *Enter Thomas Bowers* (April 26, 1964)

Credits: *Writers:* Jessica Benson, Murray Golden. *Director:* Murray Golden. *Producer:* David Dortort. **Starring:** Lorne Greene, Pernell Roberts, Dan Blocker, Michael Landon. **Supporting Cast:** William Marshall (Thomas Bowers); Ken Renard (Jed); Ena Hartman (Caroline); Kelly Thordsen (Sam); Jason Wingreen (Luke); Ray Teal (Sheriff Roy Coffee); J. Edward McKinley, Dorothy Neumann, Robert P. Lieb, Russ Bender, Jeanne Determann, Alice Frost, Don Washbrook, Robert Adler, George Petrie.

Synopsis: Three women are waiting for opera singer Thomas Bowers to arrive on the stage. When he shows up, the ladies are shocked to see that he is black. When he considers leaving town on the next stage, he is told that the next one will not leave until Monday. Bowers has trouble getting a hotel room and even a meal. Hoss asks him to stay at the Ponderosa.

After Roy Coffee receives a telegram about a runaway slave, Adam warns Hoss that Ben could go to jail if Bowers is that man. When four men come for Bowers, Roy is forced to take him into custody for his own protection.

Note: General Motors was afraid that this episode would offend some Southern viewers and wanted NBC not to air it. The network felt that the show's theme had more value than the number of car sales.

E165. *The Dark Past* (May 3, 1964)

Credits: *Writer:* William Bruckner. *Director:* Murray Golden. *Producer:* David Dortort. **Starring:** Lorne Greene, Pernell Roberts, Dan Blocker, Michael Landon. **Supporting Cast:** Dennis Hopper (Dev Farnum); Susan Seaforth (Holly Burnside); Ron Starr (Jamey Boy Briggs); Lewis Charles (Wetzell); Jim Boles (Pete Burnside).

Synopsis: Dev Farnum, a bounty hunter, shows up at the Ponderosa with an injured horse that has to be put down. Afterwards he agrees to work off the price of a new animal. The next day, Joe and Dev go to town where they find Pete Burnside drunk. They take him home to his daughter Holly. She is in trouble and wants Joe to hide her at the Ponderosa.

On the way to church, Ben and Joe look in on Pete. He is being held at gunpoint by his son-in-law, Jamie Briggs, who wants to know where Holly is. After church, the Cartwrights find Pete wounded. Before he dies, he says that he did not tell of Holly's location. Farnum makes a deal to help capture Briggs for a share of the $5,000 reward but is double-crossed.

E166. *The Pressure Game* (May 10, 1964)

Credits: *Writer:* Don Tait. *Director:* Tay Garnett. *Producer:* David Dortort. **Starring:** Lorne Greene, Pernell Roberts, Dan Blocker. **Supporting Cast:** Kathie Browne (Laura Dayton); Joan Blondell (Aunt Lil); Guy Williams (Will Cartwright); Katie Sweet (Peggy Dayton); Robert Karnes (Jeff); Charles Bateman (Rick); Bern Hoffman.

Synopsis: Adam, Peggy and Laura are talking about the Fourth of July picnic and both of the two ladies think that she will be the next Mrs. Cartwright. When they get back to her ranch, Laura's Aunt Lil is waiting for them. After Adam goes home, Laura and Lil discuss Adam and marriage.

On the Fourth, Laura, Peggy and Lil are waiting for Adam, who is in the saloon making a cattle deal. When he tells them to go on ahead, they run into Will, who stays to eat. That night, Adam arrives at Laura's ranch to apologize for not making the picnic but she is very angry. A couple of days later, Adam finds out that Laura is selling her house and moving away.

E167. *Triangle* (May 17, 1964)

Credits: *Writer:* Frank Cleaver. *Director:* Tay Garnett. *Producer:* David Dortort. **Starring:** Lorne Greene, Pernell Roberts, Dan Blocker, Michael Landon. **Supporting Cast:** Guy Williams (Will Cartwright); Kathie Browne (Laura Dayton); Katie Sweet (Peggy Dayton); Grandon Rhodes (Doctor).

Synopsis: Laura comes to the Ponderosa looking for Adam, who is not there. She has an appointment with Mr. Weems to sell her ranch. Will goes with her in place of Adam. Ben then goes to talk to Adam, who is building a house as a surprise for Laura on their wedding day. The next day, Adam leaves on a trip to San Francisco but promises to be back for Ben's party. After Adam misses the party, Will takes Laura home. They talk of his job offer in San Francisco but he gets upset.

On Sunday, Laura comes to town to talk to Will, who is selling his horse to take that job. On the way back to the Ponderosa, they stop to talk and discover that they love each other. When they go to tell Adam at the new house, he is startled and falls off the ladder.

Note: Location shooting took place at Golden Oaks Ranch.

E168. *Walter and the Outlaws* (May 24, 1964)

Credits: *Writer:* Lois Hire. *Director:* Ralph E. Black. *Producer:* David Dortort. **Starring:** Lorne Greene, Pernell Roberts, Dan Blocker, Michael Landon.

Supporting Cast: Arthur Hunnicutt (Obie); Steve Brodie (Macie); Vic Werber (Teague); James Luisi (Willard).

    Synopsis: Obie has not seen his sister in quite a while. He drops his dog Walter off at the Ponderosa so the Cartwrights can look after him during his absence. Walter prevents everyone from getting any sleep. Hoss becomes concerned when the animal disappears.

    Inept outlaws Macie, Willard and Teague are after Obie's gold. To get it, they kidnap Walter and hold him for ransom.

    Note: Location shooting took place at Iverson's Movie Ranch.

Sixth Season
(September 20, 1964–May 23, 1965)

E169. *Invention of a Gunfighter* (September 20, 1964)

    Credits: *Writer:* Dan Ullman. *Director:* John Florea. *Producer:* David Dortort. **Starring:** Lorne Greene, Pernell Roberts, Dan Blocker, Michael Landon. **Supporting Cast:** Guy Stockwell (Johnny Chapman); Valerie Allen (Olive); Ron Foster (Al Mooney); Bern Hoffman (Bartender); John Hubbard (Doctor); Ray Teal (Sheriff Roy Coffee).

    Synopsis: Al Mooney enters a Virginia City saloon where Joe and Johnny are talking to a saloon girl. After Mooney knocks Johnny down, he tries to goad him into drawing his gun. Johnny lowers his head, walking out of the door while everyone laughs. The next day, Johnny visits Joe and asks him to teach him how to handle a gun. Later Johnny shows Joe how fast he has gotten and promises that he will only use his skill in self-defense.

    When Mooney returns to town, Johnny kills him in a fair fight. Later he is told by Adam that there was a $2,000 bounty on Mooney's head. Johnny then tells Joe that he is not afraid any more. Ben tells Joe that Johnny has gotten into a new line of work — bounty hunter.

    Review: *Variety* (September 20, 1964): The critic thought that the opener "didn't show to much invention in plotting ... but it served as a good enough vehicle for the characters concerned." It was felt that "the best performance was given by guest Guy Stockwell ... and that director John Florea got the most action out of the limited tale by dispensing with extraneous shots, but without sacrificing necessary plotting."

E170. *The Hostage* (September 27, 1964)

    Credits: *Writer:* Donn Mullally. *Director:* Don McDougall. *Producer:* David Dortort. **Starring:** Lorne Greene, Pernell Roberts, Dan Blocker, Michael Landon. **Supporting Cast:** Harold J. Stone (Chad); Jacqueline Scott (Willa); Conlan Carter (Tip); Buck Taylor (Billy); Cal Bartlett (Len); Bill Clark (Jim).

    Synopsis: Ben is out riding when four men stop him, taking him hostage. He is asked to get off his horse Buck and onto another. Buck is returned to the Ponderosa with a note. Ben is then taken to an old abandoned mine and shackled to a post. When Adam, Hoss and Joe find Buck and the ransom note, Adam rides to Eagles Notch, where he finds another note demanding $100,000.

Note: Location shooting took place at Baldwin Gold Mine in Holcomb Valley, close to Big Bear. This episode was shown without commercials in order for the sponsor, Chevrolet, to introduce its new models at the end of the show.

E171. *The Wild One* (October 4, 1964)

Credits: *Writer:* Jo Pagano. *Director:* William Witney. *Producer:* David Dortort. **Starring:** Lorne Greene, Pernell Roberts, Dan Blocker, Michael Landon. **Supporting Cast:** Aldo Ray (Lafe Jessup); Kathryn Hays (Prudence).

Synopsis: Hoss has become involved with Lafe Jessup and wild horses. When they spot a black stallion, Hoss decides it is the horse he wants. Lafe thinks the animal is too fast to catch, but Hoss will not allow Lafe to wound it to slow it down. After they get into a fight, Lafe's wife Prudence shows up after six months of looking for him. He married her after being saved from a blizzard but left after a month.

The next day, Lafe and Hoss ride out to try to capture the black stallion. After lassoing the animal, they return to the cabin. Later, while Prudence says a prayer for her husband and unborn child, Hoss overhears. He agrees to keep the secret about the baby.

Note: Location shooting took place at Red Rock Canyon.

E172. *Thanks for Everything, Friend* (October 11, 1964)

Credits: *Writer:* Jerry Adelman. *Director:* Christian Nyby. *Producer:* David Dortort. **Starring:** Lorne Greene, Pernell Roberts, Dan Blocker, Michael Landon. **Supporting Cast:** Rory Calhoun (Tom Wilson); Linda Foster (Sue); Tom Skerritt (Jerry); Barbara Wilkin (Matilda); Ray Teal (Sheriff Roy Coffee); John Mitchum (Grimes).

Synopsis: Wanderer Tom Wilson comes to Adam's rescue when he nearly drowns. Tom, a ladies man, sets his sights on Sue, a friend of Adam's. However, Jerry, her fiance, takes offense. With the murder of Sue's father, Jerry takes advantage of the situation to eliminate his competition.

E173. *Logan's Treasure* (October 18, 1964)

Credits: *Writers:* Ken Pettus (Adaptation), Robert Sabaroff. *Director:* Don McDougall. *Producer:* David Dortort. **Starring:** Lorne Greene, Dan Blocker. **Supporting Cast:** Dan Duryea (Sam Logan); John Kellogg (Frank Reed); Virginia Gregg (Angie Malone); Tim McIntyre (Mike); Ray Teal (Sheriff Roy Coffee); Jack Carol, Russ Bender.

Synopsis: Ben and Hoss are waiting for Sam Logan, who has been released from prison, to arrive on the stage. Roy warns Ben that there might be trouble because the stolen gold is still missing. On the way to the Ponderosa, they talk about the night Sam was arrested: Ben was leading the posse when Logan's partner Crawford was hung. Logan still swears that Crawford was the only one who knew where the gold was buried.

At the house, Hoss tells his father that Frank Reed is looking for Logan. Ben confronts Reed, demanding to know why he is hounding Logan. He is told that he wants to return the money to Wells Fargo in order to collect the $10,000 reward and to spit in Logan's eye. When he accuses Ben of being in league with Logan, he is slugged. Things become complicated when Angie Malone, a friend of Logan's, and Crawford's son Mike arrive looking for the gold.

Note: Location shooting took place at Golden Oaks Ranch.

E174. *The Scapegoat* (October 25, 1964)

Credits: *Writer:* Rod Peterson. *Director:* Christian Nyby. *Producer:* David Dortort. Starring: Lorne Greene, Pernell Roberts, Dan Blocker, Michael Landon. Supporting Cast: George Kennedy (Waldo Watson); Sandra Warner (Nancy Collins); Richard Devon (Weaver); Jon Lormer (Collins); Troy Melton (Reese); Bill Catching (Pitts).

Synopsis: Hoss prevents Waldo Watson from committing suicide. He empathizes with the man, who is similar in size to him. Waldo, an ex-boxer, is fleeing his promoters after failing to take a dive. They believe he received a payoff and are after him to get their money.

E175. *A Dime's Worth of Glory* (November 1, 1964)

Credits: *Writers:* Richard Shapiro, Esther Mayesh. *Director:* William F. Claxton. *Producer:* David Dortort. Starring: Lorne Greene, Pernell Roberts. Supporting Cast: Walter Brooke (Tobias Finch); Bruce Cabot (Sheriff Reed Laramore); Charles Maxwell (Pickard); Dal Jenkins (Raymond); Preston Pierce (Mike); Anthony Jochim (Deputy); John Harmon (Telegrapher); James Bell.

Synopsis: After catching Ben and Adam thwarting a stage robbery, Tobias Finch plans to novelize their heroic deed. The Cartwrights want nothing to do with the idea. Finch gets Sheriff Reed Laramore to arrest Ben and Adam so they cannot prevent him from getting his story.

E176. *Square Deal Sam* (November 8, 1964)

Credits: *Writers:* Jessica Benson, Murray Golden. *Director:* Murray Golden. *Producer:* David Dortort. Starring: Lorne Greene, Pernell Roberts, Dan Blocker, Michael Landon. Supporting Cast: Ernest Truex (Sam Washburn); Nydia Westman (Martha Washburn); Victor Sen Yung (Hop Sing); Danny Flower (Danny); Sandy Kenyon (Gibson).

Synopsis: Elderly con man Sam Washburn scams the Cartwrights and Hop Sing when he sells each of them the deed to the same property.

E177. *Between Heaven and Earth* (November 15, 1964)

Credits: *Writer:* Ed Adamson. *Director:* William Witney. *Producer:* David Dortort. Starring: Lorne Greene, Dan Blocker, Michael Landon. Supporting Cast: Richard Jaeckel (Mitch); Bob Biheller, Bill Moss.

Synopsis: Joe wakes up from a nightmare where he falls from a mountain he is climbing. The next day, Joe and Mitch spot a mountain lion. Joe climbs the same mountain to get a better look, panics and leaves his rifle at the top.

Later, when Joe tries to get the rifle, Hoss tells him that he is needed back at the ranch to break in a new horse. After he gets thrown, Joe storms off. When he

Looking from the living room into the dining room. (Photograph by Linda F. Leiby.)

runs into Mitch, he jumps down his throat. He then rides to the mountain, but he tells himself that he has nothing to prove.

Note: Location shooting took place at Vasquez Rocks.

E178. *Old Sheba* (November 22, 1964)

Credits: *Writer:* Alex Sharp. *Director:* John Florea. *Producer:* David Dortort. **Starring:** Lorne Greene, Pernell Roberts, Dan Blocker, Michael Landon. **Supporting**

Cast: William Demarest (Tweedy); Henry Kulky (Bearcat); Clegg Hoyt (Barney); Phil Chambers (Anderson); Ray Teal (Sheriff Roy Coffee).

Synopsis: The circus is coming to town and Hoss is in training for a wrestling match with Bearcat Sampson. The winner will get $100. At the contest, Adam bets Ben that Hoss will lose. After squeezing Bearcat, cracking five ribs, Hoss agrees to take his place for three weeks.

After that time period, Hoss and Joe arrive home with Old Sheba, an elephant, instead of the $400 in back pay. When they arrive home, they tell their father that they have signed a paper stating that they would take the elephant instead of the money. Ben gets into trouble when he rides Old Sheba into town, trying to return her to Tweedy.

E179. *A Man to Admire* (December 6, 1964)

Credits: *Writer:* Mort R. Lewis. *Director:* John Florea. *Producer:* David Dortort. **Starring:** Lorne Greene, Pernell Roberts, Dan Blocker, Michael Landon. **Supporting Cast:** James Gregory (Whitney Parker); Hal Baylor (Ev Durfee); Booth Colman (Flint Durfee); Ray Teal (Sheriff Roy Coffee); Michael Petit (Benjie); William Mims (Evans); Jason Johnson (Doctor); Dave Willock, Jonathan Hole, Bern Hoffman.

Synopsis: Hoss is arrested for Flint Durfee's murder. Attorney Whitney Parker, although brilliant, maintains friendship with Abraham Lincoln and has taken to the bottle. Hoss is determined to have Parker defend him despite the reservations of his family.

With the arrival of the prosecutor from Carson City, Hoss' chances for acquittal look doubtful because the men he prosecutes usually end up on the gallows.

*E180. *The Underdog* (December 13, 1964)

Credits: *Writer:* Donn Mullally. *Director:* William F. Claxton. *Producer:* David Dortort. **Starring:** Lorne Greene, Dan Blocker, Michael Landon. **Supporting Cast:** Charles Bronson (Harry Starr); Tom Reese (Lee Burton); Bill Clark (Warren).

Synopsis: In need of help for a roundup, Ben takes on drifter Harry Starr, who is part Comanche. The hands are unhappy about working with him. Lee Burton picks a fight with Harry. After quitting, he accuses Starr of getting him fired. In retaliation, his pals beat up Harry. When Starr plans to leave the Ponderosa, Ben persuades him to take a job at a secluded cabin. Unbeknownst to the Cartwrights, Harry and Burton are really horse thieves.

E181. *A Knight to Remember* (December 20, 1964)

Credits: *Writer:* Robert V. Barron. *Director:* Vincent McEveety. *Producer:* David Dortort. **Starring:** Lorne Greene, Pernell Roberts, Dan Blocker, Michael Landon. **Supporting Cast:** Henry Jones (King Arthur); Robert Sorrells (Cyril); Charles Watts (Sheriff Munsey); Ray Teal (Sheriff Roy Coffee); Zeme North (Pheobe); Rudolfo Acosta (Juan).

Synopsis: Adam is on his way back to Virginia City when the stage is held up. He spots the bandits being pursued by a figure wearing armor. Realizing no one would believe his story, Adam is without defense when he is found with the strongbox and taken into custody for holding up the stage.

E182. *The Saga of Squaw Charlie* (December 27, 1964)

Credits: *Writer:* Warren Douglas. *Director:* William Witney. *Producer:* David Dortort. **Starring:** Lorne Greene, Pernell Roberts, Dan Blocker, Michael Landon. **Supporting Cast:** Anthony Caruso (Charlie); Vickie Coe (Angela Hale); Don Barry (Bud); Virginia Christine (Martha); Myron Healey (Buck); William Tannen (Lem); Ray Teal (Sheriff Roy Coffee).

Synopsis: The people of Virginia City seem to take great pleasure in teasing Charlie. Later, when he frees a horse from the mud, Hoss and Joe assume he is stealing the animal. Ben gives Charlie the horse because he saved its life.

Little Angela arrives at Charlie's hut to make a basket but her mother, Mrs. Hale, threatens to horsewhip him if he tries to see her again. Mrs. Hale meets three men from town wanting to know what can be done about Charlie. After finding him with the horse, they decide to drag him. Ben rides in telling them he has given the horse to Charlie. As the three men ride away, they plot their revenge. Later at the Ponderosa, the Cartwrights are discussing Charlie when Roy arrives to tell them that Angela is missing and everyone in town is blaming Charlie.

E183. *The Flapjack Contest* (January 3, 1965)

Credits: *Writers:* Frank Cleaver, Tom Davison. *Director:* William F. Claxton. *Producer:* David Dortort. **Starring:** Lorne Greene, Pernell Roberts, Dan Blocker, Michael Landon. **Supporting Cast:** Johnny Seven (Trager); Mel Berger (Big Ed); Joan Huntington (Lily); Howard Wendell (Banker); Olan Soule (Ira); Victor Sen Yung (Hop Sing); Bern Hoffmann.

Synopsis: Hoss is having trouble waking up his little brother so he finally throws water on him. In retaliation, Joe tosses a boot at Hoss. He then tells Hoss that he was robbed last night.

When Ben sends them into town on errands, Joe hears about a flapjack eating contest. Trager is taking bets on Big Ed to win at 5 to 1 odds so Joe bets $100 on Hoss. He then tells his brother that he entered him in the contest because he needs $1,000 to pay for Adam's stolen ruby. Hoss walks back to the ranch to build up his appetite. That night at dinner, Hoss is served a salad on Joe's orders. In the middle of the night Hoss sneaks down stairs for food but triggers his little brother's booby trap.

E184. *The Far, Far Better Thing* (January 10, 1965)

Credits: *Writer:* Mort R. Lewis. *Director:* Bernard J. McEveety. *Producer:* David Dortort. **Starring:** Lorne Greene, Pernell Roberts, Dan Blocker, Michael Landon. **Supporting Cast:** Brenda Scott (Lucinda Melviney); Warren Vanders (Tuck); X Brands (Sharp Tongue); Stacy Harris (Mr. Melviney); Jack Bighead.

Synopsis: Martin Melviney, a friend of Ben's, and Lucy, his daughter, pay a visit to the Ponderosa. Joe and his friend Tuck vie to get noticed by Lucy.

Lucy longs for the romance of the West she has read about in her books. When she hears about the romantic legend of Indian's Grief, she goes to the Paiute land, where she is taken captive by the Paiutes.

Note: Location shooting took place at Iverson's Movie Ranch.

E185. *Woman of Fire* (January 17, 1965)

Credits: *Writer:* Suzanne Clauser. *Director:* William F. Claxton. *Producer:* David Dortort. **Starring:** Lorne Greene, Pernell Roberts, Dan Blocker, Michael Landon. **Supporting Cast:** Joan Hackett (Margarita); Jay Novello (Don Miguel); Cesare Danova (Don Louis Santana); Susan Silo (Elena); Valentin De Vargas, Eugene Iglesias.

Synopsis: Don Miguel, Elena and Margarita arrive on the stage. When Margarita is introduced to Ben and the boys, she thinks that Ben's sons are servants. Later at the ranch, Miguel explains to Ben and Adam that Margarita is going to meet her prospective husband.

When Margarita is breaking china and fighting with Elena's two suitors, Adam tries breaking it up. She punches him in the stomach, so he spanks her. That night, everyone begs Adam to tame Margarita's temper for Don Louis but Adam turns them down. He finally agrees after she breaks his new guitar over Hoss' head.

Note: Location shooting took place at Golden Oak Ranch.

E186. *The Ballerina* (January 24, 1965)

Credits: *Writer:* Frank Chase. *Director:* Don McDougall. *Producer:* David Dortort. **Starring:** Lorne Greene, Dan Blocker. **Supporting Cast:** Barrie Chase (Kellie Conrad); Warren Stevens (Paul Mandel); Douglas Fowley (Ned Conrad); Read Morgan (Tad Blake); Hugh Sanders.

Synopsis: Kellie Conrad dances and her father plays the fiddle to earn a living. Hoss feels a sense of guilt after he unintentionally hurts the arm that Kellie's father uses to play the fiddle. He gets them to stay at the Ponderosa while the girl's father recuperates. While there, Ben introduces Kellie to his friend Paul Mandel, a ballet star before an explosion cut short his dancing career.

Kellie persuades Paul to help her learn ballet. She soon comes to the realization that she loves both the ballet and Paul. She struggles inwardly to make a choice between her love of ballet and giving it all up for the love of her father.

Note: Frank Chase scripted the episode for his sister Barrie, who was a real ballet dancer.

E187. *The Flannel-Mouth Gun* (January 31, 1965)

Credits: *Writers:* Leo Gordon, Paul Leslie Peil. *Director:* Don McDougall. *Producer:* David Dortort. **Starring:** Pernell Roberts. **Supporting Cast:** Earl Holliman (Sherman Clegg); Robert J. Wilke (Simmons); Don Collier (Tatum); Harry Carey, Jr. (Shelton); Ray Teal (Sheriff Roy Coffee).

Synopsis: The Dentons are illegally branding calves when one of them is shot and killed. Later in town, at the Cattleman's Club, Roy Coffee is talking to some of the smaller ranchers. When Adam defends the sheriff's ability to handle the situation, Simmons wants to hire a range detective to stop the cattle losses. Adam disagrees but is out-voted. After the meeting, Shelton and the other small ranchers are upset. When a man finds Denton's body, Roy, Adam and Simmons ride to see his brother, Sam Denton. There they find Sherman Clegg, the range detective, who has arrived early.

After Clegg warns him, Holtzmeyer comes to Adam wanting him to buy his spread, but he will not help. Later, Mr. Tatum tells Adam that Holtzmeyer has sold out to Simmons. He also says that Clegg has all of the small ranchers scared.

At the Ponderosa, Clegg arrives wanting Adam to ride with him to show him a herd of Ponderosa cattle. After he helps Adam move the herd, they ride to town, finding out that Shelton has been killed. When Adam is forced to give Clegg an alibi, Tatum thinks Adam is now on the side of the association.

E188. *The Ponderosa Birdman* (February 7, 1965)

Credits: *Writers:* Blair Robertson, Hazel Swanson. *Director:* Herbert L. Strock. *Producer:* David Dortort. **Starring:** Lorne Greene, Pernell Roberts, Dan Blocker, Michael Landon. **Supporting Cast:** Ed Wynn (Prof. Phineas T. Klump); Marlyn Mason (Amanda).

Synopsis: Hoss is sent to Devil Wind Hill to visit Prof. Klump and his grand-daughter Amanda. The professor talks to Hoss about his inventions, including his latest one — a flying machine.

After Hoss goes back to the Ponderosa, Amanda arrives asking him for his help in getting her grandfather down out of a tree. When the professor is injured, Hoss is volunteered to take his place testing the flying machine.

E189. *The Search* (February 14, 1965)

Credits: *Writer:* Frank Cleaver. *Director:* William F. Claxton. *Producer:* David Dortort. **Starring:** Pernell Roberts, Dan Blocker, Michael Landon. **Supporting Cast:** Lola Albright (Ann); Kelly Thordsen (Sheriff Conners); Elaine Devry (Valerie); John Harding (Jason); Howard Wright, Phil Chambers, Lindsay Workman.

Synopsis: Abe rides to the Ponderosa demanding that Adam pay him for a horse that Adam knows nothing about. When he gets to town, Adam finds that the man also charged $200 at the store. In addition, the stranger cashed a sightdraft for $500, leaving Adam a thank-you note. Adam Cartwright then heads to Placerville on the trail of the stranger. When he arrives, he is arrested by Sheriff Connors for a murder that his lookalike committed.

E190. *The Deadliest Game* (February 21, 1965)

Credits: *Writer:* Jo Pagano. *Director:* Gerd Oswald. *Producer:* David Dortort. **Starring:** Lorne Greene, Dan Blocker, Michael Landon. **Supporting Cast:** Cesar Romero (Borelli); Ilze Taurins (Petina); Lili Valenty (Donna Luisa); Grandon Rhodes (Doctor); Ray Teal (Sheriff Roy Coffee); Fabrizio Mioni (Carlo Alfieri).

Synopsis: Everyone in town is waiting for the great Borelli Circus. Borelli is an old friend of Ben, who invites the entire troop to stay at the Ponderosa. That night after dinner, Joe takes Petina for a walk but when they get back Carlo warns Joe to stay away from her. Before turning in, Borelli tells Petina about the practice in the morning. He then warns Carlo, whose hands are shaking, to get himself under control.

The next day during practice, Donna Louisa tells Ben that she is worried about Borelli because he continues to blame himself for the fatal accident of his wife, Angelina.

After Joe and Petina go for a ride, Carlo gets upset and challenges Joe to a duel. They meet for a fistfight. After Joe wins, he walks away, leaving Carlo on the ground. Later, when a ranch hand finds Carlo with a knife in his back, Roy is forced to place Joe under arrest for attempted murder.

E191. *Once a Doctor* (February 28, 1965)

Credits: *Writer:* Martha Wilkerson. *Director:* Tay Garnett. *Producer:* David Dortort. **Starring:** Lorne Greene, Dan Blocker, Michael Landon. **Supporting Cast:** Michael Rennie (Prof. Poppy/Percival Alexander Mundy, M.D.); Ashley Cowen (Thomas Crippen); Elizabeth Rogers (Allie Lou); Bill Clark, Grandon Rhodes.

Synopsis: Hoss is late for breakfast because of his sore foot. He goes to Virginia City to see the doctor, and learns he is out on a call. He then comes to the aid of Professor Poppy, a traveling snake oil salesman. When the towns-people become upset with him over his medicine, Hoss escorts Poppy out of town. Over a bottle of his patent medicine, the professor takes care of Hoss's foot.

Thomas Grippen comes to town stirring up trouble for Dr. Mundy, whom he claims caused the death of his wife. Hoss rides to Mundy's camp, finding him passed out on the ground. He decides to spend the night in Mundy's wagon. Not know-ing this, Grippen sneaks into camp and fires a shot into the wagon.

E192. *Right Is the Fourth R* (March 7, 1965)

Credits: *Writer:* Jerry Adelman. *Director:* Virgil W. Vogel. *Producer:* David Dortort. **Starring:** Lorne Greene, Pernell Roberts, Dan Blocker, Michael Landon. **Supporting Cast:** Everett Sloane (Col. Scott); Mariette Hartley (Barbara); Ray Teal (Sheriff Roy Coffee).

Synopsis: Adam takes over for teacher Barbara while she recuperates from a riding injury. He plans a lesson on the history of the area but is turned down when he wants to talk with Col. Scott, who played a major role in discovering the region. In spite of being warned by the colonel and an old friend of his to stop his prying, Adam persists in searching for the truth.

E193. *Hound Dog* (March 21, 1965)

Credits: *Writer:* Alex Sharp. *Director:* Ralph E. Black. *Producer:* David Dor-tort. **Starring:** Lorne Greene, Pernell Roberts, Dan Blocker, Michael Landon. **Sup-porting Cast:** Bruce Yarnell (Muley Jones); Sue Ane Langdon (Tracey); Chubby Johnson (Abner); Ray Teal (Sheriff Roy Coffee).

Synopsis: The Cartwrights hear some baying hounds which overrun the house when Hoss opens the door. They are followed in by cousin Muley. He tells the Cartwrights that he traded his gold mine for the dogs. The hounds are put in the barn but by early morning they are making so much noise that Ben orders Muley to the barn, where he sings songs to try to keep them quiet. The next morning Hoss has an idea: use the dogs to hunt coyotes in order to collect the bounty.

That night the hounds begin to howl again, so Muley decides to sell them to Hoss for $50 and a squirrel rifle. The next night Hoss is forced to sleep in the barn, but they continue to howl because he refuses to sing to them. Unbeknownst to the Cartwrights, the dogs' real owner is out looking for them.

*E194. The Trap (March 28, 1965)

Credits: *Writer:* Ken Pettus. *Director:* William Witney. *Producer:* David Dortort. **Starring:** Lorne Greene, Pernell Roberts, Dan Blocker, Michael Landon. **Supporting Cast:** Steve Cochran (Boothe and Burke Shannon); Joan Freeman (Hallie Shannon); Ray Teal (Sheriff Roy Coffee); Paul Lukather (Cletus).

Synopsis: Joe and two Ponderosa hands ride into the Shannon Ranch looking for rustlers. Burke Shannon decides to join them but when the three men dismount, Burke begins stalking Little Joe. After he takes a shot at him, Joe returns fire, killing Shannon. Later, as they head to the funeral, Ben is concerned that Joe blames himself for the man's death. Roy wonders if there were any hard feelings between them. He also tells the Cartwrights that Burke's twin brother Boothe is arriving the next day.

Hallie Shannon asks Joe in for coffee and wants to know how long they should wait before they can get married. He gets upset that she could believe that he has murdered her husband so that they could be together. Trouble really begins for both Hallie and Joe when Boothe Shannon arrives in town.

E195. *Dead and Gone* (April 4, 1965)

Credits: *Writer:* Paul Schneider. *Director:* Robert Tutten. *Producer:* David Dortort. **Starring:** Lorne Greene, Pernell Roberts, Dan Blocker, Michael Landon. **Supporting Cast:** Hoyt Axton (Howard Mead); Susanne Cramer (Hilda Brunner); Steve Ihnat (Johann Brunner); Ray Teal (Sheriff Roy Coffee).

Synopsis: On the way back from town, Johann and his sister Hilda are held up by Howard Mead. Adam, who is also on the same road, rescues them.

After Mead is released from jail, he is hired on at the Ponderosa. That night Adam and Howard go to see Johann and Hilda to apologize. The next morning Adam discovers that Mead has left. He also finds that a rifle, horse and money are missing.

Note: Hoyt Axton made his first television appearance in this episode.

E196. *A Good Nights Rest* (April 11, 1965)

Credits: *Writers:* Frank Cleaver, Jeffrey Fleece. *Director:* William F. Claxton. *Producer:* David Dortort. **Starring:** Lorne Greene, Pernell Roberts, Dan Blocker, Michael Landon. **Supporting Cast:** Jean Willes (Mrs. Jenkins); Abagail Shelton (Lucy); Jay Ripley (Larey); Eddie Firestone (Potts); Robert Ridgley (Wilfred); Michael Forest (Schirmer); Lloyd Corrigan.

Synopsis: Unable to get any rest at home, Ben checks into the Virginia City Hotel. The series of events at the hotel prevent him from getting any sleep there either.

*E197. To Own the World (April 18, 1965)

Credits: *Writer:* Ed Adamson. *Director:* Virgil W. Vogel. *Producer:* David Dortort. **Starring:** Lorne Greene, Pernell Roberts, Dan Blocker, Michael Landon. **Supporting Cast:** Telly Savalas (Charles Hackett); Linda Lawson (Maria Hackett); Curt Conway (Harry Towers); John Hubbard (Carl Davis); J. Edward McKinley (Mayor).

Synopsis: Charles and Maria Hackett and aide Carl Davis arrive at the Ponderosa on lumber business. While Charles and Ben discuss a possible deal, Joe is asked to take Maria on a tour of the ranch. When they return, she tells everyone how much she loves the Ponderosa. When the Hacketts and Davis return to town after an unsuccessful lumber deal, Charles wants to buy her the Ponderosa but she turns him down.

The next morning, Ben is out riding when he finds Charles admiring the view. Charles makes an offer for the ranch but Ben is not interested. After being warned by Maria that Charles can have anything he wants, including the Ponderosa, the Cartwrights find that Hackett has begun applying pressure.

E198. *Lothario Larkin* (April 25, 1965)

Credits: *Writer:* Warren Douglas. *Director:* William Witney. *Producer:* David Dortort. **Starring:** Lorne Greene, Dan Blocker, Michael Landon. **Supporting Cast:** Noah Beery, Jr. (Lothario Larkin); Dorothy Green (Laura); Jim Davis (Johnny); Linda Bennett (Francine); Olive Sturgess (Nancy); Morgan Woodward (Gillis); Jane Norris (Meg); Frank Ferguson (Abner); Ray Teal (Sheriff Roy Coffee).

Synopsis: When Lothario Larkin arrives in Virginia City, Sheriff Roy Coffee orders him out of town. Hoss then invites him to stay at the ranch. When he gets home, Ben is upset to hear that Lothario has returned. When Lothario arrives, he brings Meg with him. Ben orders Hoss to take her home, where he is greeted by her father's shotgun.

The next day, Lothario leaves with Adam's guitar. Hoss and Joe ride out looking for him. Meanwhile, Lothario is visiting with Nancy when her father chases him off. That night, after Joe goes home, Hoss finds Lothario in the saloon with two girls. After Meg and Nancy's fathers arrive, they start a fight with Larkin, forcing Hoss to join in. When Roy Coffee arrives, he places everyone under arrest.

E199. *The Return* (May 2, 1965)

Credits: *Writers:* Ken Pettus, Frank Chase. *Director:* Virgil W. Vogel. *Producer:* David Dortort. **Starring:** Lorne Greene, Dan Blocker, Michael Landon. **Supporting Cast:** Tony Young (Trace Cordell); Joan Blackman (Clara Dorn); John Conte (Paul Dorn); Ray Teal (Sheriff Roy Coffee); Dan Riss (Latham); Phil Chambers (Hubbell); Robert J. Stevenson, Bill Clark.

Synopsis: When Trace Cordell rides into town, banker Paul Dorn believes there is a threat to him. A number of years ago, Paul was paralyzed by Trace in a gunfight. Since that time he has married Clara, who was Trace's girlfriend. He is afraid he might lose her and will do anything to get Trace out of his life.

E200. *Jonah* (May 9, 1965)

Credits: *Writer:* Preston Wood. *Director:* William F. Claxton. *Producer:* David Dortort. **Starring:** Lorne Greene, Dan Blocker, Michael Landon. **Supporting Cast:** Andrew Prine (George Whitman); Angela Clark (Teresa); Erin O'Donnell (Susan); Dean Harens (Poole); Ken Mayer (Kern); Bill Clark (Will); Troy Melton (Charlie); Martha Manor (Martha).

Synopsis: The ranch hands feel that new hand George Whitman is a jinx

Dining room. The table displays real antiques. (Photograph by Linda F. Leiby.)

and stay to themselves. Hoss tries to get George to forget talk about being jinxed but is scared when a gypsy foresees a number of incidents resulting in death.

E201. *The Spotlight* (May 16, 1965)

Credits: *Writer:* Dick Carr. *Director:* Gerd Oswald. *Producer:* David Dortort. **Starring:** Lorne Greene, Dan Blocker, Michael Landon. **Supporting Cast:** Viveca Lindfors (Angela Drake); Ron Randell (Carleton Ames); Winnie Coffin (Mrs. Brown); Jeanne Determann (Mrs. Finch); Victor Sen Yung (Hop Sing); Robert Foulk, John Fredericks, Ian Wolfe, Billy M. Greene.

Synopsis: Ben chairs a meeting for Virginia City's anniversary. The women want something other that the usual rodeo so Ben is nominated to locate some entertainment. When Ben goes to the opera house, he finds an old poster of Angela Drake. He then decides to go to San Francisco to hire the opera singer for the festivities. After agreeing to take the job, Angela arrives in Virginia City on the stagecoach.

The next day, Angela discovers that there is to be no accompanist for her performance so Ben tries to find her one. When her former accompanist, Carlton Ames, arrives in town, Angela fears he may reveal her secret.

Note: Location shooting took place at Golden Oak Ranch.

E202. *Patchwork Man* (May 23, 1965)

   Credits: *Writers:* Don Tait, William Koenig. *Director:* Ralph E. Black. *Producer:* David Dortort. **Starring:** Lorne Greene, Dan Blocker. **Supporting Cast:** Grant Williams (Albert "Patch" Saunders); Bruce Gordon (Bronson); Lane Bradford (Stimler); Sue Randall (Ann Fleming); Ray Teal (Sheriff Roy Coffee); Grandon Rhodes (Doctor).

   Synopsis: Hoss is impressed with reclusive Albert Saunders (better known as "Patch") and particularly with his ability to make apple pies. He offers him a job on the Ponderosa. Ben does not share Hoss' opinion of "Patch," especially after "Patch" shows cowardice during a confrontation between the Cartwrights and a mining boss.

Seventh Season
(September 12, 1965–May 15, 1966)

E203. *The Debt* (September 12, 1965)

   Credits: *Writer:* William Blinn. *Director:* William F. Claxton. *Producer:* David Dortort. **Starring:** Lorne Greene, Dan Blocker, Michael Landon. **Supporting Cast:** Tommy Sands (Wiley Kane); Brooke Bundy (Annie Kane); Ford Rainey (Sam Kane); Ray Teal (Sheriff Roy Coffee).

   Synopsis: When Wiley and Annie Kane ask Joe for directions to the Ponderosa, he takes them back to meet Ben. At the ranch, Wiley explains they are there to work off a debt. He also tells them their father was Sam Kane and that they have been traveling around for three years repaying all the money that their father had stolen.

   Later, in Annie's room, Joe discovers that she cannot read and offers to teach her. When Wiley finds out, he tells Joe to stay away from his sister. Wiley tells Annie that they cannot take anything from anybody.

   The next day, when Joe, Wiley and Annie go to town, they are shocked to find out that Roy Coffee has just arrested their father Sam Kane, whom they thought had died.

   Review: *Variety* (September 15, 1965) The reviewer felt that the show "was smoothly paced and aside from overly talky plot was up to *Bonanza* standards."

   Note: Location shooting took place at Incline Village.

E204. *The Dilemma* (September 19, 1965)

   Credits: *Writers:* John Hawkins, Ward Hawkins. *Director:* William F. Claxton. *Producer:* David Dortort. **Starring:** Lorne Greene, Dan Blocker, Michael Landon. **Supporting Cast:** Tom Tully (Sundown); Anthony Call (Billy); Elizabeth Perry (Ruth); Walter Sande (Hamilton); Kelly Thordsen (Drugan); John Hubbard (Snell); Dayton Lummis (Judge O'Hara); John Archer (Powell); Lincoln Demyan (Hicks); Ray Teal (Sheriff Roy Coffee).

   Synopsis: Judge O'Hara is going on vacation and Ben is sworn in as his replacement. He is then wished good luck and advised to keep a level head. Joe and Hoss escort their father to the courthouse when there is a commotion. The bank has been robbed of $256,000 and the president thinks that the bank will have to close.

When Ben returns to the ranch, he finds that Sundown Davis is waiting to talk to him. Davis tells Ben that he robbed the bank and wants to turn himself in. When asked about the money, he says that it has been hidden. Sundown agrees to turn over the money if he does not go to prison. Sundown is then taken to jail by the Cartwrights, and Hoss and Joe are made deputies.

On the day of the trial, Ben has a meeting with the two attorneys for their opinions on the case. Ben is urged to make a deal because the town is bankrupt.

E205. *The Brass Box* (September 26, 1965)

Credits: *Writer:* Paul Schneider. *Director:* William F. Claxton. *Producer:* David Dortort. **Starring:** Lorne Greene, Dan Blocker, Michael Landon. **Supporting Cast:** Ramon Novarro (Jose Ortega); Michael Dante (Miguel); Adam Williams (Muller); Sydney Smith (Ira Minton); Bill Clark (Jim); Roy Jenson (Harry); Grandon Rhodes (Doctor); Bruno Ve Sota (Bartender).

Synopsis: In the saloon, Joe is listening to Don Jose Ortega tell stories of a land grant that he has in a brass box. When Muller tries to hit Don Jose, Joe comes to his rescue.

The next morning, when Joe returns a gold chalice that Don Jose had given him, he is shocked by all the treasures that he sees in Ortega's house. Don Jose introduces Joe to his nephew Miguel, who insults him.

Miguel is later hired as a horse wrangler on the Ponderosa. After insulting six men, Ben urges him to change his attitude, so he quits. Miguel returns to his uncle's house. When he does not find Don Jose there, he begins to search for the brass box. Later that night, Miguel finds his uncle in the saloon. He produces the land grant and introduces his uncle as the patron of the entire area. According to Ben's lawyer Ira, the land grant would take almost all of the Ponderosa.

E206. *The Other Son* (October 3, 1965)

Credits: *Writer:* Thomas Thompson. *Director:* William F. Claxton. *Producer:* David Dortort. **Starring:** Lorne Greene, Dan Blocker, Michael Landon. **Supporting Cast:** Ed Begley (Clint Watson); Tom Simcox (Andy Watson); Richard Evans (Ellis Watson); Bing Russell (Sheriff Walker).

Synopsis: When Ben tries to deliver a wagon load of nitroglycerin to the Virginia City mines, he is denied access to the public roads. So Ben goes to see muler Clint Watson and his sons Andy and Ellis to ask for their help. As they start across the mountains with mules loaded with nitro, Ellis is having trouble with his animal. When Andy helps his brother, he discovers that one of the bottles has broken. Ben very carefully unloads the crate in order to remove the broken bottle.

The next day, after Andy gets into a fight with Ellis, Hoss has Joe ride into camp to meet their father. Later, as they come down a steep slope, Clint sends Andy to help his brother get his mule down. Andy apologizes to Ellis, who starts down first. Suddenly there is a huge explosion.

Note: Lorne Greene does a voice over at the beginning. Location shooting took place at Incline Village and Toiyabe National Forrest.

E207. *The Lonely Runner* (October 10, 1965)

Credits: *Writer:* Thomas Thompson. *Director:* William Witney. *Producer:* David Dortort. **Starring:** Lorne Greene, Dan Blocker, Michael Landon. **Supporting Cast:** Gilbert Roland (Jim Acton); Pat Conway (Deputy Pete); Ray Teal (Sheriff Roy Coffee); Ken Lynch (Sam Whipple); Roy Barcroft (Frank).

Synopsis: Before a court decision is read, Jim Acton leaves to join Hoss and his pregnant mare. Jim tells Hoss that he wants to give the colt to his great-nephew. Deputy Pete and Whipple ride in with the judge's decision awarding the mare to Whipple. After Hoss and Jim try to buy the horse, Jim threatens to kill Whipple. Hoss then stays with Jim while Pete goes to speak to Ben about his vote in the upcoming election.

Jim meets Whipple on the road and they get into an argument. When Whipple shoots at Jim, he fires back in self-defense, killing Whipple.

Note: Location shooting took place in Incline Village and Toiyabe National Forrest.

E208. *Devil on Her Shoulder* (October 17, 1965)

Credits: *Writer:* Suzzane Clauser. *Director:* Virgil W. Vogel. *Producer:* David Dortort. **Starring:** Lorne Greene, Dan Blocker, Michael Landon. **Supporting Cast:** Ina Balin (Sarah Reynolds); John Doucette (Rev. Evan Morgan); Peter Helm (Gwylem); Adrienne Marden (Emma Morgan); Angela Dorian (Victoria Vetri/ Essie); Karl Lukas (Brother).

Synopsis: Ben comes upon the Eternal Brethren wagon train which has broken down. Reverend Morgan's wife Emma blames Sarah for all their troubles. When Ben offers to help, he is turned down. So Sarah asks Ben for some milk for the children but Mrs. Morgan also finds fault with that.

Reverend Morgan dismisses school when he overhears Sarah teaching the children that the world is round. He will not let her teach the children any more. When Ben returns, Sarah tells him that Evan Morgan is her uncle and that he is wrong about the children. She is also sorry that she left St. Louis and civilization.

Later, at the camp, Essie collapses. Mrs. Morgan feels she had a spell put on her by Sarah. When Gwylem is told that Essie is dying, he decides to go get Sarah. Meanwhile, the Morgans' plan to rid her of Satan.

E209. *Found Child* (October 24, 1965)

Credits: *Writer:* Frank Cleaver. *Director:* Ralph E. Black. *Producer:* David Dortort. **Starring:** Lorne Greene, Dan Blocker, Michael Landon. **Supporting Cast:** Eileen Baral (Lisa); Gerald Mohr (Collins); Grandon Rhodes (Doctor); Ray Teal (Sheriff Roy Coffee); Charles Bateman (Jim); Quentin Sondergaard (Hank); H. T. Tsiang (Su Chin); Phil Chambers (Store Owner).

Synopsis: Hoss is out riding when he comes across a stage accident. After finding the bodies of two passengers and the driver, Hoss discovers a little girl in shock. Picking her up in his big arms, Hoss takes her home. Over the next few days, the little girl begins to come around. Hoss gets upset when Ben asks Roy Coffee to send telegrams to find out the identity of the people on the stage.

Roy eventually discovers that the girl's name is Lisa and that her parents were supposedly carrying a large sum of money to start a business. The next day, Hoss and Lisa go on a picnic and she is kidnapped.

E210. The *Meredith Smith* (October 31, 1965)

Credits: *Writer:* Lois Hire. *Director:* John Florea. *Producer:* David Dortort. **Starring:** Lorne Greene, Dan Blocker, Michael Landon. **Supporting Cast:** Anne Helm (Callie); Robert Colbert (Ace); Guy Lee (Ah Chow); Robert Sorrells (Swanson); Strother Martin (Little Meredith); Winnie Coffin (Widow Smith); Bert Mustin (Jake Smith); Eddie Firestone (Mr. Potts); Kam Tong (Ching); Wynn Pearce (Ozzie); Owen Bush (Ira); Howard Wright (Cal).

Synopsis: While Ben is talking to Jake Smith about renewing the water rights, Jake decides to make out his will. He thinks that Ben's lawyer could handle that while he is looking at the water rights agreement. After lunch, Jake collapses in Ben's arms. Before he dies, he asks Ben to see that his estate goes to Meredith Smith, his only living relative.

Ben's lawyer informs him that Jake's estate is worth over $160,000. Ben then finds out that he is the executor and has six months to find the heir. Ben really has trouble when the time is almost up and he has not one Meredith Smith but six who claim the estate.

E211. *Mighty Is the Word* (November 7, 1965)

Credits: *Writers:* Thomas Thompson (Teleplay), Robert L. Goodwin (Story). *Director:* William F. Claxton. *Producer:* David Dortort. **Starring:** Lorne Greene, Dan Blocker, Michael Landon. **Supporting Cast:** Glenn Corbett (Rev. Paul Watson); Michael Whitney (Cliff Rexford); Sue Randall (Sue Watson); Julie Gregg (Dolly).

Synopsis: Rev. Paul Watson, a reformed gunfighter, is arm wrestling in the saloon for $1.00 bets to raise money for his new church. When Cliff Rexford, a Ponderosa hand, challenges him, Cliff says that the next time it will be with a gun.

Paul and his wife Sue go home for dinner where she presents him with Adam's final plans for the church.

The next morning, Ben leaves for Sacramento, leaving Hoss in charge. After Hoss takes a load of lumber to the new church site, he joins Paul and Joe to work on the building. Cliff arrives, trying to goad Paul into a gunfight. When Hoss wants to fire him, Paul says no because he has killed Cliff's twin brother.

E212. *The Strange One* (November 14, 1965)

Credits: *Writers:* Jo Pagano (Teleplay), Stephen Lord (Story & Teleplay). *Director:* Gerd Oswald. *Producer:* David Dortort. **Starring:** Lorne Greene, Dan Blocker, Michael Landon. **Supporting Cast:** Louise Sorel (Marie); Willard Sage (Wyn); Robert McQueeney (Jeremy); Michael Barrier (Luke); Grandon Rhodes (Doc Martin).

Synopsis: On their way to New Orleans, a wagon train heads across the Ponderosa. Feeling she is a witch, Marie is left behind. Finding the hurt girl, Hoss and Joe take her to the ranch. Joe shows her a music box that had been his mother's. She places her hands on the box and becomes aware of events in the lives of the Cartwrights.

Ben attempts to make Marie see she is not the witch everyone thinks she is. When the diphtheria epidemic foreseen by Marie comes to pass, her fellow journeymen and even her parents are determined to see her hanged.

Note: Location shooting took place at Iverson's Movie Ranch.

E213. *The Reluctant Rebel* (November 21, 1965)

Credits: *Writer:* Wally George. *Director:* R. G. Springsteen. *Producer:* David Dortort. **Starring:** Lorne Greene, Dan Blocker, Michael Landon. **Supporting Cast:** Tim Considine (Billy Penn); Royal Dano (Hank Penn); Keith London (Sam Cotterfield); Craig Curtis (Sport); Janis Hansen (Millie); Mike Ragan (Burkhart); Ray Hemphill (Shale).

Synopsis: Billy Penn and his friends are rustling cattle on the Ponderosa. Billy is knocked over the head when he prevents Hoss from being shot. When he comes to, Billy refuses to tell Hoss who the other gang members are. Hoss takes Billy home to his father Hank, who wants to know what happened. After Hoss leaves, Billy gets upset because his father is proud of being a pig farmer. Billy runs away to the Ponderosa, where Hoss finds him hiding in the barn. In order to help, Hoss hires Billy to take care of Macho, a prize bull, that he plans to enter in the town fair.

E214. *Five Sundowns to Sunup* (December 5, 1965)

Credits: *Writer:* William L. Stuart. *Director:* Gerd Oswald. *Producer:* David Dortort. **Starring:** Lorne Greene, Dan Blocker, Michael Landon. **Supporting Cast:** Ray Teal (Sheriff Roy Coffee); Marie Windsor (Ma Lassiter); Douglas Henderson (The Rev. Mr. Holmes); John Hoyt (Major Sutcliffe); Jack Chaplain (Harry Lassiter); G.B. Atwater (Merrick); Bruce Mars (Deputy John Maddock); Stacy Harris (Judge Simpson); Tom Drake (Kirt); John Alderson (Gwylnedd); Bruce Mars (Johnny); William Tannen (Albee); Dan White (Weems); K. L. Smith (Deets).

Synopsis: Ben and Hoss ride into Virginia City, where they find Roy shot. He was wounded while the Lassiters were trying to free Harry Lassiter. The town wants Ben to take Roy's place with Hoss as his deputy. Judge Simpson's daughter says that the Lassiters have taken her father. Mrs. Lassiter tells the judge that he will hang if her son Harry is not released.

The next day the district attorney, Merrick, is taken off the stage. When the stage arrives in town, the hangman gives Ben a note from the Lassiters. Ben is feeding Harry Lassiter, who keeps laughing because he does not believe that he will hang. Things really turn desperate for Ben when Joe is also taken hostage.

E215. *A Natural Wizard* (December 12, 1965)

Credits: *Writers:* William Blinn (Teleplay), Suzanne Clauser (Story). *Director:* Robert Totten. *Producer:* David Dortort. **Starring:** Lorne Greene, Dan Blocker. **Supporting Cast:** Eddie Hodges (Skeeter Dexter); Karl Swenson (Dr. Woods); Jacqueline Scott (Joy Dexter); Douglas Kennedy (Stoney); Victor Sen Yung (Hop Sing); Robert Rothwell (Ranch Hand).

Synopsis: When young Skeeter tries to free a fox from a trap, he steps in one himself but is rescued by Hoss. Hoss then tells Stoney, the boy's stepfather, about

Skeeter being injured. At the ranch, Stoney threatens Skeeter for emptying his trap line and that he is leaving forever.

Later Hoss demands that Skeeter take him to see his mother. They find her sleeping off a drunken binge. Joy does not want anything to do with Skeeter because she blames him for her current situation. Hoss continues to help Skeeter in the hope that Joy Dexter will change her mind.

E216. *All Ye His Saints* (December 19, 1965)

Credits: *Writer:* William Blinn. *Director:* William F. Claxton. *Producer:* David Dortort. **Starring:** Lorne Greene, Dan Blocker, Michael Landon. **Supporting Cast:** Clint Howard (Michael Thorpe); Leif Erickson (Caine); Rudolfo Acosta (Lijah); Simon Scott (Evan Thorpe); Harvey Stephens (Dr. Randall).

Synopsis: Hoss and Joe ride onto the Thorpe farm, where Hoss hand-wrestles Michael and loses. While Mr. Thorpe and Lijah are looking for barn owls, Evan Thorpe is seriously wounded when his gun goes off by accident. He soon slips into a coma. Then Michael asks Lijah who God is and if He caused his father's accident. Lijah tells him that God is a big man who lives high in the mountains all alone. That night, while everyone is asleep, Michael decides to go find God. When they discover that the boy is missing, Joe starts the search while Hoss goes to town for deputies and the doctor to care for Mr. Thorpe.

After finding Michael's mule, Joe continues to look for the boy. Later Joe takes care of Michael, who fell after seeing a mountain man whom he thinks is God. Tom Caine, the mountain man, arrives in camp taking Joe and Michael captive.

Note: Location shooting took place at Toiyabe National Forest and Incline Village.

E217. *The Dublin Lad* (January 2, 1966)

Credits: *Writer:* Mort Thaw. *Director:* William F. Claxton. *Producer:* David Dortort. **Starring:** Lorne Greene, Dan Blocker, Michael Landon. **Supporting Cast:** Liam Sullivan (Terrence O'Toole); Maggie Mahoney (Molly Dimmer); Tim McIntyre (Jeb Dimmer); Paul Birch (Mr. Porter); Paul Genge (Judge); Bern Hoffman (Bartender); Robert Carson (Jury Foreman); Ray Teal (Sheriff Roy Coffee).

Synopsis: Terrence O'Toole is on trial for murder and robbery. Joe is the only hold-out against conviction. The foreman eventually consents to review the evidence one more time. Joe is finally persuaded to change his mind. As the verdict is announced, something in Terrence's eyes assures Joe that he is innocent. With the man's impending hanging, Joe is determined to learn what really happened.

Note: Location shooting took place at Incline Village.

E218. *To Kill a Buffalo* (January 9, 1966)

Credits: *Writer:* Michael Fisher. *Director:* William F. Claxton. *Producer:* David Dortort. **Starring:** Lorne Greene, Dan Blocker, Michael Landon. **Supporting Cast:** Jose De Vega (Tatu); Steven Gravers (Martinez); Grandon Rhodes (Doctor); Sarah Selby (Mrs. Flanner); Ralph Moody (Old Indian); Trudy Ellison (Julie); Victor Sen Yung (Hop Sing).

Synopsis: Hoss is out riding when he spots circling vultures above an injured

Ute Indian boy. Hoss is forced to knock him out to disarm him and to look at his leg. In the struggle, the boy's medal comes off.

Back at the ranch, Joe and Ben are counting horses when Hoss arrives with the boy. When the doctor comes, Martinez tells Ben that the boy's name is Tatu and he is the son of a war chief. When Hoss goes back to find Tatu's medal, the boy crawls out of his room. He manages to get into Ben's room, taking his gun. Tatu continues to crawl to the top of the stairs where he starts shooting at the Cartwrights.

*E219. *Ride the Wind* [Part I] (January 16, 1966)
E220. *Ride the Wind* [Part II] (January 23, 1966)

Credits: *Writer:* Paul Schneider. *Director:* William Witney. *Producer:* David Dortort. **Starring:** Lorne Greene, Dan Blocker, Michael Landon. **Supporting Cast:** Rod Cameron (Curtis Wade); Victor Jory (Charles Ludlow); Tom Lowell (Jabez Ludlow); DeForrest Kelley (Tully); Bill Clark (Wilson); Wolfe Barzell (Bornstein); Stewart Moss (Aaron); Warren Banders (Hoke); Richard Hale (Winnemucca); Clay Tanner (Herb); Jack Bighead (Bear Dance); James Noah (Sykes); Robert Brubaker (DeVere); Gilbert Green (Jensen); Roger Etienne (Fontaine); David Pritchard (Pat); S. Newton Anderson (Gus); Tom Lutz (Emmett); Raymond Guth (Homer); Peter Ritter (Hank); Ben Wright (Spires); Bill Edwards (Hoffman).

Synopsis: The Cartwrights attend a meeting with Pony Express owner Charles Ludlow, who is asking for everyone's support. After Ben pledges $6,000, he is asked to serve on the board of directors.

The next day, as men are signing on as Pony Express riders, Joe also decides to sign up. When Ben finds out, he becomes angry but finally agrees to let him ride. The riders are watched by Winnemucca and his braves. Ben and Hoss decide to pay a visit to Winnemucca, who refuses to sign a treaty and threatens to kill any riders that cross his land.

Tully, a reporter, arrives in town to write an article on Ludlow but realizes the real story lies with Curtis Wade. He decides to show Tully information about Ludlow in order to remove him from the presidency. At the board meeting, Wade says that the express will not shut down nor detour. Everyone except Ben votes Wade in as president of the company.

A rider tells Ben that Joe is trapped in a way station. After Joe is rescued, they find Charles Ludlow murdered because he was trying to deliver a peace treaty to the Indians. At Ludlow's funeral, Ben and Wade vow that the Pony Express will flourish but disagree about crossing Winnemucca's land.

As part of his plans, Wade has decided to fortify the Indian Wells station with Hoss manning it. Wade then goes to Ben, asking him for $5,000 and more horses. Tully then tells Wade that Wade might be in for a political nomination. When he is told that more money is needed for political lobbies, Wade gives him the money that was intended as the riders' back pay. Trouble really begins when Joe is taken captive by the Paiutes and Wade threatens to hang Winnemucca's son.

Note: Location shooting took place at Vasquez Rocks and Red Rock Canyon. The United States Post Office honored this episode with a citation. Lorne Greene did voiceovers during this episode. In 1967, this episode was released in overseas theaters.

E221. *Destiny's Child* (January 30, 1966)

Credits: *Writer:* Robert V. Barron. *Director:* Gerd Oswald. *Producer:* David Dortort. **Starring:** Lorne Greene, Dan Blocker, Michael Landon. **Supporting Cast:** Richard Peabody (Sonny); Walter Burke (Jesse Pherson); Tim Stafford (Jamie); Steve Raines (Darrel); Lindsay Workman (Badgett); Grandon Rhodes (Doctor); Chris Anderson (Hunter); Ray Teal (Sheriff Roy Coffee).

Synopsis: Jesse Pherson and Sonny come along just in time for Sonny to lift Ben's wagon out of the mud. A grateful Ben treats them to dinner at the Ponderosa. After dinner, Jesse and Sonny talk to the Cartwrights about their travels, doing odd jobs, trying to earn enough money to go to Oregon.

The next morning, as they chop wood, Joe rides in and tells Jesse about a possible job at the town livery stable. Leaving Sonny with Hoss, Jesse goes to town. He manages to talk Brightman into letting him try the only job available, that of breaking wild horses. Jesse is fatally injured by a horse. Before he dies, he asks Ben to take care of Sonny. After the funeral, Sonny helps with ranch chores but he keeps wanting to go look for Jesse. As Hoss and Joe are having lunch, Ben tells them that Sonny knows deep down that Jesse is really dead. After they discover that Sonny is gone, Roy tells them that he is wanted for murder in Arizona.

E222. *Peace Officer* (February 6, 1966)

Credits: *Writer:* Donn Mullally. *Director:* William Witney. *Producer:* David Dortort. **Starring:** Lorne Greene, Dan Blocker, Michael Landon. **Supporting Cast:** Eric Fleming (Wes Dunn); Ron Foster (Dave Morissey); Ray Stricklyn (Cliff); Dee Pollack (Chuck); Ted Knight (Mayor); Clyde Howdy (Deputy Bill Harris); Grandon Rhodes (Doc Brown); I. Stanford Jolley (Jonesy); Roy Barcroft (Deputy Hacker); Lorna Thayer (Mrs. Roberts).

Synopsis: When Deputy Bill Harris tries to stop five young teenagers from drinking and breaking up the saloon, he is hit over the head and killed. As the five young men ride off, Joe jumps Cliff, who is then placed in a cell.

Major Garrett decides to hire Wes Dunn, who is famous for cleaning up towns. After Dunn is sworn in, he establishes a nine P.M. curfew. He almost kills Cliff when he demands to know where the other four boys are.

While Hoss is on a cattle drive, he comes upon Chuck, one of the wanted boys. When Hoss goes for Chuck's gun, he is accidentally shot.

E223. *The Code* (February 13, 1966)

Credits: *Writer:* Sidney Ellis. *Director:* William F. Claxton. *Producer:* David Dortort. **Starring:** Lorne Greene, Dan Blocker, Michael Landon. **Supporting Cast:** George Montgomery (Dan Taggert); Robert Ellenstein (Fitts); Jan Shepard (Sally); Gordon Wescourt (Win); Zalman King (Pete); Charles Wagenheim (Felger); Bruno Ve Sota (Tucker); Martha Manor (Martha).

Synopsis: An Easterner, Mr. Fitts, is fascinated by the fast draw and Little Joe is the fastest. At the saloon, Dan Taggert, who has been watching the target shooting, starts a fight with Joe. After Dan challenges Joe to a gunfight at 6:30 the next morning, Fitts bets $5,000 that Joe will not show up for the gunfight.

Ben and Hoss enter the saloon and soon find out what has been going on.

When Ben finally finds Joe, he demands that his son try to apologize. Taggert refuses his gesture, claiming that the townspeople will call Joe a coward.

Note: Location shooting took place at Incline Village.

E224. *Three Brides for Hoss* (February 20, 1966)

Credits: *Writer:* Jo Pagano. *Director:* Ralph E. Black. *Producer:* David Dortort. **Starring:** Lorne Greene, Dan Blocker, Michael Landon. **Supporting Cast:** Stuart Erwin (Jester); Majel Barrett (Annie Slocum); Danielle Aubry (Yvette); Mitzi Hoag (Libby Spencefield); Sharyl Locke (Jenny); Claude Hall (Ned); Wynn Pearce (Jed); Orville Sherman (Matt); Grandon Rhodes (Doctor); Victor Sen Yung (Hop Sing).

Synopsis: Annie Slocum and her brothers Jed and Ned arrive at the Ponderosa looking for Hoss. They are there because of a marriage contract which he knows nothing about. Annie's brothers think that Hoss is trying to back out of the arrangement. There is a knock at the door. Opening it, they find Yvette, who also claims to be Hoss' finacée.

Ben and Hoss contact their lawyer, who tells them that the two women have a very good case. After sending Hoss home, Ben asks the storekeeper, who also handles the mail, if he remembers either of the women's names.

Meanwhile, Hoss is trying to get Joe to help him with the two women who are fighting over him. As if things were not complicated enough, Libby Spencefield arrives at the ranch looking for her fiancé Hoss.

E225. *The Emperor Norton* (February 27, 1966)

Credits: *Writers:* Robert Sabaroff (Teleplay & Story), Gerry Prince Young (Story). *Director:* William F. Claxton. *Producer:* David Dortort. **Starring:** Lorne Greene, Dan Blocker, Michael Landon. **Supporting Cast:** Sam Jaffe (Emperor Joshua Norton); Victor Sen Yung (Hop Sing); Ray Teal (Sheriff Roy Coffee); Parley Baer (Harry Crawford); John Napier (Chris Milner); William Challee (Mark Twain); Charles Irving (Judge); Tom Palmer (George Harris); Audrey Larkin (Woman).

Synopsis: Joshua Norton, the emperor of the United States and the Protector of Mexico (and an old friend of Ben's,) has come to the Ponderosa. He needs a place to stay because some powerful men in San Francisco want him committed.

Later, there is a mine explosion. After the miners are rescued, Norton is upset because the owners did not use canaries to alert miners of gas. That night at dinner, the emperor appoints Hop Sing as the Ambassador for Oriental Affairs. Norton then shows everyone his drawing of a suspension bridge which will someday be built across the Golden Gate in San Francisco.

The next day, the emperor goes to town and tries to arrest Mr. Crawford, the mine owner, for murder. When Crawford is released, he sends a telegram to San Francisco. After Roy Coffee brings Norton home, he tells Ben that Crawford is circulating a petition for a sanity hearing.

Note: In real life, Emperor Joshua Norton lived in San Francisco.

E226. *Her Brother's Keeper* (March 6, 1966)

Credits: *Writers:* Mort Thaw (Teleplay), Lee Pickett (Story). *Director:* Virgil W. Vogel. *Producer:* David Dortort. **Starring:** Lorne Greene, Dan Blocker, Michael

Landon. **Supporting Cast:** Nancy Gates (Claire Amory); Wesley Lau (Carl Amory); Grandon Rhodes (Doctor); Ralph Montgomery (Charlie); Norman Leavitt (Clerk).

Synopsis: Ben is helping Carl with repairs to his roof when Joe and Hoss bring in a load of new shingles. As they unload the wagon, Carl has an attack, so they send for the doctor. The Cartwrights insist that Carl should send for his sister, Claire, in San Francisco. Carl asks Ben to entertain Claire, so he meets her at the stage and drives her to Carl's house after showing her some beautiful scenery.

Over the next several days, Ben continues to see a great deal of Claire. Later she tells him that she has fallen in love with him. Trouble begins when her brother makes her feel responsible for his condition.

Note: Lorne Greene wore a black eye patch as a result of an actual injury. Location shooting took place at Golden Oak Ranch.

E227. *The Trouble with Jamie* (March 20, 1966)

Credits: *Writer:* Helen B. Hicks. *Director:* R. G. Springsteen. *Producer:* David Dortort. **Starring:** Lorne Greene, Dan Blocker, Michael Landon. **Supporting Cast:** Michael Burns (Jamie); Ross Elliott (Matthew); Tracy Olsen (Elizabeth); Ray Teal (Sheriff Roy Coffee); Victor Sen Yung (Hop Sing).

Synopsis: Ben's cousin Matthew arrives with his ward Elizabeth and his extremely rude son Jamie. That night at dinner, Jamie tells everyone that his mother died in childbirth but his father just ignores him.

The next morning, Jamie goes riding with Elizabeth and Joe but soon returns with a very lathered horse. When he tries to take Chub, Hoss dumps him in the water trough.

Matthew talks to Ben about his son and asks for his help. When Matthew has to make a business trip to San Francisco, he tells Jamie that he is going to stay at the Ponderosa. When Jamie keeps causing trouble on the ranch and in Virginia City, Ben puts him to work as a hired hand to work off the damages.

E228. *Shining in Spain* (March 27, 1966)

Credits: *Writer:* Elliot Gilbert. *Director:* Maury Geraghty. *Producer:* David Dortort. **Starring:** Lorne Greene, Dan Blocker, Michael Landon. **Supporting Cast:** Judi Rolin (Wendy Daniels); Woodrow Parfrey (Huber); Gene Lyons (Taylor Daniels); Hal Baylor (Drummer); Robert B. Williams (Hotel Clerk); Grandon Rhodes (Doctor); Clint Sharp (Stage Driver).

Synopsis: After stopping a runaway stage, Joe escorts one of the passengers, Wendy Daniels, to the hotel. She is in town to meet her father, whom she has not seen in five years. At the hotel Hoss is celebrating his birthday when Joe invites Wendy to join them. She tells them that her father is attempting to set up another stage line. She then proposes a very long toast to Hoss and her father.

The next day when Ben goes to the bank, he finds Wendy. The bank president, Mr. Huber, tells Ben that she is broke so Ben places $300 into her account just until the bank draft arrives from her father. After Joe takes Wendy on a buggy ride, Mr. Huber comes to the ranch to tell Ben that Wendy found out about the money. He also says that he received a telegram from Denver about Mr. Daniels' lack of funds and that he also had checked out of his hotel three days earlier.

E229. *The Genius* (April 3, 1966)

Credits: *Writer:* Donn Mullally. *Director:* R. G. Springsteen. *Producer:* David Dortort. **Starring:** Lorne Greene, Dan Blocker, Michael Landon. **Supporting Cast:** Lonny Chapman (Will Smith); Jorja Curtwright (Lydia Evans); Salvador Baguez (Jesus); Troy Melton (Draves); Raymond Mays (Joel); Grandon Rhodes (Doctor); Bruno Ve Sota (Bartender).

Synopsis: Mr. Smith, a drunk, recites poetry in the saloon. When a fight breaks out, Hoss comes to his rescue. In the morning, Ben catches him with a basket of food that he is taking out to Smith in the barn.

After Will is hired, Joe finds him asleep under a bush. When Hoss comes along, he tells Smith that he believes that there is a man in there somewhere. After Smith searches the bunk house for a bottle, he is caught and fired by Ben. When Hoss takes him to the doctor's office, he finds out that Smith's real name is William Warloc Evans, the famous poet.

E230. *The Unwritten Commandment* (April 10, 1966)

Credits: *Writers:* Joe Pagano (Teleplay), William Blinn (Teleplay and Story), Dan Ullman (Story). *Director:* Gerd Oswald. *Producer:* David Dortort. **Starring:** Lorne Greene, Dan Blocker, Michael Landon. **Supporting Cast:** Wayne Newton (Andy Walker); Ann Jeffreys (Miss Lily); Malcolm Atterbury (Willard Walker); Jerry Newton (Mike).

Synopsis: Andy Walker is singing while loading sacks of grain he is going to take to town. On the way he stops at the Ponderosa to give them one of the bags. Joe offers to ride into town with him and to buy him a beer. At the saloon, Andy tells Joe that Miss Lily is singing "Scarlet Ribbons" completely wrong and proceeds to sing the song correctly. When he gets home, he tells his father, Willard, that Lily has offered him a job singing in the saloon, but his father refuses to give his permission. Andy gets mad and storms out, going to the Ponderosa where he sings "Danny Boy." He tells the Cartwrights that he is taking vocal lessons and will start his singing job on Friday night.

On Friday night, Andy performs two songs, "Scarlet Ribbons" and "Old Joe Clark." When his father enters the saloon, Andy stops singing. After Willard expresses his humiliation, he is punched by the bartender. Andy, feeling guilty, leaves with his father.

Note: Location shooting took place at Incline Village. Wayne Newton also sang "The Old Rugged Cross." As "Danny Boy" and "The Old Rugged Cross" were written in 1913 and "Scarlet Ribbons" in 1949, they would not have been around at the time of this episode.

E231. *Big Shadow on the Land* (April 17, 1966)

Credits: *Writers:* William F. Leicester, Richard Barrett. *Director:* William F. Claxton. *Producer:* David Dortort. **Starring:** Lorne Greene, Dan Blocker, Michael Landon. **Supporting Cast:** Jack Kruschen (Giorgio Rossi); Brioni Farrell (Regina Rossi); Michael Stephani (Lorenzo Rossi); Penny Santon (Maria Rossi); Hoke Howell (Billy); Robert Foulk (Seth); Robert Corso (Tonio).

Synopsis: While Joe is out riding, he comes across Giorgio Rossi and his family camped on the Ponderosa. When he tries to tell them that they cannot stay,

Hop Sing's Stove. (Photograph by Linda F. Leiby.)

Giorgio pulls a gun, ordering him off the land. After Joe gets home, he tells Hoss what has happened. Hoss decides to pay the Rossis a visit. He tries to explain things but ends up in a fight with the son, Lorenzo.

When Ben gets back to town, he discovers what has been going on. Joe takes him to see Giorgio Rossi. After an exchange of words, Ben gives Rossi one week to leave.

Note: Location shooting took place at Incline Village.

E232. *The Fighters* (April 24, 1966)

Credits: *Writer:* Robert L. Goodwin. *Director:* R. G. Springsteen. *Producer:* David Dortort. **Starring:** Lorne Greene, Dan Blocker, Michael Landon. **Supporting Cast:** Michael Conrad (Hank Kelly); Phillip Pine (Ross Dugan); Mari Aldon (Ruby Kelly); Cal Bolder (Charlie); Grandon Rhodes (Doctor); Bruce Mars (Bert); Gene Tyburn (Smitty).

Synopsis: There is a professional exhibition fight in Virginia City between Hank Kelly and Charlie. After a wager is offered to anyone who can remain standing after four rounds, Hoss is pulled into the ring to fight Charlie. When he will not fight Hoss, the older fighter Hank is forced to take his place. At the start of the second round, Hoss keeps getting hit but finally knocks out Kelly, almost killing him. When Hoss tries to apologize to Ruby Kelly, she calls him an animal. At the ranch, Hoss tries to explain to his father that he had lost his temper, wanting to kill the fighter. He also agrees with Mrs. Kelly that he truly is an animal.

Fight promoter Ross Dugan arrives to try to arrange another fight between Charlie and Hoss. After Ben throws him out of the house, Dugan vows to get Hoss into the ring.

Note: Location shooting took place at Incline Village.

E233. *Home from the Sea* (May 1, 1966)

Credits: *Writers:* George E. Slavin, Stanley Adams. *Director:* Jean Yarbrough. *Producer:* David Dortort. **Starring:** Lorne Greene, Dan Blocker, Michael Landon. **Supporting Cast:** Alan Bermann (Gilly Maples); Ivor Barry (Morgan); Margaret Shinn (Saloon Girl); Wayne Heffley (Andy); Victor Sen Yung (Hop Sing).

Synopsis: After the stage arrives with Gilly Maples, a friend of Adam's, Hoss and Joe take him back to the Ponderosa. When Ben comes home, he mistakes Gilly for Adam. Over dinner, they talk about Adam and the sea.

Joe later asks Ben about the Mendoza herd which had been delayed two weeks and about the payment that must be paid in gold.

When Gilly decides to return to town, the Cartwrights ask him to stay on the Ponderosa. After Ben tells Gilly that he has written Adam a letter, Maples goes to the hotel to visit Morgan, the other man on the stage. He tells him about the letter and voices a change of heart. Morgan then reminds him that he owes him.

That night, while the Cartwrights think that Gilly reminds them of Adam, Gilly rides back to the hotel. He tells Morgan that the gold will be delivered the next day and about the Cartwrights' plans.

E234. *The Last Mission* (May 8, 1966)

Credits: *Writers:* William Douglas Langsford (Teleplay), S. S. Schweiter (Story & Teleplay). *Director:* R. G. Sprinsteen. *Producer:* David Dortort. **Starring:** Lorne Greene, Dan Blocker, Michael Landon. **Supporting Cast:** R. G. Armstrong (Col. Keith Jarrell); Tom Reese (Sergeant Devlin); Brendon Boone (Lowell); Ken Mayer (Poker); George Keymas (Chief Elkoro); Clay Tanner (Wiggins); Victor Sen Yung (Hop Sing).

Synopsis: The Cartwrights ride back to the Ponderosa and find a cavalry patrol in their yard. When they enter the house, they discover Col. Keith Jarell waiting for his old friend Ben. He has come to ask Ben's help to find Elkoro, a war chief of the Paiutes, in order to talk peace. When Ben finally agrees to go, Hoss and Joe draw cards to see who will accompany their father. At first Ben will not let Hoss go but finally agrees. The patrol mounts up and rides out, leaving a worried Joe behind. As they continue to ride they are followed by Indians. At Ben's suggestion, the colonel sends a man out on point with a white flag. When the pointman is found dead, Hoss volunteers to take his place. Unbeknownst to the Cartwrights, the colonel and his patrol are not on a peaceful mission.

Note: Location shooting took place at Vasquez Rocks.

E235. *A Dollar's Worth of Trouble* (May 15, 1966)

Credits: *Writer:* Robert L. Goodwin. *Director:* Don Daves. *Producer:* David Dortort. **Starring:** Lorne Greene, Dan Blocker, Michael Landon. **Supporting Cast:** Sally Kellerman (Kathleen Walker); Hampton Fancher III (Craig Bonner); Mabel Albertson (Mme. Adella); Elisha Cook, Jr. (John Walker); Robert Foulk (Seth).

Synopsis: Fortune teller Madame Adella predicts Hoss will meet a tall blonde woman who will immediately become infatuated with him. Joe feels the whole idea is ridiculous until the prediction comes true when Hoss meets Kathleen Walker.

That evening, Madame Adella arrives at the ranch trembling. She warns Hoss to be careful of Craig Bonner, a gunslinger, responsible for the deaths of 13 men.

Eighth Season
(September 11, 1966–May 14, 1967)

E236. *Something Hurt, Something Wild* (September 11, 1966)

Credits: *Writers:* Jerry Adelman, William Driskill. *Director:* Lewis Allen. *Producer:* David Dortort. **Starring:** Lorne Greene, Dan Blocker, Michael Landon. **Supporting Cast:** Lynn Loring (Laurie Ferguson); Lyle Bettger (Jed Ferguson); Erik Holland (Cleve Ferguson); Ron Foster (Stark); David Pritchard (Bret); Bruno Ve Sota (Sam the Bartender); Bruce MacFarlane (Clerk).

Synopsis: Joe is entertaining Laurie Ferguson, who has been away for six years, while Ben is in the house talking with her father, Jed. When Joe kisses her, she screams, slapping his face. Her father, Ben and Hoss come running out of the house.

In the morning, Hoss and Joe discover a fence being built between the two ranches. Ben then goes to talk to Jed, who warns him that there will not be any trouble if no one crosses the property line.

The next day two Ponderosa hands load a wagon in order to go branding. Ben warns them not to cross Ferguson's land but they do it anyway. Four of Ferguson's men fire on the wagon. When Hoss and Joe ride up, they too are shot at.

Note: Location shooting took place at Golden Oak Ranch.

E237. *Horse of a Different Hue* (September 18, 1966)

Credits: *Writer:* William R. Cox. *Director:* William Witney. *Producer:* David Dortort. **Starring:** Lorne Greene, Dan Blocker, Michael Landon. **Supporting Cast:**

Charlie Ruggles (Colonel Fairchild); Julie Parrish (Patty Lou Fairchild); Skip Homeier (Jack Geller); Johnny Silver (Snowden); Joe Haworth (O'Leary); Steven Marlo (MacKaye); Bing Russell (Deputy Clem Foster).

Synopsis: Joe owns a very fast race horse named Clancey. Ben's friend Colonel Fairchild and his granddaughter, Patty Lou, also own a race horse, Jeff Davis. They try to arrange a race between the two horses, which Ben finally agrees to. Fairchild next meets with Jack Geller about the con game that they will be running on the race.

Joe goes into town and bets $5,000 on the race. When Ben hears about the bet, he gets very upset. When he tries to pay the bet, Ben gets conned into doubling it. When Colonel Fairchild and Patty Lou try to talk to Geller about stopping the race, he threatens their lives and those of the Cartwrights.

Review: *Variety* (September 21, 1966): "[P]roduction credits are exceptional and the two-horse race was excellently staged for excitement. ...Charles Ruggles and Julie Parish were fine."

Note: Location shooting took place at Golden Oak Ranch.

E238. *A Time to Step Down* (September 25, 1966)

Credits: *Writer:* Frank Chase. *Director:* Paul Henreid. *Producer:* David Dortort. **Starring:** Lorne Greene, Dan Blocker, Michael Landon. **Supporting Cast:** Ed Begley (Dan Tolliver); Audrey Totter (Beth Riley); Donald "Red" Barry (Temple); Sherwood Price (Sand); Renny McEvoy (Flint); Bruno Ve Sota (Bartender).

Synopsis: Joe finds Dan Tolliver sleeping on horseback during a cattle drive. He also finds Sand and Temple drinking when they should have been on watch. When he fires them, they start a fight and Dan saves Joe's life.

After Hoss is injured in a branding accident, Joe tries to explain to his father that Dan should step down. Ben finally agrees. When Dan hears this, he gets mad and quits. The next morning, Dan returns to the Ponderosa to collect his wages, telling Joe that he hopes that Joe will someday know how it feels to be old.

Later, at the hotel, Sand and Temple pay a visit to Dan to tell him of a way to make money. Their plan is to rob Ben of the payroll money and to take Joe hostage.

E239. *The Pursued* [Part I] (October 2, 1966)
E240. *The Pursued* [Part II] (October 9, 1966)

Credits: *Writers:* Thomas Thompson (Teleplay & Story), Mark Michaels (Story). *Director:* William Witney. *Producer:* David Dortort. **Starring:** Lorne Greene, Dan Blocker, Michael Landon. **Supporting Cast:** Eric Fleming (Heber Clawson); Dina Merrill (Susannah); Lois Nettleton (Elizabeth Anne); Vincent Beck (Grant Carbo); Booth Colman (Parson Parley); Robert Brubaker (Menken); Jean Inness (Mrs. Lang); Donald Elson (Lang); Clay Tanner (Tex); Bill Clark (Dave); Nelson Leigh (Dr. Bingham); Byron Morrow (Rev. Mr. Blaisdale); Dee Carroll (Mrs. Blaisdale).

Synopsis: The Cartwrights head for Beehive, Nevada, to purchase some horses from a Mormon, Herber Clawson. Herber refuses to let the townspeople deter him from following his religious views.

When fire destroys Heber's ranch, one of his two wives needs a doctor and they set out to find her medical help.

Note: Location shooting took place at Lone Pine's Anchor Ranch.

E241. *To Bloom for Thee* (October 16, 1966)

Credits: *Writer:* June Randolph. *Director:* Sutton Roley. *Producer:* David Dortort. **Starring:** Lorne Greene, Dan Blocker, Michael Landon. **Supporting Cast:** Geraldine Brooks (Carol Attley); Don Haggerty (Demers); Bing Russell (Deputy Clem Foster); Robert B. Williams (Hotel Clerk); Paul Micale (Barber); Phil Chambers (Storeman); Clint Sharp (Stage Driver).

Synopsis: A woman gets off the stage and checks into the Palace Hotel under the name of Carol Attley. When she leaves the hotel, Hoss follows Carol to the cemetery to visit the grave of Kate Attley. After she cries, Hoss offers his help and drives her back to town.

Meanwhile, at the ranch, Joe is complaining that Hoss is not doing his chores, and Ben warns him not to tease his brother about courting a girl. After Hoss returns from a picnic with Carol, he informs Joe and Ben that he intends to marry her. Unbeknownst to the Cartwrights, Carol is wanted on murder charges.

Note: Location shooting took place at Golden Oak Ranch.

E242. *Credit for a Kill* (October 23, 1966)

Credits: *Writer:* Frederic Louis Fox. *Director:* William F. Claxton. *Producer:* David Dortort. **Starring:** Lorne Greene, Dan Blocker, Michael Landon. **Supporting Cast:** Don Collier (Sheriff Fenton); Luana Patten (Lorna); Dean Harens (Morgan Tanner); Regina Gleason (Martha Tanner); Charles Maxwell (Virgil); Ed Faulkner (Casey); Ted Markland (Boone); Troy Melton (Walt).

Synopsis: After working hard at branding, Joe is given a week off. He decides to visit his friends Morgan and Martha Tanner. When a man tries to steal a horse, the two men shoot at the same time, killing the thief. When they take the body to Sheriff Fenton, he identifies the man as Luke Jordan, who happens to have a $2,000 bounty on his head.

Luke's three brothers arrive in town looking for their brother's killer. To protect his friend, Joe claims that he alone killed Luke Jordan and wants all of the reward money.

E243. *Four Sisters from Boston* (October 30, 1966)

Credits: *Writer:* John M. Chester. *Director:* Alan Crosland, Jr. *Producer:* David Dortort. **Starring:** Lorne Greene, Dan Blocker, Michael Landon. **Supporting Cast:** Vera Miles (Sarah Lowell); Lyn Edgington (Gabrielle); Madeline Mack (Lorraine); Melinda Plowman (Heather); Morgan Woodward (Catlin); Ray Teal (Sheriff Roy Coffee); Victor Sen Yung (Hop Sing); Owen Bush (Billings); Quentin Sondergaard (Crocker); Rand Brooks (Cowboy); Raymond Guth (Toothless).

Synopsis: Sarah Lowell arrives in town with her three sisters and goes to the sheriff's office to prevent her property from being sold on the auction block because of $2,800 back taxes. Billings, the auctioneer, goes to see Mr. Catlin, who needs and intends to buy the ranch. The auction begins with the Land Castle property and, before bidding ends, Ben pays the back taxes.

Sara and Lorraine Lowell stop at the Ponderosa with legal papers for Ben to repay his loan. After Sheriff Roy Coffee checks on the sisters, their shed catches fire. Roy then tells Ben that Sarah blames him for setting the fire. When Lowell's well is poisoned, causing Heather Lowell to become ill, Roy is forced to arrest Joe because he was seen on the ranch.

E244. *Old Charlie* (November 6, 1966)

Credits: *Writers:* Robert and Wanda Duncan. *Director:* William F. Claxton. *Producer:* David Dortort. **Starring:** Dan Blocker. **Supporting Cast:** John McIntire (Charlie); Jeanette Nolan (Annie); Hal Baylor (Jack Barker); Tim McIntire (Billy and George Barker); Ray Teal (Sheriff Roy Coffee); Bill Fletcher (Sam); Bruno Ve Sota (Bartender); Dick Winslow (Heckler).

Synopsis: Charlie is a likable old gent who stretches the truth when he tells stories about his accomplishments. The townspeople find him funny but indulge him.

Stranger Billy Barker holds Charlie up at knifepoint and hits him over the head. Hoss hits Billy and he is killed unintentionally by his own knife.

When Charlie come to, he thinks he was responsible for Billy's death. George and Jack seek retribution against Charlie for their brother's murder.

E245. *Ballad of the Ponderosa* (November 13, 1966)

Credits: *Writers:* Michael Landon (Teleplay), Ric Vollaerts (Story). *Director:* William F. Claxton. *Producer:* David Dortort. **Starring:** Lorne Greene, Dan Blocker, Michael Landon. **Supporting Cast:** Randy Boone (Colter Preston); Ann Doran (Lisa Stanley); Roger Davis (Harold Stanley); John Archer (D.A. Dave Sinclair); Charles Irving (Judge Borman); Robert Foulk (Sheriff); Robert B. Williams (Simpson); Will J. White (Hank); Lane Bradford (Charlie).

Synopsis: On his way to town, Ben comes across a young man in need of water and directions to Virginia City.

Later Ben is having lunch with District Attorney Dave Sinclair and Judge Borman when the young man comes in. After he finishes singing his "Ballad of the Ponderosa," he introduces himself as Colter Preston. He is the son of Doug Preston, a man the town hanged for murder years before. Colter continues to sing his song around town because he believes that his father was innocent. He also blames Ben, Dave Sinclair and Judge Borman for his father's death.

E246. *The Oath* (November 20, 1966)

Credits: *Writer:* Martha Wilkerson. *Director:* Gerd Oswald. *Producer:* David Dortort. **Starring:** Lorne Greene, Dan Blocker, Michael Landon. **Supporting Cast:** Tony Bill (Charlie Two); Douglas Kennedy (Big Charlie); Dallas McKennan (Jenkins); Rusty Lane (Fielding); Ben Gage (Sheriff Calvin); Howard Wright (Sam); Bing Russell (Deputy Clem Foster).

Synopsis: The father of Charlie Two, a half-breed, is sent to the gallows after being found guilty of murder. Just prior to the hanging, he gets Charlie to promise to avenge his death by killing Ben.

While heading to the Ponderosa, Charlie comes across Joe. Not realizing that he is Ben's son, Charlie tells him he is going to kill Ben. Joe does not let on who he is and tries to talk Charlie out of his plans. Being unsuccessful, he must stop him; a fight ensues.

Note: Location shooting took place at Vasquez Rocks.

E247. *A Real Nice, Friendly Little Town* (November 27, 1966)

Credits: *Writer:* Herman Hoffman. *Director:* Herman Hoffman. *Producer:* David Dortort. **Starring:** Lorne Greene, Dan Blocker, Michael Landon. **Supporting Cast:** Louise Latham (Willie Mae Rikeman); Mark Slade (Judd Rikeman); Robert Doyle (Jeb Rikeman); Robert Foulk (Deputy); Burt Mustin (Old Man); Herb Vigran (Card Player); Billy M. Greene (Freddie); Clegg Hoyt (Sheriff); Vaughn Taylor (C. R. Lively); Bobby Byles (Skinny).

Synopsis: Joe, out searching for strays, returns home after being shot in the rear end. Since the Virginia City sheriff is busy, Hoss is deputized to look into the shooting. The only evidence he has to go on is a hat dropped at the scene with the name J. Rikeman inside.

After Hoss arrives in the next town, he finds that the people are not very cooperative, especially when he tries to arrest the Rikemans. He also finds no help when he goes to the town sheriff. When Hoss finally gets directions to the Rikeman ranch, he walks into a trap.

E248. *The Bridegroom* (December 4, 1966)

Credits: *Writer:* Walter Black. *Director:* William F. Claxton. *Producer:* David Dortort. **Starring:** Lorne Greene, Dan Blocker, Michael Landon. **Supporting Cast:** Joanne Linville (Maggie Dowling); Jeff Corey (Tuck Dowling); Ron Hayes (Jared Wilson).

Synopsis: Tuck Dowling and his daughter Maggie are visiting Ben and Joe at the Ponderosa. Joe then goes with the Dowlings to see Jared about buying horses. Tuck tries pushing his daughter on Wilson. Upset, Maggie asks Joe to take her for a ride. When they stop for a chat, she tells him that she knows that she is plain. After she decides to walk home, Joe returns the horse to Jared, who had sold it to her father.

Tuck later talks to Jared about his owing $600 to the bank. Tuck suggests that he will pay the debt if Jared will marry Maggie. That night, Tuck holds a party where he announces the couple's engagement. Maggie gets upset, running outside. The next morning she is still upset and tells Tuck that she cannot live with him any more.

E249. *Tommy* (December 18, 1966)

Credits: *Writers:* Mort Thaw (Teleplay), Mary Teri Taylor (Story), Thomas Thompson (Teleplay & Story); *Director:* William Witney. *Producer:* David Dortort. **Starring:** Lorne Greene, Dan Blocker, Michael Landon. **Supporting Cast:** Janet de Gore (Allie Miller); Michael Whitney (Jess Miller); Teddy Quinn (Tommy); Frank Puglia (Padre); Jorge Moreno (Waiter); Grandon Rhodes (Doctor); Rudolfo Hoyos (Police Chief); Ray Teal (Sheriff Roy Coffee); Victor Sen Yung (Hop Sing).

Synopsis: Hoss gets a package on the stage: a little boy who cannot hear or talk. When they arrive at the Ponderosa, Ben is given a letter from the boy's mother

Allie, asking them to take care of him for a while. Ben decides to go get Allie but finds her outlaw husband Jess hiding in her house. Before Ben arrives, Jess demands that she accompany him to Mexico but she refuses to go.

Ben returns to the Ponderosa with Allie. She tells him how much Jess has changed since they were married.

The Cartwrights soon find fences down and cattle stampeded. Later, when Joe rides back to the ranch, he is shot in the back. Allie, feeling responsible, decides to leave with Jess in order to protect the Cartwrights.

E250. *A Christmas Story* (December 25, 1966)

Credits: *Writer:* Thomas Thompson. *Director:* Gerd Oswald. *Producer:* David Dortort. **Starring:** Lorne Greene, Dan Blocker, Michael Landon. **Supporting Cast:** Wayne Newton (Andy Walker); Jack Oakie (Thadeus Cade); Mary Wickes (Mainwary); Dabbs Greer (Sam); Dean Michaels (Mike); Ray Teal (Sheriff Roy Coffee); Victor Sen Yung (Hop Sing).

Synopsis: Andy Walker along with his uncle and manager Thadeus Cade arrive in Virginia City to perform a benefit at an orphan's party. Hoss is left in charge of the benefit while Ben is in San Francisco closing a lumber deal, and he needs to raise $20,000 by Christmas Eve. When widow Hattie Mainwary, a wealthy socialite, hears that Hoss is in charge, she is not happy about the idea. Thadeus approaches her about taking over, and she consents.

Ben returns and gets mad when he finds out that Thadeus is collecting money instead of pledges. He is especially upset when he hears that Cade is getting a ten percent commission.

Note: Songs sung in this episode included "Sweet Betsy from Pike," "Home Is where I Want to Be on Christmas" and "Silent Night."

E251. *Ponderosa Explosion* (January 1, 1967)

Credits: *Writer:* Alex Sharp. *Director:* William F. Claxton. *Producer:* David Dortort. **Starring:** Lorne Greene, Dan Blocker, Michael Landon. **Supporting Cast:** Dub Taylor (Barlow); Chubby Johnson (Clyde); Chick Chandler (Nate); Phil Chambers (Storekeeper); Victor Sen Yung (Hop Sing).

Synopsis: Hoss and Joe are conned into purchasing two rabbits for $50. They plan to breed them for their fur to make coats. They take in a partner who agrees to provide them with a horse as a present for their father's birthday. Complications begin when the rabbits multiply in leaps and bounds and they cannot force themselves to skin the adorable little animals.

E252. Justice (January 8, 1967)

Credits: *Writer:* Richard Wendley. *Director:* Lewis Allen. *Producer:* David Dortort. **Starring:** Lorne Greene, Dan Blocker, Michael Landon. **Supporting Cast:** Beau Bridges (Horace); Shirley Bonne (Sally Bristol); Lurene Tuttle (Mrs. Cutler); Bing Russell (Deputy Clem Foster); Roy Roberts (Mr. Bristol); Antony Costello (Cliff).

Synopsis: Joe becomes engaged to Sally Bristol, the banker's daughter, much to the unhappiness of Horace, who also works at the bank.

Joe takes Sally to the dance and Horace comes to her rescue when Cliff tries to force himself on her. Horace later gets embarrassed and leaves, going to a saloon to get drunk. When the dance is over, Joe and Sally see Horace staggering down the street. After Joe goes home, Horace comes to tell Sally how he feels and that he is sorry.

When Sally is found murdered, Joe is determined to find out who committed the crime.

E253. *A Bride for Buford* (January 15, 1967)
Credits: *Writer:* Robert V. Barrow. *Director:* William F. Claxton. *Producer:* David Dortort. **Starring:** Lorne Greene, Dan Blocker, Michael Landon. **Supporting Cast:** Lola Albright (Dolly Bantree); Jack Elam (Buford Buckalew); Richard Devon (Blackie Wells); Paul Brinegar (Rev); Robert B. Williams (Searcy); Ray Teal (Sheriff Roy Coffee); Victor Sen Yung (Hop Sing).

Synopsis: Hoss, Joe and the townspeople are welcoming Dolly Bantree to town and are introduced to her manager Blackie Wells. Hoss gets volunteered by Joe to carry all of her luggage into the hotel. Meanwhile Buford and his brother Lev come into town, announcing that they just hit a big strike.

That night, Wells urges Dolly to pay attention to Buford so he can get his hands on the money. Hoss later finds Buford in the saloon with Dolly and gambling with Wells. Suspecting that something is wrong, Hoss decides to try to help Buford.

At the Ponderosa, Hoss comes down all dressed in a new suit to go to town. When Buford comes to escort Dolly, he finds Hoss there having dinner. Blackie Wells tells Dolly to go after Hoss instead of Buford or he will mar her face.

Note: Lola Albright sings "Allouette," "At the Fair" and "Aura Lee."

E254. *Black Friday* (January 22, 1967)
Credits: *Writers:* Herbert Kastle, John Hawkins. *Director:* William F. Claxton. *Producer:* David Dortort. **Starring:** Michael Landon. **Supporting Cast:** John Saxon (Friday); Ford Rainey (Judge Wyllit); Robert Phillips (Jakes); James Davidson (Cole Berry); Robert McQueeney (Enos Low); Robert Christopher (Clerk); Willard Sage (Sheriff); Nelson Leigh (Dr. Geis); Ken Drake (Charlie).

Synopsis: Joe rides into the small town of Chiso on a cattle buying trip. He runs into gunslinger Steve Friday, who used to work on the Ponderosa. Joe finds his friend sick and being held captive in his hotel room. The young Cartwright decides to help but neither the townspeople nor the sheriff give him any assistance. He is then asked to leave town. When he does not, his room is rented, forcing him to move in with Friday. Judge Wyllit tells Joe that he holds Friday responsible for the death of his son. He has hired a gunfighter to even the score on Friday the Thirteenth.

E255. *The Unseen Wound* (January 29, 1967)
Credits: *Writer:* Frank Chase. *Director:* Gerd Oswald. *Producer:* David Dortort. **Starring:** Lorne Greene. **Supporting Cast:** Leslie Nielsen (Sheriff Rowan); Nancy Malone (Catherine Rowan); Bill Fletcher (Tollar); Douglas Henderson (Dr. Evens); Jack Lambert (Landers); Cal Bartlett (Garrett); Frankie Kabott (Timmy); Percy Helton (Bleeker).

Synopsis: Ben rides into the town of Concho to visit his old friend Paul Rowan, the town marshall. He seems to be suffering from severe headaches which bring on violent mood swings.

Paul keeps a tight rein on the town by keeping all the firearms in his office. When he and his deputy attempt to arrest an old man for being drunk, both the old man and the deputy are killed. Paul cracks, taking refuge in an old building. He starts shooting and wounds several townspeople, including Ben.

E256. *Journey to Terror* (February 5, 1967)

Credits: *Writer:* Joel Murcott. *Director:* Lewis Allen. *Producer:* David Dortort. **Starring:** Lorne Greene, Michael Landon. **Supporting Cast:** John Ericson (Wade Hollister); Jason Evers (Tom Blackwell); Elizabeth Rogers (Ellie Sue Blackwell); Lory Patrick (Rita); Robert Hale (Neal); Kevin Hagen (Sheriff King); Lindsay Workman (Doc Jensen); Kerry McLain (Benjie).

Synopsis: Joe leaves on the stage to visit some old friends, the Blackwells. Before Joe can rent a horse, Sheriff King questions him about a bank robbery in Tucson. He then drives Joe to their ranch to make sure that Tom and Ellie Blackwell know him.

As Joe and Ellie reminisce about old times, Tom comes in, held at gunpoint by the Hollisters, one of whom is badly wounded. They are worried because the sheriff is coming in the morning to bring the Blackwells some water because of the drought. Joe and Tom Blackwell are tied up and forced to sit on the floor.

E257. *Amigo* (February 12, 1967)

Credits: *Writers:* John Hawkins (Adaptation), Jack Turley (from his book). *Director:* William F. Claxton. *Producer:* David Dortort. **Starring:** Lorne Greene, Michael Landon. **Supporting Cast:** Henry Darrow (Amigo); Gregory Walcott (Cap Fenner); Ray Teal (Sheriff Roy Coffee); Grandon Rhodes (Dr. Martin); Anna Navaro (Consuela); Warren Kemmerling (Hartley); Tim Herbert (Mosquito); Robert J. Stevenson (Benton); Troy Melton (Carson).

Synopsis: When Ben brings home a wanted outlaw named Amigo, he tells Joe to get the doctor and sheriff. After Roy arrives, he asks Amigo where Cap Fenner and the rest of his gang is hiding. Roy also asks Ben to put the money that Amigo was carrying in his safe.

Joe tells his father that he feels that Amigo should hang. After Joe brings him food, Amigo tells him how everybody sees him as a dirty Mexican.

The next day, some men tell Roy that a ranch was raided the night before. When they go to the Ponderosa looking for Amigo, Joe releases him while the posse is allowed to search the house. Amigo finds his way to Fenner's camp, where he is told to return to the Ponderosa. Fenner also tells him to give the stolen money back or Amigo's pregnant wife will be harmed.

Note: Sammy Davis, Jr., was first considered for the part of Amigo, but Henry Darrow replaced him.

E258. *A Woman in the House* (February 19, 1967)

Credits: *Writer:* Joel Murcott. *Director:* Gerd Oswald. *Producer:* David

Dortort. **Starring:** Lorne Greene, Dan Blocker, Michael Landon. **Supporting Cast:** Paul Richards (Russ Wharton); Diane Baker (Mary Farnum Wharton); Dennis Cross (Monk); Raymond Guth (Goliath); Robert Brubaker (Lassiter); Victor Sen Yung (Hop Sing).

Synopsis: The Cartwrights are hiring men for a roundup. Russ Wharton, who is slightly hung over, arrives needing a job. He gets hired because he is married to an old family friend, Mary Farnum.

Ben pays a visit to Mary and they talk of old times. She tells him that they have lost their ranch. Russ comes into the small cabin asking Ben for supplies, but Ben will not advance him any money in order to buy whiskey.

That night, one of the hands informs the Cartwrights that the bunkhouse has been robbed of $6 and a bottle of whiskey. When Ben finds Russ drunk and slapping his wife, he fires him.

Several days later, Russ stumbles in, demanding to see his wife. When Russ draws a gun on her, Joe and Hoss take him to jail. Before Russ leaves, he threatens to kill Ben.

E259. *Judgment at Red Creek* (February 26, 1967)

Credits: *Writer:* Robert Sabaroff. *Director:* William F. Claxton. *Producer:* David Dortort. **Starring:** Dan Blocker, Michael Landon. **Supporting Cast:** John Ireland (Will Rimbau); Harry Carey, Jr. (Mapes); Martin West (Hill); James Sikking (Jack Rimbau); Bartlett Robinson (Willow).

Synopsis: Hoss and Joe arrive at a way station by stagecoach. When they enter, they find Tom Delaney, the station agent, dead and Jack Rimbau badly wounded. Jack's brother Will, who rides shotgun, gets a description from his brother of the two men responsible. While Hoss stays with the wounded man, Joe rides out with the other men on the stage to look for the suspects.

They come upon two men, Stub and Johnny, who admit they were at the station for a meal but know nothing about any robbery. After Joe takes control of the posse, they return to the station, finding out that Jack has died. Hoss and Joe decide to find out who really committed the crime.

E260. *Joe Cartwright, Detective* (March 5, 1967)

Credits: *Writers:* Michael Landon (Teleplay), Oliver Crawford (Story). *Director:* William F. Claxton. *Producer:* David Dortort. **Starring:** Lorne Greene, Dan Blocker, Michael Landon. **Supporting Cast:** Mort Mills (Perkins); Ken Lynch (Simms); Ed Prentiss (Barnes); Herb Vigran (Charlie); Robert B. Williams (Clerk); Bing Russell (Deputy Clem Foster); Victor Sen Yung (Hop Sing).

Synopsis: Joe is reading a book called *How to Solve Crimes* at the breakfast table. Ben gets upset, accusing him of reading those books all of the time. He then sends Hoss and Joe to town on errands and also asks his younger son not to buy any more detective novels.

Hoss and Joe go to the bank where Simms and Perkins talk to the bank president, Mr. Barnes, about seeing the vault because of a large deposit they will be making. After Joe overhears the conversation, he is determined to thwart their plans with his brother's help.

The famous map behind Ben's desk. (Photograph by Linda F. Leiby.)

E261. *Dark Enough to See the Stars* (March 12, 1967)

Credits: *Writer:* Kelly Covin. *Director:* Don Daves. *Producer:* David Dortort. **Starring:** Lorne Greene, Dan Blocker, Michael Landon. **Supporting Cast:** Richard Evans (Billy); Linda Foster (Jennifer); Richard Eastham (Tom Yardley); Victor Sen Yung (Hop Sing); Willard Sage (Denton); Grandon Rhodes (Dr. Martin); Rita Lynn (Angel); Steven Marlo (Barclay); Baynes Barron (Marshal).

Synopsis: Ben is out riding when he comes across a young drifter who collapses from hunger. Back at the ranch, the doctor treats the boy. In the morning, Ben talks to the boy, who says his name is Billy Wilcox, about his past. After being hired, Billy, Ben and Hoss go to town to pick up Ben's friend Tom Yardley and his daughter Jennifer. That night, Ben and Tom talk about raising children and of old times.

The next day, Hoss and Billy are working when Jennifer comes along. She and Billy go for a ride. Later, Sam Denton, a Texas ranger, rides into the Ponderosa looking for a young man named Aaron Mendoza who is wanted for murder.

Note: Location shooting took place at the Golden Oak Ranch.

E262. *The Deed and the Dilemma* (March 26, 1967)

Credits: *Writer:* William F. Leicester. *Director:* William F. Claxton. *Producer:* David Dortort. **Starring:** Lorne Greene, Dan Blocker, Michael Landon.

Supporting Cast: Jack Kruschen (Georgio Rossi); Brioni Farrell (Regina Rossi); Michael Stephani (Lorenzo Rossi); Peggy Santon (Maria Rossi); Donald Woods (Gurney); Robert F. Lyons (Sandy); Chris Alcaide (Blake); Bing Russell (Deputy Clem Foster).

Synopsis: The Cartwrights are having lunch with the Rossis and they toast each other. Ben presents Georgio with the deed to 80 acres of land. When Mr. Rossi starts the cistern to irrigate the land, the water soon stops flowing. Everyone rides to the top of the hill to find three armed men guarding the water. When Mr. Gurney says that he will lease the water for $20 a month, Rossi gets mad and storms off. When Ben offers to pay the money, Georgio gets even madder.

Gurney and his son Sandy get into an argument over the water and Sandy storms out. He soon runs into the foreman, Jim Blake, who warns him to stay out of his way. Sandy then rides to the Rossis' place to apologize and is introduced to the entire family.

The next day, Georgio Rossi shows Ben a law book about water cases. They decide to visit Gurney about the water. They arrive to sign the water lease but Gurney now wants 50 percent of the wine profits. Georgio gets very mad, threatening Gurney.

E263. *The Prince* (April 2, 1967)

Credits: *Writers:* John Hawkins (Teleplay), Melvin Levy (Story); *Director:* William F. Claxton. *Producer:* David Dortort. **Starring:** Lorne Greene, Dan Blocker, Michael Landon. **Supporting Cast:** Lloyd Bochner (Prince Vlady and Peters); Warren Stevens (Count Alexis); Claire Griswold (Countess Elena); Adam Williams (Hardesty); Noah Keen (Dixon); Jerry Summers (Rivers); Clyde Howdy (Sgt. Bell); Gil Perkins (Porter); Bill Hickman (Ketch); Victor Sen Yung (Hop Sing).

Synopsis: A cavalry patrol escorts Mr. Dixon, Count Alexis and Countess Elena to the Ponderosa, where they are greeted by the Cartwrights. (Their father used to work for Ben.) Later Dixon discusses security with the Cartwrights because Elena brought her jewels.

Prince Vlady next arrives at the Ponderosa, telling Joe that he is a prince and an old friend of the count and countess. At dinner, Vlady toasts the Cartwrights and Elena and speaks of old times in Russia. Then Alexis talks to Vlady about cutting his visit short and about the 21 crimes with which Vlady was charged. Alexis also promises not to tell Elena the truth if Vlady leaves in three days.

The next day, Vlady and Alexis go for a ride, losing the cavalry escort. With the escort gone, Vlady takes Alexis hostage for personal satisfaction and the jewels.

E264. *A Man Without Land* (April 9, 1967)

Credits: *Writer:* Steven McNeil. *Director:* Don Daves. *Producer:* David Dortort. **Starring:** Lorne Greene, Dan Blocker, Michael Landon. **Supporting Cast:** Jeremy Slate (Ed Phillips); Royal Dano (Matt Jeffers); Joan Marshall (Millie Perkins); James Gammon (Harry Jeffers); Bing Russell (Clem); Dorothy Neuman.

Synopsis: The Jeffers and their foreman, Ed Phillips, try to hold onto their land but it will be sold for back taxes. Later Ed goes to see Millie, who works in the tax office. His plan is to pay the back taxes because he knows about an underground river on the ranch.

Joe goes into the saloon, where Harry Jeffers picks a fight with him. After Joe leaves, Harry claims that someday he will kill Joe.

Matt Jeffers visits Ben so that he can pay him $5,000, enabling him to pay the back taxes (with Ben getting to keep the ranch as a result). Ben comes up with the idea of an irrigation ditch between the Ponderosa and the Jeffers ranch. After Matt pays the taxes, Ed claims that he will get the land even if he has to cause trouble between Ben and Matt.

E265. *Napoleon's Children* (April 16, 1967)

Credits: *Writers:* Judith and Robert Burroy. *Director:* Christian Nyby. *Producer:* David Dortort. **Starring:** Lorne Greene, Dan Blocker, Michael Landon. **Supporting Cast:** Robert Biheller (Napoleon); Michael Burns (Donny); Woodrow Parfrey (Professor); Phyllis Hill (Grace); Bing Russell (Deputy Clem Foster); Eugene Martin (J. W); Kevin O'Neal (Reb); Ken Del Conte (Sampson); Victor Sen Yung (Hop Sing).

Synopsis: When Joe catches a young man, Sampson, trying to steal horses, he knocks him out and takes him to jail. Later Napoleon is planning to raid the Ponderosa during a Friday night social. At the social, Donny and his mother arrive as Napoleon and his gang sneak up on the ranch. Clem tells Ben that Sampson is wanted in Carson City and will be moved the next day. The gang then attacks, stealing the donation money.

After Clem learns the identity of the gang leader, he and Ben pay a visit to the boy's uncle. It seems that he used to teach at Harvard and his nephew is very interested in the Napoleonic Wars. Soon Napoleon and his gang strike again by ambushing Hoss and severely beating him.

E266. *The Wormwood Cup* (April 23, 1967)

Credits: *Writers:* Joy Dexter, Michael Landon (Adaptation); *Director:* William F. Claxton. *Producer:* David Dortort. **Starring:** Lorne Greene, Dan Blocker, Michael Landon. **Supporting Cast:** Judi Meredith (Linda Roberts); Frank Overton (Amos Crenshaw); Bing Russell (Deputy Clem Foster); Clay Tanner (Dewitt); Will J. White (Flores); Victor Sen Yung (Hop Sing); Myron Healey (Sam); Robert B. Williams (Clerk); Quentin Sondergaard (Luke); Walter Kray (Caleb).

Synopsis: After Joe is cleared of the murder charges of Zack Crenshaw, Linda Roberts walks around town hanging $1,000 wanted posters. She will pay that money to anyone who will kill Joe. When Hoss and Joe learn of the posters, they go to the hotel to talk to Linda. Joe was questioned about killing her brother Billy Roberts, but she thinks that Joe killed him.

Clem puts Linda in jail for attempting to incite a murder. Hoss then sends Joe home to keep him out of trouble. Later Linda is released and accosted in her hotel room by a masked man who says he will do the job only if he is paid in advance.

E267. *Clarissa* (April 30, 1967)

Credits: *Writer:* Chester Krumholtz. *Director:* Lewis Allen. *Producer:* David Dortort. **Starring:** Lorne Greene, Dan Blocker, Michael Landon. **Supporting Cast:** Nina Foch (Clarissa); Roy Roberts (George Bristol); Robert Foulk (Peterson); Ray Teal (Sheriff Roy Coffee); Victor Sen Yung (Hop Sing); Louise Lorimer (Mrs. Peterson); Ken Mayer (Baker); Norman Leavitt (Telegrapher).

Synopsis: Cousin Clarissa arrives at the Ponderosa for a visit and begins changing the normal routine of the household. She has the house redecorated with doilies and requires that Ben, Hoss and Joe wear slippers when they enter the house. Clarissa even meddles in Hop Sing's kitchen.

Clarissa even interferes in Ben's bank business and the running of Roy's re-election campaign. The hands threaten to quit when she hangs curtains in the bunkhouse and throws out all of their whiskey.

E268. *Maestro Hoss* (May 7, 1967)

Credits: *Writer:* U. S. Anderson. *Director:* William F. Claxton. *Producer:* David Dortort. Starring: Lorne Greene, Dan Blocker, Michael Landon. Supporting Cast: Zsa Zsa Gabor (Mme. Morova); Kathleen Freeman (Miss Hibbs); Del Moore (Hank); Doodles Weaver (Barney); Ray Teal (Sheriff Roy Coffee); Victor Sen Yung (Hop Sing).

Synopsis: Madame Morova, a gypsy fortune teller, cons Hoss into believing he will become a famous violinist. She gives him a Stradivarius and tells him she had taken a loan out on the instrument. Hoss offers to give her the money to pay off her debt.

Hoss' practicing cannot be deterred and he drives Ben and Joe to distraction. Ben and Joe learn that Madame Morova has conned others, but Hoss is not swayed.

Ben brings a music teacher to the ranch hoping that she will discourage Hoss from following his desire to become a violinist. But things do not work out because when she sees Hoss, she becomes infatuated with him.

Note: Location shooting took place at the Golden Oak Ranch.

E269. *The Greedy Ones* (May 14, 1967)

Credits: *Writer:* James Amesbury. *Director:* Don Daves. *Producer:* David Dortort. Starring: Lorne Greene, Dan Blocker, Michael Landon. Supporting Cast: Robert Middleton (Shasta); George Chandler (Gus); William Bakewell (Henshaw); Ray Teal (Sheriff Roy Coffee); Grandon Rhodes (Doctor); Lane Bradford, Phil Chambers.

Synopsis: When Gus, an old prospector, comes into town with ore samples, the assayer says that he has made a big gold strike. Everyone thinks the strike has to be on the Ponderosa. Ben worries that if the gold strike was on the ranch, the property will be overrun.

Shasta and Henshaw are plotting to get their hands on Gus and the gold. First he is wined and dined and asked to sign an agreement for 25 percent of the profits. The next day, Shasta goes to see Gus to sweeten the deal, but Gus turns him down.

Ben asks Gus whether his claim is on the ranch, but he will not tell anyone where it is located. Shasta and Henshaw visit Ben to offer him a partnership deal. Ben says no because he is aware that Shasta's mining practices would turn the Ponderosa into a wasteland.

Note: Lorne Greene did a voiceover in this episode.

Ninth Season
(September 17, 1967–July 28, 1968)

E270. *Second Chance* (September 17, 1967)

Credits: *Writers:* John Hawkins (Adaptation), Paul Schneider. *Director:* Leon Benson. *Producer:* David Dortort. **Starring:** Lorne Greene, Dan Blocker, Michael Landon. **Supporting Cast:** James Gregory (Mulvaney); Bettye Ackerman (Estelle); Joe DeSantis (Dawson); Douglas Kennedy (Frazier); Jane Zachary (Anna); Ken Drake (Breck); James Beck (Lt. Marsh); Martin Eric (Telegrapher); Olan Soule.

Synopsis: Joe and Hoss are on their way home from Sweetwater when they are attacked by Indians. When Joe is hit in the shoulder with an arrow which breaks off when Hoss tries to take it out. Leaving Joe behind, Hoss spies a campfire and goes for help. When Joe hears shots, he manages to get on Cochise. He rides into the camp, thinking that his brother is in trouble. As luck would have it, one of the passengers is a doctor. With the help of his wife, he operates on Joe. To repay the favor, Hoss offers to lead the wagon train to safety.

E271. *Sense of Duty* (September 24, 1967)

Credits: *Writers:* John Hawkins (Adaptation), Gil Lasky, Abe Polsky. *Director:* William Witney. *Producer:* David Dortort. **Starring:** Lorne Greene, Dan Blocker, Michael Landon. **Supporting Cast:** Gene Rutherford (Sergeant Ankers); David Canary (Candy); Michael Forest (Wabuska); Peter Deull (Hack); Ron Foster (Steve); Richard Hale (Chief Winetka); Ben Gage (Deputy); John Matthews (Col. Brill); Kip Whitman (Tim Kelly).

Synopsis: The Cartwrights run into a cavalry patrol escorting a Paiute prisoner, Wabuska. the sergeant has orders to turn him over to Ben, who has just been reactivated as a major in the 116th militia.

In Virginia City, Ben asks for volunteers to escort the prisoner through Indian territory to Fort Churchill. That night, Candy appears in camp and agrees to help. Soon the men find themselves under full attack by Chief Winetka and his braves.

Note: Location shooting took place at Red Rock Canyon. This was the first appearance of David Canary as Candy.

E272. *The Conquistadors* (October 1, 1967)

Credits: *Writer:* James Amesbury. *Director:* Leon Benson. *Producer:* Robert Blees. *Executive Producer:* David Dortort. **Starring:** Lorne Greene, Dan Blocker, Michael Landon. **Supporting Cast:** John Saxon (Blas); John Kellogg (Bill Anderson); Ray Teal (Sheriff Roy Coffee); Eddie Ryder (Perkins); Mike DeAnda (Quail); Carlos Rivas (Miguel); Rudolfo Hoyos (Emiliano); King Moody (Charlie); Clyde Howdy (Boke); Jim Boles (Aldrich).

Synopsis: On his way home from Carson City, Joe is kidnapped by four Mexicans. Blas decides to ask for $100,000 in gold but settles for $25,000.

After Ben, Hoss and Roy go to the bank to arrange for the ransom, teller Perkins overhears the conversation. Perkins reports to John Kellogg and, along with some more men, decide to follow Blas.

Ben and Hoss ride out after the Mexican with Roy telling them about Kellogg and his friends. When Blas returns to camp after hiding the gold, he and Joe are captured by Kellogg and his men.

E273. *Judgment at Olympus* (October 8, 1967)

Credits: *Writer:* Walter Black. *Director:* John Rich. *Producer:* Robert Blees. *Executive Producer:* David Dortort. **Starring:** Lorne Greene, Dan Blocker, Michael Landon. **Supporting Cast:** David Canary (Candy); Barry Sullivan (Fuller); Arch Johnson (Wheelock); Brooke Bundy (Mary Elizabeth); Vaughn Taylor (Eggers); Robert Brubaker (Sheriff Henning); James Griffith (Deputy Gibbs); Dabbs Greer (Dawes); Rusty Lane (Judge Beckert); Olan Soule (Telegrapher).

Synopsis: A deputy from Olympus arrives at the Ponderosa with an arrest warrant for Candy on murder charges. Joe, Candy and Deputy Gibbs go to Olympus where they are met by Mr. Fuller, an attorney, who agrees to defend Candy.

When Joe tries to send a telegram, it is intercepted and burned. At the hearing, Mr. Eggers claims that he saw Candy leaving the scene of the crime. After the hearing, Eggers is found murdered and Joe is arrested for the crime.

E274. *Night of Reckoning* (October 15, 1967)

Credits: *Writer:* Walter Black. *Director:* Leon Benson. *Producer:* Robert Blees. *Executive Producer:* David Dortort. **Starring:** Lorne Greene, Dan Blocker, Michael Landon. **Supporting Cast:** Richard Jaeckel (Dibbs); Ron Hayes (Buckler); Joan Freeman (Kelly); Eve McVeagh (Harriet); Teno Pollick (Carew); William Jordan (Rusher); David Canary (Candy); Grandon Rhodes (Dr. Martin); James Wainwright (Webster).

Synopsis: Joe rides to a line shack and finds a wounded man named Buckler. Before he was found, Buckler managed to hide the stolen money that he was carrying. After Joe brings the man to the Ponderosa, Dibbs and three other men burst in, demanding the money. Hoss and Joe are taken captive.

E275. *False Witness* (October 22, 1967)

Credits: *Writer:* Eric Norden. *Director:* Michael Moore. *Producer:* Robert Blees. *Executive Producer:* David Dortort. **Starring:** Dan Blocker, Michael Landon. **Supporting Cast:** Davey Davison (Valerie Townsend); Michael Blodgett (Billy Slader); Frederick Downs (Matt Haskell); Bill Fletcher (Doug Slader); Ross Conway (Judge Wheeler); David Canary (Candy); Jerry Douglas (Jeremiah); Len Hendry (Jensen); Frank Gerstle (Strand); Bill Henry (Farrell).

Synopsis: After Hoss, Joe, Candy and Valerie Townsend witness a murder, they are put under a round-the-clock guard by Sandy Dust's sheriff. The brothers of murderer Billy Slader are determined to see that there are no witnesses around to convict their brother.

E276. *The Gentle Ones* (October 29, 1967)

Credits: *Writer:* Frank Chase. *Director:* Harry Harris, Jr. *Producer:* David Dortort. **Starring:** Lorne Greene, Dan Blocker. **Supporting Cast:** Robert Walker,

Jr. (Mark); Lana Wood (Dana Dawson); Pat Conway (Frank Cole); Douglas Henderson (Major Dawson); Bing Russell (Deputy Clem Foster); Stuart Anderson (Trask).

Synopsis: Ben and Frank Cole talk about the fact that Major Dawson is coming to buy horses. Frank decides to bring his horses the next morning.

When Mark, one of Frank's hired hands, quits, Ben hires him to work on the Ponderosa. After the major and Ben complete their horse deal, Frank arrives with his horses. Cole gets mad when the colonel tells him that they are not up to Army standards, except one black stallion. After Cole is thrown by the stallion, he starts whipping the animal. Mark tries to stop him but is knocked down. Before Ben orders Cole off the Ponderosa, the major agrees to buy the stallion if he can be saddle-broken before he leaves.

Dana Dawson tells Ben that she considers Mark a coward and does not like him since her husband died a coward in battle.

E277. *Desperate Passage* (November 5, 1967)

Credits: *Writer:* John Hawkins. *Director:* Leon Benson. *Producer:* Robert Blees. **Starring:** Lorne Greene, Dan Blocker, Michael Landon. **Supporting Cast:** Steve Forrest (Josh Tanner); Tina Louise (Mary Burns); James Forrest (Paul Burns); Bing Russell (Deputy Clem Foster); David Canary (Candy).

Synopsis: The Cartwrights and Candy are returning to the Ponderosa with some horses when they see a signal light. Arriving at the nearest town, they find three people dead from an Indian raid. The Cartwrights hear a noise coming from the jail, where they find Josh Tanner locked in a cell. He tells Ben what happened in town while Hoss and Joe hunt for the keys. A ledger indicates that Tanner was imprisoned for the first degree murder of Billy Colter. After they bury the dead, Mary Burns comes staggering down the street.

The next day everyone leaves for Virginia City. Joe is jumped by a Paiute and is forced to kill him. The following morning they continue on their way when a group of Indians charge at them, taking Mary hostage.

Note: Location shooting took place at the Ponderosa Ranch at Incline Village.

E278. *The Sure Thing* (November 12, 1967)

Credits: *Writers:* Sidney Ellis (Teleplay & Story); Robert Vincent Wright (Teleplay). *Director:* William Witney. *Producer:* David Dortort. **Starring:** Lorne Greene, Dan Blocker, Michael Landon. **Supporting Cast:** Kim Darby (Trudy Loughlin); Tom Tully (Burt Loughlin); William Bryant (Harper); King Moody (Carter); Duane Grey (Townsman); Matt Emery (Official); Victor Sen Yung (Hop Sing).

Synopsis: Hoss and Joe spot Trudy Loughlin trying to catch a stallion so they help her. When Joe offers to buy the horse after it has been broken in, she turns him down. Ben and Joe later ride to Trudy's place to see the stallion but again she will not sell. She tells them that her father, Burt, does not know about the horse.

The next day, Burt finds his daughter with the horse. Taking the animal to the Cartwrights, he plans to sell the stallion for $100. After Trudy beats Joe in a horse race, her father accuses Ben of cheating him. The Cartwrights offer Trudy a deal to let her ride in the Stakes Race. If she wins, she will get the horse and half the prize money when she comes of age. Meanwhile, her father makes his own deal with a gambler named Harper.

E279. *Showdown at Tahoe* (November 19, 1967)

Credits: *Writer:* Thomas Thompson. *Director:* Gerald Mayer. *Producer:* Robert Blees. *Executive Producer:* David Dortort. **Starring:** Lorne Greene, Dan Blocker, Michael Landon. **Supporting Cast:** Richard Anderson (Jamison Filmore); David Canary (Candy); Sheila Larken (Julie); Karl Swenson (Captain Larson); Kevin Hagen (Guy Gilroy); Christopher Dark (Testy); Troy Melton (Houston); Bing Russell (Clem); Bill Clark (Tucker).

Synopsis: An outlaw gang is rehearsing a stage robbery where the leader, Filmore, plans to use Ben's new paddlewheel boat as his method of escape. Later Filmore pays a visit to his former cell mate, Captain Nels Larson. Filmore wants Larson to introduce him to Ben. After the introduction, Jamison talks to Ben about buying a stand of timber.

Nels later tells Filmore that he will not stand to see Ben get hurt but Filmore has an opportunity to take $1,000,000.

When Nels goes to pay a visit to Ben, he is stopped by Filmore and killed.

Note: Location shooting took place at Incline Village and on Lake Tahoe. The M. S. Dixie II still sails on Lake Tahoe today, taking passengers on tours of the lake.

E280. *Six Black Horses* (November 26, 1967)

Credits: *Writers:* William Jerome (Story and Teleplay), Michael Landon (Teleplay). *Director:* Don Daves. *Producer:* David Dortort. **Starring:** Lorne Greene, Dan Blocker, Michael Landon. **Supporting Cast:** Burgess Meredith (Ownie Dugan); David Lewis (Giblin); Judy Parker (Julie); Richard X. Slattery (McCoy); Hal Baylor (Tierney); Don Haggerty (Patrick O'Neil); Grandon Rhodes (Dr. Martin); Liam Dunn (Father O'Brien); Victor Sen Yung (Hop Sing).

Synopsis: After Ownie Dugan and two other men arrive on the stage, Dugan goes to the saloon to wait for Ben. Back at the ranch, Dugan tells Ben that his daughter Julie is in school in San Francisco. He also asks Ben to invest the $114,000 that he has in his little black bag. They decide to purchase a tract of land for its lumber. The next day, Ben signs the papers with Mr. Giblin. Dugan receives a telegram saying that his daughter is coming.

Ben and Dugan are out walking that night when Dugan is shot. After being put to bed, he confesses to Ben that he is a scoundrel and a con man. He also says that the money was graft and asks Ben not to tell Julie. After the doctor tends Dugan, Ben urges him to return the money.

E281. *Check Rein* (December 3, 1967)

Credits: *Writers:* Robert I. Holt (Adaptation), Olney Sherman. *Director:* Leon Benson. *Producer:* Robert Blees. *Executive Producer:* David Dortort. **Starring:** Lorne Greene, Dan Blocker, Michael Landon. **Supporting Cast:** James MacArthur (Jace Fredericks); Patricia Hyland (Kathy); Ford Rainey (Bingham); Charles Maxwell

(Rio); David Canary (Candy); Robert Karnes (Sheriff Buhler); William Fawcett (Asa); Tom Fadden (Cowboy).

Synopsis: After Jace Fredericks is injured, he is unable to attend a horse auction and has Hoss represent him. He is after a certain horse and authorizes Hoss to bid no more than $500. At the auction, Hoss sees Jace's Uncle Bingham, who is after the same horse and will stop at nothing to acquire the animal.

E282. *Justice Deferred* (December 17, 1967)

Credits: *Writer:* Jack Miller. *Director:* Gerald Mayer. *Producer:* Robert Blees. *Executive Producer:* David Dortort. **Starring:** Lorne Greene, Dan Blocker, Michael Landon. **Supporting Cast:** Simon Oakland (Mel Barnes/Frank Scott); Nita Talbot (Gladys); Carl Reindel (Andy); Shannon Farnon (Eleanor Eads); Ray Teal (Sheriff Roy Coffee); John Hubbard (Eads); Claudia Bryar (Mrs. Scott); Harlan Warde (Monroe); Tol Avery (Judge); Byron Morrow (Belden).

Synopsis: Ben, Hoss and Joe are at an engagement party for Eleanor Eads, banker Andy's daughter. When Hoss and Andy go outside, they see a man strangle a girl who dies in Hoss' arms. Andy and Hoss identify Frank Scott as the attacker and testify to that at the trial. Mrs. Scott testifies that her husband was with her that night but the court still finds him guilty, sentencing him to hang.

The Cartwrights go to Carson City to close a land deal. While there, Hoss spots Mel Barnes, an exact double for Frank Scott. Fearing that he might have made a tragic mistake, Hoss sets about trying to get Barnes convicted of the crime.

E283. *The Gold Detector* (December 24, 1967)

Credits: *Writer:* Ward Hawkins. *Director:* Don Daves. *Producer:* David Dortort. **Starring:** Lorne Greene, Dan Blocker, Michael Landon. **Supporting Cast:** Wally Cox (McNulty); Paul Fix (Barney); Caroline Richter (Casey); Kelly Thordsen (Vern Higgins); Dub Taylor (Simon); Chubby Johnson (Cash); Mike deAnda (Corrales); Victor Sen Yung (Hop Sing).

Synopsis: Hoss purchases a gold detector as a sideline business. When Barney's mine runs out of gold, he comes to Hoss for help. Vern Higgins wants to buy the mine but decides to give Hoss a week to assemble his gold detector.

Albert McNulty from the Lodestar Manufacturing Company arrives in Virginia City to help Hoss assemble the machine. After it is put together, Hoss and Albert try to explain how it works to Barney and his daughter, Casey. Before the machine can be used at Barney's mine, it is stolen by two old miners.

E284. The Trackers (January 7, 1968)

Credits: *Writers:* Louis Bercovitch (Adaptation), Frederic Louis Fox. *Director:* Marc Daniels. *Producer:* Robert Blees. *Executive Producer:* David Dortort. **Starring:** Lorne Greene, Dan Blocker. **Supporting Cast:** Warren Stevens (Sam Bragan); Bruce Dern (Cully Maco); Warren Vanders (Buzz); Ted Gehring (Grifty); David Canary (Candy); Ray Teal (Sheriff Roy Coffee); Robert P. Lieb, James Sikking, Christopher Shea, Arthur Peterson.

Synopsis: Cully Maco has been in prison serving a five-year sentence for holding up a bank. After being released, he heads for Virginia City. The townspeople want him out of town but Roy Coffee's hands are tied because Cully has not committed any crime.

After the Wells Fargo drops off $121,000, cashier Evans is shot during a hold-up. At the same time, Maco skips town. Ben, Hoss and Candy join a posse to search for Cully. They apprehend him but the other posse men believes it is a waste of time to return him for trial and want to take the law in their own hands.

E285. *A Girl Named George* (January 14, 1968)

Credits: *Writer:* William H. Wright. *Director:* Leon Benson. *Producer:* Robert Blees. *Executive Producer:* David Dortort. **Starring:** Lorne Greene, Dan Blocker, Michael Landon. **Supporting Cast:** Jack Albertson (Enos Blessing); Gerald Mohr (Cato Troxell); Sheilah Wells (George); Fred Clark (Judge Neely); David Canary (Candy); Andy Devine (Roscoe); Patsy Kelly (Mrs. Neely); Steve Raines (Deputy); Harry Harvey, Sr. (Coroner).

Synopsis: Cato Troxell's brother is found guilty of murdering a Ponderosa ranch hand and sentenced to hang. Cato threatens to kill Judge Neely.

Enos Blessing and his niece George come to the Ponderosa trying to sell Ben a memorial photograph. Ben and the boys agree to have their picture taken. Taking the pictures, including one with all of the hands, takes the entire morning. Cato Troxell also pays Enos $1,000 to have his picture taken. When Judge Neely is found murdered, the Cartwrights suspect that Troxell might be responsible since he had threatened the man.

E286. *The Thirteenth Man* (January 21, 1968)

Credits: *Writer:* Walter Black. *Director:* Leon Benson. *Producer:* Robert Blees. *Executive Producer:* David Dortort. **Starring:** Lorne Greene, Dan Blocker, Michael Landon. **Supporting Cast:** Ray Teal (Sheriff Roy Coffee); Albert Salmi (Marcus Alley); Richard Carlson (Arch Holenbeck); Anna Navarro (Prudence Wells); Kenneth Tobey (Heath); Myron Healey (Johannsen); Bill Quinn (Allison); John Zaremba (Charles); John Lodge (Terry); Michael Kriss (Welles); Jon Lormer (Lamar).

Synopsis: With the current outbreak of cattle thefts, the cattlemen's group obtains the services of range detective Marcus Alley. His method of handling the situations is questionable: He gets suspects to draw and, when he shoots them, he insists he did it in self-defense. No one is ever around to dispute his claim. When he discovers rustler Heath working for the Cartwrights, Marcus seeks revenge on the man who eluded him five years earlier.

Note: Location shooting took place at Vasquez Rocks.

E287. *The Burning Sky* (January 28, 1968)

Credits: *Writers:* William H. Wright (Adaptation), Carol Saraceno. *Director:* John Rich. *Producer:* Robert Blees. *Executive Producer:* David Dortort. **Starring:** Lorne Greene, Dan Blocker, Michael Landon. **Supporting Cast:** Dawn Wells (Moon Holt); Bobby Riha (Bridger); Victor French (Aaron); Michael Murphy (Web Holt); Gregg Palmer (Muley); Robert Foulk (Deputy); Iron Eyes Cody (Long Bear); David Canary (Candy); Bill Clark.

Synopsis: Web Holt, Ben's new bronco buster, arrives on the stage with his

Indian bride Moon, After Candy takes them to their cabin, Web asks Ben for an advance on his salary. Hoss goes with him in case of any trouble in town.

While they are away, Moon comes across a small boy named Bridger. They soon become friends. She makes him a small paddle wheel and teaches him how to track. The small boy also tells Moon how much he hates his stepfather Aaron.

When the Holts are taunted in town, Aaron claims that they should not be allowed to stay.

E288. *The Price of Salt* (February 4, 1968)

Credits: *Writer:* B. W. Sandefur. *Director:* Leon Benson. *Producer:* David Dortort. **Starring:** Lorne Greene, Dan Blocker, Michael Landon. **Supporting Cast:** Kim Hunter (Ada Halle); John Doucette (Cash Talbot); James Best (Sheriff Vern Shaler); David Canary (Candy); Myron Healey (Williams); David Pritchard (Ned); Robert Patten (Pardee); Ken Drake (Jackson); John Jay Douglas (Conrad).

Synopsis: The Cartwrights and their neighbors are losing cattle as the result of the scarcity of salt. The only one with a supply of salt is Ada Halle from Spanish Wells. Taking advantage of the situation, she jacks up the price. Cattleman Cash Talbot makes a private arrangement with her to buy up the supply. The cattle owners are desperate for salt and will even kill to get their hands on it.

E289. *Blood Tie* (February 18, 1968)

Credits: *Writer:* Arthur Dales. *Director:* Seymour Robbie. *Producer:* David Dortort. **Starring:** Lorne Greene, Dan Blocker, Michael Landon. **Supporting Cast:** Robert Drivas (Tracy Blaine); Conlan Carter (Clay); Leo Gordon (Fargo); Ray Teal (Sheriff Roy Coffee); Peter Leeds.

Synopsis: After Tracy Blaine saves Joe's life in a bar fight, they both ride back to the Ponderosa, where Tracy is hired. Joe learns that the money for a cattle deal will be brought directly to the house on Thursday.

Fargo Taylor arrives at the ranch looking for Blaine. When Ben prevents Fargo from taking him, he is shot in the leg. After Taylor leaves, Joe and Blaine ride out looking for him.

E290. *The Crime of Johnny Mule* (February 25, 1968)

Credits: *Writer:* Joel Murcott. *Director:* Leon Benson. *Producer:* Robert Blees. *Executive Producer:* David Dortort. **Starring:** Lorne Greene, Dan Blocker, Michael Landon. **Supporting Cast:** Noah Beery (Johnny Mule); Coleen Gray (Marcy); Lee Patterson (Virgil Lowden); Jack Ging (Cleve Lowden); John Archer (Prosecutor); John Lodge (Deputy); Bruno Ve Sota (Bartender); David Canary (Candy).

Synopsis: Johnny Mule is being tried for the murder of Dave Lowden. While Hoss and Candy sit on the jury, they hear testimony from Cleve Lowden and Johnny, who claims that he heard another man's voice in the cabin the night of the murder.

The jury is sequestered and three days later they are still dead locked 11-1 with Hoss being the only hold-out for not guilty. Johnny is held for a new trial with a new jury. Hoss questions Johnny about what he saw the night of the murder. But Mule gets worried when Hoss tells him that he can not be on the next jury.

One of the numerous cameras used for filming, set up to show where the camerman stood. (Photograph by Linda F. Leiby.)

The deputy is warned that Cleve and Verge might try to kill Johnny Mule. When the deputy tries to put him in a solitary cell, Johnny pushes him down and escapes.

E291. *The Late Ben Cartwright* (March 3, 1968)

Credits: *Writer:* Walter Black. *Director:* Leon Benson. *Producer:* David Dortort. **Starring:** Lorne Greene, Dan Blocker, Michael Landon. **Supporting Cast:**

Sidney Blackmer (Sam Endicott); Bert Freed (Broome); William Campbell (White); Simon Scott (Farraday); George Gaynes (Purdy); David Canary (Candy); Tyler McVey.

Synopsis: Judge John Farraday is running for the governorship of Nevada. A wealthy businessman, Sam Endicott, has been supporting the campaign and wants Ben to back his candidate. Ben turns him down because he feels Sam is dishonest. Ben intends to propose the name of the current governor at the convention. Endicott must prevent Ben from making the nomination and retains the services of a hired killer to assassinate Ben.

E292. *Star Crossed* (March 10, 1968)

Credits: *Writer:* Thomas Thompson. *Director:* William F. Claxton. *Producer:* David Dortort. **Starring:** Lorne Greene, Dan Blocker, Michael Landon. **Supporting Cast:** Tisha Sterling (Laura Jean Pollard); William Windom (Marshal Passmore); Jean Willes (Mrs. O'Brien); David Canary (Candy); Bruno VeSota (Bartender); Martha Manor (Saloon Girl).

Synopsis: Laura Jean Pollard arrives in Virginia City looking for a job at the Bucket of Blood Saloon. Candy cannot keep his eyes off her and holds her in his arms when she faints. After Joe and Candy treat her to a meal, they escort her to Mrs. O'Brien's boarding house to get her a room.

The next day Ben gets her a job working for Mrs. Borden in her millinery store. Candy begins seeing Laura on a regular basis. They go on picnics and long buggy rides. Candy tells her that his life began when he met her and they kiss. Trouble begins for the couple when Marshal Passmore arrives in Virginia City.

Note: Location shooting took place at Franklin Lake.

E293. *Trouble Town* (March 17, 1968)

Credits: *Writer:* David Lang. *Director:* Leon Benson. *Producer:* David Dortort. **Starring:** Lorne Greene, Dan Blocker, Michael Landon. **Supporting Cast:** Robert J. Wilke (Sheriff Claude Booker); Elizabeth MacRae (Lila Holden); Steve Brodie (Deputy Horn); David Canary (Candy); Joseph Turkel (Lupe); James Daris (Shorty); Tol Avery (Almont); William Bakewell (Slatter); Doodles Weaver (Stableman); A. G. Vitanza (Bartender).

Synopsis: Candy is entertaining an old friend, Lila Holden, in a saloon in the town of River Bend. Ben's other drovers are shooting off their guns. When the Cartwrights come to round them up, Sheriff Booker asks Ben to pay $30 for a broken street lamp and a hole in a watering trough. He also warns Ben that if he finds any of the drovers in town, he will throw them in jail.

Candy tells Ben that he quits because his friend is in trouble and he has decided to stay. When the Cartwrights and their crew ride out of town, two of the men turn back. Candy tries to give Lila some money but she needs $50 to get out of town. After he plays roulette on a rigged wheel, he accidentally hits Sheriff Booker during a fight. When the deputy hits Candy over the head, one of Ben's wranglers manages to sneak out and back to camp. Meanwhile Candy and Lupe, the other wrangler, are arrested. When Ben comes to town to bail them out, the sheriff refuses to release Candy.

E294. *Commitment at Angelus* (April 7, 1968)

Credits: *Writer:* Peter Germano. *Director:* Leon Benson. *Producer:* David Dortort. **Starring:** Lorne Greene, Michael Landon. **Supporting Cast:** Marj Dusay (Stephanie); Peter Whitney (Hudson); Ivan Triesault (Thad); Ken Lynch (Garrett); Greg Mulleavy (Kabe); Hal Lynch (Steve); Alan Reynolds (Polk); David Canary (Candy).

Synopsis: Joe and Candy head for Angelus to get medical attention for Candy's hand, injured by a horse.

Reaching town, Joe runs into an old friend, Steve Regan. Steve explains to Joe that he has persuaded his fellow miners to strike because the mine's timber supports are not safe. Because Candy is injured, Joe hires Steve to help him move horses. Rusty at riding, Steve dies in a horse accident. Joe feels guilty for his friend's death. Widow Stephanie, who is pregnant, persuades Joe to aid the miners during their strike.

Note: Location shooting took place at Bronson Canyon.

E295. *A Dream to Dream* (April 14, 1968)

Credits: *Writer:* Michael Landon. *Director:* William F. Claxton. *Producer:* David Dortort. **Starring:** Dan Blocker. **Supporting Cast:** Julie Harris (Sarah Carter); Steve Ihnat (Josh Carter); Johnnie Whitaker (Timmy Carter); Michelle Tobin (Sally Carter); William Tannen (Bartender).

Synopsis: Josh Carter is drinking in the saloon when Hoss comes to talk to him about a horse deal. He then helps Josh home, where he stumbles into bed. The next morning, Hoss tries to make apologies to Sarah Carter but she says that it happens all the time. He then meets Timmy and Sally Carter, giving them the nicknames Little Hoss and Princess. Hoss soon finds himself taking Sarah and the children on a picnic and fishing. Sara then tells Hoss about son Michael, who died in a riding accident three years before.

Hoss and Josh ride out to look at the stock. Later, Hoss goes back to the house while Josh goes into his office to do paperwork and drink. Sarah starts sobbing, saying how unhappy she is with her life. In the morning, after Hoss takes Timmy for a horseback ride, Josh orders Hoss off the ranch.

Note: Location shooting took place at Franklin Lake. A *Little House on the Prairie* episode entitled "Someone Please Love Me" had the same theme.

E296. *In Defense of Honor* (April 28, 1968)

Credits: *Writers:* William Douglas Lansford (Adaptation), Richard Wendley. *Director:* Marc Daniels. *Producer:* David Dortort. **Starring:** Lorne Greene, Dan Blocker, Michael Landon. **Supporting Cast:** Lou Antonio (Davey); Arnold Moss (Chief Lone Spear); Cherie Latimer (Bright Moon); Ned Romero (White Wolf); Lane Bradford (Jud); Troy Melton (Skinner); John Lodge (Deputy); Arthur Peterson (Judge).

Synopsis: Davey, who tamed horses for Ben, had been deserted by his Yute tribe after his parents were killed in battle. Ben took Davey under his wing when Davey was five. Since that time, he has been living in the white man's world despite persecution and prejudice.

Davey falls for the chief's daughter, Bright Moon, who has been promised to White Wolf. The girl's intended hates Davey because he is a half-breed. A fight ensues between the two Indians with Davey coming out as the victor. When White Wolf is found dead, Davey is accused of his murder.

Note: Location shooting took place at Bronson Canyon.

E297. *To Die in Darkness* (May 5, 1968)

Credits: *Writer:* Michael Landon. *Director:* Michael Landon. *Producer:* David Dortort. **Starring:** Lorne Greene, Dan Blocker, Michael Landon. **Supporting Cast:** David Canary (Candy); James Whitmore (John Postley); Noah Keen (Warden).

Synopsis: John Postley has been in the Nevada State Prison for the past year and a half serving a sentence for robbery. When the real culprit admits his guilt, John is released. It was Ben and Candy's testimony that helped put Postley in prison. John assures Ben that he has no hard feelings and asks him and Candy to check out the headway he has made on his mine. wanting them to experience the hell he went through in jail, he imprisons them in a deserted mine shaft.

Note: Location shooting took place in Bronson Canyon.

E298. *The Bottle Fighter* (May 12, 1968)

Credits: *Writers:* John Hawkins, S. H. Barnett, Colin McKenzie. *Director:* Leon Benson. *Executive Producer:* David Dortort. **Starring:** Lorne Greene, Dan Blocker, Michael Landon. **Supporting Cast:** David Canary (Candy); Albert Dekker (Barney Sturgess); Douglas Kennedy (Sheriff); Harlan Warde (Ogleby); Alan Baxter (Becker); Robert Sorrells (Furguson); Charles Irving (Judge); Jon Lormer (Winter).

Synopsis: As Candy checks into the Salt Springs hotel, there is a fight upstairs and Hoss is found groggy, standing over the dead body of Warren Edwards. After Hoss is arrested for first-degree murder, Candy sends for Ben and Joe. Hoss does not remember what happened in the hotel.

The Cartwrights and Candy go to see Barney Sturgess, an attorney. Barney visits Hoss in jail. Joe is disgusted with the man, and the sheriff says that is not surprising with "Bottle Barney."

At Hoss' hearing, Barney's motion for a continuance is denied. The Cartwrights only chance to save Hoss' life hinges on this drunken old lawyer.

E299. *The Arrival of Eddie* (May 19, 1968)

Credits: *Writers:* Ward Hawkins (Teleplay), John M. Chester (Story). *Director:* Marc Daniels. *Producer:* David Dortort. **Starring:** Lorne Greene, Dan Blocker, Michael Landon. **Supporting Cast:** Michael Vincent (Eddie Makay); Jim Davis (Sam Butler); Bing Russell (Deputy Clem Foster); Lincoln Demyan (Amos); Francis DeSales (Major); David Canary (Candy).

Synopsis: Eddie Makay rides into town to ask Clem how his father died. After a storekeeper confiscates Eddie's horse for money that his father owed him, Hoss tries to help the boy. He feels that it was his bullet that killed the boy's father. Later, after Sam Butler accuses Eddie of having stolen $75, he tells the boy that Hoss killed his father.

Feeling sorry for the boy, Hoss gives him a job on the Ponderosa. Sam Butler tells him to take the job because he can be helpful to him. If Eddie refuses, Butler will see to it that he goes to jail. In the days that follow, he cuts wood, feeds chickens, slops hogs, and cleans out the barn. Soon Eddie decides to quit because he is tired of those jobs and wants a chance to break horses.

E300. *The Stronghold* (May 26, 1968)

Credits: *Writers:* John Hawkins (Adaptation), W. R. Burnett (Story). *Director:* Leon Benson. *Producer:* David Dortort. **Starring:** Dan Blocker, Michael Landon. **Supporting Cast:** David Canary (Candy); Michael Whitney (Josh Farrell); Paul Mantee (Mike Farrell); Lynda Day (Lisa Jackson); James Davidson (Dude O'Brien); William Bryant (Abner Jackson); Hal Baylor (Kelty); Martin Blaine (Moore); Robert Brubaker (Sheriff); Ref Sanchez (Pedro).

Synopsis: Joe and Dude ride into Dry Wells to do cattle business with the Farrell brothers. At the bank, Joe receives a cashier's check from Jackson, the teller. After Joe writes a receipt, everyone leaves as the teller puts the $15,000 into the saddle bags. He then goes out the back door, past the body of the real teller.

Later, at the Ponderosa, the Cartwrights are told that the check is a forgery and cannot be honored. Joe and Candy decide to ride back to Dry Wells to find the $15,000. When they reach the town, the sheriff tells them about his investigation. Jackson's body is brought into town and Joe finds a woman's picture in his pocket. The young Cartwright decides to pay a visit to the Farrell brothers because they were the only ones who knew he was bringing the money to the bank.

E301. *Pride of a Man* (June 2, 1968)

Credits: *Writers:* Ward Hawkins (Teleplay), Helen B. Hicks (Teleplay and Story). *Director:* William F. Claxton. *Producer:* David Dortort. **Starring:** Lorne Greene, Michael Landon. **Supporting Cast:** David Canary (Candy); Kevin Couglin (Willie McNab); Anne Helm (Abby Pettigrew); Morgan Woodward (Will McNab); Steve Cory (Billy); Barbara Hunter (Mary); Billy Corcoran (Tommy); Hedi Musselman (Kathy).

Synopsis: Schoolteacher Abby Pettigrew is involved in a horse accident. Her injuries prevent her from fulfilling her duties and Joe is forced to substitute for her.

Billy and Willy McNab arrive at school to give Joe a hard time and leave. At Abby's urging, Joe must get the boys back to school despite their father's objections as he does not believe an education is necessary for a hog farmer.

E302. *A Severe Case of Matrimony* (July 7, 1968)

Credits: *Writer:* Michael Fessier. *Director:* Lewis Allen. *Producer:* David Dortort. **Starring:** Lorne Greene, Dan Blocker, Michael Landon. **Supporting Cast:** Susan Strasberg (Rosalita); J. Carrol Naish (Anselmo); Andre Phillippe (Paco); Lili Valenty (Dolores); Victor Sen Yung (Hop Sing).

Synopsis: After Hoss breaks up an argument between Paco and Rosalita, he goes to meet her Aunt Dolores and Uncle Anselmo. Anselmo later goes to see Ben to apologize for being on the Ponderosa. The old gypsy wants to trade his old horse for a small tree to fix their wagon, but Ben says no.

Paco tries romancing Rosalita, who dreams of singing opera. She wants to take voice lessons but it takes a great deal of money, so her uncle suggests snagging a Cartwright. The next day, Rosalita runs onto the Ponderosa claiming that the gypsies are after her. Hoss lets her stay. Later, when Hoss tells Ben what happened, he tries to get rid of her but finally allows her to stay. That night Rosalita tells Ben of her dreams to sing, but he sends her home. Anselmo continues to plot to get some money from Ben.

Note: Location shooting took place at Franklin Lake.

E303. *Stage Door Johnnies* (July 28, 1968)

Credits: *Writer:* Alex Sharp. *Director:* William F. Claxton. *Producer:* David Dortort. **Starring:** Lorne Greene, Dan Blocker, Michael Landon. **Supporting Cast:** Kathleen Crowley (Miss Denise); Walter Brooke (Mr. Fillmore); Shug Fisher (Driver); Bruno VeSota (Bartender); Ted Ryan (Waiter); King Moody (Man); Victor Sen Yung (Hop Sing); Mike Mazurki (Big Man).

Synopsis: Hoss and Joe are rivals for the affections of a pretentious singer known as Miss Denise. When Andre, her small dog, runs away, Hoss feels he can get an edge on his brother if he finds the animal. He suggests Miss Denise place a notice in the paper offering a reward for the dog's return. He makes the mistake of letting her set the amount. After the paper comes out, the citizens of Virginia City race around looking for the animal. Hoss joins in as there is $1,000 on the line.

Tenth Season
(September 15, 1968–May 11, 1969)

E304. *Different Pines — Same Wind* (September 15, 1968)

Credits: *Writer:* Suzanne Clauser. *Director:* Leon Benson. *Producer:* Richard Collins. *Executive Producer:* David Dortort. **Starring:** Lorne Greene, Dan Blocker, Michael Landon. **Supporting Cast:** Irene Tedrow (Carrie Pickett); John Randolph (Doc); Herbert Voland (Milburn); G. D. Spradlin (Jenks); George Murdock (Marks); John J. Wheeler (Bartender).

Synopsis: A rich lumberman, Jason Milburn, wants to own the forest so he can strip it of its trees. The law says all he has to do to claim property is to make changes on a quarter-section and pay $200 when filing a claim. He gets his employees to make the claims and then pays them one dollar to obtain ownership. Joe sets out to thwart Jason by working a piece of land that would prevent Milburn from getting supplies through.

When Joe gets there, he finds a contrary old woman, Carrie Pickett, with an infected hand. He learns that the woman lived there for years with her husband Amos, who died a few years ago, and that the couple never made a legal claim to the land. Joe must convince the stubborn woman to file before Jason claims the land out from under her.

Review: *Variety* (September 18, 1968): "[A] sentimental affair.... Miss Tedrow delivered a most dependable stint of heart-tugging and Landon played off well as her befriender.... Suzanne Clauser's script was polished if familiar stuff.... As with any hit, they're not apt to rewrite the *Bonanza* formula and the opener reasserted the tone in okay fashion."

Note: Location shooting took place at Incline Village.

E305. *Child* (September 22, 1968)

Credits: *Writer:* Jack B. Sowards. *Director:* Leon Benson. *Producer:* Richard Collins. *Executive Producer:* David Dortort. **Starring:** Lorne Greene, Dan Blocker, Michael Landon. **Supporting Cast:** David Canary (Candy); Yaphet Kotto (Child Barnett); John Marley (Sheriff Millet); Harry Hickox (Mayor Bringham); Henry Beckman (Charlie Matson); Frank DeVol (Brother Stoner); Robert Ball (Clerk); Charles Maxwell (Buck); Bruce Kirby (Chad); E. J. Schuster (Harry).

Synopsis: When Hoss arrives in a secluded town, he finds himself charged with murdering and robbing the town's leading citizen. The townspeople are more interested in finding the man's money than his murderer. The mayor and a few other important citizens arrange to lynch Hoss in hopes that he will reveal the location of the victim's money.

E306. *Salute to Yesterday* (September 29, 1968)

Credits: *Writer:* John Hawkins. *Director:* Leon Benson. *Producer:* Richard Collins. *Executive Producer:* David Dortort. **Starring:** Lorne Greene, Dan Blocker, Michael Landon. **Supporting Cast:** David Canary (Candy); Pat Conway (Captain Harris); Sandra Smith (Ann Harris); John Kellogg (Sgt. Ordy); Carlos Rivas (Angel Montana); Richard Lapp (Trooper Kelly); Troy Melton (Cpl. Jensen); Rudy Diaz (Rio); Pepe Callahan (Rojo).

Synopsis: During a cattle drive, the Cartwrights and Candy find an injured cavalry officer. Before he dies, he tells them Captain Harris desperately needs their help.

Barn on the Ponderosa property. (Photograph by Linda F. Leiby.)

The soldiers are involved in a skirmish with Mexican outlaws who are after gold concealed in an Army ambulance. Candy is astonished to learn that the bandits' leader is an old boyhood friend and that his ex-wife Ann is married to the captain. To get Ann's attention, Candy slips into the enemy encampment to take water and other supplies.

Note: Location filming took place at Incline Village.

E307. *The Real People of Muddy Creek* (October 6, 1968)

Credits: *Writer:* Alf Harris. *Director:* Leon Benson. *Producer:* Richard Collins. *Executive Producer:* David Dortort. **Starring:** Lorne Greene, Dan Blocker, Michael Landon. **Supporting Cast:** Jo Don Baker (Luke Harper); David Canary (Candy); Jean Hale (Casey Collins); Ann Doran (Mrs. Walker); Susan Trustman (Linda); Hal Lynch (Haines); Clifton James (Lawson); Russell Thorson (Simon); Michael Vogel (Tommy); Val Bisoglio (Cliff Harper); Jon Lormer (Jody); Stuart Randall (Sheriff Walker); Ed Long (Deputy).

Synopsis: The Cartwrights and Candy are on a cattle drive when Walker, the sheriff of Muddy Creek, rides in, escorting his prisoner Luke Harper. When Luke kills the sheriff, Ben and Joe decide to take the man back to town. After they arrive, the townspeople try to prevent Luke from being put in the town jail and the two deputies resign. The Cartwrights try to get some help from the townspeople. The next morning they find the town deserted. Ben makes Joe ride out to bring Hoss and the crew back to town. After Joe leaves, Ben realizes that he might have to face the Harper gang alone.

E308. *The Passing of a King* (October 13, 1968)

Credits: *Writer:* B. W. Sandefur. *Director:* Leon Benson. *Producer:* Richard Collins. *Executive Producer:* David Dortort. **Starring:** Lorne Greene, Dan Blocker, Michael Landon. **Supporting Cast:** David Canary (Candy); Jeremy Slate (Jeremy Roman); Denver Pyle (Claude Roman); Diana Maldaur (Mary); Dan Tobin (Judge Rideout); Russ Conway (Ballenger); Jack Searl (Harrison); K. L. Smith (Sheriff); Larry Ward (Carver).

Synopsis: While the Cartwrights and Candy are escorting a $5,000 bull, they prevent a group from hanging Rodriguez, a Mexican man, for butchering a calf. After Jeremy Roman and his foreman Ballenger arrive, Joe and Candy head to town to get hotel rooms. Just as they check into the hotel, they find Rodriguez having a "trial" at which he is found guilty. When Joe and Candy try to prevent the hanging, they are knocked out.

Ben and Hoss arrive at the Roman Ranch to deliver the bull to Claude Roman. Joe and Candy tell Ben and Hoss about the hanging and that Jeremy Roman gave the orders.

Ben rides back to the ranch to receive the balance for the bull. He runs into trouble when Jeremy refuses to pay him the correct amount.

E309. *The Last Vote* (October 20, 1968)

Credits: *Writer:* Robert Vincent Wright. *Director:* Joseph Pevney. *Producer:* Richard Collins. *Executive Producer:* David Dortort. **Starring:** Lorne Greene, Dan

Blocker, Michael Landon. **Supporting Cast:** Tom Bosley (Titus Simpson); Wally Cox (Phineas Burke); Robert Emhardt (Judge Clampton); Bing Russell (Deputy Clem Foster); Don Haggerty (Pete); Lane Bradford (Tim); Bruno VeSota (Bartender); Victor Sen Yung (Hop Sing).

Synopsis: Hoss and Joe head for town to get some rest and relaxation. The topic of conversation seems to concern the mayoral race. The brothers make a wager as to which candidate will win. The prize is a free vacation to San Francisco paid for by the loser. With a lot riding on the results of the election, Hoss and Joe offer to run the candidates' campaigns. Joe backs the candidacy of Titus Simpson while Hoss champions Phineas Burke.

E310. *Catch as Catch Can* (October 27, 1968)

Credits: *Writer:* David Lang. *Director:* Robert L. Friend. *Producer:* Richard Collins. *Executive Producer:* David Dortort. **Starring:** Lorne Greene, Dan Blocker, Michael Landon. **Supporting Cast:** David Canary (Candy); Paul Richards (Parker); Slim Pickens (Sheriff Gant); Robert Yuro (Rice); Robert Eric Winter (Daley); Arthur Malet (Tingle); Peter Marland-Jones (Hollis); John Quade (Telegrapher); John Perak (Billy).

Synopsis: The Cartwrights head for Timbucket where Mr. Parker buys hides from Ben. Disaster strikes when the Cartwrights and Candy are framed for various incidents. They have no idea who is behind their troubles.

E311. *Little Girl Lost* (November 3, 1968)

Credits: *Writer:* Michael Fessier. *Director:* Don Richardson. *Producer:* Richard Collins. *Executive Producer:* David Dortort. **Starring:** Lorne Greene, Dan Blocker, Michael Landon. **Supporting Cast:** David Canary (Candy); Victor Sen Yung (Hop Sing); Linda Sue Risk (Samantha Dorcas); Antoinette Bower (Martha Cartwright Dorcas); George Mitchell (Calvin Dorcas); Bob Padillia (Charlie); Christian Anderson (Driver).

Synopsis: The Wells Fargo wagon arrives with something for Ben: It seems Martha Cartwright Dorcas has sent her daughter Samantha to the Ponderosa, asking the Cartwrights to take care of her. Ben tries to get to the bottom of things with Samantha about her mother. After a troublesome night with Samantha, Ben decides to send for the girl's mother in San Francisco.

The next day Hop Sing and his new "chief cook and bottle washer" Samantha bring grub to Ben and the boys. Martha Dorcas arrives, tells Ben about her job in a saloon and admits that she does not know where her drunken husband is.

Soon Martha's father-in-law arrives in Virginia City looking for them. Calvin Dorcas comes to the ranch with a court order stating that he has custody of the little girl.

Note: Location shooting took place at Franklin Lake and for the first time at Incline Village's Ponderosa Ranch house.

E312. *The Survivors* (November 10, 1968)

Credits: *Writers:* S. H. Barnett, Colin McKenzie, John Hawkins. *Director:* Leon Benson. *Producer:* Richard Collins. *Executive Producer:* David Dortort.

Starring: Lorne Greene, Dan Blocker, Michael Landon. **Supporting Cast:** David Canary (Candy); Mariette Hartley (Alicia Purcell); John Carter (Wayne Purcell); Martin Ashe (Major Anderson); Harriet Medin (Elizabeth Bowen); Lesley Woods (Agnes Smith); Ed Bakey (Hake); Stuart Nisbet (Paul Fletcher); Sidney Smith (Peter Green).

Synopsis: The Cartwrights and Candy are selling 48 horses to the Army. Major Anderson tells Ben about the Indians and a white woman with a baby that were taken captive. Ben tries talking to her but she wants to go to the reservation with the other Indians in order to spare her child the torment of living with the whites.

At dinner, everyone tries to make polite conversation. When the woman asks Ben what will happen to Chief Wahee, she is told that he will be executed if he is captured. After she runs out, Ben goes after her, calling her Alicia Purcell. He tells her that her husband has been searching for her for the past four years, but she wants to remain dead. Ben urges her to go back with him because of the baby.

At the ranch, Alicia waits for her husband Wayne. At first he is excited to see her but when he finds out what happened to her, he gets upset.

E313. *The Sound of Drums* (November 17, 1968)

Credits: *Writer:* William F. Leicester. *Director:* Robert L. Friend. *Producer:* Richard Collins. *Executive Producer:* David Dortort. **Starring:** Lorne Greene, Dan Blocker. **Supporting Cast:** David Canary (Candy); Jack Kruschen (Georgio Rossi); Brioni Farrell (Regina); Michael Stefani (Lorenzo); Penny Santon (Maria); Joaquin Martinez (Red Sky); Byron Morrow (Sam Kettle); Mark Tapscott (Sabin); Debra Domasin (Indian Girl); Pete Hernandez (Lame Dog).

Synopsis: Ben tries to forewarn Georgio Rossi of the dangers of allowing the Indians to make an encampment on his property. Disregarding his advice, Rossi permits them to come. Soon the Indians believe the land is theirs.

E314. *Queen High* (December 1, 1968)

Credits: *Writer:* Michael Fessier. *Director:* Leon Benson. *Producer:* Richard Collins. *Executive Producer:* David Dortort. **Starring:** Lorne Greene, Dan Blocker, Michael Landon. **Supporting Cast:** David Canary (Candy); Celeste Yarnell (Katie Kelly); Paul Lambert (Miles Renfro); Sandor Szabo (Ludwig); Dabney Coleman (Ivar Peterson); Ken Drake (Sam Jacks); Edward Schaaf (Beggs).

Synopsis: Joe and Candy are in a poker game where they win a mine and a stamp mill. The next day they ride over to see their property and get involved in a shootout. Afterwards they find out that they only own 40 percent; the other 60 percent is owned by a Katie Kelly. When she arrives in town, Joe and Candy take her to the Ponderosa. Later Miles Renfro comes by to offer to buy them out but Katie accuses him of causing some recent accidents.

Joe and Candy later entertain a group of independent mine owners. They give them 11 days to get the stamp mill running. That is when their contract with Renfro runs out. After the repairs are finished, Renfro orders his men to stop Joe and Candy.

Note: Location shooting took place at Bronson Canyon.

These wagons were actually used during filming. (Photograph by Linda F. Leiby.)

E315. *Yonder Man* (December 8, 1968)

Credits: *Writer:* Milton S. Gelman. *Director:* Leo Penn. *Producer:* Richard Collins. *Executive Producer:* David Dortort. **Starring:** Lorne Greene, Dan Blocker, Michael Landon. **Supporting Cast:** John Vernon (Beaudry); Melissa Murphy (Noreen); Rudolfo Acosta (Matar); Larry Ward (Stryker); Pepper Martin (Hawkface); Bruno VeSota (Bartender); David Canary (Candy); Ray Teal (Sheriff Roy Coffee).

Synopsis: Joe is out looking for strays when he comes upon Beaudry, who cons him out of his horse. When Beaudry arrives in town, he saves a girl's honor in the saloon. After Candy spots Joe's horse, he tries to take Beaudry to Sheriff Roy Coffee but runs into Ben, who takes the man back to the Ponderosa (he is an old friend of Ben's).

Beaudry has decided to stay put and buy a ranch. He buys $500 in cattle from his friend. Beaudry rides out to meet a Mexican who has come to warn him about a death warrant being issued for him in Mexico. Candy, suspicious of Ben's friend, follows him.

E316. *Mark of Guilt* (December 15, 1968)

Credits: *Writers:* Ward Hawkins (Teleplay), Frank Telford (Story). *Director:* Leon Benson. *Producer:* Richard Collins. *Executive Producer:* David Dortort. **Starring:** Dan Blocker, Michael Landon. **Supporting Cast:** David Canary (Candy); Victor Sen Yung (Hop Sing); Dick Foran (Giltner); Michael Vandever (Davis); Alan Bergmann (Gort); Lou Frizzell (Jackson); Gordon Dilworth (Judge); Ray Teal (Sheriff Roy Coffee).

Synopsis: When Hop Sing returns to Virginia City on the stage, he heads for the stable to pick up a gentle horse to ride back to the Ponderosa. Emo Younger cruelly chops off his pigtail. Hop Sing is devastated as the Chinese feel it is their passport to Heaven.

After finding Hop Sing in tears, Joe goes to Younger's ranch to retrieve the pigtail and a fight ensues. During the fight, Joe falls against a freshly painted table.

Emo Younger winds up dead. The murder weapon is a newly painted 2 × 4. Since Joe's hands are covered with paint, he is charged with murder and could end up on the gallows.

Note: In this episode, Hop Sing gives testimony in court. This could not have occurred because the Chinese had no legal standing in Virginia City and could not have testified.

E317. *A World Full of Cannibals* (December 22, 1968)

Credits: *Writer:* Preston Wood. *Director:* Gunnar Hellstrom. *Producer:* Richard Collins. *Executive Producer:* David Dortort. **Starring:** Lorne Greene, Dan Blocker, Michael Landon. **Supporting Cast:** James Patterson (Charles Ball); Linda March (Harriet Ball); Mark Richman (Vardeman); David Canary (Candy); John Milford (Rodgers).

Synopsis: Charles Ball was involved in illegal government activities and has consented to give evidence to the grand jury against his eight accomplices. Ben offers to give sanctuary to Ball. The dishonest accomplices will stop at nothing to prevent Charles from appearing in court.

E318. *Sweet Annie Laurie* (January 5, 1969)

Credits: *Writers:* John Hawkins (Adaptation), Jess Carneol, Kay Leonard, Jackson Gillis. *Director:* Don Richardson. *Producer:* Richard Collins. *Executive Producer:* David Dortort. **Starring:** Dan Blocker, Michael Landon. **Supporting Cast:** Joan Van Ark (Laurie Adams); James Olson (Kelly Adams); Lawrence Dane (Paul Rogers); James Jeter (Duncan); Ray Teal (Sheriff Roy Coffee); Victor Sen Yung (Hop Sing); Dean Goodhill (Clerk).

Synopsis: On his way back to the Ponderosa, Hoss finds a woman secreted in his wagon. She insists on going to Carson City, so he drives her to a deserted way station. She faints after spotting Paul Rogers, a friend of her husband's. Hoss takes her the Ponderosa where the Cartwrights learn she is trying to get away from her husband, Kelly Adams, who is wanted by the law.

When Rogers shows up at the ranch, he says Kelly has agreed to divorce her but wants to see her first. She consents to meet with him. Adams threatens to see to it that Hoss dies if she refuses to accompany him to Mexico.

E319. *My Friend, My Enemy* (January 12, 1969)

Credits: *Writers:* Jack B. Sowards (adaptation), Stanley Roberts. *Director:* Leon Benson. *Producer:* Richard Collins. *Executive Producer:* David Dortort. **Starring:** Lorne Greene, Dan Blocker, Michael Landon. **Supporting Cast:** David Canary (Candy); John Saxon (Jacova); Woodrow Parfrey (Theodore Scott); Chick Chandler (Judge Butler); Gregory Walcott (Sheriff Crowley); Ben Hammer (Quinn); Raymond Guth, Sunshine Parker, Duane Grey.

Synopsis: Candy is arrested for killing John Legett. The Cartwrights must help him out of his predicament. They find the going rough because the one person who saw what happened is a hardtofind Indian who steals horses. His defense attorney is indifferent about his job. To make matters worse, the man hearing the case has the reputation of sentencing those found guilty to the gallows.

Note: Location shooting took place at Franklin Lake.

E320. *Mrs. Wharton and the Lesser Breeds* (January 19, 1969)

Credits: *Writer:* Preston Wood. *Director:* Leon Benson. *Producer:* Richard Collins. *Executive Producer:* David Dortort. **Starring:** Lorne Greene, Dan Blocker, Michael Landon. **Supporting Cast:** David Canary (Candy); Mildred Natwick (Mrs. Elizabeth H. Wharton); Oren Stevens (Billy Buckman); Jess Pearson (Ed); Jeffrey Morris (Dunne); Chanin Hale (Laura Mae); J. S. Johnson (Carmody); Chuck Bail (Reese); Ollie O'Toole (Bartender); Bill Beckett (Drummer).

Synopsis: Candy helps out a cantankerous, old British woman, Elizabeth Wharton, in hopes of making some quick money. Her jewels are stolen when the stage is held up. Candy gets more than he bargained for when she heads for the law-breaking town to get back what is rightfully hers. Candy goes with her, fearing she will be killed.

E321. *Erin* (January 26, 1969)

Credits: *Writer:* Sandy Summerhays. *Director:* Don Richardson. *Producer:* Richard Collins. *Executive Producer:* David Dortort. **Starring:** Lorne Greene, Dan Blocker. **Supporting Cast:** Mary Fickett (Erin O'Donnell); Don Briggs (Clint Murray); Michael Keep (Bear Hunter); Joan Tompkins (Mrs. Murray); Harry Holcombe (Doctor); David Canary (Candy).

Synopsis: In need of beef, Chief Red Eagle is found with Ponderosa cattle. Hoss consents to exchange horses for steers. He spots Erin O'Donnell, the tribe's top wrangler, who had been left to the Sioux by her father following the death of her mother.

Erin was just involved in a horse accident and her shoulder becomes inflamed. Hoss takes her to the ranch. Looking after Erin, he falls in love with her and intends to make her his bride. Erin is reminded of a Paiute prophet's prediction that she will be killed in a skirmish between the red and white men.

E322. *Company of Forgotten Men* (February 2, 1969)

Credits: *Writers:* Kay Leonard, Jess Carnoel. *Director:* Leon Benson. *Producer:* Richard Collins. *Executive Producer:* David Dortort. **Starring:** Lorne Greene, Dan Blocker, Michael Landon. **Supporting Cast:** James Gregory (Sgt. Mike Russell); John Pickard (Perkins); Ken Lynch (Gibson); William Bryant (Beau); I. Stanford Jolley (Jackson); Phil Chambers (Webster); David Canary (Candy); Charles Maxwell (Jeb).

Synopsis: A group of retired Army men hold up the mint in Carson City. They take the gold to force the government to relinquish their pensions. Candy is forced to help them. The men almost succeed in carrying out their plan, but the nitroglycerin authority is determined to hang onto the gold for himself.

E323. *The Clarion* (February 9, 1969)

Credits: *Writers:* John Hawkins, Frank Chase. *Director:* Lewis Allen. *Producer:* Richard Collins. *Executive Producer:* David Dortort. **Starring:** Lorne Greene, Dan Blocker, Michael Landon. **Supporting Cast:** Phyllis Thaxter (Ruth Manning); Simon Oakland (Seth Tabor); William Jordan (Leek); Hamilton Camp (Dobbs); David Canary (Candy); Philip Kennally (Sheriff Knox); Ken Mayer (North); Connie Sawyer (Mrs. Lewis); James Jeter (Cotton); S. Newton Anderson (Sam); Arthur Peterson (Dr. Adams); Ed McCready (Purdy).

Synopsis: Ben rides into Gunlick on business. While there, he visits with an old friend, Ruth Manning, who has owned the town's paper *Clarion* since the death of her husband. Ben is surprised to learn that she wants to get out of the paper business. The only thing in town that Judge Seth Tabor does not govern is the paper. He is determined to get possession of the *Clarion* no matter what it takes.

E324. *The Lady and the Mountain Lion* (February 23, 1969)

Credits: *Writer:* Larry Markes. *Director:* Joseph Pevney. *Producer:* Richard Collins. *Executive Producer:* David Dortort. **Starring:** Lorne Greene, Dan Blocker, Michael Landon. **Supporting Cast:** Richard Haydn (Malcom the Magnificent); Alyce and Rhae Andrece (Jan and Janice); Michael Keep (Brett Rankin); Dabbs Greer (Doc Chukett); Chet Stratton (Clerk); Jack Searl (Lanky Man); Bern Hoffman (Bartender); Ray Teal (Sheriff Roy Coffee).

Synopsis: Mr. Malcom the magician and his beautiful daughter Jan arrive in Virginia City. Hoss offers to carry a trunk upstairs for them. Hoss labors up the steps with the extremely heavy trunk, not realizing that Janet's twin sister, Janice is inside.

Joe and Hoss both have dates that night and argue over who is going to take the surrey. Later Malcom and his two daughters argue about Janice having to ride in the trunk on top of the stage all of the time. Confusion continues to reign as Hoss and Joe date the twin girls.

E325. *Five Candles* (March 2, 1969)

Credits: *Writer:* Ken Trevey. *Director:* Lewis Allen. *Producer:* Richard Collins. *Executive Producer:* David Dortort. **Starring:** Lorne Greene, Dan Blocker, Michael Landon. **Supporting Cast:** David Canary (Candy); Ray Teal (Sheriff Roy Coffee); Don Knight (Bristol Toby); Scott Thomas (Jonathan Pike); Ted Gehrig (Arch Tremayne); Tiffany Bolling (Callie); Eddie Firestone (Banty); Bobbie Pickett (Gibson); Louise Fitch (Mrs. Connor); William Keene (Dr. Hill).

Synopsis: When a mine blows up, it causes the courthouse in town to collapse. Ben finds himself trapped in the basement. Along with him are Bristol Toby, a miner accused of murder, Callie, a clerk, her fiancé, and Jonathan Pike, whose testimony could put Bristol away. As the air supply becomes critically low, Jonathan and Toby must work together if the group is to make it out of their predicament alive.

E326. *The Wish* (March 9, 1969)

Credits: *Writer:* Michael Landon. *Director:* Michael Landon. *Producer:* Richard Collins. *Executive Producer:* David Dortort. **Starring:** Lorne Greene, Dan Blocker,

Michael Landon. **Supporting Cast:** Ossie Davis (Sam Davis); George Spell (John O. Davis); Roy Jenson (Craig); Harry Page (Jesse); Barbara Parrio (Beth); Charles Seel (Titus); Jerry Summers (Johnson); David Canary (Candy).

Synopsis: Hoss has accumulated vacation time and plans to spend his two months fishing. While picking up supplies in Chiso, he meets a young black boy named John Davis. The youngster has one wish — that his father become white.

Taking the boy home, Hoss discovers the farm and family are in a bad way because of the lack of rain. His father Sam and older brother Jesse are unable to get a job because of prejudice. Hoss must find a way to help the Davis family without destroying Sam's pride.

E237. *The Deserter* (March 16, 1969)

Credits: *Writers:* B. W. Sandefur, John Dunkel. *Director:* Leon Benson. *Producer:* Richard Collins. *Executive Producer:* David Dortort. **Starring:** Lorne Greene, Michael Landon. **Supporting Cast:** Ben Johnson (Sam Bellis); Ellen Davalos (Nanata); Ford Rainey (Arnholt); David Canary (Candy); Duane Grey (Henderson); Ken Drake (Leatham); Todd Martin (Denton); Lincoln Demyan (Trooper); Christian Anderson (Turner).

Synopsis: Candy comes to the aid of his friend Sam Bellis, an Army sergeant who has been labeled a coward after running off during an Indian battle. Bellis believes he was right in what he did because the Indians had first-rate fire arms. The military brass refused to accept Sam's explanation. Candy, Bellis and his Shoshone wife Nanata are determined to prove Bellis was not a coward by substantiating that the rifles exist and by discovering who is supplying the firearms to the Indians.

E328. *Emily* (March 23, 1969)

Credits: *Writers:* Eliott Gilbert (Story and Teleplay), Preston Wood (Teleplay). *Director:* Leon Benson. *Producer:* Richard Collins. *Executive Producer:* David Dortort. **Starring:** Lorne Greene, Dan Blocker, Michael Landon. **Supporting Cast:** Beth Brickell (Emily McPhail); Ron Hayes (Wade McPhail); David McLean (Marshal Calhoun); Harry Holcombe (Dr. Lewis); Byron Webster (Dr. Stebbins); Charles P. Thompson (Storekeeper); Quentin Sondergaard (Hendrix); Don Adkins (Assistant); David Canary (Candy); Bing Russell (Deputy Clem Foster)

Synopsis: Joe cannot believe his eyes when Emily Anderson, his ex-fiancée, arrives in Virginia City. They had almost married when Joe was in Monterey five years ago. Her father disliked his daughter's prospective husband and ran interference by preventing her from receiving his letters. The feelings are still there but she neglects to inform him that she is married to Deputy Marshal Wade McPhail. Wade and Marshall Calhoun are safeguarding $90,000.

Emily insists on leaving town but Wade ignores her request. When Wade discovers Joe and Emily hugging, he almost kills Joe, who now realizes Emily is married. She continues telling false stories and as a result Joe is shot and unjustly incriminated for robbery and murder.

E329. *The Running Man* (March 30, 1969)

Credits: *Writers:* Ward Hawkins, Louis Vittes. *Director:* Leon Benson. *Producer:* Richard Collins. *Executive Producer:* David Dortort. **Starring:** Lorne Greene, Dan Blocker, Michael Landon. **Supporting Cast:** Will Geer (Calvin Butler); Jennifer Douglas (Barbara Parker); Robert Pine (Stead Butler); Larry Casey (Jess Parker); Lee Farr (Torrance); Ed Long (Sheriff Daniels); David Canary (Candy); Rusty Lane (Tracy); Russ Bender (Garvey); George Sims (Casey); Donald Elson (Clerk); Don Keefer (Billy Harris).

Synopsis: Barbara Parker sends a letter to Candy, with whom she had been involved, pleading that he come to Butlerville. It seems that a number of her neighbors have been forced out of their homes by fire. Candy and Joe head for Butlerville where they learn that Barbara's husband Jess witnessed one of the fires kill a woman and her child.

E330. *The Unwanted* (April 6, 1969)

Credits: *Writers:* Thomas Thompson, Suzanne Clauser. *Director:* Herschel Daugherty. *Producer:* Richard Collins. *Executive Producer:* David Dortort. **Starring:** Lorne Greene, Dan Blocker, Michael Landon. **Supporting Cast:** David Canary (Candy); Bonnie Bedelia (Lorrie Mansfield); Charles McGraw (Luke Mansfield) Jan- Michael Vincent (Rick Miller).

Synopsis: Marshall Luke Mansfield and his daughter Laurie arrive in Virginia City to visit Luke's old friend Ben. The marshal is searching for Billy Miller, who escaped from prison and is responsible for the bullet in his leg.

Tombstones used in the TV movies. (Photograph by Linda F. Leiby.)

Rick Miller, who works for Ben, acknowledges he is Billy's cousin and insists that Billy passed away shortly after making his getaway. Luke feels Rick is covering up for his cousin. Mansfield, Joe and Candy head out to find Billy's grave in an attempt to verify Rick's claim.

E331. *Speak No Evil* (April 20, 1969)

Credits: *Writers:* B. W. Sandefur (Teleplay), Norman Katkov (Story). *Director:* Leon Benson. *Producer:* Richard Collins. *Executive Producer:* David Dortort. **Starring:** Lorne Greene, Dan Blocker, Michael Landon. **Supporting Cast:** Charles P. Thompson (Claude); Patricia Smith (Mararet Claybourne); Kevin Burchett (Coley); Dana Elcar (Caleb Melton); Chick Chandler (Judge Butler); Debbie Smaller (Beth); Ed Bakey (Luby Sains); Ed Peck (Pollard); David Canary (Candy); Gregg Palmer (Terrell).

Synopsis: Coley goes into the general store where the storekeeper will not give him any more credit. Hoss finds out that Coley's father died in a cave-in. Since Ben is the executor of the estate, Hoss decides to look after the boy until the elder Cartwright returns. Hoss, Judge Butler and the boy's Uncle Caleb try to decide what to do about the boy.

Hoss feels that Coley's mother should be notified. When she arrives in town, Coley refuses to have anything to do with her. Unbeknownst to everyone, Uncle Caleb has a meeting with a mine representative about getting the rights to Coley's gold mine.

E332. *The Fence* (April 27, 1969)

Credits: *Writers:* Ward Hawkins (adaptation), Milton S. Gelman, Alf Harris. *Director:* Lewis Allen. *Producer:* Richard Collins. *Executive Producer:* David Dortort. **Starring:** Lorne Greene, Dan Blocker. **Supporting Cast:** John Anderson (Sam Masters); J. D. Cannon (Col. Hudson); Verna Bloom (Ellen); Lawrence Linville (Will Tyler); Frank Webb (Teddy); Charles Dierkop (Sawyer); Gary Walberg (Bower); Patrick Hawley (Stubbs).

Synopsis: In the recent past, Ben sold Sam Masters a mine with the stipulation that he would purchase it back if Sam asked him to. When Ben and Hoss pay Sam and his daughter Ellen a visit, Masters takes his friend up on his offer. Ben is confused as the mine is prosperous.

The Cartwrights learn that 500 men did not survive a prison camp run by Masters during the Civil War because of disease and lack of food. The survivors, lead by Colonel Jim Hudson, are out for revenge. They soon begin firing on Sam's home to force him to give himself up.

Note: Location shooting took place at Big Bear.

E333. *A Ride in the Sun* (May 11, 1969)

Credits: *Writers:* John Hawkins (Teleplay), Peter Germano (Story, Teleplay). *Director:* Leon Benson. *Producer:* Richard Collins. *Executive Producer:* David Dortort. **Starring:** Lorne Greene, Dan Blocker, Michael Landon. **Supporting Cast:** Robert Hogan (Tobias Horn); Marj Dusay (April Horn); Anthony Zerbe (John Spain); Jack Collins (Harry Bishop); Harry Holcombe (Dr. Lewis); Ray Teal (Sheriff Roy Coffee).

Synopsis: Hoss and Joe rescue Tobias and April Horns, who are being chased by a bandit. They decide to escort the Horns to town. When they arrive at the hotel, Joe introduces Tobias to the bank president, Harry Bishop. Horn deposits $30,000 in the bank.

At the Ponderosa, April and Tobias agree to buy cattle from Ben, paying $19 cash per head. Sheriff Roy Coffee comes in with a vest which is identified as being worn by the gunman. After the deal is made, Tobias receives a wire about one of his clipper ships sinking. His bank demands immediate payment so Ben agrees to cancel the cattle deal and return the check. Ben and the Horns return to town to explain the change of plans to Harry Bishop. When the banker opens the safe to cash the check, Tobias pulls a gun on Ben and Bishop, shooting them both in the back.

Eleventh Season
(September 14, 1969–April 19, 1970)

E334. *Another Windmill to Go* (September 14, 1969)
Credits: *Writer:* Palmer Thompson. *Director:* James B. Clark. *Producer:* Richard Collins. *Executive Producer:* David Dortort. **Starring:** Lorne Greene, Dan Blocker, Michael Landon. **Supporting Cast:** David Canary (Candy); Lawrence Naismith (Don Q. Hoat); Jill Townsend (Abbey); Bart LaRue (Walters); Gregg Palmer (Benson); George Furth (Horace Keylot); Virgil Frye (Andy); Lee Jay Lambert (Shack); Bruce Watson (Clay); Foster Brooks (Judge); Remo Pisani (Bartender).

Synopsis: When Candy and Hoss come across Abbey and her father Don Q. Hoat rowing across government land, they ride to tell Ben about it. Ben and Joe ride out to find out what is going on. They soon find three drunken cowboys accosting Abbey and her father. After introductions are made, Joe decides to ride along with the Hoats to protect them.

Hoat later goes to Virginia City to see the government land agent. Ben and Joe soon find out that he has filed a claim on over 1,280 acres of government land at $1.25 an acre—land that Ben has leased to graze his cattle. As a result of this claim, Ben is forced to get an injunction against anyone else from doing the same thing until the law can be changed.

Review: *Variety* (September 24, 1969): "Lorne Greene continues to score as papa Cartwright nicely mixing frontier resolve, sagacity and manly mien. Michael Landon as Little Joe handles both the romantic chores and brief fisticuffs comfortably and Dan Blocker rounds out the program with beefy visual values. Guests Lawrence Naismith and Jill Townsend turned in firm performances."

E335. *The Witness* (September 21, 1969)
Credits: *Writer:* Joel Murcott. *Director:* Don Richardson. *Producer:* Richard Collins. *Executive Producer:* David Dortort. **Starring:** Lorne Greene, Michael Landon. **Supporting Cast:** David Canary (Candy); Melissa Murphy (Jenny Winters); Stefan Gierasch (Orvil Winters); Connie Hines (Hilda); Alan Baxter (Jim);

Bo Hopkins (Stretch); Wayne Storm (Bo); Matt Clark (Fantan); Bing Russell (Deputy Clem Foster).

Synopsis: One man is killed and another wounded during a stagecoach robbery. Jenny Winters was a witness and declares that she saw the Logan Brothers commit the crimes. Ben offers Jenny protection as the Logans are notorious for seeing to it that no witness survives to testify.

E336. *The Silence at Stillwater* (September 28, 1969)

Credits: *Writer:* Preston Wood. *Director:* Josef Leytes. *Producer:* Richard Collins. *Executive Producer:* David Dortort. **Starring:** Lorne Greene, Dan Blocker, Michael Landon. **Supporting Cast:** David Canary (Candy); Pat Hingle (Sheriff Austin); Strother Martin (Lonnie); Frank Marth (Barnum); Eddie Ryder (Vern); Dan Kemp (Jim Hale); Gene Shane (John Ferson); Gene Dynarski (Hostler); Gene Tyburn (Deputy); Teddy Quinn (Peter); John Zaremba (Doctor).

Synopsis: When Candy arrives in Stillwater, Sheriff Austin arrests him but will not tell him why. The sheriff uses the money found on Candy as evidence against him even though Candy claims the money was given to him to buy horses.

The Cartwrights arrive to meet up with Candy but are not even told he is in jail. Things look bleak for Candy, who has been accused of robbery and murder. To make maters worse, the victim's son has identified Candy as the guilty party and the sheriff impedes Candy's defense.

E337. *A Lawman's Lot Is Not a Happy One* (October 5, 1969)

Credits: *Writer:* Robert Vincent Wright. *Director:* Don Richardson. *Producer:* Richard Collins. *Executive Producer:* David Dortort. **Starring:** Lorne Greene, Dan Blocker, Michael Landon. **Supporting Cast:** David Canary (Candy); Tom Bosley (Hiram Peabody); Melinda Dillon (Cissie Summers); Robert Emhardt (Paul Forbes); Jay Novello (Fairfax); Ray Teal (Sheriff Roy Coffee); Harry Hickox (Mr. Green); Byron Morrow (Mr. Franklin); Elizabeth Talbot-Martin (Mrs. Green); Helen Kleeb (Mrs. Franklin); Bob Gravage (Elbert); Remo Pisani (Bartender).

Synopsis: Sheriff Coffee and Ben are waiting for the stagecoach to arrive so they can head for San Francisco to give evidence against a timber magnate. Coffee is concerned because his temporary replacement has not shown up. When Hoss gets off the stage, they learn that the deputy took off after Hoss beat him up. To get back at Hoss, Roy appoints him sheriff while Coffee is in San Francisco.

Hirim Peabody, who works for the stage line, has been writing Cissie Somers. When she comes to Virginia City, he gets frightened as he has not been totally honest with her. He does his best to get arrested, figuring she will go away.

Paul Forbes and Fairfax, his butler, show up in Virginia City to get investors for a resort hotel. The people take a liking to the men and become infuriated when Hoss comes across a warrant for a man fitting Paul's description and takes him into custody.

E338. *Anatomy of a Lynching* (October 12, 1969)

Credits: *Writer:* Preston Wood. *Director:* William Wiard. *Producer:* Richard Collins. *Executive Producer:* David Dortort. **Starring:** Lorne Greene, Dan Blocker,

Michael Landon. **Supporting Cast:** Guy Stockwell (John Degnan); Walter Barnes (Will Griner); Ellen Weston (Louise Thurston); Ted Gehring (Jim Fisher); Stacy Harris (Teague); Ray Teal (Sheriff Roy Coffee); David Canary (Candy); Mills Watson (Pete); Dan Scott (Stut); Tyler McVey (Al Crane); Roy Engel (Clyde Quinn); Stephen Coit (Lassen).

Synopsis: Will Griner is cleared of murder charges, but the citizens of Virginia City become riled up because they believe witnesses were paid off. Sheriff Coffee places Griner behind bars for his own safety.

Although Ben dislikes Will and thinks he is guilty, he cannot allow the town to lynch him and sets out to prove that Will has bribed the witnesses.

E339. *To Stop a War* (October 19, 1969)

Credits: *Writer:* Carey Wilbur. *Director:* Leon Benson. *Producer:* Richard Collins. *Executive Producer:* David Dortort. **Starring:** Lorne Greene, Dan Blocker, Michael Landon. **Supporting Cast:** Steve Forrest (Dan Logan); Miriam Colon (Anita); Warren Kemmerling (Slater); Bing Russell (Deputy Clem Foster); Alan Vint (Pete Hill); Chuck Bail (Ike Kels); John Tracy (Billy); Ollie O'Toole (Bartender); Richard Bull (Jes Hill); David Canary (Candy).

Synopsis: Prompted by a series of cattle thefts, the Cattleman's Association hire ex-lawman, Dan Logan, a range detective. Over Ben's objections, Frank Slader puts a bounty on the rustlers' heads, paying Dan $300 for each man he brings in regardless if they are still breathing or not.

Note: Music for this episode was composed by Harry Sukman.

E340. *The Medal* (October 26, 1969)

Credits: *Writer:* Frank Chase. *Director:* Lewis Allen. *Producer:* Richard Collins. *Executive Producer:* David Dortort. **Starring:** Lorne Greene, Dan Blocker, Michael Landon. **Supporting Cast:** Dean Stockwell (Matthew Rush); Susan Howard (Lori); John Beck (Walt); Charles Briles (Del); E. J. Schuster (Barker); William Pyfer (Cowboy); Victor Sen Yung (Hop Sing); Remo Pisani (Bartender); Sundown Spencer (Boy); James Rawley (Telegraph Clerk); David Canary (Candy); Harry Townes (Seth Nagel).

Synopsis: Ben discovers Matthew Rush intoxicated in a bar. Knowing he is a Congressional Medal of Honor winner, Ben takes him back to the Ponderosa and gives him employment.

Seth Nagel and his son Walt despise the man because their town had been set on fire by Northern forces. They want Matthew either forced to leave town or dead.

Note: Location filming took place at Los Padres National Forest.

E341. *The Stalker* (November 2, 1969)

Credits: *Writer:* D. C. Fontana. *Director:* Robert L. Friend. *Producer:* Richard Collins. *Executive Producer:* David Dortort. **Starring:** Lorne Greene, Dan Blocker, Michael Landon. **Supporting Cast:** David Canary (Candy); Charlotte Stewart (Lisa Campbell); Lloyd Battista (Jake); Bing Russell (Deputy Clem Foster); John Perak (Devlin); Dorothy Konrad (Mrs. Pardee); Harry Holcombe (Doctor); Vernon Weddle (South); Pitt Herbert (Postal Clerk); Brian Dewey (Kenny); Austin Roberts (Travis); Ed Griffith (Jim Campbell).

Synopsis: When bandit James Campbell holds up the bank, Candy is forced to kill the robber. He feels responsible and offers to help Campbell's widow, Lisa, and her son. They begin to fall in love.

Jake, Lisa's brother-in-law, responds to a letter she sent him after the shooting in which she wanted him to take Candy's life. She no longer wants Candy dead but Jake does.

E342. *Meena* (November 16, 1969)

Credits: *Writer:* Jack B. Sowards. *Director:* Herschel Daugherty. *Producer:* Richard Collins. *Executive Producer:* David Dortort. **Starring:** Lorne Greene, Michael Landon. **Supporting Cast:** David Canary (Candy); Ann Prentiss (Meena); Victor French (Jesse); Dub Taylor (Luke); Robert Donner (Owen); George Morgan (Virg); Jack Collins (Banker); Henry Oliver (Firman); John Harmon (Rider); Stu Nisbet (Charlie).

Synopsis: Joe and Candy vie for Meena Calhoun's attention. They wager on who can get the first date with her. Separately they trail her home to a lonely gold mine she shares with her father.

Joe's horse is stolen by three incompetent bandits. When he arrives at the Calhouns, he asks Luke to borrow a horse but is turned down. Meena is ready to get married and Joe happens to be on hand.

Note: Location shooting took place at Iverson's Ranch.

E343. *A Darker Shadow* (November 23, 1969)

Credits: *Writers:* John Hawkins (Teleplay), B. W. Sandefur, Jonathan Knopf (Story). *Director:* Don Richardson. *Producer:* Richard Collins. *Executive Producer:* David Dortort. **Starring:** Lorne Greene, Dan Blocker, Michael Landon. **Supporting Cast:** David Canary (Candy); Gregory Walcott (Wade Turner); Sandra Smith (Sarah); Dabney Coleman (Clyde); Bill Zuckert (Barker); Chick Chandler (Dr. Mills); Michael King (Hank); Don Melvoin (Sweeny).

Synopsis: Things could not be going better for Wade Turner, who has just been promoted at the bank and is going to marry Sarah. Then, without warning, he cancels the wedding and absconds with $5,000 from the bank.

Wade sees a doctor in Willow Bend and learns that he has a brain tumor that will render him blind if not taken care of.

When Joe sets out to help his friend, he soon realizes that Clyde, who worked with Wade at the bank, desires both Sarah and the promotion and is intent on seeing Turner dead.

Note: Location shooting took place at Los Padres National Forest.

E344. *Dead Wrong* (December 7, 1969)

Credits: *Writer:* Michael Landon. *Director:* Michael Landon. *Producer:* Richard Collins. *Executive Producer:* David Dortort. **Starring:** Dan Blocker. **Supporting Cast:** David Canary (Candy); Arthur Hunnicutt (Salty Hubbard); Mike Mazurki (Big Jack); Robert Surrells (Sid); Eric Christmas (Bobby Dann); Ivor Francis (Banker); Jim Connell (Hotel Manager); Guy Wilkerson (Sheriff); Milton Parsons (Undertaker); Sunshine Parker (Bum #1); Lee McLaughlin (Bum #2); John Carradine (Dillard).

Synopsis: Hoss and Candy arrive in Sunville. They have just finished selling some cattle and are carrying the money in a bag. When the money unintentionally spills out, teller Sally Hubbard is certain that Hoss is "Big Jack," a famous bank robber.

E345. *Old Friends* (December 14, 1969)

Credits: *Writer:* Barney Slater. *Director:* Leon Benson. *Producer:* Richard Collins. *Executive Producer:* David Dortort. **Starring:** Lorne Greene, Dan Blocker, Michael Landon. **Supporting Cast:** David Canary (Candy); Robert J. Wilke (Charlie Sheppard); Morgan Woodward (Jess Waddell); Rick Lamson (Morgan Shepperd); Victor Sen Yung (Hop Sing).

Synopsis: It has been 25 years since Jess Waddell, Charlie Shepperd and Ben have seen each other. Their reunion is not a congenial one as Jess has become a bounty hunter and is after Charlie, who has pursued a life of crime. Ben must keep Jess from killing Charlie because Hoss has been taken hostage by the outlaw.

Note: Location shooting took place at Franklin Lake and Vasquez Rocks.

E346. *Abner Willoughby's Return* (December 21, 1969)

Credits: *Writers:* Jack B. Sowards (Teleplay), Leslie McErlaine (Story and Teleplay). *Director:* Herschel Daugherty. *Producer:* Richard Collins. *Executive Producer:* David Dortort. **Starring:** Lorne Greene, Dan Blocker, Michael Landon. **Supporting Cast:** John Astin (Abner Willoughby); Emmaline Henry (Widow Sprague); Irene Tedrow (Minnie); Russell Schulman (Charlie); Walter Sande (Sheriff Brian); William Hansen (Vinson); Patrick Sullivan Burke (Stokes); Duane Grey (Captain Price); E. A. Sirianni (Clerk); David Canary (Candy).

Synopsis: After Joe finishes selling 52 horses to the Army for $1,300, he heads for home. When he stops for water, he is almost robbed by Abner Willoughby. Joe follows Abner to Glory Hole but when they get there all they find is the town of Shotgun Springs. It seems that Abner has returned to retrieve money that he buried years before.

E347. *It's a Small World* (January 4, 1970)

Credits: *Writer:* Michael Landon. *Director:* Michael Landon. *Producer:* Richard Collins. *Executive Producer:* David Dortort. **Starring:** Lorne Greene, Dan Blocker, Michael Landon. **Supporting Cast:** Michael Dunn (George Marshall); Edward Binns (John Flint); Angela Clarke (Mrs. Marshall); Bing Russell (Deputy Clem Foster); Carol Lawson (Alice); Ralph Moody (Clarke); Roy Engel (Dr. Martin); Stuart Nisbet (Wyley); Michele Tobin (Annie); David Canary (Candy).

Synopsis: George Marshall, a midget, has grown tired of the circus and wants to find a new job. He finds it difficult to get work because people are prejudiced against him due to his size. When Ben learns there is an opening for a bank teller, he tries to get banker John Flint to hire George. Flint makes excuses and will not give him the job.

Needing money, George holds up the bank but gives it back when he is caught. Flint intends to bring George up on charges.

Later, when John's daughter plunges down a shaft, George is the only one who can save her.

Note: This idea was used again in *Little House: The Next Generation* (the episode "Little Lou").

E348. *Danger Road* (January 11, 1970)

Credits: *Writers:* Milton S. Gelman (Story, Teleplay), Brian McKay (Story). *Director:* William F. Claxton. *Producer:* Richard Collins. *Executive Producer:* David Dortort. **Starring:** Lorne Greene, Dan Blocker, Michael Landon. **Supporting Cast:** David Canary (Candy); Robert Lansing (Gunny Riley); William Sylvester (Cambeau); Anna Navarro (Serafina); Jay Jones (Willard); LeRoy Johnson (Ed); Bing Russell (Deputy Clem Foster); Stuart Nisbet (Storekeeper); Ollie O'Toole (Bartender).

Synopsis: Gunny is hauling a load to Virginia City and has trouble with one of his wheels. When Joe and Candy ride in, Candy stays to help and suspects that Gunny used to be in the Army. Candy takes them to a line shack where Gunny's wife Serefina wants to stay awhile, but he wants to continue on to Canada.

Gunny goes to town in search of another load but Cambeau says no. He then goes to re-sign a freight contract but Ben will not sign. When Ben hears that Gunny is on the Ponderosa, he orders him off the ranch. It seems that Ben and Gunny knew each other in the Mexican War.

After Gunny successfully brings three 30-foot beams off the mountain for Ben, Joe and Candy get the idea to back Gunny in the freight race but he gets mad and refuses. That night, after Cambeau's men attempt to wreck Gunny's wagon, Gunny changes his mind about the race.

Note: Location shooting took place at Los Padres National Forest.

E349. *The Big Jackpot* (January 18, 1970)

Credits: *Writer:* John Hawkins. *Director:* Herschel Daugherty. *Producer:* Richard Collins. *Executive Producer:* David Dortort. **Starring:** Lorne Greene, Dan Blocker, Michael Landon. **Supporting Cast:** David Canary (Candy); Walter Brooke (Atworth Perry); Robert F. Simon (Thurston); Alan Caillou (Hare); Elizabeth Talbot-Martin (Harriet); Al Checco (Hornsby); Nelson Olmsted (Appleton); Robert Ball (Henny); Paula Mitchell (Melody); Carol Rouk (Ruth); Richard Stahl (Fiber); Leon Lontoc (Ah Yee); Remo Pisani (Bartender); Bruce Kirby (Simms).

Synopsis: Hoss and Joe watch Candy clean out a water hole. After they leave, a man tells Candy that he has inherited a gold mine worth $100,000—$50,000 in cash and the rest in stocks. Candy comes riding into the ranch, yelling at the top of his lungs. He shows Hoss and Joe the money, giving each of them a sample $500 bill. Hoss, Joe and Candy ride into town where he is harassed by everyone.

E350. *The Trouble with Amy* (January 25, 1970)

Credits: *Writers:* Jack Miller, John Hawkins. *Director:* Leon Benson. *Producer:* Richard Collins. *Executive Producer:* David Dortort. **Starring:** Lorne Greene.

Tombstone of Hop Sing. (Photograph by Linda F. Leiby.)

Supporting Cast: Jo Van Fleet (Amy Wilder); John Crawford (Barton Roberts); Donald Moffat (Judge); Linda Watkins (Margaret); Brian Wo (Fareti); Elaine Giftos (Charity); Carl Pitti (David); Harriet Medin (Mrs. Ocher); Eleanore Berry (Mrs. Eads); Harry Hickox (Mr. Eads); Gail Billings (Mary Ann); Elizabeth Thompson (Sally).

   Synopsis: Widow Amy Wilder is a lonely old woman whose only reason for living is the animals she cares for.

   When a wealthy businessman wants to buy a piece of land she does not use, she refuses to sell despite the handsome offer he has made her. She believes the land is needed by her animals. Desperate for the property, the businessman plans to get hold of the land by having her committed for incompetency.

E351. *The Lady and the Mark* (February 1, 1970)

Credits: *Writer:* Preston Wood. *Director:* Leon Benson. *Producer:* Richard Collins. *Executive Producer:* David Dortort. **Starring:** Lorne Greene, Dan Blocker, Michael Landon. **Supporting Cast:** David Canary (Candy); Christopher Connelly (Chris Keller); Elaine Giftos (Charity McGill); James Westerfield (Blackwell); Lou Frizzell (Charley); Sam Davis (Walt); Bing Russell (Deputy Clem Foster); Ralph Waite (Hoby); Ralph James (Alderman).

Synopsis: Chris Keller gets off the stage before it arrives in Virginia City and walks to the Ponderosa. When he gets there, Chris tells Ben that he made $67,000 in the gold fields. Ben warns him to be careful because there are confidence men in town.

The confidence men are having a meeting about their next "mark"—Chris. they decide to sell him stock in the Patent Reaper Company. Later Chris tells Ben about the men's offer. In town, Ben and Chris meet with Mr. Miles, who decides to sell them $71,000 in stock. Realizing that the con men are being conned, Mr. Blackwell leaves town. After the con men leave town, Ben is not sure that Chris' problems are over.

E352. *Is There Any Man Here* (February 8, 1970)

Credits: *Writer:* B. W. Sandefur. *Director:* Don Richardson. *Producer:* Richard Collins. *Executive Producer:* David Dortort. **Starring:** Lorne Greene, Dan Blocker, Michael Landon. **Supporting Cast:** Mariette Hartley (Jennifer Carlis); Burr De Benning (Tuttle Ames); John McLiam (Harry Carlis); Vaughn Taylor (Bert Taylor); Roy Engel (Dr. Thomas); Jon Lormer (Preacher); Don Melvoin (Morris); David Canary (Candy); Victor Sen Yung (Hop Sing).

Synopsis: Jennifer Carlis arrives at the Ponderosa looking for Ben. She is the daughter of Harry, an old friend of Ben's, and she has left her fiance Tuttle Ames at the altar because she really loves Ben. Harry has asked Ben to talk to her about it.

Several days later, Ben kisses Jennifer and tells Hoss and Joe that he is going to marry her. When Jennifer goes to Tuttle, he assumes that there is going to be a wedding. He then warns her that he can and will break Ben financially if she marries him.

E353. *The Law and Billy Burgess* (February 15, 1970)

Credits: *Writer:* Stanley Roberts. *Director:* William F. Claxton. *Producer:* Richard Collins. *Executive Producer:* David Dortort. **Starring:** Lorne Greene, Dan Blocker, Michael Landon. **Supporting Cast:** Mercedes McCambridge (Matilda Curtis); Les Tremayne (Doc Lyman); David Cassidy (Billy Burgess); Charles Maxwell (Billings); Sam Melville (Coulter); Bill Phipps (Tom Burgess); David Canary (Candy); James Chandler (Osgood); Harlan Warde (Nicholson); Tani Phelps (Nora Burgess); Foster Brooks (Judge Rogers); Ray Teal (Sheriff Roy Coffee); Remo

Pisani (Bartender); Lenore Stevens (Ines); Fred Gerber (Jeff); Gary Morgan (Chip); Paul Harper (Sully).

Synopsis: On the first day of the Ponderosa School, Ben is addressing the students and introduces Doc Lyman, their new teacher. Doc threatens to quit after the kids set fire to the school. The next day, Lyman continues to have more trouble — especially with Billy Burgess. Joe and Hoss keep a watch on things but Hoss finally sends Billy home for threatening the teacher.

Doc later agrees to mediate an argument between two men over the ownership of a ranch. The next morning, Candy rides into the ranch saying he found Doc's dead body.

E354. *Long Way to Ogden* (February 22, 1970)

Credits: *Writer:* Joel Murcott. *Director:* Lewis Allen. *Producer:* Richard Collins. *Executive Producer:* David Dortort. **Starring:** Lorne Greene, Dan Blocker, Michael Landon. **Supporting Cast:** David Canary (Candy); Walter Barnes (Emmett J. Whitney); Kathleen Freeman (Ma Brinker); James McCallion (Luther); Mark Tapscott (Steve Rance); Billy Greenbush (Spanier); Arthur Peterson (Lloyd Walsh); Anthony Colti (Ollie); Remo Pisani (Bartender); Ray Teal (Sheriff Roy Coffee).

Synopsis: As winter approaches, Ben and the other ranchers must get their herds to Ogden. They can load them on railroad cars headed for Chicago. With the rise in beef prices, they anticipate the best profits in some time.

When Joe informs them that Emmett J. Whitney, a meat packing business owner in Chicago, has acquired all of the available train cars, they are infuriated. Whitney offers to buy up their herd for a measly three dollars a head. to add insult to injury, he threatens to reduce the price by a dollar for every day they hold out.

E355. *Return Engagement* (March 1, 1970)

Credits: *Writer:* Stanley Roberts. *Director:* Don Richardson. *Producer:* Richard Collins. *Executive Producer:* David Dortort. **Starring:** Lorne Greene, Dan Blocker, Michael Landon. **Supporting Cast:** Sally Kellerman (Lotta Crabtree); Morgan Sterne (Stan Hope); David McLean (Marshall Fallon); Joyce Bulifant (Bonnie); Bartlett Robinson (Howell); Victor Sen Yung (Hop Sing); Ray Teal (Sheriff Roy Coffee); David Canary (Candy).

Synopsis: Actress Lotta Crabtree plays a return engagement in Virginia City. To show their appreciation, the Cartwrights throw a party at the ranch. While there, Lotta spends time with Hoss, much to her leading man's disapproval.

When the leading man becomes too drunk to rehearse, Hoss steps in. When the leading man finds out, he becomes irate. At the end of the play, Lotta is to shoot her co-star. At curtain call, the leading man is found dead. Hoss is accused of murder when Roy Coffee discovers blanks in his saddle bag.

E356. *The Gold Mine* (March 8, 1970)

Credits: *Writers:* Robert Buckner (Teleplay), Preston Wood (Story and Teleplay). *Director:* Leon Benson. *Producer:* Richard Collins. *Executive Producer:* David

Dortort. **Starring:** Lorne Greene, Dan Blocker, Michael Landon. **Supporting Cast:** David Canary (Candy); Tony De Costa (Ramon); Bruce Dern (Bayliss); Ross Hansen (Rader); Charles P. Thompson (Clerk).

Synopsis: Bayliss and Rader ride into the ranch along with a Mexican boy named Ramon. Ben allows them to stay the night in the barn. After Ramon is beaten by the two men, he tells Ben that he works for the two men. As Hoss treats the boy's back, he realizes that Ramon has been beaten before.

After unsuccessfully trying to rob the house, the two men escape with Ramon to a small cabin. They continue to threaten the boy, then send him out for firewood. When he returns with rocks, they get angry so he runs away. Bayliss and Rader soon discover that there is gold in the rocks. In town, they find out that the ore is worth $10,000 a ton.

Joe finds Ramon, taking him back to the Ponderosa. Ramon tells the Cartwrights that his father sold him for two sacks of grain and some beans. Later the two men show up at the ranch, offering Ramon $1,000 for his mine. When they threaten Joe's life, Ramon decides to go back with them. The next morning, the Cartwrights ride out looking for Ramon. After they split up, Joe is taken hostage.

Note: Location shooting took place at Vasquez Rocks.

E357. *Decision at Los Robles* (March 22, 1970)

Credits: *Writer:* Michael Landon. *Director:* Michael Landon. *Producer:* Richard Collins. *Executive Producer:* David Dortort. **Starring:** Lorne Greene, Michael Landon. **Supporting Cast:** William H. Bassett (Jed Walker); Joe De Santis (Father Xavier); Ted Cassidy (Garth); Anakorita (Maria); George Wallace (Doctor); Rico Alaniz (Ricardo); Emile Meyer (John Walker); Joaquin Martinez (Sanchez); Victor Campos (Gunman #1); Lee DeBroux (Gunman #2).

Synopsis: Ben and Joe arrive in Los Robles. When John Walker, who runs the town, gives a waitress a hard time, Ben takes her side. When he leaves the saloon, Walker fires his gun and Ben is hit in the back. Before passing out, Ben shoots and kills Walker. Jed Walker seeks revenge for his father's death and warns Joe he has 24 hours to turn over his father or he will take the life of a citizen every hour Joe fails to comply.

Note: Location shooting took place at some of *The High Chaparral* sets.

E358. *Caution: Easter Bunny Crossing* (March 29, 1970)

Credits: *Writer:* Larry Markes. *Director:* Bruce Bilson. *Producer:* Richard Collins. *Executive Producer:* David Dortort. **Starring:** Lorne Greene, Dan Blocker, Michael Landon. **Supporting Cast:** David Canary (Candy); Marc Lawrence (Red Gaskell); Art Metrano (LeRoy Gaskell); Allyn Ann McLerie (Charity Moffit); Sandy Kenyon (Elijah Meek); James Jeter (Blacksmith); Jack Williams (Stage Driver); Len Lesser (Fred); Vic Tayback (Everett).

Synopsis: A traveling salesman is robbed and hit over the head by the Gaskell brothers, but all they find are Bibles and dirty shirts. When Ben goes to town, he meets Miss Charity Moffit, who wants to buy some cattle because she has 18 children in an orphanage to feed. Hoss delivers a milk cow to her and she asks him to be a rabbit on Easter and hide the eggs for the children. The only catch is that he has to have a fitting for the bunny costume before Sunday.

The Gaskell brothers arrive in Virginia City. After one of them overhears Joe talking of a Wells Fargo silver shipment, they make plans to rob it.

Note: Location shooting took place at Iverson's Ranch.

E359. *The Horse Traders* (April 5, 1970)

Credits: *Writer:* Jack B. Sowards. *Director:* Herschel Daugherty. *Producer:* Richard Collins. *Executive Producer:* David Dortort. **Starring:** Lorne Greene, Dan Blocker, Michael Landon. **Supporting Cast:** Dub Taylor (Luke Calhoun); Ann Prentiss (Meena); George Morgan (Virgil); Victor French (Jesse); Lou Frizzell (Dusty); Robert Donner (Owen); Jack Collins (Banker); Henry Oliver (Firman); John Harman (Rider).

Synopsis: Meena tells her father that she wants her fiancé Virgil to go to work. So Luke tells Virgil and his two brothers that they have to get jobs.

Joe talks to Mr. Firman about buying some horses for $40 a head. He then hires a drifter named Dusty Rhoades to help deliver the horses. When Hoss, Joe and Dusty bring the horses to Firman's, they find Virgil's brother. When they go to the other livery stable they find Virgil's other brother as manager.

When they go to the C & P Development Company office, the Cartwright boys find out that Luke Calhoun and Virgil are the owners of all the livery stables in town. Hoss and Joe decide to open their own livery stable.

Note: Lou Frizzell appears in this episode for the first time as Dusty Rhoades.

E360. *What Are Partners For?* (April 12, 1970)

Credits: *Writer:* Jack B. Sowards. *Director:* William F. Claxton. *Producer:* Richard Collins. *Executive Producer:* David Dortort. **Starring:** Lorne Greene, Dan Blocker, Michael Landon. **Supporting Cast:** David Canary (Candy); Slim Pickens (Sheriff); John Beck (Luke); Richard Evans (John); Hamilton Camp (Calvin); Dabbs Greer (Judge); Bruce Glover (Scooter); Tol Avery (Bradley); Bob Padilla (Running Cloud); Robert Cornthwaite (Blake); Tom Peters (Ray Stahl).

Synopsis: Hoss meets two incompetent bank robbers and is accused of being an accomplice. Hoss tries to clear himself, but things only get worse: They call him partner.

E361. *A Matter of Circumstance* (April 19, 1970)

Credits: *Writer:* B. W. Sandefur. *Director:* William F. Claxton. *Producer:* Richard Collins. *Executive Producer:* David Dortort. **Starring:** Lorne Greene, Dan Blocker, Michael Landon. **Supporting Cast:** David Canary (Candy); Ted Gehring (Griffin); Vincent Van Patten (Tim); Victor Sen Yung (Hop Sing); Harry Holcombe (Doctor).

Synopsis: Ben, Hoss and Candy head out on a cattle drive, leaving Joe to join them later.

A horse is riled up during a thunderstorm. Joe attempts to settle the horse down and his arm and leg are crushed by the animal. He must stay awake to tend his wounds.

View of Lake Tahoe taken from behind the Ponderosa Ranch House. (Photograph by Linda F. Leiby.)

Twelfth Season
(September 13, 1970–April 11, 1971)

E362. *The Night Virginia City Died* (September 13, 1970)
   Credits: *Writer:* John Hawkins. *Director:* William Wiard. *Producer:* Richard Collins. *Executive Producer:* David Dortort. **Starring:** Lorne Greene, Dan Blocker, Michael Landon. **Supporting Cast:** Ray Teal (Sheriff Roy Coffee); Angel Tompkins (Janie); Bing Russell (Deputy Clem Foster); Phil Brown (Wade Tucker); Victor Sen Yung (Hop Sing); Edith Atwater (Roberta); John Shank (Tim Moss); Mark Tapscott (Hamilton); Lane Bradford (Ira); Mona Bruns (Mrs. Carter); William Fawcett (Whiskey Smith); Stuart Nisbet (Evans); Paul Kent (Dr. Martin); Lou Frizzell (Dusty Rhoades).

Synopsis: Virginia City is experiencing an outbreak of fires. Sheriff Coffee and Deputy Clem Foster arrest a known arsonist but another fire breaks out while he is in jail.

The townspeople are afraid to go to sleep at night, fearing another fire. They demand that the culprit be caught but the two lawmen have no idea who is responsible.

Note: This episode is based on fact: The fire that almost destroyed the entire town occurred in 1875.

E363. *A Matter of Faith* (September 20, 1970)

Credits: *Writers:* D. C. Fontana (Story), Jack B. Sowards, John Hawkins (Teleplay). *Director:* William Wiard. *Producer:* Richard Collins. *Executive Producer:* David Dortort. **Starring:** Lorne Greene, Dan Blocker, Michael Landon. **Supporting Cast:** Mitch Vogel (Jamie Hunter); Lou Frizzell (Dusty Rhoades); Bruce Gordon (Scott); Jack Collins (Mayor Corey); Geoffrey Lewis (Rogers); Michael Hinn (Garrison); Dabbs Greer.

Synopsis: The Cartwrights come across Jamie Hunter and their old friend Dusty Rhoades, who are on their way to Virginia City. In town two men are complaining about the price of water when Jamie and Dusty ride in. Mayor Corey agrees to pay them $5,000 if they can make it rain within two weeks. After getting $200 advance, Jamie goes to the general store for supplies.

On the Ponderosa, Jamie and Dusty start mixing the ingredients. When Ben visits their camp, Dusty tells him how he met Jamie and his father. After the man died, Dusty had promised to look after the boy. Jamie then tells Ben that he is positive that he can make it rain because his father wrote everything down in a book.

Several days later, four men from town ride into their camp, wreck it, knock out Dusty and burn Jamie's book.

E364. *The Weary Willies* (September 27, 1970)

Credits: *Writer:* Robert Pirosh. *Director:* Leo Penn. *Producer:* Richard Collins. *Executive Producer:* David Dortort. **Starring:** Lorne Greene, Michael Landon. **Supporting Cast:** Mitch Vogel (Jamie Hunter); Richard Thomas (Billy); Lee Purcell (Angie); Lonny Chapman (Colter); Elisha Cook, Jr. (Marcus); Mayf Nutter (Pelletin); Kevin Tighe (Krulak); Scott Graham (Trimble); David Hayward (Hurley); Remo Pisani (Bartender); Harry Holcombe (Doctor); Stacy Keach (Farmer); Lou Frizzell (Dusty Rhoades).

Synopsis: Three drifters resting by the lake stop a freight wagon looking for a ride to Virginia City. When the driver recognizes them as weary willies, he asks Joe and Dusty for help. When the three willies run away, they make camp on the Ponderosa. After Joe allows them to stay, the willies put out a stone marker indicating to other weary willies where the camp is located.

As more and more willies arrive in camp, the townspeople become upset. When Angie becomes infatuated with one of the willies, her father and boyfriend become angry. The situation comes to a boiling point when Angie is found unconscious near the willie's camp.

E365. *The Wagon* (October 4, 1970)

Credits: *Writer:* Ken Pettus. *Director:* James Neilson. *Producer:* Richard Collins. *Executive Producer:* David Dortort. **Starring:** Lorne Greene, Dan Blocker, Michael Landon. **Supporting Cast:** Denver Pyle (Price Buchanan); Salome Jens (Madge Tucker); George Murdock (Luis Getty); Jonathan Lippe (Kyte); Lee Jay Lambert (Jase); Stuart Randall (Sheriff Brody); Bob Vanselow (Fred Quinn).

Synopsis: When a prison wagon makes camp, one of the prisoners escapes. He soon finds Hoss making camp, so he takes his horse Chub, wounding Hoss in the process. Meanwhile, Ben and Joe are in town loading their wagon when the escaped convict rides in. They take him to jail after they find him with Chub.

Hoss comes to and starts walking. He is found unconscious by the prison wagon driver. Price Buchanan decides to use Hoss as a replacement for the missing prisoner.

E366. *The Power of Life and Death* (October 11, 1970)

Credits: *Writer:* Joel Murcott. *Director:* Leo Penn. *Producer:* Richard Collins. *Executive Producer:* David Dortort. **Starring:** Lorne Greene, Michael Landon. **Supporting Cast:** Rupert Crosse (Davis); Lou Frizzell (Dusty Rhoades); Larry Ward (Sheriff); Ted Gehring (Matt); Tina Menard (Mexican Woman).

Synopsis: Joe is loading a wagon when Davis rides into town looking for Col. Clayton. Upon entering the saloon, shots are fired. Davis then runs out and rides away. Ben and Joe join a posse and head across the desert in pursuit of Davis. Meanwhile, Davis is being chased by Utes. Eluding them, he stops off at a water hole. As Ben and Joe continue to follow, they are also being watched by the Indians. The Cartwrights soon arrive at the same water hole and take Davis captive.

The next day, Ben is shot by the Utes. After Davis drags Ben to safety, the Indians steal their horses. Joe decides to cross the desert with two canteens of water in order to get help.

Note: Location shooting took place in Old Tucson, Arizona, for the first time.

E367. *Gideon the Good* (October 18, 1970)

Credits: *Writer:* Ken Pettus. *Director:* Herschel Daugherty. *Producer:* Richard Collins. *Executive Producer:* David Dortort. **Starring:** Lorne Greene, Dan Blocker, Michael Landon. **Supporting Cast:** Richard Kiley (Sheriff Gideon Yates); Terry Moore (Lydia Yates); A. Martinez (Luis); Carmen Zapata (Maria); John Himes (Myles); Wes Bishop (Hicks); Allen Emerson (Pike Rogers).

Synopsis: After a woman in a carriage almost runs him off the road, Joe finds a dead man. He takes the body into the nearest town. Joe tells Sheriff Yates that he is on his way to War Bonnet to meet his family. He sends a telegram to his father saying he will be late. Joe then takes the sheriff to the spot where he found the body. There they find a hankerchief with an "L" on it. Back in town, the sheriff tells Joe that he can leave after signing a statement but Joe decides to stay. That night, Joe is shot from ambush.

Another shot of the Territorial Enterprise, *Nevada's first newspaper; see also page 10. (Photograph by Linda F. Leiby.)*

E368. *The Trouble with Trouble* (October 25, 1970)
Credits: *Writer:* Jack B. Sowards. *Director:* Herschel Daugherty. *Producer:* Richard Collins. *Executive Producer:* David Dortort. **Starring:** Lorne Greene, Dan

Blocker, Michael Landon. **Supporting Cast:** Gene Evans (Montana Perkins); G. D. Spradlin (Chip); E. J. Andre (Judge); Victor Sen Yung (Hop Sing); Jeff Morris (Matthew Brody); Hal Homes (Mark); Ray Young (Reverend); Edgar Daniels (Tom Blackwell); Don Hanmer (Fred); Lane Bradford (Jack Clanton); Chanin Hale (Lily); Bobo Lewis (First Lady); Athena Lorde (Second Lady); E. A. Sirianni (Jethro); Sunshine Parker (Wally); Bobby Riha (Eben).

Synopsis: Montana Perkins arrives at the Ponderosa to ask for help controlling the lawless town of Trouble. Ben volunteers Hoss for the job. He is thwarted in his attempts to end the disorder because the townspeople have a total disregard for the law.

E369. *Thornton's Account* (November 1, 1970)

Credits: *Writer:* Preston Wood. *Director:* William F. Claxton. *Producer:* Richard Collins. *Executive Producer:* David Dortort. **Starring:** Lorne Greene, Dan Blocker, Michael Landon. **Supporting Cast:** Gregory Walcott (Thornton); Carl Reindel (Frank Wells); Heather Menzies (Martha); Scott Walker (Blue); Jerry Gatlin (Harvey); Chick Chandler (Doctor); Harlan Warde (Boyle); Darrell Larson (Brian); Ken Mayer (Sheriff).

Synopsis: Ben is riding a free-spirited horse when it is startled by a falling object and bucks. Ben loses his balance and is thrown down a steep embankment, injuring his back. Joe needs a wagon and team of horses to rescue his father. He finds that people are unwilling to lend a hand because they are being harassed by three hired hands of a powerful property owner.

Note: Location shooting took place at Big Bear.

E370. *The Love Child* (November 8, 1970)

Credits: *Writer:* Michael Landon. *Director:* Michael Landon. *Producer:* Richard Collins. *Executive Producer:* David Dortort. **Starring:** Lorne Greene, Dan Blocker, Michael Landon. **Supporting Cast:** Mitch Vogel (Jamie); Carol Lawson (Etta); Michael-James Wixted (Scott); Will Geer (Zac); Josephine Hutchinson (Martha); Victor Sen Yung (Hop Sing); David Bond (Doctor).

Synopsis: When Etta learns she has leukemia and does not have long to live, she returns home with her son Scott. Her mother Martha is delighted to see her but Zak, her father, will have nothing to do with them. He has not forgiven her for being involved with a man who was married and for having Scott out of wedlock.

Note: This episode won an Emmy for David Rose's music. The same story line was used in the *Highway to Heaven* episode "Child of God."

E371. *El Jefe* (November 15, 1970)

Credits: *Writers:* Ken Petus (Teleplay), Richard P. McDonough (Story). *Director:* William F. Claxton. *Producer:* Richard Collins. *Executive Producer:* David Dortort. **Starring:** Lorne Greene, Dan Blocker, Michael Landon. **Supporting Cast:** Rudolfo Acosta (Sheriff Vincente Aranda); Warren Stevens (Owen Driscoll); Jaime Sanchez (Cardenas); Anna Navarro (Sara); Shug Fisher (Toler); Victor Sen Yung (Hop Sing); Troy Melton (Graves); Bill Shannon (Brady); Alex Sharp (Truitt); Pepe Hern (Rojas).

Synopsis: The Driscoll Mining Company has been trying to buy out Ramon Cardenas' property as well as that of his Mexican neighbors. When Ramon refuses to sell, one of Driscoll's men is sent to burn him out. To protect himself, Ramon is forced to kill him. He is then arrested for murder.

E372. *The Luck of Pepper Shannon* (November 22, 1970)

Credits: *Writers:* John Hawkins (Story and Teleplay), George Schenck, William Marks (Story). *Director:* Nick Webster. *Producer:* Richard Collins. *Executive Producer:* David Dortort. **Starring:** Lorne Greene, Dan Blocker, Michael Landon. **Supporting Cast:** Mitch Vogel (Jamie); Neville Brand (Pepper Shannon); Ray Teal (Sheriff Roy Coffee); Victor Sen Yung (Hop Sing); Walter Brooke (Corry); Dan Tobin (Mills); Arthur Peterson (Donavan); Harry Holcombe (Dr. Harris); Raymond Guth (Jones); Bing Russell (Deputy Clem Foster).

Synopsis: Outlaw Pepper Shannon, who is the subject of dime store novels, is eluding two men on his trail. When he runs into Jamie, Pepper persuades him to escort him to town and turn him over to the law. As no charges are pending, Shannon is released.

When Pepper is framed for crimes he did not commit, Jamie helps him confront those behind the frame-up.

E373. *The Impostors* (December 13, 1970)

Credits: *Writer:* Robert Vincent Wright. *Director:* Lewis Allen. *Producer:* Richard Collins. *Executive Producer:* David Dortort. **Starring:** Lorne Greene, Dan Blocker, Michael Landon. **Supporting Cast:** Strother Martin (Joad Bruder); Anthony Colti (Randy Bruder); Anthony James (Willie Bruder); Diane Shalet (Mrs. York); Jarion Monroe (Cass Bruder); William Lucking (Gabe); Jim Raymond (Deputy Harris); Harry Harvey (Bixle); Larry W. Finley (Petey); Robert Ridgely (Marley); Bing Russell (Deputy Clem Foster).

Synopsis: Hoss and Joe ride into a small town looking for Joad Bruder. They introduce themselves as the man's sons, Randy's partners. After they go upstairs to his place above the store, Hoss tells Joad about a stage hold-up and the $51,000 that was stolen.

After Joad talks to his other two sons, Cass and Willie, about giving the money to Hoss and Joe, they leave. Randy escapes from jail and his two brothers return with Mrs. York, the wife of the man that Hoss is pretending to be.

E374. *Honest John* (December 20, 1970)

Credits: *Writer:* Arthur Heineman. *Director:* Lewis Allen. *Producer:* Richard Collins. *Executive Producer:* David Dortort. **Starring:** Lorne Greene, Dan Blocker, Michael Landon. **Supporting Cast:** Mitch Vogel (Jamie); Jack Elam (Honest John); Bing Russell (Deputy Clem Foster); Victor Sen Yung (Hop Sing); Bucklind Beery (Luke).

Synopsis: Jamie seems to be having trouble getting his chores done but will not tell Hoss what is wrong. When he starts feeding the chickens, a crow flies in, so Jamie decides to take care of it.

One of the hands brings in an old man who introduces himself as Honest John and invites himself to stay a few days. Later John finds Lucifer, the crow, taking it out of the cage and claiming that the bird belongs to him. That night at dinner, Honest John tells tall tales of his past. Afterwards Jamie and John go outside, where he asks the boy about staying a while longer. He then tells Jamie that if he can arrange it, he will give him Lucifer. The Cartwrights become concerned about Honest John's influence on Jamie.

E375. *For a Young Lady* (December 27, 1970)

Credits: *Writer:* B. W. Sandefur. *Director:* Don Richardson. *Producer:* Richard Collins. *Executive Producer:* David Dortort. **Starring:** Lorne Greene, Dan Blocker, Michael Landon. **Supporting Cast:** Mitch Vogel (Jamie); Bing Russell (Deputy Clem Foster); Jewel Blanch (Carri Sturgis); Madeline Sherwood (Vella Owens); Paul Fix (Buford Sturgis); William Bramley (Gifford Owens); Harry Holcombe (Doctor); Peggy Rea (Clara); Victor Sen Yung (Hop Sing).

Synopsis: Buford Sturgis, an old miner, is injured when he falls down a hill after getting the drop on Jamie and Joe. They then take him back to his cabin. Joe goes to town for the doctor, leaving Jamie with Buford's granddaughter Carri. While Joe is gone, Carri's Aunt Bella and Uncle Gifford come to see Buford asking who is going to take care of Carri. After they go outside, Buford tells his granddaughter that it is a good idea that she go with them for a while.

The doctor decides that Buford should be moved to his office in town. Meanwhile, Carri is being treated like a slave by her aunt and uncle. The Cartwrights decide to help the girl.

E376. *A Single Pilgrim* (January 3, 1971)

Credits: *Writer:* Suzanne Clauser. *Director:* William Wiard. *Producer:* Richard Collins. *Executive Producer:* David Dortort. **Starring:** Lorne Greene, Dan Blocker, Michael Landon. **Supporting Cast:** Beth Brickell (Dilsey Brennan); Jeff Corey (Frank Brennan); John Schuck (Tom Brennan).

Synopsis: Hoss is in the mountains inspecting trees when he is shot by accident. After he is taken to a cabin, Tom Brennan is told by his father Frank to wipe out the tracks. When Hoss comes to, he asks Tom's wife Dilsey what happened to him. He also asks her to get a message to his family. When Dilsey tells her husband and Frank about Hoss, they decide to go to Genoa to learn more about him. The Brennans soon find out that the Cartwrights are rich and that people are out looking for Hoss.

Later Joe rides in looking for his brother, and he is told that they have not seen him. That night, Hoss overhears Frank telling his son that they have to kill him.

Note: Location shooting took place at Los Padres National Forest.

E377. *The Gold-Plated Rifle* (January 10, 1971)

Credits: *Writer:* Preston Wood. *Director:* Joseph Pevney. *Producer:* Richard Collins. *Executive Producer:* David Dortort. **Starring:** Lorne Greene, Dan Blocker, Michael Landon. **Supporting Cast:** Mitch Vogel (Jamie); Victor Sen Yung (Hop Sing);

Ray Teal (Sheriff Roy Coffee); Lou Frizzell (Dusty Rhoades); Jessica Myerson (Mrs. Hagen); George Paulsin (Frank Snyder); John Daniels (First Boy); Jimmy Brown (Second Boy).

Synopsis: Jamie is very upset when Ben tells him that he has to start school the next day. Jamie wants to go on the round-up and work on the ranch instead.

When Ben takes Jamie to school, he gets reprimanded by the teacher for being late. At recess, Jamie gets harassed by three boys who tease him about being an orphan. After school, everyone is so busy with the round-up to listen to Jamie, so he decides to go hunting.

Jamie continues to have troubles at school. He decides to take Ben's gold-plated rifle to impress Frank Snyder, one of the bullies. The only trouble is that on his way home, Jamie is bucked off his horse and the gold-plated rifle gets broken.

E378. *Top Hand* (January 17, 1971)

Credits: *Writers:* John Hawkins (Teleplay), Arthur Heinemann (Story). *Director:* William F. Claxton. *Producer:* Richard Collins. Executive *Producer:* David Dortort. **Starring:** Lorne Greene, Dan Blocker, Michael Landon. **Supporting Cast:** Ben Johnson (Kelly James); Roger Davis (Bert Yates); Walter Barnes (Weatherby); Jerry Gatlin (Quincy); Richard Farnsworth (Sourdough); Bill Clark (Jimpson); Ed Jauregui (Bones); Hal Burton (Smokey).

Synopsis: The Cartwrights are involved in a large cattle round-up with Weatherby and Haley. Ben introduces them to Kelly, his foreman, whom he wants to head the drive. But Weatherby wants *his* foreman, Bert Yates, for the job. Weatherby tells Ben that he fired Kelly because he drank and got into trouble with the law.

Kelly and some men round up a herd of wild horses. He then orders Yates and the men to stand guard all night, but they decide to go to Stillwater for drinks. That night a stallion stampedes the horses. The next morning, Kelly and Sourdough, the cook, ride to Stillwater to retrieve the drunk cowhands. Ben and Weatherby ride up just as Kelly carries Yates out of the saloon.

Note: Location shooting took place at Old Tucson, Arizona. The music played in the background was to become the theme for *Little House on the Prairie* and was written by David Rose.

E379. *A Deck of Aces* (January 31, 1971)

Credits: *Writer:* Stanley Roberts. *Director:* Lewis Allen. *Producer:* Richard Collins. *Executive Producer:* David Dortort. **Starring:** Lorne Greene, Dan Blocker, Michael Landon. **Supporting Cast:** Lorne Greene (Bradley Meredith); Alan Oppenheimer (Wentworth); Linda Gaye Scott (Dixie); Jeff Morris (Turk); Charles Dierkop (Nicholson); Tom Basham (Dan Fielding); Ray Teal (Sheriff Roy Coffee); Victor Sen Yung (Hop Sing); Jack Collins (Ned Blaine); Guy Wilkerson (Milt Jarvis); Stephen Coit (Mel Waters); Sam Javis (Telegraph Operator); Ralph James (First Poker Player); Bern Hoffman (Bartender); Lee McLaughlin (Second Poker Player); John Gilgreen (Desk Clerk #1)

Synopsis: Two men rob the stage, taking the mail bag to Bradley Meredith, who is an exact double for Ben. Meredith is looking for some money which is not there.

Later, Ben is discussing a lumber deal with the railroad but Dan Fielding, a forestry student, does not think that it would be a good idea and Ben agrees.

Meredith and the two men arrive in town and soon discover that he is an exact double for Ben. After some trouble in the Lucky Nugget Saloon, Roy urges Meredith over to the jail where they meet the major and Mr. Wentworth, a representative from the railroad. Bradley Meredith then agrees to the lumber deal provided he receive an additional $30,000 in cash.

E380. *The Desperado* (February 7, 1971)

Credits: *Writer:* George Lovell Hayes. *Director:* Phillip Leacock. *Producer:* Richard Collins. *Executive Producer:* David Dortort. **Starring:** Lorne Greene, Dan Blocker, Michael Landon. **Supporting Cast:** Lou Gossett, Jr. (Buck Walters); Marlene Clark (Liza Walters); Ramon Vieri (Solomon); Warren Vanders (Cal); Mike Mikler (Thad); George Dunn (Andy); Sandy Rosenthal (Davy).

Synopsis: A black couple Buck and Liza Walters, have been blamed for a murder and are trying to elude the law. The couple, Buck and Liza Walters, takes refuge on a hilltop. When Hoss comes along, the Walters fear he is after them and take him hostage.

Note: Location shooting took place at Old Tucson.

E381. *The Reluctant American* (February 14, 1971)

Credits: *Writer:* Stanley Roberts. *Director:* Phillip Leacock. *Producer:* Richard Collins. *Executive Producer:* David Dortort. **Starring:** Lorne Greene, Dan Blocker, Michael Landon. **Supporting Cast:** Daniel Massey (Leslie Harwood); Jill Haworth (Gillian Harwood); Daniel Kemp (Bolton); J. Pat O'Malley (Big Mac); Ronald Long (Gore Stanhope); Bing Russell (Deputy Clem Foster); Victor Sen Yung (Hop Sing); Mitch Vogel (Jamie); Sandra Ego (Haida); Pat Houtchens (Reverend Williams); Red Morgan (Stokely).

Synopsis: A neighboring ranch is not doing well financially and has been hit by cattle thieves. The English owner sends a representative and his expectant wife to turn profits around and discover who is stealing his cattle.

E382. *Shadow of a Hero* (February 21, 1971)

Credits: *Writers:* John Hawkins, B. W. Sandefur (Teleplay), Mel Goldberg (Story). *Director:* Leon Penn. *Producer:* Richard Collins. *Executive Producer:* David Dortort. **Starring:** Lorne Greene, Dan Blocker, Michael Landon. **Supporting Cast:** Lawrence Luckinbill (Freed); Dean Jagger (Gen. Ira Cloninger); John Randolph (Donavan); Linda Watkins (Mrs. Bertha Cloninger); Lane Bradford (Willis); Ruben Moreno (Sam Greybuck); Stuart Randall (Sheriff Baker); Steve Shemayme (Thomas Greybuck).

Synopsis: The Cartwrights are celebrating the birthday of General Ira Cloninger, an old friend of Ben's. Everyone goes to town for the celebration. Speeches are made and a statue is unveiled.

Freed, a reporter, arrives in town to get a story on the general and the Indian he killed the day before trying to steal horses. Freed convinces Joe to take him to Angel's Point to talk to Greybuck and his other son, Thomas. They then tell Freed and Joe that the horses belonged to them.

At the general's ranch, Ira gets up early and finds Greybuck and Thomas trying to steal two horses. In the ensuing gunfight, Ira is wounded but manages to kill Thomas.

Note: Location shooting took place at Vasquez Rocks.

E383. *The Silent Killer* (February 28, 1971)

Credits: *Writers:* John Hawkins (Teleplay), Edward DeBlasio (Story). *Director:* Leo Penn. *Producer:* Richard Collins. *Executive Producer:* David Dortort. **Starring:** Lorne Greene, Dan Blocker, Michael Landon. **Supporting Cast:** Mitch Vogel (Jamie); Meg Foster (Evangeline Woodtree); Louise Latham (Harriet Clinton); Harry Holcombe (Dr. Joshua Martin); Victor Sen Yung (Hop Sing); Ian Berger (Dr. Woodtree); Bing Russell (Deputy Clem Foster); Hal Burton (Barley Bates).

Synopsis: Dr. Woodtree and his wife have come from Ireland to Virginia City with plans of opening a hospital. As he comes from a small, little-known college, he believes people will not believe that he is a doctor, so he claims he is a Harvard graduate. Dr. Martin, who went to Harvard, has never heard of him and has him arrested as an impostor.

Mrs. Woodtree arrives at the Ponderosa to try and convince Dr. Martin and Ben that her husband is on the level. She is forced to stay when the Ponderosa becomes quarantined after an outbreak of influenza.

E384. *Terror at 2:00* (March 7, 1971)

Credits: *Writer:* Michael Landon. *Director:* Michael Landon. *Producer:* Richard Collins. *Executive Producer:* David Dortort. **Starring:** Lorne Greene, Dan Blocker, Michael Landon. **Supporting Cast:** Mitch Vogel (Jamie); Steve Ihnat (Gans); Dabbs Greer (Sam Dawson); Byron Mabe (Hunter); Bing Russell (Deputy Clem Foster); Chubby Johnson, Iron Eyes Cody, Helen Kleeb.

Synopsis: Ganz and two other men capture an Army wagon. They kill the two soldiers and take their cargo — a Gatling gun. Later, in Virginia City, Clem and Ben are getting ready for the signing of the Paiute peace treaty. Ben leaves to escort the Paiute chiefs.

Ganz and the two other men, posing as reporters, arrive on the stage and check into the hotel. After they set up the Gatling gun, the men go down on the street to get information.

Jamie is helping Sam Dawson, a newspaper publisher, who becomes suspicious of Ganz's man when he does not use film in his camera. He confronts Ganz in his hotel room and is taken hostage when he spots the gun. When Dawson does not return, Jamie sends Hoss to the hotel to look for him. He too is taken hostage.

E385. *The Stillness Within* (March 14, 1971)

Credits: *Writer:* Suzanne Clauser. *Director:* Michael Landon. *Producer:* Richard Collins. *Executive Producer:* David Dortort. **Starring:** Lorne Greene, Dan Blocker, Michael Landon. **Supporting Cast:** Mitch Vogel (Jamie); Jo Van Fleet (Miss Ellen Dobbs); Harry Holcombe (Doctor); Victor Sen Yung (Hop Sing); Jeannine Brown (Sally); Robert Noe (Ranch Hand).

Synopsis: Hoss and Joe are unloading nitroglycerin in a shack, and Joe is blinded when a cat knocks one of the bottles off of the shelf. A month later, Joe is still blind and the doctor says that it will take time for his sight to return. Later, Joe comes down for breakfast and is very sarcastic towards his father and brother. He agrees to go on a buggy ride with Jamie. While they are gone, Ellen Dobbs arrives from the Institute for the Blind in San Francisco. Ben and Hoss are surprised to see that she is blind. With their help she learns the layout of the house.

When Joe comes home, he tells Miss Dobbs that he does not want her there, but changes his mind after they talk. The next day she begins to teach Joe how to live with his blindness. Days later, Joe is playing a game of horseshoes when Miss Dobbs tells Ben that Joe will eventually have to face the fact that he might always be blind.

Note: This episode was filmed with the assistance of the Braille Institute of America, Inc.

E386. *A Time to Die* (March 21, 1971)

Credits: *Writer:* Don Ingalls. *Director:* Phillip Leacock. *Producer:* Richard Collins. *Executive Producer:* David Dortort. **Starring:** Lorne Greene, Dan Blocker, Michael Landon. **Supporting Cast:** Mitch Vogel (Jamie); Vera Miles (April Christopher); Henry Beckman (Dr. Phelps); Melissa Newman (Lori); Victor Sen Yung (Hop Sing); Rance Howard (Sam); Bing Russell (Deputy Clem Foster); Michael Clark (Perkins).

Synopsis: Jamie and April Christopher are collecting eggs when she is attacked and bitten by a wolf. The doctor tells Ben that he needs to know if the wolf was rabid, so Ben says he will track the animal down. Before Ben leaves, he asks the doctor not to tell April anything. Ben, Joe and Jamie track down the wolf, kill it and send the body away for testing.

The next day the house is being decorated for a party with April getting Ben and Jamie's help. When she becomes faint and almost falls, Ben takes her to the doctor, who orders her to get more rest. The doctor then tells Ben to watch her very closely for signs of rabies. On their way home, April tells Ben that she thinks that the wolf might be rabid.

E387. *Winter Kill* (March 28, 1971)

Credits: *Writers:* John Hawkins and Robert Pirosh (Teleplay). *Director:* William Wiard. *Producer:* Richard Collins. *Executive Producer:* David Dortort. **Starring:** Lorne Greene, Dan Blocker, Michael Landon. **Supporting Cast:** Mitch Vogel (Jamie); Glen Corbett (Howie Landis); Sheilah Wells (Marie Landis); Clifton James (Mr. Quarry); John Pickard (Griggs); Robert Knapp (Denman); Stuart Nisbet (Fred Tyson); Remo Pisani (Bartender); Troy Melton (Gorley).

Synopsis: Because of the brutal winter, the ranchers have been losing cattle. Ben has purchased a Montana steer he feels is the answer to their problem.

The Cattleman's Association is planning a party and Howie Landis, a neighboring foreman, says the ranch he works for will supply the needed beef. When his boss Mr. Quarry refuses to donate the steer, Howie must supply his own. Unknowingly, he shoots Ben's Montana steer. When Mr. Quarry finds out what happened, he is pleased because the bank will not give the ranchers the money they need to acquire the Montana beef and he can now get his neighbors' ranches cheaply. He tells Howie that he will see that he goes to prison if he does not tell Ben the steer succumbed due to the winter kill.

Note: Location shooting took place at Incline Village.

E388. *Kingdom of Fear* (April 4, 1971)

Credits: *Writer:* Michael Landon. *Director:* Joseph Pevney. *Producer:* Richard Collins. *Executive Producer:* David Dortort. **Starring:** Lorne Greene, Dan Blocker, Michael Landon. **Supporting Cast:** David Canary (Candy); Alfred Ryder (Judge); Luke Askew (Hatch); Richard Mulligan (Farley); Warren Finnerty (Second Gunman); Jay Jones (First Gunman); Charles Briles (Billy).

Synopsis: Hoss, Joe, Candy and Billy are camping when Ben rides in after selling a herd. They decide to head back through the high country to get Billy back earlier for his wedding. They are soon confronted by four armed men who take their guns and arrest them for trespassing. When Billy tries to protest, he is shot and killed. The Cartwrights and Candy are taken to a work camp where they are found guilty, placed in irons and sentenced to six months of hard labor.

All the next day they work with other men on a mine. That night, one of the guards talks to Ben about his bank draft of $22,000. In exchange for the money, he will bring back a posse when the judge sends him to Carson City for supplies. When the judge hears of the plan, the guard is killed. After another hard day on the chain gang, the Cartwrights devise a plan that might allow Joe to escape.

Note: Location shooting took place at Incline Village in 1967 but it was not aired until 1971.

E389. *An Earthquake Called Callahan* (April 11, 1971)

Credits: *Writer:* Preston Wood. *Director:* Herschel Daugherty. *Producer:* Richard Collins. *Executive Producer:* David Dortort. **Starring:** Lorne Greene, Dan Blocker, Michael Landon. **Supporting Cast:** Victor French (Tom Callahan); Sandy Duncan (Angeline); Lou Frizzell (Dusty Rhoades); Dub Taylor (Otto); Larry D. Mann (Alex Steiner); Ted Gehring (Marshal); Hal Baylor (Shad Willis); Roy Johnson (Barber); John Mitchum (Meyers); Beth Peters (Woman); Bing Russell (Deputy Clem Foster); Don Haggerty.

Synopsis: Dusty is trying to square a bet with Meyers but ends up in jail because Meyers claims that Dusty took the money by force. Joe decides to get the only witness, Callahan, to testify. Joe finally finds him about to engage in a prize fight with the local bouncer, Shad. When he tries talking to Callahan, Tom begins working the crowd, singing "Camptown Races." After the fight starts, Callahan is arrested for illegal prizefighting and fined $10. He is also ordered out of town.

When they leave town, Callahan refuses to go with Joe because he feels that Joe caused him to lose $150 in bet money. To help Dusty, Joe begins to follow Callahan from fight to fight.

Thirteenth Season
(September 19, 1971–April 2, 1972)

E390. *The Grand Swing* (September 19, 1971)
Credits: *Writers:* John and Ward Hawkins (Teleplay), William Koenig (Story). *Director:* William F. Claxton. *Producer:* Richard Collins. *Executive Producer:* David Dortort. **Starring:** Lorne Greene. Dan Blocker, Michael Landon. **Supporting Cast:** Mitch Vogel (Jamie); Charlotte Stewart (Betsy Rush); Med Flory (Clint Rush); Ted Gehring (Harlow); Ralph Moody (Tall Pony); Raymond Guth (Bill Cooper); Lane Bradford (Jake Rasko); Bill Shannon (Charlie Trapp); Mary Mayomi (White Squirrel); Duane Grey (Sheriff Snell); Chuck Bail (Kale).
Synopsis: Jamie sets out a wagon but disobeys Ben's orders by taking the mountain road instead of the longer, safer way. An accident kills one of the horses.
   Later, at the ranch, Ben orders Jamie to pack and he figures that he is being thrown out. He soon learns that he is leaving on a four-day pack trip with Ben. On their way around the Ponderosa, they run into cattle rustlers and miners. One day on the trail, riding through some beautiful scenery, they stop for a meal and discuss Jamie's punishment for disobedience.
Note: Filming took place at Incline Village and Old Tucson.

E391. *Fallen Woman* (September 26, 1971)
Credits: *Writer:* Ward Hawkins. *Director:* Lewis Allen. *Producer:* Richard Collins. *Executive Producer:* David Dortort. **Starring:** Lorne Greene, Dan Blocker, Michael Landon. **Supporting Cast:** Susan Tyrrell (Jill Conway); Arthur O'Connell (Dr. Hubert); Ford Rainey (Judge Simms); Lillian Field (Katie Tomlin); Johnny Lee (Petey Conway); Stuart Nisbet (Colter); Fletcher Allen (Becker); Victor Sen Yung (Hop Sing).
Synopsis: As Hoss testifies at Conway's trial, the defendant's wife screams that he is lying. After the judge sentences Conway to five years in prison, Mrs. Conway gives her son Petey to Hoss because she cannot care for him. Hoss brings Petey back to the Ponderosa.
   Hoss goes to see Mrs. Conway and finds her place a mess and her drinking. She does not seem to remember where her son is even when Hoss tells her. Judge Simms tells Hoss that Jill Conway is an unfit mother and he wants Hoss to consider adopting Petey.

E392. *Bushwacked!* (October 3, 1971)
Credits: *Writer:* Preston Wood. *Director:* William Wiard. *Producer:* Richard Collins. *Executive Producer:* David Dortort. **Starring:** Lorne Greene, Dan Blocker, Michael Landon. **Supporting Cast:** Evans Thornton (Flanders); Sandy Rosenthal (Steen); Keith Carradine (Ern); Victoria Thompson (Julia); Richard O'Brien (Griswold); Peggy McCay (Mrs. Griswold); David Huddleston (Doc Scully); Walter Barnes (Sheriff Truslow); Anthony Colti (Orv); Bill Stevens (Fenton).
Synopsis: Mr. Griswold and Ern hear shots and find a badly wounded Joe. They load him on a travois to take him back to the Griswold ranch. The Griswolds

take care of Joe by sending for the doctor. When the Cartwrights arrive at the ranch, Doc Scully informs them that he removed a bullet from Joe's leg, but is afraid to remove the bullet in Joe's back because of a high fever. With the help of Mr. Griswold, Ben and Hoss are determined to find out who shot Little Joe.

Note: Location shooting took place at Old Tucson in Tucson, Arizona.

E393. *Rock-A-Bye Hoss* (October 10, 1971)

Credits: *Writers:* Preston Wood (Teleplay), Robert Vincent Wright (Story). *Director:* Herschel Daugherty. *Producer:* Richard Collins. *Executive Producer:* David Dortort. **Starring:** Lorne Greene, Dan Blocker, Michael Landon. **Supporting Cast:** Mitch Vogel (Jamie); Victor Sen Yung (Hop Sing); Jack Manning (Henry Clagger); Patricia Harty (Cissy Porter); Edward Andrews (Bert); Ellen Moss (Elaine Summers); Darryl Sandeen (Mark Tait); Ivor Francis (Charlie); George Furth (Jim Pinder); Al Checco (Rufus); E. A. Sirianni (Lon Meecham); Remo Pisani (Joel Sawyer); Jan Burrell (Clara); Gillian Spencer (Edith); Helen Funai (Lem Toy); Joyce Perry (Rose Ann); Don Chuy (Matt Tait); Cindy Eilbacher (Cathie); Ralph James (Gambler).

Synopsis: The Virginia City Council votes to have a baby contest to raise money but they have to get judges. The first person they ask is Hoss. When he arrives back at the ranch, everybody seems to know about it. Hop Sing tries to sway his vote by showing him his second cousin.

Meanwhile, in town, Cissy is going around town boasting about her baby. When she goes to the dressmaker to have a baby dress made, she runs into Hoss and Jamie. Cissy tells the dressmaker to make the best baby dress available.

When Hoss gets home, he finds a lot of women there with their babies. Hoss and the other two judges soon find themselves pressured from all sides by people trying to influence their votes.

E394. *The Prisoners* (October 17, 1971)

Credits: *Writer:* Arthur Heinemann. *Director:* William F. Claxton. *Producer:* Richard Collins. *Executive Producer:* David Dortort. **Starring:** Lorne Greene, Dan Blocker, Michael Landon. **Supporting Cast:** Michael Witney (Hank Simmons); Morgan Woodward (Sheriff Clyde Moorehouse); Manuel Padilla (Pedro); Priscilla Garcia (Maria); Victor Sen Yung (Hop Sing); Bob Hoy (Yancy).

Synopsis: When Sheriff Clyde Moorehouse is killed, Joe is elected to see that his prisoner reaches jail. Joe finds he has his hands full as a friend of the culprit and two Mexican children are determined to see that Joe does not succeed.

Note: Location shooting took place at Los Padres National Forest.

E395. *Cassie* (October 24, 1971)

Credits: *Writer:* True Boardman. *Director:* Herschel Daugherty. *Producer:* Richard Collins. *Executive Producer:* David Dortort. **Starring:** Lorne Greene, Dan Blocker, Michael Landon. **Supporting Cast:** Mitch Vogel (Jamie); Jack Cassidy (Kevin O'Casey); Diane Baker (Mrs. Norma O'Casey); Lisa Gerrittison (Cassie O'Casey); Walker Edmiston (Auctioneer); Lindsay Workman (Kendall); Jen Arvan (Jensen); Elliot Lindsey (Larson); Harry Holcombe (Doc Martin).

Synopsis: Ben, Hoss and Jamie are at a horse auction where Hoss bids on and gets a stallion named Prince Omar for $800. Norma O'Casey plans on leaving her husband Kevin (the horse owner) because he is a con artist. He says that he will get the horse ranch that he has always promised but his daughter Cassie does not believe him any more. After Hoss pays Norma for the stallion, she and her daughter get a ride to Virginia City.

At the Ponderosa, Jamie and Cassie go riding. When they get back, Kevin O'Casey rides in to ask Ben directions. he also talks to his wife and daughter. He swears that he still loves them and wants to change but Cassie does not believe him. When Cassie goes to the barn to say goodbye to Prince Omar, she warns Hoss not to race Omar against her father's horse, Captain.

Note: Location shooting took place at Los Padres National Forest.

E396. *Don's Cry, My Son* (October 31, 1971)
Credits: *Writer:* Michael Landon. *Director:* Michael Landon. *Producer:* Richard Collins. *Executive Producer:* David Dortort. **Starring:** Lorne Greene, Dan Blocker. **Supporting Cast:** Richard Mulligan (Dr. Mark Sloan); Diana Shalet (Ruth Sloan); Dan Ferrone (Eli Johnson); Ann Whitsett (Annie Johnson); Bing Russell (Deputy Clem Foster).

Synopsis: Ben says good-bye to Dr. Mark Sloan and his expectant wife Ruthie. On their way home, the Sloans are met by a frantic Eli Johnson, whose wife Annie is in labor. As Dr. Sloan helps to deliver the Johnsons' baby, Ruthie goes home alone and goes into labor.

On a rainy day, Mark and Ruthie bury their infant son, Mark Jr. Ruthie screams at her husband, blaming him for the baby's death. Ben later calls on Mark, who assures him that everything is better but Ruth is resting. In reality, Ruthie is packing to leave him.

Dr. Sloan then goes to visit Annie Johnson, telling her to get more rest. As he goes to leave their house, he stops to see the baby, who starts crying. Mark picks up the baby and takes him home.

E397. *Face of Fear* (November 14, 1971)
Credits: *Writer:* Ken Pettus. *Director:* Chris Christenberry. *Producer:* Richard Collins. *Executive Producer:* David Dortort. **Starring:** Lorne Greene, Michael Landon. **Supporting Cast:** Mitch Vogel (Jamie); Bradford Dillman (Griff Bannon); Jewel Blanch (Neta); Bing Russell (Deputy Clem Foster); Lou Frizzell (Dusty Rhoades); Victor Sen Yung (Hop Sing); Chick Chandler (Garroway); Donald Moffatt (Thatcher); Athena Lorde (Miss Griggs); Tom Gillerman (Trumbull); Susan Joyce (Wilma).

Synopsis: Griff Bannon stumbles across Trumbull, who tells him that he has come into an inheritance. When Griff hits him over the head, he is seen by Neta. After she screams and runs away, Jamie discovers the body. When she is late from school, her father threatens her with a switch and sends her to her room. Later, when Jamie brings Joe and Ben back to see the body, they find it gone.

Meanwhile, Griff is in Virginia City at a lawyer's office, posing as Trumbull to claim the man's uncle's $42,000 estate. After the attorney tells Griff that it will take ten days to get the money, Griff says that he needs some cash. The attorney gives him Ben's name to get a job. Afterwards they head to the saloon where Griff spots Neta and her father.

E398. *Blind Hunch* (November 21, 1971)

Credits: *Writers:* John Hawkins (Teleplay), Robert Pirosh (Story and Teleplay). *Director:* Lewis Allen. *Producer:* Richard Collins. *Executive Producer:* David Dortort. **Starring:** Lorne Greene, Dan Blocker, Michael Landon. **Supporting Cast:** Mitch Vogel (Jamie); Rip Torn (Will Hewitt); Don Knight (Clayton); Loretta Leversee (Laurie Hewitt); Charles Maxwell (Keeley); James Chandler (McKay); Robert Ridgely (Bartender); Larry Ward (Deputy).

Synopsis: Jamie comes across Will Hewitt, who is looking for his brother's ranch but needs Jamie's help because he is blind. Jamie tells him that the Hewitts are at the Ponderosa but Will has come to visit his brother Sam's grave. When they arrive at the Ponderosa, Will asks his father and Joe how and where Sam died.

Will tells everyone that he has a job making harnesses. Julie and her father-in-law head for Carson City. Then Joe and Will talk to the law about the site of Sam's death. Joe takes Will to the saloon, where he talks to Keeley about Sam's body. Will tells everybody in the saloon that he will find and kill the person responsible.

E399. *The Iron Butterfly* (November 28, 1971)

Credits: *Writer:* Harold Swanton. *Director:* Leo Penn. *Producer:* Richard Collins. *Executive Producer:* David Dortort. **Starring:** Lorne Greene, Dan Blocker, Michael Landon. **Supporting Cast:** Mariette Hartley (Lola Fairmont); Mills Watson (Fontaine); Ray Teal (Sheriff Roy Coffee); Stefan Gierasch (Grady); Allen Garfield (Charlie); Jack Collins (Mayor); John McCann (Bennett); Red Currie (Driver); Peter Whitney.

Synopsis: Sheriff Roy Coffee tells the major that Carson, the senator's son, will be escorting Miss Lola Fairmont to town. When Hoss hears that the bridge is out, he rides over to take a look. He decides to build a foot bridge but the stage arrives before he finishes. After wading half way across, he introduces himself. Trying to make sure that Lola gets to town, he carries her trunk and then Lola across the creek. On the way to Virginia City, they stop at the Juniper Creek Station. They are met by Bennett, who demands that Lola ride with him. When she refuses, there is a struggle and Hoss is hit over the head. To keep Hoss from being hit again, Lola shoots and kills Bennett. Hoss then takes her gun, deciding to take the blame himself.

E400. *The Rattlesnake Brigade* (December 5, 1971)

Credits: *Writer:* Gordon T. Dawson. *Director:* William Wiard. *Producer:* Richard Collins. *Executive Producer:* David Dortort. **Starring:** Lorne Greene, Dan Blocker, Michael Landon. **Supporting Cast:** Mitch Vogel (Jamie); Neville Brand (Doyle); David Sheiner (Fancher); Steven Darden (Price); Don Keefer (Tobias Temple); Chris Beaumont (Lester); Richard Yniquez (Ricardo); Michele Nicholas (Judith); Joaquin Martinez (Chavez); Larry Finley (Centro); Biff Maynard (Suggins); Scott Walker (Amber); Bobby Hall (Goatman); John Quade (Tallman); Eleanor Berry (Emily Fancher); Bing Russell (Deputy Clem Foster).

Synopsis: A prison wagon comes to Virginia City on a Sunday. Samuel Thatcher comes out of the church to talk to the prison guards. While Fancher and the guards are inside the Sheriff's office, Mrs. Fancher follows her husband but is grabbed by the prisoners. Jamie tries to rescue her, but he too is grabbed. Ben wants the two released but the five prisoners demand to be unchained and let go. When Jamie is placed in the wagon, two other boys and a girl are also taken and put in the wagon. Doyle, the gang's leader, mounts Ben's horse, warning the people not to follow.

Later, at the Ponderosa, Ben, the fathers and Fancher are having a meeting. Doyle and another man show up, telling Ben that he wants $10,000 for each child. When Fancher shoots one of the outlaws, Doyle demands more money and will keep one child to insure their 24 hours head start.

E401. *Easy Come, Easy Go* (December 12, 1971)

Credits: *Writer:* Jack B. Sowards. *Director:* Joseph Pevney. *Producer:* Richard Collins. *Executive Producer:* David Dortort. **Starring:** Lorne Greene, Dan Blocker, Michael Landon. **Supporting Cast:** Victor Sen Yung (Hop Sing); Dub Taylor (Luke Calhoun); Ann Prentiss (Meena); Lyman Ward (Pete); Dan Scot (Dave); Channing Polluck (Carter); Robert Lussier (Garvey); Lou Frizzell (Dusty Rhoades).

Synopsis: When Luke bumps into Hoss and Joe, he asks for work because he lost all of his money. He gets hired after his daughter Meena comes along. Luke also promises that he will not be any trouble. At the ranch, Luke settles into the bunkhouse. Dusty tells him that there is no poker playing, so Luke decides to play checkers for 50¢ a game. He wins all of the games and takes all of the men's money.

The next morning Hop Sing is upset because Meena is helping in the kitchen. Not only do the Cartwrights have to deal with the Calhouns but they must also obtain a right of way that is needed desperately.

E402. *A Home for Jamie* (December 19, 1971)

Credits: *Writer:* Jean Holloway. *Director:* Leo Penn. *Producer:* Richard Collins. *Executive Producer:* David Dortort. **Starring:** Lorne Greene, Dan Blocker, Michael Landon. **Supporting Cast:** Mitch Vogel (Jamie); Will Geer (Paris Callahan); Ford Rainey (Judge Taylor); Victor Sen Yung (Hop Sing); Robert Karnes (Jess McLean); Phyllis Love (Miss Griggs); Robert Carradine (Phinney McClean).

Synopsis: While at school, Jamie has been dreaming about becoming a Cartwright and has written the name on a piece of paper to see how it looks. When Jess McLean snatches the paper, Jamie hits him and a fight ensues.

When Ben goes to see Jamie's teacher, Miss Griggs, she shows him what Jamie has written. Ben has made plans to adopt the boy but according to the law he must be sure no relatives exist. He has sent letters around the country but so far no one has responded. As the adoption is about to take place, Paris Callahan, Jamie's maternal grandfather, arrives, intending to take his grandson back to Boston.

E403. *Warbonnet* (December 26, 1971)

Credits: *Writers:* Robert Blood, Arthur Heineman, Charles Goodwin. *Director:* Arthur H. Nadel. *Producer:* Richard Collins. *Executive Producer:* David

Dortort. **Starring:** Lorne Greene, Dan Blocker, Michael Landon. **Supporting Cast:** Forrest Tucker (Frank Ryan); Chief Dan George (Red Cloud); Linda Crystal (Teresa); Patrick Adiarte (Swift Eagle); Russ Martin (Sheriff); Lee DeBroux (Elias); M. Emmet Walsh (Mattheson); John Wheeler (Hill).

Synopsis: When a Paiute boy, Swift Eagle, finds Joe unconscious in the desert, he takes his gun. Chief Red Cloud, the boy's grandfather, sees the weapon and instructs his grandson to see that the rightful owner gets his property back. Red Cloud nurses Joe back to health. After Joe feels better, Swift Eagle escorts him to town. Frank Ryan, an important resident, treats Joe well.

Red Cloud comes to town to reclaim his warbonnet. When Frank Ryan refuses to let him have it, the chief wants to fight him to the death for it.

Note: Location shooting took place at Bronson Canyon.

E404. *The Lonely Man* (January 2, 1972)

Credits: *Writer:* John Hawkins. *Director:* William F. Claxton. *Producer:* Richard Collins. *Executive Producer:* David Dortort. **Starring:** Lorne Greene, Dan Blocker, Michael Landon. **Supporting Cast:** Victor Sen Yung (Hop Sing); Kelly Jean Peters (Missy); Peter Hobbs (Judge Hill); Harry Willis (Sand); Bing Russell (Deputy Clem Foster).

Synopsis: Hop Sing has three weeks off and plans to spend it looking for gold. He meets a bewildered young lady, Missy, who at first keeps her distance but finally trusts Hop Sing. Hop Sing wants to take Missy as his bride but learns that the law prohibits interracial marriages.

E405. *Second Sight* (January 9, 1972)

Credits: *Writers:* Arthur Weingarten, Suzanne Clauser. *Director:* Lewis Allen. *Producer:* Richard Collins. *Executive Producer:* David Dortort. **Starring:** Lorne Greene, Dan Blocker, Michael Landon. **Supporting Cast:** Mitch Vogel (Jamie); Victor Sen Yung (Hop Sing); Joan Hackett (Judith); James Booth (Jess); Larry Ward (Harve); Bob Gravage (Station Master); Don Adkins (Stableman).

Synopsis: When Jamie does not come home, Joe and Hoss set out looking for him. Because there is so much ground to cover, Hoss goes to Judith Coleman, who has the power to envision things, but is turned away.

E406. *The Saddle Stiff* (January 16, 1972)

Credits: *Writers:* John Hawkins (Teleplay), Samuel A. Peoples (Story and Teleplay). *Director:* William F. Claxton. *Producer:* John Hawkins. *Executive Producer:* David Dortort. **Starring:** Lorne Greene, Dan Blocker, Michael Landon. **Supporting Cast:** Buddy Ebsen (Cactus Murphy); Don Collier (Paul Walker); Charles H. Gray (Cass Breckenridge); Jay MacIntosh (Sally); Dick Farnsworth (Tate); Henry Wills (Yokum); Hal Riddle (Tiller); Mitch Vogel (Jamie).

Synopsis: Ben is told by Cactus Murphy that he might break something if he continues to be bucked off horses. Ben later fires Cactus, who tells him that Ben cannot cut it any more. He also bets Ben that he could not get a job as "Ben Brown" and keep it for a month. Deciding to take the bet, Ben rides to a line camp where he changes clothes and horses. That night, three men come into his camp, demanding that he leave Breckenridge land. Later Ben walks his injured horse into the Walker Ranch and is given supper. After being hired, Mr. Walker explains to Ben about the range war with the Ponderosa and its owner Ben Cartwright.

Note: Location shooting took place at the Golden Oak Ranch.

E407. *Frenzy* (January 30, 1972)

Credits: *Writers:* Preston Wood (Teleplay), Karl Tunberg (Story). *Director:* Lewis Allen. *Producer:* Richard Collins. *Executive Producer:* David Dortort. **Starring:** Lorne Greene, Dan Blocker, Michael Landon. **Supporting Cast:** Kathleen Widdoes (Anna); Michael Pataki (Nick); Jason Karpf (Sandor); Bing Russell (Deputy Clem Foster); Emile Meyer (Cherokee); Troy Melton (Slim); Dave Cass (Deputy).

Synopsis: Anna and Nicholas are having an argument with him braking up the furniture. Sandor runs out the door. When he runs into Ben, who takes the boy home. Ben finds that nothing seems to be wrong so he leaves.

Later, Anna goes to Ben for help. She wants her husband locked up because she believes that he is going crazy.

When Anna sends Nicholas into Virginia City for supplies, he gets into a fight with two men in the saloon and spends the night in jail. While he is there, Anna and Sandor run away to a friend's house. Nicholas escapes from jail and begins terrorizing Ben, Anna and Sandor.

E408. *The Customs of the Country* (February 6, 1972)

Credits: *Writer:* Joseph Bonaduce. *Director:* Joseph Pevney. *Producer:* Richard Collins. *Executive Producer:* David Dortort. **Starring:** Lorne Greene, Dan Blocker, Michael Landon. **Supporting Cast:** Alfonso Arau (Simon); Alan Oppenheimer (Ernesto); Pilar Saurat (Ines); David Renard (Padre); Maria Grimm (Leonora); Mike de Anda (Blacksmith); Annette Cardona (Carmen); Mallia Saint Duval (Raquel); George Cervera (Rafael); Tony deCosta (Jose).

Synopsis: The Cartwrights head for Agua Santos. Ben tells Joe to go to town and hire some men. When he does not return, Hoss is sent to look for him. He finds Joe in jail, charged with removing his hat while in church. When Hoss tries to help his brother, he winds up in trouble himself.

Note: Dan Blocker provided a voice-over.

E409. *Shanklin* (February 13, 1972)

Credits: *Writer:* William Kelley. *Director:* Leo Penn. *Producer:* Richard Collins. *Executive Producer:* David Dortort. **Starring:** Lorne Greene, Dan Blocker, Michael Landon. **Supporting Cast:** Charles Cioffi (Shanklin); Woodrow Parfrey (Dr. Ingram); Karl Lukas (Irons); Rance Howard (Bosardus); Clark Gordon (Beasley); Victor Sen Yung (Hop Sing); Michael Clark (Brackney); Scott Walker (Grange); Dehl Berti (Ritter); Denny Hall (Beecher); Mitch Vogel (Jamie); Bing Russell (Deputy Clem Foster); E. J. Andre (Yost); Dan McGovern (Till); Sam Jarvis (McLaughlin); Bill Beckett (Asquith); Eddie Little Sky (Gaviotta); Byron Morrow (Whitlock); Shannon Christie (Mary Elizabeth).

Synopsis: A Confederate officer, Shanklin, leads a group of his men into the Ponderosa and, in a fight, Hoss is shot in the leg. Later, as the men are looting the house, Ben rides in. Shanklin tells him that he wants $25,000 in gold and silver coins. Shanklin plans to sign loan papers so that Ben can be repaid by the Confederate States of America.

Ben rides to town to get the money. Meanwhile, Dr. Ingram is escorted to the ranch, where he wants to amputate Hoss' leg because the femoral artery is lacerated.

E410. *Search in Limbo* (February 20, 1972)

Credits: *Writer:* Don Ingalls. *Director:* Leon Penn. *Producer:* Richard Collins. *Executive Producer:* David Dortort. **Starring:** Lorne Greene, Dan Blocker, Michael Landon. **Supporting Cast:** Mitch Vogel (Jamie); Albert Salmi (Sheriff); Pamela Payton-Wright (Zeena); Lucille Benson (Mrs. Melody); Gerald Hiken (Dr. Penner); Lawrence Montaigne (Sid Langley); Kenneth Tobey (Notary); Chubby Johnson (Old Man); Lee McLaughlin (Clerk).

Synopsis: Ben arrives in Mountain City to make a land deal with Sid Langley, whom he has hated for a long time. He plans to return later to sign the paperwork but collapses in his hotel room as a result of a concussion.

After he awakens, Ben goes back to Langley's office, where he finds out that the man was shot and robbed the night before. When Ben goes around asking questions, an eyewitness claims that she saw him going into Langley's office at noon and again at midnight the day before. Ben has lost an entire day, and evidence is building against him.

E411. *He Was Only Seven* (March 5, 1972)

Credits: *Writer:* Michael Landon. *Director:* Michael Landon. *Producer:* Richard Collins. *Executive Producer:* David Dortort. **Starring:** Lorne Greene (Voice-over in Introduction), Dan Blocker (Voice-over in Introduction Only), Michael Landon. **Supporting Cast:** Mitch Vogel (Jamie); Roscoe Lee Browne (Joshua Morgan); William Watson (Zack); Robert Doyle (Clem); Edward Crawford (Jonah); Jeff Morris (Hal); Joseph Perry (Sheriff Tyson); Dick Farnsworth (Troy); Claudia Bryar (Martha); Sean Kelly (Billy); Harry Holcombe (Dr. Martin); Beverly Carter (Alice); Napoleon Whiting (Bert); Bing Russell (Deputy Clem Foster).

Synopsis: Joe and Jamie discover seven-year-old Jonah begging for coins on the streets of Virginia City. Jamie takes the boy back to his crippled grandfather, Joshua Morgan. He then explains to the boy that he was wrong for doing what he did. Jamie takes the boy to the bank to put the coins in the poor box.

Joe is in the bank when the Springer gang enters to commit a robbery. Just as Jonah and Jamie enter the bank, Zack Springer turns and fires, killing Jonah. When the law is unable to cross the county line, Joe, Joshua and Jamie ride out to track down the outlaws.

E412. *The Younger Brothers' Younger Brother* (March 12, 1972)

Credits: *Writer:* Michael Landon. *Director:* Michael Landon. *Producer:* Richard Collins. *Executive Producer:* David Dortort. **Starring:** Lorne Greene, Dan Blocker, Michael Landon. **Supporting Cast:** Mitch Vogel (Jamie); Strother Martin (Cole Younger); Chuck McCann (Lonnie Younger); Ted Gehring (Bart Younger); Henry

Jones (Sheriff); Doc Severinsen (Hotel Manager); Ken Lynch (Warden); James Jeter (Stage Guard); John Steadman (Sam); William Challee (Pa Younger).

Synopsis: After serving 12 years in prison, the inept Younger Brothers are freed. They attempt to rob a stage but bungle the job, and the driver is about to take them into custody. Hoss, believing the *driver* is a thief, comes to their aid. When he does so, Hoss is arrested because he is considered to be the group's younger brother.

The brothers help Hoss escape but kidnap him for money. after Ben hands over the money, he and Joe try to get things squared away. When Ben and Joe say they are related to Hoss, the sheriff assumes they belong to the Younger gang and take them into custody too.

E413. *A Place to Hide* (March 19, 1972)

Credits: *Writers:* William P. Gordon (Teleplay and Story), Ward Hawkins (Story). *Director:* Herschel Daugherty. *Producer:* Richard Collins. *Executive Producer:* David Dortort. **Starring:** Lorne Greene, Dan Blocker, Michael Landon. **Supporting Cast:** Mitch Vogel (Jamie); Suzzane Pleshette (Rose); Hurd Hatfield (Major Donahue); Jon Sypher (Ransom); Jodie Foster (Bluebird); John Perak (McLeod); Edward Knight (Sgt. Brown); Wayne Sutherlin (Thibideaux); Stephen Coit (Plummer); Biff Manard (Harsfield); Richard Ryal (Boardman); Reid Smith (Wells); Robert Ridgely (Liscomb); Jay Jones (Twohy); Victor Sen Yung (Hop Sing); Ray Teal (Sheriff Roy Coffee).

Synopsis: Hoss is waiting for the stage. Finding Rose Beckett and her daughter Bluebird, he gets their luggage while Rose sends a telegram. Major Donahue is given a copy of the telegram. He then tells Roy Coffee that they are looking for Cody Ransom, a wanted outlaw. Donahue also feels that Ben might be involved.

Roy visits Ben, telling him what has been happening. Before leaving, he gives Rose a telegram. She then tells Ben that she really is Mrs. Cody Ransom and that she has not seen her husband for six years. After she shows Ben letters from Cody, he agrees to help. As the Cartwrights make plans, they realize that the ranch is being watched by Major Donahue's men.

Note: Location shooting took place at Franklin Lake. This episode was the final one shot by Dan Blocker and Ray Teal, although not the last one aired.

E414. *A Visit to Upright* (March 26, 1972)

Credits: *Writer:* Joseph Bonaduce. *Director:* William Wiard. *Producer:* Richard Collins. *Executive Producer:* David Dortort. **Starring:** Dan Blocker, Michael Landon. **Supporting Cast:** Alan Oppenheimer (Dalrymple); Loretta Swit (Ellen Sue); Richard Kiley (Dan Bellington); Andrew Duggan (Delando); Edmond O'Brien (Burtelson); Gene Andrusko (Eric); Anne Seymour.

Synopsis: Joe, Hoss and Jamie head for Upright. The Cartwright brothers plan to claim their shares in a saloon and put them up for sale. When they arrive, they mistake a thriving saloon for the run-down one they own. Joe and Hoss believe something is up when offers come in far above the value of the property. They discover that the previous owner, who has died, secreted something of great value on the grounds.

E415. *One Ace Too Many* (April 2, 1972)

Credits: *Writer:* Stanley Roberts. *Director:* Lewis Allen. *Producer:* Richard Collins. *Executive Producer:* David Dortort. **Starring:** Lorne Greene, Dan Blocker, Michael Landon. **Supporting Cast:** Mitch Vogel (Jamie); Victor Sen Yung (Hop Sing); Lorne Greene (Bradley Meredith); Greg Mullavey (Jordan); Kate Jackson (Ellen); Ray Teal (Sheriff Roy Coffee); Harry Holcombe (Dr. Martin); William Mims (Williams); Jack Collins (Mayor Harlow); Bill Zuckert (Mack Fowler); Harlan Warde (Osgood); Eddie Ryder (Clerk); Gene Dynarski (Wheeler); Dave Cass (Deputy Coghlan); Richard X. Slattery (Henderson).

Synopsis: The Cartwrights are packing for Carson City, leaving Hop Sing in charge. Unbeknownst to the Cartwrights, they are being watched by Bradley Meredith and Jordan.

That night, Meredith and his partner, posing as Ben and a doctor, ride into Virginia City. Jordan tells Roy Coffee that his patient wants to see his lawyer out at the ranch because Ben is dying. At the ranch, Meredith asks his lawyer, George, about changing his will in order to build schools and hospitals for the town. To raise the money, the land and stock will have to be sold. After Roy promises to bring qualified buyers the next morning. Meredith tells Jordan that they will only stay 24 hours.

Fourteenth Season
(September 12, 1972–January 16, 1973)

E416. *Forever* (September 12, 1972)

Credits: *Writer:* Michael Landon. *Director:* Michael Landon. *Producer:* Richard Collins. *Executive Producer:* David Dortort. **Starring:** Lorne Greene, Michael Landon. **Supporting Cast:** David Canary (Candy); Mitch Vogel (Jamie); Bonnie Bedelia (Alice Harper); Andy Robinson (John Harper); Larry Golden (Damion); Roy Jenson (Hanley); Lee deBroux (Kater); Robert Doyle (Sloan); Luana Anders (Julie); Jay Jones (Carver); Ivan Bonar (Minister); Joan Lemmo (Gloria); Helen Kleeb (Miss Grayson); John J. Fox (Jack); William Challee (Jake); Toby Anderson (Hotel Clerk).

Synopsis: John Harper and his sister Alice arrive in town. John has an addiction to drinking and gambling. When Alice discovers her brother has lost their savings, she wants him out of her life.

Alice and Joe fall in love, and he begins building a home for the future Mrs. Cartwright. The couple are married. Several months later, she tells Joe she is pregnant. Joe heads for the Ponderosa to pick up materials to add onto the house for the forthcoming baby. While he is gone, John shows up with Damien and his gang. When Alice will not pay off her brother's debt to Damien, the outlaw has them murdered and the house set on fire. Joe and Candy come back to see the place ablaze and John and Alice dead. Distraught, Joe and Candy set out to find those responsible.

Note: Location shooting took place at Stanislans National Forest and Burbank Studios. The original theme music returned after a two seasons. This episode was originally conceived for Dan Blocker.

E417. *Heritage of Anger* (September 19, 1972)

Credits: *Writer:* Don Ingalls. *Director:* Nick Webster. *Producer:* Richard Collins. *Executive Producer:* David Dortort. **Starring:** Lorne Greene, Michael Landon. **Supporting Cast:** David Canary (Candy); Mitch Vogel (Jamie); Robert Lansing (John Dundee); Fionnuala Flanagan (Elizabeth); Len Lesser (Francher); Roydon Clark (Bartlett); Warren Kemmerling (Sheriff Garth); Ed Long (Anders); Harry Harvey (Sangster); Henry Oliver (Telegrapher).

Synopsis: A friend of Ben's was sent to prison as a result of an unjust trial. Now, after serving a five-year sentence, he is set free. His plans to resume his life are thwarted when his wife does not want anything to do with him. His business associates want to destroy him so they do not have to split the money they earned while he was imprisoned.

Note: Location shooting took place at Senora, California.

E418. *The Initiation* (September 26, 1972)

Credits: *Writer:* Douglas Day Stewart. *Director:* Alf Kjellin. *Producer:* Richard Collins. *Executive Producer:* David Dortort. **Starring:** Lorne Greene, Michael Landon. **Supporting Cast:** Mitch Vogel (Jamie); Victor Sen Yung (Hop Sing); Ronnie Howard (Ted Hoag); William Bramley (Mueller); Ed Bakey (Lumis); Nichlas Beauvy (Ron); James Chandler (George Adams); Sean Kelly (Josh Adams); Biff Elliot (Harley Lewis); Jeff Smart (Sonny Mueller); Jimmy Van Patten (Corky Sibley); Pitt Herbert (Mr. Cropin); John Zaremba (Judge); Al Barker, Jr. (Billy Newton); Ivor Barry (Preacher); Sam Jarvis (Bailiff); William Challee (Stableman); Harry Basch (Prosecutor); Jim Moore (Ray); Phyllis Love (Miss Grigs); Ray Teal (Sheriff Roy Coffee).

Synopsis: Jamie befriends Ted Hoag. After he is fired from his store job, Ted goes to live in the livery stable. Jamie tries to get his friend a job at the Ponderosa.

That night, Jamie and Sonny Mueller are waiting to be initiated into the Vigilante Raiders, a club run by Ted. Each boy is blindfolded and tied down. Jamie volunteers to go first. When Sonny changes his mind, begins to panic and tragically dies.

The next day at school, two posse men ride up looking for Sonny because he did not come home the night before. The club members decide to keep quiet about what happened. A drifter named Lomis is charged with murder.

Note: Location shooting took place at Bronson Canyon.

E419. *Riot* (October 3, 1972)

Credits: *Writer:* Robert Pirosh. *Director:* Lewis Allen. *Producer:* Richard Collins. *Executive Producer:* David Dortort. **Starring:** Lorne Greene, Michael Landon. **Supporting Cast:** David Canary (Candy); Denver Pyle (Warden); Aldo Ray (Mr. Heiser); Tim Matheson (Griff); Marco St. John (Plank); Gregory Walcott (Will Cooper); Barney Phillips (Asa Calhoun); Bob Delegall (Willie Noon); William Patterson (Mr. Vannerman); Noble Willingham (Mr. Kirby); William Bryant (Governor); Biff Maynard (Scoggins); Morton Lewis (Idaho); Red Morgan (Kelly); Charles Wagenheim (Donovan); Nolan Leary (Old Charlie).

Synopsis: Ben is asked to be a member of the Governor's Investigating Committee. He and two other inspectors take a tour of the Nevada State Prison.

Meanwhile, Candy and Joe are in a saloon near the prison when the alarm sounds, signifying trouble. When they get there, they find out that the inmates have rioted, taking the three inspectors hostage. After a list of demands is delivered to the warden, Ben promises the men that changes will be made. The leader, Will Cooper, is killed by another con, who is bent on revenge against Ben.

Note: Nevada State Prison is located near Carson City. It still serves as a prison today.

E420. *New Man* (October 10, 1972)

Credits: *Writer:* Jack B. Sowards. *Director:* Leo Penn. *Producer:* Richard Collins. *Executive Producer:* David Dortort. **Starring:** Lorne Greene, Michael Landon. **Supporting Cast:** David Canary (Candy); Tim Matheson (Griff); Mitch Vogel (Jamie); Bing Russell (Deputy Clem Foster); Ronny Cox (Lucas); Charles Dierkop (Shorty); Jeff Morris (Tulsa); Carol Vogel (Amy); Chuck Hayward (Guard); Jac Flanders (Clerk); Bill Clark (Man).

Synopsis: Ben, Candy and Joe pick up Griff at the Nevada State Prison and ride back to the Ponderosa. On the way, they stop at a store to buy Griff some new clothes. He claims that the only thing missing is the number on the back of his shirt. That night at the ranch, Ben tells him that he has an opportunity but all Griff wants to do is leave. He eventually decides to stay. Candy takes Griff to the bunkhouse where the hands cut the strings on his bunk. When the men laugh, Griff gets into a fight.

The next morning, Clem rides into the Ponderosa to tell Ben about a robbery in town. Since Griff is an ex-convict, Clem suspects him of the crime.

E421. *Ambush at Rio Lobo* (October 24, 1972)

Credits: *Writer:* Joel Murcott. *Director:* Nicholas Colasanto. *Producer:* Richard Collins. *Executive Producer:* David Dortort. **Starring:** Lorne Greene, Michael Landon. **Supporting Cast:** Mitch Vogel (Jamie); Sian Barbara Allen (Teresa Burnside); James Olson (Vance); Murray MacLeod (Zachariah Burnside); Albert Salmi (Stretch); Douglas Dirkson (Gabe).

Synopsis: Ben tells Joe and Jamie that he will meet them in Rio Lobo, Ben first heads to the old Bartlett Ranch. When he arrives there, he feeds the stock and finds pregnant Teresa Burnside unconscious on the floor. She tells Ben that her husband Zachariah went to town for a doctor but she is worried because she knows something has happened to him.

Zachariah is on his way to town to get the doctor when he is taken by three outlaws, Vance, Stretch and Gabe. They bring him to their cabin, where they threaten him because he had testified against them three years ago.

Later the outlaws make plans for a robbery which include using Teresa to stop the stage.

E422. *The Twenty-Sixth Grave* (October 31, 1972)

Credits: *Writer:* Stanley Roberts. *Director:* Leo Penn. *Producer:* Richard Collins. *Executive Producer:* David Dortort. **Starring:** Lorne Greene, Michael Landon. **Supporting Cast:** Mitch Vogel (Jamie); David Canary (Candy); Bing

Russell (Deputy Clem Foster); Ken Howard (Samuel Clemens); Dana Elcar (Merrick); Phil Kenneally (McNabb); Walter Burke (Campbell); Staats Cotsworth (Judge Hale); Richard Bull (Goodman); Stacy Keach, Sr. (Prentiss); Wayne Heffley (Bert); Harlan Warde (Osgood); Curt Conway (Caldwell); Arthur Peterson (Martin); Britt Leach (Postal Clerk); Victor Izay (Foreman); Owen Bush (Station Agent); Sean Kelly (Petey).

Synopsis: The publisher of *The Territorial Enterprise* departs on the stage to buy a new press, leaving Sam Clemens in charge of the paper. After Ben reads an article in the paper about corruption, someone throws a rock through the window of the newspaper office.

In the saloon, Sam tells Ben about claim-jumping and five unmarked graves in the cemetery. Clem sues Sam for $10,000 for libel. On the day of the trial, Sam is put on the witness stand but he will not reveal his source. The jury then decides to award Mr. Prentiss the $10,000. They also order Sam to print an immediate retraction. Prentiss warns Ben that the next time, there will not be any lawsuit.

E423. *Stallion* (November 14, 1972)

Credits: *Writers:* Jack B. Sowards (Teleplay), Mort Zarkoff, Juanita Bartlett (Story). *Director:* E. W. Swackhammer. *Producer:* Richard Collins. *Executive Producer:* David Dortort. **Starring:** Lorne Greene, Michael Landon. **Supporting Cast:** David Canary (Candy); Tim Matheson (Griff); Clu Gulager (Billy Brenner); Mitzi Hoag (Alice Brenner); Vincent Van Patten (Tommy Brenner); Lew Brown (Seth); Michael Green (Travis); Wallace Chadwell (Doctor).

Synopsis: After Billy, Alice and Tommy Brenner move into a mountain cabin, Alice nags Billy about getting a job. He rides down to the railroad and finds that they are not hiring, but is told maybe Ben might be. Ben and Joe arrive at the train where Ben gives his son a black stallion for his birthday. After Joe saddles the stallion, he rides off along with his father.

Later Billy comes home saying he has a plan. Alice gives him her wedding ring to sell. The next morning Billy heads to the Ponderosa looking for work. When there is not any, he and Joe get into a small fight. Joe orders him off the Ponderosa. Billy later sneaks into the barn, stealing the stallion. When Joe comes in, he gets hit over the head.

Note: Location shooting took place in the Sierra foothills close to Senora, California.

E424. *The Hidden Enemy* (November 28, 1972)

Credits: *Writers:* Stanley Roberts (Story and Teleplay), Jack B. Sowards (Teleplay). *Director:* Alf Kjellin. *Producer:* Richard Collins. *Executive Producer:* David Dortort. **Starring:** Lorne Greene, Michael Landon. **Supporting Cast:** David Canary (Candy); Tim Matheson (Griff); Bing Russell (Deputy Clem Foster); Mike Farrell (Dr. Will Agar); Melissa Murphy (Nancy Agar); David Huddleston (Myles Johnson); Gary Busey (Henry Johnson); Harry Holcombe (Dr. Martin); Mons Kjellin (Chris Agar); Ayn Roymen (Nurse Evie Parker); Russell Thorson (Judge Phelps); Clifford Davi (Defense Lawyer); Jason Wingreen (Prosecutor).

Synopsis: The hands are teasing Griff by hiding his saddle at the top of the barn. When he goes up to get it, he falls, breaking his arm. Dr. Agar arrives to set Griff's arm. Henry Johnson is looking for the doctor to help his injured brother. Ben decides to drive the doctor back to town. After they get there, nurse Evie Parker cannot stop the bleeding. Agar disappears into the back office. When he returns, he seems dazed. Agar then tells Myles Johnson that his other son just died.

The next day, Ben talks to Agar about what happened to the Johnson boy. When Mrs. Agar tells Will that it has started all over again, he gets mad, storming into the back office. Ben runs into Myles who is looking for his son Henry. It seems that Henry is out to kill Agar.

Note: This episode was filmed with the assistance of the U. S. Bureau of Narcotics.

E425. *The Sound of Sadness* (December 5, 1972)

Credits: *Writer:* Michael Landon. *Director:* Michael Landon. *Producer:* Richard Collins. *Executive Producer:* David Dortort. **Starring:** Lorne Greene, Michael Landon. **Supporting Cast:** Tim Matheson (Griff); Jack Albertson (Johnathan May); Timothy Marshall (Robbie); Dan Ferrone (Mr. Holcombe); John Randolph (Dawson); Carol Lawson (Mrs. Holcombe); Marty McCall (Tim); Irene Tedrow (Miss Gaines); Jerry Harper (Silas); Harry Holcombe (Dr. Martin); Penelope Gillette (Mrs. Farmer); Bing Russell (Deputy Clem Foster).

Synopsis: Tim and Robbie are orphans who decide to leave the orphanage when the Holcombes only want to adopt the older boy, Tim. They do not want Robbie because he will not talk. The boys soon find their way to the house of Johnathan May, who takes them in. That night Johnathan goes to see Clem about the two boys. He finds Mr. Dawson, the head of the orphanage, there reporting them missing, but he says nothing.

The next day, Griff spots the two boys at May's house but he too decides to keep quiet. When Johnathan asks Mr. Dawson about adoption, he is told that he needs a working farm. Johnathan then goes home and works all day plowing but he collapses because of his age.

E426. *The Bucket Dog* (December 19, 1972)

Credits: *Writer:* John Hawkins. *Director:* William F. Claxton. *Producer:* Richard Collins. *Executive Producer:* David Dortort. **Starring:** Lorne Greene, Michael Landon. **Supporting Cast:** Mitch Vogel (Jamie); David Canary (Candy); Tim Matheson (Griff); Victor Sen Yung (Hop Sing); William Sylvester (Horace Kingston); John Zaremba (Judge Wilcox); Don Knight (Tim Riley); Ivan Bonar (Minister); Don Harris (Turner); Bing Russell (Deputy Clem Foster).

Synopsis: Jamie is walking along a stream where he meets Riley and his Irish setter, April. Riley wants to sell the dog for $100 and a lot of love but finally settles for $20. After they agree to meet the same time tomorrow, Jamie goes home to count his money. The next day, Jamie brings April back to the Ponderosa where she seems to get into a lot of trouble. One day in town, April is spotted by Horace Kingston, Riley's boss. Kingston claims that April is his dog. April is locked up in the jail while Justice Wilcox tries to decide who owns the dog.

Note: Location shooting took place at the Golden Oak Ranch.

E427. *First Love* (December 26, 1972)

Credits: *Writer:* Richard Collins. *Director:* Leo Penn. *Producer:* Richard Collins. *Executive Producer:* David Dortort. **Starring:** Lorne Greene, Michael Landon. **Supporting Cast:** Mitch Vogel (Jamie); Tim Matheson (Griff); Pamela Franklin (Mrs. Kelly Edwards); Jordon Rhoades (Dan Edwards); Lisa Eilbacher (Eloise); David Doremus (Gene); Steve Benedict (Henry); Michael Blake (Lew); Dennis Robertson (Ranch Hand); Eileen Ryan (Emily); Victor Sen Yung (Hop Sing).

Synopsis: A new teacher, Dan Edwards, arrives in town with his wife Kelly. The students dislike him because of his belittling tactics. He also uses the same tactics with his wife.

When Jamie offers to help around the Edwards farm and teaches Kelly to ride, he becomes very infatuated with her.

Note: Location shooting took place at the Golden Oak Ranch.

E428. *The Witness* (January 2, 1973)

Credits: *Writers:* Joel Murcott (Teleplay), Arthur Heineman (Teleplay and Story). *Director:* Lewis Allen. *Producer:* Richard Collins. *Executive Producer:* David Dortort. **Starring:** Lorne Greene, Michael Landon. **Supporting Cast:** David Canary (Candy); Tim Matheson (Griff); Sally Kemp (Kate Fallon); Stephen Nathan (Oscar Hamner); Byron Mabe (Lewis Gardner); William Wintersole (Schulte); Shirley O'Hara (Ella Peterson); Ross Elliott (Harvey Walters); David McLean (Sheriff Touhy).

Synopsis: Candy and Kate Fallon are having dinner in Sudsville during a bad rainstorm. As they go to their rooms, Candy is knocked over the head. After he comes to, he realizes that the envelope he was carrying for Ben is missing.

Meanwhile, in Hawthorne, Mrs. Peterson is getting $3,000 from the bank to repay a debt owed Ben. She tells Harvey Walters, the banker, that Ben's man is waiting for her at the house. As the town clock strikes 12, Candy and Kate ride into town. After Mrs. Peterson gets back to her house, she is pushed down and the money taken. She then grabs her chest and dies. When Candy arrives in her house, he is found stooping over the body by Mr. Walters. The sheriff questions Candy. After the sheriff checks out the hotel for Kate and does not find her there, he arrests Candy for Mrs. Peterson's murder.

E429. *The Marriage of Theodora Duffy* (January 9, 1973)

Credits: *Writer:* Ward Hawkins. *Director:* William F. Claxton. *Producer:* Richard Collins. *Executive Producer:* David Dortort. **Starring:** Lorne Greene, Michael Landon. **Supporting Cast:** David Canary (Candy); Tim Matheson (Griff); Mitch Vogel (Jamie); Victor Sen Yung (Hop Sing); Karen Carlson (Duffy); Ramon Bieri (Jonas Holt); Robert Yuro (Dody Hendrickson); Richard Eastham (Stanton); Rayford Barnes (Shaw); Willard Sage (Marshal Taylor); Bill Clark (Bates); Jerry Gatlin (Barnes); Hal Burton (Read).

Synopsis: When Griff comes into the ranch house, he is confronted by Duffy, who wants to know why he ran out on her after their marriage. After the Cartwrights help the couple load a wagon, they set up housekeeping in a small ranch house.

Duffy reminds Griff that this is only a game. Later as he knocks down a fence and steals cattle, two men are watching him.

That night, when four men break into their house, Jonas Holt demands that Griff work for him. He wants Griff to bring him supplies and direct other men to his camp. After Jonas leaves, Griff demands to know what is going on.

E430. *The Hunter* (January 16, 1973)

Credits: *Writer:* Michael Landon. *Director:* Michael Landon. *Producer:* Richard Collins. *Executive Producer:* David Dortort. **Starring:** Lorne Greene, Michael Landon. **Supporting Cast:** Mitch Vogel (Jamie); Tom Skerritt (Tanner); Phillip Avenetti (The Mexican); Peter O'Crotty (Old Man); Grizzley Green (Harve); Hal Burton (Man).

Synopsis: Joe rides to Fort Lowell to complete a horse deal with the Army. Meanwhile Tanner, an escaped mental patient, kills a man, taking his gear. Later, Tanner rides into Joe's camp and spends the night. The next morning, Joe wakes up to find Tanner gone along with his horse and gear. Tanner wants to prove a point, that he is a good tracker and that Joe will kill for food and a horse. So with a four-hour head start, Joe begins running.

Television Movies

*1. *Bonanza: The Next Generation* (April 20, 1988)

Credits: *Writer:* Paul Savage (Screenplay). *Director:* William F. Claxton. *Producer:* David Dortort. **Cast:** John Ireland (Aaron Cartwright); Barbara Anderson (Annabelle Cartwright); Michael Landon, Jr. (Benji Cartwright); Brian A. Smith (Josh Cartwright); Peter Mark Richman (Clel Dunston); Gillian Greene (Jennie Sills); Robert Fuller (Charlie Poke); John Amos (Mr. Mack); Robert Hoy, Rex Lynn, Jack Lilley, Gary Reed, Richard Bergman, Jerry Gatlin, Robert Jauregui, Jeff Meyer, Dabbs Greer (Mr. Sills, the Banker); William Benedict, Kevin Hagen, Jeffrey Boudov, David Q. Combs, Patrick Joseph O'Neil, Bill Anderson, Laurie Rude, Joyce Anderson, Michael Dellafemina, Clayton Staggs, Lee McLaughlin, Lloyd Dewayne Collins, Sr., Buddy Wright, John D. "Zeke" Ward, Jeannette Tedler Knight, William James Anderson, Barbara Gulling-Goff, Dean Calkins, John E. O'Leary, Jennifer Watson, Robert J. "R. J." Fuller.

Synopsis: After the death of his brother Ben, Aaron Cartwright, a former sea captain, assumes control of the Ponderosa along with other Cartwrights Annabelle, Benji (Little Joe's wife and son) and Josh (Hoss' son).

A mining company has acquired property next to the ranch. They seek access to the land by crossing the Ponderosa. Aaron grants them permission, assuming they are just there to test the land. He feels that the company would provide much-needed employment and help the economy of Virginia City.

When Aaron finds the company is using hydraulic mining, he no longer permits them access to the Ponderosa. To get even with the Cartwrights, the devious supervisor attempts to sway the residents of Virginia City to his side.

Note: Filming began on October 24, 1987. Shooting took place at Incline

Village and Spooner Lake State Park. The Story occurred around 1905 with Little Joe missing in the Spanish-American War. Gillian Greene is the daughter of Lorne Greene.

*2. *Bonanza: The Return* (November 28, 1993)

Credits: *Writers:* Michael McGreevey (Screenplay), Michael Landon, Jr., Tom Brinson, Michael McGreevey (Story). *Director:* Jerry Jameson. *Producers:* Gary Wohllenben, Kent McCray, David Dortort. **Cast:** Ben Johnson (Bronc Evans); Alistair McDougall (Adam "A. C." Cartwright, Jr.); Brian Leckner (Josh Cartwright); Michael Landon, Jr. (Benji Cartwright); Emily Warfield (Sarah Cartwright); Jack Elam (Buckshot Patterson); Dirk Blocker (Finster); Dean Stockwell (Former Ranch Hand/Tycoon); Linda Grey (Laredo Simmons); David Sage, Stewart Moss, John Ingle, Richard Roundtree (Jacob Briscoe); Charles Gunning (Slacker).

Synopsis: The Cartwright cousins gather at the Ponderosa with foreman Bronc Evans and cook Buckshot Patterson to thwart the attempts of an ex-ranch hand turned tycoon, who not only wants revenge but has plans to use the land for strip mining.

Note: Filming took place at the Ponderosa Ranch and Lake Tahoe. Flashbacks from the series were shown. The story was set around 1905 and brought in Adam's son A. C. Dirk Blocker (Dan's son) played a reporter.

A nostalgic retrospect, *Back to the Ponderosa*, was broadcast prior to the airing of the movie and centered around the series episode "The Legacy." It was hosted by Michael Landon, Jr., and Dirk Blocker.

3. *Bonanza: Under Attack* (January 15, 1995)

Credits: *Writer:* Denne Bart Petticlerc (Screenplay). *Director:* Mark Tinker. *Producer:* Kent McCray. *Executive Producer:* Thomas Sarnoff. **Cast:** Ben Johnson (Bronc Evans); Michael Landon, Jr. (Benji Cartwright); Brian Leckner (Josh Cartwright); Leonard Nimoy (Frank James); Dennis Farina (Charley Siringo); Richard Roundtree (Jacob); Jeff Phillips (Adam "A. C." Cartwright, Jr.); Emily Warfield (Sarah Cartwright); Jack Elam (Buckshot Patterson); James Karen (Mr. Stewart); Sonja Satra (Annie Stewart); Dirk Blocker (Finster); J. Bordon Indice (Black Jack); Ted Markland (Cole); Bill Yarbrough (Lucas); Kenny Call (Mears); Don Collier (U. S. Marshal); Eric Lawson (Morgan); Cal Bartlett (Sheriff); Biff Manard (Luke).

Synopsis: Relatives of the Cartwrights, who have inherited the Ponderosa, come to the aid of repentant outlaw Frank James, who is wounded while being chased by traitorous Pinkerton agents.

Note: Location filming took place in Nevada.

PART III

The Stars

In this chapter, the major cast is presented from father to youngest son. For each, a biographical essay is given first for the character, then the actor portraying the part. The actor's media credits for film, radio, television, theater and personal appearances are listed following their biography.

Lorne Greene

BEN CARTWRIGHT

Ben Cartwright, the strong and affluent patriarch of the Ponderosa, *was born in 1825 to a shop owner in Jonns Common, Massachusetts.*

At 20, he sailed from Boston aboard the Barkentine Wanderer. *Under the command of Captain Stoddard, he became the ship's third officer. A year or so later, he had a disagreement with Stoddard and became a seaman on the* Hartisbeake. *Next he served as a second mate aboard the* Pandora *and served as first officer under Captain Emil Dawson. When the* Pandora *headed for New Orleans, Ben left the ship and booked passage on the* Coastal Lugger Manhasset, *sailing back to Boston.*

Ben had had feelings for Elizabeth Eloise (Stoddard's daughter) before sailing on the Wanderer *but felt it inappropriate to express them to her as he did not know how she felt about him. He was now delighted to learn she returned his love. After receiving the blessings of Captain and Mrs. Morgan Stoddard, they were married in May by Reverend Wickstrom at the Middlesex Congregational Church.*

After a three-week honeymoon, they moved into a small house on Baldwin Lane. Stoddard offered to finance the Cartwright Chandlery. Ben had a good business sense and would manage the shop. They would split the profits fifty-fifty.

In 1842, Elizabeth gave birth to a son, Adam Milton Cartwright, and died shortly after. She was the Stoddards' only child.

When Ben and Adam left Boston, he got a job on the ship Gaynell Malone, *which hauled freight and sometimes passengers. After a boiler exploded, they headed to Galesburg, Illinois. At first, Ben was employed by McWhorter to work in his tavern. McWhorter fired him when he became jealous over Ben's attention to his fiancée, Inger. Gunnar and Inger Borgstrom then hired Ben to work in their mercantile. Inger, born in May 1822, was a tall, large-boned woman in her twenties. She and Ben fell in love and were married. In 1848, Inger gave birth to Eric Haas. Adam called him Hoss and the name stuck. Deciding to follow Ben's dream to go to California, the Cartwrights headed to Saint Joe and joined up with the Johnston wagon train. They were attacked by Indians near Denver, and Inger was killed.*

Upon seeing the beautiful Nevada territory, Ben and his sons left the California-bound wagon train and began building his dream ranch with his own hands, sweat and the help of his sons. He named it the Ponderosa after the stately Ponderosa pines. He hired Jean Pierre DeMarigny as his foreman. Jean was killed saving Ben's life and was buried on a ridge over-looking Lake Tahoe. Ben traveled to New Orleans to tell Pierre's widow Marie of her husband's death. Marie was a small, slim, pretty, dark-haired, dark-eyed woman with a temper. By the time they returned to Nevada, they had fallen in love and were married in Genoa by Justice of the Peace Lawrence Jessup.

Under Marie's guidance, a new ranch house began construction. In 1857, she gave birth to Ben's third son, Joseph Burns. By this time, Hop Sing had become the Cartwright cook, houseboy and handyman. In 1859, Marie was accidentally killed after falling from her horse and was buried near Jean Pierre.

With hard work, mining investments and the sale of timber (he believed in conservation), the Ponderosa grew into a 1000-square-mile ranch.

Ben was a tall man with snow-white hair, dark eyes and black eye-brows. He had a sense of humor and enjoyed friends and conversation. He was there to help out his friends. He had a sense of duty and was one of the volunteers who rode with Major Ormsby during the Pyramid Lake War.

He was also a well-respected and important member of the community. He was a stock holder in the High Sierra Shortline, a member of the committee of the theater, the honorary chief of the Gold Hill Volunteers, a board member of the Golden State Marine Bank and Trust and a member of the Washoe Club. He even was nominated for territorial governor.

As a father, Ben was stern but loving. His sons were the most important things in his life. The Ponderosa was to be his legacy to them. Ben died in 1903 and was buried on the ranch he loved.

Lorne Greene was born on February 12, 1915, in Ottawa, Ontario to Russian-Jewish immigrants Daniel and Dora Greene. He became an only child when his older brother died as an infant. He had a good relationship with his parents. His mother was one of 12 children. His father, a respected member of the community, was stern yet gentle. Lorne later recalled that his dad "didn't have to punish; all he had to do was look ... he thought things through."[1] Daniel earned his living in his leather shop where he made orthopedic shoes and boots, thus affording his family a comfortable living. Lorne was named after his father's first customer, Lorne MacKenzie.

His parents were interested in the theater and their passion rubbed off on Lorne. He went to high school at Lisgar Collegiate Institute. While there, his French teacher was responsible for his first stage role as one of two deaf characters in *Les Deux Sourds*. "I was more interested in basketball at the time," Greene recalled, "but I did it and I got hooked."[2]

After high school, Lorne enrolled in Queen's University (1933-1937) in Kingston, Ontario, majoring in chemical engineering. The theater once again beckoned. As there was no drama major, Lorne switched to languages (French and German), thus giving him more time to devote to the Drama Guild. His first leading role was in *The Shining Hour* and he would go on to act and direct in many other productions.

After graduating with a B. A. in 1937, he went to the Neighborhood Playhouse in New York under a fellowship. He studied with San-

Lorne Greene. (Authors' collection.)

ford Meiser and with the Martha Graham School of Contemporary Dance, which helped him with stage movement. Dennis Weaver also attended the playhouse.

The British Empire went to war in 1938, and during the war Greene flew for the Royal Canadian Air Force.

In 1939, Greene returned to Canada. There were no professional theaters in which to pursue his craft. Steve Brodie gave him an audition and he went to work for an ad agency, earning a weekly salary of $10 as a program supervisor. He began in Ottawa and met Alan McFee, the present chief announcer. Within three months, he was transferred to Toronto with an increase in salary to $25. He became the chief newscaster for the Canadian Broadcasting Corporation (1940-1943) and earned $50,000 a year doing the national news. A Winnipeg newspaper gave him the title "the voice of doom" during the Battle of Britain because he reported bad news. One night he was reporting good news in connection with the Battle of Libya and was chewed out for editorializing when he prefaced the broadcast by telling listeners he had some good news for a change. He was delighted when listeners sent him letters thanking him for the editorial comments. He did several *Voice of America* broadcasts for NBC and the U. S. aimed at nations controlled by the Nazis.

In 1940, he married Rita Hands. In 1941, he worked on a series of John Grierson film documentaries and narrated a film on Winston Churchill that received an Academy Award.

By 1942, Lorne Greene was known as the "Voice of Canada" and won NBC's Top Announcing Award (the only Canadian to be so honored). In 1943, he went to Hollywood to do 25 15-minute radio shows to help raise money for war bonds in Canada.

In 1944, when the CBC requested that earnings from narration be returned, Greene quit. He went to work for Jack Kent Cooke on station C Key in Toronto where he did a newscast twice a day. He became co-founder of the Jupiter Theatre in Toronto. He directed or acted in some 50 shows as part of a repertory group.

In 1945, Lorne and Rita became parents with the birth of twins Charles and Belinda Susan.

Greene founded the Academy of Radio Arts in 1946. Students addressed him as Dean Greene and were trained in the fundamentals of broadcasting in the areas of writing, producing and announcing. Over 400 students graduated from the Academy, among them Leslie Nielsen. The two men became friends. Lorne served as academic director, performed on 15 weekly radio shows, lectured at the university and produced for theater and radio.

"I was determined to use as much of me as possible for as long as I live.

... I keep seeking things both in my acting and my everyday life that will stretch what abilities I have."[3]

In 1950, Greene organized Canada's first television clinic. He invented a stopwatch that ran backwards from 60 to zero. His discovery was the result of taking a standard watch apart. He felt the watch would be beneficial to radio announcers so they would know how much time was left in their broadcast. In the spring of 1953, he flew to New York to demonstrate his invention to NBC executives. Rita stayed in Canada as she had little interest in show business. They had grown apart and would divorce in 1960. (She would later remarry.) While in New York, Lorne ran into Canadian producer Fletcher Markle. Markle had been a teacher in Greene's Academy. He was producing *Studio One* and hired Lorne to play a conductor in "Rendezvous." Felix Jackson hired him to play a tough policeman in George Orwell's *1984*. The experience hooked Greene and he closed his Academy.

Next he appeared in the 1953 Broadway production of the Lindsay-Crouse play *The Prescott Proposals*, playing a radio journalist opposite Katharine Cornell. Greene came to the attention of Hollywood and was offered the role of Apostle Peter in *The Silver Chalice* (1954) starring Paul Newman (in his first film). Greene would make a number of films including *Tight Spot* (1955), *Autumn Leaves* (1956), *Peyton Place* (1957) and *The Buccaneer* (1958).

In the summer of 1955, he returned to Canada and appeared as the Prince of Morocco in *The Merchant of Venice* and Brutus in *Julius Caesar*. He returned to Broadway to do *Speaking of Murder* (1956) and would tour in Jose Ferrer's *Edwin Booth* (1958).

In 1955, Greene was scheduled to star opposite Claire Bloom in the Billy Rose-Joseph Mankiewicz production *Maiden Voyage*, written by Paul Osborne. When Miss Bloom suddenly returned to England, Osborne shelved the project. Producer Kermit Bloomgraden offered Lorne the father role in *Look Homeward Angel*, in 1957, but replaced him with British actor Hugh Griffin.

In 1956, Daniel Greene died from surgery complications. "It was a small stupid accident," Greene recalled, "which never should have happened."[4]

Greene enjoyed doing movies and television more than theater. He did a few drama shows but it was his role in a 1959 episode of TV's *Wagon Train* that got him noticed by producer David Dortort. Dortort saw in him the qualities he was looking for in the character Ben Cartwright and offered him the part of the patriarch on NBC's *Bonanza*. He needed to learn to ride and took two lessons in Palm Springs, then continued to practice. At the time, there were 35 Westerns on the air. The show did poorly at the beginning. Because RCA owned NBC and were using the show (filmed in color) to push the sales of color televisions, the show was not canceled.

Lorne was instrumental in helping *Bonanza* succeed by threatening to quit, in 1961, if his character was not changed form the Bible-quoting man who was over-protective of his Ponderosa and threatened to shoot anyone coming onto his property. He also wanted a warmer relationship with his TV sons. He based the character of Ben on his father. He recalled, "At first, Ben was not a very nice person.... I worked to have him made over into a warm person, a strong man, but one with a sense of humor, a human being. I think I succeeded."[5] He represented a father figure for many fans. Chevrolet was the sponsor of *Bonanza* and was responsible for having the series moved from Saturday to Sunday night in its third season. Its popularity climbed and fans included President Johnson and Queen Elizabeth. Friend Leslie Nielsen said of Greene, "Lorne cares deeply about everything he does. He has great ability and he never has stopped using it to make a better show."[6]

Greene married Nancy Ann Deale on December 28, 1961. She was born in 1933 and was from Bethlehem, Pennsylvania, and Brooklyn. Her mother had been an Olympic swimmer and had won many meets. Nancy and Lorne had known each other for three years prior to marrying. At first they argued over acting, philosophy and politics. When they started talking, they realized they did not really disagree that much. Lorne described Nancy as an "extraordinary bright, talented individual that it would have been wicked to try and change her in any way."[7] Nancy decided to give up her acting career (billed as Lisa Cummings) as they both felt that two careers might cause problems geographically as well as emotionally. After a couple of years, Nancy did not miss acting but needed something to take its place, so she became involved with the Equal Rights Amendment. It took a little time to bring Lorne around to her way of thinking. Nancy said that her husband was "one of the best kind ... always has been and I knew he would before we were married ... he is powerful, intelligent, and a gentle man."[8]

When Queen Elizabeth visited Canada, Greene hosted the Royal Command Performance. He also emceed a TV tribute on President John F. Kennedy after his assassination.

RCA decided to take advantage of the popularity of *Bonanza* and its stars by releasing the album *Ponderosa Party Time* (1962) and *Christmas on the Ponderosa* (1963). Pernell Roberts and Dan Blocker each released an album and Michael Landon a few singles, but it was Lorne Greene who had the biggest output. It was on the album *Welcome to the Ponderosa,* that hit the music charts on November 28, 1964, and peaked at 35, that Greene recorded the song "Ringo." It was during the period when the Beatles were big in the U. S. Many thought the song was about the Beatle, Ringo. In reality, it concerned a real badman who reformed and who was portrayed by Gregory Peck in the film *The Gunfighter* (1950). The song hit the music charts on October 31, 1964, and became a number one hit for Greene (in the U.S.) and would earn him a gold record. It peaked at 22 in England. Some 50,000 orders for "Ringo" were placed before the song was even released. Greene had his own publishing company and purchased the rights to "Ringo" with plans of producing a film. He was named father of the year in the spring of 1964.

Lorne seldom talked about his first marriage out of respect for Nancy but stayed close to his twins. Linda married Robert Bennett, a TV producer, in 1966, and they lived in Santa Monica. Son Charles was an MIT graduate. In 1966, Greene sang the theme song in the film *Waco*, starring Howard Keel.

Greene offered advice to his TV sons Dan Blocker and Michael Landon. He was like a father to Michael. Lorne, Dan and Michael went together on several land deals. A typical day for Greene was rising at six and reporting to the set at 7:15. He returned home for dinner around 7:00 P.M. and stayed up until midnight, reading or talking with Nancy. He reflected on *Bonanza*, "Look, nobody claims that every script we do is great. If we get eight or ten good ones out of 34 in a year, that's a lot of good theater that there would not be without *Bonanza*."[9]

During *Bonanza*, he did variety shows, narrated TV specials, worked in films and made personal appearances at fairs, rodeos, supper clubs and holiday parades. Many of the personal appearances were done with Dan and Michael. Appearing as Ben, Greene spoofed his TV sons. Michael North was the agent who booked personal appearances for Lorne, Dan and Michael. Jay Ellen was his business manager. In 1967, Lorne, Dan Blocker and Michael Landon went into partnership with NBC and Joyce and Bill Anderson to start the Ponderosa Ranch at Incline Village, Nevada. It became a successful venture, drawing millions of visitors a year.

Nancy and Lorne became parents with the birth of Gillian Donna on January 6, 1968. She was born at Cedars of Lebanon Hospital. Gillian was one month premature. Although Lorne and Nancy tried to hide their concern, they had been worried about the birth due to Nancy's age. Lorne also became a grandfather that year when daughter Linda gave birth to Stacey. The family enjoyed charades and Gillian learned to do pantomime and play bridge. Lorne had fun watching his daughter grow up and spent more time with her than he had with his older children.

Greene co-owned Greene-Lee in Chatsworth, California. He and his partner Lee McLaughlin had 20 race horses. Their racing colors were purple and gold. Two of his favorite horses were Nancy's Protest (named after his wife) and Little Gillian (after his daughter). He liked tennis, keeping up with current events, walking, swimming and reading Housman, Keats, Shelley and Shakespeare. His taste in music included classical. He did some composing for his private pleasure and played some piano and guitar. He received praise from Omar Sharif (an international bridge master), who claimed Greene was one of the best bridge players in show business. Nancy and Lorne often played bridge with the Blockers, with whom they often socialized. Greene also enjoyed the outdoors—fishing, hunting, riding and golfing (he played in the low 80s).

Nancy, an artist and designer, helped decorate a replica of the Ponderosa they had built in Mesa, Arizona, as a getaway home. She also painted; the El Merahor Gallery, in Palm Springs, asked to show her work. Nancy was the speakers' chairman for the National Women's Political Causes in Southern California. The N.W.P.C. prepared women to enter politics.

At four, Gillian was swimming, riding and doing some French ballet. Her pony was kept at a stable at Woodland Hills, which was near Stacey. The two often rode and played together. Gillian spoke Spanish to her nurse Mary.

In 1968, Greene was bringing in nearly $32,000 an episode and $3,000,000 with his other projects. He owned apartment houses, real estate developments and land throughout California, including Malibu Beach property that stretched a half-mile and was valued at $2,000,000. He had a potato-packing plant in Oregon. In addition to his Ponderosa property in Arizona, he had a ranch in Central California, a summer home in Long Island and a 22-room home in the Brentwood section of West Los Angeles which was decorated in the modern and Spanish style. He was a partner in a traveling Ponderosa Ranch and a stockholder in a chain of Bonanza Steak Houses. He received a medal "Order of Canada" on October 28, 1969, from Governor General Roland Michener for his outstanding service to Canada.

On his many years on the show, Greene reflected, "After all these years, there are times when I'm fed up with Ben and Bonanza.... We all wake up wishing we didn't have to do what we do.... Basically I enjoy what I do. I rather suspect, when I leave the show, I'll miss it. After all, I spend more time with my *Bonanza* family than I do with my real family."[10] He had no plans to leave the show until his contract was up in 1970–71. He wanted to do more singing and dancing—perhaps a Broadway musical and a good movie.

Over the years, Lorne Greene stayed in touch with Queen's University and received an honorary doctorate in 1971.

Raising Gillian kept Nancy busy but as their daughter began to grow, Nancy enrolled in UCLA to study Chinese and Russian. She also got involved with local and national campaigns. Hubert Humphrey and the Greenes were friends and Nancy became a Humphrey delegate for the 1972 Democratic Convention and served on the policy committee of the National Women's Political Council. "Her involvement has made her happier," Lorne realized. "I've had a few moments of guilt because Nancy did have to give up something in order for us to have a good marriage. It doesn't seem quite right. What man ever gave up his career for marriage?"[11]

On a Friday night in September 1972, Lorne and Nancy were having dinner at Madame Wu's in West Los Angeles when he experienced chest pains and collapsed. He was rushed to St. John's Hospital in Santa Monica. Nancy's doctor Reox Kennamer transferred Lorne to Century City Hospital's coronary unit. Confusing reports as to his ailment surfaced but on Monday, the official account was a gastrointestinal upset which accompanied a mild disorder of the heartbeat. The Friday before, he had taped *Dinah* with hostess Dinah Shore. They had talked about acupuncture that he found helpful in curing back pain that had kept him from sleeping and sitting. They also discussed the fact that everyone on the show missed Dan Blocker, who had passed away in May 1972 from a blood clot that resulted from gall bladder surgery. The Greenes had been staying with friends in Baltimore, Maryland, when Lorne talked to his manservant, who told him to call his agent at the Blocker home. When he received no answer, he contacted his secretary Pat Evans, who told him that Blocker had died. The Greenes immediately flew home. *Bonanza* was canceled in January 1973 due to low ratings. The show had difficulty filling the void left by Blocker's death.

Greene could have taken a well-deserved break as he certainly did not need the money. "I'm a compulsive worker," he explained.[12] He turned down two Broadway musicals, feeling they were not very good. He also did not want to move his family to New York. He could have decided to do a yearly movie or a few for TV but instead he signed to do another series, *Griff* (1973–74), just a month after leaving *Bonanza*. He would play a private eye who came out of retirement to solve the murder of his son. To research his role, he observed the Footprinters, who were men who had reached the pinnacle of their law enforcement careers. The series was short-lived due in part to fans finding it hard to see Greene in a different role. He made no excuses for the show's demise. "I gave *Griff* all I had, but obviously it was not enough."[13] There had been a writers' strike and the show was forced to go on despite not being ready. Greene had gone to Israel and upon his return the show's concept had been changed entirely.

In 1974, Greene played Ava Gardner's father in the film *Earthquake*. A small tremor occurred on the first day of shooting. The process of Sensurround was used to add realism to the vibrations of the earthquake.

The IRS reported that Greene had claimed to have formed two partnerships and acquired the distributed motion pictures and claimed an investment tax credit and depreciation. The IRS disallowed such a claim, saying, "It has not been established that the partnership's activities were engaged in for profit or had economic significance other than the avoidance of the tax."[14] Lorne went on to narrate the animal series *Last of the Wild* (1974–1979), based on the German show *Animal Lexicon*, shot by Ivan Tors, who joined his show. Sir Laurence Olivier was the first choice as series host but Greene got the job.

Greene believed in ESP, which persuaded him to sign for the role of Commander Adama in *Battlestar Galactica* (1978–1979). He went on to play an arson investigator in *Code Red* (1981–1982) and do Alpo dog commercials. He made two appearances with his TV sons, the first in the season premiere of *Vegas* (1978) with Pernell Roberts, the second with Michael Landon in *Highway to Heaven* (1985).

His next series was *Lorne Greene's New Wilderness* (1982–1986). "I've been interested and concerned with wildlife for a heck of a long time," Greene said.[15] He was vice-chairman of the American Wild Horse Protection Association and honorary chairman of the Wildlife Federation. He received the Congressional Medal for Outstanding Contributions to American Agriculture. He wrote a book entitled *The Lorne Greene Book of Remarkable Animals* in 1980 for Simon and Schuster.

Greene had been experiencing 60 percent loss of hearing for about six years and tried to deny his need for a hearing aid but finally came to terms with his problem. "I've had a hearing loss for over six years. But at first I refused to admit it.... What was happening was that it was becoming increasingly more difficult ... to understand what people were saying."[16]

"When are you going to admit it," Nancy demanded, "and when are you going to do something about it?"[17] She made him an appointment and within ten days he was wearing a hearing aid. He attributed his hearing loss to several unexpected explosions during World War II service and to gunshots during his 14 years on *Bonanza*.

On February 15, 1985, Lorne Greene was honored with a star on the Hollywood Walk of Fame near the TAV Celebrity Center at 1555 Vine Street (West) for television as Ben Cartwright on *Bonanza*. In March 1985, he entered Santa Monica Hospital to undergo a three-and-a-half hour operation to remove cancer and his prostrate gland. He had trouble breathing while recovering from the surgery. His lungs were checked for a blood clot but tests proved negative.

Lorne Greene had dreamed of returning to *Bonanza* and was scheduled to start filming *Bonanza: The Next Generation* in September 1987. In June 1987, while filming an Alpo commercial, he was experiencing pain but hid it while the cameras rolled. He went to the doctors complaining of severe abdominal pains on August 19, 1987, and was immediately admitted to St. John's Hospital in Santa Monica for stomach surgery for a bleeding ulcer. After the operation, a hospital spokesman reported, "Mr. Greene is in fair condition and is resting comfortably in the intensive care unit."[18]

"He's looking better and better each time we see him. I'm not a doctor," said Nancy, "but I'm hopeful that he'll be out of the hospital soon."[19] Roseanne Lawrence, a spokesperson from *Lorne Greene's New Wilderness*, reported, "Lorne is expected to remain in the intensive care unit for about a week before being moved to a regular unit, where he will likely stay for an additional week or two."[20] Greene would have to alter his diet, eating bland foods and a number of small meals in order to ease the work of the stomach and intestines.

Six days following surgery, he was still in intensive care when he experienced a major drop in blood pressure. This led doctors to discover a blood clot in the lungs. The embolism was potentially fatal if it blocked blood flow to the lungs. The major drop in blood pressure could also cause him to go into shock. The drugs normally given to dissolve clots could not be used because they would prevent the ulcer from healing.

Those involved with *Bonanza: The Next Generation* kept hoping Greene would recover and return to the project. David Dortort made several revisions to the script, reducing the physical demands of his role, but Lorne Greene would never see his dream project fulfilled as he died at 12:14 P.M. on Friday, September 11, 1987, at St. John's Hospital and Health Center in Santa Monica from adult respiratory distress syndromes. He was buried at Hillside Memorial Park in Los Angeles, California.

Dortort rewrote the script of *Bonanza: The Next Generation* to explain Ben's passing rather than recast the role. It was felt that the project took on a special meaning — a sort of memorial to Greene's enthusiasm and spirit.

Michael Landon visited Greene for the last time on September 10 and went into seclusion after learning of Greene's passing. He later reflected, "He was Ben Cartwright to the end. He was ready to die with no complaints. The last time I saw him, he couldn't speak. I took his hand in mine and held it. He looked at me and then slowly, he began to arm wrestle with me like we

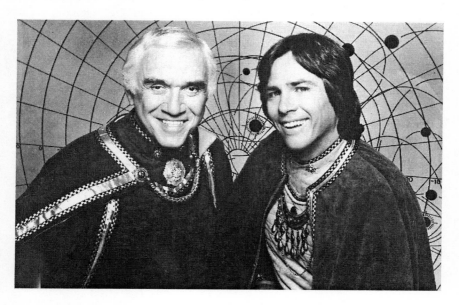

Publicity shot of Lorne Greene and Richard Hatch in the TV series Battlestar Galactica. *(Authors' collection.)*

used to. He broke into a smile then nodded. I think that he wanted me to know that everything was OK."[21]

Nancy recalled, "His brave heart just wouldn't quit. He still waved, he still smiled, he gave the OK sign in his last days. When he was still able to talk, he was able to say that all would be fine. In the last week, once when he was dreaming, he said, 'Let the old man do it his way.' I think that he finally succeeded."[22]

Movies, Telefilms, Miniseries

An asterisk (*) denotes video availability.

1. *Churchill's Island* (1941); as Narrator
2. **The Silver Chalice* (Warner Bros., 1954); as Peter
3. *Tight Spot* (Columbia, 1955); as Benjamin Costain
4. **Autumn Leaves* (Columbia, 1956); as Mr. Hanson
5. *The Hard Man* (Columbia, 1957); as Rice Martin
6. **Peyton Place* (20th Century–Fox, 1957); as Prosecutor
7. **The Buccaneer* (Paramount, 1958); as Mercier
8. *The Gift of Love* (20th Century–Fox, 1958); as Grant Allan
9. *The Last of the Fast Guns* (Universal, 1958); as Michael O'Reilly
10. **The Trap* [*The Baited Trap*-G. B.] (Parkwood Heath/Paramount, 1959); as Mr. Davis
11. **The Errand Boy* (Paramount, 1961); as Ben Cartwright
12. *Waco* (A. C. Lyles/Paramount, 1966) Sang Theme Song
13. *Destiny of a Spy* (Universal/NBC, November 27, 1969) Telefilm; as Peter Vanin
14. *The Harness* (Universal/NBC, November 12, 1971) Telefilm; as Peter Randall
15. **Earthquake* (Universal, 1974); as Sam Royce
16. **Tidal Wave* (U.S./Japan, 1975); as Warren Richards
17. *High Country Calling* (1975)
18. *Nevada Smith* (Rackin-Hayes/MGM/NBC, May 3, 1975) Telefilm; as Jonas Cord
19. *Man on the Outside* (Universal/ABC, June 29, 1975) Telefilm; as Wade Griffin
20. *George Washington—The Man* (Kidak/Bicentennial Films, April 1, 1976–October 31, 1976); as George Washington
21. *Lorne Greene's Canada* (Film Short)
22. *The Moneychangers* (Ross Hunter/Paramount/NBC, December 4, 5, 12, 19, 1976) Miniseries; as George Quartermain
23. **Roots* (David L. Wolper/ABC, January 23 1977–January 30, 1977) Miniseries; as John Reynolds
24. *SST—Death Flight* [*SST: Disaster in the Sky*] (Circle Theatre/ABC, February 25, 1977) Telefilm; as Marshall Cole
25. **The Trial of Lee Harvey Oswald* (Charles Fries Productions/ABC, September 30, 1977–October 7, 1977) Miniseries; as Matthew Arnold Warson
26. *That's Country* (1978)
27. **The Bastard* [*Kent Family Chronicles*] (Universal/Operation Prime Time, May 22, 1978–May 23, 1978) Miniseries; as Bishop Francis

28. *Battlestar Galactica* (Universal, 1979); as Commander Adama
29. *Mission Galactica: The Cylon Attack* (Glen A. Larson/Universal, 1979); as Commander Adama
30. *Conquest of the Earth* (Glen A. Larson/Universal, 1980); as Commander Adama
31. *Fever [Jack London's Klondike Fever]* (Fi Investment, 1980); as Sam Steele
32. *A Time for Miracles* (ABC/Circle Films, December 21, 1980) Telefilm; as Bishop John Carroll
33. Code Red (ABC, September 20, 1981) Telefilm; as Captain Joe Rorcheck
34. *Heidi's Song* (Hanna-Barbera/Paramount, 1982); as Grandfather
35. Police Squad! Help Wanted (1982)
36. *Vasectomy: A Delicate Matter* (1986)
37. *The Alamo: 13 Days to Glory* (NBC, January 26, 1987) Telefilm; as Sam Houston

Radio

38. Network News (CBC, 1940–1943)
39. Voice of America (NBC, Early 1940s)
40. Canadian War Bond Shows (NBC, 1943) 25 15-minute shows
41. News (C Key, Toronto, 1944)
42. Queen's Men (CBC) 30 Minutes
43. Notebook (CFRB, February 6, 1952)
44. The Sears Radio Theatre (CBS, February 5, 1979–February 11, 1980); as Host of "Monday's Western Night"
45. The Mutual Theatre (Mutual, February 14, 1980–December 19, 1981); as Host of Monday's "Western Night"

TV Series

46. Sailor of Fortune (Syndicated, 1957) 30 Minutes, 39 Episodes; as Captain Grant Mitchell
47. Bonanza (NBC, September 12, 1959–January 16, 1973) 60 Minutes, 430 Episodes; as Ben Cartwright (See Episode Guide)
48. Griff (ABC, September 29, 1973–January 5, 1974) 60 Minutes, 12 Episodes; as Wade "Griff" Griffin
49. Lorne Greene's Last of the Wild (Syndicated 1974–1979) 30 Minutes, 104 Episodes; as Host and Narrator
50. *Battlestar Galactica* (ABC, September 17, 1978–April 29, 1979) 60 Minutes, 21 Episodes; as Commander Adama
51. Galactica 1980 (ABC, January 27, 1980–May 4, 1980) 60 Minutes, 9 Episodes; as Commander Adama
52. Code Red (ABC, November 1, 1981–September 12, 1982) 60 Minutes, 18 Episodes; as Captain Joe Rorchek
53. *Lorne Greene's New Wilderness* (Syndicated, 1982–1986) 30 Minutes; as Host and Executive Producer

TV Guest Appearances

54. *Studio One* "Rendezvous" (CBS, June 1, 1953) 60 Minutes; as Symphony Orchestra Conductor
55. *Studio One* "1984" (CBS, September 21, 1953) 60 Minutes; as O'Brien
56. *Philip Morris Playhouse* "Journey to Nowhere" (CBS, October 8, 1953) 30 Minutes
57. *You Are There* "Christopher Columbus Sets Foot on San Salvador" [Columbus discovers America] (CBS, October 11, 1953); as Christopher Columbus
58. *Studio One* "A Handful of Diamonds" (CBS, April 19, 1954) 60 Minutes
59. *You Are There* "The Fall of Parnell" (CBS, June 13, 1954) 30 Minutes; as Parnell
60. *Studio One Summer Theatre* "The Cliff" (CBS, September 13, 1954) 60 Minutes; as Dr. Maddison West
61. *Danger* "Experiment With Death" (CBS, November 16, 1954) 30 Minutes
62. *You Are There* "Torment of Beethoven" (CBS, January 9, 1955) 30 Minutes; as Beethoven
63. *Climax!* "Private Worlds" (CBS, April 7, 1955) 60 Minutes; as Dr. Charles Saunders
64. *E in Hour* "Driftwood" (NBC, May 3, 1955) 60 Minutes; as Vernon Dyall
65. *Star Stage* "The Toy Lady" (NBC, September 9, 1955) 30 Minutes; as Dr. Calder
66. *Kraft Television Theatre* "Day of Judgment" (NBC, November 23, 1955) 60 Minutes; as Father Capuchin
67. *Studio 57* "Death Dream" (Dumont, November 26, 1955) 30 Minutes
68. *Alfred Hitchcock Presents* "Help Wanted" (CBS, April 1, 1956) 30 Minutes
69. *Alcoa Hour* "Key Largo" (NBC, October 14, 1956) 60 Minutes; as Sheriff Gash
70. *Armstrong Circle Theatre* "Flare-up" (NBC, October 30, 1956) 60 Minutes; as Dr. Bundesen
71. *U.S. Steel Hour* "Survival" (CBS, November 7, 1956) 60 Minutes; as Dallas
72. *Producers Showcase* "Mayerling" (NBC, February 4, 1957) 90 Minutes
73. *Kraft Theatre* "The Medallion" (NBC, April 3, 1957) 60 Minutes; as Colonel Matthews
74. *Playhouse 90* "Edge of Innocence" (CBS, October 31, 1957) 90 Minutes; as Lowell Williams
75. *Studio One* "Twenty-Four Hours to Dawn" (CBS, November 11, 1957) 60 Minutes
76. *Shirley Temple's Storybook* "Rumpelstiltskin" (ABC, February 2, 1958) 60 Minutes
77. *Shirley Temple's Storybook* "Sleeping Beauty" (ABC, June 8, 1958) 60 Minutes
78. *Suspicion* "Return From Darkness" (NBC, June 30, 1958) 60 Minutes
79. *Shirley Temple's Storybook* "The Little Prince" (ABC, July 15, 1958) 60 Minutes; as Wicked King
80. *Gale Storm Show* "Jail Mates" (CBS, February 28, 1959) 30 Minutes; as Constable Barnaby
81. *Wagon Train* "Vivian Carter Story" (NBC, March 11, 1959) 60 Minutes; as Christopher Webb

82. *Bronco* "Prairie Skipper" (ABC, May 5, 1959) 60 Minutes; as Amos Carr
83. *Mike Hammer* "A Haze on the Lake" Syndicated, July 7, 1959) 30 Minutes
84. *My True Story* (NBC, July 25, 1959) 60 Minutes; as Marion Davis
85. *The Third Man* "The Hollywood Incident" (Syndicated, 1960) 30 Minutes
86. *Cheyenne* "Gold, Glory and Custer — Prelude" [Part I] (ABC, January 4, 1960) 60 Minutes; as Colonel Bell
87. *Cheyenne* "Gold, Glory and Custer — Requiem" [Part II] (ABC, January 11, 1960) 60 Minutes; as Colonel Bell
88. *Here's Hollywood* (NBC, August 18, 1961) 30 Minutes
89. 37th Annual Macy's Thanksgiving Day Parade (NBC, November 23, 1961); as co-host with Betty White
90. *Perry Como's Kraft Music Hall* (NBC, January 3, 1962) 60 Minutes
91. 38th Annual Macy's Thanksgiving Day Parade (NBC, November 22, 1962); as co-host with Betty White
92. *The Missing Links* (NBC, 1963) 30 Minutes
93. *The Art Linkletter Show* (NBC, February 25, 1963) 30 Minutes
94. *Andy Williams Show* (NBC, May 2, 1963) 60 Minutes
95. *The International Beauty Spectacular* (NBC, August 16, 1963) 60 Minutes; as Master of Ceremonies
96. *The Tonight Show Starring Johnny Carson* (NBC, November 27, 1963)
97. 39th Annual Macy's Thanksgiving Day Parade (NBC, November 28, 1963); as co-host with Betty White
98. *Opening Night at the World's Fair* (NBC, April 22, 1964) 90 Minutes; as Host
99. *What's This Song* (NBC, October 26, 1964) 30 Minutes
100. *Memorial Tribute to President John F. Kennedy* (NBC, November 22, 1964) as Host
101. 40th Annual Macy's Thanksgiving Day Parade (NBC, November 26, 1964); as co-host with Betty White
102. *The Les Crane Show* (ABC, 1965) 90 Minutes
103. *Allan Sherman's Funnyland* (NBC, January 18, 1965) 60 Minutes
104. *The Journals of Lewis and Clark* (NBC, February 23, 1965); as Narrator
105. *Jack Paar Show* (NBC, April 23, 1965)
106. *Lorne Greene's American West* (NBC, Nay 3, 1965); as Host
107. 41st Annual Macy's Thanksgiving Day Parade (NBC, November 23, 1965) 120 Minutes; as co-host with Betty White
108. *London Palladium* (NBC, May 26, 1966) 60 Minutes; as Host
109. *It's a Dog's World* (NBC, November 1966); as Host
110. *Christmas with Lorne Greene* (NBC, December 17, 1966) 30 Minutes; as Host
111. *The Kraft Music Hall* "How the West Was Swung" (NBC, October 18, 1967) 60 Minutes; as Host
112. *World of Horses* (NBC, January 19, 1968) 60 Minutes; as Narrator
113. *America's Junior Miss Pageant* (NBC, March 15, 1968); as co-host with Joanie Sommers
114. *The Dean Martin Show* (NBC, October 3, 1968) 60 Minutes
115. *The Don Rickles Show* (ABC, November 1, 1968) 30 Minutes
116. *The Merv Griffin Show* (Syndicated, December 9, 1968) 90 Minutes
117. *The Joey Bishop Show* (ABC, December 17, 1968) 90 Minutes

118. *Dinah Shore Special* (NBC, April 13, 1969)
119. *Jimmy Durante Presents the Lennon Sisters Hour* (ABC, December 19, 1969) 60 Minutes
120. *Andy Williams Show* (ABC, January 10, 1970) Cameo
121. *American Rainbow* "Lincoln Center Children's Festival" (NBC, January 31, 1970) 60 Minutes; as Host
122. *Ice Capades* (NBC, February 11, 1970)
123. *Movin'* (CBS, February 24, 1970) 60 Minutes
124. *The Young Americans* (ABC, March 12, 1970) 60 Minutes
125. *Johnny Cash* (November 15, 1970)
126. *Sesame Street* (PBS, March 1971)
127. *Sing Out Sweet Land* (NBC, April 8, 1971)
128. *Wildfire* (NBC, June 13, 1971) 60 Minutes; as Narrator
129. *Sonny and Cher Comedy Hour* (CBS, January 24, 1972) 60 Minutes
130. *Watch Your Child/The Me Too Show* (NBC, February 14, 1972–February 18, 1972) reads *The Little Red Hen*
131. *A Special London Bridge Special* (NBC, May 7, 1972) 60 Minutes; Cameo
132. *Dinah!* (Syndicated, September 7, 1972)
133. *A Salute to Television's 25th Anniversary* (ABC, September 10, 1972) 90 Minutes
134. *Sonny and Cher Comedy Hour* (CBS, November 3, 1973) 60 Minutes
135. 49th Annual Macy's Thanksgiving Day Parade (NBC, November 1973); as co-host with Betty White
136. *The Merv Griffin Show* (Syndicated, 1974)
137. *Sandy in Disneyland* (CBS, April 10, 1974) 60 Minutes
138. *Rex Harrison Presents Short Stories of Love* "The Fortunate Painter" (NBC, May 1, 1974) 120 Minutes; as Hercule
139. *Tattletales* (CBS, March 8, 1976–March 12, 1976)
140. *Dinah!* (Syndicated, May 7, 1976)
141. *The Great American Music Celebration* (Syndicated, June 11, 1976) 60 Minutes; as Host
142. *What Do You Want to Be When You Grow Up?* (NBC, September 15, 1976) as Narrator
143. *Ballad of America* (1976)
144. *Hollywood Squares* (NBC, October 15, 1976) 30 Minutes
145. Film Documentary (November 20, 1976) as Narrator about modern contributions of horses
146. *Donny and Marie* (ABC, March 11, 1977)
147. *Hardy Boys/Nancy Drew Mysteries* "The Hardy Boys and Nancy Drew Meet Dracula" [Part I] (ABC, September 11, 1977) 60 Minutes; as Count Dracula/Inspector Stavlin
148. *Happy Days* "The Fonz in Hollywood" (ABC, September 13, 1977) as Himself
149. *Hardy Boys/Nancy Drew Mysteries* "The Hardy Boys and Nancy Drew Meet Dracula" [Part II] (ABC, September 18, 1977) 60 Minutes; as Count Dracula/Inspector Stavlin
150. *Yabba Dabba Doo!* The Happy World of Hanna Barbera (CBS, November 24, 1977) 120 Minutes
151. *A Celebration at Ford's Theatre* (NBC, February 2, 1978) 60 Minutes; as Host
152. *The Redd Foxx Special* (ABC, April 4, 1978) 90 Minutes

153. *The Love Boat* "The Wedding" (ABC, September 15, 1979) 60 Minutes; as Bride's Widowed Father
154. *Vegas* "Aloha, You're Dead" (ABC, November 5, 1980) 120 Minutes; as Remick
155. 92nd Tournament of Roses Parade (NBC, January 1, 1981) 150 Minutes; as Grand Marshall
156. *Aloha Paradise* (ABC, February 25, 1981) 60 Minutes
157. *Police Squad!* "A Substantial Gift" (ABC, March 4, 1982) 30 Minutes; Killed during opening
158. *The Love Boat* "Love Will Find a Way" (ABC, November 20, 1982) 60 Minutes; as Buck Hamilton
159. *Twenty-Five Years with Hanna-Barbera* (WUAB Channel 43, Cleveland, December 3, 1982); as co-host with Gary Coleman
160. The Thirty-Fifth annual Emmy Awards (NBC, September 25, 1983) 210 Minutes; Presented Supporting Actor and Actress Award to Christopher Lloyd and Carol Kane of *Taxi*
161. *The Nut Cracker, A Fantasy on Ice* (HBO, December 5, 1984) 85 Minutes; as Narrator
162. *Dean Martin Celebrity Roast* (NBC, December 7, 1984) Roasts Michael Landon
163. *Reading Rainbow* "Ox-Cart Man" (WNEO, Ohio, June 5, 1985); as Narrator
164. *Highway to Heaven* "The Smile in the Third Row" (NBC, November 20, 1985) 60 Minutes; as Fred Fusco
165. *NBC's 60th Anniversary Celebration* (NBC, May 12, 1986) 180 Minutes
166. *Answer America* (1986)

Stage

167. *Les Deux Sourds* (Lisgar Collegiate Institute in Ottawa, Canada, 1930s); as Deaf Character
168. *Musical Review* (Lisgar Collegiate Institute in Ottawa, Canada, 1933)
169. *A-1 Hallow's Eve* (Lisgar Collegiate Institute in Ottawa, Canada, 1933)
170. *The Shining Hour* (Queen's University in Ottawa, Canada, 1937)
171. *The Secret* (Queen's University in Ottawa, Canada, 1937)
172. *The Moneymakers* (Jupiter Theatre in Toronto, Canada, November 14, 1952–November 22, 1952); as Paul Finch
173. *Come Back Little Sheba* (Toronto, Canada, 1952)
174. *The Prescott Proposals* (Broadhurst Theatre on Broadway, December 16, 1953–April 3, 1954) 125 Performances; as Elliott Clark
175. *Julius Caesar* (Stratford Connecticut Shakespeare Festival, June 24, 1955); as Brutus
176. *The Merchant of Venice* (Stratford Connecticut Shakespeare Festival, June 30, 1955); as the Prince of Morocco
177. *The Taming of the Shrew* (Stratford Connecticut Shakespeare Festival, 1955); as Petrucchio
178. *Hamlet* (Stratford Connecticut Shakespeare Festival, 1955); as Claudius
179. *Speaking of Murder* (Royal Theatre in New York, December 19, 1956–January 19, 1957) 37 Performances; as Charles Ashton

180. *This Edwin Booth* (LaJola Playhouse in California, August 26, 1958); as Narrator/Booth's Friend
181. *Edwin Booth* (46th Street Theatre in New York, November 24, 1958) 24 Performances; as William Winter
182. *The Greatest Glory* (University of Texas in Austin, Texas, June 1966)

Personal Appearances

183. National Soap Box Derby (1964) Fires Starting Gun
184. 1964 Jamboree (Valley Forge, Pennsylvania, 1964)
185. First Canadian Royal Variety Performance (Prince Edward Island, October 1964) for Queen Elizabeth
186. Miami Stadium (Miami, Florida, 1965)
187. Australia (1965)
188. Globe Theatre (Odessa, Texas, 1965)
189. Illinois State Fair (1965)
190. 17th Annual Spindletop Charity Horse Show (Beaumont, Texas, 1965)
191. Pasadena Tournament of Roses (Pasadena, California, January 1, 1965)
192. Canadian Western Exposition (Edmonton, Alta, March 1965)
193. Nugget (Sparks, Nevada, April 29, 1965)
194. Grand National Horse Show and Rodeo (San Francisco's Cow Place, San Francisco, California, October 1965)

Book

195. *The Lorne Greene Book of Remarkable Animals* by Lorne Greene. Simon and Schuster, 1980

———— Pernell Roberts ————

ADAM CARTWRIGHT

In 1842, Adam Milton Cartwright was born to Benjamin and Elizabeth Eloise Stoddard Cartwright in Boston, Massachusetts. He received his middle name from his father's favorite writer, John Milton, who penned Paradise Lost. *He never really got to know his mother as she died shortly after giving birth. She was the only child of Captain and Mrs. Abel Morgan Stoddard. His grandfather was captain of the ship the* Wanderer, *on which his father served as third officer. His mother was a popular, pretty, dark-haired woman who had attended Mrs. Carrecker's Academy for Young Ladies.*

Ben and Adam left Boston to follow his dream westward. By the age of four, Adam had already shown signs of being inquisitive and not letting anything get by him. He proved to be a quick learner, already having learned his colors and alphabet. Ben would spend his evenings educating his son, who had already shown a fondness for all animals. It was during his travels that his father met Inger Borgstrom and they were married. When Adam's brother Eric Haas was born in 1848, Adam called him Hoss and the name stuck. Inger was later killed by Indians near Denver.

It was in Nevada that Ben decided to settle and build his Ponderosa. His father would meet Marie and bring her to the ranch. She gave birth to another brother, Joseph Burns, in 1857. One day she fell from her horse and died from her injuries. Hop Sing, who had come to work for the Cartwrights, was now in charge of running the household.

Adam would grow up to be a tall, handsome, dark-haired man with a lean but athletic build. He got his looks from his mother. He proved to be the more sensitive, serious and intellectual of the sons. He was not one to quickly hand out praise and was good at sizing up people. He readily stood by his beliefs. He enjoyed reading, the guitar, singing and dancing. His good head for business made him the most likely of the brothers to take over the running of the Ponderosa. He even became one of Virginia City's councilmen.

Adam helped his friend Phillip Deidesheimer get his square set mining system installed in Virginia City mines.

Once while hunting wolves, he accidentally shot Joe, causing him to become disillusioned with life in the West. When the Civil War approached, he and Joe became divided in their allegiance to the North and South as he was from Boston and Little Joe from New Orleans.

His inner strength was tested when a madman, Peter Kane, tortured him in an attempt to get him to kill, but he had the strength to resist.

Adam met Laura Dayton, whose husband had been accidentally killed. He fell in love with her and her daughter Peggy, and proposed. Laura began to feel neglected because Adam spent so much time away from her. She did not know he had been secretly building their new home as a wedding present. While he was away, Laura and Cousin Will fell in love. While working on the roof of the new home, Adam fell off and became temporarily paralyzed. Laura felt guilty and decided to go through with the wedding. Adam sensed her real feelings and refused to stand in her way. Will and Laura were married and moved to San Francisco.

It was the disillusionment with the West that had Adam going off to sea, traveling back East and studying abroad during his lifetime. While studying architecture in England, he had a son, Adam Cartwright, Jr. who would eventually return to the Ponderosa to help his relatives defend their land.

Pernell Roberts, an only child, was born on May 18, 1928, in Waycross, Georgia. He grew up in a poor household. His father, Pernell E. Roberts, distributed Dr. Pepper to support his family. He did well in school until about the age of 15 when his interests turned to civil rights and music. He learned to play several instruments. As a teenager, he became disillusioned with organized religion, believing it to be hypocritical. His understanding parents were not strong disciplinarians.

Upon graduating from Waycross High School, he entered Georgia Tech as an engineer major but soon became bored and flunked out in 1945. In 1946, he joined the Marine Corps. While in the service, Pernell took up the tuba. He remained in the service until his 1948 discharge. After conversing with captives of the Japanese, he became interested in philosophy and

Pernell Roberts. (Authors' collection.)

psychology, an interest he would keep throughout the years.

In 1949, Pernell enrolled at the University of Maryland to study acting. He was feeling lonely and felt the experience would enable him to meet people. While there, he appeared in four productions. Unfortunately, he flunked out twice in the same year because his mind was not on his studies. After leaving the university, he was forced to take on a variety of different jobs such as welder, railroad worker, butcher, tombstone carver and forest ranger before pursuing a career in acting.

In 1950, he packed up and headed for Washington DC's Arena Theatre, where he debuted in *The Man Who Came to Dinner* and was also cast in *The Firebrand.* During his two years there, he developed his craft. At the theater, he met Vera Mowry, who was a technical director for the arena. "There was a purity there," said Mowry. "You couldn't help but feel the truth in his acting."[23] They fell in love and were married. In 1951, son Christopher, was born. He would grow up to be a stage manager.

In 1952, the Roberts family moved to New York, where Vera took a job at Hunter College teaching acting classes. They would later divorce. He struggled to find work for the next seven years and would do a number of shows up and down the East Coast. He did four Broadway plays including *Macbeth* (1955), for which he won the Drama Desk Award as Best Broadway Actor of the Year, *Romeo and Juliet* (1956), and *Lovers* (1956) starring Joanne Woodward. Theater became his first love. Paramount caught his performance in *Lovers* and, liking what they saw, cast him in the film *Desire Under the Elms*. He moved to Hollywood in 1957 to begin filming. Actress Jan Ferrand, whom he had met while doing the play *Tonight in Samarkand* (1955), joined him on the West Coast. Before the film's release, he had gotten work guesting on such TV shows as *Gunsmoke, Have Gun Will Travel* and *Cimarron City*. His work in *Desire Under the Elms* (1958) that got him noticed by producer David Dortort, who cast him as Adam Cartwright in the long-running television series *Bonanza*.

Pernell was disillusioned with the show almost from the beginning, feeling his talent was being wasted. He thought the scripts were inferior and that, because of the time restraints, character development was almost impossible. He asked Dortort for permission to remove his toupee. The producer, unaware that Roberts had no hair, felt that without the hairpiece he looked 15 years older and refused. Dortort thought Roberts was "aloof, rebellious and outspoken."[24] However, he thought highly of his talent.

In 1962, he married actress and talented soprano Judy Le Becque and they became social activists, attending a march in Selma. He released the RCA album *Come All Ye Fair and Tender Ladies* in 1963. His musical talents also included playing the French horn and tuba. Roberts' stand-in for things such as lighting tests was Betty Endicott, because she was the same height, and had the same hair and skin color. Of the three *Bonanza* co-stars, Roberts received the most fan mail. He earned $10,000 per episode with $1,000,000 in additional benefits.

As Roberts became more and more discontented with the show, he asked for his release before 1965. Cousin Will Cartwright (Guy Williams) was brought in as a possible substitute character should Pernell make good his threat to leave. The network told him he would have to serve out the rest of his contract or he would never work again. He had no choice but to stay. He claimed, to keep his sanity, he would give only ten percent of himself and proceeded to walk through his part. The network tried to appease Roberts by holding script conferences in order for actors, directors, and producer to have input. After six weeks, the conferences were dissolved because they proved unproductive. Finally, on February 22, 1965, he was free of *Bonanza*. At first, plans were made to kill off Roberts' character, but it was finally decided to say that he was traveling about in order to leave the door open in the event Roberts changed his mind and returned. Many believed that the actor had made a big mistake. Roberts felt that, since he had found work before *Bonanza*, he would continue to do so afterwards. He believed his popularity on the show would insure him plum roles. Over the years, he has been asked if he has ever regretted leaving *Bonanza*. "God no!" he insisted. "I'm only sorry I wasn't able to get out of my contract sooner. So the others made millions. How much does one person need to live? I've never needed or wanted that much."[25]

When plans to join a Minneapolis repertory theater failed, Pernell found himself guesting on numerous television shows such as *The Big Valley* and the television adaptation of the musical *Carousel*, in which he played Jigger. He toured in many stock productions of musicals such as *The Music Man, Camelot* and *The King and I*. He went on to star in the short-lived Broadway-bound musical productions of *Mata Hari* and *Gone with the Wind* (as Rhett Butler). During this time, he divorced Judy and, in 1972, married Kara Knack. The couple resided in the Hollywood Hills. They attended a Washington fund raiser for Indians, as did Lorne Greene. Roberts has preferred to keep his personal life private and shies away from reporters and interviews. He liked to jog four miles a day and Kara came along on her bike.

In December 1978, CBS was interested in airing *Trapper John, M.D.* and programming head Bud Grant got together with producers Frank Glicksman, Don Brinkley and director Jackie Cooper to search for their lead. They decided on Pernell Roberts. "I knew he was a fine actor," said Frank Glicksman, "a first-rate dramatic actor who's got a great sense of comedy, too ... has strong opinions ... very intellectual."[26] Tony Curtis, John Forsythe, Richard Crenna, James Whitemore and Cooper himself were among the others being considered for the role. Curtis asked for too much money and Cooper preferred directing. "I got a call to come in and talk about the show. Three weeks later I was called back to do a screen test. And then I waited again until I finally got the word about a week before we shot the pilot that the network had approved me for the part."[27] Pernell accepted the role because it helped pay the bills and provided financial security. Before production started, he went to San Francisco's Mofitt General Hospital. He also spoke with nurses, interns and medical students and he even got to watch open heart surgery. It was ironic that, during this period, his father underwent successful cancer treatment. As of the fifth season, Roberts was earning $40,000 an episode. He also grew a vegetable garden near the set, which was on stage 5. He stayed with the show until it was canceled in 1986.

After *Trapper John, M.D.* (now on cable) stopped production, Roberts found time to travel and visit friends who had been vital to his development as an actor and a human being.

David Dortort asked Pernell to host *Back to Bonanza*, a tribute to precede the showing of *Bonanza: The Return*, but Roberts was not interested and turned down Dortort's request. Learning of Michael Landon's death on July 1, 1991, he was greatly saddened.

Pernell Roberts circa late 1970s. (Photofest.)

F.B.I.: The Untold Stories came his way in 1991 and became his first steady job in five years. He would spend a day in front of the cameras and a second one doing voice-overs.

When *F.B.I.: The Untold Stories* left the air, Roberts went into semi-retirement, appearing in commercials and doing occasional guest shots on such shows as *The Young Riders*, the made-for-TV movie *Doner* and, most recently, *Diagnosis Murder* starring Dick Van Dyke, where he reprised a 1973 *Mannix* role with guest star Mike Connors. When not working, he enjoys his hobbies, which have included stock car racing, swimming, photography, running, riding and tennis. Throughout his career, Roberts has valued his privacy. An announcement came in February 1995 that Pernell and Kara were divorcing due to irreconcilable differences.

Although Pernell Roberts and *Bonanza* had gone their separate ways, and each have their own stories of survival, many have stopped, along the way, and pondered what might have been had the last of the Cartwrights remained on the Ponderosa.

Movies, Telefilms, Miniseries

An asterisk (*) denotes video availability.

1. **Desire Under the Elms* (Paramount, 1958); as Peter Cabot
2. *The Sheepman* (MGM, 1958); as Choctaw
3. *Ride Lonesome* (Ranown/Columbia, 1959); as Sam Boone
4. **Errand Boy* (Paramount, 1961); as Adam Cartwright
5. *Carousel* (ABC, May 7, 1967); as Jigger
6. **Four Rode Out* (Sagitarius/AD, 1969)
7. **Kashmiri Run* (FHE, 1969); as Greg Nelson
8. *The Silent Gun* (Paramount/ABC, December 16, 1969) Telefilm; as Sam Benner
9. *San Francisco International* (Universal/NBC, September 29, 1970) Telefilm; as Jim Conrad
10. *The Bravos* (Universal/NBC, January 9, 1972) Telefilm; as Jackson Buckley

11. *The Adventures of Nick Carter* (Universal/ABC, February 20, 1972) Telefilm; as Neal Duncan
12. *Assignment: Munich* (MGM/ABC, April 30, 1972) Telefilm; as C.C. Bryan
13. *Dead Man on the Run* (Sweeney-Finnegan/ABC, April 2, 1975) Telefilm; as Brock Dillon
14. **The Deadly Tower* [The Sniper] (MGM/NBC, October 18, 1975) Telefilm; as Lieutenant Lee
15. *The Lives of Jenny Dolan* (Ross Hunter/Paramount/NBC, October 27, 1975) Telefilm; as Camera Shop Proprietor
16. **Paco* (1975)
17. *Captain and Kings* (Universal/NBC, October 7, 14, 28, 1976–November 4, 11, 1976) Miniseries; as Beaithwaite
18. *Charlie Cobb: Nice Night for a Hanging* (Universal/NBC, June 19, 1977) Telefilm; as Sheriff Yates
19. **The Magic of Lassie* (International, 1978); as Jamison
20. *Centennial* "For as Long as the Water Flows/"The Massacre" (Universal/NBC, November 4, 1978) Miniseries; as General Asher
21. *The Immigrants* (Universal/Operation Prime Time, November 20, 1978 and November 21, 1978) Miniseries; as Anthony Cassala
22. *Night Rider* (Stephen Cannell/Universal/ABC, May 11, 1979) Telefilm; as Alex Sheridan
23. **Hot Rod* (ABC Circle Films, May 25, 1979) Telefilm; as Sheriff Marsden
24. **High Noon, Part II: The Return of Will Kane* (CBS, November 15, 1980) Telefilm; as Marshal J.D. Ward
25. *Incident at Crestridge* (CBS, December 29, 1981) Telefilm; as Major David Hill
26. *Desperado* (NBC, April 27, 1987); as Marshal Dancey
27. **Night Train to Katmandu* (Disney, June 15, 1988) Telefilm; as Professor Harry Hadley-Smythe
28. **Around the World in 80 Days* (1989) Telefilm
29. *Perry Mason: The Case of the All-Star Assassin* (NBC, 1989); as Sports Entreneur/Murder Victim
30. *Donor* (1990) Telefilm; as Dr. Martingale
31. **Checkered Flag* (1990)

TV Series

32. *Bonanza* (NBC, September 12, 1959–May 23, 1965) 60 Minutes; as Adam Cartwright (See Episode Guide)
33. *Trapper John, M.D.* (CBS, September 23, 1979–September 4, 1986) 60 Minutes, 149 Episodes; as Dr. John McIntyre
34. *F.B.I.: The Untold Stories* (ABC, September 26, 1991–June 26, 1993) 30 Minutes; as Host

TV Guest Appearances

35. *Hollywood Screen Test* (ABC, 1953) 30 Minutes
36. *Kraft Television Theatre* "Shadow of Suspicion" (NBC, November 7, 1956) 60 Minutes

37. *Gunsmoke* "How to Kill a Woman" (CBS, November 30, 1957) 30 Minutes; as Nat Pilcher
38. *Sugarfoot* "Misfire" (ABC, December 10, 1957) 60 Minutes
39. *Matinee Theatre* (NBC, 1958)
40. *Trackdown* "Reward" (CBS, January 3, 1958) 30 Minutes; as Bannion
41. *Shirley Temple's Storybook* "Rumpelstiltskin" (NBC, February 2, 1958) 60 Minutes; as Count Schoenfeld
42. *Sugarfoot* "Man Wanted" (ABC, February 18, 1958) 60 Minutes; as Deuce Brade
43. *Have Gun Will Travel* "Hey Boy's Revenge" (CBS, April 12, 1958) 30 Minutes
44. *Tombstone Territory* "Pick Up the Gun" (ABC, May 14, 1958) 30 Minutes; as Johnny Coster
45. *Zane Grey Theatre* "Utopia, Wyoming" (CBS, June 6, 1958) 30 Minutes; as Jet Mason
46. *Shirley Temple's Storybook* "Sleeping Beauty" (NBC, June 8, 1958) 60 Minutes; as Theorabore
47. *Shirley Temple's Storybook* "Hiawatha" (NBC, October 5, 1958) 60 Minutes
48. *Northwest Passage* "The Assassin" (NBC, November 16, 1958) 30 Minutes; as Captain Jacques Chavez
49. *Zane Grey Theatre* "Pressure Point" (CBS, December 4, 1958) 30 Minutes
50. *Lawman* "The Posse" (ABC, March 8, 1959) 30 Minutes; as Fent Hartley
51. *Cimarron City* "Have Sword Will Duel" (NBC, March 14, 1959) 60 Minutes; as O'Hara
52. *Alcoa Presents One Step Beyond* "The Vision" (ABC, March 24, 1959) 30 Minutes; as Sergeant
53. *Bronco* "The Belles of Silver Flat" (ABC, March 24, 1959) 60 Minutes; as Rev. David Clayton
54. *77 Sunset Strip* "Abra Cadaver" (ABC, April 17, 1959) 60 Minutes
55. *Buckskin* "A Question of Courage" (NBC, May 11, 1959) 30 Minutes
56. *Buckskin* "Mary MacNamara" (NBC, May 18, 1959) 30 Minutes; as Oscar
57. *The Detectives* "House Call" (ABC, January 29, 1960) 30 Minutes
58. *Naked City* "The S.S. American Dream" (ABC, May 8, 1963) 60 Minutes
59. *Route 66* "Child of the Night" (CBS, January 3, 1964) 60 Minutes
60. *You Don't Say* (NBC, 1964/65)
61. *The Girl from UNCLE* "The Little John Doe Affair" (NBC, December 13, 1966) 60 Minutes; as Joey Celeste
62. *The Virginian* "Long Journey Home" (NBC, December 14, 1966) 90 Minutes; as Jim Boyer, Sr.
63. *The Big Valley* "Cage of Eagles" (ABC, April 24, 1967) 60 Minutes; as Patrick Maddigan
64. *The Wild Wild West* "Night of the Firebrans" (CBS, September 15, 1967) 60 Minutes; as Sean O'Reilley
65. *Mission Impossible* "Operation Heart" (CBS, October 22,1967) 60 Minutes; as President Beyron Rurich
66. *Gunsmoke* "Stranger in Town" (CBS, November 20, 1967) 60 Minutes; as Dave Reeves
67. *Ironside* "To Kill a Cop" (NBC, January 25, 1968) 60 Minutes

68. *Mission Impossible* "The Mercenaries" (CBS, October 20, 1968) 60 Minutes; as Col. Hans Krim
69. *The Big Valley* "Run of the Cat" (ABC, October 21, 1968) 60 Minutes; as Ed Tanner
70. *The Big Valley* "Hunter Moon" (ABC, December 30, 1968) 60 Minutes
71. *Name of the Game* "Chains of Command" (NBC, October 17, 1969) 90 Minutes
72. *Lancer* "Welcome to Genesis" (CBS, November 18, 1969) 60 Minutes; as Banning
73. *Mission Impossible* "Death Squad" (CBS, March 15, 1970) 60 Minutes; as Chief Manuel Corba
74. *The Bold Ones* [The Doctors] "A Matter of Priorities" (NBC, January 3, 1971) 60 Minutes
75. *Alias Smith and Jones* "Escape from Wickenburg" (ABC, January 28, 1971) 60 Minutes; as Sam Finrock
76. *Hawaii Five-O* "The Grand Stand Play" [Part 1] (CBS, March 3, 1971) 60 Minutes; as Lon Phillips
77. *Name of the Game* "Beware of the Watch Dog" (NBC, March 5, 1971) 90 Minutes
78. *Hawaii Five-O* "The Grand Stand Play" [Part 2] (CBS, March 10, 1971) 60 Minutes; as Lon Phillips
79. *Men from Shiloh* "Wolf Track" (NBC, March 17, 1971) 60 Minutes; as the Stranger
80. *Marcus Welby, M.D.* "The Tender Comrade" (ABC, September 14, 1971) 60 Minutes
81. *Night Gallery* "The Tune in Dan's Cafe" (NBC, January 5, 1972) 60 Minutes; as Joe Bellman
82. *Alias Smith and Jones* "21 Days to Tenstrike" (ABC, January 6, 1972) 60 Minutes; as Terence Tynan
83. *Owen Marshall Counselor at Law* "The Trouble with Ralph" (ABC, October 9, 1972) 60 Minutes
84. *Sixth Sense* "I Did Not Mean to Slay Thee" (ABC, November 11, 1972) 60 Minutes
85. *Banacek* "To Steal a King" (NBC, November 15, 1972) 90 Minutes; as Donneger
86. *Marcus Welby, M.D.* "The Day After Forever" (ABC, February 27, 1973) 60 Minutes
87. *Mission Impossible* "Imitation" (CBS, March 30, 1973) 60 Minutes; as Boomer
88. *Mannix* "Little Girl Lost" (CBS, October 7, 1973) 60 Minutes; as George Fallon
89. *Hawkins* "Candidate for Murder" (CBS, March 5, 1974) 90 Minutes
90. *Police Story* "Chief" (NBC, March 19, 1974) 60 Minutes
91. *The Odd Couple* "Strike Up the Band or Else" (ABC, October 17, 1974) 30 Minutes
92. *Nakia* "Roots of Anger" (ABC, November 30, 1974) 60 Minutes; as Matt Haywood
93. *Police Story* "To Steal a Million" (NBC, February 4, 1975) 60 Minutes
94. *Medical Story* "Test Case" (NBC, September 25, 1975) 60 Minutes
95. *The Adventures of Ellery Queen* "The Adventure of Colonel Niven's Memoirs" (NBC, October 23, 1975) 60 Minutes

96. *Bronk* "Deception" (CBS, December 7, 1975) 60 Minutes
97. *Cannon* "The House of Cards" (CBS, January 14, 1976) 60 Minutes
98. *Six Million Dollar Man* "Hocus Pocus" (ABC, January 18, 1976) 60 Minutes
99. *Jig Saw John* "Death of the Party" (NBC, March 22, 1976) 60 Minutes
100. *The Quest* "The Last of the Mountain Men" (NBC, 1976) 60 Minutes
101. *Barnaby Jones* "Testament of Power" (CBS, January 20, 1977) 60 Minutes as Mr. Matthews
102. *Switch* "Camera Angles" (CBS, January 30, 1977) 60 Minutes
103. *Baretta* "The Reunion" (ABC, February 2, 1977) 60 Minutes
104. *Quincy, M.E.* "Visitors in Paradise" (NBC, February 18, 1977) 60 Minutes; as Sheriff Connely
105. *Quincy M.E.* "Two Sides of Truth" (NBC, February 25, 1977) 60 Minutes
106. *Most Wanted* "The Driver" (ABC, March 14, 1977) 60 Minutes
107. *Police Woman* "Deadline Death" (NBC, March 22, 1977) 60 Minutes
108. *Streets of San Francisco* "Breakup" (ABC, May 12, 1977) 60 Minutes
109. *Feather and Father Gang* "The Golden Fleece" (ABC, May 21, 1977) 60 Minutes
110. *Westside Medical* "Risks" (ABC, June 30, 1977) 60 Minutes
111. *Man from Atlantis* "Shoot-Out at Land's End" (NBC, November 8, 1977) 60 Minutes; as Williams
112. *Rockford Files* "The House on Willis Avenue" (NBC, February 24, 1978) 60 Minutes
113. *Wide World of Mystery* "Alien Lover" (ABC, March 29, 1978)
114. *Hardy Boys/Nancy Drew Mysteries* "Arson and Old Lace" (ABC, April 1, 1978) 60 Minutes
115. *Hardy Boys Mysteries* "Assault on the Tower" (ABC, October 15, 1978) 60 Minutes
116. *Quincy, M.E.* "Death by Good Intentions" (NBC, October 26, 1978) 60 Minutes; as Dr. Charles Banning
117. *Vegas* "Milliken's Stash" (ABC, November 8, 1978) 60 Minutes.
118. *The Paper Chase* "A Case of Detente" (CBS, April 17, 1979) 60 Minutes
119. *Vegas* "Aloha, You're Dead" (ABC, November 5, 1980) 60 Minutes; as Logan
120. *The Love Boat* (ABC, November 15, 1980) 60 Minutes
121. *Battle of the Network Stars* (ABC, November 20, 1981) 120 Minutes; as CBS Team Captain
122. *Night of 100 Stars* (ABC, March 8, 1982) 180 Minutes
123. *Battle of the Network Stars* (ABC, May 7, 1982) 120 Minutes; as CBS Team Captain
124. *Hotel* "Hotel" [Premiere] (ABC, September 21, 1983) 60 Minutes
125. *Night of 100 Stars II* (ABC, March 11, 1985) 180 Minutes
126. *Circus of the Stars* (CBS, December 8, 1985) 120 Minutes
127. *National Geographic* "Realm of the Alligator" (PBS, April 17, 1986)
128. *Young Riders* "Requiem for a Hero" (ABC, November 17, 1990) 60 Minutes; as Hezekiah Horn
129. *Diagnosis Murder* (CBS, July 7, 1995) 60 Minutes
130. *Diagnosis Murder* "Hard Boiled Murder" (CBS, February 20, 1997) 60 Minutes; as George Fallon

Stage

131. *The Man Who Came to Dinner* (Arena Theatre in Washington, D.C., 1950)
132. *Firebird* (Arena Theatre in Washington, D.C., 1950)
133. *Down in the Valley* (Provincetown Playhouse, July 1, 1952)
134. *Twelfth Night* (Jan Has Auditorium in New York, November 9, 1954); as Antonio
135. *Tonight in Samarkand* (Forest Theatre in Philadelphia, Pennsylvania, January 25, 1955); as Angelo Fannacci
136. *Tonight in Samarkand* (Morosco Theatre in New York, February 16, 1955); as Angelo Fannacci
137. *Guys & Dolls* (Brattle Shakespeare Festival, 1955); as Nathan Detroit
138. *Othello* (New York City Center of Music & Drama, September 7, 1955–September 15, 1955) 15 Performances; as Montano
139. *Henry IV Part I* (New York City Center of Music & Drama, September 21, 1955–October 2, 1955) 15 Performances; as Sheriff
140. *Macbeth* (Jan Hus Auditorium in New York, October 1955); as Macbeth
141. *Romeo and Juliet* (Jan Hus Auditorium in New York, February 1956); as Escaius
142. *Lovers* (Martin Beck Theatre in New York, May 10, 1956–May 12, 1956) 4 Performances; as Austrict dela Crux
143. *King John* (Stratford Connecticut Shakespeare Festival, June 1956); as Earl of Pembroke
144. *Measure for Measure* (Stratford Connecticut Shakespeare Festival, June 1956); as Barnardine
145. *The Taming of the Shrew* (Stratford Connecticut Shakespeare Festival, August 5, 1956); as Petruchio
146. *A Clearing in the Woods* (Belasco Theatre in New York, January 10, 1957–February 9, 1957) 36 Performances; as George
147. *The Taming of the Shrew* (Phoenix Theatre in New York, February 20, 1957–March 10, 1957) 23 Performances; as Petruchio
148. *The Duchess of Malfi* (Phoenix Theatre in New York, March 19, 1957–April 7, 1957) 24 Performances; as Bosola
149. *A Thousand Clowns* (Playhouse in the Park, Philadelphia, Pennsylvania, July 1964)
150. *Night of the Iguana* (Playhouse on the Mall, Paramus, New Jersey, October 1964)
151. *The Music Man* (Playhouse in the Park in Philadelphia, Pennsylvania, mid–1960s)
152. *The King and I* (St. Louis, Missouri, 1966); as the King
153. *Camelot* (Kansas City, Kansas & Pittsburgh, Pennsylvania, 1967)
154. *Tiny Alice* (New Jersey, 1967)
155. *Two for the Seesaw* (Atlanta, Chicago, 1967)
156. *The King and I* (Miami, Florida, Summer of 1967); as King
157. *The Man Who Came to Dinner* (Olevy Theatre in Maryland, 1967)
158. *Mata Hari* (National Theatre in Washington D.C., November 18, 1967–December 9, 1967) Pre-Broadway; as Henry LaFarge
159. *Captain Brassbound's Conversion* (Ethel Barrymore Theatre in New York, April 17, 1972–April 29, 1972) 16 Performances; as Captain Brassbound

160. *Gone with the Wind* (Opened in Los Angeles, California and closed in San Francisco, California, August 28, 1973–November 24, 1973); as Rhett Butler

Personal Appearances

161. *101 Ranch Rodeo* (Ponca City, Oklahoma, September 16, 1962)

Dan Blocker

ERIC "HOSS" CARTWRIGHT

Eric Haas Cartwright was born in 1848. He got the name Eric from his maternal grandfather. When Adam called him Hoss, the name stuck. While traveling across the country, they were attacked by Indians. An arrow struck and killed the baby's Swedish mother Inger in September 1848

Hoss grew up to become a six-foot-four big man weighing between 240 and 300 pounds. He was a strong, powerful man and often feared his own strength. His face was broad and moon-shaped and he loved to eat, chicken being one of his favorite meals.

Despite his bigness and strength, he had a heart that matched his size. He loved nature, animals and small children. His kind nature often found him championing the underdog. He had a special affinity for men of his size because he could identify with them.

He was a good marksman and often used a Henry .44 caliber carbine or .44 caliber Smith and Wesson. He was also a good horseman and rode Chub.

Hoss found himself shy around women. He was sensitive, idealistic and sentimental. He could be depended upon and could not easily be swayed from his principles.

Often Hoss found himself in love but never made it to the alter. Occasionally potential wives found him by accident. Once when he ordered fireworks, Tai Li was shipped in error as a mail order bride.

Hoss was close with his family. Once he rode to Genoa to get medicine for Joe, who had accidentally been shot by Adam. He even defended Joe, with Hop Sing's help, when his brother was on trial for murdering the man who cut off Hop Sing's pigtail. While returning from a cattle sale, the Cartwrights were arrested for trespassing and sentenced to six months hard labor on a chain gang.

He was often conned into Joe's hare-brained schemes, such as being entered into a flapjack contest, going into the rabbit business and accepting an elephant as payment for wrestling in the circus. Hoss did not need

Joe to get him into trouble as problems often sought him out (spotting leprechauns on the Ponderosa, testing a flying machine, playing the violin, going into the gold detecting business, dressing as an Easter bunny, judging a baby contest).

As a favor to his father, Hoss became sheriff of the lawless town of Trouble, California. He also was once a temporary sheriff of Virginia City. He even manned a relay station for the Pony Express.

Young Josh showed up at the Ponderosa in 1905, claiming to be Hoss' son born out of wedlock. He hated his father and wanted to kill him. He was upset as his mother had just passed away. When he saw Hoss' grave, he learned that his father died in 1881 while saving his mother from drowning. Hoss had proposed to her but she turned him down. She had left without telling him she was expecting. Josh no longer hated his father and remained on the ranch with his family.

Dan Blocker was born in DeKalb, Texas, on December 10, 1928, to Ora Shack and Mary Blocker He weighed in at 14 pounds and was considered the biggest baby born in Bowie County. "We were poorer than poor," Dan said. "When my father's farm failed ... he became a blacksmith."[28]

By the time he reached first grade, Blocker already weighed 105 pounds. When he was eight, his father moved the family to O'Donnell, Texas, where he opened a grocery and market. Dan would help out around the store.

At age 12, he weighed 200 pounds and had grown to six feet. From early on, his classmates made fun of his size. At 13 Dan attended Texas Military Institute in San Antonio. He found football and boxing enjoyable but was more interested in studying and reading. As a boy, horses, hunting, and fishing never really interested him.

Dan had a sister, Ora Virginia, who died from pneumonia in 1933 at the age of 11.

He enrolled at Hardin-Simmons University, located in Abilene, in the fall of 1946 but left to enter Sul Ross State College (later University) in Alpine, Texas, in the fall of 1947. He was on an athletic scholarship to play football. He majored in physical education and minored in political theory. He joined the football team (#58). He was also elected president of the freshman class and joined the debate team. When not studying, he often played practical jokes. He roomed with Gene Hendryx, who eventually owned radio station KVLF. According to football coach Dr. Paul Pierce, he was the biggest player on the 1948 team. "He had the nickname of 'one-man gang,'" Pierce recalled. "He handled the fullback and tackle chores for us."[29] With his help, the Lobos had an undefeated season that resulted in winning two conference titles and playing in the Tangerine Bowl in Florida. He was also an impressive boxer and won a number of Golden Glove titles. "Dan could have been a heavyweight champ," friend Dennis Reed said, "but he lacked the killer instinct. He was too soft-hearted."[30]

He met 5'3" Dolphia Parker at Sul Ross and they began dating. She was born on a ranch in Oklahoma where her parents raised quarter horses. As she was on the stage crew of *Arsenic and Old Lace,* he often sat in the auditorium. Anne Kate Furguson needed someone with the strength to carry a dead body from the cellar in the play. She spotted Blocker and got him to take the part. "I did it reluctantly," he said, "and I hooked a pal into it too. Much to my surprise, we had a ball. I came back for more."[31] When Dolphia became sick, Freda Gibson Powell took over her duties. Dolphia's first encounter with Dan was not under the best circumstances because she was forced to ask him to leave the auditorium when he heckled the performers. But his feeling for Dolphia made him behave and soon he was back in good graces with Freda. She encouraged him to pursue the theater instead of football. He soon found acting enjoyable. Dolphia was the first to recognize how much Dan was into acting and got him to switch his major to speech in his junior year. As a member of the Mask and Slippers, he appeared in or directed a number of productions. As director of *Mr. Roberts,* he got the entire football team into the act, but it was for his portrayal of DeLawd in *Green Pastures* that he received the national award for Best College Acting in 1949. He appeared as Dolphia's husband in Noël Coward's *Famed Oak.* Blocker became a member of the Gamma Iota Chapter of the national fraternity of Alpha Psi Omega because of his work in drama.

After graduating with a B.S. in Speech on May 2, 1950, he was offered a chance to play professional football but turned down the offer, deciding to give acting a chance. He and his friend Dennis Reed headed East and joined the summer stock circuit starting with Boston's Brattle Hall Theatre. He also had a run on Broadway in *King Lear* in 1950.

He received his draft notice in November 1950. He was inducted into the Army and spent four months in Los Angeles at Camp Polk where he appeared in *Macbeth.* It took him four weeks to get his custom made boots size 14EEE. He joined the 179th regiment and spent nine months in Japan. The last nine months were spent in Korea. On Christmas Eve, 1951, his squad was trapped by the enemy on Hill 255 for ten hours. He was discharged on September 23, 1952. Two days later, on Thursday, September 25, 1952, Dan and Dolphia were married at noon in Carlsbad, New Mexico, by a retired Presbyterian minister, Rev. J. Dando.

He returned to Sul Ross to get his masters in drama and English as well as a teaching certificate. The couple found going rough at the beginning and Blocker took a job substituting in order to make ends meet. While at the college, he received good notices when he appeared in Shakespeare's *Othello.* He had a special affinity for the famous playwright.

Dan Blocker. (Authors' collection.)

He graduated in 1954. That same year, twin daughters Debra and Danna were born to the couple. Dan took a teaching position in Sonora, Texas, followed by one in Carlsbad, New Mexico. By this time, he had taught a little bit of everything.

Finally the family moved to California where Blocker pursued a doctorate at UCLA. They moved into a home in Northridge, located in the San Fernando Valley, a suburb of Los Angeles. The home was Early American and had a 12-foot-deep swimming pool.

Dan Blocker was still teaching at Glendale High School when he was cast in a 1956 episode of *Gunsmoke* and found that show business paid more for four days of work than teaching did in a month. This convinced him to leave education for an acting career. Also in 1956, a son David was born.

He enjoyed water sports, folk and classical music and spicy Mexican food.

Blocker continued to appear in such shows as *Richard Diamond, Maverick, The Rifleman, Jefferson Drum, The Rebel* and in a Three Stooges short, cast mainly as a heavy because of his voice and size.

In 1957, he considered leaving show business because he was unhappy about being typecast. Producer David Dortort hired him to play a deaf mute in *Restless Gun*. One time it took him five minutes to memorize six pages of lines. Dortort was impressed and now knew that Blocker could handle more than playing a heavy.

A second son Dirk, was born in 1958. In October of that year, he appeared as Tiny Budinger in the NBC series *Cimarron Strip*, which only lasted 26 episodes.

"He was very discouraged," Dortort remembered. "He and his family were living in a motel all set to pack up and leave."[32] Dortort cast him as the middle son in the TV series *Bonanza* feeling he would appeal to children of all ages. "I created the part specifically for him," Dortort said. "He was the only actor I ever had in mind."[33] Blocker appealed to many fans because of his strength and tenderness. He could be angered but also touch your heart.

Reflecting on his successful rise in the business, Blocker said, "If I had been an average-sized guy, I never would have stood a chance.... There were only a few big guys around."[34]

His father died a prosperous man in 1960. Dan's mother stayed with him but eventually moved back to DeKalb to be with her friends. He continued to support her. He bought her a Cadillac and gave her $1,000 each month.

As *Bonanza* became more popular, so did he. It became more difficult to do the everyday things a family does such as going to a ball game or getting ice-cream without being swarmed by fans. "A man never appreciates his privacy until he's lost it," he complained. "And it bugs me, it *really* bugs me. I try to keep the family normal, unaffected by father's so-called celebrity. It's a losing battle."[35] With the lack of privacy and weariness of the role of Hoss Cartwright, Dan considered returning to teaching. "He says things like that when he gets fed up with the lack of privacy and being unable to go anywhere comfortably," said Dolphia.[36]

O'Donnell wanted to put up a sign promoting the town as the place where Dan had lived but decided against the idea, feeling Blocker would not have approved.

He managed to have a life outside of *Bonanza*. He and Pernell Roberts had similar political beliefs and were both liberal Democrats. They got involved in the Civil Rights cause. Blocker supported Lyndon Johnson. At an affair honoring *Bonanza's* sponsor General Motors, he upset the network brass when he debated Hedda Hopper, who supported Republican Barry Goldwater.

Dan and his friend Bob Harris were very interested in racing cars. His love for the sport led him into a partnership in Vinegaroom Racing Associates. Blocker spent every Memorial Day at Indianapolis. In 1964, he and Bob Harris were there to watch friend Davy MacDonald, a real contender, race. To their horror, Davy was involved in one of the worst accidents ever at Indianapolis and was killed immediately during the first lap.

Blocker was also quite a businessman (as were his co-stars Lorne Greene, and Michael Landon, with whom he became close both on and off the set). The three stars invested in apartments and office buildings, land, oil and gas. Among his own investments were shares in a fertilizer company and Ole Dan's Mesquite Wood Chips (a barbecue fuel). He was also instrumental in creating the Bonanza Steak Houses. Chains sprouted up all over the country.

When the show reached its highest point of popularity, Dan earned $20,000 an episode and earned $300,000 a year. He and his co-stars also received residuals. Toward the end of the 1960s, Blocker, Greene and Landon sold their legal claims to syndicating the series in a seven-figure deal. As did his co-stars, Blocker appeared on a number of variety specials and talk shows but found the situation unpleasant. "I'm an actor," he said. "If somebody gives me something that's written down, I can act it, but I can't go on these panel shows where you have to talk."[37]

He was the most popular of the *Bonanza* stars and worked on more projects during the period than his co-stars. He liked to write, and he published a short story entitled "The Best Kept Secret" in a 1970 issue of *Playboy*. He hoped to use the story for a TV movie. He was also reported to be creating a *Bonanza* script entitled "Star." Neither project came about.

Dan, Lorne and Michael were in great demand and made many public appearances, especially in rodeos.

Toward the end of the series, his weight reached 300 pounds. With the weight came back problems, forcing him to wear a back brace so he could handle the more vigorous scenes as well as ride his Morgan horse, Chub. He also wore size 56 and needed to have his clothes hand-made. He was able to bring his weight down to 260 pounds through dieting. This helped ease his back pain.

Director Robert Altman was a friend of Blocker's from the days he worked on *Bonanza* He wanted to cast him as a lead in the 1970 film *M*A*S*H* but producers objected to the director's choice. However, he dedicated the film to Dan when it was released in 1973.

Dan was now making $30,000 an episode. When *Bonanza* reduced the number of episodes made during a season, this gave him five months off to pursue other interests. One such activity was his 74-foot luxury yacht that he docked at Marina Del Rey Harbor.

For privacy, Dan took Lorne Greene's suggestion and rented a villa on Lake Lugano, Switzerland, as the TV stations there did not carry *Bonanza*. Dan also felt that his children could get a better education there so he enrolled them in private school. He denied rumors that he went to Switzerland to avoid taxes, reminding critics that he still resided in the United States. He was only giving his children the opportunity to study there for a year before doing the same in England. Ironically, when Blocker went to Switzerland, television stations there picked up *Bonanza*, invading his privacy once more. Dan, Dolphia and Debra returned from Switzerland in the spring of 1972.

Robert Altman contacted him about playing the part of an alcoholic writer in the film *The Long Goodbye*, derived from Raymond Chandler's novel of the same title. Plans were made to sell their estate in Hancoch Park and purchase a home in Seattle, Washington, away from the influences of Hollywood.

These projects were put on hold when he experienced a touch of pancreatitis. He was told to quit smoking and drinking. He seemed to be doing fine until he felt some pain. Doctors found the problem was his gall bladder and on May 1, 1972, the organ was removed at Ingelwood's Centinela Valley Hospital. He started exercising, which was done to help keep blood clots from developing. He was home recuperating until he experienced shortness of breath. He was rushed to Daniel Freeman Hospital where Dr. Rosenberg discovered he had a deadly blood clot in his lungs. He was placed on a heart and lung machine in the intensive care unit where he died at four o'clock P.M. on May 13, 1972. His wife and daughter Debra were at his bed side when he died.

"For me, Dan's death was like losing a brother," Landon lamented.[38] "Our personal relationship was like brothers or father and son," said Lorne

Greene.[39] His body was flown to Dallas then driven to DeKalb, where his mother resided. Arrangements were taken care of by the Henner Funeral Home.

"It was a nationwide shock," said friend and funeral director Robby Bates. "A man of his size, his vitality — to die so suddenly like that."[40]

The 43-year-old actor was laid to rest in Woodman Cemetery between his father and sister, only a mile from where he was born. The ceremony took place at 2 P.M. on May 17, 1972, two hours ahead of schedule, with only 20 immediate family members present. No one from the studio or *Bonanza* cast attended the burial services at the family's request. The family asked that memorial donations be sent to Guyot Foundation Home For Girls, which had been founded anonymously by Blocker. A memorial scholarship fund was set up at Sul Ross University in Dan's name. His mother was placed in a nursing home in 1984.

Hundreds of visitors have journeyed each year to DeKalb to visit Dan Blocker's grave site. His memory has lived on through reruns of *Bonanza,* his family (especially actor Dirk Blocker, whose physical appearance resembles that of his father) and the millions of fans who each year have visited the Ponderosa Ranch at Lake Tahoe. To his many loyal fans, he will always be remembered as the gentle giant.

Movies, Telefilms, Miniseries

An asterisk (*) denotes video availability.

1. *Outer Space Jitters* (Columbia short, 1957)
2. *Gunsight Ridge* (1957)
3. *The Young Captives* (Paramount, 1959); as Oil Field Roughneck
4. **The Errand Boy* (Paramount, 1961); as Dan Blocker
5. *Come Blow Your Horn* (Paramount, 1963); as Mr. Eckman
6. **Lady in Cement* (Arcola-Millfield/20th Century–Fox, 1968); as Waldo Gronsky
7. *Something for a Lonely Man* (Universal/NBC, November 28, 1968) Telefilm; as John Killibrew
8. *The Cockeyed Cowboys of Calico County* [*A Woman for Charley*] (Universal, 1970); as Charley

Radio

9. *Tell Tale Heart* (KVLF, October 26, 1949); as Director

TV Series

10. *Cimarron City* (NBC, October 11, 1958-September 16, 1960) 60 Minutes; as Tiny Budinger
11. *Bonanza* (NBC, September 12, 1959-April 2, 1972) 60 Minutes; as Hoss Cartwright

TV Guest Appearances

12. *Gunsmoke* "Alarm at Pleasant Valley" (CBS, August, 25, 1956) 30 Minutes; as Lieutenant
13. *Cheyenne* "Land Beyond Law" (ABC, January 15, 1957) 60 Minutes; as Pete
14. *Sheriff of Cochise* "Grandfather Grandson" (Syndicated, February 11, 1957) 30 Minutes; as Bartender
15. *Sgt. Preston of the Yukon* "Underground Ambush" (Syndicated, April 25, 1957) 30 Minutes; as Mule Conklin
16. *Tales of Wells Fargo* "Renegade Raiders" (NBC, May 20, 1957) 30 Minutes; as Joe Purdy
17. *Colt .45* "A Time to Die" (ABC, October 25, 1957) 30 Minutes; as Will
18. *The Restless Gun* "Jody" (NBC, November 4, 1957) 30 Minutes; as Ike Burnett
19. *The Restless Gun* "The Child" (NBC, December 23, 1957) 30 Minutes; as El Bruto
20. *Walter Winchell File* "The Reporter (File #20)" (ABC, 1958) 30 Minutes
21. *Dick Powell's Zane Grey Theatre* "Man Unforgiving" (CBS, January 3, 1958) 30 Minutes; as Matt
22. *Wagon Train* "The Dora Gray Story" (NBC, January 29, 1958) 60 Minutes
23. *Sugarfoot* "The Deadlock" (ABC, February 4, 1958) 60 Minutes
24. *Have Gun Will Travel* "Gun Shy" (CBS, March 29, 1958) 30 Minutes
25. *The Thin Man* "The Departed Doctor" (ABC, April 4, 1958) 30 Minutes
26. *The Virginian* [Pilot] (NBC, July 6, 1958) as Salem
27. *The Restless Gun* "Mercy Day" (NBC, October 6, 1958) 30 Minutes
28. *Jefferson Drum* "Stagecoach Episode" (NBC, October 10, 1958) 30 Minutes; as Craig
29. *Gunsmoke* "Thoroughbreds" (CBS, October 18, 1958) 30 Minutes; as Keller
30. *Zorro* "The Senorita Makes a Choice" (ABC, October 30, 1958) 30 Minutes; as Blacksmith
31. *Maverick* "Jail at Junction Flats" (ABC, November 9, 1958) 60 Minutes; as Hog Nose Hughes
32. *The Rifleman* "The Sister" (ABC, November 25, 1958) 30 Minutes; as Peter Snipe
33. *The Restless Gun* "Take Me Home" (NBC, December 29, 1958) 30 Minutes; as Olaf Burland
34. *Westinghouse Desilu Playhouse* "Chez Rogue" (CBS, February 16, 1959)
35. *The Restless Gun* "The Way Back" (NBC, July 13, 1959) 30 Minutes; as Olaf Burland
36. *The Rebel* "Johnny Yuma" (ABC, October 4, 1959) 30 Minutes; as Pierce
37. *Troubleshooters* "Tiger Culhane" (NBC, October 9, 1959) 30 Minutes
38. *Here's Hollywood* (NBC, 1960) 30 Minutes
39. *Perry Como's Kraft Music Hall* (NBC, 1962) 60 minutes
40. *Henry Fonda and the Family* (CBS, February 6, 1962)
41. *The Andy Williams Show* (NBC, 1963) 60 Minutes
42. *Exploring* (NBC, 1963)
43. *I'll Bet* (NBC, March 29, 1965) 30 Minutes
44. NBC News Special
45. *The Tonight Show Starring Johnny Carson* (NBC, November 12, 1968)

46. *Rowan and Martin's Laugh-in* (NBC, 1969) 60 Minutes
47. *Jack Benny's Birthday Special* (NBC, February 17, 1969)
48. *Sesame Street* (PBS, March 1971)
49. *Swing Out, Sweet Land* (NBC, April 8, 1971)

Stage

50. Spring Varieties [Freshman Variety Show] (Sul Ross State College Auditorium, April 15, 1948)
51. *Arsenic and Old Lace* (Sul Ross State College Auditorium, June 29 and 30, 1948); as Dr. Einstein
52. *1949 Follies* [Act II Scene I "Vaudeville" as Bartender] [Scene II "Movie Lot," as Fighter]
53. *My Sister Eileen* (Sul Ross State College Auditorium, July 7-8, 1949) as The Wreck
54. *The Green Pastures* (Sul Ross State College Auditorium, November 30, December 1, 1949) as Delawd
55. *Famed Oak* (Sul Ross State College Auditorium, 1949); as Husband
56. *King Lear* (Broadway, 1950s)
57. The Tenth Intra-Mural One-Acts "Alcestis" (Sul Ross State College Auditorium, April 5, 1950); as Director
58. *Blithe Spirit* (Sul Ross State College Auditorium, (May 1950); as Dr. Bradman
59. Plymouth Drama Festival (July 1950) [It played for six weeks.]
60. *Macbeth* (Camp Polk in Louisiana [45th Army Infantry Division] 1950-51; as Macbeth
61. *The Princess and Mr. Parker* (Fine Arts Center, April 20, 1953-April 23, 1953); as a Supporter
62. *Western Star* (Sul Ross State College Auditorium, 1953); as one of the Readers
63. Fourteenth Intra-Mural One Acts "The Winslow Boy"; as Sir Robert Morton and "The Man in the Bowler Hat"; as Director (Sul Ross State College Auditorium, April 1953)
64. *The Torchbearers* (Sul Ross State College Auditorium, 1953); as Assistant to the Director
65. *Othello* (Sul Ross State College Auditorium, August 17, and 18, 1953); as Othello
66. *Mister Roberts* (Sul Ross State College Auditorium, August 1954); as one of the Radio Voices and Director
67. *Green Pastures* (Odessa College Auditorium, November 18, 1961–November 19, 1961) [three benefit performances]
68. *The Greatest Glory* (University of Texas in Austin, June 1966); as Ben Franklin and George Washington

Personal Appearances

69. Sul Ross Homecoming Parade (1960)
70. Jaycee Rodeo of Rodeos (Phoenix, Arizona, April 5, 1962)

Short Story

Michael Landon

JOSEPH BURNS CARTWRIGHT

Joseph Burns was born in 1857 to Marie Courlan DeMarigny and Benjamin Cartwright. At birth, he weighed five and three-quarter pounds. Marie grew to love and treat Adam and Hoss as if they were her own. Unlike his brothers, the young boy never really got to know his mother as she was killed in a riding mishap not long after his birth. She was buried on a small hill overlooking Lake Tahoe.

Joe grew to five-feet nine and a quarter inches. He had jet-black, curly hair. He loved the ladies and became quite a charmer with his mischievous grin and infectious laugh. Being the youngest, he was often called Little Joe. He was a proud and sensitive young man who really cared about people but was quick-tempered (a trait he inherited from his mother). Ben saw a lot of Marie in his son.

Because his mother came from New Orleans, Joe strongly identified with the South, which sometimes caused problems with Adam, who came from Boston. His affinity for the South enabled him to help Fred Kyle to acquire silver to aid the Confederate cause. On another occasion, Judge Terry, a Southern sympathizer, appointed Joe as a delegate to the Statehood Convention to further his ambitions.

He would later learn that he had a stepbrother, Clay Stafford, who was conceived two years prior to Marie's marriage to Ben. He was the son of Marie and Jean Pierre, who was Ben's foreman and who had died while saving Ben's life. Her mother-in-law took the baby and Marie was later told he had died of fever.

Little Joe enjoyed horses and became a competent rider. He rode a black and white Pinto named Cochise.

Joe sometimes became annoyed with his brothers, who were like mother hens and did not allow him to do things without them looking after him. He wanted to prove himself and took charge of a construction contract. He learned that he could handle the responsibilities. When trouble developed, he also realized that it was nice to have his family there when he needed them.

He enjoyed playing jokes on people and often involved himself and Hoss in some hare-brained money-making schemes. He and Hoss were once almost shot when they were mistaken for outlaws (the Slade Brothers). He once became Hoss' trainer so they could win $100 when Hoss wrestled Bearcat Sampson. Joe got Hop Sing to put Hoss on a vegetable diet so his brother would be starved when he competed in a pancake eating contest. Hoss and Joe went into business raising rabbits for their coats but neither was willing to skin the rabbits. Joe entered the detective business after reading How to Solve Crimes and enlisted his brother's help in preventing a bank robbery.

He was civic-minded when he took on danger while riding for the Pony Express. Along with Hoss, they became involved with Virginia City's mayoral race by backing two different candidates.

He found his hands full when a pretty teacher was injured and he was chosen to fill-in for her while she mended. Once when he and Candy were playing cards, Joe loaned Candy some money. The ranch hand won the co-ownership in a mine and stamp mill. On another occasion, Hoss, Dusty and Joe bought a livery stable business to thwart the competition. Once when Joe went to see the man who cut off Hop Sing's pigtail, they got into a fight. When the man later was found dead, Joe was arrested for the murder.

Joe had his own tragedies. When everyone had left for a cattle drive, Joe stayed behind to await the arrival of the cook. A storm developed and, when he tried to calm the horses, he was trampled on and left alone to tend his injuries. Once when moving nitroglycern, Joe was temporarily blinded in an explosion.

Little Joe fell in love with Alice Harper and they were married. Some months after the wedding, Joe took his expectant wife to their soon-to-be new home. While he was away getting something from the Ponderosa, she and her brother were murdered. Grief-stricken, Joe headed out to find the murderer.

Years later, he met and fell in love with Annabelle. They were married and had a son, Benji (named after his grandfather), and a daughter, Sarah. The Spanish-American War drew Joe into battle. He rode up San Juan Hill with Teddy Roosevelt, an action which won him a medal. Unfortunately, he was not heard from again and was listed missing in action and presumed killed in 1899. His family grieved their loss. Benji joined his cousins on the Ponderosa and took up the fight against strip miners to defend the ranch his father grew up on and loved.

Michael Landon was born Eugene Maurice Orowitz on October 31, 1936, to Eli M. and Peggy O'Neil Orowitz. Eli worked in RKO's publicity department and was responsible for handling the top movie stars of the day.

When Eli met Irish-Catholic Peggy O'Neil, she was a Ziegfeld Girl. Despite their different personalities, they were married.

Michael's older sister (by three years) was Evelyn, who had fair hair and skin. She called her little brother Ugy.

When work slowed down, Eli moved his family from Forest Hill, New York, to 632 South Newton Lake Drive in Collingswood, New Jersey, where he got a job managing several theaters. From the start, marital problems plagued the Orowitzes (primarily over their different religious beliefs and Peggy's departure from show business). She was known to often attempt suicide but not very seriously.

When Michael entered elementary school, he tried to handle his home life and the fact his father paid little attention to him. At ten his best friend was a collie named Ike. Landon was a good student, earning all A's.

He developed a bed-wetting problem and his mother made things worse by trying to embarrass him by hanging the wet sheets out the window for the neighbors to see. This practice would continue until he was 14.

At 13, he played a Japanese houseboy in *The Bat* for an amateur Haddonfield theater group. He was also in their *A Thousand Clowns*.

Michael, now 16, wanted to buy an old Studebaker but needed $150. To earn the money, he took a job in a soup cannery. His mother would not let him drive it until he was 17.

While attending Collingswood High, he took up the javelin under Coach Ritter's guidance. After seeing the film *Samson and Delilah* (1949), Michael grew long hair. While at Collingswood High he was elected class Vice-President. He did not do well in high school and had to take his sophomore year over again. He would eventually graduate 299 out of 301. Michael showed promise in high school, throwing the javelin. As a sophomore he won the regional championship. He was second in the state during his junior year and as a senior he became the best in the state. He proved himself good enough at the sport to be awarded a scholarship at the University of Southern California. In February 1955, he enrolled at USC as a speech and drama major. He kept his long hair and three football players thought he was a freak. They got him down while they shaved off his hair. Michael tried to regain his skill with the javelin by continuously throwing it but with poor results. Because of his continued efforts, his shoulder was damaged, thus ending his college career and his Olympic dreams.

Eli thought he could get a job at Paramount, so he moved the family to North Los Angeles. He was crushed when no one there remembered him. Not able to face further rejection, he got work in downtown Los Angeles at some run-down movie theaters.

After college, Landon took on several odd jobs such as working in a ribbon factory, selling blankets door to door and acting as a lifeguard at public pools. He later worked on the docks at J. J. Newberry, a local department store.

One day, Nick Venet, a friend at the docks, persuaded Michael to be his partner at a Warner Bros. audition in a scene from *Home of the Brave*. An executive liked his looks and persuaded him to enroll in the studio's acting school under a scholarship. Evelyn and her friend David Kramer also took lessons from coach Estelle Harmor. Michael liked the experience but felt the name Orowitz did not make a good stage name and decided to change it. He liked Lane but found the name was already registered with the Screen Actors Guild. He flipped through the phone book and found Landon — thus becoming Michael Landon.

Michael began seeing a 26-year-old widow named Dodie Fraser. She was a legal secretary whose husband was killed in an automobile accident. She had a seven-year-old boy named Mark. Despite Peggy's interference, they were married.

Towards the end of 1956, Michael's career started to take off with appearances on TV's *Dupont Theatre, Telephone Time, General Electric Theatre, Schlitz Playhouse of Stars* and *Tales of Wells Fargo*, to mention just a few. In 1957, producer David Dortort hired Landon to play a villain in one of his *Restless Gun* episodes. Dortort liked what he saw and thought he might be able to use him for a future project.

Producer Herman Cohen persuaded Michael to try out for the part of Tony in *I Was a Teenage Werewolf*. He offered him a contract. Cohen recalled, "Michael was a hard worker. He rehearsed with us evenings and weekends."[41] Michael's ears protruded out too far and had to be taped back — a condition he would later remedy by surgery. The film took six days to shoot and had a $100,000 budget. The film was finished on time, was released in July 1957 and grossed more than $2,000,000 and is considered a cult classic today.

In 1958, he acted in the motion picture *God's Little Acre* (as an albino, Dave Dawson). The film was based on Erskine Caldwell's novel of the same name. Again in 1958, he made *Maracaibo* starring Cornel Wilde. He also filmed *The Legend of Tom Dooley* (1959) and played the title role. With the release of these films, his box office future seemed bright.

Peggy finally accepted Dodie into the family and Michael enjoyed the role of fatherhood with his son Mark.

Michael Landon. (Photofest.)

Herman Cohen still held Michael's contract and was able to get him an agent with the William Morris Agency. When David Dortort created *Bonanza* in 1959, he wanted to cast Landon as Little Joe. He had Landon in mind for the role since he cast him in *The Restless Gun.* "The kid was good," Dortort recalled, "but for some reason no one had ever signed him for a regular series. I fixed that."[42] The only hitch was the fact that Herman Cohen still had him under contract. Herman felt bad that he had not exercised his rights much after *I Was a Teenage Werewolf* and decided not to hold back the young man's career, so he released him from his contract.

Landon could not believe his good fortune of earning $500 a week. With his first paycheck, he celebrated at his favorite Chinese restaurant. He was a skinny 132-pound young man who had to put on a bulky sweatshirt beneath his other clothes until he worked out, increasing his weight to a muscular 148 pounds.

Bonanza aired on September 12, 1959. "After I saw the pilot and the first few episodes, I thought it would be a sure flop," Landon stated.[43] However the network got behind the show and it improved and climbed in the ratings.

Now that Michael was bringing in good money, he and Dodie bought a Spanish-style home in the Hollywood Hills. Michael was pleased he could now provide security for his family. Because of Dodie's heart problems, she was discouraged from having any more children, so they adopted infant Josh Fraser.

Shortly before *Bonanza* grew in popularity, Eli passed away from a 1959 heart attack while having coffee in a shop next to the theater where he worked. Michael and Eli had grown closer in later years and, when Eli left Peggy, he became a part of the Landon household.

The four *Bonanza* stars had countless offers for personal appearances at rodeos and fairs. Landon earned around $175,000 his first year by doing weekend stints.

Singing interested Michael and he did a brief stint on the road with Jerry Lee Lewis. He also recorded "Gimme a Little Kiss" and "Be Patient with Me" for Candlelight Records. He would later sing on the *Bonanza* cast albums. He appeared on some variety shows such as *Highway of Melody* (April 22, 1962), on which he sang "There's Nothing Like a Dame" with Hugh O'Brian and Gordon MacRae. He also hosted an episode of *Hullabaloo* (November 29, 1965) and sang on *Bing Crosby's Sun Valley Christmas Show* on December 19, 1973.

Landon was frequently away, which took its toll on his marriage. He turned to alcohol and pills to help him cope. The couple adopted Jason hoping it would help their marriage but it did not make a difference. "My mother and father never loved each other, really ever, and my first wife and I never loved each other and we both knew it when we got married."[44] They had gone ahead with the wedding because neither had the heart to tell Mark they did not want to. The couple divorced amiably in 1960, with Michael still spending time with his sons. The adoption papers had not been signed for Jason and Dodie felt she could not take care of another child, so he was sent back to the adoption agency.

One day on the Paramount lot, Michael spotted a young model, Lynn Noe, born in Louisville, Kentucky. In 1940, her parents John and Virginia Noe headed for California where he started a manufacturing company. Lynn had fallen for a football player and left college to marry him. They had a daughter, Cheryl Pontrelli, born on November 16, 1953. Lynn supported her husband while he attended law school. After three years of marriage, the couple divorced with Lynn retaining custody of their daughter.

Michael finally got up the nerve to talk to Lynn and they soon fell in love. After courting her, they eloped to Mexico on January 12, 1961. The next year they had a small wedding in Reno and Dan Blocker was his best man. Because of filming demands, they delayed their honeymoon for two months when they went to Acapulco. On their return to Los Angeles, they bought a home in the San Fernando Valley. When Michael decided to adopt Cheryl, her real father refused to give his consent. Lynn would often travel with Landon on his personal appearance tours.

In 1963, Lynn gave birth to Leslie Ann at the Presbyterian Hospital in Hollywood. When Leslie was three months old, Lynn told Michael she was expecting another child. On the season's last day of shooting, Lynn started getting labor pains. He met his mother-in-law in the waiting room where they waited for the birth of Michael Graham Landon in 1964.

Peggy and her son reconciled their differences. She readily announced that she had "the greatest son anyone could have. I have no financial worries."[45] Peggy and Evelyn shared a small apartment along with Evelyn's teenage daughter. Evelyn tried her lot at acting, taking the stage name of Victoria King. Michael also helped support his mother and sister.

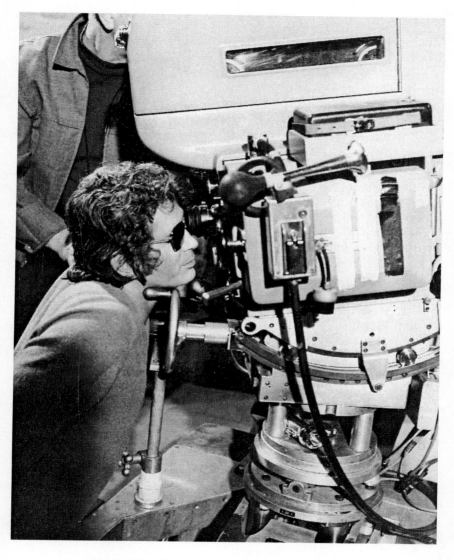

Michael Landon as director. (Authors' collection.)

Over the years, Landon made many wise investments with co-stars Lorne Greene and Dan Blocker.

He was multi-talented, wanted to learn more about the behind-the-scenes aspects of the business and used *Bonanza* to develop his writing and directing skills. Ted Voigtlander and William F. Claxton took Landon under their wings. Dortort said Michael was "a very good director who knows how to handle actors with a firm hand."[46] During the *Bonanza* years, he earned close to $500,000 acting, writing and directing and doubled that with earnings from outside interests.

With the death of Dan Blocker on May 13, 1972, and the switch from their Sunday schedule, ratings fell. Michael found the loss of Blocker hard but he remembered the fun times they had shared together. The network eventually pulled the plug on *Bonanza* and the last episode aired on January 16, 1973. Michael and Lorne were unhappy with the way the network informed them of the show's cancellation. "They told us on Monday that we would quit shooting on Wednesday, November 8, 1972," Michael recalled.[47] Landon was earning around $14,000 per episode and millions more from selling his syndication rights. He had spent 14 of his 35 years on the show. He looked forward to new projects. His spirits were lifted when Lynn revealed she was pregnant again. She carried daughter Shawna the full term and gave birth on December 4, 1971.

NBC offered him an exclusive deal, enabling him to create new projects for them.

The Landon children were not permitted to take advantage of servants and were expected to clean their rooms and pick up after themselves, for which they were given an allowance. They were also not permitted to watch a lot of television with the exception of educational programs and their father's shows.

While a freshman at the University of Arizona in 1972, Cheryl was involved in a car accident and she almost died. Fortunately she fully recovered. During her ordeal, however, she became addicted to drugs. The family learned of a program CEDU in the town of Running Hills. It was a voluntary program. Respecting Michael's advice, she joined the program. He then became a spokesman for Nancy Reagan's drug campaign.

Part of Landon's daily routine included searching for ideas for NBC. The network assigned him an anthology series and he directed and wrote the opening episode (based on the film *Love Story*). Next the network produced a biography series and Landon worked on *It's Good to Be Alive*, the story of Roy Campanella.

Ed Friendly held the rights to the *Little House on the Prairie* stories and approached Landon about being his partner in the series as well as playing Charles Ingalls. Michael loved the material as it would give him a venue to promote good family morals. NBC was not thrilled with the project but eventually agreed to back a two-hour pilot. If it did well in the ratings, they would place it on their fall schedule. As soon as Michael saw Karen Grassle, he knew he had found his Caroline. Melissa Sue Anderson was chosen to play Mary; for his Laura, he picked Melissa Gilbert. Ed Friendly and Landon were at odds from the beginning on how to develop the series. Friendly wanted

Landon removed from the series but NBC stood behind Michael. Without him, they would not back the show. The pilot aired on March 30, 1974, and earned good ratings. By August, Friendly had become a silent partner and control of the show belonged to Michael. He expected more from the adult actors but if any of the children were uptight, he would shut down production and set up a game of baseball or horseshoes until they relaxed. He also demanded good grades from the children or they would not appear on that week's episode. He tolerated no temper tantrums from the adults and dismissed anyone who could not control themselves (including some name stars). He enjoyed a happy set and often played practical jokes or threw a party or picnic. He often used actors and behind-the-scenes people from the *Bonanza* years. Landon would use the same people and crew in future shows by keeping them on retainer. He used the money that he saved by bringing the shows in under budget. He often presented his company with nice gifts or bonuses. Stories were derived from the books as well as personal experiences. He also revamped some of his *Bonanza* scripts. He was known as a perfectionist not only at work but at home. By taking control of his projects, he had only himself to blame if things did not work out.

In 1975, Lynn was expecting another child and presented Michael with a son Christopher Beau.

The topic of bed-wetting was not one openly discussed, but Michael felt that no child should go through what he did. He decided to enlighten the public by making *The Loneliest Runner* (1976) starring Lance Kerwin.

About 1980, Michael needed another project to sink his teeth into and developed the NBC series *Father Murphy*, starring Merlin Olson (who had worked on *Little House on the Prairie*). The show debuted in 1981. Michael handled the production chores and did not appear on screen as he was still doing *Little House on the Prairie*. *Father Murphy* filmed in Phoenix, Arizona, and *Little House* in Los Angeles, so Michael went back and forth between the two cities. *Father Murphy* lasted two years — until the network pitted it against *60 Minutes*.

When Landon first encountered Cindy Clerico on *Little House on the Prairie*, he was hooked. The news spread to the tabloids. Kodak decided to drop Landon as their spokesperson. Attempts to reconcile with Lynn proved fruitless. In 1980, he left Lynn. "We were together for 19 years," Michael said. "I don't consider that a failed marriage. I don't think it was a disaster. We produced some terrific kids. We just didn't grow in the same direction. We became different people. We both changed."[48] Landon started divorce proceedings on April 16, 1981, Lynn learned about it while she and the children were vacationing in Acapulco. After a lengthy battle over property, Michael gave in on April 27 and allowed her to receive $26,000,000. That included their 3.5 million dollar home. He then moved into an apartment. During

Michael Landon as Charles Ingalls on Little House on the Prairie. ***(Authors' Collection.)***

Michael's marital problems, his 71-year-old mother passed away on March 15, 1981. A couple of weeks following Peggy's death, Evelyn had a nervous breakdown and was placed in an institution. Lynn joined LADIES (Life After Divorce Is Eventually Sane) along with the wives of other celebrities. Michael and Lynn's divorce became final in December 1981.

In 1979-80, *Little House on the Prairie* became NBC's most profitable show in the prime-time schedule.

Cheryl and Jim Wilson, a manufacturer's representative, were married on December 22, 1981 and honeymooned in Hawaii thanks to Michael's wedding gift.

After the 1982-83 season, Landon informed NBC he would no longer appear as Charles Ingalls on *Little House on the Prairie*. The series would end its run on February 6, 1984.

When Leslie went to the University of Southern California, it was discovered she suffered from bulimia. Fortunately she received the proper help that aided her in overcoming the disease.

Hal Bartlett held the rights to Australian journalist John Everingham's Laos story, titled *Love Is Forever*. He had problems finding someone to do it. He contacted Landon. Michael persuaded NBC to invest in the project while Bartlett got 20th Century–Fox to join the venture. A war over control ensued between Michael and Hal. Bartlett vowed never to do another project with Landon.

Michael and Cindy chose Valentine's Day 1983 as their wedding day and the ceremonies took place at his Malibu home. Six months later, she gave birth to daughter Jennifer. Michael became a grandfather for the first time in 1983 when Cheryl and Jim became the parents of a baby boy.

Michael went to NBC with a series about an angel. They were hesitant as it did not fit the image they were seeking. However, they relented and even provided the title of *Highway to Heaven*. Michael wanted Victor French to play his sidekick. The brass at NBC thought a younger, sexier actor was more in line. Landon stood his ground. "I had to change my deal with the network from one pilot project to two to get the series on," Michael explained. "Their attitude is that they're letting me get this one out of my system."[49] *Highway to Heaven* premiered on NBC on September 19, 1984, to good responses. Landon asked Lorne Greene to guest on *Highway to Heaven*. "Mike and I had wanted to work together ever since *Bonanza* went off the air," explained Greene. "But Mike didn't want to use me on *Little House* because he said, and I agreed, that it was too much like *Bonanza*."[50] The episode was shot on November 19, 1985, and aired in 1986.

While still working on *Highway to Heaven*, Landon wrote the script for *Sam's Son* (1984), which centered around getting his father's recognition. It starred Timothy Patrick Murphy (as Gene) and Eli Wallach and Anne Jackson as his parents.

Michael and Cindy became the proud parents of Sean Matthew in 1986.

Landon smoked as much as four packs each day but after Victor French's death in July 1989, he drastically cut down and eventually quit smoking.

Highway to Heaven was the first of his projects to be produced by Michael Landon Productions. It ran until 1989.

On January 20, 1990, *Where Pigeons Go to Die* starring Art Carney was aired. It was to be Michael's last NBC project. The film received two Emmy nominations but did not win.

In June 1990, Michael attended the network's affiliates meeting in Washington, DC. He was one of the NBC stars to receive a Lifetime Achievement Award for contributions to the great programming he had made over the years. Landon soon became unhappy with NBC and moved his offices to the MGM Studio, now owned by Columbia. "I'm not going to be with NBC any more," declared Michael. "I'll be basically with CBS in terms of network affiliation, and I'll also be under contract to Columbia Studios for motion pictures and television."[51] In 1990, Michael's company joined CBS to develop the pilot *US* as a possible new series. After the pilot was completed in March 1991, Michael took his family on a skiing vacation to Park City, Utah. While there, he began to feel ill. When the pain became too great, he went to a doctor for tests but nothing was discovered. On April 3, 1991, Michael entered Cedars-Sinai Medical Center, where he was given a liver biopsy. Two days later, he was released and returned to his Malibu home. Michael was later told he had pancreatic cancer. He decided to hold a press conference and tell the world of his condition before the tabloids got hold of the news. After trying conventional treatments, he stopped them in favor of an organic diet which seemed to ease the stomach pain. Landon returned to the hospital on April 24, 1991, for a second cat scan. He was then told that the tumor had grown much larger and the cancer was now in his colon.

Landon got in touch with his friend Johnny Carson and asked if he could appear on Carson's *Tonight Show*. His May 9, 1991, appearance drew the second highest audience within the show's prior ten year period. Landon wanted to talk about his illness. As Michael left the stage, he wore a smile and waved to the audience who gave him a standing ovation. Around the same time he had also done an interview with *Life* and appeared on the cover. The tabloids were full of stories and even predicted how much time he had to live. He was deluged with cards from well-wishers.

On weekends, his children visited their father. He spent as much time with them as he could. By June, he rapidly began slipping and soon he was no longer able to keep up appearances. Michael Landon passed away on July 1, 1991, which ironically was his mother's birthday. He was cremated the next day. The funeral took place at Hillcrest Memorial Gardens in West Los Angeles. It was a private service and officiated by a rabbi. Dodie and her sons were among the family and friends in attendance; Lynn chose not to attend. His ashes were placed in a tomb some 50 yards from where Lorne Greene was buried. Landon reportedly had left behind an estate somewhere between $100,000,000 to $250,000,000.

After his death, Ashley Taylor Landon was born to Michael Landon, Jr., and his wife Sharee on August 12, 1991. On March 15, 1993, Cindy Crawford accepted, on his behalf, an award in connection with the National Children's Leukemia Foundation. He was also inducted into TV's Hall of Fame on April 18, 1996.

Michael had written a poem for a *Little House on the Prairie* episode in which Patricia Neal had appeared. Melissa Gilbert read it at his funeral because it expressed his own sentiments:

> Remember me with smiles and laughter
> for that is how I will remember you all!
> If You can only remember me with tears
> then don't remember me at all.[52]

Michael Landon had come a long way from his dysfunctional background to become one of the most versatile talents in television with major achievements as an actor, director, writer and producer. He will always be remembered for the clean, family-oriented, quality shows he worked on.

Movies, Telefilms, Miniseries

An asterisk (*) denotes video availability.

1. *These Wilder Years* (MGM, 1956); as Boy in Poolroom
2. **I Was a Teenage Werewolf* (American International Pictures, 1957); as Tony
3. **God's Little Acre* (United Artists, 1958); as Dave Dawson
4. **High School Confidential!* [*The Young Hellions*] (MGM, 1958); as Steve Bentley
5. *Maracaibo* (Theodora/Paramount, 1958); as Lago Orlando
6. **The Legend of Tom Dooley* (Columbia, 1959); as Tom Dooley
7. *The Errand Boy (Paramount, 1961); as Little Joe Cartwright
8. **Little House on the Prairie* (NBC, March 30, 1974) Telefilm; as Charles Ingalls
9. **The Loneliest Runner* (NBC, December 20, 1976) Telefilm; as John Curtis-as an Adult
10. *Killing Stone* (Universal/NBC, May 2, 1978) Telefilm; as Producer, Director, Screenwriter
11. *Love Is Forever* [*Comeback*] (20th Century–Fox/NBC, April 3, 1983) Telefilm; as John Everingham
12. *Look Back to Yesterday* (TV, 1984) Telefilm
13. **Sam's Son* (Invictus/NBC, 1984) Telefilm; as Director and Screenwriter
14. *The Last of the Great Survivors* (CBS, January 3, 1984) Telefilm
15. *Where Pigeons Go to Die* (NBC, January 29, 1990) Telefilm; as Hugh as an Adult; Producer, Director, Screenwriter
16. US (CBS, September 20, 1991) Telefilm; as Jeff Hayes; Producer, Director, Screenwriter

TV Series

17. *Bonanza* (NBC, September 12, 1959–January 16, 1973); as Little Joe Cartwright
18. **Little House on the Prairie* (NBC, September 11, 1974–May 10, 1982); as Charles Ingalls
19. *Highway to Heaven* (September 19, 1984–August 4, 1989); as Jonathan Smith

TV Guest Appearances

20. *Crossroads* (ABC, mid– to late 1950s) 30 Minutes
21. *Cavalcade of America* (ABC, Mid to Late 1950s) 30 Minutes
22. *Luke and the Tenderfoot* [Pilot] (August 6, 1955) 30 Minutes; as Tough
23. *Sheriff of Cochise* (Syndicated, Late 1950s or early 1960s) 30 Minutes
24. *Telephone Time* "The Mystery of Casper Hauser" (CBS, May 6, 1956) 30 Minutes; as Casper Hauser
25. *Stories of the Century* "Shadows of Belle Starr" (Syndicated, 1956)
26. *Adventures of Jim Bowie* "Deputy Sheriff" (ABC, September 28, 1956) 30 Minutes; as Jerome
27. *Adventures of Jim Bowie* "The Swordsman" (ABC, December 14, 1956) 30 Minutes; as Armand DeNivernais)
28. *Wire Service* "High Adventure" (ABC, December 20, 1956); as Pietro
29. *Dupont Theatre* "The Man from St. Paul" (ABC, January 29, 1957) 30 Minutes; as Frank "Tex" Benson
30. *Telephone Time* "Fight for the Title" (CBS, March 17, 1957) 30 Minutes; as Jud Lombard
31. *General Electric Theatre* "Too Good with a Gun" (Syndicated, March 24, 1957) 30 Minutes; as Claude
32. *Schlitz Playhouse of Stars* "The Restless Gun" (CBS, March 29, 1957) 30 Minutes; as Sandy
33. *Tales of Wells Fargo* "Shotgun Messenger" (NBC, May 7, 1957) 30 Minutes; as Tad Cameron
34. *Tales of Wells Fargo* "Sam Bass" (NBC, June 10, 1957) 30 Minutes; as Jackson
35. *Schlitz Playhouse of Stars* "Hands of the Enemy" (CBS, August 9, 1957) 30 Minutes; as Fred Simmons
36. *The Court of Last Resort* "The Forbes-Carol Case" (NBC, October 18, 1957) 30 Minutes; as Thomas Forbes
37. *Matinee Theatre* "The Weak and the Strong" (NBC, October 29, 1957)
38. *Tales of Wells Fargo* "The Kid" (NBC, November 18, 1957) 30 Minutes; as Tad Cameron
39. *Zane Grey Theatre* "The Gift from a Gunman" (CBS, December 13, 1957) 30 Minutes; as Dan
40. *U.S. Marshall* "The Champ" (Syndicated, 1958) 30 Minutes
41. **Cheyenne* "White Warrior" (ABC, March 11, 1958) 60 Minutes; as Alan Horn
42. *Trackdown* "The Pueblo Kid" (CBS, April 4, 1958) 30 Minutes
43. *Goodyear Theatre* "The Giant Step" (NBC, April 28, 1958) 30 Minutes
44. *Schlitz Playhouse of Stars* "Belle Starr" (a.k.a. "Way of the West") (CBS, June 6, 1958) 30 Minutes; as Don Burns

45. *Alcoa Theatre* "Johnny Risk"(NBC, June 16, 1958) 30 Minutes; as Johnny Risk
46. *Studio One* "Man Under Glass" (CBS, July 14, 1958) 60 Minutes
47. *Wanted Dead or Alive* "The Martin Poster" (CBS, September 6, 1958) 30 Minutes; as Carl Martin
48. *Tombstone Territory* "The Rose of Rio Bravo" (ABC, September 17, 1958) 30 Minutes; as Barton Clark
49. *The Rifleman* "End of a Young Gun" (ABC, October 10, 1958) 30 Minutes; as Will Fulton
50. *The Texan* "The Hemp Tree" (CBS, November 17, 1958) 30 Minutes; as Nick Ahearn
51. *Trackdown* "Day of Vengeance" (CBS, November 28, 1958) 30 Minutes; as Jack Summers
52. *Zane Grey Theatre* "Living Is a Lonesome Thing" (CBS, January 1, 1959) 30 Minutes; as Vance Coburn
53. *Frontier Doctor* "Shadows of Belle Starr" (Syndicated, January 3, 1959) 30 Minutes
54. *Wanted Dead or Alive* "The Legend" (CBS, March 7, 1959) 30 Minutes; as Clay McGarrett
55. *Tombstone Territory* "The Man from Brewster" (ABC, April 24, 1959) 30 Minutes; as Chris Anderson
56. *Playhouse 90* "The Project Immortality" (CBS, June 11, 1959) 90 Minutes
57. *Rifleman* "The Mind Reader" (ABC, June 30, 1959) 30 Minutes; as Bill Mathis
58. *Johnny Staccato* "The Naked Truth" (NBC, September 10, 1959) 30 Minutes; as Freddie Tate
59. *Tender Years* (1959–60)
60. *Here's Hollywood* (NBC, 1960)
61. *Your First Impression* (NBC, 1962)
62. *Highway of Melody* (NBC, April 22, 1962) 60 Minutes
63. *Your First Impression* (NBC, 1963)
64. *Stump the Stars* (CBS, 1963) 30 Minutes
65. *Bonanza* "Alias Joe Cartwright" (NBC, January 26, 1964) 60 Minutes; as Borden
66. *Truth or Consequences* (NBC, 1964) 30 Minutes
67. *You Don't Say* (NBC, 1964) 30 Minutes
68. *Vacation Playhouse* "Luke and the Tenderfoot" (CBS, August 6, 1965) 30 Minutes; as Tough
69. *Hullabaloo* (NBC, November 29, 1965) 30 Minutes; as Host
70. *Chain Letter* (NBC, September 5, 1966-September 9, 1966) 30 Minutes
71. *Goodyear Playhouse* "Giant Step" (NBC, April 28, 1968) 60 Minutes
72. *A Country Happening* [Pilot] (NBC, September 8, 1969)
73. *Name Droppers* (NBC, September 29, 1969) 30 Minutes
74. *Dean Martin* (NBC, November 29, 1970) 60 Minutes
75. *Sesame Street* (PBS, March 1971) 30 Minutes
76. *Swing Out, Sweet Land* (NBC, April 8, 1971) 90 Minutes
77. *Amateur's Guide to Love* [Pilot] (CBS, August 8, 1971) 30 Minutes
78. *Monsanto Presents Mancini* (Syndicated, December 1971) 60 Minutes
79. *A Special London Bridge Special* (NBC, May 7, 1972) 60 Minutes

80. *Rowan & Martin's Laugh-In* (NBC, October 9, 1972) 60 Minutes
81. *The Vin Scully Show* (CBS, January 22, 1973) 30 Minutes
82. *The Match Game* (CBS, July 2, 1973) 30 Minutes
83. *Love Story* "Love Came Laughing" (NBC, October 3, 1973) 60 Minutes
84. *Bing Crosby's Sun Valley Christmas Show* (NBC, December 19, 1973) 60 Minutes
85. *NBC Follies* (NBC, 1973) 60 Minutes
86. 17th Annual America's Junior Miss (CBS, 1974) 60 Minutes; as Host
87. *Merv Griffin Show* (Syndicated, April 9, 1974) 90 Minutes
88. *The Tonight Show Starring Johnny Carson* (NBC, December 16, 1974) 90 Minutes; as Guest Host
89. *Mitzi and a Hundred Guys* (CBS, March 24, 1975) 60 Minutes
90. *Donny and Marie* (ABC, April 30 1976) 60 Minutes
91. *Dinah!* (CBS, May 7, 1976) 90 Minutes
92. 19th Annual America's Junior Miss Pageant (CBS, May 10, 1976); as Host
93. *Hollywood Squares* (ABC, June 29, 1976) 30 Minutes
94. *Dinah!* (CBS, December 1, 1976) 90 Minutes
95. *Doug Henning's World of Magic I* (NBC, December 23, 1976) 60 Minutes; as Host
96. *Dinah!* (CBS, 1977) 90 Minutes.
97. 88th Annual Tournament of Roses Parade (NBC, January 1, 1977); as co-Host
98. *National Kid's Quiz* (NBC, January 28, 1978) 60 Minutes; as Host
99. *TV: The Fabulous 50s* (NBC, March 3, 1978) 90 Minutes; as co-Host
100. *Barbara Walters Special* (ABC, May 30, 1978)
101. *General Electric's All-Star Anniversary* (ABC, September 29, 1978) 120 Minutes
102. 92nd Annual Tournament of Roses Parade (NBC, January 1, 1981) 150 Minutes; as Host
103. *Funtastic World of Hanna-Barbera Arena Show* (NBC, June 25, 1981) 90 Minutes; as Host
104. *Father Murphy* (NBC, November 3, 1981-June 17, 1984) 60 Minutes; Creator, Executive Producer, one of the Writers and Directors
105. *Walt Disney* "One Man's Dream" (CBS, December 12, 1981) 120 Minutes; as Host
106. 25th Annual America's Junior Miss Pageant (CBS, June 22, 1982) 60 Minutes; as Host
107. *Let the Children Live* (Channel 9, August 23, 1982) 300 Minutes; as co-Host
108. *PBS Survival* "Killers of the Plain" (PBS, November 24, 1982); as Narrator
109. *When Will the Dying Stop* (WKBN-TV, January 14, 1983); as co-Host
110. The Fourth Annual *TV Guide* Special (NBC, January 24, 1983); as co-Host
111. The Twenty-Sixth Annual Junior Miss Pageant (CBS, June 21, 1983) 60 Minutes; as Host
112. The Thirty-Fifth Annual Emmy Awards (NBC, September 25, 1983); as a Presenter with Lorne Greene and Dirk Blocker
113. *An Appeal to All Americans* (PBS, October 27, 1983)
114. *The Chemical People* (PBS, November 2, 1983)
115. *Here's Television Entertainment* (NBC, December 4, 1983)

116. *Dean Martin's Celebrity Roast* (NBC, December 7, 1984); as Honored Guest
117. *Bob Hope Buys NBC* (NBC, September 17, 1985) 60 Minutes
118. NBC's 60th Anniversary Celebration (NBC, May 12, 1986) 180 Minutes; Co-Host
119. *NBC Investigates Bob Hope* (NBC, September 17, 1987) 60 Minutes
120. *Bob Hope* "Happy Birthday, Bob" (NBC, May 16, 1988) 180 Minutes
121. *Larry King Live* (1990) 90 Minutes
122. *The American Dream Contest* (Channel 29, March 1, 1990); as Host
123. **The Tonight Show Starring Johnny Carson* (NBC, May 9, 1991) 90 Minutes
124. *America's Missing Children* (CBS, May 20, 1991) 60 Minutes; as Host

Tributes, Honors and Biographies

125. **Michael Landon: Memories with Laughter and Love* (NBC, September 17, 1991) 120 Minutes
126. *Desperate Passage* (Family Channel, September 11, 1993)
127. *People's 20th Birthday* (ABC, March 7, 1994) 120 Minutes; Tribute by Melissa Gilbert
128. 11th Annual Academy of Television Arts & Sciences Hall of Fame (NBC, April 18, 1996) 90 Minutes; as Inductee
129. *True Hollywood Story* "Michael Landon" (E! Channel, June 29, 1997) 120 Minutes
130. *Michael Landon: The Father I Knew* (NBC, May 23, 1999) 120 Minutes
131. *Biography*; "Michael Landon" (A&E Network, August 8, 1999) 120 Minutes

Stage

132 *The Bat* (Haddonfield Theatre Group, 1949); as Japanese Houseboy
133. *A Thousand Clowns* (Haddonfield Theatre Group, 1949)

Personal Appearances

134. Camp Pendleton Rodeo (Orange County, California, Early 1960s)
135. Dixie National Livestock Show and Rodeo (Jackson, Mississippi, 1960s)
136. Anchorage, Alaska (1964)
137. Camdenton, Missouri (1964)
138. Fort Madison, Iowa (1964)
139. Phoenix Rodeo (Phoenix, Arizona, 1964)
140. Tampa, Florida (1964) Made Honorary Sheriff's Association Member
141. Tampa's State Fair Grounds Rodeo (1964) Sang "Tom Dooley"
142. Indiana State Fair (Indianapolis, Indians, 1965)
143. Kentucky State Fair (1965)
144. 17th Annual Spindle Top Charity Horse Show (Beaumont, Texas, 1965)
145. South Texas State Fair (1965)
146. Spindle Top Charity Horse Show (Shreveport, Louisiana, 1965)
147. Variety Village Telethon (Buffalo, New York, 1965)

148. Nugget Sparks (Reno, Nevada, April 1966)
149. Jackson Hole, Wyoming (March 1973)

NOTES

1. Shapiro, Melany. *Bonanza: The Unofficial Story of the Ponderosa*. Pioneer Books, 1993.

2. Libby, Bill. "*Bonanza's* Lorne Greene." *Coronet*. February 1968.

3. Miller, Lee O. *The Great Cowboy Stars*. Arlington House, 1979.

4. Libby, Bill. "Bonanza's Lorne Greene." *Coronet*. February 1968.

5. *Ibid.*

6. *Ibid.*

7. Holt, Toni. "A Visit with Lorne and Nancy." *Movie Life*. February 22, 1979.

8. *Ibid.*

9. Shapiro, Melany. *Bonanza: The Unofficial Story of the Ponderosa*. Pioneer Books, 1993.

10. Libby, Bill. "*Bonanza's* Lorne Greene." *Coronet*. February 1968.

11. "Irresistible Lorne Greene." *TV Star Parade*. March 1974.

12. *Ibid.*

13. Miller, Lee O. *The Great Cowboy Stars*. Arlington House, 1979.

14. "IRS Chasing Lorne Greene in Tax Shelter Case." *The Philadelphia Evening Bulletin*. January 6, 1981.

15. "He's Still Going Strong: Actor Lorne Greene Thrives on Jet Lag, Creativity." *Delaware County Times*. April 14, 1982.

16. Greene, Lorne. "I Ignored My Hearing Problems — And Hurt the Family I Loved." *National Enquirer*. November 8, 1983.

17. *Ibid.*

18. Hoffman, Greg, and Telden, Lorraine. "Lorne Greene Battles New Health Crisis." *Star*. September 8, 1987.

19. *Ibid.*

20. *Ibid.*

21. *Ibid.*

22. *Ibid.*

23. Whitney, Dwight. "What Makes Pernell Roberts So Angry?" *TV Guide*. October 30, 1982.

24. Cook, Anthony. "When Lady Luck Smiled, He Kicked Her in the Teeth." *TV Guide*. November 24, 1979.

25. Beck, Marilyn. "A New Pernell Roberts: This Time He'll Make No Waves." *The Philadelphia Sunday Bulletin*. June 3, 1979.

26. Cook, Anthony. "When Lady Luck Smiled, He Kicked Her in the Teeth." *TV Guide*. November 24, 1979.

27. Beck, Marilyn. "A New Pernell Roberts: This Time He'll Make No Waves." *The Philadelphia Sunday Bulletin*. June 3, 1979.

28. Scott, Vernon. "Blocker, *Bonanza's* Most Loveable Lout." *The Philadelphia Evening Bulletin*. January 5, 1969.

29. Kokernot, H. L. "Sul Ross Ceremonies Pay Tribute to Harley May and Dan Blocker." *Alpine (Texas) Avalance*. July 30, 1987.

30. Tusher, Bill. "Mixed Marriage Made Me a Man." *Photoplay*. April 1965.

31. Greenland, David R. *Bonanza: A Viewer's Guide to the TV Legend*. R.G. Productions, 1997.

32. *Ibid.*

33. *Ibid.*

34. "Actor's Grave is Still Visited by Hundreds." *Houston Chronicle*. December 31, 1984.

35. Greenland, David R. *Bonanza: A Viewer's Guide to the TV Legend*. R.G. Productions, 1997.

36. Tusher, Bill. "Mixed Marriage Made Me a Man." *Photoplay*. April 1965.

37. Greenland, David R. *Bonanza: A Viewer's Guide to the TV Legend*. R.G. Productions, 1997.

38. *Ibid.*

39. "Dan Blocker Dies at 43, 'Hoss' on TV's *Bonanza*." *The Philadelphia Evening Bulletin*. May 15, 1972.

40. "Actor's Grave Is Still Visited by Hundreds." *Houston Chronicle*. December 31, 1984.

41. Daly, Marsha. *Michael Landon: A-Biography*. St. Martin's Press, 1987.

42. *Ibid.*

43. *Ibid.*

44. *Ibid.*

45. *Ibid.*

46. *Ibid.*

47. Joyce, Aileen. *Michael Landon: His Triumphs & Tragedies*. Zebra Books, 1991.

48. Landon, Cheryl. *I Promised My Dad*. Simon and Schuster, 1992.

49. Daley, Marsha. *Michael Landon: A-Biography*. St. Martin's Press, 1987.

50. Joyce, Aileen. *Michael Landon: His Triumphs & Tragedies*. Zebra Books, 1991.

51. Ito, Tom. *Conversations With Michael Landon*. Contemporary Books, 1992.

52. Flynn, Harry and Flynn, Pamela. *Life, Love & Laughter*. Pomegrante Press, 1991.

PART IV

The Supporting Cast

Victor Sen Yung

HOP SING

Hop Sing was born in 1818 and spoke the Cantonese dialect. To free themselves from a land of famine, Hop Ling, his son Hop Sing and their relatives sailed to America aboard the Asian Queen. *Arriving in the American West in the 1840s, they settled in San Francisco's Chinatown.*

Leaving one of California's placer camps, five-foot, four-inch, 125-pound Hop Sing headed for Nevada, surviving on gold pieces dropped by miners. He settled in Johntown in a section reserved for the so-called "uncivilized" and "irreligious" Chinese.

Drunken miners would often beat up the Chinese and found it fun to tie their pony tails together and shoot at their feet. The Chinese accepted this as the way things were. One day, two drunken miners came to the Chinese camp and beat Hop Sing nearly to death. He was rolling on the ground trying to avoid the beating when he saw a big man climb down from a buggy and come to his aid. Hop Sing saw a woman telling the big man that he was hurt. He remembered being placed in the buggy and taken to his shack.

After he recovered, Hop Sing remembered the man who had helped him. Asking around, he learned of the Ponderosa and a family named Cartwright. He also found out the man had three sons and felt that the kind lady of the house needed help. He arrived at the Ponderosa and became the Cartwright cook, houseboy and handyman with no formal agreement or salary being decided upon. He was proud of his cooking which was as good as that of the Washoe Club. He was independent, very efficient, honest and likable.

When Mrs. Cartwright died, he felt he was needed even more. He ran the household and looked after the baby, Little Joe. He found Hoss (the middle boy) to be caring and sensitive. He learned about flowers and wildlife from him. With Adam (the oldest), he worked on his pidgin English.

He became one of the family. He loved the Cartwrights and was loyal. He frequently spoke his mind and often threatened to quit. The Cartwrights found they could not do without him. He once helped Hoss clear Little Joe of murder charges with his knowledge of the ancient Chinese art of fingerprints.

He often visited his cousin Yee Foo and niece Mai Ah Toy in San Francisco. One of his cousins filled in while he was away. While on vacation after roundup, Hop Sing would either gamble in Chinatown or go prospecting. Once while prospecting, he met a Caucasian woman whom he called Missy. They fell in love and wanted to marry, but when the couple went to Virginia City to get a license, they learned that interracial marriages were not permitted by law. Unable to find a legal way to marry, Hop Sing forced Missy to go home and he returned to the Ponderosa.

Hop Sing remained on the ranch until his death in 1885 and was buried on the Ponderosa.

Sen Yung's parents left China in the late 1890s and settled in San Francisco, where he was born on October 15, 1915, as Sen Yeu Cheung. His mother died in 1919 as a result of a flu epidemic. After his wife's death, Victor's father wanted to return to China and needed to put his son and daughter into a children's shelter. After he remarried, he returned to San Francisco in the mid-1920s and reclaimed his children. During this period, Victor began speaking Cantonese.

He attended the University of California where he majored in Animal Husbandry in the College of Agriculture. He earned money to put himself through school working as a houseboy for rich families in the area. After graduation, he planned to go to China to practice his profession. However, he would ultimately switch his major to Economics. In 1937, he was an extra in the MGM film *The Good Earth.*

Upon graduation in 1938, he was hired by a chemical company. He went to 20th Century–Fox to sell them a new flame-proofing material but wound up making a screen test as Charlie Chan's son. He was cast as Sidney Toler's number two son in *Charlie Chan in Honolulu* (1938). A novice in films, Sen Yung received some advice from Sidney Toler. He also enrolled at the California Graduate School of Cinema Arts to learn more about his craft. He would go on to appear in 19 Chan films (11 for Fox and eight for Monogram).

He also appeared in *The Letter* (1940) with Bette Davis and *Across the Pacific* (1942) with Humphrey Bogart. He had been billed as Sen Yung until the early 1940s when he added the name Victor. He went on to play a variety of roles including bankers, doctors, bartenders and spies in numerous films and television shows.

Victor had always yearned to go to China, the land of his ancestry. During World War II, whenever he learned a unit was being shipped to China, he would request to be assigned to that unit. He missed (by two days) a transfer to the 22nd field Hospital and instead was assigned to the Air Force's "Winged Victory Unit." He became a Captain in the Air Force Intelligence

Victor Sen Yung. (Photofest.)

Unit being formed for duty in China. He took a course in Madarin dialect at Berkeley but by the time he received his orders the war had ended.

His biggest break came in 1959 when he was cast as Hop Sing, the Cartwrights' Chinese cook, in *Bonanza*. He appeared frequently throughout the run of the show and occasionally had a featured segment. During the 1961–62 season, he also was a regular on ABC's *Bachelor Father*, playing Cousin Charlie Fong.

In 1971, Victor Sen Yung was in Sacramento, California for a television interview in connection with a Charlie Chan Festival. He was returning to Hollywood on Pacific Southwest Airlines when the plane was hijacked. He was seated near one of the hijackers, saw him talking to a stewardess and noticed that the hijacker had a gun. The gunfire started when F.B.I. agents stepped on board. He dropped out of his seat to avoid the shooting. He was hit in the back; one passenger stood up and was shot and killed. A hijacker asked him to move his seat but he pretended not to understand until the stewardess convinced him to leave his aisle seat.

After the hijacking incident ended, Victor Sen Yung was rushed to the Peninsula Hospital where the bullet was removed from his left side. He told reporters he was feeling better and would soon be released from the hospital. He brought a $500,000 suit against the airlines but was able to settle things before they reached court.

On *Bonanza* he did not really cook as the prop men were responsible for supplying the food. In reality, he had been quite adept at cooking since age 12. In fact, after *Bonanza* was canceled, he wrote *The Great Wok Cookbook* (published by Nash in 1974).

In 1977, Victor was the guest of honor at a dinner given by the Los Angeles Chinese Historical Society. He recalled, "I've been all over the country selling a book and everyone thinks I worked on every show [in *Bonanza*] and that I am a millionaire. The truth is that I appeared in about 20 percent of the shows over 14 years, and that was not enough to sustain myself. You do all kinds of things when someone needs a cook, I cook."[1] He supplemented his income marketing Chinese food for a public relations firm. He also gave cooking demonstrations both for department stores and television, as well as being a waiter, selling men's clothes and driving a truck. In 1980, he began writing a second cookbook.

After playing a cook on *Bonanza*, it was ironic that he died on November 9, 1980, alone and nearly broke as a result of a gas leak from his stove (used to warm his modest home in the San Fernando Valley). At the time of his death, a sister, a son (from a previous marriage) and two grandchildren resided in Ohio.

Movies, Telefilms, Miniseries

An asterisk (*) denotes video availability.

1. *The Good Earth* (MGM, 1937); as an Extra
2. *Charlie Chan in Honolulu* (20th Century–Fox, 1938); as Lee Chan
3. **Shadows Over Shanghai* (Grand National, 1938); as Wang
4. *Charlie Chan at Treasure Island* (20th Century–Fox, 1939); as Jimmy Chan
5. *20,000 Men a Year* (Cosmopolitan-Fox, 1939); as Harold Chang
6. *Charlie Chan in Reno* (20th Century–Fox, 1939); as Jimmy Chan
7. *Charlie Chan in Panama* (20th Century–Fox, 1940); as Jimmy Chan
8. **Murder Over New York* (20th Century–Fox, 1940); as Jimmy Chan
9. *Charlie Chan's Murder Cruise* (20th Century–Fox, 1940); as Jimmy Chan
10. **Charlie Chan at the Wax Museum* (20th Century–Fox, 1940); as Jimmy Chan
11. *The Letter (Warner Bros., 1940); as Ong Chi Seng
12. **Charlie Chan in Rio* (20th Century–Fox, 1941); as Jimmy Chan
13. *Dead Men Tell* (20th Century–Fox, 1941); as Jimmy Chan
14. *A Yank on the Burma Road* (MGM, 1942); as Wing
15. *Secret Agent of Japan* (20th Century–Fox, 1942); as Fu Yen
16. *Moontide* (20th Century–Fox, 1942); as Takeo

17. *Little Tokyo, U.S.A.* (20th Century–Fox, 1942); as Okono
18. *Across the Pacific* (Warner Bros., 1942); as Joe Tutsuiko
19. *Manila Calling* (20th Century–Fox, 1942); as Amando
20. *Castle in the Desert* (20th Century–Fox, 1942); as Jimmy Chan
21. *The Mad Martindales* (20th Century–Fox, 1942); as Jeff Gow
22. *Night Plane From Chungking* (Paramount, 1943); as Cpt. PO
23. *China* (Paramount, 1943); as Third Brother-in-law Wei
24. *Betrayal from the East* (RKO, 1945); as Oneya
25. *Dangerous Money* (Monogram, 1946); as Jimmy Chan
26. *Dangerous Millions* (20th Century–Fox, 1946)
27. *Shadows Over Chinatown* (Monogram, 1946); as Jimmy Chan
28. *Intrigue* (United Artists, 1947); as Cable Clerk
29. *The Web of Danger* (Republic, 1947); as Sam
30. *The Trap* (Monogram, 1947); as Jimmy Chan
31. *The Chinese Ring* (Monogram, 1947); as Tommy
32. *The Crimson Key* (20th Century–Fox, 1947); as Wing
33. *The Flame* (Republic, 1947); as Chang
34. *The Feathered Serpent* (Monogram, 1948); as Tommy Chan
35. *Half Past Midnight* (20th Century–Fox, 1948)
36. *Rogues Regiment* (Universal, 1948); as Rickshaw Boy
37. *The Mystery of the Golden Eye* (Monogram, 1948); as Tommy Chan
38. *Docks of New Orleans* (Monogram, 1948); as Tommy Chan
39. *The Shanghai Chest* (Monogram, 1948); as Tommy Chan
40. *Boston Blackie's Chinese Venture* (Columbia, 1949)
41. *Oh You Beautiful Doll* (20th Century–Fox, 1949); as Houseboy
42. *And Baby Makes Three* (Columbia, 1949)
43. *State Department— File 649* (Film-Classics, Inc., 1949); as Johnny Hamm
44. *A Ticket to Tomahawk* (20th Century–Fox, 1950); as Long Time, the Laundryman
45. *The Breaking Point* (Warner Bros., 1950); as Mr. Sing
46. *Key to the City* (MGM, 1950); as Chinese MC
47. *Women on the Run* (Universal, 1950); as Sammy
48. *The Groom Wore Spurs* (Universal, 1951); as Ignacio
49. *The Law and the Lady* (MGM, 1951); as Chinese Manager
50. *Peking Express* (Paramount, 1951); as Chinese Captain
51. *Valley of Fire* (Columbia, 1951); as Ching Moon
52. *The Sniper* (Kramer/Columbia, 1952); as Waiter
53. *Target Hong Kong* (Columbia, 1952); as Johnny Wing
54. *Forbidden* (Universal, 1953); as Allan
55. *Jubilee Trail* (Republic, 1954); as Mickey, the Chinese Man
56. *The Shanghai Story* (Republic, 1954); as Sun Lee
57. *Port of Hell* (Allied Artists, 1954); as Enemy Radio Operator
58. *The Left Hand of God* (20th Century–Fox, 1955); as John Wong
59. *Blood Alley* (Batjac/Warner Bros., 1955); as Cpl. Wang
60. *Soldier of Fortune* (20th Century–Fox, 1955); as Goldie
61. *Accused of Murder* (Republic, 1956); as Houseboy
62. *Men in War* (United Artists, 1957); as Korean Sniper
63. *The Hunters* (20th Century–Fox, 1958); as Korean Farmer
64. *Jet Attack* (American International Pictures, 1958); as Chon

65. *The Saga of Hemp Brown* (Universal, 1958); as Chang
66. **She Demons* (Astor Pictures, 1958); as Sammy Ching
67. **Flower Drum Song* (Universal, 1961); as Frankie Wing
68. *Confessions of an Opium Eater* (Allied Artists, 1962); as Wong Young
69. *A Flea in Her Ear* (20th Century–Fox, 1968); as Oke Saki
70. *The Hawaiians* (United Artists, 1970); as Chun Fat
71. *Kung Fu* (TV-Warner Bros./ABC, February 22, 1972); as Chuen
72. *The Red Pony* (Universal/Omnibus, 1973); as Mr. Sing/Mr. Green
73. **The Killer Elite* (MGM, 1975); as Chinese Underworld Tough
74. **The Man with Bogart's Face* (20th Century–Fox, 1980); as Mr. Wing

Radio

75. *Lux Radio Theatre* "The Letter" (CBS, April 21, 1941); as Lawyer's Assistant

TV Series

76. *Bonanza* (NBC, September 12, 1959-January 9, 1973) 60 Minutes; as Hop Sing.
77. *Bachelor Father* (ABC, 1961-62) 30 Minutes; as Cousin Charlie Fong

TV Guest Appearances

78. *Stories of the Century* "Black Bart" (Syndicated, May 6, 1954) 30 Minutes
79. *Alias Mike Hercules* (ABC, July 31, 1956); as Charlie
80. *The Lone Ranger* "The Letter Bride" (ABC, November 15, 1956) 30 Minutes
81. *Death Valley Days* "Quong Kee" (Syndicated, December 9, 1957)
82. *Broken Arrow* "The Courage of Ling Tang" (ABC, May 20, 1958) 30 Minutes; as Ling Tang
83. *Man Without a Gun* "Daughter of the Dragon" (Syndicated, June 22, 1959) 30 Minutes
84. *The Rifleman* "The Querie" (ABC, May 16, 1961) 30 Minutes; as Wang Chi
85. *Hawaiian Eye* "Blow Low, Blow Blue" (ABC, March 3, 1963) 60 Minutes
86. *I Spy* "Pinwheel" (NBC, April 15, 1968) 60 Minutes
87. *Wild Wild West* "The Night of the Camera" (CBS, November 29, 1968) 60 Minutes; as Baron Kyosai
88. *Hawaii Five-O* "Face of the Dragon" (CBS, January 22, 1969) 60 Minutes; as Dr. Kuri
89. *Hawaii Five-O* "The Box" (CBS, January 29, 1969) 60 Minutes
90. *Rod Serling's Night Gallery* "Rare Object" (NBC, October 22, 1972) 60 Minutes; as Joseph, the Butler
91. *Kung Fu* "A Praying Mantis Kills" (ABC, March 22, 1973) 60 Minutes; as Master Ling
92. *Kung Fu* "The Squaw Man" (ABC, November 1, 1973) 60 Minutes; as Farmer
93. *Kung Fu* "The Way of Violence Has No Mind" (ABC, January 24, 1974) 60 Minutes; as Chu

94. *Kung Fu* "Besieged: Death on Cold Mountain [Part 1]" (ABC, November 15, 1974) 60 Minutes; as Tamo
95. *Kung Fu* "Besieged: Cannon at the Gates [Part 2]" (ABC, November 22, 1974) 60 Minutes; as Tamo
96. *Kung Fu* "The Raiders" (ABC, November 24, 1974) 60 Minutes; as Chu
97. *Kung Fu* "The Demon God" (ABC, December 13, 1974) 60 Minutes; as Old Mandarin
98. *How the West Was Won* "The Chinese Girl" (ABC, April 16, 1979) 60 Minutes; as Hospital Worker

Book

99. *The Great Wok Cookbook* (Nash, 1974)

Ray Teal

ROY COFFEE

Roy Coffee was the capable sheriff of Virginia City for some ten years. Prior to taking office, he had experienced tragedy in his personal life. Outlaw Wharton ambushed Coffee's family at his home, killing his only child. While coming to her husband's aide, Roy's daughter-in-law was struck down. Suffering a broken heart, his wife died a few weeks later, leaving him to raise his granddaughter Sara Ann.

He was now in his mid-fifties with thin graying hair and deafness in his right ear caused from years of gunfights. His easy going nature often caused outlaws and those who did not know him to feel he was indecisive and too old for the job. In reality, he was quite competent and could still handle his duties and was not easily scared.

Coffee and Ben Cartwright were old friends and he would not hesitate to ask for his friend's help. Ben was often asked to run his re-election campaigns for sheriff.

When Coffee felt he had been sheriff long enough, his deputy Clem Foster replaced him as Virginia City's main lawman.

Ray Teal was born in Grand Rapids, Michigan, on January 12, 1902. He furthered his education at the Universities of Texas and California. He helped pay his way through college by playing the saxophone and would form his own small band after graduation.

He would spend some 20 years playing the saxophone in dance bands. Eventually worked in stock until making his Hollywood debut in 1938. He

Ray Teal. (Photofest.)

would spend the next 32 years as a very busy character actor in scores of films, often playing a villain or corrupt lawman.

Ray was a man with a solid build, fatherly face, thin brown hair and a thick mustache. He joined the cast of the hit TV series *Bonanza* in 1960, as Sheriff Roy Coffee. He had finally gotten to play an honest man. He would remain with the show until the end of its 1971–72 season.

In the mid–1960s, he played Sheriff Snead on *Walt Disney's Wonderful World of Color* (in the series *Gallagher Goes West*). He continued making TV guest appearances and films. His last — *The Hanged Man* — aired on ABC on March 13, 1974.

After suffering from a long illness, the 74-year-old actor died on April 2, 1976.

Movies, Telefilms, Miniseries

An asterisk (*) denotes video availability.

1. *Zorro Rides Again* (Republic, 1937); as Pete
2. *Western Jamboree* (Republic, 1938); as McCall
3. *Edison the Man* (MGM, 1940)
4. *Cherokee Strip* (Paramount, 1940); as Smokey Morrell
5. *I Love You Again* (MGM, 1940); as Watchman
6. *Prairie Schooners* [Through the Storm] (Columbia, 1940); as Wolf Tanner
7. *Kitty Foyle* (RKO, 1940); as Saxophonist
8. *Pony Post* (Universal, 1940); as Claud Richards
9. *Florian* (MGM, 1940)
10. *Adventures of Red Ryder* (1940); as Shark
11. *Viva Cisco Kid* (1940); as Josh
12. *The Trail Blazer* (Republic, 1940)
13. *Trail of the Vigilantes* (1940); as Deputy Sheriff
14. *New Moon* (MGM, 1940); as Bondsman
15. *Northwest Passage* (MGM, 1940); as Bradley McNeil
16. Third Finger Left Hand (MGM, 1940); as Cameraman

17. *Strange Cargo* (MGM, 1940); as a Guard
18. *They Met in Bombay* (MGM, 1941)
19. *They Died with Their Boots On* (Warner Bros., 1941); as Barfly
20. *Badmen of Missouri* (Warner Bros., 1941)
21. *Honky Tonk* (MGM, 1941); as Poker Player
22. *The Bugle Sounds* (MGM, 1941)
23. *Outlaws of the Pan Handle* (Columbia, 1941); as Walt Burnett
24. *Sergeant York* (Warner Bros., 1941)
25. *Wild Bill Hickok Rides* (Warner Bros., 1941); as Jack Henley
26. *Billy the Kid* (MGM, 1941)
27. *Shadow of the Thin Man* (MGM, 1941); as Cab Driver
28. *Ziegfeld Girl* (MGM, 1941); as Pawnbroker
29. *Apache Trail* (MGM, 1942); as Ed Cotton
30. *Juke Girl* (Warner Bros., 1942); as Man
31. *Prairie Chickens* (1942)
32. *Nazi Agent* (MGM, 1942); as Officer Graves
33. *Secret Enemies* (Warner Bros., 1942); as a Motor Cop
34. *Tennessee Johnson* (MGM, 1942)
35. *Woman of the Year* (MGM, 1942); as a Reporter
36. *Northwest Rangers* (MGM, 1942)
37. *Captain Midnight* (1942)
38. *Escape from Crime* (Warner Bros., 1942)
39. *Lost Angel* (MGM, 1943)
40. *Gentle Gangster* (Republic, 1943); as Joe Barton
41. *Madame Curie* (MGM, 1943); as Driver
42. *The North Star* (Goldwyn/RKO, 1943); as German Motorcycle Officer
43. *The Chance of a Lifetime* (Columbia, 1943)
44. *She Has What It Takes* (Columbia, 1943); as a Cop
45. *Song of Russia* (MGM, 1943)
46. *Slightly Dangerous* (MGM, 1943); as a Pedestrian
47. *Thousands Cheer* (MGM, 1943); as Ringmaster
48. *The Youngest Profession* (MGM, 1943); as Taxi Driver
49. *Barbary Coast Gentleman* (MGM, 1944)
50. *Wing and a Prayer* (20th Century–Fox, 1944); as Executive Officer
51. *Strange Affair* (Columbia, 1944); as a Truck Driver
52. *An American Romance* (MGM, 1944)
53. *None Shall Escape* (Columbia, 1944); as Oremski
54. *Gentle Annie* (MGM, 1944); as Expressman
55. *The Home Front* (1944)
56. *Hollywood Canteen* (Warner Bros., 1944); as Captain
57. *Maisie Goes to Reno* (MGM, 1944)
58. *Nothing but Trouble* (MGM, 1944); as Officer
59. *Mr. Co-ed* (1944)
60. *Once Upon a Time* (Alexandra Hall/Columbia, 1944); as Shipyard Worker
61. *Raiders of Ghost City* (Universal, 1944)
62. *The Princess and the Pirate* (RKO, 1944); as a Guard
63. *The Thin Man Goes Home* (MGM, 1944); as a Man
64. *Captain Kidd* (United Artists, 1945); as Michael O'Shawn
65. *Circumstantial Evidence* (20th Century–Fox, 1945); as a Policeman

66. *Along Came Jones* (Cinema Artists/Fox, 1945); as Kriendler
67. *The Runaround* (Universal, 1945)
68. *The Fighting Guardsman* (Columbia, 1945); as Albert
69. **The Clock* (MGM, 1945)
70. *Strange Voyage* (Signal, 1945); as Captain Andrews
71. *A Gun in His Hands* (1945)
72. **Anchors Aweigh* (MGM, 1945); as Assistant Movie Director
73. *Snafu* (Columbia, 1945)
74. **Back to Bataan* (RKO, 1945); as Lt. Col. Roberts
75. *Three Wise Fools* (MGM, 1945)
76. *Keep Your Powder Dry* (MGM, 1945); as Army Captain
77. *Sudan* (Universal, 1945); as Slave Trader
78. **Wonder Man* (Goldwyn/RKO, 1945); as Ticket Taker
79. **Ziegfeld Follies* (MGM, 1945); as Special Officer
80. *Adventure* (MGM, 1945)
81. *Shady Lady* (Universal, 1945)
82. **The Best Years of Our Lives* (Goldwyn/RKO, 1946); as Mr. Mollett
83. *Bandit of Sherwood Forest* (Columbia, 1946); as Little John
84. *Blonde Alibi* (Universal, 1946)
85. *Blondie Knows Best* (Columbia, 1946)
86. *Canyon Passage* (Universal, 1946); as Neil Howlson
87. *A Dangerous Business* (Columbia, 1946)
88. *Decoy* (Monogram, 1946); as a Policeman
89. *A Letter for Evie* (MGM, 1946)
90. *Deadline for Murder* (20th Century–Fox, 1946); as Frank
91. **The Harvey Girls* (MGM, 1946); as Conductor
92. *Tenth Avenue Angel* (MGM, 1946)
93. *The Missing Lady* (Monogram, 1946)
94. **Till the Clouds Roll By* (MGM, 1946); as Orchestra Conductor
95. *Deep Valley* (Warner Bros., 1947); as Prison Official
96. *Desert Fury* (Paramount, 1947); as Bus Driver
97. **Road to Rio* (Paramount, 1947); as Buck
98. *The Fabulous Texan* (Republic, 1947)
99. *Unconquered* (Paramount, 1947); as Soldier at Gilded Beaver
100. *The High Wall* (MGM, 1947); as Lt. of Police
101. **The Michigan Kid* (Universal, 1947); as Sergeant
102. *Brute Force* (Universal, 1947); as Jackson
103. *Cheyenne* (Warner Bros., 1947); as a Gambler
104. **Ramrod* (Enterprise/United Artists, 1947); as Burma
105. **Dead Reckoning* (Columbia, 1947); as Motorcycle Policeman
106. *Driftwood* (Republic, 1947); as Perkins
107. *The Long Night* (RKO, 1947); as Hudson
108. **The Man from Colorado* (Columbia, 1947)
109. *Roses Are Red* (20th Century–Fox, 1947)
110. **My Favorite Brunette* (Paramount, 1947); as Trooper
111. *Louisiana* (Monogram, 1947)
112. **Northwest Outpost* (Republic, 1947); as Wounded Trapper
113. *The Swordsman* (Columbia, 1947)
114. **Pursued* (United States Pictures/Warner Bros., 1947); as Army Captain

115. *The Sea of Grass* (MGM, 1947); as a Cattleman
116. *The Mating of Millie* (Columbia, 1948)
117. *The Black Arrow* (Columbia, 1948)
118. *Countess of Monte Cristo* (Universal, 1948); as Charlie
119. *Whispering Smith* (Paramount, 1948); as Seagrue
120. *Raw Deal* (Eagle-Lion/Reliance, 1948)
121. *Road House* (20th Century–Fox, 1948); as a Policeman
122. *Black Bart* (Universal, 1948)
123. *Joan of Arc* (RKO, 1948); as Bertrand de Poulengy
124. *Hazard* (Paramount, 1948)
125. *Walk a Crooked Mile* (Columbia, 1948); as Police Sergeant
126. *An Act of Murder* (Universal, 1948)
127. *Daredevil of the Clouds* (Republic, 1948); as Mitchell
128. *Mr. Soft Touch* (Columbia, 1948)
129. *Fury at Furnace Creek* (20th Century–Fox, 1948); as Sergeant
130. *I Wouldn't Be in Your Shoes* (Monogram, 1948); as a Guard
131. *The Miracle of the Bells* (RKO, 1948); as Koslick
132. *The Snake Pit* (20th Century–Fox, 1948)
133. *One Sunday Afternoon* (Warner Bros., 1948)
134. *Oh You Beautiful Doll* (20th Century–Fox, 1949)
135. *Bad Boy* (Allied Artists/Monogram, 1949)
136. *Once More, My Darling* (Neptune/Universal, 1949); as a Truck Driver
137. *Kazan* (Columbia, 1949); as McCready
138. *The Great Gatsby* (Paramount, 1949)
139. *It Happens Every Spring* (20th Century–Fox, 1949)
140. *Ambush* (MGM, 1949); as Captain J.R. Wolverson
141. *Streets of Laredo* (Paramount, 1949); as Cantrel
142. *Scene of the Crime* (MGM, 1949); as a Patrolman
143. *Blondie Hits the Jackpot* (Columbia, 1949); as Gus
144. *Rusty's Birthday* (Columbia, 1949); as Virgil Neeley
145. *Samson and Delilah* (Paramount, 1949)
146. *No Way Out* (20th Century–Fox, 1950); as Day Deputy
147. *Convicted* (Columbia, 1950); as a Guard
148. *Our Very Own* (RKO, 1950); as Mr. Lynch
149. *The Men* (United Artists, 1950); as Man at Bar
150. *Where Danger Lives* (RKO, 1950); as Joe Borden
151. *The Redhead and the Cowboy* (Paramount, 1950); as Brock
152. *Davy Crockett, Indian Scout* (United Artists, 1950); as Captain McHale
153. *Harbor of Missing Men* (Republic, 1950); as Frank
154. *The Kid from Texas* (Universal, 1950); as Sheriff Rand
155. *Edge of Doom* (RKO, 1950); as Ned Moore
156. *Petty Girl* (Columbia, 1950); as Policeman
157. *When You're Smiling* (Columbia, 1950); as Steve
158. *Winchester 73* (Universal, 1950); as Marshall Noonan
159. *Fort Worth* (Warner Bros., 1951); as Gabe Clevenger
160. *Lorna Doone* (Columbia, 1951); as Farmer Ridd
161. *Tomorrow Is Another Day* (Warner Bros., 1951)
162. *The Big Carnival* [Ace in the Hole] (Paramount, 1951); as Sheriff
163. *Distant Drums* (Warner Bros., 1951); as Pvt. Mohair

164. *The Flaming Feather* (Paramount, 1951)
165. *The Lion and the Horse* (Warner Bros., 1952); as Dave Tracy
166. *Captive City* (United Artists, 1952); as Chief Gillette
167. *Montana Belle* (RKO, 1952); as Emmett Dalton
168. *The Turning Point* (Paramount, 1952); as Clint
169. *Jumping Jacks* (Paramount, 1952); as General Timmons
170. *Carrie* (Paramount, 1952); as Allan
171. *Hangman's Knot* (Columbia, 1952); as Quincey
172. *The Wild North* (MGM, 1952); as Ruger
173. *Cattle Town* (Warner Bros., 1952); as Judd Hastings
174. *The Wild One* (Columbia, 1953)
175. *Ambush at Tomahawk Gap* (Columbia, 1954); as Doc
176. *The Command* (Warner Bros., 1954); as Dr. Trent
177. *Lucky Me* (Warner Bros., 1954); as a Crony
178. *About Mrs. Leslie* (Paramount, 1954); as Barney
179. *Rogue Cop* (MGM, 1954); as Patrolman Mullins
180. *Rage at Dawn* (RKO, 1955); as Constable Brant
181. *The Indian Fighter* (United Artists, 1955); as Morgan
182. *Run for Cover* (Paramount, 1955); as Sheriff
183. *The Desperate Hours* (Paramount, 1955); as Fredericks
184. *The Man from Bitter Ridge* (Universal, 1955); as Shep Bascom
185. *Apache Ambush* (Columbia, 1955); as Sgt. O'Roarke
186. *The Young Guns* (Allied Artists, 1956)
187. *The Burning Hills* (Warner Bros., 1956); as Joe Sutton
188. *Canyon River* (Allied Artists, 1956)
189. *Band of Angels* (Warner Bros., 1957); as Mr. Calloway
190. *Utah Blaine* (Columbia, 1957); as Russ Nevers
191. *The Phantom Stagecoach* (Columbia, 1957); as Sheriff Ned Riorden
192. *The Oklahoman* (Allied Artists, 1957); as Jason, the Stableman
193. *The Wayward Girl* (Republic, 1957); as Sheriff
194. *The Tall Stranger* (Allied Artists, 1957); as Cap
195. *Decision at Sundown* (Columbia, 1957); as Morley Chase
196. *The Guns of Fort Petticoat* (Columbia, 1957); as Salt Pork
197. *Saddle the Wind* (MGM, 1958); as Brick Larson
198. *Gunmen's Walk* (Columbia, 1958); as Jensen Sieverts
199. *Inherit the Wind* (United Artists, 1960); as Dunlap
200. *Home from the Hill* (MGM, 1960); as Dr. Reuben Carson
201. *One-Eyed Jacks* (Paramount, 1960); as Bartender
202. *Girl on the Run* (Rose Tree/Astor, 1961)
203. *Posse from Hell* (Universal, 1961); as Larson
204. *Judgment at Nuremberg* (United Artists, 1961); as Judge Curtiss Ives
205. *Ada* (MGM, 1961)
206. *A Girl Named Tamiko* (Paramount, 1962)
207. *Cattle King* [Guns of Wyoming] (MGM, 1963); as Ed Winters
208. *Bullet for a Badman* (Universal, 1964)
209. *Taggart!* (Universal, 1964); as Ralph Taggart
210. *The Liberation of Lord Byron Jones* (Columbia, 1970); as Police Chief
211. *Chisum* (Warner Bros., 1970); as Justice Wilson
212. *The Hanged Man* (Fenady Assoc./Bing Crosby Productions/ABC, March 13, 1974); as Judge Homer Bayne

TV Series

213. *Bonanza* (NBC, 1960-1972) 60 Minutes; as Sheriff Roy Coffee
214. *Walt Disney's Wonderful World of Color* "Gallagher Goes West" (NBC, October 30, 1966-April 7, 1968) 60 Minutes; as Sheriff Snead

TV Guest Appearances

215. *The Lone Ranger* "Never Say Die" (ABC, April 6, 1950) 30 Minutes
216. *The Lone Ranger* "Ex-Marshall" (ABC, September 16, 1954) 30 Minutes
217. *The Lone Ranger* "The Too Perfect Signature" (ABC, March 31, 1955) 30 Minutes
218. *The Lone Ranger* "Adventure at Arbuckle (ABC, July 14, 1955) 30 Minutes
219. *Cheyenne* "Julesburg" (ABC, October 11, 1955) 60 Minutes; as McCanles
220. *Lux Video Theatre* "The Human Jungle" (NBC, October 20, 1955) 60 Minutes; as Chief Rowan
221. *Frontier* "Cattle Drive to Casper" (NBC, November 27, 1955) 30 Minutes
222. *Cheyenne* "The Black Hawk War" [Decision] (ABC, January 24, 1956) 60 Minutes; as Major Heffler
223. *Broken Arrow* "Hermano" (ABC, November 20, 1956) 30 Minutes; as Col. McBride
224. *Circus Boy* "The Remarkable Ricardo" (ABC, January 20, 1957) 30 Minutes; as Sheriff Green
225. *Tales of Wells Fargo* "Sam Bass" (NBC, June 10, 1957) 30 Minutes; as Capt. McNelly
226. *Wagon Train* "The Les Rand Story" (NBC, October 16, 1957) 60 Minutes
227. *Maverick* "Stage West" (ABC, October 27, 1957) 60 Minutes; as Mart Fallon
228. *Broken Arrow* "The Bounty Hunters" (ABC, November 26, 1957) 30 Minutes; as Fenster
229. *Trackdown* "Look for the Woman" (CBS, December 6, 1957) 30 Minutes; as Sheriff Michael
230. *Zorro* "Slaves of the Eagle" (ABC, January 23, 1958) 30 Minutes
231. *The Restless Gun* "Hang and Be Damned" (NBC, January 27, 1958) 30 Minutes; as Sheriff
232. *The Restless Gun* "The Hand Is Quicker" (NBC, March 17, 1958) 30 Minutes; as Sheriff Lander
233. *Man Without a Gun* "The Day the West Went Wild" (Syndicated, March 18, 1958) 30 Minutes
234. *Gunsmoke* "Carmen" (CBS, May 24, 1958) 30 Minutes; as Sgt. Jones
235. *Maverick* "The Day They Hanged Bret Maverick" (ABC, September 21, 1958) 60 Minutes; as Sheriff Chick Tucker
236. *77 Sunset Strip* "The Girl on the Run" (ABC, October 10, 1958) 60 Minutes; as Lt. Harper
237. *77 Sunset Strip* "The Bouncing Chip" (ABC, November 7, 1958) 60 Minutes; as Pete Collier
238. *The Californians* "Hangtown" (NBC, November 18, 1958) 30 Minutes; as Yotts Meyer

239. *Trackdown* "Three Legged Fox" (CBS, December 5, 1958) 30 Minutes; as Ward
240. *Wanted Dead or Alive* "Die by the Gun" (CBS, December 6, 1958) 30 Minutes; as Nebro
241. *The Texan* "No Tears for the Dead" (CBS, December 8, 1958) 30 Minutes; as Dave Travers
242. *Maverick* "Two Beggars on Horseback" (ABC, January 8, 1959) 60 Minutes; as Stryker
243. *Bronco* "Riding Solo" (ABC, February 10, 1959) 60 Minutes; as Tom Biggert
244. *Desilu Playhouse* "Two Counts of Murder" (CBS, August 10, 1959) 60 Minutes; as Sheriff Blaney
245. *Laramie* "Glory Road" (NBC, September 22, 1959) 60 Minutes
246. *Maverick* "A Tale of Three Cities" (ABC, October 18, 1959) 60 Minutes; as Sheriff Murray
247. *Bat Masterson* "No Funeral for Thorn" (NBC, October 22, 1959) 30 Minutes; as Vergil Gardiner
248. *The Rifleman* "Eddie's Daughter" (ABC, November 3, 1959) 30 Minutes; as Albie Finley
249. *Wagon Train* "The Jess MacAbbee Story" (NBC, November 25, 1959) 60 Minutes; as Jed Culpepper
250. *Bronco* "The Devil's Spawn" (ABC, December 1, 1959) 60 Minutes; as Jeb Donner
251. *The Alaskans* "The Abominable Snowman" (ABC, December 13, 1959) 60 Minutes; as Ezra Granit
252. *Walt Disney Presents* "El Fego Baca: Friendly Enemies at Law" (ABC, March 18, 1960) 60 Minutes; as Frank Oxford
253. *Colt .45* "The Trespasser" (ABC, June 21, 1960) 30 Minutes; as Mike O'Tara
254. *Bat Masterson* "Law of the Land" (NBC, October 6, 1960) 30 Minutes; as H.G. Cogswell
255. *Cheyenne* "Counterfeit Gun" (ABC, October 10, 1960) 60 Minutes; as Sheriff
256. *Klondike* "Klondike Fever" (NBC, October 10, 1960) 30 Minutes; as Augie Teejen
257. *Riverboat* "Zigzag" (NBC, December 26, 1960) 60 Minutes; as Sheriff Clay
258. *Lawman* "The Trial" (ABC, May 7, 1961) 30 Minutes; as Judge Whitehall
259. *Rawhide* "Judgment at Hondo Seco" (CBS, October 20, 1961) 60 Minutes; as Hennegan
260. *Maverick* "Mr. Muldoon's Partner" (ABC, April 15, 1962) 60 Minutes; as Sheriff Bundy
261. *Wide Country* "Straight Jacket for an Indian" (NBC, October 25, 1962) 60 Minutes; as Harry Kemper
262. *Wide Country* "A Devil in the Chute" (November 8, 1962) 60 Minutes; as Frank Higgins
263. *Empire* "The Tall Shadow" (CBS, November 20, 1962) 30 Minutes; as Mr. Todd
264. *Cheyenne* "Showdown at Oxbend" (ABC, December 17, 1962) 60 Minutes; as Sheriff Ben Jethro
265. *Wide Country* "Speckle Bird" (NBC, January 31, 1963) 60 Minutes; as Charlie

266. *The Twilight Zone* "The Printer's Devil" (CBS, February 28, 1963) 60 Minutes; as Mr. Franklin
267. *The Fugitive* "The Witch" (ABC, September 24, 1963) 60 Minutes; as McNary
268. *77 Sunset Strip* "Bonus Baby" (ABC, December 20, 1963) 60 Minutes
269. *Walt Disney's Wonderful World of Color* "Bristle Face [Part 1]" (NBC, January 26, 1964) 60 Minutes; as Justice Mackley
270. *Walt Disney's Wonderful World of Color* "Bristle Face [Part 2] (NBC, February 2, 1964) 60 Minutes; as Justice Mackley
271. The Monroes "Silent Night, Deadly Night" (ABC, November 23, 1966) 60 Minutes; as Laif Goff
272. Wonderful World of Disney "Hacksaw [Part 1]" (NBC, September 26, 1971) 60 Minutes; as Rancher
273. Wonderful World of Disney "Hacksaw [Part 2]" (NBC, October 3, 1971) 60 Minutes; as Rancher

Bing Russell

CLEM FOSTER

Clem Foster was the tall, husky, nice-looking, dark-haired deputy of Virginia City. He was quite competent and dedicated to his work and was a big help to Sheriff Roy Coffee. He would often fill in when Roy was out of town on business. The Cartwrights would depend on him in the absence of Coffee.

Clem attended church and sang in the choir. He eventually met a girl named Janie, whose mother died in childbirth. Her father blamed Janie for her mother's death. During one of the fires that nearly destroyed Virginia City, she was trapped and burned. Clem was knocked out while trying to save her.

When Roy Coffee decided to give up his office, Clem became sheriff of Virginia City.

Bing Russell was born in 1928 and became a baseball player before turning his talents to character acting in films in 1953. In 1956, he began playing the same character roles in television, where he was a natural for Westerns.

In 1963, he was hired to play Deputy Sheriff Clem Foster in the hit television series *Bonanza* and would become Virginia City's sheriff during the end of the series after Ray Teal left the show.

"*Bonanza* is the only show of the thousands I did," he recalled, "that I truly missed after finishing." He felt that the cast, crew and production company were "great." He said of his co-stars, "Lorne could walk on water.

Mike was an extreme talent, acting, writing and *directing*! And Dan a wonderful actor and friend." He thought that Pernell was "a consummate professional."[2]

After *Bonanza*, Russell continued working in crime series and telefilms into the mid-1970s, including Michael Landon's *Loneliest Runner* (December 20, 1976). Bing has appeared with his son, actor Kurt Russell, in Disney's *The Computer Wore Tennis Shoes* (1970) and as Vernon Presley in the TV movie *Elvis* (1979). He has since retired from show business.

Movies, Telefilms, Miniseries

An asterisk (*) denotes video availability.

 1. *The Big Leaguer* (MGM, 1953)
 2. **Tarantula* (Universal, 1955); as Deputy
 3. *Behind the High Wall* (Universal, 1956); as a Guard
 4. **Fear Strikes Out* (Paramount, 1957)
 5. **Gunfight at the OK Corral* (Paramount, 1957); as Bartender
 6. *Ride a Violent Mile* (Regal Films/20th Century–Fox, 1957); as Norman
 7. *Teenage Thunder* (Howco International, 1957); as Used Car Salesman
 8. *Cattle Empire* (20th Century–Fox, 1958); as Douglas Hamilton
 9. *Good Day for a Hanging* (Columbia, 1958); as George Fletcher
10. **Suicide Battalion* (American International, 1958); as Lt. Chet Hall
11. **The Horse Soldiers* (United Artists, 1959); as Dunker
12. **Last Train from Gun Hill* (Paramount, 1959); as Skag
13. **Rio Bravo* (Warner Bros., 1959); as Cowboy Murdered in the Saloon
14. **The Magnificent Seven* (United Artists, 1960); as Robert
15. **Stakeout* (Crown International, 1962); as Joe
16. **The Stripper* (20th Century–Fox, 1963); as Mr. Mulvaney
17. **A Gathering of Eagles* (Universal, 1963)
18. **Cheyenne Autumn* (Warner Bros., 1964); as Telegrapher
19. *One Man's Way* (United Artists, 1964); as Tom Rayburn
20. **The Hallelujah Trail* (United Artists, 1965); as Horner
21. **Billy the Kid versus Dracula* (Circle/Embassy, 1966)
22. *An Eye for an Eye* (Circle/Embassy, 1966)
23. **Madame X* (Universal, 1966); as Sgt. Riley
24. *The Ride to Hangman's Tree* (Universal, 1967); as Keller
25. *Journey to Shiloh* (Universal, 1968); as Grey Beard
26. **The Computer Wore Tennis Shoes* (Disney/Buena Vista, 1970); as Angelo
27. **Million Dollar Duck* (Disney/Buena Vista, 1971)
28. **Yuma* (Aaron Spelling/ABC, March 2, 1971); as Rol King
29. *A Taste of Evil* (Aaron Spelling/ABC, October 12, 1971); as the Sheriff
30. **Now You See Him, Now You Don't* (Disney/Buena Vista, 1972); as Alfred
31. *Set This Town on Fire* (Public Arts Production/Universal TV, January 8, 1973); as Chuck
32. **Satan's School for Girls* (Spelling/Goldberg/ABC, September 19, 1973); as Sheriff
33. *Runaway!* (Universal/ABC, September 29, 1973); as Fireman

34. *A Cry in the Wilderness* (Universal/ABC, March 26, 1974); as Griffey
35. *The Sex Symbol* (Screen Gems/Columbia/ABC, September 17, 1974); as Public Relations Man
36. **Death Sentence* (Spelling/Goldberg/ABC, October 2, 1974); as Trooper
37. **The Apple Dumpling Gang* (Buena Vista, 1975); as Herm Dally
38. **The Loneliest Runner* (NBC, December 20, 1976)
39. *The Moneychangers* (Ross Hunter Productions/Paramount, December 4, 5, 12, 19, 1976); as Timberwell
40. *The New Daughters of Joshua Cabe* (Spelling/Goldberg/ABC, May 29, 1976)
41. *Elvis* (Dick Clark Productions/ABC, February 11, 1979); as Vernon Presley
42. **Sunset* (Columbia/Tri Start, 1988); as Studio Guard

TV Series

43. *Bonanza* (NBC, 1963-1973) 60 Minutes; as Deputy Clem Foster

TV Guest Appearances

44. *Gunsmoke* "Mr. and Mrs. Amber" (CBS, April 4, 1956) 30 Minutes; as Simon
45. *Cavalry Patrol* [Pilot] (CBS, 1956/1957); as Jenner
46. *Tombstone Territory* "Guns of Silver" (ABC, November 27, 1957) 30 Minutes; as Ollie Williams
47. *Wagon Train* "The Charles Avery Story" (NBC, November 13, 1957) 60 Minutes; as Cullen
48. *Maverick* "The Naked Gallows" (ABC, December 15, 1957) 60 Minutes; as Tyler Brink
49. *Wyatt Earp* "The General's Lady" (ABC, January 14, 1958) 30 Minutes; as Sgt. Turner
50. *Colt .45* "Ghost Town" (ABC, February 21, 1958) 30 Minutes; as Jack Lowden
51. *Tales of Wells Fargo* "Special Delivery" (NBC, March 31, 1958) 30 Minutes; as Capt. Maynard
52. *Maverick* "Seed of Deception" (ABC, April 13, 1958) 60 Minutes; as Ross Aikens
53. *Sugarfoot* "Guns for Big Bear" [Contraband Cargo] (ABC, April 15, 1958) 60 Minutes; as Sgt. McKinnock
54. *Northwest Passage* "Break Out" (NBC, October 19, 1958) 30 Minutes; as Ben Smith
55. *Have Gun Will Travel* "A Sense of Justice" (CBS, November 1, 1958) 30 Minutes
56. *Gunsmoke* "Lynching Man" (CBS, November 15, 1958) 30 Minutes; as Ed Shelby
57. *Zane Grey Theatre* "Deadfall" (CBS, February 19, 1959) 30 Minutes; as Deputy Stover
58. *Black Saddle* "Client Robinson" (NBC, February 21, 1959) 30 Minutes; as Ken Wilson
59. *Colt .45* "Dead Aim" (ABC, April 12, 1959) 30 Minutes; as Jed Coy
60. *Bronco* "Prairie Skipper" (ABC, May 5, 1959) 60 Minutes; as Jeb
61. *The Rifleman* "A Matter of Faith" (ABC, May 19, 1959) 30 Minutes; as Hode Evans

62. *The Texan* "The Dishonest Posse" (CBS, October 5, 1959) 30 Minutes; as Larry Boland
63. *Tales of Wells Fargo* "The Train Robbery" (NBC, October 12, 1959) 30 Minutes; as Gig
64. *Black Saddle* "The Long Rider" (NBC, October 16, 1959) 30 Minutes
65. *Wanted Dead or Alive* "Desert Seed" (CBS, November 14, 1959) 30 Minutes
66. *Maverick* "A Fellow's Brother" (ABC, November 22, 1959) 60 Minutes; as Sheriff Jed Hanes
67. *Walt Disney Presents* "Wild Horse Revenge" [The Code] (ABC, December 11, 1959) 60 Minutes; as Arne
68. *Tales of Wells Fargo* "Wanted Jim Hardie" (NBC, December 21, 1959) 30 Minutes; as Tom
69. *The Alaskans* "The Trial of Reno McKee" (ABC, January 10, 1960) 60 Minutes; as Edward Carse
70. *Laramie* "Company Man" (NBC, February 9, 1960) 60 Minutes; as Tex
71. *Wanted Dead or Alive* "Triple Vise" (CBS, February 27, 1960) 30 Minutes; as Billy Hemp
72. *Laramie* "Men of Defiance (NBC, April 19, 1960) 60 Minutes; as Reb O'Neil
73. *Tate* "The Reckoning" (NBC, August 4, 1960) 30 Minutes; as Corey
74. *The Rifleman* "Seven" (ABC, October 11, 1960) 30 Minutes; as Sanchez
75. *Gunsmoke* "Don Matteo" (CBS, October 22, 1960) 30 Minutes; as Grave Tabor
76. *Maverick* "A Bullet for the Teacher" (ABC, October 30, 1960) 60 Minutes; as Luke Storm
77. *Zane Grey Theatre* "The Mormons" (CBS, December 15, 1960) 30 Minutes; as Cole
78. *Maverick* "The Bold Fenian Men" (ABC, December 18, 1960) 60 Minutes; as Orson Holt
79. *Bronco* "Stage to the Sky" (ABC, April 24, 1961) 60 Minutes; as Johnny Rawlins
80. *Twilight Zone* "The Arrival" (CBS, September 21, 1961) 30 Minutes
81. *Gunsmoke* "Old Yellow Boots" (CBS, October 7, 1961) 60 Minutes; as Head
82. *Death Valley Days* "The Watch" (Syndicated, December 4, 1961) 30 Minutes; as Jack Short
83. *Laramie* "The Lawless Seven" (NBC, December 26, 1961) 60 Minutes
84. *Loggers* [Pilot] (NBC, 1961/1962)
85. *Bonanza* "The Long Night" (NBC, May 6, 1962) 60 Minutes; as Poindexter
86. *Rawhide* "Abilene" (CBS, May 18, 1962) 60 Minutes; as Jack Harris
87. *Have Gun Will Travel* "Memories of Monica" (CBS, October 27, 1962) 30 Minutes; as Sheriff Reagan
88. *The Virginian* "Riff Raff" (NBC, November 7, 1962) 90 Minutes
89. *Stoney Burke* "To Catch the Kaiser" (ABC, March 11, 1963) 60 Minutes; as Neeley
90. *Laramie* "The Sometime Gambler" (NBC, March 19, 1963) 60 Minutes; as Reeves
91. *G.E. True* "Five Tickets to Hell" (CBS, March 24, 1963) 30 Minutes
92. *Ben Casey* "In the Name of Love, a Small Corporation" (ABC, May 27, 1963) 60 Minutes

93. *Death Valley Days* "Measure of a Man" (Syndicated, October 1, 1963) 30 Minutes; as Jack Alvord
94. *The Fugitive* "The Girl from Little Egypt" (ABC, December 17, 1963) 60 Minutes; as Officer Westphal
95. *Twilight Zone* "Ring-a-Ding Girl" (CBS, December 27, 1963) 30 Minutes
96. *The Virginian* "The Invaders" (NBC, January 1, 1964) 90 Minutes
97. *The Fugitive* "Nemesis" (ABC, October 13, 1964) 60 Minutes; as Matt Davis
98. *The Fugitive* "Runner in the Dark" (ABC, March 30, 1965) 60 Minutes; as Sgt. Eggins
99. *Branded* "Very Few Heroes" (NBC, April 11, 1965) 60 Minutes; as Thomas Teal
100. *Combat* "Odyssey" (ABC, April 20, 1965) 60 Minutes
101. *The Fugitive* "Wings of an Angel" (ABC, September 14, 1965) 60 Minutes; as Officer No. 1
102. *Bonanza* "The Other Son" (NBC, October 3, 1965) 60 Minutes; as Sheriff Walker
103. *A Man Called Shenandoah* "The Verdict" (ABC, November 1, 1965) 30 Minutes; as Clem
104. *Branded* "The Golden Fleece" (NBC, January 2, 1966) 30 Minutes; as Sheriff Gorman
105. *The Big Valley* "Barbary Red" (ABC, February 16, 1966) 60 Minutes; as Clint
106. *The Virginian* "The Wolves Up Front, The Jackals Behind" (NBC, March 23, 1966) 90 Minutes; as Donovan
107. *The Fugitive* "In a Plain Paper Wrapper" (ABC, April 19, 1966) 60 Minutes; as First Officer
108. *The Virginian* "The Challenge" (NBC, October 19, 1966) 90 Minutes; as Sam Fuller
109. *The Monroes* "The Hunter" (ABC, October 26, 1966) 60 Minutes; as Aaron
110. *The Big Valley* "The Man from Nowhere" (ABC, November 14, 1966) 60 Minutes; as Rancher
111. *Gunsmoke* "Mail Drop" (CBS, January 28, 1967) 60 Minutes; as Walsh
112. *The Big Valley* "Cage of Eagles" (ABC, April 24, 1967) 60 Minutes; as Mac
113. *The Big Valley* "Turn of a Card" (ABC, March 20, 1967) 60 Minutes; as Joe Garrett
114. *The Virginian* "The Deadly Past" (NBC, September 20, 1967) 90 Minutes; as Ned Smith
115. *The Big Valley* "A Flock of Trouble" (ABC, September 25, 1967) 60 Minutes; as Matt Kelsey
116. *The Guns of Will Sonnett* "A Son for a Son" (ABC, October 20, 1967) 30 Minutes
117. *Dundee and the Culhane* "The 1000 Feet Deep Brief" (CBS, October 25, 1967) 60 Minutes; as H.P. Graham
118. *Hondo* "Hondo and the Hanging Town" (ABC, December 8, 1967) 60 Minutes; as Thompson
119. *The Guns of Will Sonnett* "And He Shall Lead the Children" (ABC, January 19, 1968) 30 Minutes; as Charlie
120. *Death Valley Days* "By the Book" (Syndicated, May 10, 1968) 30 Minutes; as Rogers
121. *The Big Valley* "The Profit and the Lost" (ABC, December 2, 1968) 60 Minutes; as Sheriff

122. *The Guns of Will Sonnett* "The Fearless Man" (ABC, December 13, 1968) 30 Minutes
123. *The Guns of Will Sonnett* "Robber's Roost" (ABC, January 17, 1969) 30 Minutes
124. *The Big Valley* "The Secret" (ABC, January 27, 1969) 60 Minutes; as Slade
125. *The Outcasts* "The Glory Wagon" (ABC, February 3, 1969) 60 Minutes; as Grainer
126. *The Big Valley* "Point and Counterpoint" (ABC, May 19, 1969) 60 Minutes; as Sheriff Jim Dolan
127. *Death Valley Days* "Son of Thunder" (Syndicated, October 26, 1969) 30 Minutes
128. *Adam-12* "Log 124 — Airport" (NBC, February 28, 1970) 30 Minutes
129. *O'Hara, U.S. Treasury* "Operation Crystal Springs" (CBS, December 3, 1971) 60 Minutes
130. *Streets of San Francisco* "Shield of Honor" (ABC, November 15, 1973) 60 Minutes
131. *Gunsmoke* "The Iron Blood of Courage" (CBS, February 18, 1974) 60 Minutes; as Rolfing
132. *Rockford Files* "The Dexter Crisis" [Find the Woman] (NBC, November 15, 1974) 60 Minutes; as Lieutenant
133. *Mannix* "Picture of a Shadow" (CBS, November 24, 1974) 60 Minutes
134. *Streets of San Francisco* "Labyrinth" (ABC, February 27, 1975) 60 Minutes
135. *Petrocelli* "Terror By the Book" (NBC, December 10, 1975) 60 Minutes
136. *Rockford Files* "To Protect and Serve [Part 1]" (NBC, March 11, 1977) 60 Minutes; as Wes Wesley
137. *Rockford Files* "To Protect and Serve [Part 2]" (NBC, March 18, 1977) 60 Minutes; as Wes Wesley

David Canary

CANDY CANADAY

Candy Canaday was born on an army post and grew up under the influence of the military. His father was often gone on army business, causing his mother to be alone frequently. It was her loneliness and the hardships of life on the frontier that caused her death when Candy was only four. He was only seven when his father died a war hero. He was now alone in the world.

He had met a girl by the name of Ann while growing up; her father also was in the army. They fell in love and were married. Ann's father disapproved of the couple's union, feeling Candy was not good enough for his daughter. He sent Candy away and annulled the marriage. Ann would later marry Captain Harris.

Candy became a drifter, moving about as the mood struck him. Inde-

pendent and with no one to help him with his problems, he did not hesitate to use his fists and consider the consequences later.

Candy, in search of food, came across the campsite of Ben Cartwright, who was in charge of a military expedition sent out to take a trouble-making Indian to prison. Candy hung around and helped Ben and the soldiers ward off friend Chief Wennemuca, who had come to free the prisoner, believing him to be a god. In appreciation for his help, Ben offered Candy a job on the Ponderosa. Candy accepted with the stipulation that he could leave any time he wanted or that Ben could send him packing at a moment's notice.

Because of his unconventional ways, Candy got away with things that the Cartwrights could not have. After a few years, the wanderlust forced Candy to move on to new adventures. The Cartwrights were the family he never had and soon the feeling of belonging overpowered his need to roam. He returned to the Ponderosa, where he was accepted with open arms and became like one of the family.

David Canary was born on August 25, 1938, in Elwood, Indiana. The family moved to Masillon, Ohio, where he spent most of his childhood years. His father was a store manager for J. C. Penny. Canary and the family claimed to have a link to the Old West as descendants of Calamity Jane, whose real name was Martha Jane Canary. In high school, he joined the football team. This led to his receiving a football scholarship to the University of Cincinnati. His major was music with particular attention being given to his baritone voice. He was able to take advantage of a program the university had with the Cincinnati Conservatory of Music.

He played football and broke his nose in his sophomore year. In his senior year, the Denver Broncos scouted him and wanted him to play left end for them. His father advised him to choose the career he really wanted. David turned down the Broncos and, after receiving his Bachelor's degree, moved to New York to pursue an acting career. He took acting classes, did some chorus work in an off–Broadway show and had a small part in *The Happiest Girl in the World*. He made his Broadway debut in Jose Quintero's *Great Day in the Morning* starring Colleen Dewhurst. Before being drafted in the Army in 1962, he got the lead in the off–Broadway production *The Fantasticks*.

While in the Army, he directed a version of *The Fantasticks* for them and appeared in nine more shows. In 1963, he won the "All Army Entertainment Contest" as Best Popular Singer.

In 1964, he was released from the Army and headed for San Francisco, where he resumed his career in *The Fantasticks* in December.

His big break came in 1965, when he was cast as Dr. Russ Gehring for six months in ABC's *Peyton Place*. He also did some TV work on *Gunsmoke* and *Cimarron Strip.* 20th Century–Fox cast him in *The St. Valentine's Day Massacre* (1967) and *Hombre* (1967) with Paul Newman. It was during a barroom scene in *Hombre* that Canary came to producer David Dortort's attention and was cast as Candy in NBC's *Bonanza.* Dortort described him as "the kind of kid who comes on and suddenly there's nobody else on screen."[3] He was a regular from 1967–1970, when he left the show to pursue writing and directing his own films. He soon realized he had made a mistake. Two things convinced him to return to the show. "First, a pilot called *The Young Prosecutors* didn't get sold," he

David Canary. (Photofest.)

stated. "Then I heard that one of the very top filmmakers was having trouble raising money for his next picture. If he couldn't do it, I sure as hell wasn't going to be able to."[4] This time he remained on the show until it was canceled in 1973.

After leaving *Bonanza,* he did a number of commercials for such products as bread and television sets. He guested on a few television shows and made some TV-movies during the 1970s but devoted most of his time to theater work.

In 1981, he ventured into daytime soap operas and spent two years as Stephen Frame on NBC's *Another World.*

In 1982, he married Maureen, with whom he had two children — Chris and Katie. He had a daughter, Lisa, from his first marriage to Julie. He left *Another World* in 1983, and for his next project that same year, he took on the dual role as twins Adam and Stuart Chandler in ABC's *All My Children.* His father became a fan of the show and his brother John played Dr. Voight. He has received much acclaim for his work in the series. He has won four Emmys for Outstanding Lead Actor. It was during the 1987-88 *Emmy Awards* that he got a standing ovation while accepting his second award. "I am painfully aware that this belongs to my brother Stuart," he joked.[5]

When not acting, he spends his time refinishing furniture and enjoying health foods. Over the years, he has recorded a number of albums using his gifted voice. He has also developed his talents by writing plays, some of which he has done with Robert Lupone's Manhattan Class Co. Maureen and David reside in a little Connecticut town.

Movies, Telefilms, Miniseries
An asterisk (*) denotes video availability.

1. *Hombre* (20th Century–Fox, 1966); as Lamar Dean
2. *The St. Valentine's Day Massacre* (20th Century–Fox, 1967); as Frank Gusenberg
3. *Incident on a Dark Street* (20th Century–Fox/NBC, January 13, 1973); as Pete Gallagher
4. *Melvin Purvis: G-Man* (American International Pictures/ABC, April 9, 1974); as Eugene Farber
5. *Posse* (Paramount, 1975); as Pensteman
6. *Shark's Treasure* (United Artists, 1975); as Larry
7. *Johnny Firecloud* (1975)
8. *The Dain Curse* (Martin Poll Productions/CBS, May 22, 1978–May 29, 1978) Miniseries; as Jack Santos

TV Series

9. *Peyton Place* (ABC, 1965–1966) 30 Minutes; as Dr. Russ Gehring
10. *Bonanza* (NBC, 1967–1970) 60 Minutes; as Candy Canaday
11. *Bonanza* (NBC, 1972–1973) 60 Minutes; as Candy Canaday
12. *Search for Tomorrow* (CBS) 30 Minutes; as Arthur Bensen
13. *The Doctors* (NBC, 30 Minutes; as Warren
14. *Another World* (NBC, 1981–1983) 60 Minutes; as Stephen Frame
15. *All My Children* (ABC, 1983–Present) 60 Minutes; as Adam and Stuart Chandler

TV Guest Appearances

16. *Gunsmoke* "Nitro [Part I]" (CBS, April 8, 1967) 60 Minutes; as George McClaney
17. *Gunsmoke* "Nitro [Part II]" (CBS, April 15, 1967) 60 Minutes; as George McClaney
18. *Dundee and the Culhane* "The Dead Man's Brief" (CBS, October 4, 1967) 60 Minutes; as Charlie Montana
19. *Cimarron Strip* "Knife in the Darkness" (CBS, January 25, 1968) 60 Minutes; as Tal St. James
20. *The F.B.I.* "The Last Job" (ABC, September 26, 1971) 60 Minutes
21. *Hawaii Five-O* "3000 Crooked Miles to Honolulu" (CBS, October 5, 1971) 60 Minutes; as George
22. *Bearcats* "Hostages" (CBS, October 14, 1971); as Joe Bascom
23. *Alias Smith and Jones* "Everything Else You Can Steal" (ABC, December 16, 1971) 60 Minutes; as Sheriff Coffin

24. *Alias Smith and Jones* "The Strange Fate of Conrad Meyer Zulick" (ABC, December 2, 1972) 60 Minutes; as Doc Donovan
25. *The Rookies* "Down Home Boy" (ABC, November 19, 1973) 60 Minutes
26. *Police Story* "Death on Credit" (NBC, November 27, 1973) 60 Minutes
27. *Kung Fu* "The Elixer" (ABC, December 20, 1973) 60 Minutes; as Frank Grogan
28. *The Rookies* " A Test of Courage" (ABC, December 2, 1974) 60 Minutes
29. *S.W.A.T.* "Kill S.W.A.T." (ABC, September 20, 1975) 60 Minutes
30. *American Playhouse* "Kind of America" (PBS, January 19, 1982)
31. *Michael Landon Memories with Laughter and Love* (NBC, September 17, 1991) 120 Minutes
32. *QVC* (QVC, October 25, 1996) in phone conversation with guest Susan Lucci
33. *Oprah Winfrey Show* (ABC, October 30, 1996) 60 Minutes
34. Daytime Emmy Awards (NBC, May 15, 1998)
35. *Law & Order* (NBC, November 18, 1998) 60 Minutes; as Jeremy Orenstein
36. 15th Annual *Soap Opera Digest* Awards (NBC, February 26, 1999)
37. Daytime Emmy Awards (ABC, May 19, 2000)

Stage

38. *Kittiwake Island* (Martinque Theatre in New York, October 12, 1960); as Rusty Swallow
39. *The Happiest Girl in the World* (Martin Beck Theatre in New York, April 3, 1961–June 24, 1961) 96 Performances; as Hector
40. *Hi Paisano* (York Playhouse in New York, September 30, 1961) 3 Performances; as Dino
41. *Great Day in the Morning* (Henry Miller Theatre in New York, March 28, 1962–April 7, 1962) 13 Performances; as Owen Brady
42. *The Fantasticks* (Off-Broadway, 1962)
43. *The Fantasticks* (Tour in San Francisco, California, December 1964)
44. *I Do! I Do!* (1970s); as Michael
45. *That's Entertainment* (Edison Theatre Middle in New York, April 14, 1972–April 16, 1972); as Greg
46. *Macbeth* (Actors' Theatre of Louisville/Macauley Theatre in Louisville, Kentucky, March 22, 1973) 27 Performances
47. *Kiss Me Kate* (Playhouse in the Park in Philadelphia, Pennsylvania/Robert S. Marx Theatre in Cincinnati, Ohio, June 21, 1973) 22 Performances
48. *Jacques Brel Is Alive and Well and Living in Paris* (Actors' Theatre of Louisville/Victor Jory Theatre, March 2, 1975) 37 Performances
49. *Gone With the Wind* (June 14, 1976); as Rhett Butler
50. *The Sea Gull* (Pittsburgh Public Theatre: Main Stage/Allegany Theatre in Pittsburgh, Pennsylvania, November 8, 1979) 54 Performances
51. *Clothes for a Summer Hotel* (John F. Kennedy Center/Eisenhower Theatre in Washington, D.C., January 29, 1980) 39 Performances; as Edourd/Intern
52. *Summer* (Hudson Guild Theatre, September 17, 1980) 35 Performances
53. *Blood Moon* (Production Company, January 5, 1983)

Personal Appearances

———————— Mitch Vogel ————————

Jamie Hunter Cartwright

Jamie Hunter Cartwright was a slender, red-headed, freckle-faced lad of average height. He was born to Elizabeth and Tom Hunter. Elizabeth married Tom at the age of 20 and died when her son was only two.

Tom was a rain maker and was tarred and feathered by a mob from Grass Flatt while Jamie was forced to watch. He later died from a fever, thus making Jamie a teenage orphan.

Dusty Rhoades came across Jamie and his father and promised Tom to look after his son. Dusty and Jamie arrived in Virginia City where Dusty made a deal with the mayor and the town to make it rain in two weeks. For their services, they were paid $5,000 with an advance of $200 for supplies. They get it to rain two hours before their deadline. Jamie convinced the town to attribute the deed to his father.

Dusty and Jamie moved to the Ponderosa, where the boy liked fishing and helped out with ranch chores. Jamie loved animals and once purchased April, an Irish setter, from Tim Riley, who worked for the dog's owner Horace Kingston. They entered April in field trials. Jamie was once taken hostage by escaped outlaws and held for $10,000 ransom. He was also credited with the capture of an outlaw, Pepper Shannon. He was once initiated into a boy's club, the Vigilante Raiders, during which one of the boys died. The boys tried to stick together and not tell what happened. Jamie realized they could not keep quiet when an innocent man was accused of the boy's death.

Jamie had an affinity for getting into trouble. He was asked to take a wagon to town and thought he was old enough to take a more dangerous route after Ben had forbid him to do so. He ended up killing a horse and wrecking the wagon. Ben took him on a four-day pack trip to get him to realize what he had done.

Ben made Jamie go to school against his wishes instead of going on a roundup. When bullied and teased about being an orphan, he took Ben's gold-plated rifle to impress his school mates and accidentally broke it. After admitting what he had done, he ran away to Mill City to work at a livery stable. He returned home only after he realized Ben was right in disciplining him.

Another time at school, he fell in love with Mrs. Kelly Edwards, the wife of his teacher Dan Edwards, after he had helped out at their ranch. He played the guitar and sang "Camptown Races" to her. He learned that Dan was beating his wife and came to her defense.

When adoption of Jamie was first mentioned, he became irritated because he felt that Ben and the boys were doing it out of pity, but was appeased when Ben told him proceedings had started six months earlier. Jamie was 15 when adopted. Barris Callahan, Jamie's maternal grandfather, arrived in Virginia City from Boston, where he was a rich ship builder. Callahan challenged the adoption and wanted to take the boy back to Boston. Ben claimed that the boy's roots were on the Ponderosa. However, Jamie was forced to go with his grandfather. In an accident along the way, Callahan's leg was broken and his grandson attended his injuries. Callahan came to his senses and agreed to let Jamie remain with the Cartwrights with the stipulation that he would be permitted to visit him in Boston. Thus the adoption went through, making Jamie Ben's fourth son and a welcome addition to the Cartwright clan.

He was born Mitchell Vogel on January 17, 1956, in Alhambra, California. He became an avid rock collector, swimmer and horseback rider and developed into an expert horseman.

In 1966, at the age of ten, he was given the choice of taking guitar or acting lessons. He chose acting after he and his mother had gone to see *Peter Pan*. This led to starring roles in *Tom Sawyer, Heidi* and *The Wizard of Oz* at the Orange County Performing Arts Foundation, a local community theater. It was there that he was noticed by an agent and was taken on professional auditions. This led to his film debut in *Yours, Mine and Ours* starring Lucille Ball and Henry Fonda and future *Bonanza* castmate Tim Matheson. He received particular notice in *The Reivers* and he would go on to appear in two Disney anthology series, *Bayou Boy* (1971) and *Menace on the Mountain* (1972), where David Dortort took notice of him. His first appearance on *Bonanza* was as Tommy in the episode "The Real People of Muddy Creek" (October 10, 1968) and he took on the role of Jamie in 1970 at the age of 13. Dortort felt that he would fill the youth void and give Ben someone to listen to his fatherly words of wisdom.

Mitch resided with his mother, half-sister and grandmother. His grandmother also served as his business manager and put him on an allowance of three dollars per week.

The child labor laws limited his work day to four hours with three hours devoted to his on-set schooling. His work day started at 8 A.M. in makeup and wardrobe and was followed by tutoring which also occurred between scenes.

"I think I would like to be an actor all my life," Vogel said in early 1971. "But maybe by the time I turn 16, there won't be any parts for me."[6]

Vogel had the sense to pursue a college education so that he had something else to fall back on should his acting career come to an end.

Mitch Vogel. (Photofest.)

In 1971 he said, "I would like to play a bad kid, maybe one from the ghetto who is an addict."[7] He turned 17 the night *Bonanza*'s final episode aired.

He continued to appear in guest spots on television, including Michael Landon's *Little House on the Prairie* (1974) as well as several other films.

Mitch has since left the industry to pursue other interests outside of show business.

Movies, Telefilms, Miniseries

An asterisk (*) denotes video availability.

1. *Yours, Mine and Ours* (United Artists, 1968); as Tommy North
2. *The Reivers* (Duo-Solar/National General, 1969); as Lucius McCaslin
3. *Quarantined* (Paramount/ABC, February 24, 1970); as Jimmy Atkinson
4. *Born Innocent* (Tomorrow Entertainment/NBC, September 10, 1974); as Tom Parker
5. *Texas Detour* (1978)

TV Series

6. *Bonanza* (NBC, 1970–1973) 60 Minutes; as Jamie Hunter Cartwright

TV Guest Appearances

7. *Dundee and the Culhane* "The Thy Brother's Keepers Brief" (CBS, November 22, 1967) 60 Minutes; as Jeffrey Bennett
8. *Bonanza* "The Real People of Muddy Creek" (NBC, October 6, 1968) 60 Minutes; as Tommy
9. *The Virginian* "The Storm Gate" (NBC, November 13, 1968) 90 Minutes; as Boy
10. *Death Valley Days* "The Tenderfoot" (Syndicated, October 9, 1969) 30 Minutes; as Jerry
11. *The Wonderful World of Disney* "Menace on the Mountain [Part 1]" (NBC, March 1, 1970) 60 Minutes; as Jamie McIver
12. *The Wonderful World of Disney* "Menace on the Mountain [Part 2]" (NBC, March 8, 1970) 60 Minutes; as Jamie McIver
13. *Here Come the Brides* "Absalom" (ABC, March 20, 1970) 60 Minutes; as Absalom
14. *Two Boys* (NBC, July 1970); as Jud Thomas
15. *Gunsmoke* "McCabe" (CBS, November 30, 1970) 60 Minutes; as Dobie
16. *The Wonderful World of Disney* "Bayou Boy [The Boy from Deadman's Bayou] [Part 1]" (NBC, February 7, 1971) 60 Minutes; as Jeannot
17. *The Wonderful World of Disney* "Bayou Boy [Part 2]" (NBC, February 14, 1971) 60 Minutes; as Jeannot
18. *Gunsmoke* "Lynch Town" (CBS, November 19, 1973) 60 Minutes; as Rob Fiedler
19. *Little House on the Prairie* "The Love of Johnny Johnson" (NBC, October 9, 1974) 60 Minutes; as Johnny Johnson
20. *Streets of San Francisco* "Jacobs Boy" (ABC, October 24, 1974) 60 Minutes
21. *Gunsmoke* "The Hiders" (CBS, January 13, 1975) 60 Minutes; as Dink
22. *State Fair* (CBS, May 14, 1976); as Wayne Bryant
23. *The Quest* "Seventy-Two Hours" (NBC, November 3, 1976) 60 Minutes; as Jess

Stage

24. *Tom Sawyer* (Orange County Performing Arts Foundation, Late 1960s)
25. *Heidi* (Orange County Performing Arts Foundation, Late 1960s)
26. *The Wizard of Oz* (Orange County Performing Arts Foundation, Late 1960s)

Lou Frizzell

DUSTY RHOADES

Dusty Rhoades was a short, stocky drifter who arrived in Virginia City and met Hoss and Joe. The two Cartwrights were upset with Calhoun's monopoly in the livery business. Dusty suggested they go into a partnership and set up their own livery business in an attempt to give Calhoun competition. They signed a year's lease to help deliver horses. When things got slow, Dusty suggested providing services for free to get business away from Calhoun.

After they succeeded, Dusty headed for Montana's gold fields. On a return trip, he came across Jamie Hunter and his father Tom, who was sick with fever. Dusty stayed with them until Tom died. Keeping the promise he had made to the boy's father, he took Jamie under his wing. In Virginia City, he posed as rainmaker Garabaldy. He helped Jamie prove his father's formula could really make it rain.

Jamie and Dusty moved to the Ponderosa where Dusty became a trusted, hard-working ranch hand. He and Jamie remained close.

Lou Frizzell was born on June 10, 1920, and was educated at UCLA. He developed into one of America's leading character actors. He made his Broadway debut in 1949, appearing in *Oklahoma!* He would continue to appear in New York and regional theatres throughout the 1950s and 1960s in such productions as *Great Day in the Morning* (1962) with future *Bonanza* co-star David Canary and *Desire Under the Elms* (1963). He often played a townsman.

He made numerous film and television appearances in the 1960s and 1970s, often playing country citizens or minor officials. He next joined the cast of the hit television series *Bonanza* (1970), playing drifter Dusty Rhoades, who later became the Cartwrights' faithful trusted ranch hand.

After leaving *Bonanza* in 1973, he became a regular on the 1974 series *Chopper One* (playing Mitch) and *The New Land* as Bo.

He remained busy until he suffered from a long illness which resulted in his death in Los Angeles on June 17, 1979. The 59-year-old actor was survived by his father.

Movies, Telefilms, Miniseries

An asterisk (*) denotes video availability.

1. *The Reivers* (Duo Solar/National General, 1969); as Doyle
2. *The Stalking Moon* (National General, 1969); as Station Master
3. *Tell Them Willie Boy Is Here* (Universal, 1969); as Station Agent
4. *Halls of Anger* (United Artists, 1970); as Stewart
5. *Lawman* (United Artists, 1971); as Cobden
6. *Summer of '42* (Warner Bros., 1971); as Druggist
7. *Banacek* "Detour to Nowhere" (Universal/NBC, March 20, 1972); as Denny
8. *Streets of San Francisco* (Quinn Martin/Warner Bros./ABC, September 16, 1972); as Lou
9. *Footsteps* (CBS/Metro Media Productions, October 3, 1972); as Meat Inspector
10. *Hickey and Boggs* (United Artists, 1972); as Lawyer

11. *The Other* (20th Century–Fox, 1972); as Uncle George
12. *Rage* (Warner Bros., 1972); as Spike Boynton
13. *Runaway!* (Universal/ABC, September 29, 1973); as Brake Man Herb Elkhart
14. *Letters from Three Lovers* (Spelling/Goldberg Productions/ABC, October 3, 1973); as Eddie
15. *Money to Burn* (Universal/Silvertone Productions/ABC, October 27, 1973); as Guard Sergeant
16. *Manhunter* (Quinn Martin/CBS, February 26, 1974); as Scofield
17. *The Crazy World of Julius Vrooder* (20th Century–Fox, 1974); as Fowler
18. *The Front Page* (Universal, 1974); as Endicott
19. *The Nickel Ride* (20th Century–Fox, 1974); as Paulie
20. *Crossfire* (Quinn Martin/NBC, March 24, 1975); as Arthur Peabody
21. *Returning Home* (Lorimar/Samuel Goldwyn/ABC, April 29, 1975); as Butch Cavendish
22. *Farewell to Manzanar* (Korty Films/Universal/NBC, March 11, 1976); as Lou Frizzell
23. *Lucan* (MGM/ABC, May 22, 1977); as Casey
24. *Ruby and Oswald* (Alan Landsburg Productions/CBS, February 8, 1978); as Capt. J. Will Fritz
25. *Devil Dog: The Hound of Hell* (Zeitman, Landers, Roberts Production/CBS, October 31, 1978); as George
26. *Capricorn One* (Warner Bros., 1978); as Man on Launch Gantry
27. *Steel Cowboy* (Roger Gimbel/EMI Television/NBC, December 6, 1978); as Arky
28. *Centennial* (Universal/NBC, October 1978–February 1979); as Mr. Norris

TV Series

29. *Bonanza* (NBC, 1970–1972) 60 Minutes; as Dusty Rhoades
30. *Chopper One* (ABC, January 17, 1974–July 11, 1974) 30 Minutes; as Mitch, the Mechanic
31. *The New Land* (ABC, September 14, 1974–October 19, 1974) 60 Minutes; as Mr. Murdock
32. *Forever Fernwood* (Syndicated, 1977) 30 Minutes; as Nat Deardsen
33. *Alice* (CBS, 1978–1979) 30 Minutes; as Bubba Norris

TV Guest Appearances

34. *Armstrong Circle Theatre* "The Antique Swindle" (CBS, November 9, 1960) 60 Minutes
35. *Armstrong Circle Theatre* "Moment of Panic" (CBS, May 10, 1961) 60 Minutes; as Lou Alison
36. *East Side/West Side* "No Wings at All" (CBS, October 28, 1963) 60 Minutes
37. *Profile in Courage* "The Robert Taft Story" (NBC, January 3, 1965) 60 Minutes
38. *Run for Your Life* "The Company of Scoundrels" (NBC, October 18, 1967) 60 Minutes

39. *The F.B.I.* "Crisis Ground" (ABC, January 28, 1968) 60 Minutes
40. *Daniel Boone* "Faith's Way (NBC, April 4, 1968) 60 Minutes
41. *The F.B.I.* "The Quarry" (ABC, October 6, 1968) 60 Minutes
42. *The Outcasts* "The Heady Wine" (ABC, December 2, 1968) 60 Minutes; as Dr. Traynor
43. *Bonanza* "The Mark of Guilt" (NBC, December 15, 1968) 60 Minutes; as Jackson
44. *The High Chaparral* "The Brothers Cannon" (NBC, October 3, 1969) 60 Minutes; as Jeff Patterson
45. *The High Chaparral* "A Piece of Land" (NBC, October 10, 1969) 60 Minutes; as Jeff Patterson
46. *Bonanza* "The Lady and the Mark" (NBC, February 1, 1970) 60 Minutes; as Charley
47. *Owen Marshall, Counselor at Law* "Eulogy for a Wide Receiver" (ABC, September 30, 1971) 60 Minutes
48. *Rod Serling's Night Gallery* "Dr. String Fellow's Rejuvenator" (NBC, November 17, 1971) 60 Minutes; as Man
49. *Owen Marshall, Counselor at Law* "Until Proven Innocent" (ABC, December 9, 1971) 60 Minutes
50. *Sarge* "A Party to a Crime" (NBC, December 28, 1971) 60 Minutes
51. *Nicols* "Eddie Joe" (NBC, January 4, 1972) 60 Minutes; as Warden
52. *The F.B.I.* "The Runner" (ABC, September 17, 1972) 60 Minutes
53. *Hawaii Five-O* "Chain of Events" (CBS, October 24, 1972) 60 Minutes; as Mr. Phil Rynack
54. *Hawaii Five-O* "Little Girl Blue" (CBS, February 13, 1973) 60 Minutes
55. *Cannon* "The Seventh Grave" (CBS, February 28, 1973) 60 Minutes
56. *The Waltons* "The Bicycle" (CBS, March 1, 1973) 60 Minutes; as Joe Murdock
57. *Barnaby Jones* "Murder Go-Round" (CBS, April 15, 1973) 60 Minutes
58. *Marcus Welby, M.D.* "A Question of Fault" (ABC, October 16, 1973) 60 Minutes
59. *The Streets of San Francisco* "The Victims" (ABC, November 29, 1973) 60 Minutes
60. *Barnaby Jones* "Programmed for Killing" (CBS, January 27, 1974) 60 Minutes
61. *Chase* "Out of Gas" (NBC, February 20, 1974) 60 Minutes
62. *Biography* "The Man from Independence" (ABC, March 11, 1974); as Quilling
63. *Harry-O* "Forty Reasons to Kill [Part 1]" (ABC, December 5, 1974) 60 Minutes
64. *Harry-O* "Forty Reasons to Kill [Part 2]" (ABC, December 12, 1974) 60 Minutes
65. *The Streets of San Francisco* "The Glass Dart Board" (ABC, September 18, 1975) 60 Minutes; as Martin Trueax
66. *Hawaii Five-O* "Death's Name Is Sam," (October 10, 1975) 60 Minutes; as Sam
67. *Harry-O* "Portrait of a Murder" (ABC, November 20, 1975) 60 Minutes
68. *The New Mickey Mouse Club* "The Mystery of Rustler's Cove" (Syndicated, 1976) 30 Minutes; as Buzy
69. *Barnaby Jones* "Dead Heat" (CBS, January 1, 1976) 60 Minutes; as Sid

70. *Police Story* "Odyssey of Death" (NBC, January 9, 1976) 60 Minutes
71. *The Streets of San Francisco* "No Minor Vices" (ABC, November 4, 1976) 60 Minutes
72. *Barnaby Jones* "The Inside Man" (CBS, March 3, 1977) 60 Minutes
73. *Barnaby Jones* "Shadow of Fear" (CBS, November 24, 1977) 60 Minutes
74. *Lou Grant* "Renewal" (CBS, January 30, 1978) 60 Minutes
75. *Project U.F.O.* "Sighting 4004: The Howard Crossing Incident" (NBC, March 19, 1978) 60 Minutes
76. *Colorado CI* [Pilot] (CBS, May 26, 1978); as Frank Bannock
77. *Jackie and Darlene* [Pilot] (ABC, July 8, 1978); as Sgt. Gutherie
78. *The Waltons* "The Empty Nest" (CBS, September 21, 1978) 60 Minutes; as Joe Murdock

Stage

79. *Red Roses for Me* (Booth Theatre, December 28, 1955) 29 Performances; as Second Railway Man
80. *The Quare Fellow* (Circle in the Square in New York, November 27, 1958); as Donnelly
81. *Great Day in the Morning* (Henry Miller Theatre, March 28, 1962–April 7, 1962) 13 Performances; as Shultz
82. *Pullman Car Hiawatha* (Circle in the Square in New York, December 3, 1962); as Stage Manager
83. *Desire Under the Elms* (Circle in the Square in New York, January 10, 1963); as Peter Cabot
84. *After the Fall* (Repertory Theatre of Lincoln Center, January 23, 1964) 59 Performances; as Chairman
85. *Marco Millions* (Repertory Theatre of Lincoln Center, February 20, 1964); as Marco's Father
86. *A Moon for the Misbegotten* (Studio Arena Theatre in Buffalo, New York, October 7, 1965) 15 Performances
87. *Muzeeka* (Mark Taper Forum in Los Angeles, 1967–1968)

Tim Matheson

GRIFF KING

Griff King was a thin, good-looking young man. He was only 15 when he and Candy worked together in Billings, Montana. He wound up in the Nevada State Prison because he nearly killed his abusive stepfather. He was sentenced to prison for a two-to-five year term and had four years left to serve. He was assigned to the prison kitchen.

As Ben Cartwright inspected the prison, a riot broke out and Griff came to Ben's rescue, keeping him from being killed. The other prisoners got him to write down their demands. After the riot was quelled, Ben persuaded the governor to release Griff in his custody.

He acquired a new set of clothes and a pair of size 11 boots (at a cost of $8.63). No one consulted him about the parole and he felt unhappy with being forced to stay at the ranch. He wanted to leave but had to stay or he would break parole. He regarded the Ponderosa as the fanciest prison he had ever been in. He was always one to speak his mind.

Deputy Clem Foster was not pleased about Griff's being out on parole. When Griff was accused of robbing a store, a man named Lucas provided him with an alibi. While in town picking up a purchase for Lucas at the Wells Fargo Office, Griff discovered that the office had been robbed. Fearing blame, he fled. After the real culprit was apprehended, Griff was proven innocent.

Griff considered everything a matter of life and death because it meant survival in prison. He overreacted when the men in the bunk house cut the ropes of his bunk. He got mad and a fight ensued.

Eventually he learned to trust the Cartwrights and to adapt to the civilian way of life and soon became a welcomed addition to the Ponderosa.

Tim Matheson was born in Glendale, California, on December 31, 1947. The acting bug bit him in grade school after one of his friends introduced him to his producer-father Mike Stokey. Within a year, he was cast on Robert Young's series *Window on Main Street* (1961–62). He went on to be educated at California State University. He continued to work steadily in episodic TV on such shows as *Leave It to Beaver* (1962) and *The Farmer's Daughter* (1964). He also provided the voices for a number of Hanna-Barbera cartoons, including that of Jonny in Jonny Quest (1964–1965)

In 1968 he appeared in the film *Yours, Mine and Ours* starring Henry Fonda and Lucille Ball. Also in the cast was future *Bonanza* co-star Mitch Vogel.

Tim joined *Bonanza* during its last season to help fill the void left by the death of Dan Blocker. At first, he felt awkward but soon was able to adjust.

Tim Matheson. (Photofest.)

On September 22, 1976, Matheson co-starred with Kurt Russell as Quentin Beaudine in the NBC series *The Quest*. They played two brothers who set out to locate their sister, who had been captured by Cheyenne Indians. The show lasted until December 29, 1976.

In 1985, he started directing various episodes of television series as well as music videos. In 1989, he became the chairman and chief executive officer of the National Lampoon Company.

Through the years, Tim Matheson has continued working steadily and has made a number of made-for-TV movies. On September 29, 1999, he started playing the semi-regular character Vice-President John Hines on the NBC series *West Wing*.

Movies, Telefilms, Miniseries

An asterisk (*) denotes video availability.

1. *Divorce American Style* (Columbia, 1967); as Mark Harmon
2. **Yours, Mine and Ours* (Desilu–Walden/United Artists, 1968); as Mike
3. **How to Commit Marriage* (Cinerama, 1969); as David Poe
4. *Owen Marshall, Counselor at Law* "A Pattern of Morality" (Universal/ABC, September 24, 1971); as Jim McGuire
5. *Lock, Stock and Barrel* (Universal/ABC, September 24, 1971); as Clarence Bridgeman
6. **Magnum Force* (Warner Bros., 1973); as Sweet
7. *Hitched* (Universal/NBC, March 13, 1973); as Clarence Bridgeman
8. *Remember When* (Danny Thomas Productions/Raisin Co./ABC, March 23, 1974); as Warren Thompson
9. *The Last Day* (Paramount/A.C. Lyles Productions/NBC, February 15, 1975); as Emmet Dalton
10. **The Runaway Barge* (Lorimar/NBC, March 24, 1975); as Danny Worth
11. *Best Sellers*: "Captains and Kings" (Universal, September 30, October 7, 14, 28, November 4, 11, 1976)
12. *The Quest* "Listen to Your Heart" (David Gerber Production/Columbia Pictures/NBC, May 13, 1976); as Quenton Baudine
13. **Mary White* (Radnitz/Mattel/ABC, November 19, 1977); as William L. White
14. *Almost Summer* (Universal, 1978); as Kevin Hawkins
15. **National Lampoon's Animal House* (Universal, 1978); as Eric "Otter" Stratton
16. **1941* (Universal, 1979); as Berkhead
17. **The Apple Dumpling Gang Rides Again* (Disney/Buena Vista, 1979); as Private Jeff Reid
18. **Dreamer* (20th Century–Fox, 1979); as Dreamer
19. *The House of God* (1979)
20. **A Little Sex* (MTM/Universal, 1982); as Michael Donovan
21. **Listen to Your Heart* (CBS, January 14, 1983); as Josh Stern
22. **To Be or Not to Be* (Brooks Films/20th Century–Fox, 1983); as Lt. Ande Sobenski

23. *Impulse* (20th Century–Fox, 1984); as Stuart
24. *Up the Creek* (Orion, 1984); as Bob McGraw
25. *The Best Legs in the 8th Grade* (HBO, 1984); as Mark Fisher
26. *Fletch* (Universal, 1985); as Alan Stanwyk
27. *Obsessed with a Married Woman* (Sidaris-Oamhe/Feldman Meeker Co./ABC, February 11, 1985); as Tony Hammond
28. *Blind Justice* (CBS, March 9, 1986); as Jim Anderson
29. *Eye of the Demon* (NBC, 1987)
30. *Warm Hearts, Cold Feet* (CBS, 1987)
31. *The Littlest Victims* (CBS, 1989)
32. *Little White Lies* (NBC, 1989); as Dr. Harry McCrae
33. *Blind Fury* (1989) [Also Produced]
34. *Speed Zone* (Orion, 1989); as Jack
35. *Buried Alive* (USA, 1990); as Clint Goodwin
36. *Solar Crisis* (Trimark Pictures, 1990); as Captain Steve Kelso
37. *Joshua's Heart* (1990); as Tom
38. *Drop Dead Fred* (1991)
39. *Quicksand: No Escape* (1991)
40. *Sometimes They Come Back* (1991); as James Norman
41. *Mortal Passion* (1991)
42. *The Woman Who Sinned* (1991); as Michael
43. *Starfire* (1992)
44. *Those Bedroom Eyes* (Made for Cable, 1993); as Psychology Professor
45. *Dying to Love You* (1993); as Roger Paulson
46. *Robin Cook's Harmful Intent* (CBS, 1993); as Dr. Rhodes
47. *Going Underground* (1993); as Daniel Tate
48. *Relentless: Mind of a Killer* (1993); as Dr. Peter Hellman
49. *A Kiss to Die For* (1993); as William Tauber
50. *Trial and Error* (Made for Cable, 1993); as Peter Hudson
51. *Target of Suspicion* (1994); as Nick Matthews
52. *While Justice Sleeps* (1994); as Winn Cook
53. *Fast Company* (1995); as Lt. Jack Matthews
54. *Tails You Live, Heads You're Dead* (Made for Cable, October 18, 1995); as Detective McKinley
55. *Jonny Quest vs. Cyber Insects* (TNT Made for Cable, November 19, 1995); as Voice of Dac the Robot
56. *A Very Brady Sequel* (Paramount, 1996) as Roy Martin and Trevor Thomas
57. *Buried Secrets* (1996); as Clay
58. *An Unfinished Affair* (ABC, May 5, 1996) as Professor Alex Connor
59. *Black Sheep* (1996); as Al
60. *Christmas in My Hometown* (CBS, December 10, 1996); as Jake Peterson
61. *Buried Alive II* (USA, February 4, 1997); as Clint Goodwin [Also Directed]
62. *Sleeping with the Devil* (CBS, April 22, 1997); as Dick Strang
63. *Rescuers: Stories of Courage—Two Families* (Showtime, September 27, 1998)
64. *Forever Love* (CBS, September 27, 1998); as Alex
65. *Catch Me If You Can* (Fox Family, November 22, 1998); as Detective Norm Gannon
66. *At the Mercy of a Stranger* (CBS, November 3, 1999); as John Davis

67. *Navigating the Heart* (Lifetime, February 14, 2000) as John Daly
68. *Hell Swarm* (UPN, March 17, 2000) as Kirk Bluedorn [Also Directed]

TV Series

69. *Window on Main Street* (CBS, October 2, 1961–September 12, 1962) 30 Minutes; as Roddy Miller
70. *The Alvin Show* (CBS, October 4, 1961–September 12, 1962) 30 Minutes; as Voice of Sinbad, Jr.
71. **Jonny Quest* (ABC, September 18, 1964–September 9, 1965) 30 Minutes; as Voice of Jonny Quest
72. *Space Ghost* (CBS, September 10, 1966–September 7, 1968) 30 Minutes; as Voice of Jayce
73. *Samson and Goliath* (ABC, September 6, 1967–September 7, 1968) 30 Minutes; as Voice of Samson
74. *The Virginian* (NBC, September 17, 1969–March 18, 1970) 90 Minutes; as Jim Horn
75. *Bonanza* (NBC, September 23, 1972–January 16, 1971) 60 Minutes; as Griff King
76. *The Quest* (NBC, September 22, 1976–December 22, 1976) 60 Minutes; as Quentin Baudine
77. *Tucker's Witch* (CBS, October 6, 1982–May 5, 1983) 60 Minutes; as Rick Tucker
78. *Just in Time* (ABC, April 6, 1988–May 18, 1988) 30 Minutes; as Harry Stadlin
79. *Charlie Hoover* (Fox, November 9, 1991–February 2, 1992) 30 Minutes; as Charlie Hoover
80. *The West Wing* (NBC, September 29, 1999) 60 Minutes; as Vice President John Hines

TV Guest Appearances

81. *Leave It to Beaver* "Tell it to Ella" (ABC, 1962) 30 Minutes
82. *Leave It to Beaver* "The Clothing Drive" (ABC, 1963) 30 Minutes
83. *The Farmer's Daughter* "The Morley Report" (ABC, April 15, 1964) 30 Minutes
84. *Thompson's Ghost* (ABC, August 5, 1966); as Eddie Thompson
85. *The Hardy Boys* [Pilot] (NBC, September 8, 1967); as Joe Hardy
86. *Weekend* (NBC, September 9, 1967); as Randy
87. *Adam-12* "Grand Theft Horse" (NBC, January 18, 1969) 30 Minutes
88. *Bracken's World* "The Country Boy" (NBC, December 18, 1970) 60 Minutes
89. *Matt Lincoln* "Karen" (ABC, January 7, 1971) 60 Minutes
90. *Room 222* "The Long Honeymoon" (ABC, January 27, 1971) 30 Minutes
91. *The D.A.* "The People vs. Slovick" (NBC, October 22, 1971) 30 Minutes
92. *Bold Ones: The Lawyers* "By Reason of Insanity" (NBC, November 28, 1971) 60 Minutes
93. *Night Gallery* "Logoda's Heads" (NBC, December 29, 1971) 60 Minutes; as Henley

94. *Here's Lucy* "Kim Moves Out" (CBS, January 24, 1972) 30 Minutes; as Kim's Boyfriend
95. *Ironside* "His Fiddlers Three" (NBC, March 2, 1972) 60 Minutes
96. *The Smith Family* "Father-in-Law" (ABC, June 7, 1972) 30 Minutes
97. *Owen Marshall, Counselor at Law* "Why Is a Crooked Letter" (ABC, February 7, 1973) 60 Minutes
98. *Medical Center* "Impasse" (CBS, October 1, 1973) 60 Minutes
99. *Kung Fu* "The Soldier" (ABC, November 29, 1973) 60 Minutes; as Lt. Bill Wyland
100. *Owen Marshall, Counselor at Law* "A Killer with a Badge" (ABC, February 9, 1974) 60 Minutes
101. *The Magician* "The Illusion of the Fatal Arrow" (NBC, March 4, 1974) 60 Minutes
102. *Police Story* "Fingerprint" (NBC, March 12, 1974) 30 Minutes
103. *Three for the Road* "Match Point" (CBS, 1975) 60 Minutes
104. *Jigsaw John* "Thicker Than Blood" (NBC, February 23, 1976) 60 Minutes
105. *Hollywood Television Theatre* "The Hemingway Play" (PBS, March 11, 1976)
106. *Visions* "The War Window" (PBS, October 28, 1976); as Voice
107. *Battle of the Network Stars* (ABC, November 13, 1976) 120 Minutes
108. *Hawaii Five-O* "Deadly Doubles" (CBS, November 17, 1977) 60 Minutes; as Brent Sunders
109. *What Really Happened to the Class of '65* "Everybody's Girl" (NBC, December 8, 1977) 60 Minutes
110. *Hawaii Five-O* "East Wind, I'll Wind" (CBS, December 29, 1977) 60 Minutes
111. *Black Sheep Squadron* "Wolves in the Sheep Pen" (NBC, January 4, 1978) 60 Minutes
112. *How the West Was Won* (ABC, February 9, 26, March 5, 1978) 60 Minutes; as Clint Grayson
113. *Bus Stop* (HBO, August 22, 1982) 60 Minutes; as Bo Decker
114. *Trying Times* "Get a Job" (PBS, 1988)
115. *USA Live* (USA, January 23, 1997) Interviewed
116. *Intimate Portrait of Melissa Gilbert* (Lifetime, July 26, 1998) 60 Minutes; as Narrator
117. *Regis & Kathie Lee* (ABC, October 18, 1999) 60 Minutes

Guy Williams

WILL CARTWRIGHT

Will Cartwright was a tall, well-built, dark-headed man with a black mustache. He was the son of Ben's brother, John.

While drifting around the country, he often got involved with the wrong kind of people. After stealing some engraving plates from his employer Butler, he faked his death in order to escape him. With Ben's help, he turned over the plates and decided to remain on the Ponderosa for a while with his uncle and cousins.

After Ben and the boys had gone on a cattle drive, Will decided to pull up stakes and head off again. His plans were delayed when some men attempted to rob the ranch and were thwarted by him.

When an old friend, Mateo Ibara, was wounded on the Ponderosa, he and his wife Carla stayed on the ranch while Mateo recuperated. The two men had fought together in Juarez, Mexico, and Mateo had saved him from a firing squad. Will was tempted to return with his friend to Mexico but had a change of heart.

Adam was courting Laura Dayton but was often away on ranch business. As a result of Adam's neglect, Will and Laura grew closer and soon realized they had fallen in love. Adam sensed the couple's true feelings for each other and persuaded Laura to marry Will. Leaving, the couple headed for San Francisco where Will had taken a job in the import business.

Guy Williams was born Armando Catalano in New York City on January 14, 1924. His father Attilio and many of his uncles were trained in the art of fencing. His father, an insurance agent, felt his son should also learn the sport, and lessons began when Guy was only seven. He also learned to play the guitar and became a competent horseman. He went to school at Peekskill Military Academy with plans to go on to West Point.

However, Williams became interested in acting and went to the neighborhood playhouse to learn his craft. Modeling enabled him to support himself. "It required little time and paid well," Williams recalled.[8]

He decided to change his name to Guy Williams because he felt his real name sounded too foreign and would limit his opportunities by typecasting him.

Signing a contract with MGM, he headed for California in 1948. He was not pleased with the roles he received and moved back to New York to do such shows as *Studio One*. He was forced to model between jobs to support himself. It was during this time he met and fell in love with model Janice Cooper, whom he married in the 1950s.

One day he was seen by an agent walking down Fifth Avenue. The pictures of him taken by the agent helped him win a contract with Universal-International. He and Janice returned to California where Guy filmed *Bedtime for Bonzo* (1952) for the studio.

In the mid–1950s, Williams was experiencing frequent highs and lows in his career and thought about changing occupations. "There were times when I seriously doubted if I were cut out for this business."[9]

His left shoulder and arm were severely hurt in a riding accident. Guy began taking fencing lessons under the expert leadership of Aldo Nadi. The exercise helped heal his injuries and six months later he was as good as new. He had also become an expert fencer.

When work slowed, the couple moved back to New York until 1957, when he headed back to California and appeared in *I Was a Teenage Werewolf* starring Michael Landon.

An announcement ran in the April 19, 1957, issue of *Daily Variety* stating that director Norman Foster was holding auditions for the part of Don Diego for the Disney production of *Zorro*. They were interested in hiring a little-known actor.

Guy Williams. (Authors' collection.)

Before he screen-tested for the part, Guy had worked at a soda fountain and as a garment worker and model.

Williams was athletically built and stood six foot three. He had dark hair and his handsome face often wore a nice smile. He also had a perfect Spanish accent.

"Guy fit Zorro to a T," Foster claimed.[10] He was quickly signed to a one-year contract with the option to extend it to seven years. Buddy Van Horn was his double, but Guy handled his own sword fighting.

When not promoting the show, Guy and his family could be found sailing their yacht, the Oceana. Guy and Janice asked Norman Foster and his wife to be the godparents for their son Steve and daughter, Toni.

Disney wanted to move *Zorro* from ABC to NBC because of a more lucrative deal. NBC was moving in the direction of color shows. Since *Zorro* was filmed in black-and-white, a deal could not be made. Rather than staying with ABC, Disney canceled the show, shutting down production on February 17, 1959, despite good ratings.

"Cancellation was a particular blow," Janice recalled. "He was so frustrated because the show was going beautifully and he was enjoying it so much."[11] He went on to film *Captain Sinbad* in 1963.

Williams had originally been considered for the part of Adam but could not accept it as he had signed for *Zorro* by the time *Bonanza* got underway. It was ironic that in 1964, he appeared in five episodes of *Bonanza* as cousin Will Cartwright. He had been hired as a possible replacement for Pernell

Roberts, who wanted to leave the series. When Roberts remained with the show, there was no longer a need for his character. It was reported that Guy did not enjoy his *Bonanza* experience because he felt he was being used as leverage between the network and Roberts.

On September 15, 1965, CBS premiered the series *Lost in Space* on which Williams starred as Professor John Robinson. The show ran until September 11, 1968, when it was canceled due to low ratings. Williams reportedly was unhappy with the show because he felt his character had been overshadowed by the Robot and Dr. Zachary Smith characters.

In 1973, reruns of *Zorro* aired in Argentina. When the show became extremely popular, Williams made promotional appearances for Channel 13 in Buenos Aires.

During the last years of his life, he divided his time between Buenos Aires and Los Angeles. Guy had financial troubles due in part to money he lost on the ponies and his divorce from Janice. His money problems forced him to sell his estate in California and his cherished yacht. After Williams had a stroke, he became reclusive. On May 6, 1989, he was discovered in his apartment in Buenos Aires, where he had died from a heart attack at age 65. The police felt that Williams had passed away a week prior to discovery of this body.

Movies, Telefilms, Miniseries

An asterisk (*) denotes video availability.

1. *Bonzo Goes to College* (Universal, 1952); as Ronald Calkins
2. *Willie and Joe Back at the Front* [Back at the Front] (Universal, 1952)
3. *All I Desire* (Universal, 1953)
4. *The Golden Blade* (Universal, 1953); as Tom Cries
5. **The Man from the Alamo* (Universal, 1953); as Sgt. McCully
6. *The Mississippi Gambler* (Universal, 1953); as Andie
7. *Take Me to Town* (Universal, 1953); as Hero
8. *The Last Frontier* (Columbia, 1955); as Lt. Benton
9. *Seven Angry Men* (Allied Artists, 1955); as Simon
10. **Sincerely Yours* (Warner Bros., 1955); as Dick Cosgrove
11. **I Was a Teenage Werewolf* (American International, 1957); as Chris Stanley
12. *Zorro the Avenger* (Disney/Buena Vista, 1959); as Don Diego de la Vega/ Zorro
13. **The Sign of Zorro* (Disney/Buena Vista, 1960); as Don Diego de la Vega/ Zorro
14. **The Prince and the Pauper* (Disney/Buena Vista, March 11, 18, 25, 1962); as Miles Hendon
15. *Damon and Pythias* (MGM, 1962); as Damon
16. **Captain Sinbad* (MGM, 1963); as Captain Sinbad
17. *General Massacre* (U.S./Bel., 1973); as the General as a Young Man

TV Series

18. *Zorro* (ABC, October 10, 1957–September 24, 1959) 30 Minutes; as Don Diego de la Vega/Zorro
19. *Bonanza* (NBC, March 22, April 5, 19, May 10, 17, 1964) 60 Minutes; as Will Cartwright
20. **Lost in Space* (CBS, September 15, 1965–September 11, 1968) 60 Minutes; as Professor John Robinson

TV Guest Appearances

21. *Hey Mulligan* (NBC, August 28, 1954) 30 Minutes
22. *Four Star Playhouse* "Trudy" (CBS, May 26, 1955) 30 Minutes
23. *The Lone Ranger* "Six Gun Artist" (ABC, June 23, 1955) 30 Minutes
24. *Disneyland: Fourth Anniversary Show* (ABC, September 11, 1957); as Zorro
25. *Sergeant Preston of the Yukon* "The Generous Hobo" (CBS, January 2, 1958) 30 Minutes; as Jim Lorane
26. *Iron Horseman* (NBC, 1959); as a Railroad Detective
27. *Kodak Presents Disneyland '59* (ABC, June 15, 1959) 90 Minutes
28. *Walt Disney Presents* "Zorro: El Bandito" (ABC, October 30, 1960) 60 Minutes; as Don Diego de la Vega/Zorro
29. *Walt Disney Presents* "Zorro: Adios el Zuchlillo" (ABC, November 6, 1960) 60 Minutes; as Don Diego de la Vega/Zorro
30. *Here's Hollywood* (NBC, 1961) 30 Minutes
31. *Walt Disney Presents* "Zorro: The Postponed Wedding" (ABC, January 1, 1961) 60 Minutes; as Don Diego de la Vega/Zorro
32. *Walt Disney Presents* "Zorro: Auld Acquaintance" (ABC, April 2, 1961); as Don Diego de la Vega/Zorro
33. *Maverick* "Dade City Dodge" (ABC, September 24, 1961) 60 Minutes
34. *You Don't Say* (NBC, 1966)

Stage

35. *A Midsummer Night's Dream* (July 1963)

Personal Appearances

36. Disneyland Weekend Promotional Appearances (1958–1959)
37. Flint, Michigan, on a float commemorating the 50th Anniversary of General Motors
38. *Buenos Aires* (1973) Publicizing *Zorro* for Channel 13
39. *Real Madrid Circus* (Mid–1970s) Performed with Argentine fencing champion, Fernando Lupiz
40. Own Circus (Mid–1970s) Routine based on that performed at the Madrid Circus

NOTES

1. Laredo, Joseph F. *One Man with Courage.* Bear Family Records, 1993.
2. Bing Russell's response to letter from authors.
3. Shapiro, Melany. *Bonanza: The Unofficial Story of the Ponderosa.* Pioneer Books, Inc., 1993.
4. *Ibid.*
5. O'Neil, Thomas. *The Emmy.* Penguin Books, 1992.
6. Greenland, David R. Bonanza: *A Viewer's Guide to the TV Legend.* R & G Productions, 1997.
7. *Ibid.*
8. Curtis, Sandra. *Zorro Unmasked: The Official History.* Hyperion, 1998.
9. *Ibid.*
10. *Ibid.*
11. *Ibid.*

APPENDIX A

Awards, Honors and Memberships

This appendix lists all known awards, honors and memberships for each of the stars and supporting cast. Awards and honors are given chronologically and memberships alphabetically.

Bonanza

Awards

1. All-American Award for Best Show of the Year (1961)
2. Limelight's Best Western Series Award (1961)
3. TV Editors Award of Achievement (1961)
4. Edward Ancona won Emmy for Color Consultant (1965)
5. Award from U.S. Postal Service for the episode "Ride the Wind" (1966)
6. Emmy Award Nomination for Outstanding Dramatic Series (1966)
7. Emmy Award Awarded to Marvin Coil, Everett Douglas, Ellsworth Hoagla for Editing (1966)
8. Emmy Award Awarded to David Rose for Best Music for a Series for episode "The Love Child" (1970)

Honors

9. *TV Guide*'s Viewers Choice as #1 Western (November 1993)
10. *TV Guide*'s #29 of 100 Most Memorable Moments in TV History [*Bonanza* debut] (1966)

David Dortort

Awards

11. Emmy Nomination for Best Written Dramatic Material for *Climax* (1954)
12. Emmy Nomination for Best Television Adaptation of *20th Century–Fox Hour: "The Ox-Bow Incident"*

Memberships

13. Writers Guild of America, West (TV Branch)
14. President for three consecutive years of Writers Guild of America, West (TV Branch)

Lorne Greene

Awards

15. National Broadcasting Company Award for Announcing (1942)
16. John Swett Award from California Teachers' Association (1960s)
17. Foreign Press Association Award as Best Actor (1960s)
18. *Radio and Television Mirror Award* as Most Popular TV Star (1960s)
19. Variety Club of America Heart Award (1960s)
20. RIAA Gold Record Award for "Ringo" (1964/1965)
21. Canadian Man of the Year (1965)
22. Father of the Year Award (1965)
23. 50th Anniversary Medal [Authorized by Congress and the President] (1970s)
24. Order of Canada Award (1971)
25. Congressional Medal for Outstanding Contribution to American Agriculture (1980s)
26. Grand Marshall Award — Tournament of Roses Parade (1981)
27. John Macoun Award for Efforts to Protect Wildlife (1983)

Honors

28. Made Honorary Citizen of Nevada (1964)
29. Honorary Doctorate of Law from Queen's University, Ontario (1971)
30. Honorary Doctorate of Humane Letters from Missouri Valley College (1981)
31. Key to the City (Ottawa, Canada, October 1983)
32. Lorne Greene Day (Ottawa, Canada, 1983)
33. Hollywood Walk of Fame for *Bonanza* (February 12, 1985)

Memberships

34. Actors Equity Association
35. American Federation of Television and Radio Artists
36. American Freedom from Hunger Foundation (also former Chairman)
37. American Wild Horse Protection Association (Served as Vice President)
38. American Wildlife Association (Honorary Chairman)

39. National Wildlife Foundation (Former Chairman)
40. Order of Canada
41. Pritikin Research Center (Served as Member of the Board of Directors)
42. Screen Actors Guild

Pernell Roberts

Awards

43. Drama Desk Award as Best Off-Broadway Actor for Macbeth (1955)
44. Vernon Rice Award for Off-Broadway Performance with Shakespearites (1956)
45. Emmy Nomination for Outstanding Lead Actor in a Drama Series [*Trapper John, M.D.*] (1981)

Honors

46. Made Honorary Citizen of Nevada (1964)

Memberships

47. Actors Equity Association
48. American Federation of Television and Radio Artists
49. Screen Actors Guild

Dan Blocker

Awards

50. National Award for Best College Acting as DeLawd in *Green Pastures* (1949)
51. Texan of the Year from Texas Newspapers (Early 1960s)
52. Distinguished Alumni Award from Sul Ross University Ex- Student Association (August 8, 1987) presented to Mrs. Dan Blocker and family

Honors

53. Guest of Honor at Sul Ross Homecoming (1961)
54. Honorary Citizen of Nevada (1964)
55. Honorary Member of Tampa's Sheriff's Association (1964)

Memberships

56. American Federation of Television and Radio Artists
57. Screen Actors Guild

Michael Landon

Awards

58. Best Athlete of the Year for New Jersey by *Scholastic Magazine* (1953)
59. Golden Boot Award (1960s)

60. Silver Spurs Award from Reno Chamber of Commerce, presented by Governor Grant Sawyer. It was given each year to the most popular Western Television Personality as voted by over 600 entertainment and television writers (1964)
61. Academy Founder's Award from the National Academy of Television Arts and Sciences (1982)
62. Director of the Year (1985)
63. Two Emmy Nominations for *Where Pigeons Go to Die* (1990)
64. Washington, D.C. Lifetime Achievement Award from NBC (June 1990)
65. National Children's Leukemia Foundation Award [accepted by Cindy Crawford] (March 15, 1993)

Honors

66. Marine For a Day when visiting a Marine Base (October 1962)
67. Honorary Citizen of Nevada (1964)
68. Honorary Member of Tampa's Sheriff's Association (1964)
69. Honored by Collingswood, New Jersey, Women Against Rape (1980s)
70. Hollywood Walk of Fame for TV Actor (August 15, 1984)
71. Tribute by Melissa Gilbert on *People's 20th Birthday* (March 7, 1994)
72. Inducted into TV Hall of Fame (April 18, 1996)
73. One of *TV Guide*'s 50 Greatest TV Stars of All-Time (1996)

Memberships

74. American Federation of Television and Radio Artists
75. Directors Guild of America
76. National Academy of Television Arts and Sciences
77. National Association of Television Producers and Executives
78. Screen Actors Guild
79. Writers Guild-West

Victor Sen Yung

Memberships

80. American Federation of Television and Radio Artists
81. Screen Actors Guild

Ray Teal

Memberships

82. American Federation of Television and Radio Artists
83. Screen Actors Guild

Bing Russell

Memberships

84. American Federation of Television and Radio Artists
85. Screen Actors Guild

David Canary

Awards

86. All Army Entertainment Award as Best Popular Singer (1963)
87. Emmy Nomination for Outstanding Actor in a Daytime Drama (1985)
88. Emmy Award for Outstanding Lead Actor in a Daytime Drama (1986)
89. Emmy Award for Outstanding Lead Actor in a Daytime Drama (1988)
90. Emmy Award for Outstanding Lead Actor in a Daytime Drama (1989)
91. Emmy Nomination for Outstanding Lead Actor in a Daytime Drama (1990)
92. *Soap Opera Digest* Award for Outstanding Villain
93. Emmy Nomination for Outstanding Lead Actor in a Daytime Drama (1991)
94. *Soap Opera Digest* Award for Outstanding Lead Actor (1992)
95. Emmy Award for Outstanding Lead Actor in a Daytime Drama (1993)
96. Emmy Nomination for Outstanding Lead Actor in a Daytime Drama (1997)
97. Emmy Nomination for Outstanding Lead Actor in a Daytime Drama (1998)
98. *Soap Opera Digest* Award for Best Couple with Jennifer Bassey (1999)
99. Emmy Nomination for Outstanding Lead Actor in a Daytime Drama (2000)

Memberships

100. Actors Equity
101. American Federation of Television and Radio Artists
102. Screen Actors Guild

Mitch Vogel

103. American Federation of Television and Radio Artists
104. Orange County Performing Arts Foundation (1966)
105. Screen Actors Guild

Lou Frizzell

106. Actors Equity
107. American Federation of Television and Radio Artists
108. Screen Actors Guild

Tim Matheson

109. American Federation of Television and Radio Artists
110. Screen Actors Guild

Guy Williams

111. Actors Equity
112. American Federation of Television and Radio Artists
113. Screen Actors Guild

APPENDIX B

Bonanza Collectibles

This appendix documents all known *Bonanza* collectibles. They are subdivided into the following categories: Books; Comics; Dolls, Horses and Wagons; Guns and Holsters; Lunch Boxes and Thermoses; Paper Products; Records; Tin Cups; Toys and Games; TV Guides; Miscellaneous Magazines, and Miscellaneous Items.

Books

1. *Bonanza*, a novel by Noel Lewis, 1960
2. *Bonanza* "One Man with Courage" by Thomas Thompson. Media Books, September 1966. Lorne Greene wrote a letter to Media Books as an introduction.
3. *Bonanza* "Black Silver" by William R. Cox. Media Books, May 1967.
4. *Bonanza* #1 "Winter Grass" by Dean Owen. Paperback Library, Inc., July 1968.
5. *Bonanza* #2 "Ponderosa Kill" by Dean Owen. Paperback Library, Inc., September 1968.
6. *Bonanza* #1 "The Pioneer Spirit" by Stephen Calder. Bantam Books, September 1992. This book was dedicated to Michael Landon.
7. *Bonanza* #2 "The Ponderosa Empire" by Stephen Calder. Bantam Books, November 1992.
8. *Bonanza* #3 "The High-Steel Hazard" by Stephen Calder. Bantam Books, February 1993.
9. *Bonanza* #4 "Journey of the Horse" by Stephen Calder. Bantam Books, June 1993.
10. *Bonanza* #5 "The Money Hole" by Stephen Calder. Bantam Books, October 1993.
11. *Bonanza* #6 "The Trail to Timberline" by Stephen Calder. Bantam Books, February 1994.

12. *Bonanza* "Killer Lion" by Steve Frazee. Illustrated by Jason Studios. Whitman Publishing Company, 1966.
13. *Bonanza* "Treachery Trail" by Harry Whittington. Illustrated by Al Anderson & Richard Moore. Whitman Publishing Company, 1968.
14. *Bonanza* "The Bubble Gum Kid" by George S. Elrick. A Big Little Book. Whitman Publishing Company, 1967.
15. *Bonanza* "Heroes of the Wild West." Whitman Publishing Company, 1970.

Comics

16. Dell #1110 June–August 1960. Cover with Michael Landon, Dan Blocker, Pernell Roberts and Lorne Greene.
17. Dell #1221 September–November 1961. Cover with Roberts, Greene, Blocker, and Landon.
18. Dell #1283 February–April 1962. Cover with Landon, Roberts, Blocker, Greene, (and colt).
19. Dell #01070-207 May–July 1962. Cover with Roberts, Landon, Greene, and Blocker.
20. Dell #01070-210 August–October 1962. Cover with Blocker, Greene, Roberts, and Landon kneeling.
21. Gold Key #1 December 1962. Cover with Roberts, Blocker, Greene, and Landon (with their horses).
22. Gold Key #2 March 1963. Cover with Landon, Roberts, Blocker, and Greene with guns drawn as the Cartwrights.
23. Gold Key #3 June 1963. Cover with Greene, Blocker, Landon, and Roberts with guns drawn. Stories: "Stage Robber," "Bullets in Black Canyon."
24. Gold Key #4 September 1963. Cover with Landon and head shots of Greene, Blocker, and Roberts. Stories: "The Blood Debt," "The Miser."
25. Gold Key #5 December 1963. Cover with Greene, Roberts, Landon, and Blocker holding rifles. Stories: "Black Day at Virginia City," "Caught Red-Handed."
26. Gold Key #6 February 1964. Cover with Landon, Greene, Roberts and Blocker walking with guns drawn. Stories: "The Caballero," "Threat of War."
27. Gold Key #7 April 1964. Cover with Roberts and Blocker, on horseback and head shots of Greene and Landon.
28. Gold Key #8 June 1964. Cover with Blocker, Greene and Landon (guns drawn) and head shot of Roberts. Stories: "The Hatchet Man," "The Living Nightmare."
29. Gold Key #9 August 1964. Cover with Landon and Blocker kneeling and head shots of Greene and Roberts.
30. Gold Key #10 October 1964. Cover with Greene and an insert of the four in a fight scene.
31. Gold Key #11 December 1964. Cover with Blocker, Roberts and an insert of the four on horseback. Stories: "The Money Makers," "Feud Fury."
32. Gold Key #12 February 1965
33. Gold Key #13 April 1965. Cover with three inserts, one showing all four reading, another showing Greene and Landon on horseback and the third showing Greene, Roberts and Landon in a gunfight.
34. Gold Key #14 June 1965. Cover with Landon, Blocker, Greene and Roberts. There were two inserts, one with Blocker, Landon and Roberts on horseback and the other with Greene holding a rifle.
35. Gold Key #15 August 1965. Cover with Landon and an insert of Greene, Roberts, and Blocker holding guns.

36. Gold Key #16 October 1965. Cover with Roberts with outlaw and a head shot of Greene.
37. Gold Key #17 December 1965. Cover with three poses of Greene and head shots of Landon and Blocker.
38. Gold Key #18 February 1966. Cover with Landon on Cochise and a head shot of Greene as the Cartwrights.
39. Gold Key #19 April 1966. Cover with Blocker in a fight and head shots of Greene and Landon.
40. Gold Key #20 June 1966. Cover with Greene holding a gun and an insert of Landon in a fight.
41. Gold Key #21 August 1966. Cover with Blocker holding a rifle and inserts of Landon and Greene.
42. Gold Key #22 November 1966. Cover with Landon with gun drawn and an insert of Blocker firing a gun on top of the Overland stage.
43. Gold Key #23 February 1967. Cover with Landon, Blocker, Greene and a colt.
44. Gold Key #24 May 1967. Cover with Landon on Cochise leading a pack mule and an insert of Greene and Blocker with guns drawn.
45. Gold Key #25 August 1967. Cover with Blocker, Greene and Michael with guns drawn.
46. Gold Key #26 November 1967
47. Gold Key #27 February 1968
48. Gold Key #28 May 1968. Cover with Landon pouring water at a well and insert of Greene on Buck.
49. Gold Key #29 August 1968. Cover with Blocker and Greene eating with an insert of the Ponderosa map.
50. Gold Key #30 November 1968. Cover with Blocker, Landon and Greene leaning on a wagon.
51. Gold Key #31 February 1969. Cover with Landon and Blocker on horseback and an insert of Greene, also on horseback.
52. Gold Key #32 May 1969. Cover with Greene and an insert of Landon tied up on the floor.
53. Gold Key #33 August 1969. Cover with Blocker and Greene on horseback and an insert of Landon.
54. Gold Key #34 November 1969. Cover with Greene on Buck, Landon on Cochise and Blocker on Chub.
55. Gold Key #35 February 1970. Cover with Greene and Blocker on horseback and a head shot of Landon.
56. Gold Key #36 May 1970. Cover with Blocker on buckboard and head shots of Greene and Landon.

Note: Comics were also available in other countries, including France, Spain and England.

Dolls, Horses and Wagons

57. #4020 Ben and Buck Figure Kit by American Character, 1966 with 8" figure of Ben and box made to look like a stable. Accessories include hat, canteen, six-gun, gun belt and holster, rifle, rifle holster, lariat, vest and bandanna, spurs and straps, saddlebags, saddle, bridle, bit, reins and bed roll.
58. #4021 Little Joe and Cochise Figure Kit by American Character, 1966 includes all of the above accessories.
59. #4022 Hoss and Chub Figure Kit by Palitoy of England, 1966 includes all of the above accessories.

60. #4010 *Bonanza* Range Horse — Ben's Palamino by American Character, 1966 with bed roll, saddle bags, bridle, bit, reins, saddle and cinch strap.
61. #4011 *Bonanza* Range Horse — Little Joe's Pinto by American Character, 1966 includes all of the above accessories.
62. #4012 *Bonanza* Range Horse — Hoss's Chestnut Stallion by American Character, 1966 includes all of the above accessories.
63. #4013 *Bonanza* Range Horse — Outlaw's Gray Mustang by American Character, 1966 includes all of the above accessories.
64. #4000 *Bonanza* Action Doll — Ben by American Character, 1966 8" fully posable with vest, canteen, lariat, spurs, spur straps, gun, holster and gun belt, bandanna, rifle, rifle holster and hat.
65. #4001 *Bonanza* Action Doll — Little Joe by American Character, 1966 8" fully posable with all of the above accessories except the vest.
66. #4002 *Bonanza* Action Doll — Hoss by American Character, 1966 8" fully posable with all of the above accessories except bandanna.
67. #4003 *Bonanza* Action Doll — Outlaw by American Character, 1966 8" fully posable with all of the above accessories. As Pernell Roberts had left the show, his doll may have been changed, by adding a mustache, to make him an outlaw.
68. #4031 *Bonanza* Four in One Wagon by American Character, 1966 over 25" long easily changed into ore wagon, chuck wagon, ranch wagon and covered wagon. It came with two work horses and more than 70 accessories.

Guns and Holsters

69. *Bonanza* Double Gun and Holster Set by Halpern Company (Halco), 1965 with caricatures of the Cartwrights in black on light tan background. Also two silver-toned 9½" cap guns with green handles.
70. *Bonanza* Holster Set by Halpern-Nichols, 1965 with faux dark brown holster and leather belt in black with 9½" white metal cap gun.
71. *Bonanza* Gun and Holster by Halpern Company, 1965 with faux leather holster and etching of *Bonanza* logo, which also appears on the two silver cap guns.
72. *Bonanza* Guns Outfit by Marx Toys, 1966 contains 24" rifle that fires caps by pulling down the magazine to load and a 9" western hand gun that shoots toy ammunition.
73. *Bonanza*— The Hoss Range Pistol by Marx Toys, 1966 constructed of metal and plastic and on a 9 × 13" blister card featuring Dan Blocker as Hoss.
74. *Bonanza* Spanish 9½" Nickel Gun by Pilsen, early to mid–1960s with brown checkered handles and capable of shooting caps. Box features Lorne Greene, in full color, as Ben Cartwright.
75. *Bonanza* 9" Hand Gun by Leslie-Henry, 1959–65 with a gray surface and black handle.
76. *Bonanza* Hand Gun by Leslie-Henry, 1959–65 with nickel surface and white handle.
77. *Bonanza* Hand Gun by Hubley-Halco, 1963–65 with nickel surface and reddish-brown and tan handle.
78. *Bonanza* 10½" Hand Gun by Leslie-Henry, Circa 1965 with nickel surface and black handle.
79. *Bonanza* .44 Hand Gun by Leslie-Henry, Circa 1965 with matte silver surface and horse head decorating the handles.
80. *Bonanza* Double Holster Set by Leslie-Henry, 1965 done in dark brown leather with conchos containing golden horseheads. (See BC79 for gun description).
81. *Bonanza* Gun and Holster Set by Halco, 1960–65 .45 hand gun with a cylinder that turns, done in brown and black leather adorned with raised coins of gold.

82. *Bonanza* Holster and Gun Set by Leslie-Henry, 1960–65 holster done in reddish-brown leather. (See BC78 for gun description).

Lunch Boxes and Thermoses

83a. Lunch Box by Aladdin Industries, 1965–66 with Landon on Cochise and Greene and Blocker with guns drawn.
83b. Thermos by Aladdin Industries, 1965–66 with Greene, Blocker and Landon — included with above box.
84a. Lunch Box by Aladdin Industries, 1968 with Blocker, Greene and Landon on horseback with guns drawn. Artwork by Elmer Lenhardt.
84b. Thermos pictures the Cartwrights being captured by Indians and is included with above box.
85a. Lunch Box by Aladdin Industries, first produced in 1963 with Landon, Blocker, Roberts and Greene on horseback. Artwork by Elmer Lenhardt.
85b. Thermos depicts the Cartwrights with guns drawn.
86. Lunch Box by Aladdin Industries, second production in 1965 showing the Cartwrights defending Virginia City. Artwork by Elmer Lenhardt.

Paper Products

87. Publicity Poster by National Broadcasting Company, 1965 measures 21" × 24" and features large head shots of Blocker, Greene and Landon with shots of Joe and Hoss on horseback superimposed.
88. German Publicity Poster, circa 1967 in connection with release of "Ride the Wind" as full-length film.
89. *Bonanza: The Return* Publicity Poster, circa 1993 measures 15" × 27" and is in full color with full cast on horseback above blazing map.
90. *Bonanza* Map by Ponderosa Ranch, 1967 tan map, measuring 16¾" × 22½"; shows ranch and surrounding area.
91. *Bonanza* Publicity Poster measures 22½" × 35" and is in black-and-white with Greene, Blocker and Landon pictured.
92. *Bonanza* Card measures 5" × 7" with picture of the four Cartwrights standing in front of the ranch house.
93. *Bonanza* Card measures 5" × 7" with picture of Blocker, Greene and Landon standing in front of the ranch house.
94. The Ponderosa Ranch Story, 1966 6" × 9" small color paper book with Blocker, Greene and Landon on horseback.

Records

95. Ben Cartwright Chevrolet Promotion Record 6" × 6" cardboard sheet in 6½" × 6½" mailing envelope. 33⅓ RPM has a musical message by Greene and Bill and Glen used to promote test drives of Chevrolet's 1964 models.

Note: See Discography

Tin Cups

96. Tin Cup: 2¾" tall by 3½" diameter. Front has the four heads of the Cartwrights and the back has view of ranch house with stagecoach in front.
97. Tin Cup: 2¾" tall by 3½" diameter. Front has the heads of the four Cartwrights and the back has the view of the ranch without the stagecoach.
98. Tin Cup: 2¾" tall by 3½" diameter. Front has the heads of Blocker, Greene and Landon. Back has view of the ranch with visitors riding on a flatbed truck.
99. Tin Cup: 2¾" tall by 3½" diameter. Front has Greene as Ben Cartwright. Back has view of ranch with less of the truck showing.

Note: The Tin Cups were made by Schlueter Manufacturing Company, St. Louis.

Toys and Games

100. Coloring Book No. 4535 by Saalfield, 1960 measures 8½" × 11" with Ben, Adam and Little Joe on cover.
101. Coloring Book No. 1617 by Saalfield, 1965 measures 8½" × 11" with Ben, Hoss and Little Joe on cover.
102. Coloring Book by Saalfield, 1967 measures 8½" × 11" with Ben, Hoss and Little Joe on cover.
103. School Tablet, Late 1960s with Ben, in color, on cover.
104. Foto Fantastiks by Eberhard Faber Company, 1966 boxed set of 6 photos, measuring 9½" × 16½" × 1", featuring Little Joe. With materials for coloring.
105. Foto Fantastiks by Eberhard Faber Company, 1966 boxed set of 6 photos, measuring 9½" × 16½" × 1", featuring Ben. With materials for coloring.
106. Stardust Touch of Velver Art By Numbers, 1965 craft kit with two pictures.
107. Model Kit by Revell Plastics, 1966 pieces snap together to make 9" character figures of the three Cartwrights.
108. *Bonanza* Movie Viewer by K-Kids, 1961 complete with two films included.
109. *Bonanza* Tru-Vue Magic Eyes Set by Gaf, 1964 contains three stereo picture cards.
110. *Bonanza* Michigan Rummy Game by Parker Bros., 1964 box shown with Roberts, Landon, Greene and Blocker playing the game. Artwork by Jack McMann.
111. *Bonanza* Woodburning Kit by American Toy & Furniture Co., 1965 comes complete with eight wooden pictures, Model #94B tool and paints.
112. *Bonanza* #4426 Jigsaw Puzzle by Milton Bradley, 1964 with Landon, gun drawn, and Blocker, Roberts and Greene on horseback. Puzzle has 125 pieces.
113. *Bonanza* #7042 Inlay Jigsaw Puzzle by Saalfield Co., 1963 features Greene, Blocker, Landon and Roberts with horses.
114. *Bonanza* View-Master, 1964 The 21 pictures are in stereo. The front package shows Landon, Roberts, Blocker and Greene on their horses.
115. *Bonanza* View-Master, 1971 The 21 pictures are in stereo. The front of the package shows Landon, Greene, Blocker and Mitch Vogel.
116. German *Bonanza* Board Game, circa 1966 with four different scenes of the Cartwrights on the box.

TV Guides

117. Week of June 25, 1960, with Blocker, Greene, Roberts and Landon on cover.
118. Week of May 13, 1961, with Greene on cover.

119. Week of September 8, 1962, with Greene, Landon and Blocker on cover.
120. Week of March 30, 1963, with Blocker, Roberts, Landon and Greene on cover.
121. Week of January 18, 1964, with Roberts and Katie Browne on cover.
122. Week of September 26, 1964, with Blocker riding Chub on cover.
123. Week of March 13, 1965, with Landon, Blocker, Greene and Roberts on cover.
124. Week of September 4, 1965, with caricatures of Blocker, Greene and Landon on cover.
125. Week of July 22, 1967, with Landon, Blocker and Greene on cover.
126. Week of March 3, 1968, with David Canary and Greene on cover.
127. Week of November 29, 1969, with caricatures of Landon, Greene, Blocker and David Canary on cover.
128. Week of March 27, 1971, with Landon, Blocker, Greene and Mitch Vogel on cover.
129. Week of October 14, 1971, with caricature of Blocker. Those of Mitch Vogel, Greene and Landon are in the background.
130. Week of October 7, 1972, with caricatures of Landon, David Canary, Mitch Vogel, Greene and Tim Matheson on cover.

Miscellaneous Magazines

131. *TV Magazine — The Cincinnati Enquirer*, Week of June 11, 1961, cover with Roberts, Landon, Greene and Blocker.
132. *TV People Collector's Edition #1*, September 1964 with Greene, Blocker, Landon and Roberts on cover.
133. *Bonanza the Official Magazine* Vol. 1, No. 1 by Twin Hits, Inc., 1965 cover with Greene, Landon, Roberts, Blocker on their horses.
134. *The Saturday Evening Post*, December 4, 1965, with Blocker, Greene and Landon on cover.

Miscellaneous Items

135. *Bonanza* Two Sets of Ponderosa Playing Cards, 1965–66 with Blocker, Greene and Landon in front of the ranch house.
136. *Bonanza* Ashtray, Late 1960s measures 4" in diameter and features in segments Blocker, the ranch house, Greene and Landon.
137. *Bonanza* Wood Plaque of Ben Cartwright, 1960s made of pine and measures 8" × 11".
138. *Bonanza* Wood Plaque of Hoss Cartwright, 1960s made of pine and measures 8" × 11".
139. *Bonanza* Days Button, 1964 red, white and blue button measures 3" and features Landon, Greene, Roberts and Blocker.
140. *Bonanza* Stick Pin, Early 1960s measures 2½" and features Roberts as Adam Cartwright.
141. *Bonanza* Stick Pin, Early 1960s measures 2½" and features Landon as Little Joe Cartwright.
142. *Bonanza* Booster Button, 1960s with Greene in one corner and Roberts, Blocker and Landon in the others.
143. *Bonanza* Glazed Bottle, by James B. Beam Distilling Company, 1969 made in shape of Ponderosa.
144. *Bonanza* Glazed Bottle, by James B. Beam Distilling Company made in shape of a horseshoe with Ponderosa Ranch around edge, a pine tree in the center and topped with a hat.

145. *Bonanza* Unlidded Stein with Ponderosa Ranch House in relief
146. *Bonanza* Glasses from Denmark one with Greene and the other with Blocker.
147. *Bonanza* Collector's Plate, Circa 1983 with Ponderosa Ranch House bordered in white.
148. *Bonanza* Collector's Plate by Hamilton Collection, 1990 plate measures 8½" in diameter and has Greene and Blocker.

Note: Modern-day souvenirs are available at the Ponderosa Ranch including tin cups, coffee mugs, tree ornament, T-shirts, sweatshirts, playing cards, videos, glasses, etc. These may become tomorrow's collectibles.

APPENDIX C

Discography

This appendix chronicles the numerous recordings of the *Bonanza* Theme, giving the title of the record on which it appeared, label, artist, date and whether the recording was instrumental [I] or vocal [V]. It is also noted if the release was a 45, LP, CD or Cassette. If charted information is applicable, it too is given. Following the theme song, the cast albums are chronicled as well as the discography of the stars. If a recording date is known, it too is noted.

Bonanza Theme

45s

1. *Bonanza* RCA 47-7687 [I] (1960). Recorded by Buddy Morrow
2. *Bonanza* Capitol 4986 [V] (1963). Performed by Ralph Paulsen in German
3. *Bonanza* Columbia 4-42512 [V] (1962). Performed by Johnny Cash
4. *Bonanza* American Pie 9033 [I]. Performed by Al Caiola and His Orchestra
5. *Bonanza* Deep Water DW 45-1001 [I] (1984). Performed by Eddys in a Saddle-Up Medley
6. *Bonanza* MacGregor 1037. Recorded by Frank Messina and the Mavericks
7. *Bonanza* RIK S-139 [I] (1964). Recorded by Shorty Lavendar
8. *Bonanza* United Artists XW-060 [I] (1973). Performed by Al Caiola and His Orchestra
9. *Bonanza* United Artists 1601 [I]. Performed by Al Caiola and His Orchestra
10. *Bonanza* United Artists 1548 [I]. Performed by Al Caiola and His Orchestra
11. *Bonanza* United Artists 3023 [I] (1961). Performed by Al Caiola and His Orchestra

LPs

12. *Adolph's Music to Barbeque By* Adolph P4RN-9169/9170 [I]
13. *All Hopped Up* Rounder 3029 [I] (1977). Performed by NRBQ
14. *American Bandmasters Association—38th Annual Convention* Crest ABA-5 [I] (1972). Performed by U.S. Army Band in a TV Fantasy Medley
15. *American Salute* RCA LM/LSC-3277 [I] (1965). Performed by Arthur Fiedler and the Boston Pops
16. *American Salute* RCA Victor AGLI 3965 [I] (1972). Performed by Arthur Fiedler and the Boston Pops
17. *As You Remember Them Volume 7—Great Instrumentals and other Favorites* Time-Life STL 3-247 [I] (1972). Recorded by Billy May
18. *Best of Al Caiola* United Artists UAL-3310/UAS-6310 [I] (1963). Performed by Al Caiola and His Orchestra
19. *Best of the Mummers: 19th Annual Musical Salute* Sure 64-2 [I] (1980). Recorded by Fralinger String Band in Show Time at the OK Corral Medley
20. *Best of the West* RCA AHLI-4119 [I] (1981). Recorded by Floyd Cramer
21. *Blockbuster Movie/TV Themes* Two Worlds TW-9102 [I] (1972). Al Caiola and His Orchestra performed the second *Bonanza* Theme
22. *Chapel By the Sea* Dot DLP 3424/25424 [I] (1962). Performed by Billy Vaughn
23. *Double Impact* RCA LPM/LSP-2180 [I] (1960). Recorded by Buddy Morrow
24. *The Electric-Twelve String Guitar* Imperial LP-9263/12263 [I] (1964). Performed by Tom Tedesco
25. *Faron Young Aims at the West* Mercury MG-20840/SR-60840 [V] (1963). Performed by Faron Young
26. *Fabulous Favorites of Our Time* Liberty LRP-3223/LST-7223 [I] (1962)
27. *Golden Hit Instrumentals* United Artists UAL-3142/UAS-6142 [I] (1961). Performed by Al Caiola and His Orchestra
28. *Good and Plenty* Buddah 5727 [I] (1980). Performed by Jon Faddis in Western Omelette Medley
29. *Great Themes from Movies and TV* Dot DLP-3450/25450 [I] (1962). Performed by Eddie Baxter
30. *Great TV Themes* London SP-44077 [I] (1966). Recorded by Frank Chacksfield and His Orchestra. Note: It was re-released as *TV's Golden Hits*
31. *Great Western Themes* GNP Crescensdo GNPS-2046 [I] (1968). Performed by Billy Strange
33. *Hit Instrumentals from TV Western Themes* United Artists Ual-3161/Uas 6161 [I]. Performed by Al Caiola and His Orchestra
34. *King Guitar* United Artists MX-89/MS-189 [I] (1967). Performed by Al Caiola
35. *More Great Motion Picture Themes* United Artists Ual-3158/Uas-6158 [I] (1961). Performed by Al Caiola and His Orchestra
36. *More Hit TV Themes* Capitol T/ST-1869 [I] (1963). Performed by Nelson Riddle
37. *Peyton Place and Other Film and TV Themes* Spin-o-Rama S-161 [I] (1965)
38. *The Pop Goes West* RCA LM/LSC-3008 [I] (1964). Recorded by Arthur Fiedler and the Boston Pops Orchestra
39. *Pops Roundup* RCA LM/LSC-2595 [I] (1962). Recorded by Arthur Fiedler and the Boston Pops Orchestra
40. *Ringo* Wyncote W-8055 [V] (1964). Performed by Deputies
41. *Ring of Fire—Best of Johnny Cash* Columbia CL-2053/CS-8853 [V] (1963). Performed by Johnny Cash. Note: Also available on CD CK-66890
42. *Round-Up* Telarc DG-10141 [I] (1987). Performed by Erich Kunzel and the Cincinnati Pops
43. *Swingin West* RCA LPM/LSP-2163 [I] (1960). Recorded by Marty Gold Orchestra
44. The Theme from *Ben Casey* Carlton 143 [I] (1962)

45. Theme from *The Magnificent 7 Ride* United Artists/Avalanche AV-LA-058-F [I] (1973). Al Caiola and His Orchestra performed the 2nd *Bonanza* Theme
46. *Themes from TV's Top 12* Reprise R/RS-6018 [I] (1962). Recorded by Neal Hefti
47. *The TV Theme Song Sing-Along Album* Rhino RNLP-703 [I] (1985). Performed by Al Caiola
48. *The Touch of Gold* Columbia CL-2504/CS-9304 [I] (1966). Performed by Charlie Byrd
49. *TV Potpourri* Audio Fidelity AFLP-2146/AFSD-6146 [I] (1963)
50. *TV's Top Themes* Mercury MG-20706/SR-60706 [I] (1962)
51. *Western Movie's Greatest Hits* Paramount PAS-6045 [I] (1973). Recorded by Frank Pourcel
52. *Western Themes Vol. 1* Alshire S-5269 [I] (1972). Performed by 101 Strings
53. *The Wide Open Spaces* Kapp KL-1306/KS-3306 [I] (1962). Recorded by Pete King
54. *Young America Dances to TV's Greatest Themes* 20th Century–Fox TFM-3109/TFS-4109[I] (1963). Performed by Bill Ramal and His Orchestra

Cassettes and CDs

55. *All-Time Country Hits* Dominion 3128. Performed by the Western Themes Orchestra
56. *All-Time Great Instrumental Hits* Curb Records (CD/Cassette) D2-77403 [I] (1990). Performed by Al Caiola
57. *The Best Band You Never Heard in Your Life* Barking Pumpkin (CD) D2-74233 [I] (1991). Performed briefly by Frank Zappa
58. *Fantastic Television* Crescendo Record Co. (CD) GNPD-8051 (1996). Performed by Billy Strange
59. *Good and Plenty* Del Rack (CD) DRZ-908 [I] (1986). Performed by Jon Faddis in Western Omelette Medley
60. *The Greatest Western Themes* K-Tel (CD and Cassette) 0652-4 [I] (1992)
61. *Great Original TV Themes* Capitol Records, Inc. (Cassette) SM-4XL-9451 [I] (1986). Performed by Al Caiola
62. *Great TV Western Themes* EMI America (Cassette) 4Xll-9453 [I] (1986). Performed by Al Caiola
63. *The Great Western Film Themes* K-Tel (CD) 6523 [I] (1986).
64. *Gunfight at O.K. Corral* Bear Family (CD) 15429. Performed by Johnny Western
65. *Hot Songs from Motion Pictures* Curb (CD) D256-76894 [I] (1992). Performed by Mike Curb Congregation
66. *The New Nashville Cats* Warner Bros. (CD) 26509-2 [I] (1991). Performed in Medley by Mark O'Connor
67. *North* Epic (CD/Cassette) 66151 [V]. Performed by Reba McIntyre and Dan
68. *The Pop Goes West* RCA (Cassette) 4595-4-RV [I] (1986). Recorded by Arthur Fiedler and the Boston Pops Orchestra
69. *Pops Round-Up* RCA (CD) 61666-2 [I] (1993). Recorded by Arthur Fiedler and the Boston Pops Orchestra
70. *Small Screen Cowboy Heroes* Risky Business (CD/Cassette) 57474 [V]. Performed by Johnny Cash
71. *Songs of the West* Rhino Records (CD) 71451. Performed by Al Caiola and His Orchestra
72. *Songs of the West (Box Set) Vol 4.* Rhino Records (CD/Cassette) R2-71263 [I] (1993). Performed by Al Caiola and His Orchestra
73. *Tee Vee Toons Presents Television's Greatest Hits — 65 TV Themes* TVT (CD/Cassette) 1100 [I] (1985).

74. *Television's Greatest Hits* Long Island Music Co. LTD (Cassette) GRF 198. MCPS Double Play
75. *Television's Greatest Hits* Retro Music SHO 19202 [V & I] (1995). Performed by The Golden State Orchestra and Singers
76. *Triple Feature* Telarc Records (3-CD Set) 89006 [I] (1989). Performed by Erich Kunzel and the Cincinnati Pops
77. *TV Classic Themes: 25th Anniversary Edition* 2 CD Set DBDPM01062/2 Cassette Set DBDPM01064 [I]
78. *TV's Golden Hits* Compleat Records (Cassette) 671020-4 [I] (1986). Performed by Frank Chacksfield and Orchestra
79. *TV Western's Theme Songs* Laserlight/Delta Music Inc. (CD) [I] (1993).
80. *Western Film Themes* Stage & Screen Productions (Cassette) XSSC-711 [I] (1983). Performed by The Cinema Soundstage Orchestra
81. *The Western Themes: Once Upon a Time in the West* Retro Music SLD 13822 (1994).

Cast Albums

LPs

82. *Bonanza: Christmas on the Ponderosa* RCA LPM/LSP-2757 [V] (1963). Side One: "Hark! The Herald Angels Sing"— Ken Darby Singers (1); "Deck the Halls"— Blocker (1); "The New Born King"— Roberts; "The First Christmas Tree" (Story)— Blocker (1); "Oh Fir Tree Dear"— Landon (3); "Christmas is A-Comin' (May God Bless You)"— Greene (2); "O' Come, All Ye Faithful"— Greene, Blocker, Landon, Ken Darby Singers (2). Side Two: "Jingle Bells"— Greene, Blocker, Landon, Ken Darby Singers (2); "Santa Got Lost in Texas"— Landon (3); "Stuck in the Chimney"— Greene (2); "Why We Light Candles on the Christmas Tree" (Story)— Greene; "Merry Christmas Neighbor"— Greene, Blocker, Landon (3); "Merry Christmas and Goodnight (Silent Night)"— Greene, Blocker, Landon (3). Notes: Joe Reisman, Producer. John Norman, Recording Engineer. Ken Darby, Writer, Arranger, Conductor. Hank Levine, Orchestrator. Art Say, Cover Photo. Recording Dates: (1) June 27, 1963; (2) June 28, 1963; (3) April 8, 1963).
83. *Bonanza: Ponderosa Party Time* RCA LPM/LSP-2583 [V](1962). Side One: "*Bonanza*"— Greene, Roberts, Blocker, Landon (4); "Skip to My Lou"— Greene, Roberts, Blocker, Landon (4); "Sourwood Mountain"— Greene, Roberts, Blocker, Landon (4); "In the Pines"— Roberts (3); "Sky Ball Paint"— Blocker (5); "Early One Morning"— Roberts (3); "Ponderosa"— Greene (1); "Careless Love"— Landon (2). Side Two: "Happy Birthday"— Blocker (5); "My Sons, My Sons"— Greene (1); "The Hangin' Blues"— Blocker (5); "Shenandoah"— Landon (2); "Miss Cindy"— Greene, Roberts, Blocker, Landon (4); "The Place Where I Worship"— Greene (1). Note: Darol Rice, Producer. Barbara and Frank Cleaver, Dialogue Writers. Billy Liebert, Musical Director. Al Schmitt, Recording Engineer. John Norman, Comosite & Recorder. Dave Hassinger, Dialogue Recorder. Recording Dates: (1) June 20, 1962; (2) June 21, 1962; (3) June 22, 1962; (4) June 25, 1962; (5) June 26, 1962; Dialogue was recorded on June 29, 1962.
84. *Christmas with Colonel Sanders* RCA Victor PRS-291 [V]. "Merry Christmas Neighbor"— Greene, Blocker, Landon.

CDs

85. *A TV Family Christmas* Scotti Bros. 72392-75271-2 [V] (1992). "Merry Christmas Neighbor"— Greene

86. *Bonanza* (4-CD Set). Bear Family (Germany) BCD-15684 DI V](1993). CD-1 *Ponderosa Party Time/Christmas on the Ponderosa* (See D 82 & D 83). CD-2 *Lorne Greene's American West/Welcome to the Ponderosa* (See D114 & D121). CD-3 *Portrait of the West/The Man* [Also 45 in French] (See D118 & D115). CD-4 *Come All Ye Fair and Tender Ladies/ Our Land, Our Heritage* (See D142 & D145).
87. *Yules of Yore: TV Land Tunes From Christmas Past* Nick at Night Records BK 67435 [V](1995). "Merry Christmas Neighbor"— Greene, Blocker, Landon

David Rose

LPs

88. *Bonanza* TV Soundtrack MGM E/SE-3960 [I] (1958).
89. *Music from Bonanza and the High Chaparral* (2-LP Set). Capitol Records STBB-626 [I](1970). Side One: "The Big *Bonanza*"; "How Can I Leave You?"; "The Cartwright Brothers"; "I Won't Be Very Long"; "Jamie." Side Two: "Blood Brothers"; "The Big Man"; "Jim Along Rosy"; "Man Passing Through"; "*Bonanza*." Notes: Joe Lubin, Producer. Sydney Dale, Conductor, Arranger. Robin Phillips, Music Coordinator. John Richards, Recording Engineer.

CDs

90. *Treasury of the West* (2-CD Set). Time Life/Sony Music A2-33721/R124-06 (1979/1998). *Bonanza*
91. *The Very Best of David Rose* Taragon Records (Cassette/CD) Tarcs-1015 (1996). *Bonanza*, Ponderosa, Hoss

Lorne Greene

45s

92. *Artists of America 1776: The Spirit of America* National Glass Casket Company (1976).
93. *Canta en Español* (Mexico) RCA Victor EP-10161 (1965). Note: Lorne Greene sings in Spanish. The song was recorded in Mexico.
94. *Daddy's Little Girl/I Love a Rainbow* RCA Victor 47-8819 (1966).
95. *Five Card Stud/Shadow of the Cactus* RCA Victor 45-8757 (1965).
96. *I Love a Rainbow/Daddy I'm Proud to Be Your Son* GRT Music Productions GRT-32 (1969).
97. *I Love a Rainbow/The First Word* GRT Music Productions GRT-37 (1970).
98. *I'm the Same Old Me/Love Finds a Way* RCA Victor 47-8229 (1963). Note: Also available with picture sleeve with same number.
99. *It's All in the Game/The Perfect Woman* Columbia 4-44971 (1969).
100. *The Man/Pop Goes the Hammer* RCA Victor 47-8490 (1964). Note: "The Man" reached the charts on January 30, 1965, peaking at position 72. It remained on the charts for three weeks.
101. *My Sons, My Sons/The Place Where I Worship* RCA Victor 47-8113 (1962).
102. *An Ol' Tin Cup/Sand* RCA Victor 47-8554 (1965). Note: Also available with picture sleeve with same number.
103. *National Wildlife Federation Announcements* Ads/Audio (1964). Note: It was not

for sale but was used for promotion. Picture sleeve with Lorne Greene, Andy Griffith and Ernie Ford.

104. *One Solitary Life* RCA Victor 47-9037 (1966). "Must Be Santa"—with Jimmy Joyce Children's Choir

105. *Ringo/Bonanza* RCA Victor 47-8444 (1964). Note: "Ringo" reached the charts on October 31, 1964, and peaked at position 1 and remained on the charts for 12 weeks. It was awarded a RIAA Gold Record in 1964/1965.

106. *Ringo/An Ol' Tin Cup (and a Battered Ol' Coffee Pot).* RCA Victor 7-0745 (Recorded November 1, 1963).

107. *Ringo/Ponderosa* Collectable Record Corp. DPE1.1033 (1986).

108. *Ringo/Sand (Du Sable) [in French]* RCA Victor 86-498 (1965). Note: It had a picture sleeve. It was recorded on October 29, 1963, and over-dubbed on December 22, 1964.

109. *Waco/All But the Remembering* RCA Victor 47-8901 (1966).

LPs

110. *Battlestar Galactica* Soundtrack MCA 3051-with the Los Angeles Philharmonic Orchestra (1978). Note: Sony Burke, Producer. It appeared on the charts on October 21, 1978, and peaked at 144 and remained charted for six weeks. It is also available on CD (Varese Sara-Blande VSD-5949 (1999).

111. *Five Card Stud* RCA Camden CAS 2391 (1970). Side One: "Five Card Stud"; "Wagon Wheels"; "Destiny"; "Nine Pound Hammer"; "Cool Water." Side Two: "Sixteen Tons"; "The Ol' Chisholm Trail"; "End of Track"; "Twilight on the Trail."* Note: Conducted and arranged by Joe Reismo. *Conducted and arranged by Mike Lipskin

112. *Have a Happy Holiday* RCA Victor LPM/LSP-3410 (1965). Side One: "'Twas the Night Before Christmas"— Story Read by Greene; "The Gift of the Magi"— Story Read by Greene. Side Two: "Home for the Holidays"; "Jingle Bells"; "Christmas is A-Comin'"; "We Wish You a Merry Christmas"; "The Nativity"— Read by Greene; "O Little Town of Bethlehem"; "The Friendly Beasts"; "Hark! The Herald Angels Sing"; "Silent Night"; "Joy to the World"; "We Three Kings"; "O Come, All Ye Faithful." Note: Joe Reisman produced and conducted the orchestra and chorus. Wayne Robinson, Dick Reynolds and Reisman arranged the music.

113. *Heidi's Song* K-Tel NU-5310 (1982).

114. *Lorne Greene's American West* RCA Victor LPM/LSP-3409 (1966). Side One: "Five Card Stud" (June 3, 1965); "Cool Water "(May 19, 1965); "The Devil's Grin" (May 24, 1965); "Pretty Horses" (June 3, 1965); "Devil Cat" (June 3, 1965); "The Ol' Chisholm Trail" (May 24, 1965). Side Two: "Wagon Wheels" (May 20, 1965); "Frightened Town" (May 20, 1965); "Shadow of the Cactus" (June 3, 1965); "Tumbling Tumbleweeds" (May 19, 1965); "Gold" (May 20, 1965); "Whoopee Ti Yi Yo" (May 19, 1965). Note: John Norman, Recording Engineer. Joe Reisman, Producer, Arranger, Conductor. Dan Blocker wrote the back of the album.

115. *The Man* RCA Victor LPM/LSP-3302 Side One: "Pop Goes the Hammer" (July 16, 1964); "End of Track" (July 16, 1964); "Nine Pound Hammer" (July 16, 1964); "Bring on the Dancin' Girls" (July 15, 1964); "Oh! What a Town" (July 24, 1964); "Fourteen Men" (July 24, 1964). Side Two: "Destiny" (July 24, 1964); "Sixteen Tons" (July 15, 1964); "Trouble Row" (July 24, 1964); "Chickasaw Mountain" (July 15, 1964); "Darling, My Darling" (July 15, 1964); "The Man" (July 16, 1964). Note: Lorne Greene introduces each song. Joe Reisman, Producer, Arranger, Conductor. Ken Whitmore, Cover Photo. John Norman, Recording Engineer. Henry Mancini wrote the back notes.

116. *Palaver with the Man* RCA Victor SP-33-327 (1965). Side One: Interview/"The Man"; Interview/"Ringo"; Interview/"Pop Goes the Hammer"; Interview/"Young

at Heart." Side Two: Interview/"Nine Pound Hammer"; Interview/"I'm Getting Sentimental Over You"; Interview/"Destiny"; Interview/"*Bonanza*." Note: This album was not for sale, and was used by Disc Jockeys. It comes complete with written script. Songs were taken from the albums *Young at Heart, Welcome to the Ponderosa,* and *The Man.*

117. *Peter and the Wolf* RCA LM/LSC-2783 (Stereo) (1964).
118. *Portrait of the West* RCA LPM/LSP-3678 (1966). Side One: "The Search" (July 28, 1966); "Dig, Dig, Dig (There's No More Water in the Well)" (August 2, 1966); "Ol' Cyclone" (July 27, 1966); "Twilight on the Trail" (July 28, 1966); "Geronimo" (August 1, 1966); "Mule Train" (August 1, 1966). Side Two: "I'm a Gun" (July 28, 1966); "Gun-slinger's Prayer" (July 27, 1966); "Nellie Cole" (August 2, 1966); "Home on the Range" (August 11, 1966); "Virginia Town" (August 2, 1966). Note: Anita Kerr, Conductor, Arranger. Joe Reisman, Producer. Dick Bogert, Recording Engineer.
119. *The Robin Hood of Eldorado/The Legend of Joaquin Murieta* MGM Records YDS 303/MGS 2494. Side One: "Come One Come All"; "Dona Elisa Martinez"; "Background Music: El Camino Real." Side Two: "Arroyo Cantuva"; "Was It Love?"; "Background Music: El Camino Real."
120. *The Saga Battlestar Galactica* Soundtrack MCA 3078 (1978). Note: Narrative with dialogue. Lorne Greene narrated. Music by the Los Angeles Philarmonic Orchestra. Glen A. Larson and Guy Magar, Narration Writers. Glen A. Larson, Producer.
121. *Welcome to the Ponderosa* RCA LPM/LSP-2843 (1964). Side One: "*Bonanza*" (November 14, 1963); "Alamo" (November 1, 1963); "Pony Express" (November 1, 1963); "An Ol' Tin Cup (and a Battered Ol' Coffee Pot)" (November 1, 1963); "Endless Prairie" (June 17, 1963). Side Two: "Ghost Riders in the Sky" (November 1, 1963); "Ringo" (October 29, 1963); "Blue Guitar" (November 1, 1963); "Sand" (October 29, 1963); "Saga of the Ponderosa" (November 14, 1963). Note: It reached the charts on November 28, 1964, peaking at position 35, and remained charted for 19 weeks. Lorne Greene introduced each of the songs. Don Ralke, Conductor, Arranger. John Norman, Recording Engineer. Art Say, Cover Photo. William Claxton, Liner Photo. On the back cover of the album, Ben Cartwright wrote a letter to his sons about the songs.
122. *Young at Heart* RCA LPM/LSP 2661 (1963). Side One: "I'm Glad I'm Not Young Anymore"; "September Song"; "Young at Heart"; "You Make Me Feel So Young"; "Hello Young Lovers"; "Something's Gotta Give." Side Two: "I'm Getting Sentimental Over You"; "Just in Time"; "Young and Foolish"; "Speak Low"; "As Time Goes By"; "The Second Time Around." Note: Joe Reisman and Steve Sholes, Producers. Hank Levine Arranger, Conductor. Dave Hassinger, Recording Engineer. Ken Whitmore, Cover Photo.

Anthologies

123. *American Spirit* Decca/London Sp-44242 (1975).
124. *The Best of the Best* RCA LPM/LSP-3632 (1966).
125. *Fantastic Country* RCA PRS-387 (1966).
126. *Golden Throats* Rhino R2-71867 (1995). Greene sings "Ringo" in French
127. *Happy Holidays Vol. 16* RCA Special Products DPL1-0501. Greene sings "'Twas the Night Before Christmas"
128. *Joyous Noel* Reader's Digest RDAS-57A. Greene sings "We Wish You a Merry Christmas"
129. *The People's Choice of Great Talent* RCA Camden Cal/Cas 946 (1964)
130. *RCA Victor Presents Music for the Twelve Days of Christmas* RCA PRS-188
131. *Threads of Glory: Two Hundred Years of America in Words and Music* 6 LP Set 6 SP-14000 (1975) as President Franklin D. Roosevelt he does "Four Freedoms Speech," "Pearl Harbor Speech," and "Jefferson Day Speech"

Cassettes and CDs

132. *Hooray for Santa Claus* Scotti Brothers (Cassette/CD) 75469. Greene sings "Must Be Santa"
133. *Lorne Greene Lassoes 'n Spurs* BMG Music (CD) 06192 17225-2 (1991). "The Man"; "Saga of the Ponderosa"; "Cool Water"; "Mule Train"; "Ringo"; "Ghost Riders in the Sky"; "Five Card Stud"; "Sixteen Tons"; "Bring on the Dancin Girls"; "Nine Pound Hammer."
134. *My Rifle, My Pony and Me* Bear Family Records (Germany) (CD) BCD 15625 (1993). Greene sings *"Bonanza"*
135. *Nipper's Greatest Hits 60s Vol. 2* RCA Records (CD Only) 8475 (1988). Greene sings "Ringo"
136. *Nipper's #1 Hits 1956–1986 (The Best of RCA Victor).* BMG (CD) 9902-2-R (1989). Greene sings "Ringo"
137. *On the Ponderosa: Lorne Greene & His Western Classics* BMG Razor & Tie Entertainment RE 2157-2 (1997). *"Bonanza"*; "Ponderosa"; "Skip to My Lou" — with Roberts, Blocker, Landon; "The Ol' Chisholm Trail"; "Five Card Stud"; "Ringo"; "Riders in the Sky"; "Cool Water"; "Whoopi Ti Yi Yo"; "Pretty Horses"; "The Devil's Grin"; "The Man"; "An Ol' Tin Cup (And a Battered Ol' Coffee Cup)"; Sixteen Tons"; "Endless Prairie"; "Mule Train"; "Tumbling Tumbleweeds"; "Waco"; "My Sons, My Sons"; "Saga of the Ponderosa"
138. *We Wish You a Merry Christmas* BMG Music (CD) 2294-2-R. Greene sings "We Wish You a Merry Christmas." Note: Also available on cassette 2294-4-R
139. *White Men Can't Wrap* Capitol (CD) 07 7779908745 (1992). Greene sings "Ringo"

Pernell Roberts

140. *Abilene* RCA Victor (Unreleased) (Recorded June 22, 1962).
141. *Carousel* (TV Musical). Columbia Special Product (LP) CSM/CSP-479 (1967). Roberts sings "Blow High, Blow Low"
142. *Come All Ye Fair and Tender Ladies* RCA (LP) LPM/LSP-2662 (1963). Side One: "The Bold Soldier" (January 2, 1963); "Mary Ann" (January 14, 1963); "They Call the Wind Maria" (January 2, 1963); "Sylvie" (January 10, 1963); "Lily of the West"; "The Water is Wide" (January 2, 1963). Side Two: "Rake and a Ramblin' Boy" (January 10, 1963); "A Quiet Girl" (January 15, 1963); "Shady Grove" (January 14, 1963); "Alberta" (January 10, 1963); "Empty Pocket Blues" (January 15, 1963); "Come All Ye Fair and Tender Ladies" (January 14, 1963).
143. *Gone with the Wind* Original San Francisco/Los Angeles Cast. Private Tape
144. *Mata Hari* Original Cast. Private Tape

Dan Blocker

LPs

145. *Our Land and Heritage* RCA Victor LPM/LSP 2896 (1964). Side One: "Springfield Mountain" (June 25, 1964); "Roll Out, Heave That Cotton" (June 25, 1964); "The Battle Hymn of the Republic" (October 1, 1963). Side Two: "The Erie Canal" (June 25, 1964); "Paiute Sunrise Chant" (June 25, 1964); "Charles: Steal Away; He Never Said a Mumblin Word" (October 1, 1963)
146. *Tales For Young 'Uns* Trey TLP-602 (1965).

Anthologies

147. *Christmas with Colonel Sanders* RCA Victor PRS-291. (See D84).
148. *RCA Presents Music for the Twelve Days of Christmas* RCA PRS-188 (See D130).

CD

149. *A TV Family Christmas* Scotti Bros. 72392-75271-2 (See D85)

Michael Landon

45s

150. *Be Patient with Me/Gimme a Little Kiss* Candlelight 1017 (1960).
151. *Be Patient with Me/Gimme a Little Kiss* Fondo/Graf 1240 (1960). Note: Also available with picture sleeve with same number.
152. *Darlin I Can't* RCA Victor (Unreleased) Recorded June 21, 1962
153. *Linda Is Lonesome/Without You* RCA 47-8330 (1964). Note: Also available with picture sleeve with same number.

Anthologies

154. *Christmas with Colonel Sanders* RCA Victor (LP) PRS-291 (See D84)
155. *RCA Victor Presents Music for the Twelve Days of Christmas* RCA (LP) PRS-188 (See D130)

CD

156. *A TV Family Christmas* Scotti Bros. 72392-75271-2 (See D85)

Victor Sen Yung

LP

157. *Flower Drum Song* Decca DL79098 Reissued MCA 2069 (1961). Sen Yung sings "Gliding Through My Memories." Note: The soundtrack appeared on the charts on December 25, 1961, and peaked at number 15 and remained charted for 35 weeks.

David Canary

LP

158. *Kittiwake Island* Adelphimx AD-2015/6 Original Production. Note: Alex Wilder (Music); Arnold Sundgaard (Words); Jack Martin (Orchestra); Joseph Stecko (Conductor).

Guy Williams

45s

159. *Autographs & Pictures/Little Girl* Assault 1905
160. *Disney Heroes* Golden 485 (Extended Play)
161. *I Cried Over You/Foolin' Around* Romano 20837

LPs

162. *The Adventures of Zorro* Golden 448
163. *Four Adventures of Zorro* Disneyland 8601
164. *Garcia's Lament/Zorro* Disneyland 62
165. *Presenting Señor Zorro* Disneyland 501
166. *The Prince and the Pauper* (TV Soundtrack) Pickwick SPC-3204. Note: George Fischoff (Music), Verna Thomasson (Words).
167. *Zorro* Cadence 1349
168. *Zorro* Disneyland 77
169. *Zorro Frees the Indians* Disneyland 502
170. *Zorro's Daring Rescue/Zorro and the Ghost* Disneyland 504

APPENDIX D

Endorsements

This appendix lists known products and causes for which advertisements were made by the *Bonanza* cast. The endorsements are listed alphabetically by star.

Lorne Greene
1. Alpo
2. American Cancer Society
3. Chevrolet
4. Coors Light
5. Del Monte
6. RCA Victor Color Televisions
7. Williams Luxury Shaving Cream

Pernell Roberts
8. Chevrolet
9. Coors Light
10. Folonari Soave Wine
11. RCA Victor Color Televisions

Dan Blocker
12. Chevrolet
13. Coors Light
14. RCA Color Televisions

Michael Landon

15. Chevrolet
16. Coors Light
17. Del Monte
18. Free Arts for Abused Children
19. Kodak Ektra Camera
20. Kodak Ektralite 10 Camera
21. RCA Victor Color Televisions
22. Where There's a Will There's an A (Study Tapes)
23. Women Against Rape Ad for Collingswood, New Jersey

APPENDIX E

Ratings

This appendix lists the A.C. Nielsen's Top Ten shows, by season, for every year that *Bonanza* appeared. It also gives the Nielsen rankings of Westerns, by season. Also provided are how Westerns appearing on the Nielsen lists ranked with each other.

Top-Ten Shows by Season

1. 1961–1962 Season: *Wagon Train* (1); *Bonanza* (2); *Gunsmoke* (3); *Hazel* (4); *Perry Mason* (5); *The Red Skelton Show* (6); *The Andy Griffith Show* (7); *The Danny Thomas Show* (8); *Dr. Kildare* (9); *Candid Camera* (10).
2. 1962–1963 Season: *The Beverly Hillbillies* (1); *Candid Camera, The Red Skelton Show* (Tie 2); *Bonanza, The Lucy Show* (Tie 4); *The Andy Griffith Show* (6); *Ben Casey, The Danny Thomas Show* (Tie 7); *The Dick Van Dyke Show* (9); *Gunsmoke* (10).
3. 1963-1964 Season: *The Beverly Hillbillies* (1); *Bonanza* (2); *The Dick Van Dyke Show* (3); *Petticoat Junction* (4); *The Andy Griffith Show* (5); *The Lucy Show* (6); *Candid Camera* (7); *The Ed Sullivan Show* (8); *The Danny Thomas Show* (9); *My Favorite Martian* (10).
4. 1964-1965 Season: *Bonanza* (1); *Bewitched* (2); *Gomer Pyle, U.S.M.C.* (3); *The Andy Griffith Show* (4); *The Fugitive* (5); *The Red Skelton Show* (6); *The Dick Van Dyke Show* (7); *The Lucy Show* (8); *Peyton Place* (9); *Combat!* (10).
5. 1965-1966 Season: *Bonanza* (1); *Gomer Pyle, U.S.M.C.* (2); *The Lucy Show* (3); *The Red Skelton Show* (4); *Batman* [Thursday] (5); *The Andy Griffith Show* (6); *Bewitched, The Beverly Hillbillies* (Tie 7); *Hogan's Heroes* (9); *Batman* [Wednesday] (10).
6. 1966-1967 Season: *Bonanza* (1); *The Red Skelton Show* (2); *The Andy Griffith Show* (3); *The Lucy Show* (4); *The Jackie Gleason Show* (5); *Green Acres* (6); *Daktari, Bewitched* (Tie 7); *The Beverly Hillbillies* (9); *The Virginian, The Lawrence Welk Show, Gomer Pyle, U.S.M.C.* (Tie 10).

316

7. 1967-1968 Season: *The Andy Griffith Show* (1); *The Lucy Show* (2); *Gomer Pyle, U.S.M.C.* (3); *Family Affair, Gunsmoke, Bonanza* (Tie 4); *The Red Skelton Show* (7); *The Dean Martin Show* (8); *The Jackie Gleason Show* (9); *Saturday Night at the Movies* (10).
8. 1968-1969 Season: *Rowan & Martin's Laugh-In* (1); *Gomer Pyle, U.S.M.C.* (2); *Bonanza* (3); *Mayberry R.F.D.* (4); *Family Affair* (5); *Gunsmoke* (6); *Julia* (7); *The Dean Martin Show* (8); *Here's Lucy* (9); *The Beverly Hillbillies* (10).
9. 1969-1970 Season: *Rowan & Martin's Laugh-In* (1); *Gunsmoke* (2); *Bonanza* (3); *Mayberry R.F.D.* (4); *Family Affair* (5); *Here's Lucy* (6); *The Red Skelton Show* (7); *Marcus Welby, M.D.* (8); *Walt Disney's Wonderful World of Color* (9); *The Doris Day Show* (10).
10. 1970-1971 Season: *Marcus Welby, M.D.* (1); *The Flip Wilson Show* (2); *Here's Lucy* (3); *Ironside* (4); *Gunsmoke* (5); *ABC Movie of the Week* (6); *Hawaii Five-O* (7); *Medical Center* (8); *Bonanza* (9); *The F.B.I.* (10).

Western Shows by Season

11. 1960-1961 Season: *Gunsmoke* (1); *Wagon Train* (2); *Have Gun Will Travel* (3); *Rawhide* (6); *Bonanza* (17).
12. 1961-1962 Season: *Wagon Train* (1); *Bonanza* (2); *Gunsmoke* (3); *Rawhide* (13).
13. 1962-1963 Season: *Bonanza* (4); *Gunsmoke* (10); *Rawhide* (22); *Wagon Train* (25). Note: *Startime* voted *Bonanza* the nation's favorite series.
14. 1963–1964 Season: *Bonanza* (1); *The Virginian* (17); *Gunsmoke* (20).
15. 1964-1965 Season: *Bonanza* (1); *Branded* (14); *The Virginian* (22).
16. 1965-1966 Season: *Bonanza* (1); *The Wild Wild West* (23); *The Virginian* (25).
17. 1966-1967 Season: *Bonanza* (1); *The Virginian* (11); *Daniel Boone* (25).
18. 1967-1968 Season: *Gunsmoke* (4); *Bonanza* (6); *The Virginian* (14).
19. 1968-1969 Season: *Bonanza* (3); *Gunsmoke* (6); *The Virginian* (17); *Daniel Boone* (21).
20. 1969-1970 Season: *Gunsmoke* (2); *Bonanza* (3).
21. 1970-1971 Season: *Gunsmoke* (5); *Bonanza* (9); *The Men from Shiloh* (18).
22. 1971-1972 Season: *Gunsmoke* (4); *Bonanza* (20).
23. 1972-1973 Season: *Bonanza* (40) by the first week of October 1972.
24. 1993-1994 Season: *Back to Bonanza, Bonanza: The Return* (Top 10).

Over-All Western Ratings

25. *Gunsmoke* (1); *Bonanza* (2); *Wagon Train* (3); *Have Gun Will Travel* (4); *The Virginian* (5); *Rawhide* (6); *Tales of Wells Fargo* (7); *The Life and Legend of Wyatt Earp* (8); *The Rifleman* (9); *Cheyenne* (10); *Wanted: Dead or Alive* (11); *Maverick* (12); *The Lone Ranger* (13); *The Restless Gun* (14); *Dick Powell's Zane Grey Theatre* (15); *Hopalong Cassidy* (16); *How the West Was Won* (17); *Branded* (18); *The Texan* (19); *The Lawman* (20); *The Men from Shiloh* (21); *Sugarfoot* (22); *Daniel Boone* (23); *The Wild Wild West* (24).

Appendix F

Sheet Music

This appendix lists sheet music on which each cast member is pictured. The titles are arranged alphabetically with year.

Lorne Greene

1. Alamo (1964 & 1965)
2. *Bonanza* Theme (1959 & 1960)
3. Bring on the Dancing Girls (1965)
4. Daddy [I'm Proud to Be Your Son] (1970)
5. End of Track (1965)
6. The Man (1965)
7. Nine Pound Hammer (1947)
8. Oh! What a Town (1964 & 1965)
9. An Ol' Tin Cup (1963 & 1964)
10. Ringo (1963 & 1964)
11. Sixteen Tons (1947)
12. Trouble Row (1965)

Pernell Roberts

13. *Bonanza* Theme (1959 & 1960)

Dan Blocker

14. *Bonanza* Theme (1959 & 1960)

Michael Landon

15. *Bonanza* Theme (1959 & 1960)

APPENDIX G

Videolog

This appendix documents all known videos for both *Bonanza* and the main and supporting cast. For the show, the episodes are listed alphabetically followed by the various videos on which that title is found. The TV films are listed separately from the episodes. The stars are presented in the order originally covered. Under each, the video is listed alphabetically and includes different formats and releasing companies. The entries include the release date of the video and for those not available the show's production year is used. All videos are VHS except where noted.

Bonanza Television Episodes

1. "Any Friend of Walter's" *The Best of Bonanza Vol. 8* [The 1962 Season] (1991); Republic Pictures Home Video 0361
2. "The Ape" *Bonanza Collector's Edition* (1998); Madacy Entertainment Bon-3-0265
3. "The Avenger" *The Best of Bonanza* (1997); UAV Entertainment 6643. *Bonanza Vol. 2* (1997); Alpha Video 35102. *Television Classics Bonanza* (1996); Diamond Entertainment Corporation 18035. *Television Classics Bonanza* (1996); Diamond Entertainment Corporation 42003
4. "Badge Without Honor" *Bonanza Collector's Edition* (1998); Madacy Entertainment Bon-3-0264. Madacy Entertainment DVD 9-9100 (1999). Madacy Entertainment DVD 9-9047-2 (1998); [Part of 5 Disc Set]
5. "Bitter Water" *The Best of Bonanza* (1997); UAV Entertainment 6643. *Bonanza Vol. 5* (1997); Alpha Video 35105
6. "The Blood Line" *Bonanza Collector's Edition* (1998); Madacy Entertainment Bon-3-0266. Madacy Entertainment DVD 9-9047-4 (1998); [Part of 5 Disc Set]

7. "Blood on the Land" *The Best of Bonanza* (1997); UAV Entertainment 6644. *Television Classics Bonanza* (1996); Diamond Entertainment Corporation 18036. *Television Classics Bonanza* (1996); Diamond Entertainment Corporation 42002
8. "The Boss" *The Best of Bonanza Vol. 4* (1990); Republic Pictures Home Video 7163
9. "Bullet for a Bride" *Bonanza Vol. 2* (1990); Republic Pictures Home Video 0366
10. "The Cheating Game" *Bonanza Vol. 3* (1990); Republic Pictures Home Video 0365
11. "The Crucible" *The Best of Bonanza Vol. 7* [The 1961 Season] (1991); Republic Pictures Home Video 0362
12. "The Dark Gate" *The Best of Bonanza* (1997); UAV Entertainment 6641. *The Best of Bonanza Vol. 2* (1987); Republic Pictures Home Video 7167
13. "Day of Reckoning" *Bonanza Collector's Edition* (1998); Madacy Entertainment Bon-3-0264
14. "Death at Dawn" *The Best of Bonanza* (1997); UAV Entertainment 6642. *Bonanza* (1996); Quality Video 20613
15. "Desert Justice" Madacy Entertainment Bon-3-0263 (1998). Madacy Entertainment DVD 9-9100 (1999). Madacy Entertainment DVD 9-9047-1; [Part of 5 Disc Set]
16. "Enter Mark Twain" *The Best of Bonanza* Vol. 5 [The 1959 Season] (1991); Republic Pictures Home Video 0363
17. "Escape to the Ponderosa" *The Best of Bonanza* (1997); UAV Entertainment 6644. *Television Classics Bonanza* (1996); Diamond Entertainment Corporation 42000
18. "The Fear Merchants" *Televison Classics Bonanza* (1996); Diamond Entertainment Corporation 18035. Diamond Entertainment Corporation 42001
19. "Feet of Clay" *The Best of Bonanza* (1997); UAV Entertainment 6642
20. "The Gunman" *The Best of Bonanza* (1997); UAV Entertainment 6641d. *Bonanza* (1996); Quality Video 20613
21. "The Honor of Cochise" *The Best of Bonanza Vol. 2* (1987); Republic Pictures Home Video 7161
22. "Hoss and the Leprechauns" *The Best of Bonanza Vol. 3* (1987); Republic Pictures Home Video 7162
23. "The Last Viking" *Bonanza Collector's Edition* (1998); Madacy Entertainment Bon-3-0265. Madacy Entertainment DVD 9-9047-3 (1998); [Part of 5 Disc Set]
24. "The Pure Truth" *Bonanza Vol. 1* (1990); Republic Pictures Home Video 0367
25. "Ride the Wind" Republic Pictures Home Video 7690 (1989); Republic Entertainment/Artison Home Entertainment (1999)
26. "A Rose for Lotta" *The Best of Bonanza Vol. 1* (1987); Republic Pictures Home Video 7160
27. "Silent Thunder" *Bonanza Collector's Edition* (1998); Madacy Entertainment Bon-3-0267. *The Best of Bonanza Vol. 6* [The 1960 Season] (1991); Republic Pictures Home Video 0364
28. "The Spanish Grant" *Bonanza Vol. 6* (1997); Alpha Video 35106
29. "The Spitfire" *Bonanza Collector's Edition* (1998); Madacy Entertainment Bon-3-0266. *Televison Classics Bonanza* (1996); Diamond Entertainment Corporation 18036. Diamond Entertainment Corporation 42204
30. "The Stranger" *Bonanza Collector's Edition* (1998); Madacy Entertainment Bon-3-0263
31. "To Own the World" *The Best of Bonanza Vol. 4* (1987); Republic Pictures Home Video 7163
32. "The Trail Gang" *Bonanza Collector's Edition* (1998); Madacy Entertainment Bon-3-0267
33. "The Trap" *Bonanza Vol. 4* (1990); Republic Pictures Home Video 0368
34. "The Truckee Strip" *The Best of Bonanza Vol. 3* (1987); Republic Pictures Home Video 7162
35. "The Underdog" *The Best of Bonanza Vol. 1* (1987); Republic Pictures Home Video 7160

Bonanza Films

36. "Bonanza: The Next Generation" (1991) Goodtimes Home Video 9197
37. "Bonanza: The Return" (1994) Pioneer Artists Inc. LD Cum 5878 Laserdisc. V&E Entertainment VM 5878. V&E Entertainment VM 5910s

Bonanza Miscellaneous Video

38. "TV's Western Heroes" (1983) Goodtimes Home Video 05-09329. Contains *Bonanza* bloopers

Lorne Greene

39. "The Alamo: Thirteen Days of Glory" (1991) Fries Home Video 90250 & Beta. Movies Unlimited 279107. Starmaker Entertainment 1201 (1995)
40. "All-Star Hollywood Christmas" (1991) Goodtimes Home Video 8271
41. "Arizona Highways Presents the Grand Canyon"
42. "Autumn Leaves" (1958) Columbia/Tri Star Home Video. Facets Video S10382; Goodtimes Home Video 4428 & Beta
43. "The Bastard" (1978) MCA Home Video 8186 & Laserdisc. Movies Unlimited 071723
44. "Battlestar Galactica" (1978) MCA/Universal Home Video 45-19007 (CED, 1983); MCA/Universal Home Video 66011 & Beta & Laserdisc. MCA/Universal Home Video DVD 20570 (1999) Widescreen
45. *Battlestar Galactica*—"Baltar's Escape" (1979); MCA/Universal Home Video 80240
46. *Battlestar Galactica*—"Galactica 1980" (1987); Goodtimes Home Video 4124
47. *Battlestar Galactica*—"Conquest of the Earth"
48. *Battlestar Galactica*—"The Cylon Attack" (1981); MCA Video Cassette, Inc. 66035
49. *Battlestar Galactica*—"Fire in Space" (1985); MCA Home Video 80238
50. *Battlestar Galactica*—"The Long Patrol" (1978); MCA/Universal Home Video 80233
51. *Battlestar Galactica*—"The Lost Warrior" (1978); MCA Home Video 80235
52. *Battlestar Galactica*—"The Magnificent Warriors" (1978); MCA/Universal Home Video 80236
53. *Battlestar Galactica*—"The Man with Nine Lives" (1979); MCA/Universal Home Video 80237
54. *Battlestar Galactica*—"Murder on the Rising Star" (1979); MCA/Universal Home Video 80239
55. *Battlestar Galactica*—"Starbuck Returns"
56. *Battlestar Galactica*—"The Young Lords" (1978); MCA/Universal Home Video 80234
57. "The Buccaneer" (1958) Facets Video S13782 & Beta & Laserdisc. Movies Unlimited 061844. Paramount Home Video 5809 & Beta
58. "Earthquake" (1990) MCA/Universal Home Video 55034 & Beta. MCA/Universal Home Video 42072 Laserdisc & Letterbox. Movies Unlimited 071060
59. "The Errand Boy" (1961) Image Entertainment, Inc. ID664. Image Entertainment, Inc. ID6271V Laserdisc. Live Home Entertainment 62088 & Beta & Laserdisc. Movies Unlimited 276154
60. "The Fifth Pritkin Promise"

61. "Greatest Adventure Stories From the Bible — Noah's Ark" Best Film Video Corp. 254. Junior Home Video 1279. Turner Home Entertainment 2001
62. "Heidi's Song" (1982) Republic Pictures Home Video 1031 & Beta. Turner Home Entertainment 1031 (1982)
63. "High Country Calling" (1974) Video Gems & Beta
64. "Klondike Fever" (1980) HBO 90604
65. "Lorne Greene's New Wilderness: Ascent of the Chimps" (1987); Prism Entertainment 3655
66. "Lorne Greene's New Wilderness: Close Encounters of Deep Kind" (1987); Prism Entertainment 3657
67. "Lorne Greene's New Wilderness: Devil Island" (1987); Prism Entertainment 3664
68. "Lorne Greene's New Wilderness: The Enchanted Forest" (1987); Prism Entertainment 3661
69. "Lorne Greene's New Wilderness: Frozen Eden" (1987); Prism Entertainment 3654
70. "Lorne Greene's New Wilderness: Golden Eagle: Death on the Wing" (1987); Prism Entertainment 3663
71. "Lorne Greene's New Wilderness: Hunter of the Chubat" (1987); Prism Entertainment 3651
72. "Lorne Greene's New Wilderness: Huntress" (1987); Prism Entertainment 3662
73. "Lorne Greene's New Wilderness: Inky, Dinky Spider" (1987); Prism Entertainment 3660
74. "Lorne Greene's New Wilderness: It's a Male's World" (1987); Prism Entertainment 3666
75. "Lorne Greene's New Wilderness: Kindness Kills" (1987); Prism Entertainment 3667
76. "Lorne Greene's New Wilderness: A Love Story: The Canadian Goose" (1987); Prism Entertainment 3658
77. "Lorne Greene's New Wilderness: Master Hunter of the Night" (1987); Prism Entertainmnet 3652
78. "Lorne Greene's New Wilderness: Old Dog New Tricks" (1987); Prism Entertainment 3653
79. "Lorne Greene's New Wildernnss: Pretty Poison" (1987); Prism Entertainment 3656
80. "Lorne Greene's New Wilderness: Tales of the Snow Monkey" (1987); Prism Entertainment 3659
81. "Lorne Greene's New Wilderness: White Lightning" (1987); Prism Entertainment 3668
82. "Lorne Greene's New Wilderness: Yesterday's Heroes" (1987); Prism Entertainment 3665
83. "Peyton Place" (1957) CBS/Fox Video 1855. Movies Unlimited 042422
84. "The Pritkin Promise" (1984) Media Home Entertainment M445
85. "Rand McNally Alaska: Video Trip 458"
86. "Roots Vol. 1" (1977) Warner Home Video 11111 & Beta
87. "Roots Vol. 2" (1977) Warner Home Video 11112 & Beta
88. "Roots Vol. 3" (1977) Warner Home Video 11113 & Beta
89. "Roots Vol. 4" (1977) Warner Home Video 11114 & Beta
90. "Roots Vol. 5" (1977) Warner Home Video 11115 & Beta
91. "Roots Vol. 6" (1977) Warner Home Video 11116 & Beta
92. "Silver Chalice" (1954) Republic/Warner Home Video 11560 & Beta
93. "Tidal Wave" (1975) New World Entertainment
94. "Time for Miracles" (1980) Charter Entertainment 90169
95. "The Trap" (1959) Barr Entertainment
96. "The Trial of Lee Harvey Oswald" (1977) Republic Home Video 3014
97. "Vasectomy — a Delicate Matter" (1986) Republic Home Video 6003 & Beta
98. "The Wizard of Oz" (1982) Paramount Home Video 2322

Pernell Roberts

99. "Around the World in 80 Days" (1989) Art & Entertainment E8857. Best Film & Video Corp. 918. Well Spring Media Vol. 4 E18857
100. "Best of Mission Impossible: The Mercenaries" (1966); Paramount Home Video 154233
101. "Checkered Flag" (1990) Movies Unlimited 155206. Rhino Video 17906
102. "Desire Under the Elms" (1958) Movies Unlimited 061821. Paramount Home Video 5712 & Beta & Laserdisc. Republic Pictures Home Video PA 5712
103. "Errand Boy" (1961) Image Entertainment, Inc., ID664. Image Entertainment, Inc. ID62718 Laserdisc. Live Home Entertainment 62088 Beta & Laserdisc. Movies Unlimited 276154
104. "Four Rode Out" (1969) Live Home Video 62592 & Beta. Power Sports International Dist. P886
105. "High Noon Part II: The Return of Will Kane" (1980); Fries Home Video 93400 & Beta. Live Home Video 62988 & Beta. Nova Entertainment, Inc. NO37405. Video Trends, Inc. MN7566
106. "Hot Rod" (1979) Charter Entertainment 90105 & Beta
107. "Kashmiri Run" (1969) Live Home Video 63600 & Beta. USA Home Video 214-200
108. "Magic of Lassie" (1978) MGM/UA Home Video M300729
109. "The Night Train to Katmandu" (1988) Paramount Home Video 12605. Pioneer Artists, Inc. LV12605
110. "Paco" (1976) General Video GV27 & Beta
111. "Sniper" (1975) Xenon Entertainment Group XA2005

Dan Blocker

112. "The Errand Boy" (1961) Image Entertainment, Inc. ID644. Image Entertainment, Inc. ID62718 Laserdisc. Live Home Entertainment 62088 & Beta & Laserdisc. Movies Unlimited 276154
113. "Lady in Cement" (1968) Facet Multimedia, Inc. S12522. Facet Multimedia LD71821 Laserdisc. Fox Video 1167

Michael Landon

114. "Cheyenne: White Warrior" (1986) Warner Home Video 12495
115. "The Errand Boy" (1961) Image Entertainment, Inc. ID664. Image Entertainment, Inc. ID62718 Laserdisc. Live Home Entertainment 62088 & Beta & Laserdisc. Movies Unlimited 276154
116. "God's Little Acre" (1984) Memory Lane Video 07250
117. "High School Confidential" (1958) Facets Multimedia, Inc. S00568. Movies Unlimited 631051 Letterbox. Pioneer Entertainment 21808. Republic Pictures Home Video 1808
118. "I Was a Teenage Werewolf" (1991) Facets Multimedia, Inc. S146275. Movies Unlimited 020274. RCA/Columbia Pictures Home Video 60906. Republic Pictures Home Video Co60906. Sinister Cinema S179
119. "Johnny Carson: His Favorite Moments '80s & '90s — "The King of Late Night" (1994); Buena Vista Home Video 2781
120. "The Legend of Tom Dooley" (1987) Columbia/Tristar Home Video 03973
121. "Little House on the Prairie" [Premiere] (1988); Warner Home Video 29006 & Beta

122. "Little House on the Prairie: Afternoon" (1994); Goodtimes Home Video 9132
123. "Little House on the Prairie: Christmas at Plum Creek" (1991); Goodtimes Home Video 9125
124. "Little House on the Prairie: The Christmas They Never Forgot" (1989); Goodtimes Home Video 9124
125. "Little House on the Prairie: The Collection" (1991); Goodtimes Home Video 9128
126. "Little House on the Prairie: The Craftsman" (1991); Goodtimes Home Video 9139
127. "Little House on the Prairie: The Creeper of Walnut Grove" (1991); Goodtimes Home Video 9129
128. "Little House on the Prairie: A Harvest of Friends" (1994); Goodtimes Home Video 05-09341
129. "Little House on the Prairie: Injun Kid" (1993); Goodtimes Home Video 9123
130. "Little House on the Prairie: Laura Ingalls Wilder" (1993); Goodtimes Home Video 9253
131. "Little House on the Prairie: The Lord is My Shepherd" Columbia/Tristar Home Video 60431
132. "Little House on the Prairie: The Man Inside/A Most Perfect Gift" (1995); Goodtimes Home Video 0507197
133. "Little House on the Prairie: A Matter of Faith/The Gift" (1992); Goodtimes Home Video 7025
134. "Little House on the Prairie: Remember Me" Warner Home Video 29008 & Beta
135. "Little House on the Prairie: Survival" (1991); Goodtimes Home Video 9131
136. "Little House on the Prairie: There's No Place Like Home"
137. "The Loneliest Runner" (1990) Goodtimes Home Video 9109. Movies Unlimited 191375. Warners Home Video 29014 & Beta
138. "Memories with Laughter and Love" (1993) Genesis Entertainment 1001. (A Michael Landon Tribute)
139. "Passion and Valor/Fight For the Title (1995). Quality Video 20503
140. "Sam's Son" (1982) Worldvision Home Video 4100

Victor Sen Yung

141. "Across the Pacific" (1942) Facets Multimedia, Inc. S14304. MGM/UA Home Video M201853. Movies Unlimited 222228. Republic Pictures Home Video M6201853
142. "Betrayal From the East" (1945) Turner Home Entertainment
143. "Blood Alley" (1955) Warner Home Video 11559 & Beta & Laserdisc & Letterbox
144. "Castle in the Desert" (1942) CBS/Fox Video 1705
145. "Charlie Chan at the Wax Museum" (1940) CBS/Fox Video 1704 & Laserdisc
146. "Charlie Chan in Rio" (1941) CBS/Fox Video 1706 & Laserdisc. Republic Pictures Home Video KV1706
147. "The Feathered Serpent" (1948) Lionel Video Publishing 1014
148. "The Flower Drum Song" (1961) MCA/Universal Home Video 80198 & Laserdisc. Republic Pictures Home Video MC80198
149. "The Groom Wore Spurs" (1951) Movies Unlimited 108250. Nostalgia Family Video 1009
150. "The Hunters" (1958) 20th Century–Fox Film Corp.
151. "Jet Attack" (1958) Columbia/Tristar Home Video 51043. A second video, *Paratroop Command*, is on the tape
152. "Jubilee Trail" (1954) Facets Multimedia, Inc. S11403. Republic Pictures Home Video 2137

153. "The Killer Elite" (1975) Image Entertainment, Inc. ID64MG & Laserdisc. Key Video 4683 & Beta. MGM/UA Home Video M301304
154. "The Left Hand of God" (1955) CBS/Fox Video 1304
155. "The Letter" (1940) Facet Multimedia, Inc. S01757. Key Video 4684 & Beta. Key Video 46840 Laserdisc. MGM/UA Home Video M301315. Movies Unlimited 121783
156. "The Man with Bogart's Face" (1980) CBS/Fox Video 1113
157. "Men in War" (1957) Congress Video Corp. 3070 & Beta. Interglobal Video 1023. Movies Unlimited 595000. Prism Entertainment 1865. Western World Video 1019
158. "Murder Over New York" (1940) CBS/Fox Video 1707. Republic Pictures Home Video KV1707
159. "Shadows Over Shanghai" (1938) Loonic Video. Nostalgia Family Video 2968
160. "She Demons" (1958) Admit One Video AF148. Rhino Video 1946. Sinister Cinema S104. Summit Video V. Video Yesteryear 1165 & Betas & 8 Millimeter
161. "Soldier of Fortune" (1955) Grapevine Video SOF
162. "State Department-File 649" (1949) Nostalgia Family Video 3341. Sinister Cinema M080
163. "A Ticket to Tomahawk" (1950) 20th Century–Fox Film Corp.
164. "Women on the Run" (1950) Movies Unlimited 108256. Nostalgia Family Video 1804

Ray Teal

165. "Adventures of Red Ryder" (1940) Video Treasures 0200 & Beta
166. "Along Came Jones" (1945) Key Video 4671 & Beta. MGM/UA Home Video 203039
167. "Along the Great Divide" (1951) Facet Multimedia, Inc. S03433. Warner Home Video 11678 & Beta
168. "Ambush at Tomahawk" (1954). Goodtimes/Kids/Classics Distribution Corp.
169. "Anchors Aweigh" (1945) MGM/UA Home Video M202678. MGM/UA Home Video M100309 Laserdisc. Movies Unlimited 50606
170. "Back to Bataan" (1945) Facet Multimedia, Inc. S03243. Fox Hill Video 8073 & Beta. Image Entertainment, Inc. ID6541TU Laserdisc. Nova Entertainment, Inc. 21498. Republic Pictures Home Video 7041. Turner Home Entertainment 6026 (Colorized); Turner Home Entertainment 2081
171. "The Best Years of Our Lives" (1946) Facet Multimedia, Inc. S03117. Festival Films V. HBO 90657 & Beta. Movies Unlimited 441837. New Line Home Video 3031 & Beta
172. "The Black Arrow" (1948) Columbia/Tristar Home Video 60998. Facet Multimedia, Inc. S0911. Movies Unlimited 021914
173. "The Burning Hills" (1956) Warner Home Video 11149
174. "Captain Kid" (1945) Allied Artists Entertainmnet Group 4066. Barr Films & Video HM0046. Cable Films & Beta. Congress Video Group 03200 & Beta. Hollywood Home Theatre & Beta. Movies Unlimited 102043. Nostalgia Family Video 2433. Starr Classics 3154. UAV Corp. 1035. Video Yesteryear 361
175. "Carrie" (1952) Facet Multimedia, Inc. S13791. Movies Unlimited 061819
176. "Chism" (1970) Warner Home Video 11089 & Beta & Laserdisc
177. "The Clock" (1945) Facet Multimedia, Inc. S13356. MGM/UA Home Video M200890. MGM/UA Home Video ML100890 Laserdisc
178. "Dead Reckoning" (1947) Columbia/Tristar Home Video 60641. Columbia/Tristar Home Video 6041 Laserdisc. Facet Multimedia, Inc. S06547. Movies Unlimited 021826

179. "Desperate Hours" (1955) Facet Multimedia, Inc. S09566. Movies Unlimited 061667. Paramount Home Video 5509 & Beta. PI-E LV5509 Laserdisc
180. "Distant Drums" (1951) Facet Multimedia, Inc. S03504. Facet Multimedia, Inc. LD71457 Laserdisc. Republic Pictures Home Video 1035. Republic Pictures Home Video RP1035. Republic Pictures Home Video LV 21035 Laserdisc
181. "Edison the Man" (1940) Facet Multimedia, Inc. S15017. MGM/UA Home Video M202346. Movies Unlimited 122286
182. "The Hanged Man" (1974) King of Video 9145
183. "Hangman's Knot" (1952) Goodtimes/Kids/Classics Distribution Corp.
184. "The Harvey Girls" (1946) Facet Multimedia, Inc. S04985. MGM/UA Home Video M301003. MGM/UA Home Video ML101003 Laserdisc. Republic Pictures Home Video MG301003
185. "Hollywood Canteen" (1944) MGM/UA Home Video M302309. Pioneer Artists ML10309 Laserdisc. Republic Pictures Home Video MG302309
186. "Home From the Hill" (1960) Facet Multimedia, Inc. S11436. MGM/UA Home Video M300802. MGM/UA Home Video M102080 Laserdisc & Letterbox
187. "Honky Tonk" (1941) Facet Multimedia, Inc. S15259. MGM/UA Home Video M202369
188. "I Love You Again" (1940) MGM/UA Home Video 202865. Movies Unlimited 122729
189. "The Indian Fighter" (1955) MGM/UA Home Video 203122
190. "Inherit the Wind" (1960) Facet Multimedia, Inc. S02341. MGM/UA Home Video M201649. MGM/UA Home Video ML1011649 Laserdisc. Movies Unlimited 122235. Republic Pictures Home Video MG201649
191. "Joan of Arc" (1948) Facet Multimedia, Inc. S04391. Movies Unlimited 151031. UAV Corp. 18007. Vid-America 80007 & Beta. Vid-America 899 Laserdisc
192. "Judgement at Nuremberg" (1961) CBS/Fox Video Video 4682 & Beta. Festival Films V & Laserdisc. MGM/UA Home Video M301536. MGM/UA Home Video M305512 Letterbox. MGM/UA Home Video M305481. MGM/UA Home Video ML105512 Laserdisc & Letterbox. MGM/UA Home Video ML101536 Laserdisc. Movies Unlimited 121887. Republic Pictures Home Video MG301536
193. "Jumping Jacks" (1952) Movies Unlimited 061996. Paramount Home Video 5732 & Beta. Paramount Home Video LV5732 Laserdisc
194. "Kitty Foyle" (1940) Facet Multimedia, Inc. S00688. Fox Hill Video 8076 & Beta. Image Entertainment, Inc. ID8296TU Laserdisc. Movies Unlimited 051343. Nova Entertainment, Inc. N064318. Republic Pictures Home Video THE6204. Turner Home Entertainment 6327. Vid-America 893 & Beta
195. "Liberation of Lord Byron Jones" (1970) Columbia/Tristar Home Video 60381 & Beta. Facet Multimedia, Inc. S06177
196. "Lucky Me" (1954) Warner Home Video 12265
197. "Madame Curie" (1943) MGM/UA Home Video 202054. MGM/UA Home Video ML10254 Laserdisc. Movies Unlimited 122372
198. "The Man from Colorado" (1949) Columbia/Tristar Home Video 60962
199. "The Men" (1950) Movies Unlimited 631026. Republic Pictures Home Video 2710
200. "The Michigan Kid" (1947) Grapevine Video
201. "The Miracle of the Bells" (1948) Movies Unlimited 631034 (Colorized). Movies Unlimited 631037 (45th Anniversary Edition). Republic Pictures Home Video 2766. Republic Pictures Home Video 2767 (Colorized). Republic Pictures Home Video 5553 (45th Anniversary Edition)
202. "Montana Belle" (1952) Turner Home Entertainment 6122
203. "My Favorite Brunette" (1947) Barr Entertainment 11026. Cable V & Beta. Congress Video Group 13700 & Beta; Film Classics 146 & Beta; Hollywood Home Theatre & Beta. Image Entertainment, Inc. 136882NE Laserdisc. Interglobal Video 1044. Loonic Video. Movies Unlimited 102008. Nostalgia Family Video 239. Sinister Cinema JR03. Starr Classics 3144. Timeless Video, Inc. 5135. UAV Corporation 0011. Video Yesteryear 428 & Beta

204. "New Moon" (1940) MGM/UA Home Video M30138 & Laserdisc. Republic Pictures Home Video MG301381
205. "The North Star" (1943) A&E Home Video 4092. Barr Entertainment HM0114. Cable & Beta. Congress Video Group 14400 & Beta. Hollywood Home Theatre & Beta. Movies Unlimited 088068. Nostalgia Family Video 1311. Republic Pictures Home Video 0156. Timeless Video, Inc. 51193. UAV Corporation 4049. Video Yesteryear 460 & Beta
206. "Northwest Outpost" (1947) Republic Pictures Home Video 3040
207. "Northwest Passage" (1940) MGM M301132. Movies Unlimited 121964. Republic Pictures Home Video MG301132.
208. "Nothing But Trouble" (1944) MGM/UA Home Video 20806. Movies Unlimited 122547
209. "The Oklahoman" (1957) Fox V7470
210. "One-Eyed Jacks" (1961) Facet Multimedia, Inc. S02558. Movies Unlimited 061104. Paramount Home Video 6537 & Beta. Pioneer Artists, Inc. LV6537-2 Laserdisc. Pioneer Artists, Inc. LV6537 Letterbox. UAV Corp. 5459
211. "The Princess and the Pirate" (1944) HBO 90666. Movies Unlimited 441832. Newline Home Video 3057 & Beta & Laserdisc
212. "Pursued" (1947) Facet Multimedia, Inc. S04297. Republic Pictures Home Video 3326
213. "Rage at Dawn" (1955) A&E Home Video 4179. General Video & Beta. Timeless Video, Inc. 2134. World Artists Home Video 1068
214. "Ramrod" (1947) Republic Pictures Home Video 3370
215. "Road House" (1948) Facet Multimedia, Inc. S13615. Fox Video 1848. Movies Unlimited 2409
216. "Road to Rio" (1947) Columbia/Tristar 60870. Movies Unlimited 021816. Republic Pictures Home Video C060870
217. "Samson and Delilah" (1949) Facet Multimedia, Inc. S04340. Magnum Entertainment, Inc. G100 & Beta. Paramount Home Video 6726 & Beta. Paramount Home Video LV6726 Laserdisc
218. "Sergeant York" (1941) Facet Multimedia, Inc. S01868. Facet Multimedia, Inc. LD71642 Laserdisc. Key Video 4580 & Beta. MGM/UA Home Video M301758. MGM/UA Home Video ML101758 Laserdisc. Republic Pictures Home Video MG301758
219. "Shadow of the Thin Man" (1941) MGM
220. "The Snake Pit" (1948) Fox Video V1982. Fox Video V198280 Laserdisc. Movies Unlimited 042623
221. "Strange Cargo" (1940) MGM/UA Home Video M301589. Movies Unlimited 122008. Republic Pictures Home Video MG200793
222. "They Died with Their Boots On" (1941) MGM/UA Home Video M201473. MGM/UA Home Video M201857 Colorized); Movies Unlimited 122036. Republic Pictures Home Video MG201473
223. "The Thin Man Goes Home" (1944) MGM/UA Home Video M300970. Republic Pictures Home Video M970
224. "Thousands Cheer" (1943) MGM/UA Home Video M300984. MGM/UA Home Video ML100984 Laserdisc
225. "Till the Cloud Rolls By" (1946) A&E Entertainment 4027. Discount Video Tapes 20170R9134 & Beta. Film Classics 108 & Beta. General Video GV64. Media Home Entertainment M128 & Beta. MGM ML10094 Laserdisc. MGM/UA Home Video M700094. Nostalgia Family Video 1844. Republic Pictures Home Video MG700094. UAV Corporation 4023. Video Yesteryear 134 & Beta. Volencia Entertainment Corporation V708
226. "The Wild One" (1954) Columbia/Tristar 6623. Columbia/Tristar 78413. Columbia/Tristar 3623 Laserdisc. Columbia/Tristar 79636 Laserdisc restored
227. "Winchester '73" (1950) MCA/Universal Home Video 80325. MCA/Universal Home Video 40325 Laserdisc. Movies Unlimited 071389

228. "Wing and a Prayer" (1944) Fox Video V1910. Movies Unlimited 042459
229. "Woman of the Year" (1942) Facet Multimedia, Inc. S04741. Facet Multimedia, Inc. LD70710 Laserdisc. MGM/UA Home Video M600093. MGM/UA Home Video M100093 Laserdisc. Movies Unlimited 121092
230. "Wonder Man" (1945) HBO 90663 & Beta. Movies Unlimited 441843. MLHV 3078 & Beta. Pioneer Artists, Inc. PSE94-46LD Laserdisc
231. "Ziegfeld Follies" (1945) Facet Multimedia, Inc. S4407. MGM/UA Home Video M600173. MGM/UA Home Video M204761. MGM/UA Home Video M304978 (Collector's Edition & CD); MGM/UA Home Video ML100173 Laserdisc. Republic Pictures Home Video 600173
232. "Ziegfeld Girl" (1941) MGM/UA 301585
233. "Zorro Rides Again" (1937) Captain Bijou 020V. Nostalgia Family Video 1273. Pioneer Artists, Inc. 24770 Laserdisc. Republic Pictures Home Video 4770. Vid-America, Inc. Video Yesteryear 199 & Beta

Bing Russell

234. "The Apple Dumpling Gang" (1975) Walt Disney Home Video 4133. Walt Disney Home Video 018 Beta. Walt Disney Home Video 018 ASLD Laserdisc
235. "Billy the Kid vs. Dracula" (1966) Facet Multimedia, Inc. S05483. Movies Unlimited 0915540. Newline Home Video 2099 & Beta. Nostalgia Family Video 2363. Something Weird Video V. Video Yesteryear 146 & Beta
236. "Cheyenne Autumn" (1964) Facet Multimedia, Inc. S04195. Movies Unlimited 191465. Warner Home Video 11052 & Beta
237. "The Computer Wore Tennis Shoes" (1970) Walt Disney Home Video 151 & Beta (1970); Walt Disney Home Video 9839 (1998)
238. "Death Sentence" (1974) Prism Entertainment 1915. Timeless Video, Inc. 98233
239. "Fear Strikes Out" (1957) Movies Unlimited 061706. Paramount Home Video & Beta. Paramount Home Video LV5607 Laserdisc
240. "A Gathering of Eagles" (1963) MGM/UA Home Video
241. "Gunfight at the O.K. Corral" (1957) Facet Multimedia, Inc. S10837. Paramount Home Video 6218 & Beta & Laserdisc
242. "The Hallelujah Trail" (1965) Facet Multimedia, Inc. S14098. Facet Multimedia, Inc. LD7053 Laserdisc. MGM/UA Home Video M302176. MGM/UA Home Video M102176 Laserdisc. Republic Pictures Home Video MG302176
243. "The Horse Soldiers" (1959) Facet Multimedia, Inc. S12138. Facet Multimedia, Inc. LD71664 Laserdisc. MGM/UA Home Video M201772. Pioneer Artists, Inc. ML 101772 Laserdisc & Letterbox. RCA 01438 (CED); Republic Pictures Home Video MG201772
244. "Last Train from Gun Hill" (1959) CBS/Fox Video 2018 & Beta
245. "The Loneliest Runner" (1990) Goodtimes Home Video 9109. Movies Unlimited 191375. Warner Home Video 29014 & Beta
246. "Madame X" (1966) MCA/Universal Home Video 80154. Movies Unlimited 071290
247. "The Magnificent Seven" (1960) CBS/Fox Video & Beta & CED. CBS/Fox Video 55380 Laserdisc. Columbia/Tristar 7082. MGM/UA Home Video M201268. MGM/Universal Video M101563 Laserdisc & Letterbox. Movies Unlimited 121766. Republic Pictures Home Video MG201258. Vid-America, Inc. 7082 & Beta
248. "Million Dollar Duck" (1971) Walt Disney Home Video 57 & Beta
249. "Now You See Him Now You Don't" (1972) Walt Disney Home Video 80 & Beta
250. "Rio Bravo" (1959) Facet Multimedia, Inc. S035588. Facet Multimedia, Inc. LD1679 Laserdisc. RCA CED. Republic Pictures Home Video UA11050 & Laserdisc

251. "Satan's School for Girls" (1973) Prism Entertainment 1912. Timeless Video, Inc. 98313
252. "Stakeout" (1962) Loonic Video. Movies Unlimited 688839. Sinister Cinema M218
253. "The Stripper" (1963) Fox Video V1500. Movies Unlimited 041990
254. "Suicide Battalion" (1958) Columbia/Tristar Home Video 51053. Movies Unlimited 022182. Double set includes *Hell Squad*
255. "Sunset" (1984) Columbia/Tristar Home Video 27009. Columbia/Tristar Home Video 67009. Facet Multimedia, Inc. S07950. Movies Unlimited 502050. Movies Unlimited 021874
256. "Tarantula" (1955) MCA/Universal Home Video 45026
257. "Yuma" (1971) Fox Video V8093

David Canary

258. *All My Children* "Behind the Scenes" (1994) ABC 42120
259. *All My Children* "Daytime's Greatest Weddings" (1993); ABC
260. "The Dain Curse" (1972) Enterprise Home Video 2011 (10th Anniversary of Dashiell Hammett); Newline Home Video 1800 & Beta
261. "Hombre" (1967) Fox Video V1012. Fox Video V1012 Laserdisc & Letterbox
262. "Johnny Firecloud" (1975) Prism Entertainment 1652
263. "Melvin Purvis: G-Men" (1974) HBO 90012. Movies Unlimited 441484
264. "Memories with Laughter and Love" (1993) Genesis Entertainment 1001
265. "Posse" (1975) Paramount Home Video 8316. Paramount Home Video LV8316 Laserdisc
266. "Shark's Treasure" (1975) MGM/UA Home Video M600406
267. "The St. Valentine's Massacre" (1967) Facet Multimedia, Inc. S13617. Fox Video V1153. Movies Unlimited 041924

Mitch Vogel

268. "Born Innocent" (1974) Movies Unlimited 595023. UAV Corporation 5919. Western World Video, Inc. 1008
269. "The Reivers" (1969) Fox Video V7153. Movies Unlimited 041821
270. "Texas Detour" (1978) Prism Entertainment 1955
271. "Yours, Mine and Ours" (1968) MGM/UA Home Video M201702. MGM/UA Home Video M101702 Laserdisc. Movies Unlimited 121912

Lou Frizzell

272. "Capricorn One" (1978) CBS/Fox Video 9007 & Beta. CBS/Fox Video 900780 Laserdisc. Live Home Entertainment 51090. UAV Corporation 5991
273. "Devil Dog: The Hound of Hell" (1978) Live Home Entertainment 9505
274. "The Front Page" (1974) Facet Multimedia, Inc. S16152. MCA/Universal Home Video 66036. MCA/Universal Home Video 16002 Laserdisc. Movies Unlimited 071798
275. "Lawman" (1971) MGM/UA Home Video 202960

276. "Manhunter" (1974) Movies Unlimited 143107. Republic Pictures Home Video 4048 & Beta. Trans-world Entertainment V. Warner Home Video 411 & Beta & Laserdisc
277. "The Other" (1972) Fox Video V1729
278. "Rage" (1972) Movies Unlimited 191523. Warner Home Video 11428 & Beta
279. "The Reivers" (1969) Fox Video V7153. Movies Unlimited 041821
280. "The Stalking Moon" (1969) Ace Video. Warner Home Video
281. "Steel Cowboy" (1978) Interglobal Video 1369. M.C.E.G./Sterling. VCL VL9046 & Beta
282. "Summer of '42" (1971) Movies Unlimited 191047. Warner Home Video 1033 & Beta & Laserdisc
283. "Tell Them Willie Boy is Here" (1965) MCA/Universal Home Video 55084. MCA/Universal Home Video 41398 Laserdisc & Letterbox

Tim Matheson

284. "The Apple Dumpling Gang Rides Again" (1979) Walt Disney Home Video 26 & Beta
285. "The Best Legs in the 8th Grade" (1984) Live Home Entertainment 9025. Movies Unlimited 473057
286. "Black Sheep" (1996) Paramount Home Video 33242
287. "Blind Justice" (1986) Fox Video V6163. Movies Unlimited 041058
288. "Buried Alive" (1990)
289. *Classic Jonny Quest* "Adventures Best Friend" (1996)
290. *Classic Jonny Quest* "An Army of One" (1996) Turner Home Entertainment H1189
291. *Classic Jonny Quest* "Master of Evil" (1996); Turner Home Entertainment H1187
292. *Classic Jonny Quest* "Mysteries of the East" (1996); Turner Home Video H1188
293. "Dreamer" (1979) CBS/Fox Video 1096 & Beta
294. "Drop Dead Fred" (1990) Live Home Entertainment 68954 & Laserdisc. Movies Unlimited 276724
295. "Eye of the Demon" (1981) V&E Entertainment 5305. V&E Entertainment (Spanish dubbed)
296. "Fletch" (1985) MCA/Universal Home Video 80190. MCA/Universal Home Video 40190 Laserdisc. Movies Unlimited 071324
297. "How to Commit Marriage" (1969) Columbia/Tristar Home Video. Movies Unlimited 022386
298. "Impulse" (1984) Paramount Home Video 41059. Vestron Video 5066 & Laserdisc
299. "Jonny Quest" (1964) Image Entertainment, Inc. ID6610HA Laserdisc. Junior Home Video 131811
300. "Jonny Quest" (1964) "Artic Splash Down," "The Curse of Anufis," "Mystery of the Lizard Man"; Republic Pictures Home Video 1083 & Beta
301. Jonny's Golden Quest; Turner Home Entertainment H1020
302. Jonny Quest Volume 1 "Pirates from Below" (1964) "Invisible Monster," "Pirates from Below," "Werewolf of the Timberland"; Turner Home Entertainment 1225 & Beta
303. Jonny Quest Volume 2 "Tur the Terrible" (1964); Turner Home Entertainment 1305 & Beta
304. Jonny Quest Volume 3 "The Q Missle Mystery" (1964) Turner Home Entertainment 1306 & Beta
305. Jonny Quest Volume 4 "Monsters in the Monastery" (1964); Image Entertainment, Inc. ID8386 HA Laserdisc; Turner Home Entertainment 1307 & Beta
306. Jonny Quest vs. the Cyber Insects (1996); Turner Home Entertainment H1120
307. Listen to Your Heart (1983); Fox Video V7058; Movies Unlimited 041677
308. A Little Sex (1982); MCA/Universal Home Video 55079. Movies Unlimited 071118

309. Little White Lies (1989); Movies Unlimited 155213. Rhino Video 7914
310. The Longest Drive (1985); V&E Entertainment 5233 & Laserdisc
311. Magnum Force (1973); Movies Unlimited 191010. RCA CED. Warner Home Video 1039 & Beta & Laserdisc. Warner Home Video 6022 Spanish Subtitles
312. Mary White (1977); Movies Unlimited 061283. Paramount Home Video 2377 & Beta
313. National Lampoon's Animal House (1978); MCA/Universal Home Video 66000 & Spanish Subtitles. MCA/Universal Home Video 16007 Laserdisc. Movies Unlimited 071013
314. 1941 (1979); MCA/Universal Home Video 66007. MCA/Universal Home Video 16014 Laserdisc. Movies Unlimited 071024
315. Quicksand: No Escape (1991); MCA/Universal Home Video 81275. MCA/Universal Home Video 41275 Laserdisc
316. The Runaway Barge (1975); Live Home Entertainment 66372 & Beta
317. Solar Crisis (1992); CVM 5622 WS Laserdisc. Movies Unlimited 681255. Pioneer Artists, Inc. Laserdisc. V&E Entertainment 5622.
318. Sometimes They Come Back (1991); V&E Entertainment 5506 & Spanish Subtitles. V&E Entertainment LD5506 Laserdisc.
319. Speed Zone (1989); Media Home Entertainment MO 12392 & Beta
320. Tails You Live, Heads You're Dead (1995); Paramount Home Video 83469 & Beta
321. To Be or Not to Be (1983); Fox Video V1336; Fox Video V133680 Laserdisc. Movies Unlimited 041688.
322. Up the Creek (1984); Live Home Entertainment 5043 & Laserdisc
323. A Very Brady Sequel (1996); Paramount Home Video 332443
324. Yours, Mine and Ours (1968); MGM/UA Home Video M201702; MGM/UA Home Video M101702 Laserdisc; Movies Unlimited 121912

Guy Williams

325. Captain Sinbad (1963); Facet Multimedia, Inc. S16846; MGM/UA Home Video 200630
326. I Was a Teenage Werewolf (1957); Facet Multimedia, Inc. S146275; Movies Unlimited 020274; RCA/Columbia Pictures Home Video 60906; Republic Pictures Home Video CO60906; Sinister Cinema S179
327. Lost in Space "The Derelict" (1997); 20th Century–Fox Home Entertainment 6673
328. Lost in Space "The Hungry Sea" (1998); 20th Century–Fox Home Entertainment 0398
329. Lost in Space "Island in the Sky" (1997); 20th Century–Fox Home Entertainment 6674
330. Lost in Space "The Reluctant Stowaway" (1997); 20th Century–Fox Home Entertainment (1997)
331. Lost in Space "There Were Giants in the Earth" (1998); 20th Century–Fox Home Entertainment 0346
332. Lost in Space "Welcome Stranger" (1998); 20th Century–Fox Home Entertainment 0347
333. The Man from the Alamo (1981); Kartes 329-0 & Beta; MCA/Universal Home Video 80629; Nova Entertainment, Inc. NO5189
334. Prince and the Pauper (1962); Walt Disney Home Video 0179 & Beta; Walt Disney Home Video Spanish Dubbed
335. Sincerely Yours (1955); Movies Unlimited 191574; Warner Home Video 11733 Beta & laserdisc
336. The Sign of Zorro (1958); Walt Disney Home Video 47 & Beta

Bibliography

This chapter is divided into two sections. The first includes newspaper and magazine articles. The second includes books.

Newspapers and Magazines

"Actor's Grave Is Still Visited by Hundreds." *Houston Chronicle*. December 31, 1984
"The All-Time Best TV Readers' Edition." *TV Guide*. June 19, 1993.
Amory, Cleveland. "*Little House on the Prairie* Review." *TV Guide*. January 4, 1975.
_____. "Review — Griff." *TV Guide*. December 15, 1973.
Appelo, Tim. "The Sons Also Ride." *Entertainment Weekly*. July 16, 1993.
Ardmore, Jane. "Adorable? That's the Story of My Life!" *Photoplay*. February 1961.
Atkinson, Brooks. "Theatre: *Edwin Booth*." *New York Times*. November 2, 1958.
_____. "Theatre: *The Lovers*." *New York Times*. May 12, 1956.
_____. "Theatre: *Magic Fails the Magician*." *New York Times*. September 17, 1955.
_____. "Theatre: New Shylock." *New York Times*. July 1, 1955.
Beck, Marilyn. "After 20 Years on TV, Landon has Changed A Lot." *The Evening Bulletin*.July 29, 1978.
_____. "Kindness of Strangers." *TV Guide*. October 6, 1990.
_____. "Next: *Bonanza* Junior" *TV Guide*. February 8, 1992.
_____. "This Time He'll Make No Waves." *The Sunday Bulletin*. June 3, 1979.
Bianculli, David. "Nice Job, Michael — Landon's Legacy of Good Work." *New York Post*. July 2, 1991.
"*Bonanza*." *Entertainment Weekly*. July 20, 1990.
Breig, James. "TV at 50: Assessing the Golden Jubilarian." *Our Sunday Visitor*. July 23, 1989.
Brenna, Tony, and Donna Rosenthal. "Michael Landon and Wife Split." *National Enquirer*. July 8, 1980.

Buck, Jerry. "Familiar Characterizations in *Trapper John*." *The Gloucester County Times.* September 23, 1979.

Bury, Lee. "Michael Landon to Rescue in Real Fire Drama." *The Star.* January 22, 1980.

Caldwell, Kate, Diane Manning, Dave LaFontaine. "Landon Widow's $50M Promise: I'll Keep His Dream Alive." *Star.* July 23, 1991.

Callum, Myles. "The Totally Surprising *Bonanza* Photo Quiz." *TV Guide.* November 27, 1993.

Canape, Charlene. "*Bonanza's* Little Joe Still a Hero." *Daily Times.*

Carlson, Timothy. "How Michael Landon's Brave Struggle with Cancer Has Inspired America." *TV Guide.* June 8, 1991. [Landon on Cover]

_____. "Little Michael Is Little Joe." *TV Guide.* June 27, 1992.

_____. "Michael Landon's Final Days." *TV Guide.* July 20, 1991. [Landon on Cover]

_____. "What Michael Means to Us." *TV Guide.* July 13, 1991. [Michael on Cover]

Case, Beverly. "Archive Notes." *Museum Life.* Summer 1984.

Castleman, Deke. "Virginia City." *Historic Traveler.* May/June 1995.

Chapman, Francesca. "TV's Landon Dead at 54." *The Philadelphia Daily News.* July 2, 1991.

Cook, Anthony. "When Lady Luck Smiled, He Kicked Her in the Teeth." *TV Guide.* November 24, 1979.

Coole, Amy. "Michael Landon in Shock." *TV Star Parade.* March 1975.

"Dan Blocker Dies; Buried at DeKalb." *Alpine Avalanche.* May 18, 1972.

Davidson, Bill. "Michael Landon General Contractor." *TV Guide.* December 7, 1974.

De la Vina, Mark. "His Early Days Were Fun, Pals Recall." *Philadelphia Daily News.* July 2, 1991.

"Died, Lorne Greene." *Time.* September 21, 1987.

Dubrow, Rick. "A New *Bonanza* Joins an Array of Shows That Ailing NBC Let Get Away." *The Philadelphia Inquirer.* October 27, 1992.

"Dum-Tiddle-Dum." *Newsweek.* April 23, 1962.

Dunne, John Gregory. "…And Now to the Nugget." *TV Guide.*

"Dying Landon Reconciled with Ex-Wife and Changed His $250M Will." *Globe.* July 23, 1991.

"Earthquake!" *Screen Stories.* February 1975.

Elkin, Michael. "Landon Travels *Highway to Heaven*." *Jewish Exponent.* March 15, 1985.

_____. "TV: Michael Landon Lands a Winner." *Jewish Exponent Extra.* January 26, 1990.

Esterly, Glenn. "From Grandfather to Grandson." *TV Guide.* January 27, 1990.

"Exes Honor Blocker, May." *President's Perspective.* September 1987.

"Farewell." *People Weekly.* December 30, 1991–January 6, 1992.

Farr, Louise, "Michael Landon." *Ladies' Home Journal.* June 1979.

"50 Greatest TV Stars of All Time." *TV Guide.* December 14- 20, 1996.

"The First Look at Michael Landon's Last TV Show." *TV Guide.* September 7, 1991.

Flannery, Mary. "He Fought a Good Fight." *Philadelphia Daily News.* July 2, 1991.

Flint, Peter. D. "Michael Landon, 54, Little Joe on *Bonanza* for 14 Years, Dies." *The New York Times.* July 2, 1991.

"For Michael Landon Happiness Is a Slice of Salami." *TV Guide.* November 29, 1969.

Fowler, Glenn. "Guy Williams, TV and Film Actor Who Played Zorro Is Dead at 65." *The New York Times.* May 1989.

Freeman, Donald. "Mike Landon Daydreams. If the Boys from the Ponderosa Met the *High Chaparral* Guys…" *The Philadelphia Evening Bulletin.* June 22, 1969.

Furse, Jane. "Michael Landon Dead." *New York Post.* July 2, 1991.

Gardella, Kay. "All's Angelic on New Landon Series." *Philadelphia Daily News.* July 25, 1984.

_____. "Heaven's Third Year." *Philadelphia Daily News.* June 26, 1986.

"The Gift of Laughter." *People Weekly.* September 23, 1991.

Gliatto, Tom, Kristina Johnson, and Vicki Sheff. "Michael Landon's Legacy of Love." *People Weekly.* February 10, 1992.

Goodman, Mark, Lois Armstrong, Joyce Wagner, and Jack Kelley. "Michael Landon." *People Weekly.* July 15, 1991. [Cover Story]

Graham, Jefferson, and Karen Thomas. "America's Family Man to the End." *USA Today.* July 2, 1991.

Greene, Lorne. "I Ignored My Hearing Problems and Hurt the Family I Loved." *National Enquirer.* November 8, 1983.

Grehen, Ellen. "Dying Michael Landon Begs Daughter, 20, Not to Marry." *Globe.* June 4, 1991.

_____. "So Long Little Joe." *Globe.* July 16, 1991.

Haley, Larry. "Michael Landon's Dying Wish." *National Enquirer.* June 4, 1991.

_____. "Who Gets What in His New $100 Million Will." *National Enquirer.* July 23, 1991.

Harris, Harry. "Ever the Dad, on the Range or in Space." *The Philadelphia Inquirer TV Week.* September 17, 1978.

_____. "Is It All That Warm on Landon's Prairie?" *The Philadelphia Inquirer TV Week.* December 22, 1974.

Hastings, Deborah. "Landon Eulogized as Man of Integrity." *Chicago Sun Times.* July 6, 1991.

_____. "Landon Loses War." *Delaware County Daily Times.* July 2, 1991.

Hawkins, Dan. "A Very Public Death." *The Philadelphia Daily News.* July 2, 1991.

"He's Still Going Strong, Actor Lorne Greene Thrives on Jet Lag, Creativity." *Delaware County Daily Times.* April 14, 1982.

Hoffman, Greg, and Lorraine Tilden. "Lorne Greene Battles New Health Crisis." *Star.* September 8, 1987.

Holt, Toni. "A Visit with Lorne and Nancy Greene." *Movie Life.* February 22, 1979.

Hudson, Edward. "Lorne Greene, TV Patriarch, Is Dead." *The New York Times.* September 12, 1987.

Humphrey, Hal. "Freedom Is Better Than Riches, Says *Bonanza* Dropout Roberts." *The Philadelphia Sunday Bulletin.* April 30, 1967.

_____. "Lorne Greene, Man of All Causes." *The Philadelphia Evening Bulletin.*

"IRS Chasing Lorne Greene in Tax Shelter Case." *The Philadelphia Evening Bulletin.* January 6, 1981.

Johnson, John J. "*I Was a Teenage Werewolf!* A Tribute to Michael Landon." *Movie Collector's World.* August 2, 1991.

Kain, Larry. "Mike Landon Confesses: I'm so Jealous I Won't Even Leave Wife Alone Overnight!" *Screen Stars.*

Keyes, Stacie. "Little Joe's Beautiful Baby Girl." *TV Radio Mirror.*

Kleiner, Dick. "Cops, Crooks, Are Taking Over TV Season." *Delaware County Daily Times* September 5, 1973.

Klemesrud, Judy. "The Man Who Struck It Rich with *Bonanza.*" *New York Times.* October 8, 1972.

Kluge, P. K. "Lunch Is 7/10ths of an Hour. A Day on the Set of *Little House on the Prairie.*" *TV Guide.* July 5, 1980.

Kogan, Rick. "Actor, Director Michael Landon, 54." *Chicago Tribune.* July 2, 1991.

LaFontaine, Dave. "Landon's Legacy to the Children of America." *Star.* September 24, 1991.

_____. "Son Waged Secret Battle with Stingy NBC to Air 2-Hour Tribute. *Star.* September 24, 1991.

Landon, Cindy. "Life Without Michael." *Ladies' Home Journal.* May 1992.

Landon, Michael. "If I'm Going to Die, Death's Gonna Have to Fight to Get Me." *Life.* June 1991.

_____. "Why Christmas Is Special to Me." *National Enquirer.* December 25, 1979.

"Landon's a Nice Guy." *The Philadelphia Bulletin.* August 4, 1980.

Larson, Peter. "Hundreds Visit the Texas Grave of Hoss Cartwright." *The Philadelphia Inquirer.* January 20, 1985.

Levy, Paul F. "Nice Guy Michael Landon Becomes a Nasty Wise Guy." *National Enquirer.* August 19, 1980.

Lewis, Dennis. "The Night Mike Landon Went After His Wife with a Gun!" *TV and Movie Screen.*

Licklider, Deborah. "Landon and Co-stars Were a *Bonanza* for '60s Families." *Philadelphia Daily News.* July 2, 1991.

"Lorne Greene: God Gave Me a Second Chance!" *TV and Movie Screen.*

Lowry, Cynthia. "Cartwrights Build 20th Century Ponderosa." *Philadelphia Evening Bulletin.* December 29, 1968.

Lynne, Jerrie. "I Had a Sex Operation and Almost Destroyed My Wife!" *TV Radio Talk.* November 1974.

Markfield, Alan. "Michael Landon: I Work for My Wife and Kids — Not for Money or Glory." *National Enquirer.* January 6, 1976.

Marvin, Murray. "Landon Directs 1st *Bonanza.*" *Philadelphia Inquirer.* May 3, 1968.

Mays, Doug, Sammie Mays, and Martin Drydan. "Star's Funeral Filled with Love and Laughter." *National Enquirer.* July 23, 1991.

McGovern, Michael. "Michael Landon Rides Off." *Daily News.* July 2, 1991.

"Michael Landon." *Movie Life Yearbook.* 1968.

"Michael Landon, Jr.— A Tough Trail to Follow." *TV Guide.* August 7, 1993.

"Michael Landon: My Parents' Fighting Led Me Into Acting." *National Enquirer.* February 22, 1983.

"Michael Landon Tops Parade of Superstars." *Star.* August 27, 1991.

"Michael Landon's Fight to Live with Courage and Character." *People Weekly.* May 6, 1991.

"Michael Landon's Happiest Family Memories." *Star.* July 16, 1991.

"Michael Landon's Intimate Life Story: How TV Superstar Escaped Crazy Mom and Taunts of School Pals." *Star.* July 2, 1991.

"Michael Landon's Secret Dream That Never Came True." *National Examiner.* July 23, 1991.

"Mickey Mouse Thrills Michael Landon's Son." *National Enquirer.* July 25, 1978.

Mitchell, Lisa. "Michael Landon: Big Man in a Little House." *The Saturday Evening Post.* September 1980.

Murdock, Henry T. "*Tonight in Samarkand* at Forrest." *The Philadelphia Inquirer.* January 26, 1955.

Murphy, Mary. "Michael Landon — The Star Who Must Have Control." *TV Guide.* January 9, 1982. [Landon on Cover]

_____. "What Michael Landon Left Behind." *TV Guide.* June 27, 1992.

"My Darkest Hours — And How I Licked Drink and Drugs." *Star.* July 9, 1991.

"My Three Prayers Were Answered." *Screen Play.* September 1964.

Nelander, John. "Michael Landon's Son Brings TV's Little Joe Back to Life!" *Globe.* March 10, 1992.

New York Times. August 27, 1958. [Review of Lorne Greene in *This Is Edwin Booth*]

Nicholis, Nick, C. "Lorne Greene." *Classic Images.*

Nolan, Patricia. "The Way They Were ... Michael Landon." *Rona Barrett's Hollywood.* 1979.

Norbom, Mary Ann. "Landon Is Expanding His Power Base." *Philadelphia Inquirer.* August 10, 1982.

"100 Most Memorable Moments in TV History." *TV Guide.* June 29, 1996.

"On Location with ... *Little House on the Prairie*" *Rona Barrett's Gossip.* April 1975. [Landon on Cover]

"Our 40th Anniversary Show: A Special Celebration." *TV Guide*. December 18, 1993.

Pearson, Jennifer, Roger Hitts, Dave LaFontaine, and Diane Mannino. "Michael Landon: Bury Me Next to Lorne Greene." *Star*. June 11, 1991.

Perel, David, Barbara Sternig, and Ed Susman. *"Bonanza* Star's Last, Courageous Days — Gutsy Lorne Greene Refused Pain Killers to Die with Dignity." *National Enquirer*. September 29, 1987.

Polier, Rex. "It's Hard to Get Fired Up Over This One." *The Philadelphia Bulletin*. September 23, 1981.

_____. *"Little House* Was Built from Landon's Blueprint." *The Philadelphia Sunday Bulletin TV Time*. January 5, 1975.

Poppy, John. "The Worldwide Lure of *Bonanza*." *Look*. December 1, 1964.

"Raised Ranch." *Entertainment Weekly*. November 26, 1993.

Reilly, Sue. "Michael Landon's Amazing Kids." *People Weekly*. September 11, 1978.

Resnick, Sylvia. "Landons Lose Expected Baby." *Photoplay*. July 1969.

"Reunion in Arizona — The Professor and 2 of His Boys'." *The Alpine Avalanche*. April 5, 1962.

"The Role Michael Landon Wants to Forget." *Globe*. August 31, 1982.

"Scholarship Honors Blocker." *Alpine Avalanche*. May 18, 1972.

Schwarzbaum, Lisa. "A Hero with Heart." *Entertainment Weekly*. July 12, 1991.

Scott, Vernon. "Big Dan Blocker, *Bonanza*'s Most Lovable Lout." *The Philadelphia Evening Bulletin*. January 5, 1969.

Seay, Sue. "Dan Blocker, TV's Gentle Giant." *Look*. January 30, 1962.

"Secret Story Behind Michael Landon's Brave Interview with Johnny Carson." *Star*. May 28, 1991.

Sensenderfer, R. E. P. *"Tonight in Samarkand* Is New Play at Forrest." *The Philadelphia Evening Bulletin*. January 26, 1955.

Shea, Kathleen. *"Bonanza* Slips in Appeal." *The Philadelphia Daily News*. November 26, 1993.

Shull, Richard K. "Little Joe Writes and Directs to Keep Mind off Small Worries." *The Philadelphia Inquirer*. March 7, 1969.

Sobelle, Edy. "The Woman Who Gave Lorne Greene a Heart Attack!" *TV Radio Show*.

Sternig, Barbara. "Michael Landon Compares His Two Wives." *National Enquirer*.

_____. "Michael Landon — His Brave Final Days at Home with His Loving Family." *National Enquirer*. June 25, 1991.

_____. "Michael Landon Tries Last-Ditch Cancer Vaccine — The Untold Story." *National Enquirer*. May 28, 1991.

_____. "Michael Landon's Courageous Final Hours." *National Enquirer*. July 16, 1991.

_____. "Michael Landon's Smile Hides a Tragic Past." *National Enquirer*. January 3, 1979.

_____, and Tony Brenna. "Landon's Widow Reveals Michael's Inspiring Last Message." *National Enquirer*. July 23, 1991.

Storm, Jonathon. "Actor Michael Landon, 54, Dies of Cancer." *The Philadelphia Inquirer*. July 2, 1991.

_____. "Family Tale Is Landon's Final Movie." *The Philadelphia Inquirer*. September 20, 1991.

"Sul Ross Ceremonies Pay Tribute to Harley May and Dan Blocker." *Alpine Avalanche*. July 30, 1987.

"Sul Ross Play Well Received." *El Paso Times*.

"The Sunny Life of Mike Landon." *Movie Life Yearbook*. 1966.

Thall, Bernice. "Lorne Greene Barred from Mike Landon's Show." *Movieland and TV Time*.

"They Landed in the Hoosegow." *The Alpine Avalanche*. May 28, 1948.

Tilden, Lorraine. "Lorne's Last Wish." *Star*. September 29, 1987.

Trebbe, Ann, and Jefferson Graham. "TV's 'Dear Friend' Landon Dies." *USA Today.* July 2, 1991.

Tucker, Ken. "Landon and 'US'." *Entertainment Weekly.* September 20, 1991.

_____. "Promised Landon." *Entertainment Weekly.* July 11, 1997.

Tusher, Bill. "Mixed Marriage Made Me a Man." *Photoplay.* April 1965.

TV Guide. May 21, 1997. [Color Photo of David Canary with Small Article]

Unger, Arthur. "*Last of the Wild* Helps Greene Forget *Griff.*" *The Philadelphia Inquirer TV Week.* March 16, 1975.

Variety. September 25, 1963 [Review of "She Walks in Beauty" Episode]

_____. September 20, 1964. [Review of "Invention of a Gunfighter" Episode]

_____. May 5, 1965. [Review of Lorne Greene's Act at Nugget Sparks, Nevada]

_____. September 15, 1965. [Review of "The Debt" Episode]

_____. April 13, 1966. [Review of Michael Landon's Act at Nugget Sparks, Nevada]

_____. September 21, 1966. [Review of "A Horse of a Different Hue" Episode]

_____. March 22, 1967. [Review of Dan Blocker's Act at Nugget Sparks, Nevada]

_____. September 18, 1968. [Review of "Different Pines — Same Wind" Episode]

_____. September 24, 1969. [Review of "Another Windmill to Go" Episode]

_____. September 23, 1970. [Review of "The Night Virginia City Died" Episode]

_____. September 19, 1971. [Review of "The Grand Swing" Episode]

_____. September 20, 1972. [Review of "Forever" Episode]

Von Furstenberg, Betsy. "My Favorite Summer Vacation." *Good Housekeeping.* September 1980.

Weston, Wilma. "Irresistible Lorne Greene What's the Secret of His Sex Appeal?" *TV Star Parade.* March 1974.

Whitney, Dwight. "Patriarch of the Ponderosa." *TV Guide.* 1961.

_____. "What Makes Pernell Roberts So Angry?" *TV Guide.* October 30, 1982. Roberts is on cover]

Wilcox, Janie. "Michael Landon's Prayers Come True!" *TV Picture Life.*

Wright, David, and Bennet Bulton. "Landon's Widow in Tears." *National Enquirer.* August 27, 1991.

Books

Aaker, Everett. *Television Western Players of the Fifties: A Biographical Encyclopedia of All Regular Cast Members in Western Series 1949–1959.* NC: McFarland, 1997.

Adams, Les, and Buck Rainey. *The Complete Reference Guide to Westerns of the Sound Era Shoot-em Ups.* NY: Arlington House, 1978.

Baker, Mark Allen. *Collector's Guide to Celebrity Autographs.* WI: Krause Publications, 1996.

Barabas, Suzanne, and Gabor Barabas. *Gunsmoke: A Complete History.* NC: McFarland, 1990.

Big Book of Movie and TV Themes. Hal Leonard Publishing Corp., 1993.

Book of Knowledge. "Television Starts in Canada" [Entry Written by Lorne Greene], 1951.

Brooks, Tim. *The Complete Directory to Prime Time TV Stars 1946–Present.* NY: Ballantine Books, 1987.

Burlingame, Jon. *TV's Biggest Hits: The Story of Television Themes from Dragnet to Friends.* NY: Schirmer Books, 1996.

Buscombe, Edward, editor. *The BFI Companion to the Western.* NY: Atheneom, 1988.

Castleman, Deke. *Nevada Handbook* [3rd Edition]. CA: Moon Publications, 1993.

Castleman, Harry, and Walter J. Podrazik. *Watching TV: Four Decades of American Television.* NY: McGraw-Hill, 1982.

Corey, Melinda, and George Ochoa. *A Cast of Thousands: A Compendium of Who Played What in Film. Volume One: The Cast A–L. Volume Two: The Casts M–Z & Index of Directors. Volume Three: Index of Actors.* NY: Facts on File, 1992.

Cotter, Bill. *The Wonderful World of Disney.* NY: Hyperion, 1997.

Curtis, Sandra. *Zorro Unmasked: The Official History.* NY: Hyperion, 1998.

Cusic, Don. *Cowboys and the Wild West: An A–Z Guide from the Chisholm Trail to the Silver Screen.* NY: Facts on File, 1994.

Daly, Marsha. *Michael Landon: A Biography.* NY: St. Martin's Press, 1987.

D'Angelo, Rudy A. *Television's Cowboys, Gunfighters & Cap Pistols.* VA: Antique Trader Books, 1999.

Denis, Christopher Paul, and Michael Denis. *Favorite Families of TV.* NJ: Citadel Press, 1992.

Dimmitt, Richard Bertrand. *An Actor Guide to the Talkies.* NJ: Scarecrow Press, 1967.

Flynn, Harry, and Pamela Flynn. *Michael Landon: Life, Love and Laughter.* CA: Pomegranite Press, 1991.

Gardfield, Brian. *Western Films: A Complete Guide.* NY: Rawson Associates, 1982.

Gianakos, Larry James. *Television Drama Series Programming: A Comprehensive Chronicle 1947–1959* (1980). *...1959–1975* (1978). *...1975–1980* (1981). *...1980–1982* (1983). *... 1982–1984* (1987). *...1984–1986* (1992). NJ: Scarecrow Press.

Gimarc, George, and Pat Reeder. *Hollywood HiFi Over 100 of the Most Outrageous Celebrity Recordings Ever.* NY: St. Martins, 1996.

Godin, Seth. *The Encyclopedia of Fictional People the Most Important Characters of the 20th Century.* NY: Boulevard Books, 1996.

Goldberg, Lee. *Unsold Television Pilots, 1955 Through 1988.* NC: McFarland, 1990.

Golden, Fran Wenograd. *TVacations: A Fun Guide to the Sites, the Stars, and the Inside Stories Behind Your Favorite TV Shows.* NY: Pocket Books, 1996.

Golden, J. David. *The Golden Age of Radio.* CT: Radio Yesteryear, 1998.

Goldstein, Fred, and Stan Goldstein. *Prime-Time Television: A Pictorial History from Milton Berle to "Falcon Crest."* NY: Crown Publishers, 1983.

Greenland, David R. *Bonanza: A Viewer's Guide to the TV Legend.* IL: R & G Productions, 1997.

Hale, Lee, and Richard D. Neely. *Backstage at The Dean Martin Show.* Taylor Publishing Co., 2000.

Hardy, Phil. *The Film Encylopedia—The Western.* NY: William Morrow, 1983.

Huxford, Sharon, and Bob Huxford. *Collector Books.* KY: Schroeder Publishing Co., 1995.

_____, and _____. *Schroeder's Collectible Toys, Antique to Modern Price Guide.* KY: Schroeder Publishing Co., 1995.

Inman, David. *The TV Encyclopedia: The Most Comprehensive Guide to Everybody Who's Anybody in Television.* NY: Perigee Books, 1991.

Ito, Tom. *Conversations with Michael Landon.* IL: Contemporary Books, 1992.

Jackson, Ronald. *Classic TV Westerns.* NY: Citadel Press, 1994.

Joyce, Aileen. *Michael Landon: His Triumph and Tragedy.* NY: Zebra Books, 1991.

Katz, Ephraim. *The Film Encyclopedia,* 3rd ed. NY: Harper-Collins, 1998.

Key, Donald R.. *The Round-Up: A Pictorial History of Western Movie & Television Stars Through the Years.* NC: Empire Publishing, 1995.

Kwas, Michael H. *Hollywood Walk of Fame Directory.* CA: Curtis Management Group, 1993.

Lance, Steven. *Written Out of Television: A TV Lover's Guide to Cast Changes 1945–1994.* MD: Madison Books, 1996.

Landon, Cheryl. *I Promised My Dad.* NY: Simon and Schuster, 1992.

Leiby, Bruce R. *Gordon MacRae: A Bio-Bibliography.* CT: Greenwood Press, 1991.
_____. *Howard Keel: A Bio-Bibliography.* CT: Greenwood Press, 1995.
Lentz, Harris M., III. *Television Westerns Episode Guide: All United States Series 1949–1996.* NC: McFarland, 1997.
_____. *Western and Frontier Film and Television Credits, 1903–1995. Vol. 1 Actors and Actresses, Directors, Producers, and Writers. Vol. 2 Film Index, Television Index.* NC: McFarland, 1996.
Leonard, William Torbert. *Once Was Enough.* NJ: Scarecrow Press, 1986.
Lofman, Ron. *Celebrity Vocals: Attempts at Musical Fame from 1500 Major Stars and Supporting Players.* WI: Krause Publications, 1994.
Marc, David, and Robert J. Thompson. *Prime Time Primemovers — From* I Love Lucy *to* L.A. Law — *America's Greatest TV Shows and the People Who Created Them — Television Series.* NY: Syracuse University Press, 1995.
Marschall, Rick. *The Golden Age of Television.* NY: Exeter Books, 1987.
McCall, Michael. *The Best of 50's TV.* NY: Mallard Press, 1992.
McNeil, Alex. *Total Television: The Comprehensive Guide to Programming from 1948 to the Present.* 4th ed. NY: Penguin Books, 1996.
McNeil, Bill, and Morris Wolfe. *Signing on the Birth of Radio in Canada.* NY: Doubleday.
Miller, Lee O. *The Great Cowboy Stars of Movies and Television.* NY: Arlington House, 1979.
Morino, Marianne. *The Hollywood Walk of Fame.* CA: Ten Speed Press, 1987.
Nowlan, Robert, and Gwendolyn Wright Nowlan. *Cinema Sequels and Remakes, 1903–1987.* NC: McFarland, 1989.
O'Neil, Thomas. *The Emmys: Starwars, Showdowns, and the Supreme Test of TV's Best.* NY: Penguin Books, 1992.
Parish, James Robert, and Vincent Terrace. *The Complete Actors' Television Credits, 1948–1988.* 2nd ed. *Vol. I Actors.* NJ: Scarecrow Press, 1989.
Perry, Jeb H. *Universal Television: The Studio and Its Programs, 1950–1980.* NJ: Scarecrow Press, 1983.
Pilato, Herbie J. *Kung Fu Book of Caine.* VT: Charles E. Tuttle Co., 1993.
Pitts, Michael R. *Western Movies: A TV and Video Guide to 4200 Genre Films.* NC: McFarland, 1986.
_____, and Louis H. Harrison. *Hollywood on Record: The Film Stars' Discography.* NJ: Scarecrow Press, Inc., 1978.
Polizzi, Rick. *Baby Boomer Games.* KY: Schroeder Publishing Co., 1995.
Quinlan, David. *Quinlan's Illustrated Directory of Film Character Actors.* London: B.T. Batsford, 1995.
Ragan, David. *Who's Who in Hollywood.* 2 vols. NY: Facts on File, 1992.
Robertson, Ed. *Maverick Legend of the West.* CA: Pomegranite Press, 1994.
Sackett, Susan. *Prime-Time Hits.* NY: Billboard Books, 1993.
Schleyer, Jim. *Backyard Buckaroos: Collecting Western Toy Guns.* Krause Publications, 1996.
Schwartz, David, Steve Ryan, and Fred Westbrook. *The Encyclopedia of TV Game Shows.* 2nd ed. NY: Facts on File, 1995.
Shapiro, Melany. *Bonanza: The Definitive Ponderosa Companion.* CA: Cyclone Books, 1997.
_____. *Bonanza — The Unofficial Story of the Ponderosa.* NV: Pioneer Books, 1993.
Sheward, David. *The Big Book of Show Business Awards.* NY: Billboard Books, 1997.
Shulman, Arthur, and Roger Youman. *How Sweet It Was — Television: A Pictorial Commentary.* NY: Bonanza Books, 1966.
Simas, Rick. *The Musicals No One Came to See: A Guide Book to Four Decades of Musical Comedy Casualties on Broadway, Off-Broadway, and in Out-of-Town Try Outs, 1943–1983.* NY: Garland Publishing, 1987.
_____. *The Soap Opera Book: Who's Who in Daytime Drama.* NY: Todd Publications, 1992.

Stubblebine, Donald J. *Cinema Sheet Music: A Comprehensive Listing of Published Film Music from* Squaw Man *(1914) to* Batman *(1989)*. NC: McFarland, 1991.

Summers, Neil. *The First Official TV Western Book*. WV: Old West Shop Publishing, 1987.

Terrace, Vincent. *Encyclopedia of Television Series, Pilots and Specials 1974-1984 Vol. II*. NY: New York Zoetrope, 1985.

_____. *Television Specials: 3,201 Entertainment Spectaculars, 1939 through 1993*. NC: McFarland, 1995.

Walker, John, editor. *Halliwell's Filmgoer's and Video Viewer's Companion 10th Edition*. NY: Harper Perennial, 1993.

_____. *Halliwell's Filmgoer's Companion*. NY: Harper Collins, 1997.

Ward, Jack. *The Supporting Players of Television, 1959–1983*. OK: Lakeshore West Publishing Company, 1996.

_____. *Television Guest Stars: An Illustrated Career Chronicle for 678 Performers of the Sixties and Seventies*. NC: McFarland, 1993.

Warner, Gary. *All My Children — The Complete Family Scrapbook. Special 25th Anniversary Collector's Edition*. CA: General Publishing Group, 1994.

Weaver, John T. *Forty Years of Screen Credits, 1929–1969. Volume 1: A–J. Volume 2: K–Z*. NJ: Scarecrow Press, 1970.

Weiner, Ed, and the Editors of *TV Guide*. *The TV Guide TV Book: 40 Years of the All-Time Greatest: Television Facts, Fads, Hits, and History*. NY: Harper Collins, 1992.

West, Richard. *Television Westerns: Major and Minor Series, 1946–1978*. NC: McFarland, 1987.

Wilkins, Mike, Ken Smith and Doug Kirby. *The New Roadside America*. NY: Fireside Simon and Schuster, 1992.

Willis, John. *John Willis Theatre World Vol. 44, 1978–1988*. NY: Crown Publishers, 1989.

Yoggy, Gary A. *Riding the Video Range: The Rise and Fall of the Western on Television*. NC: McFarland, 1995.

Index

Numbers not preceded by letters refer to page numbers. Those preceded by E refer to their entry numbers in the Episode Guide (pages 25–189).

341

Index